The Complete Walt Disney World® 2016

Julie and Mike Neal

About this book

Your best vacation ever. The Complete Walt Disney World is a tool for planning your trip to Walt Disney World as well as fully enjoying your vacation once you arrive. It provides helpful information that is easy to find, clear and accurate. Whether you're seeking general information, looking for answers to specific questions ("Is my daughter tall enough to ride Space Mountain?" "How far is Animal Kingdom Lodge from Epcot?") or insightful advice, this book can help. Many parents like to look at it with their children, as its abundance of photos appeals to all ages.

Qualified authors. The Complete Walt Disney World is the only major Disney guide written by authors who live in Orlando; it's also the only one ever honored by the Disney company. Main author Julie Neal used to work in the Disney hotel system as a concierge supervisor, and has appeared on radio and television shows for decades. In 2015 she lead CNN correspondent Richard Quest through the Magic Kingdom in an episode of "CNN Business Traveler."

Finding information. The book starts with articles on Disney World's history, Best Bets, news for 2016, MyMagic+ and Fastpass and Planning Your Trip. Color-coded chapters cover the major areas of Walt Disney World—its theme parks, water parks, Disney Springs and ESPN Wide World of Sports—then deal with Accommodations and Characters. To make detailed planning easy, practical information is all in one place: in the chapter Walt Disney World A–Z. Categories in it include Airports, Fastpass and Tickets.

Attraction reviews. In each theme park chapter, each attraction gets its own page or two filled with helpful content, including:

Magic Kingdom | Attractions

The entrance of Disney's Pirates of the Caribbean ride recalls an actual Spanish fort—El Morro, a 16th-century fortress in San Juan, Puerto Rico.

Clockwise from top left: Jailed pirates beg a dog for a key. Capt. Jack listens in as a drunken pirate reveals the location of the town's treasure, the ride's infamous bridal auction.

Pirates of the Caribbean

Immersive slow boat ride has plundering, plastered pirates

★★★★ ✓ FastPass+ Drunk pirates "pillage and plunder… rifle and loot… kidnap and ravage and don't give a hoot" in this rowdy, rum-soaked attraction, a dark indoor boat ride which takes you through the robotic ransacking of a Spanish port. There's plenty to look at, as you pass dozens of vignettes and sight gags. Special effects simulate fire, lightning, wind and, best of all, splashing cannon balls. The inspiration for the "Pirates of the Caribbean" movies, the ride keeps a lightweight tone; its pirates have such caricatured features they seem straight from a cartoon. Updated in 2006, it now features Capt. Jack Sparrow and other characters from those films. Its cool, dim queue winds through a stone fort.

Aye, a tale there be. The attraction's storyline is a morality tale, told in flashback form. It begins in the present, as you pass through a watery grotto lined with pirate (and mermaid) skeletons, then goes back in time to show what led the pirates to their doom. Scenes include Capt. Barbossa attacking a Caribbean port as he and his men search for Capt. Jack, and later Jack himself lounging smugly among the town's riches, having outsmarted them all.

Historic it be. The last ride Walt Disney helped design, the attraction combines a farm boy's view of high-seas adventure with a Hollywood showman's use of theatrics. Conceived as a wax museum, the attraction became an Audio-Animatronics boat ride after the success of two Disney-designed efforts at the 1964 New York World's Fair. It drew from Carousel of Progress, with its then-revolutionary robotic characters, and It's a Small World, which debuted a water-jet system that propelled boats through scenes.

PC it be not. The ride's story is all in good fun, but even the most carefree parent may wonder if scenes showing torture, heavy drinking and the selling of women send the best messages to a wide-eyed child. "There is nothing politically correct about Pirates of the Caribbean," admits Imagineer Eric Jacobson. "In fact, much of it is patently offensive."

In fairness, the ride does imply the consequences of such behavior; its first scene shows that the pirates end up murdered, their bodies left behind to rot. And it's more sensitive than it used to be. A barrel that today hides Capt. Jack (see above) once contained a scared-yet-titillated young woman who was nearly naked. Holding her slip, a pirate in front of her yearned to "hoist me colors on the likes of that shy little wench. I be willin' to share, I be!"

Tips. *When to go:* Early in the morning or late at night, when lines are short. *Which line to pick:* The right one. Its sights include some chess-playing skeletons. *Where to sit:* Ask for the front row. You'll have a clear view of everything, and lots of legroom.

Fun finds. At the bridal auction, the first woman in line is beaming, happy to be sold. Referring to her portly figure as "stout-hearted and corn-fed" the auctioneer asks her to "shift yer cargo, dearie. Show 'em yer larboard side." As an impatient buxom redhead lifts her skirt, he calls "Strike yer colors you brazen wench! No need to expose yer superstructure!"… Frustrated that the dog in front of them won't bring them a key, one jailed prisoner tells another "Hit him with the soup bone!" As the dog glances at your boat, another captive says "Rover, it's us what needs yer ruddy help, not them blasted lubbers"… Painted on the exit ramp, "shoe prints" that indicate where to step consist of a normal right shoe and peg-leg left mark.

Hidden Mickeys. In the gift shop, the three-circle shape appears as three coins among a group of coins on a scale near the ride exit, and on the left shoulder of woman in a painting on the back wall.

Fun facts. A fog screen showing the face of Blackbeard is made of microscopic water droplets held in place by columns of air… The voices of Blackbeard, Capt. Barbossa and Capt. Sparrow are those of actors Ian McShane, Geoffrey Rush and Johnny Depp; the auctioneer is voiced by Paul Frees, the Haunted Mansion's ghost host.

Key facts. *Best for:* Ages 10 and up. *Duration:* 9 minutes. *Capacity:* 330 (15 per boat). *Queue:* Indoor, air-conditioned. *Fear factor:* Dark, spooky start; cannon fire may scare toddlers. *Debuted:* 1973, revised 2006, 2012 (Disneyland 1967). *Access:* ECV and wheelchair users must transfer. *Disability services:* Handheld captioning, Audio Description. *Location:* Adventureland.

Average wait times

9am	10am	11am	Noon	1pm	2pm	3pm	4pm	5pm	6pm	7pm	8pm	9pm
5m	5m	20m	25m	45m	30m	25m	40m	30m	30m	20m	20m	5m

62 THE COMPLETE WALT DISNEY WORLD 2016 | THE COMPLETE WALT DISNEY WORLD 2016 63

A **Photos.** To give you a sense of the ride or show, each review includes at least one image, usually taken by co-author Mike Neal.

B **Rating.** The attraction is rated from one to five stars (★) (see criteria below), and gets a checkmark (✔) if it's an author favorite. The Fastpass+ logo (FastPass+) appears if it can be reserved in advance.

C **A description and review.** A brief summary explains the attraction, its appeal factors, media tie-ins, history (if it's interesting) and the author's opinion of it.

D **Tips.** Author Julie Neal offers insight on everything from when to go and where to sit to how romantic couples can enjoy a ride.

E **Fun finds and fun facts.** Disney rides often hide in-jokes or Hidden Mickeys, and often are the source of interesting trivia.

F **Key facts.** Found at the end of the article, these include length of the ride or show, its capacity, whether its waiting area is inside or outside, how old it is, its disabled access, health warnings and weather issues.

G **Average wait times.** For rides where waiting lines are common, a timetable show how long guests wait for each hour of the day.

Special information for families. Scary and teachable moments in rides and shows, Disney policies that affect children and fun ways to spend family time at Disney hotels are found in Family Matters areas of this book's park and accommodation chapters; "Fear Factors" appear in attraction specs. Toward the front of the book, the article Planning Your Trip includes bonding activities in a section titled Involving Your Children. Toward the back, the A–Z chapter covers topics such as Babysitters, Birthday Parties, Childcare Centers and Lost Children.

About our ratings. We rate an attraction based on how well it lives up to its promise. That's not just a phrase; it's how the late critic Roger Ebert rated movies. And it leads to ratings that are often different than you may expect, but we believe more helpful. For example, we judge the show Festival of the Lion King on how well it lives up to its promise that (1) it's festive, (2) it's about the Lion King and (3) it's worth the time it takes out of a day that's costing you about $100 a person. That show is nothing but festive and completely about the Lion King—so there are a few stars right away. Add in Broadway-quality singers, creative costumes, killer music and a fire-baton guy and yes it's certainly worth the hour or so it will take out of your day to see it. So, five stars. Note that this method ignores an attraction's size and scope, so in some cases a slight experience will have a higher rating than an elaborate one. Also note that we believe that for our ratings to have validity we have to have some that are one or two stars. So we do, and when we do we tell you why. Overall we give 31 percent of Disney attractions 5 stars, 25 percent 4 stars, 25 percent 3 stars, 12 percent 1 or 2 stars.

Contents

A world
of its own

TWICE THE SIZE OF MANHATTAN, Walt Disney World is the world's largest collection of theme parks, water parks and resorts. It's truly a world of its own unlike anything else.

A trip to Disney is not just a way to spend time with your children, nor merely an escape from day-to-day doldrums. It's a reawakening of that free-spirited, good-natured soul who lives deep inside you—the one your spouse married, the one you want your kids to emulate. Yes it can be crowded, yes it can be expensive, yes it takes a good plan to see it all, but no other man-made vacationland so deliberately embraces creativity, optimism and a sense of wonder about the world.

Populated daily by more than 100,000 visitors as well as 57,000 employees (Disney calls them "cast members"), the 47-square-mile property is the No. 1 vacation destination on the planet. It includes four theme parks, two water parks, a sports complex, a shopping and entertainment district and 20 resort hotels.

Magic Kingdom. It's only 122 acres, just 0.5 percent of Disney property, but to many folks this park *is* Walt Disney World. Similar to California's Disneyland, it re-imagines Main Street U.S.A., Adventureland, Fantasyland, Frontierland and Tomorrowland. A family favorite, it has more than 40 attractions, including classics such as Peter Pan's Flight and Space Mountain. It's the most popular theme park in the world.

Epcot. A sort of permanent World's Fair, this 300-acre park is divided into science-themed Future World and internationally focused World Showcase. Future World attractions include simulators that offer realistic sensations of hang gliding (Soarin') and astronaut training (Mission Space). World Showcase is highlighted by its memorable entertainment, dining and shopping.

Disney's Hollywood Studios. The front of this 135-acre show-biz-themed park is a tribute to Old Hollywood, with re-created icons

such as Hollywood Boulevard and Grauman's Chinese Theatre. The rear was once an actual studio and still looks the part. The park has two of Disney's best thrill rides—the Twilight Zone Tower of Terror and the Rock 'n' Roller Coaster Starring Aerosmith.

Disney's Animal Kingdom. This theme park combines exotic live animal exhibits with high-quality attractions. Top stops include Expedition Everest, a roller coaster that travels backward into a mountain cave; Kilimanjaro Safaris, an exploration through a replicated African wildlife preserve aboard an open-sided truck; and Festival of the Lion King, a show with energetic acrobats, dancers, singers and stilt walkers. The centerpiece of the 500-acre park is the Tree of Life, a 145-foot-tall man-made sculpture.

Other parks and activities. On a summer morning it's hard to beat the family fun at Disney's Blizzard Beach and Typhoon Lagoon. Disney also has four championship golf courses as well as a 9-hole, two miniature golf courses and many tennis courts, and offers organized fishing, horseback riding, water sports and other activities.

Disney Springs. A revamp of Downtown Disney, this dining, entertainment and shopping area sits on the eastern edge of Disney World. It should be finished in August, 2016.

ESPN Wide World of Sports. This complex is 220 acres of stadiums, fieldhouses, outdoor fields and other facilities that host amateur and some professional competitions.

Resort hotels. Distant lands and forgotten eras are recalled at most of Disney's 20 hotel properties. Accommodations range from campsites to multilevel suites.

Project X. In 1964, the Walt Disney Company began secretly buying up parcels of land southwest of Orlando, using false names and dummy corporations to keep prices low. In October, 1965, the Orlando Sentinel-Star identified the buyer; a month later Walt Disney and his brother, Roy, confirmed the existence of their "Project X," a plan for a futuristic city—the Experimental Prototype Community of Tomorrow (EPCOT)—where solutions to the urban problems of the day could be explored. To help fund itself, the area would include a theme park, an East Coast version of California's Disneyland.

Walt dies. After Walt's sudden death the next year, Roy decided to go ahead with the idea, at least the theme-park portion for right then, but changed the project's name from EPCOT to Walt Disney World to honor his brother. The largest private construction project in the history of the United States, it broke ground in 1969. Development was led by two military men. Former Army general Joe Potter had overseen operations at the Panama Canal and the 1964 World's Fair; former Navy

admiral Joe Fowler had supervised the building of Disneyland. Potter, Fowler and 9,000 workers moved 8 million cubic yards of dirt, built 47 miles of canals and 22 miles of levees, dredged the 406-acre Bay Lake and created a 172-acre "Seven Seas Lagoon." They also built roads, maintenance shops, a phone company, power plant, sewage plant and tree farm.

Disney World opened to the public on Oct. 1, 1971. It consisted of the Magic Kingdom, the Contemporary and Polynesian Village resorts and the Fort Wilderness Resort & Campground. Disney's Golf Resort (today's Shades of Green) was built in 1973, and the Lake Buena Vista Village (today's Disney Springs Marketplace) opened in 1975.

EPCOT becomes Epcot. Disney executives wrestled with Walt's EPCOT idea through the early 1970s, but the vision for an experimental city just wasn't clear without its visionary. Instead, in 1976 the company announced plans for EPCOT Center, a theme park with "demonstration concepts" and an "international people-to-people exchange" located in the center of what was to be Walt Disney's city. It opened in 1982, and later became the lowercase "Epcot" in 1994.

A total vacation destination. For all that Disney created in Florida during the '70s and early '80s, it has built far more since. In 1988, when arch-rival Universal Studios announced plans to built a movie-studio theme park just

down the road, Disney quickly put together Disney-MGM Studios (today's Disney's Hollywood Studios). It opened a year later, along with the Typhoon Lagoon water park and the since-closed Pleasure Island nightclub complex. A second water park, Blizzard Beach arrived in 1995. Disney's Animal Kingdom had its grand opening in 1998. Downtown Disney's West Side and the Wide World of Sports complex arrived in 1999.

During that same period the number of hotel rooms on Disney property grew from 2,000 to 33,000. The Caribbean Beach and Grand Floridian resort hotels opened in 1988; 13 more debuted in the 1990s—the Yacht and Beach Club and Walt Disney World Swan and Dolphin (1990), Port Orleans French Quarter and Old Key West (1991), Dixie Landings (now Port Orleans Riverside, 1992), All-Star Sports and Wilderness Lodge (1994), All-Star Music and BoardWalk (1995), and Coronado Springs (1997) and All-Star Movies (1999). Disney's newest hotels are Animal Kingdom Lodge (2001), Pop Century (2003), Saratoga Springs (2004) and Art of Animation (2012).

Finally, a community. Disney developed the southwest corner of its property as a residential area, complete with its own downtown, school and post office. Named Celebration, the planned community broke ground in 1996. Today 7,500 people live there; the authors of this book did for a decade.

Best bets

It's like Christmas. You plan and save and anticipate for months. You yearn for a magical time with your family, full of memories and unforgettable moments. It certainly runs up the balance on your credit cards, but when it's over you're glad you did it. Yes, a vacation to Walt Disney World has a lot in common with Christmas, at least the secular American version. But how do you decorate your particular tree? Which presents do you choose? Here are the authors' Best Bets; two dozen of Disney's most seminal experiences:

Best thrill ride. An indoor roller coaster, Magic Kingdom's Space Mountain fills you with joy as you zip past twinkling stars and shooting comets. The low-sided, one-person-wide rocket is one of the narrowest coaster vehicles ever built, which enhances the feeling of flying solo through the cosmos.

Best princess attraction. A dazzling musical stage show, Beauty and the Beast—Live on Stage is both touching and laugh-out-loud funny. While romantics will swoon over the love story between Belle and her Beast, everyone will laugh at the cartoonish slapstick humor. And the music! It's comprised of some of Disney's best songs, the Howard Ashman classics "Belle," "Gaston," "Be Our Guest," "Something There," "The Mob Song" and "Beauty and the Beast." Villain Gaston is a hoot, funnier and less threatening than in the movie. When bookworm Belle and her resurrected Beast finally embrace, the happy ending makes some onlookers cry. The show plays daily at Disney's Hollywood Studios.

Best theatrical show. Energetic performers bring to life the best songs from Disney's 1994 movie "The Lion King" in the Festival of the Lion King, an in-the-round musical spectacle at Disney's Animal Kingdom. Creative costumes turn dancers into antelopes, warthogs, zebras and other beasts. Similar to a good circus, there is almost too much to look at; during the joyful finale singers belt out their numbers center stage while a human bird soars overhead, wisecracking host Timon mimes his reactions, animal dancers and

stilt-walkers circle the action and four huge puppets react in each corner of the theater. In 2014, the show moved to the park's Africa area.

Best vintage ride. You'll fly over London and head off to Never Land on Peter Pan's Flight, a classic dark ride at Magic Kingdom. Dusted with pixie dust by Tinker Bell, you fly a pirate ship from Wendy Darling's home toward and through scenes from the 1953 animated film, "Peter Pan." Designed more than 60 years ago, the ride's imaginative engineering and overdose of black lights conjure an experience that still charms all ages.

Best toddler attraction. Classic Magic Kingdom boat ride It's a Small World creates a child's view of our planet, one filled with colors, patterns, shapes, sparkles, textures and twinkly lights. Nearly 300 smiling dolls sing and play music while animals with flower-shaped spots and jeweled eyes dance and spin. Butterflies, clowns, jugglers and magic carpets float overhead like giant crib mobiles.

Best animal attraction. Nirvana for animal lovers, Kilimanjaro Safaris is a bouncy, open-air truck ride that offers unpredictable beastly sightings as it roams through real grasslands and forests. Each "two-week" tour is different, as the scores of animals feed, fight, graze, nurse, play and run.

Best educational attraction. President Obama speaks, as do George Washington and Abe Lincoln at Magic Kingdom's Hall of Presidents. Lifelike Audio-Animatronic versions of all 43 American leaders are represented as breathing, fidgeting, murmuring individuals... a mirror of our unsettled selves, the American people. Before they appear, a high-definition, ultra-widescreen film tells the illuminating tale of our country's origins.

Best fireworks. You're likely to tear up as you watch Wishes. Not the typical reaction to a fireworks show, perhaps, but this Magic Kingdom evening extravaganza is anything but typical. Though often understated, its synchronized starbursts, music and character dialogue pack an emotional punch for all ages; adults can't help but recall childhood dreams and memories. The show begins quietly as a lone shooting star arches over Cinderella Castle, and slowly builds to a spectacular finish that will be a highlight of your trip.

Best special event. This one's a three-way tie. Epcot's annual Flower and Garden Festival combines beauty with brains—flowers on walkways, seminars on gardening techniques. Fans of the Force love the Studios' Star Wars Weekends for their characters and special guests. For extra-cost events you can't beat the Mickey's Not-So-Scary Halloween

parties at Magic Kingdom, which young cosplay couples seem to enjoy as much as kids. It has its own special parade, and now a new stage show.

Best movie. Donald Duck finds himself in the dining hall from "Beauty and the Beast," the undersea grotto of "The Little Mermaid" and other classic Disney settings in the 3-D Mickey's PhilharMagic, a dazzling Magic Kingdom experience that all ages will love. When the duck steals a magical sorcerer's hat that Mickey Mouse needs to conduct a musician-free orchestra, the foul-minded fowl gets swept up into a long, strange trip. Don't miss his attempt to kiss Ariel, the Little Mermaid—it's electrifying.

Best scary attraction. "The next time you check into a deserted hotel on the dark side of Hollywood, make sure you know just what kind of vacancy you're filling." That's the lesson host Rod Serling teaches you at the Twilight Zone Tower of Terror, a remarkable ride at Disney's Hollywood Studios. From its abandoned, weed-filled grounds to its eerie music to its cobweb-covered lobby to its unwelcoming boiler room, the Tower of Terror is designed expressly to freak you out. And all that is before you board the creaky freight elevator for a randomly-selected series of violent plunges and sudden ascents.

Best ride at night. Magic Kingdom's "wildest ride in the wilderness," Big Thunder Mountain Railroad is even wilder at night, as its scenery is lit but its track is so pitch black that each curve and dip comes as a surprise. Crystals glow in its bat cave, and sulphur pools swirl in vivid colors. At the mining town of Tumbleweed, sharp-eyed riders will spot drunks and dance-hall dames partying upstairs at the Gold Dust Saloon.

Best character meal. It says a lot that Cinderella is *not* the most entertaining character at Cinderella's Happily Ever After Dinner, a dinner experience at the Grand Floridian hotel. Little girls love the princess, of course, but for adults the real treat is her supporting cast—regal Prince Charming proposes to moms and young women (swoon and his smile will grow); squabbling stepsisters Anastasia and Drizella flirt with little boys; haughty Lady Tremaine disapproves of everything. And the buffet is delicious.

Best night spot. Located right in the middle of a huge construction project, spirited Emerald Isle restaurant and pub Raglan Road features no-cover entertainment (step-dancers and a live band) a lavish stock of Irish beers and whiskeys and sophisticated comfort food. Most decor, including four antique grand bars, was imported

from Ireland. Children are welcome—and strangely, fit right in—and the menu offers something for every taste.

Best bands. The exceptional Mariachi Cobre was formed in Tucson, Ariz., way back in 1971 and played with Linda Ronstadt on her Spanish-language albums. Led by trumpets, violins and exuberant vocals backed by harmonizing guitars, the band expresses the romantic soul of Mexico in a way even the most whitebread gringo can appreciate. The group plays at Epcot's Mexico pavilion. Two other Disney bands are also outstanding. Underrated rockers Mulch Sweat and Shears (shown at right) tear up the Streets of America at Disney's Hollywood Studios. At Disney's Animal Kingdom, the infectious Afro-pop of Burudika (above) will lift the spirits of anyone no matter how Grumpy. Both Mulch Sweat and Shears and Burudika interact with their audiences as they perform; Mulch leader Morris Mulch even brings a female audience "volunteer" up with him to dance and sing.

Best improv troupe. Street performers who channel the mythical residents of a 1940s Tinseltown, the Citizens of Hollywood perform in Disney's Hollywood Studios, using guest "volunteers" in makeshift dating games, spelling bees and other silly setups.

They include frustrated director Alberto Dante, sassy script girl Paige Turner and dumb-blond starlet Evie Starlight.

Best Pixar attraction. You don't have to be a child to love Finding Nemo—The Musical. Playing at Disney's Animal Kingdom, the stage show taps into the bonds between fathers and sons and is a visual delight. Costumed singers act out their roles as they operate large puppets, some the size of cars.

Best water park ride. There's nothing quite like Crush 'n' Gusher, a Typhoon Lagoon water coaster that powers its riders up lifts and down dips, tunnels and many tight turns. The ride is great for couples and families, as each tube seats two, or even three people. Those with three people *fly*.

Best place to meet locals. Have the town mayor serenade you with "Happy Birthday," gossip with Hildegard Olivia Harding, learn to sing from ebullient voice teacher Victoria Trumpetto. It's all possible at Magic Kingdom's Main Street U.S.A., thanks to the Citizens of Main Street, the living, breathing embodiment of the almost-real town.

Best parade. Accompanied by colorful stilt-walkers, dancers and a catchy soundtrack, the stars of some of Disney's most beloved films ride on towering floats in its Festival of Fantasy Parade, a wildly creative procession through Magic Kingdom. Its stunning floats include a fire-breathing steampunk dragon.

Best restaurant. No, it doesn't serve roast zebra. Ignore the misconceptions about the food at Boma, a beautiful buffet restaurant at Animal Kingdom Lodge; the fare is a mix of non-exotic African dishes with traditional American comfort food. The artistic decor features hand-cut tin, hand-blown glass and thatched roofs. Servers are outstanding.

Best refurbished ride. During Disney's recent expansion of Fantasyland, the world's most adorable baby-elephant ride was moved, beautifully repainted, and doubled. Now the park's Storybook Circus area sports two Dumbo the Flying Elephants. Disney added a pool for the pachyderms to fly over and multi-colored lights that make a fountain-ringed pool underneath them glow at night. The attraction also includes a great waiting line, with its own indoor playground.

Best meet-and-greet. Audience volunteers help the heroine of "Beauty and the Beast" act out her tale as old as time in Enchanted Tales with Belle, an intimate storytelling show. Everyone who wants to participate can—including parents—and all participants meet the mademoiselle afterward. The child who is picked to play the Beast gets to dance with her, and is rewarded with a kiss on the cheek.

Best new ride. Everyone digs-digs-digs the Seven Dwarfs Mine Train, a smooth (if way too short) indoor-outdoor roller coaster at Magic Kingdom. Inside it coasts by Audio-Animatronic dwarfs; outside it picks up speed and swerves around curves. Designed for young families, it has a fear factor that falls somewhere between nearby kiddie coaster The Barnstormer and the ever-popular Big Thunder Mountain Railroad. An innovative ride system allows each mine cart to sway from side to side, which keeps its passengers from falling into each other. Expect a very long wait unless you have a Fastpass.

What's new

One thing that's always true at Walt Disney World: something is always being enhanced, improved or expanded. Here's what's happened lately and what's happening soon:

Magic Kingdom. The Harmony Barber Shop has a spiffed-up interior with more decor on its walls... The plaza in front of Cinderella Castle is much bigger now, as additional walkways and plazas have replaced hills and trees. The reason: to alleviate congestion, especially during fireworks shows... A new restaurant themed to the Jungle Cruise ride opens near the Adventureland entrance in late 2015; the Skipper Canteen... That land's Island Supply shop is now a Sunglass Hut... Totally devoted to The Haunted Mansion, new shop Memento Mori offers more than 100 Mansion items...Astro Orbiter's rockets have new paint jobs and fly by more colorful planets... The Sanderson Sisters from Disney's 1993 comedy "Hocus Pocus" star in a new show at Mickey's Not-So-Scary Halloween Party, the Hocus Pocus Villain Spelltacular... "Frozen" characters Anna, Elsa, Kristoff and Olaf now appear in Mickey's Once Upon a Christmastime Parade.

Epcot. Soarin' becomes Soarin' Around the World in 2016, as its journey changes from one over California to one that takes you over natural wonders and landmarks of many continents. It also gets new digital screens and projection systems and a third theater... Norway's Maelstrom attraction has been *sendt pakking,* to be replaced in mid-2016 by Frozen Ever After (shown on page 21), a journey through the kingdom of Arendelle. Princess Anna and Queen Elsa will greet fans in an adjacent Royal Sommerhus... New World Showcase entertainment includes the Paul Bunyan Lumberjack Show at the Canada pavilion, the Moroccan female song-and-dance troupe B'net Al Houwariyate, the a cappella American Music Machine at the American Adventure and Sbandieratori Di Sansepolcro, an Italian flag-throwing troupe... A new Taste Track food stand in front of Test Track offers elaborate grilled-cheese sandwiches.

Disney's Hollywood Studios. What's new at this park is for the most part simply news, and a lot of it: that over the next few years it will add two significant lands, one themed to the Star Wars saga, the other to the equally mythical world of the Toy Story movies.

Star Wars land. Disney says this "authentic, jaw-dropping" area (above) will "transport guests to a never-before-seen Star Wars planet," a remote trading port populated with droids, aliens and roaming beasts. Stores and dining areas will be run by "local inhabitants," and may include a Mos Eisley-style Cantina.

Two signature attractions will include an "epic adventure that puts you in the middle of a climactic battle between the First Order and the Resistance" as well as one that puts you "behind the controls of one of the most recognizable ships in the galaxy, the Millennium Falcon" as you take on a customized secret mission (left). Rumored to replace the Streets of America section of the park, the 14-acre land is scheduled to open in 2018.

Toy Story Land. Designed for families with children between age 4 and 11, this area (see next page) will be a way-larger-than-real-life version of the backyard of Andy, the boy who owns Woody the Sheriff, Buzz Lightyear and most of the other toys seen in the "Toy Story" movies. Built way larger than scale so that guests who enter it feel as if they're the size of a toy, the land will include two new

attractions. The headliner will be a roller coaster, one where the coaster itself is Slinky Dog, the toy dachshund who has a Slinky for a body. The family-family coaster will roam throughout the new land as it coasts, plunges, zips and zooms. A spinning saucers ride will be nearby, themed to Toy Story's little green aliens. Riders will spin under a looming Claw as special lighting, music and sound effects add to the experience. The saucers will be covered, so they can be ridden in a rain.

The expansion will also make it easier to ride Toy Story Mania, as it includes an update to that popular video-game ride that will give it a third track, increasing its capacity by 50 percent, and include a fast-food restaurant, a store (Al's Toy Barn) and a play area.

The 11-acre Toy Story Land will be built behind the existing theme park, up against the back of the Toy Story Mania building, an area that once contained the offices of Disney's East Coast Animation Studio and was seen on the Studios Backlot Tour.

Toy Story Land should open in 2018.

New at the Studios this year. In general what's new is what's been taken away, most in preparation of the two expansions—in the past 18 months the park has closed its American Idol Experience, Magic of Disney Animation, Studio Backlot Tour, Legend of Capt. Jack Sparrow, and for unrelated reasons removed its Sorcerer's Hat at the end of Hollywood Boulevard that served for ages as its icon and for totally unrelated reasons removed the bust of Bill Cosby from its small Hall of Fame Plaza of the Academy of Television Arts and Sciences... As for what's been added for 2016: Star Tours will have a new adventure featuring locations and characters from the upcoming film "Star Wars: The Force Awakens"... Starting in early 2016, a Season of the Force seasonal event will close out weekend nights with a new fireworks show set to the iconic Star Wars score... Replacing the Magic of Disney Animation, the Star Wars Launch Bay will be an interactive area that at first will promote the new movie "Star Wars: The Force Awakens" and later focus on the Star Wars films in general, as well as the park's upcoming Star Wars land. Expect a variety of character meet-and-greets, lots of exhibits, props, costumes and art, custom Disney Infinity video game content, and unique Star Wars merchandise and food... The Jedi Training Academy gets redesigned with new characters and a new villain to battle from the popular Disney XD series "Star Wars Rebels"... A sponsorship by Turner Classic Movies has updated The Great Movie Ride with an interactive queue, a documentary-style preshow film, a pre-recorded narrator (TCM's Robert Osborne) who sets up comments by the tram operators and some new clips to the ride's montage of them at its end... A Starbucks (the Trolley Car Café) has opened at the corner of Hollywood and Sunset Boulevards, replacing a childrenswear shop... Sunset Boulevard store Villains in Vogue has been restocked and renamed;

it's now Reel Vogue, a generic merchandise shop... Disney can't let it go: though the nearby Legends of Hollywood store has not changed its name, it's now a "Frozen" shop.

Disney's Animal Kingdom. The park will begin to stay open after dark, with a street party on a new open plaza in front of the Tree of Life, a twilight version of Kilimanjaro Safaris and an evening spectacle.

Rivers of Light. Debuting in the spring of 2016, this nighttime spectacle promises to be unlike anything ever seen in a Disney park. Held on the pond-like area of the Discovery River between Discovery Island and the park's Asia section, it's said to "celebrate the beauty and special nature of the animals in the park" in a way that combines floating lanterns, live performers, water screens and swirling animal imagery. Disney says the show starts humbly, grows elaborate as more lanterns appear and huge curtains of water and light emerge from the river with animals within them, and for its finale "takes off into the sky."

Also at Animal Kingdom. A new Harambe Market area of Africa offers a modern take on African street foods and drink. Diners sit around shaded tables... A daytime macaw show (Winged Encounters) takes place on Discovery Island, at the same plaza as the street party ... The Kilimanjaro savanna gets two new species: African wild dogs and

hyenas... The cotton-top tamarins have a new home, on the walkway to Africa just past the otters... Lavender waxbills, speckled paradise whydah and other small birds now have a home at the Pangani Forest aviary, thanks to a 2015 remodel... Births at the park in 2015 included a white rhino and two gorillas... A Starbucks has taken over Creature Comforts, the Discovery Island building that used to be a childrenswear shop... Donald's Safari Dinner debuted in 2015 at Tusker House, making that buffet restaurant all-characters all-the-time.

Other news. Downtown Disney is no more, replaced by the way-bigger Disney Springs (see our Disney Springs chapter)... Selfie-sticks are no longer allowed in Disney theme or water parks... the Walt Disney World Speedway has closed to make way for more Magic Kingdom parking, and with it the Richard Petty driving experiences... Disney food menus now list the allergen content of each menu item... "Contactless payments" (i.e., Apple Pay) are now accepted at many Disney shops, stores and snack stands... The Polynesian Village Resort has a new pool area, new Trader Sam's Grog Grotto bar, and a slew of Disney Vacation Club timeshare units... Perhaps the best new restaurant at Disney is where you'd least expect it: on Hotel Plaza Boulevard. It's American Q, an imaginative barbecue spot inside the B Hotel.

MyMagic+ and Fastpass+

Developed by Disney at a cost of reportedly close to $1 billion, MyMagic+ is a high-tech "vacation management system" that can help you make the most of your Disney stay. You can use it to schedule attractions days in advance, make dining reservations, buy food and merchandise, even open the door to your hotel room. It consists of three things: a wristband, an app, and a new Fastpass+ system that lets you book your attraction times before you leave home. All three debuted in 2014, and Disney has been tweaking them since. Here's how they worked as of August 2015:

What is a MagicBand? What appears to be a plain rubber wristband is actually a high-tech device. A radio-frequency identification (RFID) chip inside it stores an encrypted code that identifies its wearer's personal profile in a backstage Disney database, which itself stores information on the guest, such as his or her park and Fastpass+ privileges, hotel

room access and credit card data. This lets the band function as a park ticket, room key and charge card. An online system lets you decide how much information to give it. (While you can use a MagicBand as a charge card, it doesn't store your credit-card information on it. A handy safety precaution requires you to provide your PIN to make a purchase that totals more than $50.)

MagicBands are available in seven colors: red, blue, green, pink, yellow, orange and gray; replacement bands are gray by default. Bands can withstand hot and cold temperatures; are waterproof but don't float and have three-year batteries. They can be customized with trinkets called MagicBandits.

One of the most noticeable changes brought about by the addition of MagicBands is that Disney has done away with turnstiles at the entrances to its theme and water parks. Now, you line up in front of waist-high posts called "touch points," which scan your

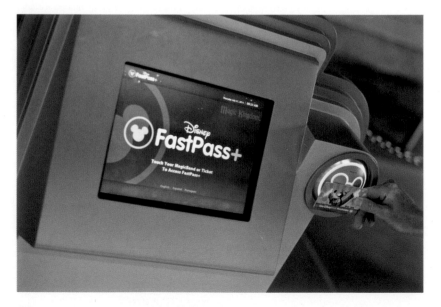

fingerprints and check to make sure your MagicBand (or park ticket) is valid. When it turns green, you're good to go.

Why should I wear a MagicBand? Because it can make your Disney stay more efficient, as it replaces cards and papers that you'd otherwise have to carry. You could potentially visit a park bag-free, with nothing but your band, your smartphone and an ID. As Disney continues to add to its technology, a guest's theme-park experience will likely become more tailored to his or her individual preferences. Though at press time (August 2015) it wasn't happening yet, in the future Disney says that Audio-Animatronics robots in waiting lines may greet guests by name, and live meet-and-greet characters such as Cinderella may offer unprompted greetings such as "So Maddie, I hear it's your birthday!"

What are its drawbacks? Mainly that it tracks you in ways you may not care for, as it lets Disney monitor which characters you meet, which souvenirs you buy and which attractions you visit and when. At its best, this information helps the company respond to shifts in crowd patterns, sending out additional staff and entertainment to busy areas, and adding ride vehicles to overwhelmed attractions. However it's possible—perhaps inevitable—that Disney will also collect personal data in other ways in an attempt to maximize guest spending. A band isn't

required to get into a theme park or to use the Fastpass+ system, as Disney also offers credit-card-like plastic tickets.

How do I get a MagicBand? MagicBands are free for Disney hotel guests and annual passholders. Other guests can buy them for $12.95 each. If you're planning to stay at a Disney hotel and reserve it at least 10 days early, Disney will ship your MagicBand(s) to you before you leave home; otherwise you'll get them when you check in. Disney ships the bands free to annual passholders upon request at 407-560-7277 or disneyworld. disney.go.com. Disney sells the bands in all of its theme parks, Disney Springs and other locations, at its Magic Band Service Centers. MagicBand shipping is only available to addresses in the United States.

What if I lose it? If you misplace your MagicBand, you don't have to worry about someone else using it to get into your hotel room or make purchases under your name. As soon as you report it as missing, a Disney cast member will deactivate it. Replacement bands are free for Disney hotel guests; others pay $12.95. If you can't get one right away you can still use the My Disney Experience app to access your Disney information, including your Fastpass+ reservations.

What is My Disney Experience? My Disney Experience is a free app for iPhones,

iPads and Android devices. Using it lets you view attraction wait times and park maps, make and modify your Fastpass+ reservations, schedule restaurant reservations and over time, Disney says, many more things. To use the app properly, you create a Disney account and link your park ticket to it.

What is Fastpass+? Fastpass+ is an attraction reservation system that lets you avoid waiting in long lines for rides or getting stuck with lousy viewing spots for shows and parades, and allows you to make and modify these reservations months in advance—before you leave home. It replaced Disney's Fastpass—no "plus"—which used paper tickets that could only be obtained at the ride or show they were good for on the day they were issued, and once issued couldn't be changed or modified. The new system has no paper tickets; everything is handled electronically. As part of the change, more than twice as many Disney attractions accept Fastpasses.

Like before, each Fastpass you reserve assigns you a window of time for you to arrive at a particular attraction. Most rides give you a one-hour window; some parades and shows require you to arrive no later than a particular time. Also like before, Disney's Fastpasses are completely free of charge.

You reserve attractions through either the Disney website (disney.com), the My Disney Experience app or at a theme-park kiosk. Disney accesses your reservation data through your MagicBand or plastic ticket and stores it in a database. At a Fastpass+ attraction you tap your band or ticket against a Touchpoint to enter its Fastpass line.

How does it work? For each day of your visit you can book three Fastpasses for you or your group, at your choice of any one theme park. If you have a Disney resort room booked and have bought park tickets as part of that package, you can reserve rides and shows 60 days in advance. If not, you can do so 30 days out. Magic Kingdom and Disney's Animal Kingdom let you freely choose any attractions you want; Epcot and Disney's Hollywood Studios divide your choices into two tiers, and restrict you to one from column A (the most popular attractions) and two from column B.

Disney hotel guests can reserve attractions for each day of their stay; other guests can schedule up to seven days of Fastpasses at a time. If you have Fastpasses reserved at one park and decide to go to a different park that day, you can cancel your reservations and rebook new ones through the app, website, or at a MyMagic+ Service Center.

Once you use your three Fastpasses (or after they expire) you can get another one for that day at a Fastpass+ kiosk, and then continue to book same-day Fastpasses one-at-a-time. *Note: you may soon be able to book four Fastpasses a day in advance, instead of three.*

What are these kiosks? Walk-up touch-screens that are clustered together in many theme-park lands. If you want to tweak the times or locations of your Fastpasses while you're in a theme park, or add more rides or shows to your schedule, you can make same-day, same-park Fastpass reservations at in-park kiosks, with the hands-on assistance of a knowledgeable Disney cast member. Need to schedule other Fastpasses, for other days and other parks? MyMagic+ Service Centers can schedule those.

What if I don't show up on time? Though Disney doesn't publicize it, its 1-hour Fastpass window has a grace period. Typically, you can arrive up to 5 minutes early, or 15 minutes late, and still enter a Fastpass line. If you miss your designated Fastpass window for an attraction due to circumstances beyond your control (weather, Disney transportation issues), cast members will usually try to accommodate you. However, the later you are, the less helpful they'll be.

How do I take advantage of Fastpass+? Look through this book before you schedule your Fastpasses. Note the hourly wait times for attractions you want to experience, so you don't waste a pass on a ride or show that doesn't need one. Other tips:

Reserve your rides and attractions as soon as you can, so you create theme-park days that best suit your needs. Morning reservation times usually go quickly, especially for the more popular attractions.

If you're part of a family or group that's visiting the parks together, add each member to your Family & Friends list on your Disney account so that your Fastpass times will sync together. Once you've booked your group's Fastpasses, they can be changed and tweaked just like those for an individual.

At a park, use the Fastpass+ kiosks when they're convenient. Doing so not only gets you the help of someone who knows what they're doing, it lets you avoid any Wi-Fi reception problems. Though it employs an innovative AT&T system, Disney's service isn't always available, especially inside buildings, remote park areas, and during heavy-use times such as right before a parade. Kiosks near park entrances tend to be the most crowded; to avoid a long wait

visit one deep in the park, such as those in Magic Kingdom's Storybook Circus.

After you make your reservations, use your phone to take a photo of its screen, or the screen of the computer or kiosk you used to make them. This makes it easy to remember your reservation times, and, when you show up at an attraction, serves as proof that you do indeed have Fastpasses for it.

If you're a parent, consider using Disney's unpublicized Child Swap service, which can be used with or without a Fastpass. You'll find information on it in our chapter Walt Disney World A–Z, under Children's Services.

What if I don't want any of this 'magic'?

If you decide you don't feel comfortable using MyMagic+, don't worry; you aren't required to participate in it to visit Walt Disney World. However, Disney has made the system so convenient, efficient and widespread that you'll probably feel compelled to be part of it. If you don't, you'll probably have to deal with Standby lines that are longer than ever, especially at popular attractions such as the new Seven Dwarfs Mine Train roller coaster at Magic Kingdom, Soarin' at Epcot, and Toy Story Mania at Disney's Hollywood Studios.

What if I don't have a smartphone?

You need one (or a tablet) for the app, but not to use MyMagic+. The system's planning and reservation tools are available at mydisneyexperience.com and can be accessed through MyMagic+ kiosks (see the overview pages of this book's theme park chapters for locations).

Ready… get set… plan. If you take the time to plan for your trip properly, MyMagic+ can be a useful tool. However, if you aren't familiar with the system and don't use it to reserve your Fastpasses ahead of time, you could easily find yourself spending much of your Disney vacation waiting in line—to choose among "leftover" attractions at in-park Fastpass kiosks, and then in long Standby lines for the rides and shows you most wanted to experience. Standby lines during the summers of 2014 and 2015 set record levels. At one, the character meet-and-greet Princess Fairytale Hall in Magic Kingdom, parents and their "Frozen"-obsessed offspring waited in line for six hours—six hours!—to meet that movie's Princess Anna and Queen Elsa.

Needless to say, using MyMagic+ makes your Disney visit much less spontaneous and the advanced planning can be a real pain. For what it's worth, though the authors of this book go to Disney nearly every day we never wear MagicBands (we think they're a little dorky); instead we carry the plastic tickets. But we use the Fastpass+ system on almost every visit, often booking our passes just as we're getting to a park.

Photo © Disney

Planning your trip

With just a little bit of preparation, it's easy to put together a terrific Walt Disney World vacation. Planning one isn't brain surgery—all you need is this book, access to the Internet and a phone; a Disney telephone directory appears at the back of this book. Ideally you should start putting your plan together a year in advance. For basic planning, here's a simple 12-step plan:

❶ **Decide when to go.** You can have a good time at Disney any day of the year, but if you've got the flexibility, the first two weeks of December is the best time to go. It's not terribly crowded, and there's more to see and do than any other time, thanks to the holiday decor and entertainment. Crowds are light and hotel rooms less expensive from mid-January to Valentine's Day, the first half of May and between Labor Day and mid-November. The least crowded, least expensive week of the year is the one after Labor Day. The worst times to visit? July and early August, when crowds are thick and the air thicker; and the week between Christmas and New Year's, when crowds are horrid and temperatures can be near freezing.

❷ **Decide how long to stay.** Want to see the best of everything Disney has to offer? You'll need at least a week.

❸ **Build your budget.** Add up your estimated daily expenses, including less-obvious spending like spur-of-the-moment snacks, souvenirs and gifts for the folks back home.

❹ **Decide where to stay.** Disney operates 20 resorts, and nearly every hotel chain known to man has at least one property within 10 miles. Disney hotels are most convenient, of course, and offer other benefits such as Extra Magic Hours (time in the parks before or after closing time), free transportation and packaged dining and recreation options.

❺ **Buy your airline tickets.** The Orlando International Airport is 19 miles east of Walt Disney World, about a 30-minute drive.

Driving to Disney? It's smack dab in the middle of Florida alongside Interstate 4, 15 miles southwest of downtown Orlando, 70 miles northeast of Tampa.

6 Decide what you want to do. Thumb through this book and check out the official Disney website disneyworld.com. If you have children, let them pick out their favorites.

7 Choose your park tickets. Disney offers a variety of options, including packages with pre-paid dining and recreation if you stay at a Disney resort hotel. Tickets are priced by the number of days they are good for; the more days the better the value.

8 Make a plan. Check the calendar at disneyworld.com for park hours, fireworks schedules and special events. Talk with your family about having a day or two when you don't visit a park (after all, this is a *vacation*). If you will be staying at a Disney hotel, check Extra Magic Hours at disneyworld.com.

9 Book it. Purchase your park tickets and reserve your Disney room through Disney at 407-934-7639 or disneyworld.com. Call between 7 a.m. and 10 p.m. Eastern time.

10 Reserve your restaurants. Character meals, dinner shows and key dining times for regular restaurants fill up months in advance. The restaurant that books the quickest is Cinderella's Royal Table, inside Cinderella Castle. You can book a Disney table as early as 190 days out if you're staying at a Disney hotel, 180 days if you're not (407-939-3463, disneyworld.com). Many entertainment and recreation choices require reservations, too.

11 Reserve your rides. Choose your Fastpass+ times on the very first day you can, so you'll have the most variety to pick from. Disney hotel guests can reserve Fastpasses 60 days in advance; others can do so 30 days out. Be obsessive with this; key times for popular rides, shows and character greetings often go on the first day they're available.

12 Rent a car, maybe. Disney has such an extensive transportation system that you may not want to rent a car. Its complimentary Magical Express buses shuttle Disney hotel guests from the Orlando airport, and its boats, buses and monorails move guests around Disney property free of charge. However, guests with cars get around faster, and have the option to visit areas outside Disney. You can rent a car at the airport or at most hotels on Disney property.

We say get a car, specifically a Ford Mustang convertible, from either Hertz at the airport or a Hertz Local Edition (HLE) spot. It has room for two adults and two children, a driving position that's pretty easy to see out from, not a lot of room in the trunk (in other words, pack light) and most importantly, a top that's amazingly easy to put up and down. Drop your top as you leave the airport and you will instantly feel like you are officially

on vacation. You'll feel the warmth of Florida air, really notice the rows of palms that line local interstate exchanges, and once you're at Disney you'll smell all the freshly cut grass. It's a splurge, yes, but one that you'll enjoy every day of your trip and your kids will long remember.

What to pack. Disney World visitors often underestimate the heat and humidity of Central Florida, and are unprepared for the outdoor exposure a Disney vacation includes.

For all ages. Musts include T-shirts, loose-fitting cotton tops, capris and shorts with large pockets, baseball caps and swimsuits, and broken-in walking shoes (pack two pair per person, so if it rains everyone still has a dry pair). Flip-flop sandals with a strap between the toes are a bad idea; they create blisters when used this intensely. In the winter guests need clothes to layer, such as jackets, sweaters and sweatshirts, as days start off cool but warm quickly. January mornings can be below freezing at 9 a.m. but 60 degrees by noon. Temperatures at 7 p.m. should be no higher than the 50s through March. From May through August, the heat index is usually at least 105 degrees by noon. For detailed weather data log on to weather.com and type in the ZIP code 32830.

Smart snacks
Nut packs, fruit and nut bars and raisin boxes are easy to stuff into a backpack or fanny pack, offer tasty and nutritious energy, and can help avoid expensive and time-consuming stops at snack stands.

Other essentials include an umbrella or rain poncho, sunglasses and sunscreen. Keep your hands free on your trip by using a backpack instead of a purse. Don't forget tickets, reservation confirmations and all the various battery chargers a modern life requires. And don't splurge on those specs—sunglasses are the No. 1 item guests lose at Disney. Cast members find hundreds of pairs a day.

For children. Dress your children like you dress yourself—casually, comfortably—but with more protection from the sun (i.e., wide-brimmed hats). Bring snacks (granola bars, raisin boxes) and, for autographs, a Sharpie (a thick one so fur characters can hold it easily).

Most forgotten item. The most common item Disney World visitors mistakenly leave at home—and at the end of the trip the one they most often leave in their hotel rooms—is the charger for their phone.

Involving your children

Announcing the trip. "We're going to Disney World!" Here are some creative ways to spring that good news:

Quiz cards. Create a quiz about Disney characters, movies or Disney World itself. Each question is on the front of a card laid face up on a table; its answer is on the back with one letter written larger, with a thick marker. When a child answers a question correctly, he or she turns over that card. When all the cards are revealed, they spell out a message such as: "We Are Going to Disney World on Tuesday!" For help coming up with questions see this book's theme-park and character chapters.

Scavenger hunt. Create a scavenger hunt that uses clues about Disney characters or quotes from Disney movies. Make each "find" a Disney trinket that has a card attached with the next clue. Attach the final card (announcing the trip) to a helium-filled Mickey balloon tucked inside a new suitcase. When the suitcase is opened, the balloon floats up.

Letter from Mickey. Mail your child a letter or postcard that appears to be from Mickey Mouse, Cinderella or another Disney character and reads "can't wait to meet you at Disney World!" Mickey could add "See ya real soon!"

Disney World backpack. As a present, fill a new backpack with Disney World items such as an autograph book or a T-shirt. Your child will quickly figure out what it mean.

Jigsaw puzzle. Create one that, when assembled, announces your vacation. Use paint or felt-tip markers to write "We're going to Walt Disney World tomorrow!" ("next week!" etc.) on the pieces. Give it to your boy or girl as a surprise present.

Sources for these materials. Disney items, including theme-park merchandise, for these ideas are available at disneystore.com or at 407-363-6200 (choose option 3 to reach a live operator). Uninflated Disney Mylar balloons are sold on Amazon.com for less than $10; the balloons can be inflated at most any florist or card shop for a token fee. Dick Blick Art Supplies (800-828-4548, dickblick.com) sells pre-cut Create-A-Puzzle kits.

Saving for your trip. Want to teach your kids the value of a dollar? A Disney trip can help. The more involved they are in the

Sun protection
Use a sunscreen with a high SPF and quality ingredients. Aloe after-sun products ease pain, help repair skin.

budgeting for one, the more they'll learn the benefits of saving and wise spending. Once your trip is in the works, create a "Disney Fund" to help pay for all of it or just special parts, such as a character meal, backstage tour or horseback ride. Start with a large can (a large Tupperware bowl will do), then decorate it and label it "Disney Fund." Put the bowl in a visible spot in your kitchen, so it's easy for everyone in your family to toss in extra money and change. Another idea: Use the fund to save up for kids' spending money.

Anticipating your trip. Like looking forward to Christmas day, anticipating a Walt Disney World vacation can be nearly as much fun as the event itself. Build your family's excitement with these ideas:

Countdown meals. Count down the days to your trip by creating Disney-themed meals and snacks that you enjoy at regular intervals (90 days before your trip, 60 days before, etc.). One of the easiest meals to make is Mickey Mouse pancakes; see the instructions on the next page. Other ideas: Making Alice in Wonderland tea sandwiches (ham and cheese, or PB&J) with Cheshire Cat smiles (slices of melon); cooking an Unbirthday Cake and presenting it to the family member whose birthday is the furthest away; setting your

Create a Disney Fund
Help pay for your trip, or special parts of it, by creating a special family savings account that everyone can contribute to. Start with a large can (a large Tupperware bowl will do), then decorate it and label it "Disney Fund."

dining table Beauty and the Beast style, with a single red rose; flying kites or feeding birds Mary Poppins style; creating Pirates of the Caribbean fruit swords on wooden skewers, perhaps with an accompanying treasure hunt.

Countdown chain. "How long 'til Disney?" Having a countdown chain is a fun way to answer that question, especially when everyone in your family teams up to make one together. Here's what you do:

Using construction paper, create a chain that has the same number of links as the number of days until your trip. Number the links consecutively on one side; decorate the other side with glitter, markers, paint and stickers. Perhaps give each link its own theme, such as a particular Disney character or Walt Disney World attraction. Make special links for birthdays and holidays, as well as countdown milestones such as "One Month To Go" and "One Week To Go." Hang the chain in a conspicuous spot, then tear off one of its links at the same time each day, perhaps first thing in the morning or just before bedtime. Remove the last link just before you set off on your trip.

Disney World movie nights. Sitting down with your family to watch a few Disney films will not only help get everyone in the proper frame of mind, it will also make your vacation itself more fun, as it will get you familiar with the characters, music and stories that form the basis of so many of Walt Disney World's rides, shows and other experiences.

To make your movie nights truly special, follow these four tips: First, schedule them at times when everyone can be home and agree to relax together. Before you hit play, have everyone get all of their chores and homework out of the way and put down their phones—no emails, no texting! Third, set a start time, turn down the lights and make sure everyone has a comfortable seat. And finally, schedule an intermission in advance for bathroom runs and snack grabs.

Not every movie night has to feature a Disney movie. Some Disney attractions are based on films from other studios, such as the Indiana Jones and Star Wars series.

Make Mickey pancakes

Spoon some pancake batter into the center of a wide pan, leaving lots of room on its top and sides. Then spoon out two smaller cakes, each an inch or two away from the first one so they spread out and touch it. Later, with a wide spatula, lift and flip your Mickey with one confident move of your wrist.

Walt Disney World

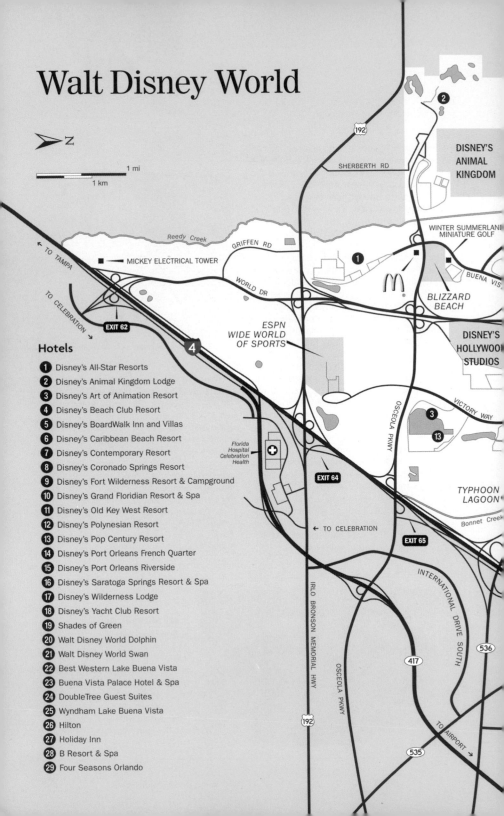

N

1 mi
1 km

MICKEY ELECTRICAL TOWER

TO TAMPA
TO CELEBRATION

EXIT 62

Reedy Creek

GRIFFEN RD

WORLD DR

192

SHERBERTH RD

DISNEY'S ANIMAL KINGDOM

WINTER SUMMERLAND MINIATURE GOLF

BUENA VIS

BLIZZARD BEACH

DISNEY'S HOLLYWOOD STUDIOS

ESPN WIDE WORLD OF SPORTS

VICTORY WAY

OSCEOLA PKWY

TYPHOON LAGOON

Bonnet Creek

Florida Hospital Celebration Health

EXIT 64

EXIT 65

← TO CELEBRATION

INTERNATIONAL DRIVE SOUTH

IRLO BRONSON MEMORIAL HWY

OSCEOLA PKWY

417

536

192

TO AIRPORT →

535

Hotels

1. Disney's All-Star Resorts
2. Disney's Animal Kingdom Lodge
3. Disney's Art of Animation Resort
4. Disney's Beach Club Resort
5. Disney's BoardWalk Inn and Villas
6. Disney's Caribbean Beach Resort
7. Disney's Contemporary Resort
8. Disney's Coronado Springs Resort
9. Disney's Fort Wilderness Resort & Campground
10. Disney's Grand Floridian Resort & Spa
11. Disney's Old Key West Resort
12. Disney's Polynesian Resort
13. Disney's Pop Century Resort
14. Disney's Port Orleans French Quarter
15. Disney's Port Orleans Riverside
16. Disney's Saratoga Springs Resort & Spa
17. Disney's Wilderness Lodge
18. Disney's Yacht Club Resort
19. Shades of Green
20. Walt Disney World Dolphin
21. Walt Disney World Swan
22. Best Western Lake Buena Vista
23. Buena Vista Palace Hotel & Spa
24. DoubleTree Guest Suites
25. Wyndham Lake Buena Vista
26. Hilton
27. Holiday Inn
28. B Resort & Spa
29. Four Seasons Orlando

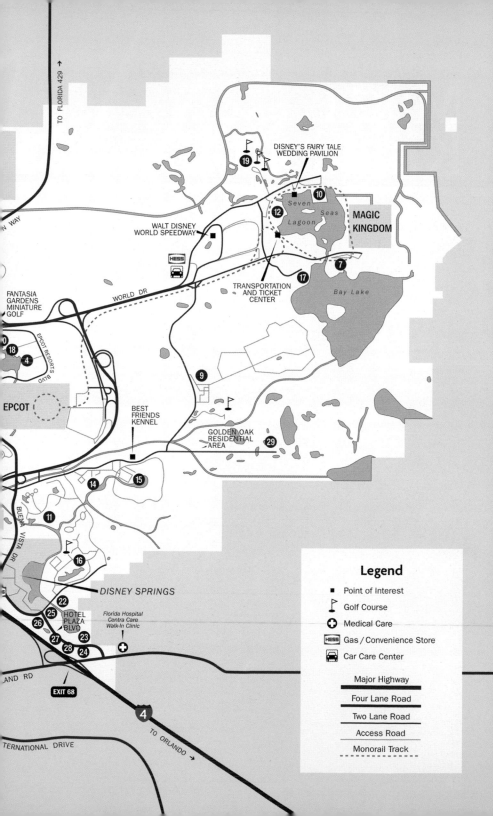

DISNEY'S FAIRY TALE
WEDDING PAVILION

19

10

12

Seven
Seas
Lagoon

MAGIC
KINGDOM

WALT DISNEY
WORLD SPEEDWAY

TO FLORIDA 429 →

N WAY

HESS

7

17

TRANSPORTATION
AND TICKET
CENTER

Bay Lake

FANTASIA
GARDENS
MINIATURE
GOLF

WORLD DR

EPCOT RESORTS BLVD

18

4

EPCOT

9

BEST
FRIENDS
KENNEL

GOLDEN OAK
RESIDENTIAL
AREA

29

14

15

BUENA VISTA DR

11

16

DISNEY SPRINGS

22

25

HOTEL
PLAZA
BLVD

Florida Hospital
Centra Care
Walk-In Clinic

26

27

23

28

24

LAND RD

EXIT 68

4

TO ORLANDO →

TERNATIONAL DRIVE

Legend

■ Point of Interest

⚑ Golf Course

✚ Medical Care

HESS Gas / Convenience Store

🚗 Car Care Center

Major Highway

Four Lane Road

Two Lane Road

Access Road

- - - **Monorail Track**

Magic Kingdom

"Partners"

We believe in our idea: a family park where parents and children could have fun... together.

The world's most popular theme park

A place for adventure, fantasy and nostalgia; a place to celebrate "Once upon a time…" and "…happily ever after," Magic Kingdom appeals to memories and imagination, childhood dreams, the wish to be the prettiest girl at the ball. Its idealized world includes the friendliest small town ever, an achingly beautiful castle, flying elephants and pirate ships.

The first park to open at Walt Disney World, Magic Kingdom started off as a larger, more spacious version of California's Disneyland. Though Walt Disney unexpectedly died just before construction began, his brother Roy ensured that his dream park was completed. It opened October 1, 1971.

Best of the park. The most child-focused Disney park, Magic Kingdom is easy to navigate, with attractions placed closely together. **It has lots of rides and shows,** more than twice that of any other Disney World park. There's a **cornucopia of characters**—in parades, shows and attractions, a street party, character meals, and at many meet-and-greet spots. A small-town American

boulevard from a century ago, **Main Street U.S.A.** is the heart of all things Disney, a dreamlike lane that's lovingly detailed, from its architecture and ambient music to the costumes of its citizens. Finally, the park has **the master's touch.** Although he didn't live to see Walt Disney World completed, Walt Disney was deeply involved in its planning as well as in several of its attractions. In a way, his spirit lives on through rides and shows such as the Carousel of Progress, the Enchanted Tiki Room, the PeopleMover, Peter Pan's Flight, Pirates of the Caribbean and the Walt Disney World Railroad.

Worst of the park. Magic Kingdom is far from perfect. Among its issues: **Crowds.** Attraction capacity: 9,750. Park capacity: 60,000. You do the math. **Inconvenience.** Getting to the park can be an adventure in itself, as its parking lot is more than a mile away. And oh those **sunny days in Tomorrowland!** Apparently the future holds little shade but lots and lots of asphalt. Not good when it's 90 degrees.

Dressed for the occasion. Performers in the Main Street Trolley Parade have different routines for Spring, Summer, Fall (above), Winter and Christmas. At left, the Dapper Dans.

Getting oriented. Magic Kingdom is divided into six distinctly themed areas:

Main Street USA. After entering the park under a train station, guests find themselves in the bustling Town Square of a turn-of-the-century American town. A boulevard leads to the new Cinderella Castle Plaza Gardens, a maze of landscaped walkways which triple the size of open areas in that space, greatly easing congestion during Wishes fireworks shows. From there, walkways spoke out to five attraction-packed lands.

Adventureland. A mix of African jungles, Arabian nights, British explorers and Caribbean and South Seas architecture.

Liberty Square. Federal and Georgian architecture bring back the Colonial era.

Frontierland. Twangin' banjo and fiddle music welcomes you to this look at 19th-century rural America.

Fantasyland. The park's largest land, its original area resembles a Renaissance fair. A recent expansion added an Enchanted Forest and a Storybook Circus area.

Tomorrowland. An intergalactic spaceport, today's Disney view of tomorrow is the future of the 1930s. Except for some of it, which is the future of the 1990s as seen from the 1970s, or other parts which are just sorta in outer space. Confused? You betcha.

Where to meet characters. More than 60 Disney characters appear at the park.

Aladdin. Near Magic Carpets of Aladdin, Adventureland.

Alice. Mad Tea Party, Fantasyland.

Anastasia and Drizella. Along the Great Wall behind Cinderella Castle, Fantasyland.

Anna and Elsa. At Princess Fairytale Hall, Fantasyland (at least through June 2016).

Ariel. At Ariel's Grotto, Fantasyland; Cinderella's Royal Table, Cinderella Castle.

Aurora. Town Square, Main Street U.S.A.; Cinderella's Royal Table breakfast, lunch (often), Cinderella Castle.

Baloo. Move It! Shake It! Dance & Play It! Street Party, Cinderella Castle hub.

Beast. Be Our Guest dinner, Fantasyland.

Belle. Stars in Enchanted Tales with Belle, Fantasyland; also at Cinderella's Royal Table, Cinderella Castle.

Buzz Lightyear. Alongside Carousel of Progress, Tomorrowland.

Chip 'n Dale. Rivers of America Crossing, Liberty Square; Move It! Shake It! Dance & Play It! Street Party, Cinderella Castle hub.

Cinderella. Princess Fairytale Hall; also Cinderella's Royal Table, Cinderella Castle.

Country Bears. Dance with them at the Frontierland Hoedown Happening, outside The Country Bear Jamboree, Frontierland.

A crowd of park guests enter Adventureland at the start of a Magic Kingdom day. The tropical area represents everywhere in the world that isn't the United States or Europe.

Daisy Duck. As Daisy Fortuna, Pete's Silly Sideshow, Storybook Circus, Fantasyland.

Donald Duck. As The Great Donaldo, Pete's Silly Sideshow, Storybook Circus, Fantasyland; Move It! Shake It! Dance & Play It! Street Party, Cinderella Castle hub.

Eeyore. Outside the Many Adventures of Winnie the Pooh, Fantasyland; also at Crystal Palace meals, Main Street U.S.A.

Fairy Godmother. At the Cinderella Castle fountain, Fantasyland.

Frozone. In Tomorrowland at that land's #INCREDIBLESSUPERDANCEPARTY.

Gaston. Gaston's Tavern, Fantasyland.

Genie. Near Magic Carpets of Aladdin, Adventureland (occasionally); Move It! Shake It! Dance & Play It! Street Party, Cinderella Castle hub.

Goofy. Pete's Silly Sideshow, Storybook Circus, Fantasyland; Move It! Shake It! Dance & Play It! Street Party, Cinderella Castle hub.

Jack Sparrow. Stars in Captain Jack's Pirate Tutorial, outside of Pirates of the Caribbean, Adventureland.

Jasmine. Near Magic Carpets of Aladdin, Adventureland; Cinderella's Royal Table breakfast, lunch (often), Cinderella Castle.

Jessie. Splash Mountain exit, Frontierland.

King Louie. Move It! Shake It! Dance & Play It! Street Party, Cinderella Castle hub.

Lady Tremaine. Outside Cinderella Castle, Fantasyland—and she's not happy about it.

Mad Hatter. Mad Tea Party, Fantasyland.

Marie. Town Square, Main Street U.S.A.

Mary Poppins. Town Square near the Town Square Theater, Main Street U.S.A.

Merida. Fairytale Garden, Fantasyland.

Mickey Mouse. Inside Town Square Theater (sometimes with the ability to speak); Move It! Shake It! Dance & Play It! Street Party, Cinderella Castle hub.

Minnie Mouse. Pete's Silly Sideshow, Fantasyland; Move It! Shake It! Dance & Play It! Street Party, Cinderella Castle hub.

Mister Incredible. In Tomorrowland at the #INCREDIBLESSUPERDANCEPARTY.

Mrs Incredible. In Tomorrowland at the #INCREDIBLESSUPERDANCEPARTY.

Penguins. Town Square, Main Street U.S.A. (often appear with Mary Poppins).

Peter Pan. Peter Pan's Flight, Fantasyland.

Phineas and Ferb. Dancing at the Move It! Shake It! Dance & Play It! Street Party, Cinderella Castle hub.

Piglet. Outside the Many Adventures of Winnie the Pooh, Fantasyland; Crystal Palace meals, Main Street U.S.A.

Pluto. Town Square, Main Street U.S.A.

Rapunzel. Inside Princess Fairytale Hall, Fantasyland.

A family crosses a bridge into Liberty Square, a Colonial village at the dawn of America's independence. A plaque reads "Past this gateway stirs a new nation waiting to be born."

Snow White. Town Square Theater porch, Main Street U.S.A.; Cinderella's Royal Table meals (often), Cinderella Castle.

Stitch. Near the Carousel of Progress, Tomorrowland; Move It! Shake It! Dance & Play It! Street Party, Cinderella Castle hub.

Tiana and Prince Naveen. Tiana's Garden Glen, behind the Ye Olde Christmas Shoppe, Liberty Square.

Tigger. Outside the Many Adventures of Winnie the Pooh, Fantasyland; Crystal Palace meals, Main Street U.S.A.

Tinker Bell. Town Square Theater, Main Street U.S.A.

Tweedledee, Tweedledum. Mad Tea Party, Fantasyland (occasionally).

Wendy. Close to Peter Pan's Flight, Fantasyland (occasionally).

White Rabbit. Mad Tea Party, Fantasyland.

Winnie the Pooh. Crystal Palace meals, Main Street U.S.A.; The Many Adventures of Winnie the Pooh, Fantasyland.

Woody. At the Splash Mountain exit courtyard, Frontierland.

Street performers. The park offers a wide variety of live entertainment:

★★★★★ ✔ **Captain Jack Sparrow's Pirate Tutorial.** Comical Capt. Jack and first mate Mack recruit aspiring young pirates from the crowd—administering the Pirate Oath, teaching them how to be rescued from a desert island, use a swordplay trick to flee an enemy and sing the Pirates of the Caribbean song "Yo Ho (A Pirate's Life for Me."). *20-min. shows. Across from Pirates of the Caribbean.*

★★★★ ✔ **Casey's Corner Pianist.** A skilled player bangs out honky tonk, rag and Disney tunes on a white upright. *20-min. shows. Casey's Corner patio, Main Street U.S.A.*

★★★★★ ✔ **Citizens of Main Street.** A troupe of improvisational actors portray the boulevard's turn-of-the-century townsfolk, strolling the street to chat, dance, joke, sing and pose for photos. Characters include Mayor Weaver, Fire Chief Smokey Miller, voice instructor Victoria Trumpetto, socialite suffragettes Hildegard Olivia Harding and Bea Starr and Main Street Gazette reporter (and avid pin-trader) Scoop Sanderson. *20-min. appearances. Main Street U.S.A.*

★★★★★ ✔ **Dapper Dans.** This barbershop quartet mixes a harmonically perfect old-time repertoire with chimes, tap dancing, and corny humor. Point it out to them—they're 5-star rated! *20-min. shows. Main Street U.S.A.*

★★ **Flag Retreat.** A security color guard lowers the park's U.S. flag, often with a guest vet. Sincere. *20-min. ceremony. 5 p.m. daily. Town Square flagpole, Main Street U.S.A.*

Lashed together by rope, a wooden sign welcomes you to Frontierland, a rural American settlement straight out of the 1800s.

★★★ **Frontierland Hoedown.** The park's Country Bears play washboard and spoons as guests square dance with friendly country-western couples. *20-min. shows. In front of Country Bear Jamboree, Frontierland.*

★★★★ ✔ **Main Street Philharmonic.** This 12-piece comedic brass and percussion ensemble plays Disney hits and Americana favorites. *20-min. shows. Main Street U.S.A. and Storybook Circus.*

★★★★ ✔ **Main Street Trolley Parade.** Gay '90s couples hop off a horse trolley to perform a soft-shoe pantomime with lots of lip-syncing. The troupe changes its show for every season. So strange, but so Disney. *3 5-min. shows per parade. Main Street U.S.A.*

★★★★ ✔ **The Notorious Banjo Brothers and Bob.** Two banjo pickers and a tuba player play Disney tunes, bluegrass and cowboy melodies. *20-min. shows. Frontierland.*

★★★ **Royal Majesty Makers.** A retired knight, etiquette diva, squire and lady-in-waiting conduct Knight School, deliver ball invitations and lead dances. *Castle Courtyard, Fantasyland.*

★★★★★ ✔ **Magic Kingdom Welcome Show.** The park opens with a song-and-dance hello from some very happy Main Street residents, who usher in a train-full of characters. *Train station, entrance plaza.*

Family matters. Many attractions have height minimums—44 inches for Space Mountain, 40 for Big Thunder Mountain Railroad and Splash Mountain; 38 for the Seven Dwarfs Mine Train; 35 for Barnstormer. Children need to be 54 inches tall to drive a Tomorrowland Speedway car; 32 to ride in one. Stitch's Great Escape has a height minimum of 40 inches. Except for the Speedway, all of these attractions could frighten children. Others that could: Astro Orbiter (high, tilted flight); The Haunted Mansion (dark ominous atmosphere, some screams, pop-up heads); and Pirates of the Caribbean (dark, short drop, realistic cannon battle, simulated fire).

If it rains. Ducking out of the rain is pretty easy, as stores and fast-food spots line most walkways. Big Thunder Mountain Railroad and the Seven Dwarfs Mine Train close when it rains, and parades, street parties, outdoor shows and fireworks can be shortened or cancelled. Eleven attractions close when lightning is in the area—Astro Orbiter, Dumbo the Flying Elephant, Jungle Cruise, Liberty Square Riverboat, Magic Carpets of Aladdin, Main Street Vehicles, Splash Mountain, Swiss Family Treehouse, the Tomorrowland Speedway, Tom Sawyer Island and the Walt Disney World Railroad.

Fantasyland represents Europe... for the most part. Its Storybook Circus area is set in a small American town, hosting a traveling show during the 1940s.

Fun finds and Hidden Mickeys.

Many things are scattered throughout the park's grounds, shops and eateries: *Main Street U.S.A.:* ❶ "Well, howdy!" a statue of Goofy says every 30 seconds, on a bench in front of Tony's Town Square Restaurant. ❷ The stars of 1955's "Lady and the Tramp" have put their paw prints in the sidewalk in front of the restaurant's patio. ❸ Inside Tony's, a window in the back right corner looks into the alley where the movie's iconic "spaghetti kiss" took place. ❹ A singer and dancer can be heard from two Center Street windows marked "Voice and Singing Private Lessons" and "Music and Dance Lessons, Ballet, Tap & Waltz." *Liberty Square:* Streams of brown pavement symbolize the sewage that often flowed down 18th-century streets. ❺ A 1987 cast of the Liberty Bell sits across from the Hall of Presidents. ❻ Two lanterns in a Hall of Presidents window facing The Haunted Mansion recall the 1860 Longfellow poem "Paul Revere's Ride." *Fantasyland:* ❼ In the mosaic in the castle breezeway, stepsister Drizella's face is green with envy, stepsister Anastasia's is red with anger. ❽ Cinderella's wishing well is to the right of the castle, on a walkway that leads to Tomorrowland. ❾ A statue of her stands in a small fountain behind the castle to the left. Thanks to a sketch of a crown on the wall behind it, toddlers who stand in front of the fountain see the princess wearing her crown. ❿ Luggage carts outside the Storybook Circus restroom include bags for Hyacinth Hippo from 1940's "Fantasia" ⓫ the Big Bad Wolf and ⓬ Red's Amazing Juggling Unicycles, referencing Pixar's 1987 short "Red's Dream," about a red unicycle ridden by a circus clown as part of a juggling act. ⓭ Another bag is marked "Melody Time brand Brass Horns," a reference to Disney's 1948 animated movie "Melody Time." ⓮ Hat boxes are from Ten Schillings and Sixpence Ltd., a nod to the number on the Mad Hatter's hat brim in the 1951 movie "Alice in Wonderland." *Hidden Mickeys:* Landscape, restaurant and shop Mickeys can be found ⓯ in Tony's Town Square restaurant, as bread loaves in a basket on a server; ⓰ on the bridge to Adventureland, as white flowers on the first shield on both sides; ⓱ in the Columbia Harbour House restaurant, as circular wall maps in a room across from the order counter; ⓲ on Gaston's statue in front of his tavern, formed by impressions in the rock below his left leg near the water line; ⓳ in a mural inside Mickey's Star Traders as loops of a highway, train headlights, glass domes, satellite dishes, clear domes covering a city and Mickey ears on top of two windows.

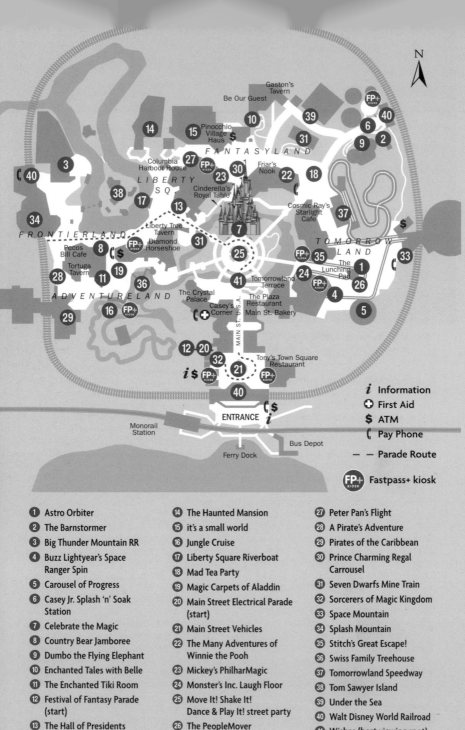

N

Gaston's Tavern

Be Our Guest

Pinocchio Village Haus

Columbia Harbour House

FANTASYLAND

LIBERTY SQ.

Friar's Nook

Cinderella's Royal Table

FRONTIERLAND

Liberty Tree Tavern

Diamond Horseshoe

Pecos Bill Cafe

Tortuga Tavern

ADVENTURELAND

Cosmic Ray's Starlight Cafe

TOMORROWLAND

The Lunching Pad

Tomorrowland Terrace

The Crystal Palace

The Plaza Restaurant
Main St. Bakery

Casey's Corner

MAIN ST. U.S.A.

Tony's Town Square Restaurant

i **$**

ENTRANCE

Monorail Station

Bus Depot

Ferry Dock

i Information

✚ First Aid

$ ATM

℄ Pay Phone

— — Parade Route

FP+ Fastpass+ kiosk

1. Astro Orbiter
2. The Barnstormer
3. Big Thunder Mountain RR
4. Buzz Lightyear's Space Ranger Spin
5. Carousel of Progress
6. Casey Jr. Splash 'n' Soak Station
7. Celebrate the Magic
8. Country Bear Jamboree
9. Dumbo the Flying Elephant
10. Enchanted Tales with Belle
11. The Enchanted Tiki Room
12. Festival of Fantasy Parade (start)
13. The Hall of Presidents
14. The Haunted Mansion
15. it's a small world
16. Jungle Cruise
17. Liberty Square Riverboat
18. Mad Tea Party
19. Magic Carpets of Aladdin
20. Main Street Electrical Parade (start)
21. Main Street Vehicles
22. The Many Adventures of Winnie the Pooh
23. Mickey's PhilharMagic
24. Monster's Inc. Laugh Floor
25. Move It! Shake It! Dance & Play It! street party
26. The PeopleMover
27. Peter Pan's Flight
28. A Pirate's Adventure
29. Pirates of the Caribbean
30. Prince Charming Regal Carrousel
31. Seven Dwarfs Mine Train
32. Sorcerers of Magic Kingdom
33. Space Mountain
34. Splash Mountain
35. Stitch's Great Escape!
36. Swiss Family Treehouse
37. Tomorrowland Speedway
38. Tom Sawyer Island
39. Under the Sea
40. Walt Disney World Railroad
41. Wishes (best viewing spot)

Cool characters. The park has three indoor character-greeting spots: Main Street U.S.A.'s Town Square Theater, and Fantasyland's Princess Fairytale Hall and Pete's Silly Sideshow.

Know before you go. Need cash? A stroller? Help with MyMagic+? Read on:

ATMs. The park has five: At the entrance by the lockers, at City Hall, in the breezeway between Adventureland and Frontierland, near the Pinocchio Village Haus restroom and inside the Tomorrowland arcade.

Baby Care Center. To the left of the Crystal Palace on Main Street U.S.A., this indoor spot has changing rooms, nursing areas, a microwave and playroom. It sells diapers, formula, pacifiers and over-the-counter meds.

Electrical Water Pageant. When the park is open late, this classic Seven Seas Lagoon light parade passes in front of it at 10:20 p.m.

FastPass+ kiosks. Cast members help you book Fastpasses at City Hall and Town Square Theater (Main Street U.S.A.), Jungle Cruise and the Adventureland breezeway (Adventureland); near Buzz Lightyear's Space Ranger Spin and Stitch's Great Escape (Tomorrowland) and Mickey's PhilharMagic and Pete's Silly Sideshow (Fantasyland).

First aid. By the Baby Care Center, nurses treat minor issues, call EMTs for serious ones.

Guest Relations. Cast members answer questions, make reservations, exchange currency, hand out maps and times guides for all parks, and store items found in the park that day. At walk-up windows outside the park entrance on the right, and inside City Hall on Town Square .

Locker rentals. Just inside the park on the right ($7 a day, $5 deposit).

MyMagic+ Service Center. Where to get help with the My Disney Experience website and app, MagicBands and the FastPass+ service. Town Square Theater.

Package pickup. Anything you buy in the park can be sent to the park entrance for you to pick up later at no charge. Allow three hours. Packages can also be delivered to Disney hotels or shipped nationally.

Parking. $17 a day per car. Free for Disney hotel guests and annual passholders.

Stroller rentals. Just inside the park entrance on the right, the Stroller Shop has single strollers for $15 a day ($13 length of stay), doubles for $31 ($27 length of stay). Get replacements at the Trading Post in Frontierland or the Tomorrowland Arcade.

Disney transportation. Buses serve theme parks, hotels and Blizzard Beach. Monorail s serve Epcot and the Contemporary, Grand Floridian and Polynesian Village hotels. Boats serve Ft. Wilderness, the Grand Floridian, Polynesian Village and Wilderness Lodge.

Wheelchair and ECV rentals. Chairs are $12 a day ($10 length of stay), scooters $50 a day (with a $20 deposit). At the Stroller Shop.

Attractions at a Glance

Five-star attractions ★★★★★

The Barnstormer. ✔ FastPass+ Zippy kiddie coaster is not threatening. Min. height 35 in. Fantasyland, Storybook Circus.

Big Thunder Mountain Railroad. ✔ FastPass+ Outdoor coaster twists and turns through mountains and a mining town. No steep drops. Min. height 40 in. Frontierland.

Disney's Festival of Fantasy Parade. ✔ FastPass+ New in 2014, creative procession stars "Sleeping Beauty" villain Maleficent as fire-breathing dragon. Travels Frontierland, Liberty Square, Main Street U.S.A.

Dumbo the Flying Elephant. ✔ FastPass+ Two-seat baby elephants circle. Indoor playground queue. Fantasyland, Storybook Circus.

The Hall of Presidents. ✔ FastPass+ A widescreen film is followed by robotic versions of all U.S. presidents. Washington, Obama speak. Liberty Square.

The Haunted Mansion. ✔ FastPass+ "Doom buggies" tour ghostly retirement home. Silly spooky. Liberty Square.

It's a Small World. ✔ FastPass+ Dark gentle ride starring singing dolls and whimsical animals tours world cultures. Fantasyland, Castle Courtyard.

Mickey's PhilharMagic. ✔ FastPass+ Donald Duck stumbles through classic Disney films in this delightful 3-D movie. Fantasyland, Castle Courtyard.

Peter Pan's Flight. ✔ FastPass+ Vintage dark ride has aerial views of London, Never Land. Fantasyland, Castle Courtyard.

Prince Charming Regal Carrousel. ✔ Pretty canopy-covered antique merry-go-round. Fantasyland, Castle Courtyard.

Pirates of the Caribbean. ✔ FastPass+ Classic dark indoor boat ride is filled with rowdy pirates. Adventureland.

Space Mountain. ✔ FastPass+ The world's first indoor roller coaster is very dark, simulates space flight. Unexpected drops. Min. height 44 in. Tomorrowland.

Wishes. ✔ FastPass+ Creative, emotional fireworks show launches behind and beside Cinderella Castle; syncs with music.

Four-star attractions ★★★★

Astro Orbiter. ✔ Elevated hub-and-spoke rockets circle at a 45-degree angle. Lousy long queue. Tomorrowland.

Enchanted Tales with Belle. ✔ FastPass+ Volunteers help "Beauty and Beast" heroine tell her story. Fantasyland, Enchanted Forest.

Casey Jr Splash 'n' Soak Station. Splash zone with the "Dumbo" circus train and animals. Fantasyland, Storybook Circus.

Mad Tea Party. ✔ FastPass+ Outdoor spinning teacups are covered with a canopy. Fantasyland, Castle Courtyard.

Main Street Vehicles. ✔ Horse trolleys and motorized vehicles shuttle you up and down Main Street U.S.A.

The Many Adventures of Winnie the Pooh. FastPass+ Indoor dark ride recalls Blustery Day. Fantasyland, Castle Courtyard.

Monsters Inc Laugh Floor. FastPass+ This interactive video improv show uses animated characters. Funny when full. Tomorrowland.

Move It! Shake It! Dance & Play It! Street Party. ✔ Street party with characters, dancers. In front of Cinderella Castle.

Seven Dwarfs Mine Train. FastPass+ A mild indoor–outdoor coaster with swaying cars, Audio-Animatronic dwarfs. Min. height 38 in. Fantasyland, Enchanted Forest.

Swiss Family Treehouse. Climb-thru "Swiss Family Robinson" home. Adventureland.

Three-star attractions ★★★

Buzz Lightyear's Space Ranger Spin. ✔ FastPass+ Dated ride-through shooting gallery uses laser beams. Tomorrowland.

Celebrate the Magic. Creative projected light show onto Cinderella Castle.

The Enchanted Tiki Room. ✔ Vintage Audio-Animatronic revue stars robotic birds, flowers and tikis. Adventureland.

Liberty Square Riverboat. Paddlewheeler circles Tom Sawyer Island. Liberty Square.

Main Street Electrical Parade. FastPass+ Retro night procession has floats, characters in lights. Travels Frontierland, Liberty Square, Main Street U.S.A.

Circus girl. A ride operator controls the action at Dumbo the Flying Elephant. All Disney cast members wear costumes; at Storybook Circus they dress as circus emcees.

Magic Carpets of Aladdin. ✔ FastPass+ Four-seat Dumbo-like ride. Adventureland.

The PeopleMover. ✔ Elevated indoor-outdoor tour of Tomorrowland.

A Pirate's Adventure. Scavenger hunt uses treasure map to trigger hidden special effects in the landscape of Adventureland.

Sorcerers of the Magic Kingdom. ✔ Spell cards vanquish video villains in this scavenger hunt. Sign up on Main Street U.S.A.

Splash Mountain. FastPass+ Soggy flume ride travels indoors and outdoors, passing Audio-Animatronic scenes that tell Brer Rabbit's story, ending in a steep splashdown. Min. height 40 in. Frontierland.

Tom Sawyer Island. A walk-through cave, mine, cavalry fort; little chance to explore off walkways. You get there via raft. Frontierland.

Tomorrowland Speedway. ✔ FastPass+ Kiddie race cars from Yesterdayland are still fun. Tomorrowland.

Walt Disney World Railroad. ✔ Steam train circles the park. Stations at Main Street U.S.A., Frontierland, Fantasyland.

Walt Disney's Carousel of Progress. ✔ Audio-Animatronics stage show takes a robotic family through the ages as they extoll the joys of electricity. A five-star General Electric show in 1964, today a lame-yet-fascinating unsponsored historic relic that cries out for restoration. Tomorrowland.

Two-star attractions ★★

Jungle Cruise. ✔ FastPass+ Some skippers are so fun they make this outdoor boat ride a must. Requires you're in on the joke: see how lame we are? Adventureland.

Under the Sea—Journey of the Little Mermaid. FastPass+ Budget slow-moving dark ride goes past scenes from Ariel's story. Children may it, adults will notice its cheapness. Fantasyland, Enchanted Forest.

One-star attractions ★

Country Bear Jamboree. Low-brow robotic bears sing cornball song snippets. Created by legendary Imagineers using hee-haw humor that hasn't aged well. Frontierland.

Stitch's Great Escape. In-the-round show sort of creates the illusion of Experiment 626 skittering around you, definitely makes you forget why you liked "Lilo & Stitch." You wear a harness, and the theater goes dark. Min. height 40 in. Tomorrowland.

© Disney

Be Our Guest. Filled with detail and decorated to the nines, the Beast's castle holds an elaborate restaurant. The food is routine at breakfast and lunch, outstanding at dinner.

Restaurants and food

Below, each Magic Kingdom eatery is rated from one to five stars (★) based on the quality of its food, service and atmosphere. A five-star spot fully lives up to its promise; a one-star place should be avoided. A checkmark (✔) indicates an author personal favorite. The price of a typical adult dinner entree is summarized by dollar signs as follows:

$ less than $10
$$ less than $15
$$$ less than $20
$$$$ less than $25
$$$$$ more than $25

To reserve a table at any Walt Disney World restaurant call Disney at 407-939-3463.

Table service. Almost guaranteed to be both better and more expensive than you expected, the table-service restaurants at Magic Kingdom will irritate your credit card but please your palate. A quick summary: The best food is at Be Our Guest, for dinner. The best value: lunch at Liberty Tree Tavern.

★★★★★ ✔ $$$$$ **Be Our Guest.** Boasting a stunning dining hall that recalls the 1991 movie "Beauty and the Beast," this contemporary French-American restaurant is beautiful, and filled with lovely special effects. A prix-fixe breakfast debuted in 2015; the eatery's fast-food lunch is mostly sandwiches and salads. Dinner is an enchanting experience that features a creative menu, an inspired wine list and impressive service. Some dishes are prepared tableside, and the Beast himself greets guests in a side chamber. Special decor effects add charm throughout the day. *Fantasyland, Enchanted Forest. Breakfast 8 a.m.–10 a.m., $20 (children $13). Lunch 10:30 a.m.–2:30 p.m., $9–$14 (children $7–$8). Dinner 4 p.m.–10 p.m., $18–$33 (children $9–$11). Reservations taken for all meals. Seats 546 for breakfast and lunch, 340 dinner.*

★★★★ $$$$$ **Cinderella's Royal Table.** Snow White, Jasmine and other Disney princesses greet guests at their tables at this regal restaurant, which hides up on the second floor of Magic Kingdom's iconic Cinderella Castle. No one comes for the food; the ridiculously overpriced *prix-fixe* menus offer French-American fare that's worth about half its tab. Instead, the draw here is location, location, location—your child will never forget that you ate inside this world-famous landmark—as well as the bevy of impossibly poised young women who embody their princess roles to perfection.

A best bet. You're almost guaranteed a relaxing, hearty meal at Liberty Tree Tavern, which resembles a Colonial home that's been turned into a restaurant. Best is its ala carte lunch; there's a Thanksgiving-style feast for dinner.

The medieval dining hall seems authentic; its stone walls, sky-high ceiling and stained glass windows fit for royalty. Though the experience may be too corny if you're an adult couple eating on your own, it's a magical moment for many young girls. Unlike the other princesses, Cinderella does not appear in the dining room. She's in the lobby. Note: Cinderella's Royal Table is the toughest restaurant reservation to nab in all of Disney World; its tables often book to capacity 190 days early, on the first day they're available to Disney-hotel guests. Meals are paid for at the time they're reserved. *Cinderella Castle. Breakfast 8:05 a.m.–10:40 a.m., $55 (children $35). Lunch 11:45 a.m.–2:40 p.m., $58 (children $36). Dinner 3:50 p.m.-park close, $68 (children $42). Prices include trinkets for children and a photo of each diner with Cinderella. Seats 184. A Disney Signature Restaurant.*

★★ **$$$$$ Crystal Palace.** Even adorable Winnie the Pooh, Eeyore, Piglet and Tigger can't redeem this character buffet. It's just too crowded, overpriced and loud. Tables are packed together, with little room between them, which makes it a chore to squeeze back and forth to the food lines, where there are decent meats and salads but salty soups and vegetables. High ceilings and marble tabletops make for a pretty decor, but amplify the noise. Characters often can't linger at your table, so when you meet one it's just for a moment. For the most time with them reserve a table for the first or last breakfast seating or the first dinner seating. *Main Street U.S.A. Breakfast 8 a.m.–10:45 a.m., $29 (children $17). Lunch 11:30 a.m.–2:45 p.m., $31 (children $17). Dinner 3:15 p.m.–10 p.m., $44 (children $21). Seats 400.*

★★★★ ✔ **$$$$$ Liberty Tree Tavern.** Hearty comfort food and a cozy atmosphere make this unpretentious New England eatery a relaxing break. Resembling a large, Colonial house, it has six separate little dining rooms, which keeps its noise level low. Despite its name, no liquor flows. Best choice for lunch: the tender pot roast. Dinner is a fixed-price, family-style Thanksgiving feast. Window-side tables overlook the park's parade route. *Lunch 11:30 a.m.–3 p.m., $13–$23 (children $9); Dinner 4 p.m.–park close, $38 (children $19). Seats 250.*

★★★ ✔ **$$$ The Plaza.** The food at this Victorian café screams diner—good hamburgers, sandwiches and sundaes—but the quiet atmosphere fits a more upscale eatery. Carpeted floors, padded wrought-iron chairs and faux-marble tabletops add to the charm. Hand-dipped ice cream treats come from the adjacent parlor. *Main Street U.S.A. 11 a.m.–park close. $12–$19 (children $9). Seats 94.*

NEW! Skipper Canteen. Jungle Cruise skippers are your servers at this new restaurant, which serves "World Famous Jungle Cuisine" in several unique dining rooms, including the crew mess hall and a once-hidden secret meeting area of the Society of Explorers and Adventurers. Run by the Jungle Navigation Company. Adventureland. Opens late 2015.

★★★★ ✔ **$$$$ Tony's Town Square.** Fans of 1955's "Lady and the Tramp" may not recognize this comfortable café as the Tony's from that film—it's not overly themed—but that's about its only weakness. The menu offers generous portions of Italian comfort food; the shrimp scampi has roasted tomatoes. A lovely glass-ceiling solarium can be

In the Big Top. Situated in the center of the Big Top Souvenirs gift shop, Big Top Treats makes mouth-watering concoctions in front of your eyes, including elaborate caramel apples.

too sunny but there are many indoor tables; ask for one by the fountain. The authors eat lunch here often. *Main Street U.S.A. Lunch 11:30 a.m.–2:45 p.m. $13–$22 (children $9). Dinner 4:30 p.m.–park close. $18–$33 (children $9). Seats 286.*

Counter service. The top choice: Columbia Harbour House. Stay away from Pecos Bill's but embrace (if it's open) the little Tortuga Tavern, a spot right around the corner.

★★★ ✔ $ **Casey's Corner.** A recent re-do improved this little hot dog spot by replacing its bleachers and low-res video screen with tables and chairs, creating a dining area that's clean and relatively peaceful. The hot dogs and fries remain the same: decent, satisfying and overpriced. *Main Street U.S.A. $5–$10. 11 a.m.–park close. Seats 48 inside, 80 outside.*

★★★★★ ✔ $ **Columbia Harbour House.** Focused on chicken and seafood, this fresh, healthy eatery is one of Magic Kingdom's gems. Its grilled salmon is as good as fast-food fish gets, served with moist couscous and steamed broccoli. The dinner menu includes a creamy shrimp-and-lobster mac and cheese and a chicken pot pie which tastes nearly homemade, with big chunks of white meat and crisp veggies. Served

all day, a hearty vegetarian chili is a steal at less than $5. The restaurant straddles the border between Liberty Square and Fantasyland; sit upstairs over the walkway to people-watch. *Liberty Square. Lunch $8–$12 (children $5–$6). Dinner $9–$16 (children $5–$6). Seats 593.*

★★★ ✔ $$ **Cosmic Ray's Starlight Cafe.** This sprawling spot has improved over the past few years. Dinner includes a rib-and-rotisseried half-chicken combo with green beans; a condiment bar is expansive. On the downside, the ordering system still requires you to wait in different lines to order different items, the cheap 1970s Six Flags decor still features tiresome robotic lounge singer Sonny Eclipse, and new menu items often focuses on bland choices such as hot dogs. The midday rush is a noisy, crowded madhouse, otherwise the place is calm. *Tomorrowland. $8–$15 (children $5–$6). 10:30 a.m.–park close. Seats 1,162.*

★★★ $ **Diamond Horseshoe.** This old-time saloon and dance hall opens as a restaurant during peak periods, with food from the kitchens of the nearby Liberty Tree Tavern. There's no drinking or dancing, but for Frontierland fast food it can't be beat. *Frontierland. $7–$9 (children $5–$7). Open seasonally. Seats 300.*

★★ $ **Friar's Nook.** It's mostly mac and cheese at this outdoor fast-food window—you can get it on a hot dog, pot roast, a bacon cheeseburger or all by its lonesome, and it's always bland. For breakfast there are equally challenged French toast sticks and sausage dogs. *Fantasyland, Castle Courtyard. $7–$9. Park hours. No seating.*

★★★ ✔ $ **Gaston's Tavern.** Living up to its name in ways that aren't always good, this heavily themed little spot has the mark of its buffoonish he-man owner (the villain of 1991's "Beauty and the Beast") all over it. It uses antlers in all of its decorating, serves beer (or at least a sweet slushy kids' drink that certainly looks like beer) and has as its only entree a pork shank, which unfortunately is just a tasteless hunk of fatty meat. Fans of the film love the decor; few leave without taking a selfie or two in a fireside faux-fur chair. The authors eat here often, not for the food, but because it's the only indoor fast-food spot in the park that's open in the morning and has seats. We order a cinnamon roll, and always ask for a warm one with lots of icing. *Fantasyland, Enchanted Forest. $3–$10. Park hours. Seats 70 inside, 32 outside.*

★★★ $ **The Lunching Pad.** Pricey hot dog creations from walk-up windows. Forget the cost and they're not bad. *Tomorrowland. $8–$9. 11 a.m.–park close. Seats 83 outside.*

★★★ $ **Main Street Bakery.** Reopened in 2013 as a Starbucks, this former Disney-run bakery still has a Disney touch to its decor, but other than that it's the same as any other Starbucks anywhere. Except there's no place to sit, and lines are often ridiculous. *Main Street U.S.A. $4–$5. Park hours. No seating.*

★ $ **Pecos Bill Cafe.** Expect to be disappointed at this uninspired spot, where the focus is on meat—burgers, chicken, pork, ribs, even steak—but not on quality. A toppings bar includes freshly grilled onions and hot faux cheese. Back dining rooms are the quietest. *Frontierland. 10:30 a.m.–park close, $10–$14 (children $5–$6). Seats 1,107.*

★★ $ **Pinocchio Village Haus.** Located right in the middle of Fantasyland just behind Cinderella Castle, this Italian-themed spot is as unreliable as its namesake's ability to tell the truth—sometimes its generous flatbreads are full of sharp flavor; at other times they're barely cooked. Lined with murals that depict scenes from Disney's 1933 movie "Pinocchio," its Old World interior is charming as long as it's vacant; unfortunately the tables are often packed with screaming children. To avoid the ruckus, eat here very early or very late. Nab a window-side table in the far left dining room and you'll look down into the boarding area of It's a Small World *Fantasyland, Castle Courtyard. 10:30 a.m.–park close. $8–10. Seats 400.*

★ $ **Tomorrowland Terrace.** This perfect outdoor location is, over the last few years, being ruined by lousy food. Its menu changes often, but most recently has included a lobster roll with no taste, ho-hum salads with no thought, and pastas that were worse than the frozen ones you can buy at Walmart for $1. *Tomorrowland. $8–$12 (children $5–$6). Open seasonally. Seats 500.*

★★★ ✔ $ **Tortuga Tavern.** Take advantage of the topping bar at this breezy outdoor café and no matter what you get it will be better than anything you could have gotten at the adjacent Pecos Bill Café. Best bets are the burritos, which overflow with quality ingredients and come with a side of delicate cilantro rice. Ask for a complimentary side of salsa when you order; the one from the kitchen is a pico de gallo. The best tables are those on a back patio that's sheltered by tropical foliage. Ambient fiddle music adds some life, as do signs and posters that reveal a back story: the place is run by a teenage girl, Arabella Smith from the young-adult book series "Pirates of the Caribbean: Jack Sparrow." And she has her rules. *Adventureland. $8–$9 (children $5–$6). 11 a.m.–4 p.m. Seats 240, including 12 seats at the bar and seven umbrella-covered tables. Open seasonally.*

Snacks. Creating temptations before your eyes, **Big Top Treats** (★★★★★ ✔) serves up concoctions that are fresher and more varied than those of the similar **Confectionery** near the park entrance. Located in Fantasyland's Storybook Circus inside Big Top Souvenirs, it often sends its bakers strolling through the store with free samples. Guests rave about Big Top's chocolate-covered bananas; the authors love the elaborate caramel apples and the caramel corn, especially when it's fresh. You can sit under an outdoor tent nearby.

Other worthwhile Magic Kingdom treats include the Dole Whip soft-serve at **Aloha Isle** (★★★) in Adventureland, the hand-dipped real ice cream at the **Plaza Ice Cream Parlor** (★★★) on Main Street U.S.A., and the waffles and funnel cakes at **Sleepy Hollow** ★★★★ in Liberty Square.

See also **Restaurant Policies** in the chapter **Walt Disney World A–Z.**

Friends Jennifer and Jenny wear personalized Mickey Mouse and Minnie Mouse ear hats, an iconic park souvenir. You'll find them at the Chapeau and Big Top Souvenirs.

Shops and salons

It's not all Mickey Mouse stuff. Many Magic Kingdom stores offer quality merchandise that goes beyond typical theme-park items. The best are summarized below. Stores are rated from one to five stars (★) based on the quality of their merchandise, service and atmosphere; one- and two-star stores are not listed. A checkmark (✔) indicates that the store is one of the authors' personal favorites.

★★★★ **Bibbidi Bobbidi Boutique.** If your little girl is into the princess look you'll be tempted to spend a good chunk of her college savings at this makeover salon. Depending on how much you'd like to draw out of that account, she can get her hair and nails done, her cheeks and lips made up, a princess costume and sash, even a photo session. The room is a shrine to princess glamour. Elaborate tiaras sparkle in glass domes; frothy princess gowns hang on the walls as if they're works of art. Little boys can get their hair glittered and spiked; those who do get a toy sword and shield. *Girls $55–$190 and up; boys $16. Ages 3–12. 8 a.m.–7 p.m.; allow 30–60 minutes. Reservations: 407-939-7895 available 6 months in advance. Inside Cinderella Castle.*

★★★★★ ✔ **Big Top Souvenirs.** A hidden oasis at the back of Fantasyland, this giant circus tent offers a huge variety of apparel, plush, toys and dolls; features a watch-them-make-it sweet shop right in the middle; and has a terrific atmosphere—cast members often juggle scarves, spin plates or play games with kids as they work the floor, and sometimes give away candy samples. Merchandise includes Storybook Circus souvenirs; a side station embroiders Mickey ear hats while you wait. The store's heavenly aroma, jaunty circus music and cool air-conditioning tempt you to stay forever. Disney geeks will drool over hidden tributes to obscure Disney characters such as Salty the Seal. *Storybook Circus, Fantasyland.*

★★★ **Bonjour Village Gifts.** Cozy but charmless, this upscale boutique sells china, housewares and other high-end stuff themed to the 1991 Disney film "Beauty and the Beast" that you won't find anywhere else. Stone arches and a wood-beamed ceiling add a rustic feel. *Fantasyland.*

★★★★ **Castle Couture.** Wanna-be princesses squeal over the sparkly ball gowns and costumes at this cramped little shop, and tap out their parents' credit cards as they insist on all the accessories Disney ruthlessly displays right alongside the outfits — tiaras, white gloves, plastic high heels, even faux fur stoles. Have a boy? Rest easy. There's almost nothing for princes. The store is supposedly the dressmaker's shop for the adjacent castle's royalty; sewing materials fill the top shelves. A hidden antechamber serves as a Photopass studio for little princesses, though anyone who asks can have their picture taken in it at no extra charge. A professional backdrop and overhead soft boxes help create a perfect portrait. *Directly behind Cinderella Castle, Castle Courtyard.*

★★★ **The Emporium.** Though it looks like a line of little stores from the outside, The Emporium is really one big long shop that takes up nearly the entire left side of Main Street. Inside is a huge selection of all kinds of merchandise; it's Magic Kingdom's biggest store, with a little of everything but unfortunately few items that are all that special. *Main Street U.S.A.*

★★★ ✓ **Fantasy Faire.** An angry Donald Duck glares down at you from the ceiling of this small store; maybe he's mad because a slew of parked strollers usually blocks its entrance and he hates seeing the place empty, which it often is. Underneath him are some unique Donald T-shirts (an author favorite) and impulse items, as well as Mickey Mouse ear hats. Orchestral ambient music adds to a relaxing atmosphere. *At the exit to Mickey's PhilharMagic, Fantasyland.*

★★★★★ ✓ **Harmony Barber Shop.** This iconic old-fashioned barber shop specializes in a child's first haircut, with a package that includes a commemorative pair of Mickey ears and a certificate. Other services include adult cuts and beard and moustache trims. There's no shampooing; come with clean dry hair. The Dapper Dans sometimes appear; a potbelly stove adds to the illusion of timelessness, as does the pleasant unhurried banter of your barber. *Between the Car Barn and the Emporium, Town Square, Main Street U.S.A. 9 a.m.–5 p.m. First haircuts $19, other services $11–$19. Reservations at 407-939-7529. Walk-ins welcome. Refurbished and redecorated in 2015.*

★★★★ ✓ **Hundred Acre Goods.** Head to this teeny shop for cute-as-a-button Pooh apparel, plush and toys for infants and preschoolers. A cute decor features giant storybook pages on the walls and ceiling; shelves appear to be dripping honey onto the floor. The store is almost always crowded; Disney's Pooh ride exits into it. *At The Many Adventures of Winnie the Pooh, Fantasyland.*

★★★★ ✓ **Pirate's Bazaar.** This sprawling open-air shop offers pirate booty galore, including fashion apparel, toys and a bunch of Jake and the Never Land Pirates stuff. *At exit to Pirates of the Caribbean, Adventureland.*

NEW! ★★★★★ ✓ **Memento Mori.** You won't find princess dresses here; this spooky shop is completely dedicated to The Haunted Mansion. Shelves are packed with over 100 items inspired by the attraction, including action figures of its famous hitchhiking ghosts, tombstone-shaped coasters and fashion apparel inspired by its demonic wallpaper. Visitors can also purchase ghostly portraits of themselves that are taken in a small Spirit Photography studio. The shop is intended to be the former home of the Haunted Mansion's spiritualist Madam Leota; her spirit visits from time to time, causing eerie effects. *At the Haunted Mansion, Liberty Square.*

★★★★ ✓ **Pirates League.** This salon transforms adults and children into swashbucklers, swashbucklerettes and mermaids. Packages can include facial effects, a reversible bandana, a false earring and eye patch, a sword, a temporary tattoo, a pirate coin necklace, an official pirate name and a personalized oath. Costumes, headwear and photo packages are also available. Participants can join an Adventureland Pirate Parade daily at 4 p.m. *Packages $30–$75. Ages 3 and up. At the exit of Pirates of the Caribbean. Reservations up to 180 days in advance: 407-939-2739.*

★★★★ ✓ **Sir Mickey's.** Despite its name, this longtime menswear shop has responded to the opening of the Princess Fairytale Hall character spot next door by dumping its guy gear and going female. Nearly the entire store is filled with clothing for girls and women, most of it themed to Disney princesses, much of it unexpectedly creative. Fashion T-shirts feature haughty sketches of Ariel, Aurora and other Disney teen queens as grown women; the store's infant wear is often both adorable and classy. The holdover male decor is based on two classic cartoons: "The Brave Little Tailor" and "Mickey and the Beanstalk." Look around to see tailoring references, large vines and the "Beanstalk" giant peeking in from outside. *Directly behind Cinderella Castle, Castle Courtyard.*

★★★★ **Ye Olde Christmas Shoppe.** This cute spot sells Christmas items year-round, with oodles of ornaments, nutcrackers, stockings and other festive gear. *Liberty Square.*

See also **Shopping** in the chapter **Walt Disney World A–Z.**

A steam engine pulls an open-air passenger train around Magic Kingdom. The park uses four such locomotives, all of which were built between 1916 and 1928.

Walt Disney World Railroad

Smart steam-train rides are marred by dopey details

★★★ ✔ A relaxing way to get around Magic Kingdom, this authentic narrow-gauge railroad circles the park. Antique steam locomotives pull street-trolley passenger cars down a track lined with bamboo, palms, pines and live oaks. Two or three trains run continuously, so there's rarely much of a wait.

It's a nice ride. You're out of the sun, there's a nice breeze and unlike walking you can't get lost; hop on a train at Frontierland and you will go directly to Dumbo and his circus even if you have no idea how to get there. But it's not perfect; a hokey pre-recorded narrator drops every "G" as if he's ridin' the rails at Dollywood. Alongside the track, fake alligators and deer never have a hankerin' to move.

Tips. *When to go:* Anytime. *Where to sit:* On the right for the best views, though riders on the left sometimes spot live alligators in a canal behind Fantasyland.

Fun facts. ❶ Built by Baldwin Locomotive Works of Philadelphia between 1916 and 1928, the four engines hauled passengers, jute, sisal and sugar cane for the United Railway of the Yucatán for decades. ❷ They take on water at the Fantasyland station every third loop, and get serviced every few hours.

Fun finds. ❶ Mutoscopes and a few other antique amusements line the waiting room of the Main Street station; some still work.

Key facts. *Best for:* All ages. *Duration:* 20-min. round trip (1.5 miles). *Capacity:* 360. *Queues:* Outdoor, covered. *Operating hours:* Idle during parades, fireworks. *Weather issues:* Closed during thunderstorms. *Debuted:* 1971. *Access:* Guests may stay in wheelchairs, ECVs. No Disney strollers. *Disability services:* Handheld captioning. *Location:* Stations at Main Street U.S.A., Frontierland, Fantasyland.

Average wait times

9am	10am	11am	Noon	1pm	2pm	3pm	4pm	5pm	6pm	7pm	8pm	9pm
5m	5m	5m	5m	5m	5m	5m	5m	5m	5m	5m	5m	5m

Hitched to his Main Street trolley, 'Queasy' the Clydesdale waits for the park to open. Once his trolley fills with riders, he'll pull it down a track embedded in the pavement.

Main Street Vehicles

Just hop on one of these quaint replicas and feel special

★★★★ ✓ It's too bad they're out only in the mornings, because these old-fashioned vehicles are a true Disney treasure. Shuttling passengers either way between Town Square and Cinderella Castle, they offer simple old-school fun. Just hop on and off you go… no wait, Fastpass or extra charge required.

Riding one gives you a taste of a bygone era. The vehicles look completely authentic, with their uncushioned metal dashes, worn leather and wood benches, and their sounds only reinforce that notion. Bells ding. Engines chug. Horns honk. Horses clop.

You also feel special. As you are driven down Main Street the masses part for you, then smile and wave to you as you pass.

The fleet consists of four horse trolleys, three horseless carriages, two jitneys, a miniature fire truck and a double-decker bus. The trolley runs on a track embedded in the street; its driver operates a set of reins, a brake pedal and a foot bell. The Dapper Dans barbershop quartet often hop on and sing.

Tips. *When to go:* Immediately after you enter the park. *Where to sit:* Up front, for the best view and to chat with your driver. *For families:* Ask ahead of time and your child might be able to honk a horn, ring the trolley's bell or crank the fire truck's siren.

Fun facts. ❶ Built for Disney, the vehicles debuted at Magic Kingdom the day it opened. ❷ They run on natural gas. ❸ License plates are dated "1915," the first year Florida issued automobile tags.

Key facts. *Best for:* All ages. *Duration:* 3–4 min. *Capacity:* 6–40 depending on vehicle. *Operating hours:* Typically park open—late morning. *Weather issues:* Closed during rain. *Debuted:* 1971. *Access:* Must be ambulatory. *Location:* Main Street U.S.A.

Average wait times

9am	10am	11am	Noon	1pm	2pm	3pm	4pm	5pm	6pm	7pm	8pm	9pm
0m	0m	0m	0m	n/a	n/a	n/a	n/a	n/a	n/a	n/a	n/a	n/a

Two scavenger hunts. Top row: Sorcerers of the Magic Kingdom players sign up on Main Street U.S.A., then search for hidden videos. Above row: Odd finds on A Pirate's Adventure.

Magic Kingdom interactive games

Easy-to-play adventures feature high-tech effects

★★★ ✔ **Sorcerers of the Magic Kingdom.** You play this game on hidden video screens throughout the park. Recruited by Merlin the Magician (from 1963's "The Sword in the Stone"), you stop Hades (1997's "Hercules") from making Magic Kingdom his summer home. You do it by casting spells on Disney villains, who appear on the screens and react when you hold up an RFID-embedded card, a packet of which you get when you sign up. Play the game long enough (think a full day) and you'll send Hades back to H-E-double-hockey-sticks. The cards are free, and Pokémon quality. The video animation, however, is beneath Disney's standards, and some characters don't have their well-known voices.

★★★ **A Pirate's Adventure.** You trigger special effects throughout Adventureland in this game, as you use a treasure map to help Capt. Jack Sparrow lift a curse. There's never much of a line to play, and the effects are pretty cool—you may fire a cannon, or raise a sunken skeleton out of its water. But there are no cards to collect.

Tips. *Sorcerers:* Get your cards as soon as you enter the park, while it's convenient. Play the game as it fits into your attraction schedule. *A Pirate's Adventure:* Play the game during the morning or late afternoon, when the weather is relatively cool. If you get lost, touching your MagicBand to any game station will tell you where you should be.

Key facts. *Best for:* Children. *Duration:* Allow 5 min. per portal or effect. *Debuted:* Sorcerers: 2012, Pirate's Adventure 2013. *Access:* Guests may stay in wheelchairs, ECVs. *Disability services:* Sorcerers: Video captioning. *Sign-up location:* Sorcerers: Main Street firehouse. Pirate's Adventure: Next to Pirates of the Caribbean, Adventureland.

Average wait times

9am	10am	11am	Noon	1pm	2pm	3pm	4pm	5pm	6pm	7pm	8pm	9pm
5m	15m	15m	20m	10m	10m	5m	5m	5m	5m	5m	5m	5m

A family crosses a suspension bridge on their way to the Swiss Family Treehouse, an improvised home made from items scavenged from a shipwreck.

Swiss Family Treehouse

Dated but detailed walk-through home takes a tiring trek

★★★★ You'll climb six stories at this outdoor attraction, a self-guided walking tour through the improvised home of a shipwrecked father, mother and three sons. Various rooms display ingenious contraptions (a water-wheel system lifts bamboo buckets, a barrel in the kitchen cools a refrigerator) but have no interactive elements. The tree's 62 steps can challenge overweight adults, but offer healthy kids an easy way to burn off energy.

Though the tree pales as an attraction based on modern standards, from a 1960s perspective it's pretty cool. Remnants of the ship are everywhere, and include its lantern, log book and captain's wheel. Ropes from the ship appear to hold the home together, while its rooms adapt found objects into everyday effects. Giant clamshells form sink basins.

Tip. *When to go:* At night, when the heat's died off and the tree looks the most realistic.

Fun facts. ❶ Based on a banyan tree—a tropical fig that grows aerial roots to support its outlying branches—the 200-ton, 60-foot-tall, 90-foot-wide *Disneyodendron eximus* ("out-of-the-ordinary Disney tree") is made of concrete, stucco and steel. ❷ Its 330,000 leaves are polyethylene, but its Spanish moss is real, as are its lush surroundings.

Fun finds. ❶ There's a bible in the living room (one of the few in Disney attractions, a sticking point for some), with ❷ some brandy right above it. ❸ Wild hummingbirds and butterflies flutter among the flowers; ❹ huge bullfrogs live under the tree's bridges.

Key facts. *Best for:* Children. *Duration:* Unlimited, allow 20 min. *Capacity:* 300. *Queue:* Outdoor, shaded. *Operating hours:* Park hours. *Debuted:* 1971 (Disneyland 1962). *Access:* Guests must be ambulatory to enter. *Location:* Adventureland.

Average wait times

9am	10am	11am	Noon	1pm	2pm	3pm	4pm	5pm	6pm	7pm	8pm	9pm
0m	0m	0m	0m	0m	0m	0m	0m	0m	0m	0m	0m	0m

"If you want to take pictures go ahead," Jungle Cruise skippers tell guests as they pass a pool of playful pachyderms. "All the elephants have their trunks on."

Jungle Cruise

With the right skipper, this tropical boat ride is hilarious

★★ ✔ **FastPass+** Elephants squirt water from their trunks, headhunters shake their spears, hungry hippos threaten to attack... and they're all fodder for jokes on this ancient outdoor boat ride, as a crazed skipper rattles off corny puns and one-liners at every turn. You tour four mighty rivers: the Amazon, Congo, Nile and Mekong. Is it worth your time? If you get a good skipper, yes.

Tips. *When to go:* At night. The line might be shorter and the boat's spotlight adds to the fun. *Where to sit:* Ask to sit on the left for the best views, ideally next to the skipper. *For families:* Ask nicely as you board and your child may be able to "steer" the boat.

Fun facts. ❶ The water is dyed its murky color. **❷** The boats are on a track; skippers control their speed but not their course.

Fun finds and Hidden Mickeys. ❶ A sign in the queue honors the Jungle Cruise

company's latest Employee of the Month: E.L. O'Fevre. **❷** Along the covered exitway, a list of missing persons includes "Ilene Dover" followed by "Ann Fellen." **❸** The queue radio plays Cole Porter's 1935 hit tune "You're the Top," which includes the lyrics *"you're a Bendel bonnet, a Shakespeare sonnet, you're Mickey Mouse!"* **❹** Three-circle Mickey shapes hide as lichen on the side of a tree across from the boarding dock and **❺** on the ride on the side of a crashed plane between and below its windows.

Key facts. *Best for:* All ages. *Duration:* 10 min. *Capacity:* 310. *Queue:* Outdoor, covered. *Operating hours:* Park hours. *Weather issues:* Closed during thunderstorms. *Debuted:* 1971 (Disneyland 1955). *Access:* Guests may remain in wheelchairs, ECVs. *Disability services:* Assistive listening, handheld captioning. *Location:* Adventureland.

Average wait times

9am	10am	11am	Noon	1pm	2pm	3pm	4pm	5pm	6pm	7pm	8pm	9pm
5m	20m	35m	45m	40m	30m	20m	40m	65m	25m	25m	20m	30m

58 THE COMPLETE WALT DISNEY WORLD 2016

Couples sit side-by-side and families of four ride together on Magic Carpets of Aladdin, a carnival-style ride that circles in a tropical setting.

Magic Carpets of Aladdin

Colorful carnival ride is simple, satisfying

★★★ ✔ FastPass+ Inspired by Disney's 1992 animated feature "Aladdin," this carnival-style hub-and-spoke ride is a fun diversion. Circling around a giant genie bottle, guests fly magic carpets which climb, dip and dive at their command. It's a nice use of 90 seconds, especially early in the morning or late at night when its waiting line is short.

Just another Dumbo? Not really. Each carpet seats four, not two, so small families can ride together. The carpets ride rougher than Dumbo, too. Tall palms lend a tropical air.

Tips. *When to go:* At night, when lines are short and the weather cool. *Where to sit:* In front, so you can control the height of your carpet. The back seat controls the pitch, but its "magic scarab" rarely works. *While you fly:* Flp the front-seat lever up and down to bounce your carpet. Fly about halfway up to be in the line of fire of a spitting golden camel.

Fun finds and Hidden Mickeys. ❶ The carpets travel over a pool of water (little camel heads drool into it) so as you fly you can look down at your reflection just as Aladdin and Jasmine do in the film. ❷ On the ride's genie-bottle hub, cart-wheeling images of Aladdin's pet monkey Abu recall early zoetrope animation. ❸ A second spitting camel targets passersby from behind the ride's sign. ❹ Mickey's three-circle shape appears twice in the surrounding walkway, behind the camel statue that faces the ride on two yellow stones of a faded four-piece bracelet and ❺ nearby on a small teardrop-shaped silver charm.

Key facts. *Best for:* Children, couples. *Duration:* 90 seconds. *Capacity:* 64. *Queue:* Outdoor, shaded. *Operating hours:* Park hours. *Weather issues:* Closed during thunderstorms. *Debuted:* 2001. *Access:* ECV users must transfer. *Location:* Adventureland.

Average wait times

9am	10am	11am	Noon	1pm	2pm	3pm	4pm	5pm	6pm	7pm	8pm	9pm
10m	10m	15m	30m	30m	35m	20m	25m	30m	25m	20m	15m	10m

A **vintage show** created in 1963, The Enchanted Tiki Room was designed during the height of "Tiki culture," an American fantasy of Polynesian food, drinks and style.

Walt Disney's Enchanted Tiki Room

Woefully dated birds, flowers, tikis somehow still enchant

★★★ ✔ "All the birds sing words and the flowers croon" in this sweet yet woefully dated musical revue, a 1960s Disney icon which stars over 200 robotic birds, flowers and carved tikis. Young children may like the show's vintage songs and corny jokes; others will yawn at its slow pace. The performance takes place in-the-round in an air-conditioned theater. You sit on a bench.

Perched above the audience, birds sing "Let's All Sing Like the Birdies Sing," "The Hawaiian War Chant" and "The Tiki, Tiki, Tiki Room." Flowers warble from hanging baskets; tiki statues come to life on the walls. Hosting the revue are four macaws—German Fritz, Mexican José, Irish Michael and French Pierre—all stereotyped beyond anything that would be created today: the show begins with José waking up and complaining that "my siestas are getting *chorter* and *chorter*."

Two toucans recount how they migrated to the Tiki Room from the Jungle Cruise in the show's vintage preshow, which takes place alongside the outdoor waiting area. As Claude—voiced by Sebastian Cabot, Mr. French the butler on the 1960s sitcom "Family Affair"—tells the story, his friend Clyde supplies the sounds of an elephant, lion and lurking crocodile ("Lurk! Lurk!").

Disney's first robots. Conceived by Walt Disney as a restaurant with a coffee bar in its center, the Tiki Room became a show before it debuted at California's Disneyland in 1963. Its new Audio-Animatronics technology stunned audiences, as hundreds of tiny movements in its birds, flowers, and tiki idols were synchronized to its audio, and triggered by hidden pneumatic valves that opened and closed at the perfect times—creating a life-like effect that seemed almost real.

Average wait times

9am	10am	11am	Noon	1pm	2pm	3pm	4pm	5pm	6pm	7pm	8pm	9pm
n/a	5m	5m	5m	5m	5m	5m	5m	5m	5m	5m	5m	5m

© Disney

Walt Disney poses inside Disneyland's The Enchanted Tiki Room in 1963. The attraction featured Disney's first Audio-Animatronics figures.

Hunky tuna tostada. A duplicate version opened at Walt Disney World in 1971. The Disney company redid it in 1998, creating a sarcastic storyline starring hornbill Zazu from 1994's "The Lion King" and parrot Iago from 1992's "Aladdin" (who misinterprets a reference to *hakuna matata*). In 2011 Disney restored the show to a shorter version of the original, with modern lighting and audio.

Tips. *When to go:* In the afternoon when other attractions have long lines, or during a rain. There's never a crowd. *Where to sit:* Halfway down on the left side of the room; the host birds will often face you. Kids may like to sit in a back corner to be near the tikis.

Fun fact. ❶ The show's bird calls and whistles were all voiced by one man. A. Purvis Pullen was also the voice of the birds in Disney's 1937 movie "Snow White and the Seven Dwarfs" as well as those in 1959's "Sleeping Beauty," Cheetah the chimp in the 1930s Johnny Weissmuller Tarzan films and Bonzo the chimp in the 1951 Ronald Reagan flick "Bedtime for Bonzo." Using the stage name Dr. Horatio Q. Birdbath, he performed with novelty band Spike Jones and His City Slickers, providing its bird calls and dog barks. Despite all that, Pullen called his Tiki Room work "my favorite accomplishment... The one that's gonna last."

Fun finds and Hidden Mickeys. ❶ José asks "I wonder what happened to Rosita?" as female cockatoos start to warble "Let's All Sing Like the Birdies Sing," though a bird with that name has never been in the show. ❷ During that song, the four host macaws do impressions of vintage crooners Louis Armstrong, Maurice Chevalier, Bing Crosby and Jimmy Durante. ❸ The *"phew! phew!"* sounds of the pressurized air that animates the birds and flowers are easy to hear. Though modern Audio-Animatronic figures use hydraulic oil-filled valves, those in the Tiki Room still use air valves, to ensure they don't leak on their audience. ❹ Mickey's shape hides on the entrance doors, as 2-inch berries on a stem underneath a bird's tail, 4 feet off the ground.

Key facts. *Best for:* Young children, seniors, Disney enthusiasts. *Duration:* 13 min. *Capacity:* 250. *Queue:* Outdoor, shaded. *Fear factor:* A simulated thunderstorm outside the room's "windows" seems real and can startle timid toddlers. *Operating hours:* Typically opens at 10 a.m. *Debuted:* 1971 (Disneyland 1963); updated 1998, 2011. *Health advisories:* None. *Access:* Guests may remain in wheelchairs, ECVs. *Disability services:* Audio Description, assistive listening, hand-held captioning. *Location:* Adventureland.

The exterior of Disney's Pirates of the Caribbean attraction recalls an actual Spanish fort—El Morro, a 16th-century fortress in San Juan, Puerto Rico.

Pirates of the Caribbean

Immersive slow boat ride has plundering, plastered pirates

★★★★★ ✔ FastPass+ Drunk pirates "pillage and plunder... rifle and loot... kidnap and ravage and don't give a hoot" in this rowdy, rum-soaked attraction, a dark indoor boat ride which takes you through the robotic ransacking of a Spanish port. There's plenty to look at, as you pass dozens of vignettes and sight gags. Special effects simulate fire, lightning, wind and, best of all, splashing cannon balls. The inspiration for the "Pirates of the Caribbean" movies, the ride keeps a lightweight tone; its pirates have such caricatured features they seem straight from a cartoon. Updated in 2006, it now features Capt. Jack Sparrow and other characters from those films. Its cool, dim queue winds through a stone fort.

Aye, a tale there be. The attraction's storyline is a morality tale, told in flashback form. It begins in the present, as you pass through a watery grotto lined with pirate (and mermaid) skeletons, then goes back in time to show what led the pirates to their doom. Scenes include Capt. Barbossa attacking a Caribbean port as he and his men search for Capt. Jack, and later Jack himself lounging smugly among the town's riches, having outsmarted them all.

Historic it be. The last ride Walt Disney helped design, the attraction combines a farm boy's view of high-seas adventure with a Hollywood showman's use of theatrics. Conceived as a wax museum, the attraction became an Audio-Animatronics boat ride after the success of two Disney-designed efforts at the 1964 New York World's Fair. It drew from Carousel of Progress, with its then-revolutionary robotic characters, and It's a Small World, which debuted a water-jet system that propelled boats through scenes.

Average wait times

9am	10am	11am	Noon	1pm	2pm	3pm	4pm	5pm	6pm	7pm	8pm	9pm
5m	5m	20m	25m	45m	30m	25m	40m	30m	30m	20m	20m	5m

Clockwise from top left: Jailed pirates beg a dog for a key, Capt. Jack listens in as a drunken pirate reveals the location of the town's treasure, the ride's infamous bridal auction.

PC it be not. The ride's story is all in good fun, but even the most carefree parent may wonder if scenes showing torture, heavy drinking and the selling of women send the best messages to a wide-eyed child. "There is nothing politically correct about Pirates of the Caribbean," admits Imagineer Eric Jacobson. "In fact, much of it is patently offensive." In fairness, the ride does imply the consequences of such behavior; its first scene shows that the pirates end up murdered. And it's more sensitive than it used to be. A barrel that today hides Capt. Jack once contained a titillated young woman who was nearly naked. Holding her slip, a pirate in front of her yearned to "hoist me colors on the likes of that shy little wench. I be willin' to share, I be!"

Tips. *When to go:* Early in the morning or late at night, when lines are short. *Which line to pick:* The right one. Its sights include some chess-playing skeletons. *Where to sit:* Ask for the front row. You'll have a clear view of everything, and lots of legroom.

Fun facts. ❶ A fog screen of Blackbeard's face consists of microscopic water droplets held in place by columns of air. **❷** The voices of Blackbeard, Barbossa and Sparrow are those of actors Ian McShane, Geoffrey Rush and Johnny Depp; **❸** the auctioneer is voiced by Paul Frees, the Haunted Mansion's ghost host.

Fun finds and Hidden Mickeys. ❶ At the bridal auction, the first woman is beaming, happy to be sold. **❷** Referring to her portly figure as "stout-hearted and corn-fed" the auctioneer asks her to "shift yer cargo, dearie. Show 'em yer larboard side." **❸** As an impatient buxom redhead lifts her skirt, he calls "Strike yer colors you brazen wench! No need to expose yer superstructure!" **❹** Frustrated that the dog in front of them won't bring them a key, one jailed prisoner tells another "Hit him with the soup bone!" As the dog glances toward your boat, another captive says "Rover, it's us what needs yer ruddy help, not them blasted lubbers" **❺** Painted on the exit ramp, "shoe prints" that indicate where to step consist of a normal right shoe and peg-leg left mark. **❻** In the gift shop, the Mickey's three-circle shape appears as coins on a scale near the ride exit, and **❼** on the left shoulder of a woman in a painting on the back wall.

Key facts. *Best for:* Ages 10 and up. *Duration:* 9 min. *Capacity:* 330 (15 per boat). *Queue:* Indoor, air-conditioned. *Fear factor:* Dark, spooky start; cannon fire may scare toddlers. *Debuted:* 1973, revised 2006, 2012 (Disneyland 1967). *Access:* ECV and wheelchair users must transfer. *Disability services:* Handheld captioning, Audio Description. *Location:* Adventureland.

The exterior of the Hall of Presidents resembles Independence Hall in Philadelphia. The "1787" atop the building refers to the year of its Constitutional Convention.

The Hall of Presidents

A civil civics lesson with robotic commanders-in-chief

★★★★★ ✔ FastPass+ A robotic version of President Obama speaks in this uplifting theatrical show, which also features Abraham Lincoln standing up to recite the Gettysburg Address, a short speech by George Washington and an appearance by every U.S. president. Fans of American history, parents wanting to inspire their children or perhaps just anyone longing for a return to civility in American politics should love every minute. It's really good.

The show begins with a large-format film. Starting with Washington's struggle to build a new nation, the movie scans our country's history, its focus on presidents who reached out to Americans during times of strife—Franklin Roosevelt, John F. Kennedy, Lyndon Johnson, Bill Clinton, George W. Bush.

Later, a curtain rises to show every president on stage simultaneously—43 life-sized animated figures, three-deep across the 100-foot-wide podium. Each president nods at the audience as he is introduced, and fidgets, looks around and sometimes whispers to his colleagues as the roll call continues.

Soon Washington stands to explain the importance of the oath of office, then Obama offers his thoughts on the American dream.

Updated often, lobby exhibits include the Eagle Scout medal of Gerald Ford, a roto-gauge used by FDR for his stamp-collecting hobby, and the incredibly gaudy boots George W. Bush wore during his first inauguration. A Caroline Herrera dress worn by Laura Bush hangs next to a photograph of her wearing it. Reproductions of other First Ladies' dresses show Martha Washington's tiny height and Edith Roosevelt's svelte waistline.

Tips. *When to go:* In the afternoon. Rarely crowded and providing lots of time out of

Average wait times

9am	10am	11am	Noon	1pm	2pm	3pm	4pm	5pm	6pm	7pm	8pm	9pm
10m	10m	10m	10m	10m	10m	10m	10m	10m	10m	10m	10m	10m

A robotic President Obama speaks in The Hall of Presidents, which includes Audio-Animatronic versions of every commander-in-chief. Below, a replica of the Liberty Bell in front of the attraction; a still from its movie.

the sun, the show offers a great way to beat the heat. *Where to sit:* Front row center. The closer you are to the presidents, the more you can catch their gestures and facial expressions. *For families:* The show provides a great starting point to talk with your child about the next presidential election, and how it fits in with the attraction's premise that our president should be "one of us." Is that a good idea? Would he or she like to be president?

Fun facts. ❶ The show's widescreen projection system was invented by Ub Iwerks, the original animator of Mickey Mouse. ❷ Disney combed the National Archives, Library of Congress, museums and private collections to find more than 130 historical images that appear in the film. ❸ The Lincoln figure is a simplified remake of Disney's first Honest Abe that debuted at the Illinois pavilion at the 1964 New York World's Fair, "Great Moments with Mr. Lincoln," and didn't exactly work that well. With any spike in current, it would flail its arms, hit itself repeatedly in the head and then slam itself down in its chair, confusing audiences who wondered if the bizarre routine was part of

the show. The malfunction inspired a scene in a 1993 episode of "The Simpsons." In "Selma's Choice," Aunt Selma takes Bart and Lisa to the Disney World-like Duff Gardens, where every attraction is themed to Duff Beer. At the Duff Hall of Presidents, Lincoln holds up a Duff can and takes a swig, then mindlessly smashes it onto his head. Today's Lincoln uses the original World's Fair recording when the robot recites the Gettysburg address. ❹ A Disney publicist used to mischievously tell visiting reporters that some of the show's presidents were played by real people—that since there were always a few robots out for repairs, each performance had at least one human stand-in. When he asked the late Walter Cronkite to spot the live actor, the veteran newsman just laughed. A minute later he turned back and said, "Jefferson?"

Key facts. *Best for:* Children through seniors. *Duration:* 20 min. *Capacity:* 740. *Queue:* Indoor. *Operating hours:* May open at 10 a.m. *Debuted:* 1971, revised 2009. *Access:* Guests may stay in wheelchairs, ECVs. *Disability services:* Assistive listening, reflective captioning. *Location:* Liberty Square.

An actual paddle-driven steamboat, the Liberty Square Riverboat takes riders on a tour of Magic Kingdom's "Rivers of America," a wide waterway that circles Tom Sawyer Island.

Liberty Square Riverboat

Real paddlewheeler is interesting, but its sights are snoozers

★★★ "Steady as she goes!" With recorded narration by an actor playing the role of Mark Twain, this three-tiered steamship offers a taste of life on the Mississippi. Circling Tom Sawyer Island, its peaceful half-mile journey passes scenes that depict the rural America of the 1800s. Unfortunately the sights are nothing special: a wilderness cabin, a small Native American camp and a few remarkably stoic woodland creatures. Voyages at dusk offer a nice diversion from thrill rides, but early afternoon trips are often hot and crowded. The boat has only a handful of seats.

Despite its flaws as a ride, the boat itself offers a decent look at a forgotten aspect of American history. Though guided by an underwater rail, it's true steam wheeler. Pumped full before each trip, a diesel boiler turns river water into steam, then pipes it to an engine which drives a large wheel as well

as the electrical system. A working whistle and smokestack top the boat.

Tips. *When to go:* Just before dusk when the weather is cool and lines are long elsewhere. *Where to stand:* On mild days head to the top deck for the best view; on hot days try the covered second floor. Need to sit? A second-floor lounge has cushioned benches, as well as authentic maps, etchings, photos and a display of playing cards and poker chips. *What to notice:* The lovely wildflowers that border Tom Sawyer Island, the respectful talk about American Indians, and as you exit, the huge sweaty steam engine and its crew on the first floor. They'll talk with you.

Key facts. *Best for:* Kids, seniors. *Duration:* 13 min. *Capacity:* 400. *Queue:* Outdoor, covered. *Operating hours:* 10 a.m.–dusk. *Debuted:* 1971, updated 2007. *Access:* Guests may stay in wheelchairs, ECVs. *Location:* Liberty Square.

Average wait times

9am	10am	11am	Noon	1pm	2pm	3pm	4pm	5pm	6pm	7pm	8pm	9pm
n/a	15m	15m	15m	15m	15m	15m	15m	15m	15m	15m	n/a	n/a

Especially spooky at night, The Haunted Mansion grounds include a toppled garden planter, a ghostly hearse with an invisible horse and the sounds of a howling wolf.

The Haunted Mansion

A charmingly creepy tour of a ghostly retirement home

★★★★★ ✓ FastPass+ Ghosts drink, duel, fly, play music, sing, sip tea, waltz and even hitchhike in this dark indoor ride, which is never truly scary. Touring a ghostly retirement home, you creep room-by-room past its inhabitants, who are brought to life by age-old visual tricks as well as modern effects. Highlights include Madame Leota, a psychic medium who appears twice—as a head in a floating crystal ball and as an eerie tiny bride just before the end of the ride, who urges you to "Hurry back… Hurry back…"

Tips. *When to go:* At night, when lines are usually short. *Where to sit:* It doesn't matter. Your "Doom Buggy" ride vehicle rotates to line you up perfectly with every sight.

Fun facts. ❶ The ride's music focuses on just one song: "Grim Grinning Ghosts" is performed in eight styles, including a dirge that plays as you enter. ❷ The mansion's "dust" is made from fuller's earth, an ingredient in kitty litter. ❸ You never go in the home; the entire ride takes place in a building behind it.

Fun finds and Hidden Mickeys. ❶ The Standby queue has crypts that when touched squirt water, play music and reveal messages. ❷ Dining hall ghosts include Julius Caesar at the table, on the chandelier Marc Antony and Cleopatra. ❸ Mickey's three circles are in the dining hall as the left-most place setting on the near side of the banquet table, and ❹ toward the end of the ride's graveyard as a silhouette at the end of the arm of the Grim Reaper.

Key facts. *Best for:* Ages 5 and up. *Duration:* 11 min. *Capacity:* 320. *Queue:* Outdoor, mostly covered. *Fear factor:* Dark, some screams and pop-up heads. *Restraint:* Lap bar. *Debuted:* 1971, revised 2007. *Access:* Must be ambulatory. *Disability services:* Handheld captioning, Audio Description. *Location:* Liberty Square.

Average wait times

9am	10am	11am	Noon	1pm	2pm	3pm	4pm	5pm	6pm	7pm	8pm	9pm
5m	15m	20m	25m	35m	30m	30m	40m	25m	15m	15m	20m	10m

Country Bear Jamboree band the Five Bear Rugs includes (clockwise from left) "thing" player Tennessee, mouth-harpist Big Fred, jug blower Ted, fiddler Zeb and banjo player Zeke.

Country Bear Jamboree

Goofy stupid bears ain't worth seein'

★ Idiotic mechanical bears sing snippets of old-time country and cowboy songs in this indoor stage show, a corn-pone piece of Disney kitsch that somehow manages to have no appealing elements behind its historic value. Devoid of wit and downright insulting to rural America, women and, yes, even bears, the show is a total waste of time. Watching it is like watching the worst rerun ever of the 1960s variety TV show "Hee Haw." And who would want to do that? Set in the union hall of an 1880s lumber camp, it features 18 life-sized performers. A 2013 revision made it shorter.

Tips. *When to go:* Mid-afternoon, when other lines are lengthy and you're desperate to get out of the sun. *Where to sit:* In the middle of a middle row. You'll be able to see the bears' faces well, and hear them okay. *For families:* Have your kids make the silly bear faces. That will be funny.

Fun facts. ❶ Two songs come from legendary cowboy star Tex Ritter: 1950's "My Woman Ain't Pretty (But She Don't Swear None)" and 1937's "Blood On the Saddle," which in its day was known as the goriest country song of all time. **❷** The show's bear faces were designed by Marc Davis, the animator who created Cruella De Vil, Maleficent and Tinker Bell, the faces on the Pirates of the Caribbean and the animals in It's a Small World. **❸** The show was meant to be part of a never-built 1960s Disney resort in California's Sequoia National Forest, and was said to be Walt Disney's favorite attraction. Of course, he was old then.

Key facts. *Best for:* Children. *Duration:* 11 min. *Capacity:* 380. *Queue:* Indoor. *Operating hours:* 10 a.m.–park close. *Debuted:* 1971. *Access:* Guests may stay in wheelchairs, ECVs. *Disability services:* Assistive listening, reflective captioning. *Location:* Frontierland.

Average wait times

9am	10am	11am	Noon	1pm	2pm	3pm	4pm	5pm	6pm	7pm	8pm	9pm
n/a	10m	10m	10m	10m	10m	10m	10m	10m	10m	10m	10m	10m

No spell check, no problem. Tom Sawyer himself appears to have written the signs that direct guests around Tom Sawyer Island.

Tom Sawyer Island

Who knew trails, forts and caves could be so dull?

★★★ Though it has its fans, as it is certainly a break from theme-park madness and is rarely crowded, Tom Sawyer would be bored to death on this small wooded island, which is meant to recall the classic 1876 novel by Mark Twain, "The Adventures of Tom Sawyer." Though children have plenty of things to walk through—a meandering cave, a mine, a windmill and a charming watermill—they have little chance for free-spirited adventure, as they're rarely allowed off the sidewalks. Across a footbridge a second island leads to frontier outpost Fort Langhorn, toy rifles in its towers can fire at Big Thunder Mountain Railroad trains and the passing riverboat. You get to the islands via powered raft (see below).

Tips. *When to go:* In the morning or about 90 minutes before dusk, when it's not so hot out. *Hidden things to do:* Play checkers at the island dock, at a landing down the left trail from it or at Fort Langhorn; cross over a bouncy barrel bridge along the right side of the island; worm your way through the "secret" escape tunnel at the back of the fort.

Fun fact. ❶ The bird trapped in the mill's cogs re-creates a scene from the landmark 1937 Disney short "The Old Mill."

Fun finds. ❶ The mill's various creaks and groans subtly create the tune "Down By The Old Mill Stream." ❷ Water in the mine appears to run uphill. ❸ Water appears to run uphill in the mine. The women's restroom at Fort Langhorn is labeled "Powder Room."

Key facts. *Best for:* Children. *Duration:* Allow 1.5 hrs. *Capacity:* 400. *Queue:* Outdoor, covered. *Fear factor:* Toddlers can get lost in the cave's side niches. *Operating hours:* Closes at dusk. *Weather issues:* Rafts don't operate in thunderstorms. *Debuted:* 1973. *Access:* Must be ambulatory. *Location:* Frontierland.

Average wait times (for raft trips, each direction)

9am	10am	11am	Noon	1pm	2pm	3pm	4pm	5pm	6pm	7pm	8pm	9pm
n/a	5m	5m	15m	20m	20m	20m	15m	5m	5m	5m	n/a	n/a

Scaredy-cats can watch Splash Mountain riders take the big plunge from a stone overpass. The 52-foot drop is one of Disney World's most thrilling moments.

Splash Mountain

Elaborate log-flume ride recalls controversial Disney film

★★★ FastPass+ You plunge 52 feet into a soaking splashdown during this half-mile flume ride, which recalls Disney's controversial 1946 film "Song of the South." A hollowed-out log takes you through bayous, swamps, a cave and a flooded mine as you witness a fox and bear's attempts to snare a wily rabbit. The ride's bright colors, many Audio-Animatronics characters and peppy music will appeal to young children; its many false drops and one big fall to thrill-seekers.

Weak versus strong. A vague storyline demonstrates how the weak can outwit the strong. Based on folk tales popular with slaves in the antebellum South, it portrays how tiny Brer ("brother") Rabbit is continually threatened by Brer Fox and Brer Bear, but always outsmarts them. In his final escape, the hare tricks the fox into tossing him safely back home, where he is welcomed by his friends.

Three tales in one. The attraction combines elements from three Brer Rabbit folk tales. In "Mr. Rabbit and Mr. Bear," he gets out of a rope trap by convincing the bear to switch places with him, saying he's earning a dollar a minute as a scarecrow. In "Brother Rabbit's Laughing Place," he leads the bear and fox to what he says is an ideal spot—his "laughing place." When it turns out to be a hollow tree full of stinging bees (from which only he escapes) he reminds them that it is *his* laughing place, not theirs. In "How Mr. Rabbit Was Too Sharp for Mr. Fox," Brer Rabbit escapes being cooked by the fox by urging the fox to cook him, as anything would be better than being thrown in a nearby briar patch. So the fox does just that, and the rabbit, who lives in the briar patch, gets away scot free.

'Pleasant memories of slavery.' Though the Brer Rabbit stories are not racist, the

Average wait times

9am	10am	11am	Noon	1pm	2pm	3pm	4pm	5pm	6pm	7pm	8pm	9pm
5m	20m	45m	35m	60m	55m	45m	70m	40m	45m	40m	30m	20m

A view from the top of Splash Mountain's Chickapin Hill, just before splashdown. Below: the Briar Patch gift shop; on the ride, Brer Fox captures Brer Rabbit by slamming a beehive over his head.

way they became widely known has some ugly overtones. They were first published in "The Complete Tales of Uncle Remus," an 1895 compilation in which its white author, Atlanta newspaper columnist Joel Chandler Harris, added a freed-slave narrator whom he described as having "nothing but pleasant memories of the discipline of slavery." At the time, the word "uncle" was often a patronizing term for an elderly black man. Disney's movie featured Uncle Remus, and did little to convey that being a slave caused him hardship.

Tips. *When to go:* With a Fastpass, during the hottest part of the day. *Where to sit:* The front seat for the best view and to get soaked, the back seat to stay relatively dry. *How to make sure you stay dry:* Choose the left side of the back seat, duck down before the splash and stay down until after the slosh (though this will ruin your souvenir ride photo).

Fun facts. ❶ Because of the movie's racist overtones, Disney does not sell "Song of the South" on DVD, show it in theaters or on television, or sell any merchandise related to it, or even the folk tales, at Walt Disney World. The gift shop offers Thumper dolls instead.

Fun finds and Hidden Mickeys. ❶ "Fleas, flat feet and furballs" are cured by the Critter Elixir trumpeted on a wagon past the second lift hill. **❷** At the start of the flooded Laughing Place, two gophers pop out of the ceiling to cheer "FSU!"—a nod to their designer's alma mater Florida State University. **❸** Just before the big drop, vultures above you ask "If you've finally found your laughing place, how come you're not laughing?" **❹** Mickey shows up as stacked barrels on the right side of the second lift hill, **❺** a hanging rope in the flooded cavern, past a turtle, **❻** and in a cloud to the right of the riverboat, a full figure reclining in the sky.

Key facts. *Best for:* All ages. *Duration:* 12 min. *Capacity:* 440. *Queue:* Indoor. *Fear factor:* A small drop is completely dark; the big one can scare adults. *Restraint:* Lap bar. *Operating hours:* Park hours. *Weather issues:* Closed during thunderstorms. *Debuted:* 1992 (Disneyland 1989). *Health advisories:* Guests should be free from motion sickness; pregnancy; high blood pressure; heart, back or neck problems. *Access:* Height min. 40 in. Must be ambulatory. *Location:* Frontierland.

All curves all the time, Big Thunder Mountain Railroad trains jostle riders into each other. The coaster is wilder than the new Seven Dwarfs Mine Train, tamer than Space Mountain.

Big Thunder Mountain Railroad

Thrilling runaway mine train has super swerves, no scares

★★★★★ ✔ **FastPass+** Full of fun, this rollicking roller coaster is ideal for those who like fast turns but not big drops. A trip through a Utah desert, this "wildest ride in the wilderness" travels around and into a mountain and passes through the flooded town of Tumbleweed and a collapsing mine shaft. Sights include hot springs, geysers and a dino skeleton. Like many coasters, it runs faster late in a day, after its track grease fully melts. A new queue lets you set off explosives and spy on miners working underground.

Tips. *When to go:* At night. The scenery is lit but the track is pitch black, which makes every swerve a surprise. *Where to sit:* For the wildest ride ask for the back seat.

Fun fact. ❶ The ride's "Howdy partners!" announcer is Dallas McKennon, the voice of Zeke in the Country Bear Jamboree and Ben Franklin at Epcot's American Adventure.

Fun finds and Hidden Mickeys. ❶ Some crates in the queue are from the "Lytum & Hyde" explosives company. ❷ An empty bird cage is labeled "Rosita," a reference to a long-lost Tiki Room songbird. ❸ In Tumbleweed, a prospector on the right has washed into town while still in his bathtub. ❹ Mickey's three-circle shape appears toward the end of the ride as rusty gears laying on the ground.

Key facts. *Best for:* Ages 8 and up. *Duration:* 4 min. *Capacity:* 150. *Queue:* Outdoor, covered. *Fear factor:* Jerky, violent turns toss riders in their seats. *Restraint:* Lap bar. *Top speed:* 36 mph. *Weather issues:* Closed during thunderstorms. *Debuted:* 1980 (Disneyland 1979). *Health advisories:* Guests should be free from motion sickness; pregnancy; high blood pressure; heart, back or neck problems. *Access:* Height min. 40 in. Must be ambulatory. *Location:* Frontierland.

Average wait times

9am	10am	11am	Noon	1pm	2pm	3pm	4pm	5pm	6pm	7pm	8pm	9pm
5m	20m	30m	40m	40m	50m	40m	40m	40m	30m	30m	30m	30m

One of the largest vintage merry-go-rounds still operating today, the Prince Charming Regal Carrousel has five rows of horses in five sizes. The largest steeds line the outer rim.

Prince Charming Regal Carrousel

Charming antique merry-go-round recalls forgotten era

★★★★★ ✔ It's a basic pleasure, but one children today rarely get to enjoy: the fun of straddling an almost life-size horse which glides up and down as it circles, a gentle breeze on your skin, the sounds of a calliope in the air. Designed to fit every member of the family, this large outdoor merry-go-round has five sizes of horses. Each horse is unique.

Tips. *When to go:* Early in the morning (you can easily pick your horse) or after dark (when the ride is lit by 2,300 tiny white lights). *Where to sit:* On the outside ring for the fastest ride, on the inside ring for the slowest.

Fun facts. ❶ The ride was built in 1917 by the Philadelphia Toboggan Co., a roller coaster shop that sold hand-carved merry-go-rounds on the side. **❷** One of only four five-row units the company ever built, it was made for Detroit's Palace Garden Park and spent time in Olympic Park in Maplewood, N.J.

Fun finds. ❶ Disney says Cinderella's horse is the one with a golden ribbon around its tail, in the second row. **❷** The namesake of the carrousel when it was built, dignified blonde Miss Liberty adorns the side of the ride's lone chariot, clad in a pink robe and sandals that were originally red, white and blue; her face appears in the top rounding boards. **❸** Some horses carry medieval weapons, including a battle axe, lance, war hammer and a one-handed flail with a spiked steel ball. **❹** Eighteen hand-painted illustrations recount the story of Cinderella on the ride's inner rounding board.

Key facts. *Best for:* Toddlers, children. *Duration:* 90 sec. (4 revolutions). *Capacity:* 91 (87 horses, 1 4-seat chariot). *Queue:* Outdoor, shaded. *Restraint:* Safety belt. *Top speed:* 7 mph. *Debuted:* 1971. *Access:* Must be ambulatory. *Location:* Fantasyland, Castle Courtyard.

Average wait times

9am	10am	11am	Noon	1pm	2pm	3pm	4pm	5pm	6pm	7pm	8pm	9pm
0m	0m	0m	0m	5m	5m	5m	5m	5m	5m	0m	0m	0m

© Disney

Donald Duck finds himself in key musical moments of classic Disney films in Mickey's PhilharMagic. The 3-D movie is shown on one of the world's widest movie screens.

Mickey's PhilharMagic

Delightful 3-D tribute to Disney musicals stars Donald Duck

★★★★★ ✔ FastPass+ Donald Duck steals a kiss from the Little Mermaid, battles the brooms from "Fantasia" and causes chaos in the dining room of the Beast in this terrific 3-D movie. Action-packed yet never scary, funny but also touching, it's a treat for any age. The plot? When maestro Mickey Mouse runs late for a performance of his musician-free orchestra, Donald's attempt to replace him leads to a madcap adventure, as he gets swept into the signature moments of six musical Disney movies, all of them classics. Hidden odorizers, air guns and water misters immerse you in the action, as do innovative lighting effects and a terrific wrap-around sound system. The 3-D images aren't razor sharp but plenty bright.

Tips. *When to go:* In the afternoon when other attractions have long lines. *Where to sit:* In the middle of a back row, where the 3-D effects have the most impact.

Fun fact. ❶ For the most part Donald's words come from old cartoons, voiced by the original Donald, Clarence "Ducky" Nash.

Fun finds and Hidden Mickeys. ❶ Before the film, Goofy walks behind the curtain and steps on a cat ("Sorry little feller!"). **❷** As you exit, he says goodbye to you in five languages ("Sigh-a-NAIR-ee!"), a reference to the last scene in the nearby attraction It's A Small World. **❸** Mickey hides on the theater's right stage column, in the French horn tubing and **❹** as a hole that Aladdin's carpet makes in a cloud as he and Jasmine fly through it.

Key facts. *Best for:* All ages. *Duration:* 12 min. *Capacity:* 450. *Queue:* Indoor, air-conditioned. *Fear factor:* Sudden images, briefly totally dark. *Debuted:* 1971. *Access:* Viewers may stay in wheelchairs, ECVs. *Disability services:* Assistive listening, reflective captioning. *Location:* Fantasyland.

Average wait times

9am	10am	11am	Noon	1pm	2pm	3pm	4pm	5pm	6pm	7pm	8pm	9pm
10m	10m	10m	10m	10m	10m	10m	10m	10m	10m	10m	10m	10m

Head to Peter Pan's Flight to fly off to Never Land in a miniature pirate galleon. Loaded with timeless charm, the classic indoor dark ride hasn't changed since it opened in 1971.

Peter Pan's Flight

Vintage flying pirate ships take you off to Never Land

★★★★★ ✔ FastPass+ You'll fly over London and swoop through Never Land on this indoor dark ride, which uses an overhead track to suspend two-seat pirate ships. Designed 60 years ago and essentially unchanged since, the attraction has a throwback charm that just gets sweeter with age.

The ride depicts key moments of Disney's 1953 movie "Peter Pan." You start off in the Darling nursery, then fly over nighttime London—its roads filled with moving vehicles—as you head off to Never Land. Passing the Lost Boys, Princess Tiger Lily and a trio of mermaids, you eventually sail through Capt. Hook's ship, and witness his battles with Peter and a ticking crocodile.

Tips. *When to go:* First thing in the morning or anytime with a Fastpass. *Where to look:* Up and down. You fly through the scenes, so there are sights all around you.

Fun finds. ❶ In the queue, a bedside calendar from December 1904 has the 27th circled—the date of the first stage performance of J.M. Barrie's novel "Peter Pan." ❷ Nearby, your shadow can ring the shadow of a bell; have the shadow of a butterfly land on it; tap the shadow of Tinker Bell, which will cause her to take flight; be topped by the shadow of a top hat or by the shadow of Capt. Hook's feathered hat—and if that last one happens the shadow of your hand will become a hook. ❸ On the ride, the glow from a volcano comes from visible sheets of aluminum foil. One of the mermaids looks like Ariel.

Key facts. *Best for:* Children. *Duration:* 3 min. *Capacity:* 60. *Queue:* Indoor, covered. *Restraint:* Safety bar. *Debuted:* 1971 (Disneyland 1955). *Access:* Must be ambulatory. *Disability services:* Handheld captioning, Audio Description. *Location:* Fantasyland.

Average wait times

9am	10am	11am	Noon	1pm	2pm	3pm	4pm	5pm	6pm	7pm	8pm	9pm
5m	35m	45m	50m	35m	45m	35m	65m	40m	70m	40m	35m	35m

Nearly three hundred singing dolls populate the It's a Small World landscape, representing the cultures of Europe, Asia, Africa, Latin America and Polynesia.

it's a small world

Colorful classic boat ride offers hope of world peace

★★★★★ ✓ **FastPass+** Promoting world harmony with dolls that sing in unison, this indoor boat ride takes you on a colorful, cultural trip around the globe. Abstract sets, whimsical animals and hundreds of singing dolls fill your field of vision in six huge dioramas, each of which represents a different region of the world.

"The happiest cruise that ever sailed" starts off in Europe, then crosses through Asia, Africa, Latin America and Polynesia. The finale returns to Europe, to Copenhagen's Tivoli Gardens (Walt Disney's inspiration for the look of his theme parks) where all the planet's children unite to celebrate the "world that we share" by dressing in white, singing in unison and enjoying the carnival together.

As for flaws...the dolls' lips barely move, the short song repeats ad nauseum (though in different languages and usually as an instrumental), the Latin American and South Pacific sets are skimpy compared to the others and the ride concludes with glitter-board good-byes that seem like a hasty addition to the more elaborate earlier scenes.

But get past all that and there's a lot to like:

As a ride. To infants, the ride is a wide-eyed journey filled with happy faces, funny animals, gentle music and the largest crib mobiles they've ever seen. To older children it's a place to bond with their parents, as there's no narration and lots of time to chat. ("Where are we now, mom?" "Hawaii!").

As a political statement. It's a Small World argues that you can honor diversity while still celebrating the commonality of mankind. Though the dolls speak different languages they all sing the same song, and though they wear different costumes, their faces are nearly identical.

Average wait times

9am	10am	11am	Noon	1pm	2pm	3pm	4pm	5pm	6pm	7pm	8pm	9pm
10m	10m	15m	25m	20m	25m	20m	20m	40m	15m	20m	15m	10m

© Disney

"The happiest cruise that ever sailed," It's a Small World takes guests on a celebratory tour of the globe. Stylized landscapes form a collage of color.

As a piece of art. As designed by illustrator Mary Blair—she did the backgrounds for the Disney movies "Cinderella" (1950) and "Alice in Wonderland" (1951)—the modernist sets have a sophisticated sensibility, forming a playful pop-art collage that combines organic and geometric shapes as well as cultural motifs. For ideas, Blair tried different combinations of wallpaper cuttings, cellophane and acrylic paint.

As a piece of history. The ride was initially created for the UNICEF pavilion at the 1964 New York World's Fair. One of 50 attractions that charged a fee, It's a Small World accounted for 20 percent of paid admissions, more than any other attraction. It also inspired some political merchandise, as The Women's International League for Peace and Freedom sold It's a Small World-style dolls to help fund protests against the Vietnam War.

Tips. *When to go:* Early, late or with a Fastpass. *Where to sit:* Ask for the front row of the first boat for the best view and the most legroom. Sit on the left for the best views of Don Quixote, Cleopatra and the flower-spotted kangaroos, or on the right to get an up-close look at the French can-can girls, the yodeling Swedish bell shakers and the winking hippo. *Where to look:* Up. Lots of stuff hangs from the ceilings. *Tips for families:* Compete with your kids: Who can identify the most countries? Who can spot the most animals?

Fun facts. ❶ Jungle Cruise skippers tell their passengers that children left on their boats will be taken to It's a Small World, have their feet glued to its floor and be forced to sing its theme song "over and over for the rest of their lives." ❷ During the finale of Jim Henson's MuppetVision 3-D, Small World dolls join in to help destroy the theater.

Fun finds and Hidden Mickeys. ❶ In the boarding area, a giant clock comes to life every 15 minutes. ❷ In the first room a pink poodle ogles the can-can girls, a crazy-eyed Don Quixote tilts at a windmill while Sancho Panza looks on in alarm, and a Swiss yodeler wields an ax. ❸ In the Middle Eastern room, one of the flying carpets has a steering wheel. ❹ In the African room, Cleopatra winks at you. ❺ Mickey's three-circle shape appears as purple flower petals in Africa, along a vine between the giraffes on your left.

Key facts. *Best for:* Toddlers, children, young women, families, Disney enthusiasts. *Duration:* 11 min. *Capacity:* 600. *Queue:* Indoor. *Debuted:* 1971, renovated 2010 (New York World's Fair 1964, Disneyland 1966). *Access:* ECV users must transfer. *Disability services:* Handheld captioning, Audio Description. *Location:* Fantasyland.

A surreal hefflalump-and-woozle nightmare highlights The Many Adventures of Winnie the Pooh, an old-fashioned ride that includes many special effects.

The Many Adventures of Winnie the Pooh

Charming dark ride tells tale of chubby little cubby

★★★★ FastPass+ You bounce with Tigger, float in a flood and see Pooh drift off to dreamland on this dark indoor ride, which uses imaginative effects to create a memorable experience. Traveling in a four-person "Hunny Pot," you enter a storybook to witness the weather woes and hefflalump-and-woozle nightmare of the 1968 featurette "Winnie the Pooh and the Blustery Day." Hidden behind swinging doors, each scene comes as a surprise. A standby queue has an interactive playground; children (and adults) can draw on video walls that appear to drip honey.

Tips. *When to go:* Before 10 a.m. *Where to sit:* The front seat of your Pot has the best view. Children in back can't see over adults in front of them. *For families:* The ride gives parents a chance to talk to kids about fear. Scenes depict Pooh characters afraid of two things they should be (a windstorm and flood) and one thing they shouldn't (rumored truths).

Fun finds and Hidden Mickeys. ❶ A mirror in the boarding makes riders appear to disappear into a storybook. ❷ Words on its first page blow off of it; ❸ words on its Floody Place page wash off. ❹ Mickey hides at the ride's entrance, on the transom of the door in Mr. Sanders' treehouse. ❺ On the ride, look for him on the radish marker in Rabbit's garden.

Key facts. *Best for:* Children. *Duration:* 3 min. 30 sec. *Capacity:* 48. *Queue:* Outdoor, covered. *Fear factor:* A clap of thunder and an odd dream sequence may startle timid toddlers. *Restraint:* Lap bar. *Debuted:* 1999. *Access:* ECV users must transfer. *Disability services:* Audio Description. *Location:* Fantasyland.

Average wait times

9am	10am	11am	Noon	1pm	2pm	3pm	4pm	5pm	6pm	7pm	8pm	9pm
5m	25m	35m	35m	30m	40m	35m	35m	35m	25m	25m	25m	20m

Micaela Neal

Orlando's Kisha and Jay Garcia spin their teacup on the Mad Tea Party. The ride is one of the few Disney World attractions in which guests totally control their experience.

Mad Tea Party

Simple spinning teacups leave you giddy and grinning

★★★★ ✔ FastPass+ "If I had a world of my own, everything would be nonsense," says schoolgirl Alice, in Disney's 1951 movie "Alice in Wonderland." "Nothing would be what it is because everything would be what it isn't. And contrary-wise; what it is it wouldn't be, and what it wouldn't be, it would. You see?"

You'll be as confused as Alice as you leave this classic carnival ride, which puts you in an oversized teacup that spins as it circles on a floor that circles too. Most guests get dizzy, and most love it. "My favorite Disney World ride has always been the teacups," NASCAR driver Kyle Petty tells us. "From the time I was little I've loved to jump in and make people sick."

A wheel in the center of your cup lets you control how fast you spin, and which direction. Covered by a huge canopy, the Mad Tea Party operates in any weather.

Tips. *When to go:* Morning, late afternoon or evening… anytime it's not crowded. *Where to sit:* Pick a cup. Any cup. *How to get really dizzy:* Spin your cup's wheel first one direction, then the other, as fast as you can. *How not to get dizzy:* Don't spin the wheel. Instead, hold onto it tightly so it doesn't move, and stare at it as the ride itself rotates and turns. *For families:* The teacups give parents an excuse to get silly with their children. Most kids love it when their mom or dad slides into them or playfully twirls the wheel.

Fun finds. ❶ The movie's soused mouse pops out of the ride's central teapot. **❷** The film's Japanese tea lanterns hang overhead.

Key facts. *Best for:* Teens, young adults, small families. *Duration:* 2 min. *Capacity:* 72 (18 4-person teacups). *Queue:* Outdoor, shaded. *Debuted:* 1971 (Disneyland 1955). *Access:* Must be ambulatory. *Location:* Fantasyland.

Average wait times

9am	10am	11am	Noon	1pm	2pm	3pm	4pm	5pm	6pm	7pm	8pm	9pm
5m	5m	10m	25m	20m	20m	20m	20m	15m	15m	15m	10m	5m

After re-enacting the story of how she and the Beast met and fell in love, Belle poses for photos with her castle guards—volunteer dads from the audience.

Enchanted Tales with Belle

Audience volunteers help the princess act out her story

★★★★ ✔ **FastPass+** This wonderful little attraction is Disney's ultimate character meet-and-greet, with a live show to boot. Belle, engaging and lovely in her golden gown, acts out the story of how she met the Beast with the help of eye-popping re-creations of Madame Wardrobe and Lumiere as well as audience volunteers. Ladeling a small experience with what seems like an unlimited budget, Disney has put a sincere effort into this, and created a great experience.

Tips. *When to go:* In the morning, as soon as the park opens. Disney needs at least 20 people to present a show, so you might wait a few moments if you're first in line. But you'll avoid having to wait outside—and you'll get a fresh, lively Belle. *Where to sit:* Front and center if you can. *For families:* Encourage your children to volunteer. Everybody who wants to be in the show can be, and usually they're the only ones who get a photo with Belle. *Have your own princess?* In the first room of the cottage, take a photo of her in front of little Belle's height chart on the right wall.

Fun finds and Hidden Mickeys. ❶ A French book telling the Cinderella tale lies open on a table in Belle's cottage. ❷ A book near the door to Maurice's workshop is titled "La Belle au Bois Dormant"—Sleeping Beauty. ❸ Maurice's blueprints for the wood-chopping machine seen in the film "Beauty and the Beast" hang on his workshop's wall. ❹ Mickey's three circles appear as roses at the neckline of Belle's gown.

Key facts. *Best for:* Children. *Duration:* 20 min. *Capacity:* 45. *Queue:* Unshaded, outdoor. *Debuted:* 2012. *Access:* Guests may remain in wheelchairs, ECVs. *Disability services:* Assistive listening, handheld captioning. *Location:* Fantasyland, Enchanted Forest.

Average wait times

9am	10am	11am	Noon	1pm	2pm	3pm	4pm	5pm	6pm	7pm	8pm	9pm
15m	30m	30m	50m	30m	40m	20m	65m	70m	20m	30m	30m	40m

All ages enjoy the Seven Dwarfs Mine Train. The coaster's carts swing independently from side to side, creating a smooth journey that doesn't toss riders into each other.

Seven Dwarfs Mine Train

Ingenious combo of coaster and dark ride delights all

★★★★ ✔ FastPass+ This musical indoor/outdoor coaster is ideal for families. It gives the right amount of thrills—more than Barnstormer, less than Big Thunder Mountain Railroad—making it a perfect fit for kid-friendly Fantasyland. Better still, the ride appeals to both sexes, even though it's based on a princess story, as it focuses its attention on the dwarfs rather than Snow White. She appears only at the end of the ride, and only if you're looking for her.

Tips. *When to go:* The very, very first thing in the morning or anytime with a Fastpass. *Where to sit:* In the front seat for the best views and the mildest ride; in back for a more thrilling experience.

Fun finds and Hidden Mickeys. ❶ The image of Walt Disney's first cartoon character, Oswald the Lucky Rabbit, appears in the mine, on a beam to your left past the crest of the second lift hill. ❷ You'll find Mickey as a three-circle shape on the loading area on the back wall above the podium, and three times inside the mine: ❸ just to the left of Dopey (level with his head, on a support beam), ❹ as three jewels slightly to the right of Grumpy, and ❺ as a full-bodied figure atop the second lift down low on your right, across from the hidden image of Oswald, holding a pickaxe.

Key facts. *Best for:* All ages. *Duration:* 2.5 min. *Capacity:* 20 (4 per mine cart, 2 per row) *Queue:* Outdoor, tree-lined path leads into an indoor queue. *Fear factor:* Tight speedy turns may frighten preschoolers, especially in the back rows. *Restraint:* Lap bar. *Weather issues:* Closed during thunderstorms. *Debuted:* 2014. *Health advisories:* Expectant mothers should not ride. *Access:* Height minimum 38 in. Wheelchair and ECV users must transfer. *Location:* Enchanted Forest, Fantasyland.

Average wait times

9am	10am	11am	Noon	1pm	2pm	3pm	4pm	5pm	6pm	7pm	8pm	9pm
60m	90m	90m	75m	75m	75m	75m	90m	90m	120m	90m	90m	75m

© Disney

Creepy villain Ursula the Sea Witch belts out "Poor Unfortunate Souls" as a video image of Ariel appears on a crystal ball on the ride Under the Sea—Journey of the Little Mermaid.

Under the Sea— Journey of the Little Mermaid

Gut the Haunted Mansion and you're left with this

★★ **FastPass+** Pardon the pun, but this headliner has no legs to stand on. Based on Disney's charming 1989 film "The Little Mermaid," its charm-free, an unmemorable indoor dark ride that creeps past scenes from the movie that are distinctly lackluster, with uninspired hard-plastic figures, little detail and dull-as-sea-muck scene transitions. No wonder Ariel wanted to get out of this place.

On the plus side, the ride *sounds* great. In the "Under the Sea" scene you drift through a fish band and hear its individual instruments. Sound effects like water splashing, a breeze through trees and fireworks bursting in a night sky are crisp and clear.

Tips. *When to go:* Before 10 a.m. or after dark. *For families:* Play the crab game in the queue; it's more fun than the ride itself. Wave your hand to help a crab sort Ariel's collection of human gadgets and gizmos.

Fun finds and Hidden Mickeys. ❶ A reference to the ride that used to be on this spot, an image of the Nautilus submarine from the movie "20,000 Leagues Under the Sea" hides on the left side of the queue, in rocks along the side of a pool. ❷ Mickey's three circles appear in the queue as sunlight on a wall past a carved ship's figurehead, from holes in a rock above. But only on Nov. 18, the character's birthday.

Key facts. *Best for:* Children. *Duration:* 7 min. *Capacity:* 4 per clamshell. *Queue:* Indoor. *Fear factor:* Ursula may scare toddlers. *Restraint:* Lap bar. *Debuted:* 2012. *Access:* ECV users must transfer. *Disability services:* Handheld captioning, Audio Description. *Location:* Enchanted Forest, Fantasyland.

Average wait times

9am	10am	11am	Noon	1pm	2pm	3pm	4pm	5pm	6pm	7pm	8pm	9pm
5m	15m	30m	40m	40m	30m	50m	40m	30m	30m	40m	20m	10m

Appealing to riders of all ages, Dumbo the Flying Elephant puts its guests in single-bench baby pachyderms that circle slowly. The ride recalls the finale of the classic 1941 film.

Dumbo the Flying Elephant

New and improved carnival ride is better than ever

★★★★★ ✔ FastPass+ Flying baby elephants become cozy ride vehicles on this classic hub-and-spoke ride. Since the attraction's move to Storybook Circus in 2012 it's gotten much better—it now has two Dumbo rides, one that moves clockwise, the other counterclockwise. Each has a pool for Dumbo to fly over and multi-colored, changing lights that, at night, make the water glow. The queue includes an indoor playground. When there's a wait to ride Dumbo, parents sit on benches while children play. When it's time, a restaurant-style pager sounds an alert.

Couples will enjoy the ride almost as much as children; its small seat requires scootching together and sharing one big seatbelt.

Tips. *When to go:* Before 11 a.m. for the shortest lines of the day, or use a Fastpass. If you can, ride at night, when the attraction glows with brilliant lights. *For families:* Snap a pic of your children in a stationary Dumbo between the two rides. *Other tips:* Ask for the Dumbo on the right (i.e., the one closest to the rest of the park) to get a terrific view of Magic Kingdom. The Dumbo on the left mostly just views the adjacent Barnstormer ride.

Fun finds. ❶ Flying storks deliver baby Dumbos along the top of each hub. **❷** Golden peanuts adorn the hubs, almost as if the legume was an object of worship.

Key facts. *Best for:* Families, couples. *Duration:* 2 min. (6 revolutions). *Capacity:* 64 (32 per Dumbo ride, in 16 2-seat vehicles); play area capacity 175. *Queue:* Indoor, includes large, elaborate play area; leads to outdoor shaded queue. *Restraint:* seatbelt. *Weather issues:* Closed in thunderstorms. *Debuted:* 1971, redone 2012 (Disneyland 1955). *Access:* Wheelchair and ECV users must transfer. *Location:* Storybook Circus, Fantasyland.

Average wait times

9am	10am	11am	Noon	1pm	2pm	3pm	4pm	5pm	6pm	7pm	8pm	9pm
10m	15m	45m	25m	30m	30m	35m	25m	45m	15m	15m	20m	15m

A **family rounds a curve** on The Barnstormer, a junior roller coaster themed to the stuntman adventures of "The Great Goofini."

The Barnstormer

Brief, cheerful kiddie coaster packs punch, is fun for all ages

★★★★★ ✔ **FastPass+** A perfect first coaster for children, this little biplane is also fun for couples and friends. Though its turns last only 20 seconds, its planes zip around a tight track at 25 mph, about as fast as the rockets inside Space Mountain. Constantly leaning into each other, riders sit two abreast in a cozy seat.

The Great Goofini. Adding to the fun is a witty backstory—the tale of an aerial mishap of the Great Goofini, the stage name Goofy gave himself during his stint as a circus daredevil. Taxiing a crop duster out of an old barn, he climbed up into the air perfectly straight... straight into a signal tower. Immediately losing control, he swooped and swayed back to the barn, crashing through his billboard on the way.

Tips. *When to go:* First thing in the morning; when cast members will often let you stay in your seat for multiple flights. *Where to sit:* For the wildest ride ask for the back seat (Row 8); for the best view the front seat.

Fun finds and Hidden Mickey. ❶ Goofy's "Canine Cannonball" cannon is next to the Fastpass queue. ❷ Its fuse flickers now and then; ❸ one of its balls is Goofy's bowling ball. ❹ Mickey hides on the right of the billboard, in the blades of an airplane propeller.

Key facts. *Best for:* Toddlers, children, couples. *Duration:* 1 minute. *Capacity:* 32 (16 per plane; 2 planes). *Queue:* Outdoor, mostly unshaded. *Fear factor:* The coaster's tight turns could scare preschoolers. *Restraint:* Lap bar. *Top speed:* 25 mph. *Track:* Steel, height 28 feet, distance 790 feet. *Weather issues:* Closed during thunderstorms. *Debuted:* 1996, revised 2012. *Health advisories:* Expectant mothers should not ride. *Access:* Height minimum 35 inches. ECV and wheelchair users must transfer. *Location:* Fantasyland, Storybook Circus.

Average wait times

9am	10am	11am	Noon	1pm	2pm	3pm	4pm	5pm	6pm	7pm	8pm	9pm
5m	5m	15m	35m	25m	35m	25m	25m	30m	25m	20m	20m	15m

A co-star of the 1940 Disney movie "Dumbo," the Casey Jr. locomotive pulled the circus train. Fantasyland's version of the train sprays water from its smokestack and animals.

Casey Jr. Splash 'n' Soak Station

Beat the heat at this jolly circus-themed splash zone

★★★★ It's more soak than splash, but that's part of the fun. Kids have a blast trying to dodge the intermittent sprays, especially if parents join in. Surrounding little locomotive Casey Jr. from Disney's 1941 film "Dumbo" are several boxcars holding faux circus animals that shoot, spit and squirt water. Oddly, the pavement is brick, not the typical squishy soft stuff water-play areas usually have. Few kids seem to have trouble with it, though.

Tips. *When to go:* Anytime. *Where to play:* If your youngsters want a light spray instead of a drench, have them play in front of the boxcar with the monkeys on top. *Other tips:* To dry off, a cart just out of range of the water sells $20 beach towels.

Fun fact. ❶ The area and its adjacent restroom are a 1940s railroad turntable and "roundhouse" storage shed: surrounded by his animal-filled boxcars waiting to be unloaded, Casey Jr. sits on the turntable, tracks from the Disney World railroad leading up to it. For most of their history locomotives did not have a reverse gear, so in order to turn around a locomotive would pull onto a piece of track that was mounted on a circular turnabout, and be twirled around on it.

Fun finds. Numbers on the train cars and clown wagon refer to the opening years of the four Walt Disney World theme parks. ❶ A "71" on the elephant car refers to 1971, the year Magic Kingdom debuted. ❷ An "82" on the clown wagon refers to 1982, the year Disney added Epcot. ❸ On the giraffe car, "89" refers to the 1989 debut of Disney's Hollywood Studios, then known as Disney-MGM Studios. ❹ On the camel car, "98" refers to 1998, the opening year of Disney's Animal Kingdom. Numbers on ❺ the nearby merchandise cart ("7") and ❻ locomotive ("9") are those of the engines of the Casey Jr. Circus Train ride at California's Disneyland. ❼ Mrs. Jumbo (Dumbo's mom) peeks out of the elephant car. ❽ The locomotive puffs steam from his smokestack and toots it from his whistle.

Key facts. *Best for:* Children. *Duration:* Allow 15 min. *Weather issues:* Closed during thunderstorms. *Debuted:* 2012. *Access:* Guests may remain in wheelchairs, ECVs. *Location:* Storybook Circus, Fantasyland.

© Disney

Experiment 626 is one steamed Stitch, unhappy with his detainment at Planet Turo's Prisoner Teleport Center. When the lights go out, the mischievous alien appears to escape.

Stitch's Great Escape

Cheap, confusing theatrical show is only for Stitch fans

★ Stitch burps in your face in this in-the-round theatrical show, geared to those familiar with the early moments of the 2002 movie "Lilo & Stitch." A low-budget makeover of the attraction that preceded it (The ExtraTERRORestrial Alien Encounter), the show is confusing and dull, and relies on cheaply animated video to tell its story—one which assumes you already know that Stitch can trick DNA-tracking cannons into tracking spit—and isn't really scary. A shoulder harness locks you in your seat, not because there's some risk you'll fall out (there's not) but to project sounds and smells behind you.

The host of the preshow, however, is great. Trying to train audience members how to guard prisoners as he chats with his wife on the phone, a sarcastic skinless robocop channels Jim Carrey's Fire Marshall Bill, from the 1990s television series "In Living Color."

Tips. *When to go:* When you're down to either this or Country Bear Jamboree and you really hate stupid bears. *Where to stand for the preshow:* Front row center (as you leave the indoor queue, choose the door to the left); the cop will look right at you. *Where to sit:* In one of the back rows. The Stitch character sits too high above the front rows. *How to deal with the shoulder harness:* If you've got bony shoulders, shrug them as the harness lowers over you and adjusts itself. Otherwise it will hurt. *How to hear the sound effects:* Lean back into your seat.

Key facts. *Best for:* Stitch fans. *Duration:* 18 min. *Capacity:* 240 (2 120-seat theaters). *Queue:* Indoor. *Fear factor:* Ominous harnesses, dark periods scare some children. *Restraint:* Shoulder harness. *Debuted:* 2004. *Access:* Height min. 40 in. ECV users must transfer. *Location:* Tomorrowland.

Average wait times

9am	10am	11am	Noon	1pm	2pm	3pm	4pm	5pm	6pm	7pm	8pm	9pm
10m	10m	10m	10m	10m	10m	10m	10m	10m	10m	10m	10m	10m

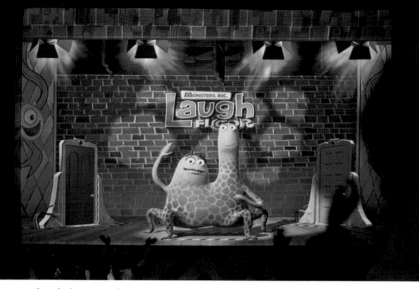

A two-headed animated monster—Sam 'n' Ella—asks for audience volunteers during a performance of the Monsters Inc Laugh Floor, an interactive comedy show.

Monsters Inc Laugh Floor

Hilarious animated creatures interact with their audience

★★★★ FastPass+ An animated monster may pick you out of the crowd to chat with or might tell your joke during this high-tech improvisational comedy show. Three large video screens front a club-style theater, where characters from the "Monsters, Inc." world tease and talk with audience members in real time. The host is Mike Wazowski, who wants to generate electricity for his utility company by gathering laughter in bulk.

The show pulls off its magic through the use of hidden cameras, powerful animation software and talented backstage actors.

Most shows are surprisingly funny. Every one is different, as the characters base much of their humor (and anti-humor) on audience members. You can text a joke to the performers ahead of time from the waiting area.

Tips. *When to go:* In the middle of day, so you see a show with a full house. The actors feed off the audience. *How to have a character talk to you:* Wear a colorful shirt or a big hat. *How to get your texted joke read:* Make it simple and Disney-based. "Where did Captain Hook get his hook? The second-hand store!"

Fun finds. ❶ As you enter the second holding room, a vending machine immediately to your left offers such treats as a Same Old Raccoon Bar and Polyvinyl Chloride Bar—the second of which is artificially flavored. **❷** In that room's pre-show video, the first child Mike Wazowski makes laugh has a poster of Tomorrowland on his bedroom wall.

Key facts. *Best for:* All ages. *Duration:* 15 to 20 min. *Capacity:* 400. *Queue:* Indoor. *Operating hours:* Park open to one hour before park close. *Debuted:* 2007. *Access:* Guests may remain in wheelchairs, ECVs. *Disability services:* Reflective captioning, assistive listening. *Location:* Tomorrowland.

Average wait times

9am	10am	11am	Noon	1pm	2pm	3pm	4pm	5pm	6pm	7pm	8pm	9pm
5m	10m	10m	10m	10m	10m	10m	20m	10m	10m	10m	10m	10m

Need to get off your feet? It's easy to relax and chat with your group on the PeopleMover, a small automated train that takes you on an elevated tour of Tomorrowland.

PeopleMover

Breezy tour of Tomorrowland offers a nice way to unwind

★★★ ✔ Zip around above Tomorrowland on this breezy and remarkably relaxing tour, as an elevated track snakes you alongside, around and through four buildings.

Tips. *When to go:* During a rain (the track is covered), at night (red lights illuminate your path) or when Space Mountain is closed (its work lights may be on). Want to go twice? Ask. *What to do:* Take photos of each other. PeopleMover is one of the few Disney rides where you can face each other.

Fun fact. ❶ While planning his dream city of EPCOT, Walt Disney thought a system of small electric trains would give people a way to get around without creating pollution or traffic. The Disney company brought the idea to life with this ride, and attempted to sell the system to cities. The idea bombed, its only sale made to the Houston airport, where a PeopleMover train still runs today.

Fun finds and Hidden Mickeys. ❶ You'll pass the center of Progress City, Walt Disney's model for his Experimental Prototype City of Tomorrow in the building that holds the Stitch's Great Escape theaters. ❷ Those theaters' original 1971 show, its host and the host of their second shows are all referenced in a page asking Mr. Tom Morrow to "contact Mr. Johnson in the Control Tower to confirm your Flight to the Moon." ❸ Mickey's in the building that holds Buzz Lightyear's Space Ranger Spin, on a belt buckle in a beauty salon.

Key facts. *Best for:* Couples, friends. *Duration:* 10 min. *Capacity:* 900 (4 per car). *Queue:* Outdoor, covered. *Fear factor:* A stretch through Space Mountain is pitch dark. *Top speed:* 7 mph. *Debuted:* 1975, revised 1996, 2009. *Access:* Must be ambulatory. *Disability services:* Audio Description, handheld captioning. *Location:* Tomorrowland.

Average wait times

9am	10am	11am	Noon	1pm	2pm	3pm	4pm	5pm	6pm	7pm	8pm	9pm
0m	0m	0m	0m	0m	0m	0m	0m	0m	0m	0m	0m	0m

Astro Orbiter's machine-age rockets circle high above Tomorrowland. The ride was dismantled, totally refurbished and reassembled in 2014.

Astro Orbiter

Thrilling retro rockets fly twice as fast as Dumbo

★★★★ ✔ Fast, high and a little bit scary, open-air rockets twirl five stories above Tomorrowland on this hub-and-spoke ride. Perched atop the boarding station of the already-elevated PeopleMover ride, Astro Orbiter lifts you 55 feet off the ground. Guests take an elevator to reach it. But there's more to this ride than height. Top speed is 20 mph—plenty zippy when you're in a tight circle and your rocket tilts at 45 degrees. Flying within a huge kinetic model of rings, planets and moons, riders make about 20 revolutions around a Buck Rogers-style antenna. At night the rockets' nose cones glow green, their exhaust fires red. The ride was dismantled and refurbished in 2014, it's now much more colorful.

Unfortunately, the waiting line is usually awful. The line moves very slowly, and those in line wait on hot asphalt with nothing to do.

Tips. *When to go:* First thing in the morning. You'll get right on and can ride two, sometimes even three times in a row. *It's a must for:* Young thrill-seekers who are too short for the roller coasters. Astro Orbiter is Walt Disney World's only thrill ride that doesn't have a height minimum.

Fun fact. ❶ The ride's orange steel-mesh elevator resembles the rocket gantries used at launchpads in early 1960s manned space missions at nearby Cape Canaveral, Fla.

Key facts. *Best for:* Children, teens, young adults, couples. *Duration:* 2 min. *Capacity:* 32. *Queue:* Outdoor, partially shaded. *Fear factor:* Height, angle can bother all ages. *Restraint:* Safety belt. *Top speed:* 20 mph. *Weather issues:* Runs during light rains; grounded by downpours, lightning. *Debuted:* 1971; updated 1994, 2015. (Disneyland 1955). *Access:* Must be ambulatory. *Location:* Tomorrowland.

Average wait times

9am	10am	11am	Noon	1pm	2pm	3pm	4pm	5pm	6pm	7pm	8pm	9pm
5m	10m	25m	40m	25m	25m	25m	40m	35m	45m	30m	35m	20m

A Rock 'Em Sock 'Em-style robot defends the home planet of the evil emperor Zurg in Buzz Lightyear's Space Ranger Spin. Riders rack up points by hitting targets marked with "Z."

Buzz Lightyear's Space Ranger Spin

Ride-through laser-gun game is a blast if you aim well

★★★ ✔ FastPass+ You use a laser gun to shoot at over a hundred cartoon targets at this video arcade, which turns the idea of a shooting gallery inside out: here the targets stay in one place while you move on a track. Riding in a two-seat space cruiser, you fire at silly cartoon aliens, black-lit targets that often move, light up or make noise if you hit them. A dashboard display tracks your score. Though the ride is low-tech by today's standards, kids and gamers should still enjoy it.

Everything takes place in a world of toys. Buzz gets his information from a Viewmaster; your space cruiser gets power from a backpack of batteries. The ride depicts an epic battle between Buzz and the Evil Emperor Zurg, who's out to become all-powerful by stealing all the world's power—its batteries.

Though it is fun, the ride does have drawbacks. Every player's laser light is the same color (red), which makes it tough to get feedback on your aim. Targets are not labeled with point values, so serious gamers waste a lot of shots. And instead of being rewarded by working together—as players are at Toy Story Mania at Disney's Hollywood Studios—here you compete against each other. Whoever controls a vehicle's joystick gets a huge advantage.

Tips. *Where to sit:* On the right. You'll face the most targets. *For Buzz fans:* The space ranger often meets guests nearby, in front of Walt Disney's Carousel of Progress.

How to get a high score. The maximum point total possible on the ride is 999,999. Here's how your score can get close to that:

1. Call dibs on the joystick, so you can keep your vehicle facing the right targets.

2. Sit on the right side of your vehicle. That side has two-thirds of the targets.

Average wait times

9am	10am	11am	Noon	1pm	2pm	3pm	4pm	5pm	6pm	7pm	8pm	9pm
5m	5m	25m	35m	40m	35m	25m	50m	45m	30m	30m	25m	20m

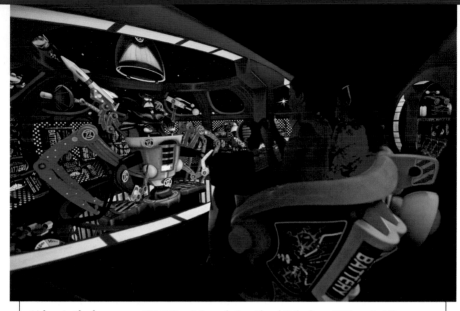

Riders in the know earn 100,000 points each time they hit the lone "Z" target at the bottom center of Zurg's space scooter. Other targets in the scene are worth far less.

3. Once your gun is activated, pull the trigger and hold it in for the entire ride. The flashing laser beam will help you track your aim. It will fire about once a second.

4. Aim only at targets with big payoffs: As you enter Room 1, aim for the left arm of the left robot (each hit is 100,000 points).

5. As you pass that robot, turn your vehicle to the left and hit the other side of that same arm (25,000 points).

6. As you leave the first room, turn backwards and aim at the overhead claw of the other robot (100,000 points).

7. As you enter the second room, aim at the top and bottom targets of the large volcano (25,000 points).

8. As soon as you see Zurg, hit the bottom target of his space scooter (100,000 points) by firing early and late; you can't aim low enough to hit it straight on.

9. As you enter the third room, aim about six feet to either side of the top of the exit to hit an unmarked target in the middle of a rectangular plate (25,000 points).

10. If the ride stops, find a high-value target and keep firing. You'll rack up points.

Fun fact. ❶ The track layout is unchanged from the ride's days as "If You Had Wings," a 1970s attraction that took passengers through a series of sets that portrayed Caribbean and Latin American countries served by Eastern Airlines. One area created the sensation of speed by combining wraparound point-of-view video clips with a slight breeze. As the ride didn't require one of the park's various "A" through "E" tickets, it was a guest favorite.

Fun finds and Hidden Mickeys. ❶ As you enter Planet Z the bendy snake from the "Toy Story" movies appears in front of you. **❷** Man-eating plant Audrey 2 from the 1986 movie "Little House of Horrors" circles to your right. **❸** "Guards! Seize them! And their little green friends, too." Zurg orders as you cruise through his spaceship. **❹** As you exit the ride, the spaceship of Stitch flies on the first mural on your right. It's tiny. **❺** A green land mass forms a Mickey profile on the planet Pollost Prime. It appears four times: on a poster in the queue, to the left of the Viewmaster in the queue, on the ride in front of you as you fight the video version of Zurg and to your left in the final battle scene. **❻** Another Mickey profile appears on your left as you enter Zurg's spaceship, under the words "Initiate Battery Unload."

Key facts. *Best for:* Children. *Duration:* 5 min. *Capacity:* 201. *Queue:* Indoor. *Debuted:* 1998. *Access:* ECV users must transfer. *Disability services:* Audio Description, handheld captioning. *Location:* Tomorrowland.

A fascinating relic from the 1964 World's Fair, the Carousel of Progress explores how a typical American family lives better with electricity throughout the 20th century.

Walt Disney's Carousel of Progress

A confused look at yesterday's great big beautiful tomorrow

★★★ ✔ Disney's first Audio-Animatronics family welcomes you into their home as they live through the ever-changing 20th century in this vintage theatrical show, which demonstrates how electricity has improved everyday life. Four scenes depict the 1900s, 1920s, 1940s and 1990s. The show is way past its prime, and cries out for either an update or total restoration. But even as it is, it's a fascinating look at the optimism of the past.

A great big all-electric tomorrow. First presented at the 1964 New York World's Fair at the General Electric pavilion, the attraction used a unique circular theater in which the seating area rotated from scene to scene. In each one, the family marveled about how great things were in "today's world," thanks to electricity and GE appliances. A finale showed the family in the future at Christmas in their stylish all-electric GE Medallion home, opening presents such as a GE portable television. To bridge the scenes, songwriters Robert and Richard Sherman ("It's a Small World") composed "There's a Great Big Beautiful Tomorrow." After the fair Disney moved the show to California's Disneyland, when its script was changed to keep pace with GE's products and marketing.

That '70s show. When the show moved to Disney World in 1975, a third version of its script tied it to the women's movement. Wife Sarah now cheerfully talked back to her husband through the ages, and demanded equal pay for wallpapering the rumpus room. An all-new finale showed John acting as the bumbling family cook. As part of the move GE insisted the show no longer focus on the future, but the present. "We're not interested in selling light bulbs tomorrow," one executive groused, "we want to sell them right

Average wait times

9am	10am	11am	Noon	1pm	2pm	3pm	4pm	5pm	6pm	7pm	8pm	9pm
5m	5m	5m	5m	5m	5m	5m	5m	5m	5m	5m	5m	5m

"We've now got gas lamps, and the latest design in cast-iron stoves," the show's father raves in the first scene. Other sets place him at a 1940s kitchenette, and his entire family at a 1990s Christmas dinner.

now!" As a result, the show got a new theme song, "The Best Time of Your Life" (*Now is the time, now is the best time...*). Disney updated this version in 1981, so its finale family was using a video-cassette recorder.

Lumbago and laser discs. In 1994 Disney revised the show yet again, bringing back its '60s song, keeping its '70s script (adding in some old-time sayings—husband John knows it won't rain because "my lumbago isn't acting up") and redoing the finale yet again—as dad fumbles with a voice-activated oven, Grandpa longs for the days before "car phones and laser discs." This version still plays today.

Tips. *When to go:* During a hot afternoon. *Where to sit:* Second or third row center. Any farther back and the dialogue from the stage will be too faint and the background music (from the back of the room) will be too loud. *For families:* Children will like watching Rover, the family dog, who glances at the audience, wags his tail and barks.

Fun facts. ❶ The auditoriums rotate at 2 feet per second on large steel wheels and tracks, just like railroad cars. ❷ The show's grandma also rocks in front of the Haunted Mansion ballroom fireplace. ❸ As part of the move to Florida, Disney returned to using wigs made from human hair. Nylon versions had been used at the World's Fair and at Disneyland, but over time klieg lights above the father had melted his hair into what one imagineer described as "a sticky pile of goo." ❹ The Carousel of Progress is the only attraction at Walt Disney World that was touched by Walt Disney himself.

Hidden Mickeys. ❶ In the 1940s scene, the sorcerer's hat from 1940's "Fantasia" sits near an exercise machine. ❷ Mickey items in the finale include a nutcracker on the mantel, ❸ a plush under a Christmas tree, ❹ a salt shaker on the bar, ❺ an abstract painting on the wall and at the start of a video game the son and grandma play, ❻ the engines of a spaceship.

Key facts. *Best for:* Seniors, Disney history buffs. *Duration:* 21 min. Capacity: 240 per theater, 6 theaters. *Queue:* Outdoor, uncovered. *Debuted:* 1964 World's Fair, Walt Disney World 1975. *Access:* Guests may remain in wheelchairs, ECVs. *Disability services:* Assistive listening, handheld and activated video captioning. *Location:* Tomorrowland.

In a subtle tribute to the 1968 movie "2001: A Space Odyssey," the ride's angled clapboard walls replicate those of that film's transport interior. Fastpass riders use the line at the right.

Space Mountain

Walt Disney World's first roller coaster is still its best

★★★★★ ✔ FastPass+ "Daddy, did you hear me scream?!" beamed the 6-year-old girl, hopping out of her rocket. "That! Was! Cool!" said her 10-year-old brother. The parents shared a look. "Let's ride again!" exclaimed the wife.

Open-air rockets zoom through a dark universe inside this circular building, which holds the world's oldest, and arguably still best, roller coaster in the dark. Sitting in low-slung ride vehicles that are just a single seat wide, guests hurtle through an inky abyss filled with shooting stars. Every dip, drop and turn comes as a surprise. Top speed is 28 miles per hour, plenty fast in the dark.

Have a nice flight. The ride's story begins as you enter the building, a futuristic spaceport and repair center that's orbiting above the earth. Passing the departure board, a long tunnel leads to a launch platform. Once you board a rocket, a sign urges you to "Check

Invisible Oxygen Dome," another flashes "Have a Nice Flight" and then off you go—into the flashing blue "energizing portal" that powers your machine. Climbing the launch tower (the chain lift), you pass under a large ship that's in for service. Then you blast off, on a journey through what an early Disney press release called "the void of the universe." As you come back to earth, you trigger a sonic boom in a red "de-energizing" tunnel.

A few years ago Disney made the ride darker and smoother and added ambient techno music and sound effects. It also added a bank of video games to its standby queue as well as a few knowing references to the 1970s.

'Where's Mr. Smee?' With astronauts Scott Carpenter, Gordon Cooper and Jim Irwin as its first passengers, Space Mountain opened on Jan. 15, 1975. Though Disney promoted it as "the nation's most breathtaking thrill

Average wait times

9am	10am	11am	Noon	1pm	2pm	3pm	4pm	5pm	6pm	7pm	8pm	9pm
10m	15m	45m	45m	70m	55m	45m	45m	55m	50m	50m	55m	30m

Space Mountain riders zoom through an "energizing portal" before their launch into space. Florida's oldest operating roller coaster, its open-air rockets are one-person wide. Waiting lines form early each morning.

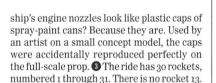

ride," not every guest got the message. As they climbed in their rockets many expected something along the lines of Peter Pan's Flight, since back then Disney parks didn't have roller coasters. Moments later, up came their lunches and out flew their hats, purses, eyeglasses and, more than once, false teeth. Disney's response included discreetly ironing out some of the most violent jerks and jolts.

Though it opened during a recession, Space Mountain was an instant smash. When summer came, families with teens, many of whom would have not considered a Disney vacation before, began crowding Magic Kingdom turnstiles early each morning. The recession, in Orlando at least, ended.

Tips. *Where to sit:* The front row of a front rocket gives you the most immersive experience, the most breeze and the most surprises, Row 1 on the boarding platform. Riders with long legs will prefer either Row 1 or 4. Back seats go faster through turns and down drops.

Fun facts. ❶ The ride's blue "energizing portal" has a practical function: its flashing lights shrink your pupils, so your flight seems darker than it really is. ❷ Why do the docked ship's engine nozzles look like plastic caps of spray-paint cans? Because they are. Used by an artist on a small concept model, the caps were accidentally reproduced perfectly on the full-scale prop. ❸ The ride has 30 rockets, numbered 1 through 31. There is no rocket 13.

Fun finds. ❶ Panels just inside the building refer to it as "Star Port Seven-Five," a nod to the ride's opening year. ❷ Intergalactic route maps along the queue contain references to the Little Mermaid, Mickey's pet dog and the 1937 movie "Snow White and the Seven Dwarfs." ❸ The spaceship alongside the chain-lift is labeled MK-1, a hint that this Magic Kingdom version of Space Mountain is the original ride; similar versions have since been built in four other Disney parks.

Key facts. *Best for:* Ages 9 and up. *Duration:* 2 min. 30 sec. *Capacity:* 180. *Queue:* Indoor. *Fear factor:* Constant surprising drops and turns. *Restraint:* Lap bar. *Top speed:* 28 mph. *Debuted:* 1975, revised 2009. *Health advisories:* Guests should be free from motion sickness; pregnancy; high blood pressure; heart, back or neck problems. *Access:* Height min. 44 in. Must be ambulatory. *Location:* Tomorrowland.

Two sisters prepare to take off at the start of the Tomorrowland Speedway, as an attendant gives the younger one instructions. Other racers wait for her to move.

Tomorrowland Speedway

Slow smelly race cars are horribly dated, surprisingly fun

★★★ ✓ FastPass+ Sounding and smelling like Harleys that desperately need tune-ups, small-scale race cars rumble down a half-mile track at this vintage attraction, children behind their wheels. Meandering past beautiful live oaks and magnolias, riders wind around five turns and under and over a bridge. Some cars are left-hand drive, some right.

Straight out of Six Flags, the ride's sun-baked waiting line is one of Disney's worst. Umbrellas offer some shade; a covered grandstand gives those not riding a way to sit down.

Tips. *When to go:* First thing in the morning, or after dark with a Fastpass when the ride is breezy. *Where to sit:* In the passenger seat if you have a child, or aren't as child-like as your companion. *Want to race?* Ask for two cars side by side. *Not riding?* Take a starting-line snapshot from a footbridge above the track, just past the boarding area.

Fun facts. ❶ Why is this old-time attraction in Tomorrowland? For a reason that could only make sense to Disney: When it opened in 1971, the track was a version of the Disneyland attraction Autopia, which, when that California ride premiered in 1955, was a simulation of the limited-access highways destined for that era's future. ❷ A 1994 redo as an alien Indy-style race confused the theme further. Today's ride has remnants of that, but officially has no futuristic theme at all.

Key facts. *Best for:* Children, couples, families. *Duration:* 5 min. *Capacity:* 292 (146 cars). *Queue:* Outdoor, partially shaded. *Restraint:* Lap belt. *Top speed:* 7.5 mph. *Weather issues:* Closed during thunderstorms. *Debuted:* 1971 (Disneyland 1955). Revised 2011. *Access:* Height minimum: 54 inches to take car out alone, 32 inches to ride. Must be ambulatory. *Location:* Tomorrowland.

Average wait times

9am	10am	11am	Noon	1pm	2pm	3pm	4pm	5pm	6pm	7pm	8pm	9pm
5m	20m	20m	30m	40m	30m	40m	30m	20m	20m	20m	20m	20m

Phineas dances with park visitors during the Move It! Shake It! Dance & Play It! street party. The Disney Channel star is one of 10 Disney characters who dance with guests.

Move It! Shake It! Dance & Play It!

Dance with Disney characters in this lively street party

★★★★ ✔ You can dance with a Disney character in this colorful street party, which takes place a few times a day in front of Cinderella Castle. If you're not shy about dancing in public, it's an easy way to have a fun character experience.

Beginning in Town Square as a five-float parade, the procession turns into an interactive party when it reaches the Cinderella Castle hub, as hosts Mickey Mouse, Minnie Mouse, Donald Duck, and Goofy invite you to snap a few selfies of yourself dancing. Soon you're urged into the street to dance with other Disney characters, and perhaps join in a conga line. Finally, you and the rest of the crowd choose a current pop tune to be the show's finale.

Dancing characters include Baloo and King Louie (from the 1967 movie "The Jungle Book"), cartoon chipmunks Chip 'n Dale, Genie (from the 1992 film "Aladdin"), Disney Channel stars Phineas and Ferb, and Stitch (from 2002's "Lilo & Stitch"). The show is an update of the former Move It! Shake It! Celebrate It! show. Gone are characters Frozone, Lumiere, Mad Hatter, Mr. Incredible, Sebastian the crab, and Woody and Jessie.

The street party takes place in direct sunlight, and the asphalt really reflects the heat; privately some performers refer to the show as "Shake It Bake It." Whenever the heat index is above 105 degrees—that's nearly every afternoon between May and September, Disney cuts the conga line.

Tips. *When to go:* See the first or last show of the day, when the weather's cooler. *How to get your selfies on the screens on the floats:* Text them to Twitter or Instagram with the hashtag #MOVEITSHAKEITPICS.

Key facts. *Best for:* Toddlers, children, teens, young adults, adults. *Duration:* 12 min. *Weather issues:* Cancelled during rain. Shortened when the heat index is above 105 degrees (most shows May through August); the conga-line segment is cut. *Debuted:* 2009. *Access:* Special areas for guests in wheelchairs, ECVs. *Location:* Proceeds down Main Street U.S.A., stops at the Cinderella Castle plaza for the show, then returns.

© Disney

Perched on an oyster shell, Ariel rides above the crowd in the Disney Festival of Fantasy Parade. Peter Pan and Wendy follow, behind Skull Rock on the Jolly Roger pirate ship.

Disney Festival of Fantasy Parade

Disney's best parade has beautiful floats, costumes, music

★★★★★ ✔ FastPass+ Magic Kingdom's new-for-2014 parade is truly new—nothing is re-used from past parades, nothing has been patched together. The performers wear fantastic costumes, bursting with color. Floats celebrate Disney princesses, "Tangled," "The Little Mermaid," "Peter Pan," and "Brave." The eye-popper is the "Sleeping Beauty" segment, which stars the evil Malificent as a giant fire-breathing Steampunk dragon. Unfortunately, some characters (including Mickey Mouse) are high in the air, making it tough for children to interact with them.

On rainy days Disney runs an alternate procession, the brief "Rainy Day Cavalcade" with an assortment of classic characters waving from Main Street Vehicles.

Tips. *When to go:* Arrive 45 minutes early to get a great viewing spot (with a Fastpass, 15 minutes). *Where to stand:* The best spot is in front of the Emporium in Town Square, in the middle of Main Street U.S.A., facing the castle. Fastpass viewers watch from the inner side of the castle hub; Disney gives out a maximum of 350 Fastpasses for this spot.

Magic Kingdom's sound system was upgraded for the parade, adding more musical zones and improving the equipment. The procession's music was composed by Mark Hammond, who also wrote the score for the popular Mickey's Soundsational Parade at California's Disneyland. Trumpets were used as a key instrument, to give the parade a regal, celebratory feel.

Hidden Mickeys. ❶ The three-circle shape appears as balloons in the upper left corner of the parade banner, ❷ as a blue jewel and two smaller white jewels in the center of a large snowflake above "Frozen's" Queen Elsa, ❸ as indentations on a gear on the belly of the dragon Maleficent ❹ and as three bolts on the elbow of its left fore-leg.

Key facts. *Best for:* All ages. *Duration:* 12 min. *Fear factor:* The dragon occasionally breathes bursts of fire. *Showtime:* Daily at 3 p.m. *Weather issues:* During rain replaced by short procession. *Debuted:* 2014. *Access:* Guests may stay in wheelchairs, ECVs. *Location:* Travels through Frontierland, Liberty Square, Main Street U.S.A.

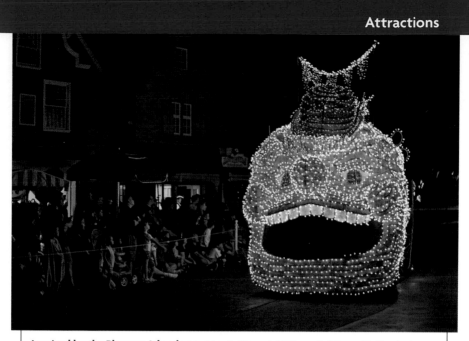

Inspired by the Pleasure Island sequence in Disney's 1940 movie "Pinocchio," a giant smiling head lights up like a Christmas tree in the Main Street Electrical Parade.

Main Street Electrical Parade

Light-bright retro floats form a cheesy, charming trip

★★★ FastPass+ Shimmering with light, everything—floats, characters, twirling snails—is covered with tiny colored bulbs in this Moog-music nighttime parade, which is either wonderful, weird or wonderfully weird, depending on your point of view. It's the one Disney parade where guests clap along to its music (the manic 1966 synthesizer ditty "Baroque Hoedown") and applaud its floats, most of which honor classic Disney movies (as well as, since it was new at the time the procession debute here, 1977's "Pete's Dragon."

Tinker Bell kicks things off, sprinkling pixie dust that leaves a golden swirl on all the floats that follow. Goofy is next, driving a train that holds Mickey and Minnie Mouse. Other characters include Alice, who chats with guests as she sits perched atop a giant mushroom, and Dopey, who drives a gem-filled mine train. Donkey-eared boys dance in front of the Pinocchio float, a decadent Pleasure Island carnival setting. Bringing up the rear is a long, bright patriotic flag straight out of Vegas, supported by saluting, high-stepping red-white-and-blue chorus girls.

Tips. *When to go:* Arrive 30 minutes early to get a decent viewing spot. *Where to stand:* On Main Street U.S.A. You'll see the parade with a great backdrop, and if you're leaving the park afterward you'll have just a short walk to the exit.

Fun finds. ❶ A caterpillar smokes a hookah on the "Alice in Wonderland" float. ❷ Cinderella's two stepsisters awkwardly hold their legs up high in front of Prince Charming, giving him views of their bloomers as they beg to try on his glass slipper. ❸ Played by grown men, Peter Pan's Lost Boys hold each other's tails as they twirl in a circle. Not that there's anything wrong with that. ❹ Huge cigar-store Indians line the back of Pinocchio's float, a giant smirking head.

Key facts. *Best for:* Toddlers, children, seniors, Disney enthusiasts. *Duration:* 20 min. *Weather issues:* Cancelled during rain. *Debuted:* 1977, revised 1999, 2010 (Disneyland 1972). *Access:* Special viewing areas for guests in wheelchairs and ECVs. *Location:* Travels Main Street U.S.A., then Liberty Square, Frontierland.

Unseen projectors bathe Cinderella Castle in brilliant, eye-popping light during Celebrate the Magic, bringing the building to life with moving images and video.

Celebrate the Magic

Stunning high-tech light show transforms Cinderella Castle

★★★ Using projected animated images and video, Cinderella Castle appears to transform during this nighttime show. Some of the visuals are truly bizarre. At one point the star of the 2012 movie "Wreck it Ralph" appears on the structure, which morphs it into an 8-bit brick version of itself that Ralph proceeds to wreck until hero Fix-It Felix saves the day. Later the castle becomes Buzz Lightyear's rocket ship and appears to blast off. Disney updates the show a few times each year; the version playing in the summer of 2014 included a frosty segment from the movie "Frozen," complete with Queen Elsa belting out the Academy Award-winning song "Let It Go." One of the more moving moments of the show is when Walt Disney himself appears on the castle, with his "It all started with a mouse" quote. Mickey Mouse as Steamboat Willie also makes an appearance.

Tips. *When to go:* Show up in front of the castle about 15 minutes before the show begins to get a good spot to watch it (however you may already be there, as this projection show is sandwiched between the end of the Main Street Electrical Parade and the start of the Wishes fireworks show; Celebrate the Magic sometimes plays twice a night, before the fireworks and then again before the nighttime parade). *Where to stand:* In the center of the castle hub, no closer than the statue of Walt Disney. From this spot you'll be far enough away to see the front of the castle and its angled sides, all of which have different images and special effects projected onto them, but still be close enough to see all of the effects' details. If viewed from an angle, the projections become distorted and skewed. *For families:* The segment featuring Maleficent could frighten your toddlers; you may want to distract them during its appearance.

Key facts. *Best for:* All ages. *Duration:* 10 min. *Fear factor:* The Maleficent moment has scary music and images. *Showtimes:* Typically twice a night; once before Wishes, once before the nighttime parade. *Weather issues:* Cancelled during rain. *Debuted:* 2012 (revised often). *Access:* Guests may remain in wheelchairs, ECVs. *Location:* Projected onto the front of Cinderella Castle.

Dozens of rockets and nearly 700 explosions light up the sky during Wishes, Walt Disney World's signature fireworks show. The visuals synchronize to a symphonic score.

Wishes

Synchronized fireworks are breathtaking, inspiring, touching

★★★★★ ✔ FastPass+ Tinker Bell flies from Cinderella Castle in Disney's signature fireworks show. It starts with a lone glowing star arching through the night sky. After narrator Jiminy Cricket (from 1940's "Pinocchio") talks about wishing on a star, $200,000 worth of pyro explode in sync with the voices of beloved Disney characters and the beats and rhythms of classic songs. Far more sophisticated than you might expect, Wishes paints delicate strokes as well as bold. Sometimes the sky sparkles, sometimes it flashes. The show packs an emotional punch too, as it teaches a heart-tugging lesson about believing in yourself. Parents often tear up during the finale.

Tips. *When to go:* 20 minutes before showtime. *Where to stand:* On the crest of the Main Street U.S.A. bridge, between the ice cream parlor and the castle hub. You'll be far enough away to see all the fireworks, but also close enough to see the castle's lighting effects. *For families:* Instead of fighting the huge crowd that leaves the park right after the show, get some ice cream and ask your children about their dreams and wishes. Tell them yours.

Fun fact. ❶ Tinker Bell is sometimes a man. The role's physical requirements are only that the performer weigh less than 105 pounds and be no taller than 5 foot 3 inches.

Fun finds. ❶ Fireworks form stars during the opening verse of "When You Wish Upon a Star." ❷ Hearts appear at the end of a "Beauty and the Beast" segment; ❸ a frowning face during the villains portion. ❹ As each Disney character says their wish, the accompanying fireworks are the color of his or her signature wardrobe. ❺ During the "Sorcerer's Apprentice" sequence, the castle is lit to resemble the blue hat Mickey Mouse wore in that segment from 1940's "Fantasia," with its white stars and moons. ❻ Images of the Evil Queen's mirror appear on the castle as she commands "Slaves in the magic mirror, come from the farthest space…"

Key facts. *Best for:* Families. *Duration:* 12 min. *Fear factor:* Loud. *Weather issues:* Cancelled for thunderstorms. *Debuted:* 2003. *Access:* Special viewing areas for guests in wheelchairs, ECVs. *Location:* The fireworks explode far behind and alongside the castle.

Epcot

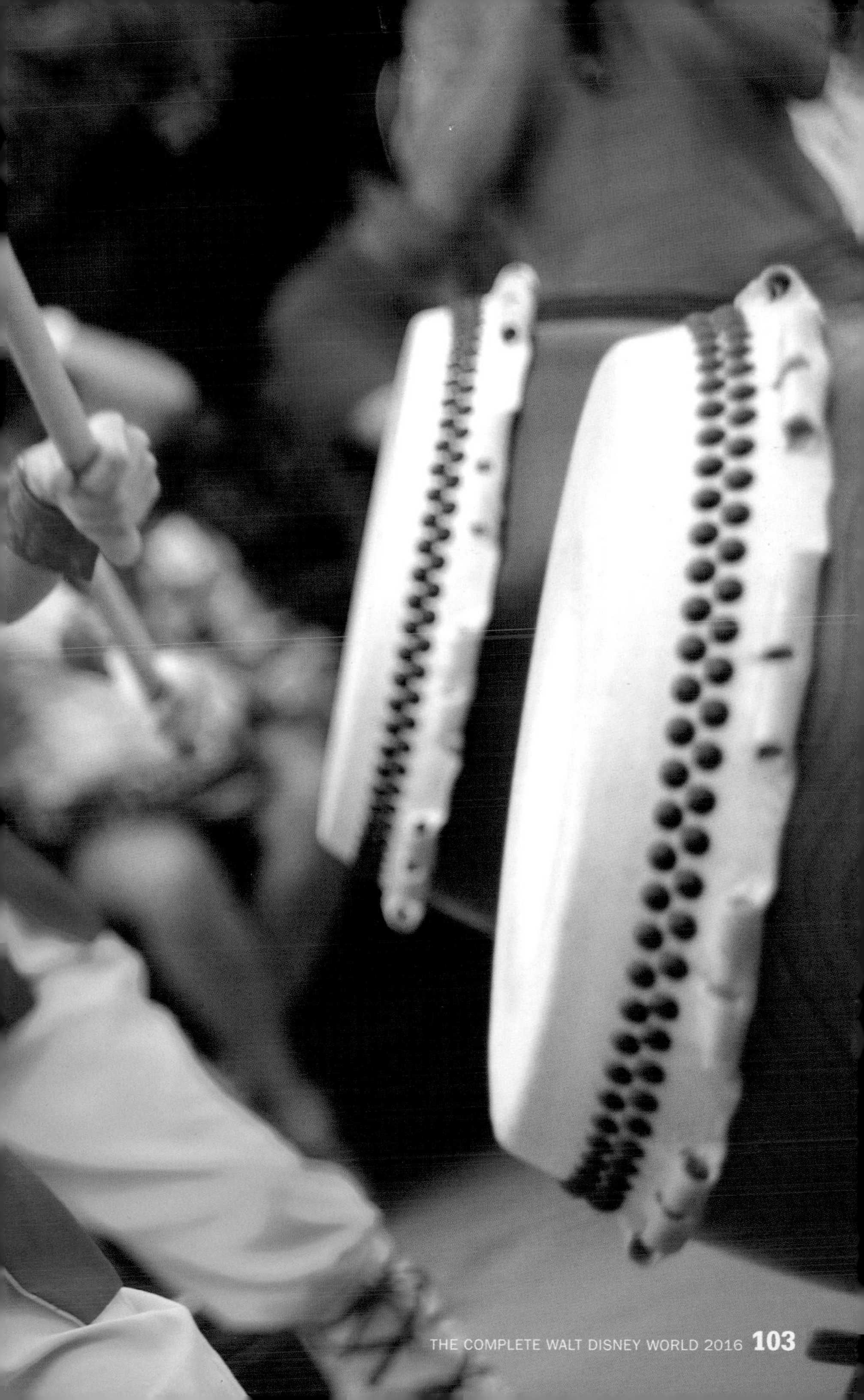

A world view. The torii gate of Japan's Itsukushima Shrine fronts Epcot's Japan pavilion. It's shown exposed at low tide, just like the real one is. At left the park icon, Spaceship Earth.

Disney's World's Fair

Human achievement rules at this inspiring park, which celebrates science, technology and cultural diversity. Like a World's Fair, Epcot's rides and shows are grouped into pavilions and focus on subjects such as communication, energy, agriculture, transportation and world cultures. Appealing most to the curious and educated, the park tends to be more interesting than thrilling.

Divided into two distinct sections—Future World and World Showcase—Epcot has a split personality. With its abundance of concrete buildings and scientific themes, Future World is a logical thinker, a corporate nerd with a pocket protector. World Showcase, on the other hand, is a people person, a music-loving shopaholic with a margarita in her hand.

Best of the park. You'll journey to far-flung lands and fly above some of the world's most unique natural landscapes and man-made wonders when the new high-definition **Soarin' Around the World** makes its debut in 2016... A quartet of **bottlenose dolphins** live at The Seas pavilion; training sessions spotlight their intelligence... Each World Showcase pavilion is staffed by **natives of its country**.

Hand-picked by Disney and flown to the United States on one-year visas, these young friendly people seem to love talking to guests about their homelands... Good food and drink, and lots of variety of both, set Epcot apart; no other spot lets you "**drink around the world**"... World Showcase shops brim with **unique wares** found nowhere else at Disney.

Worst of the park. Curiously lacking in Disney cast members, the wide walkways and public spaces in **impersonal Future World** are almost free of Disney smiles... With its emphasis on science, technology and international culture, Epcot has relatively **few child-focused experiences...** The only table-service **restaurants that serve breakfast** are character meals... Many attractions have blatant **corporate sponsorships**, leading you to wonder why Disney is charging you if it's also charging them... And finally, **the walking**. Hike through Future World out to the start of World Showcase and you've still got 1.3 miles to get around it, little of which is in the shade.

Getting oriented. Epcot consists of two separate areas, which have little to do with

The future of the '80s. A young couple strolls toward a breezeway in Future World's Innoventions Plaza, which leads to the area's Seas, Land and Imagination pavilions.

each other. The front area is Future World, with six pavilions circling a central plaza. It holds most of the park's rides and shows. In back is World Showcase, 11 pavillions that circle a lake. It holds most of the restaurants, shops and live entertainment. The two areas keep separate hours. Most of Future World opens at 9 a.m. and closes at 7 p.m. World Showcase opens at 11 a.m. and closes at 9 p.m.

Where to meet characters. Nearly two dozen characters appear at the park. It's the only place at Disney to meet Duffy or Mulan.

Aladdin. Morocco pavilion.

Alice. Tea garden, United Kingdom pavilion; Akershus Royal Banquet Hall meals (often), Norway pavilion.

NEW! Anna and Elsa. Fastpass+ Royal Sommerhus, Norway pavilion as of May 2016.

Ariel. Akershus Royal Banquet Hall meals (often), Norway pavilion.

Aurora. France pavilion fragrance garden; Akershus Royal Banquet Hall meals (often), Norway pavilion.

Belle. France pavilion, on the promenade; Akershus Royal Banquet Hall meals (often), Norway pavilion.

Chip 'n Dale. On the walkway behind Innoventions West. Garden Grill character meals, The Land pavilion.

Cinderella. Akershus Royal Banquet Hall meals (often), Norway pavilion.

Daisy Duck. Entrance Plaza.

Donald Duck. Mexico pavilion (in garb from 1944's "The Three Caballeros").

Duffy the Disney Bear. World Showcase Friendship Ambassador Gazebo, in front of the Disney Traders East gift shop.

Goofy. Fastpass+ Epcot Character Spot, Innoventions Plaza.

Jasmine. Morocco pavilion; also in the Akershus Royal Banquet Hall character meals (often), Norway pavilion.

Marie. France pavilion (sporadically).

Mary Poppins. In front of tea garden, United Kingdom pavilion; Akershus Royal Banquet Hall meals (often), Norway pavilion.

Mickey Mouse. Fastpass+ Character Spot, Innoventions Plaza; Garden Grill character meals, The Land pavilion.

Minnie Mouse. Fastpass+ Character Spot, Innoventions Plaza.

Mulan. China pavilion behind the formal gardens; Akershus Royal Banquet Hall (often), Norway pavilion.

Pluto. Entrance Plaza; Garden Grill character meals, The Land pavilion.

Snow White. Germany pavilion wishing well; Akershus Royal Banquet Hall meals (often), Norway pavilion.

Walking the world. A wide promenade circles the World Showcase Lagoon, traveling past 11 international pavilions. More than a mile long, it offers little shade on sunny afternoons.

Tigger. Inside the Toy Soldier shop, United Kingdom pavilion.

Winnie the Pooh. Inside the Toy Soldier shop, United Kingdom pavilion.

See also the chapter **Characters**.

Street performers. Every World Showcase pavilion except Germany offers live outdoor entertainment; see the upcoming World Showcase pages for details. There's also a live percussion group in Future World:

Jammitors. When a group of Innoventions Plaza janitors take a break, they transform into these witty drummers (★★★★★ ✓), using their trash cans and pails as drums.

Family matters. Four rides have height minimums—44 inches for Mission Space, 40 inches for Soarin' and Test Track, 48 inches for The Sum of All Thrills at Innoventions. Other attractions that might scare children include Ellen's Energy Adventure (loud noises, bright flashes, darkened dinosaur habitat); IllumiNations (loud explosions, fire); and Journey Into Imagination with Figment (loud noises, a sudden flash).

Every restaurant has a children's menu. There are two character meals: in Future World at the Garden Grill and in the World Showcase at the in the Norway pavilion.

Each pavilion holds a Kidcot Fun Stop, places to progressively decorate a free cardboard mask. Masks resemble either Duffy the Disney Bear or Perry, the pet platypus of Disney Channel faves Phineas and Ferb.

If it rains. Epcot is a mixed blessing on wet days—though it's comprised of indoor pavilions with multiple activities, those pavilions are spread out. Test Track closes when lightning is nearby. IllumiNations can get cancelled due to rain, as can all the park's outdoor concerts and street entertainment.

Fun finds in Future World. ① The layout of Future World mimics the left-right division of the human brain. As you enter the park, pavilions on the left are themed to analytical, linear or engineering issues and sit within a landscape of straight-lined walkways. Those on the right cover more natural topics in a hilly, meandering, watery landscape. ② Voices inside a trash can talk to you inside the Electric Umbrella restaurant. Swing open the lid of the only receptacle marked "Waste Please" (it's usually sitting next to a topping bar to the left of the order counter) and you may hear a surfer dude complain *"Like, your trash just knocked off my shades!"* or a Frenchman exclaim *"Zis ees my lucky day!*

© Disney

Epcot, 1981. The park begins to take shape in this construction photo. Opened to guests a year later, EPCOT Center was one of Walt Disney's ideas for his "Florida Project."

French fries!" ❸ Three drinking fountains imitate submarine sounds, sing opera and offer wisecracks such as "Hey, save some for the fish!" when water hits their drains. One sits in front of MouseGear along the east side of the Innoventions fountain. A second is near the play fountain between Future World and the World Showcase. A third sits close to the restrooms behind Innoventions West. ❹ Fiber-optic lights are embedded in the sidewalks in front of the Innoventions buildings. Pinpoints of shimmering, flickering stars hide in dozens of small squares. Larger, colorful changing patterns appear in three 6-foot squares in front of Innoventions West. The lights are on all day, but most noticeable at night. ❺ Thirty-eight discoveries and inventions are honored in the rarely noticed Epcot Inventor's Circle, five concentric rings embedded into the walkway that leads from Innoventions Plaza to The Land pavilion. Inner-ring discoveries lead to outer-ring ones. For example, the inner Alphabet leads to the outer World Wide Web.

Fun facts. ❶ The park has 3.5 acres of flowers and plants, 70 acres of lawns, 12,500 trees and 100,000 shrubs. ❷ There are nearly 300 optical, motion and sound effects at Epcot, more than five times the number in Magic Kingdom. ❸ The construction of Epcot was the largest private construction job in U.S. history up to that point. The $1 billion project involved 7,500 people (3,000 designers and 4,500 construction workers), and the movement of 54 million cubic feet of dirt.

Know before you go. Need a stroller? Cash? MyMagic+ help? Here's where to find it:

ATMs. There's one at the entrance on the far left, another on the bridge between Future World and World Showcase, and one near the American Adventure restrooms.

Baby Care Center. Situated at the Odyssey Center between Future World and World Showcase, this indoor spot has changing rooms, nursing areas, a microwave and a playroom. It sells diapers, formula, pacifiers and over-the-counter meds.

FastPass+ kiosks. Cast members help you book and reschedule Fastpasses at these walk-up touchscreens. You'll find them on the East and West breezeways in Future World, at Innoventions East, in the center of Innoventions Plaza and at the International Gateway, the park's back entrance.

First aid. An indoor clinic is between Test Track and World Showcase in the Odyssey Center, next to the park's Baby Care Center. Registered nurses treat minor emergencies. They call EMTs for serious issues.

Guest Relations. Located at the entrance to the park on the far right, this office has walk-up windows outside the touchpoint scanners, a walk-in lobby inside to the left of Spaceship Earth. Cast members answer general questions, make dining reservations, exchange currency, hand out maps and times guides for all Disney World parks, and store lost items found in the park that day.

Locker rentals. They're inside the park at the Camera Center in Future World, and also at the International Gateway in World Showcase ($7 a day, $5 deposit).

MyMagic+ Service Center. Cast members inside Innoventions East help with anything related to the MyMagic+ system, including the My Disney Experience website and app, the MagicBand ticketing system and the FastPass+ service.

Package pickup. Anything you buy in the park can be sent to the main park entrance or the International Gateway entrance for you to pick up later at no charge. Allow three hours. Packages can also be delivered to Disney hotels or shipped nationally.

Parking. $17 a day per car. Free for Disney hotel guests and annual passholders.

Stroller rentals. A stroller shop at the front entrance on the left—and also at the International Gateway entrance—rents single strollers for $15 a day ($13 length of stay), doubles for $31 ($27 length of stay). Get replacements at the Germany pavilion.

Disney transportation. Monorails run to the Transportation and Ticket Center (TTC), then connect to the Contemporary, Grand Floridian, Polynesian Village resorts and the Magic Kingdom park. Buses serve all other Disney resorts and theme parks as well as the Blizzard Beach water park; there's no direct service to Disney Springs, Typhoon Lagoon or ESPN Wide World of Sports. Boats serve Disney's Hollywood Studios and Epcot-area resorts from the park's International Gateway entrance in World Showcase.

Wheelchair and scooter rentals. Each entrance rents wheelchairs for $12 a day ($10 length of stay). EVCs are $50 ($20 deposit).

A closer look. In 1965, flush with success after decades in the entertainment industry, 63-year-old Walt Disney still had one dream left to explore: he wanted to find a fix for America's urban areas.

His idea: Combine corporate sponsorships with the gobs of money he had just made from the movie "Mary Poppins," and then—using 43 square miles of land he had secretly just purchased in central Florida—build an experimental city that, filled with technological advancements, would demonstrate how communities could solve their housing, pollution and transportation problems. He called the project the Experimental Prototype Community of Tomorrow. "EPCOT" for short.

The design called for a 50-acre town center enclosed in a dome, an internationally themed shopping area, a 30-story hotel and convention complex, office space, apartments, single-family homes, monorail and PeopleMover systems, an airport, underground roads for cars and trucks, even a nuclear power plant. There would be a theme park, too, a larger version of Disneyland.

On Nov. 15, 1965, Walt and his brother, Roy, held a press conference in Orlando to announce the project. "I'm very excited about it," he said, "because I've been storing these things up over the years. I like to create new things."

"We think the need is for starting from scratch on virgin land, building a community that will become a prototype for the future," Disney said in a videotaped sales pitch to potential corporate sponsors. "EPCOT will be a community of tomorrow that will never be completed, but will always be introducing and testing and demonstrating new materials and new systems."

Monsanto was interested. General Electric too. But little more than a year later, Walt Disney suddenly died. Smoking had caught up with him.

After Walt's death, the Disney company slowly abandoned his idea for an experimental city, but took two aspects of it—a corporate-sponsored science center and an international expo showcasing other cultures—and eventually turned them into a theme park. EPCOT Center (later just "Epcot") opened on October 1, 1982.

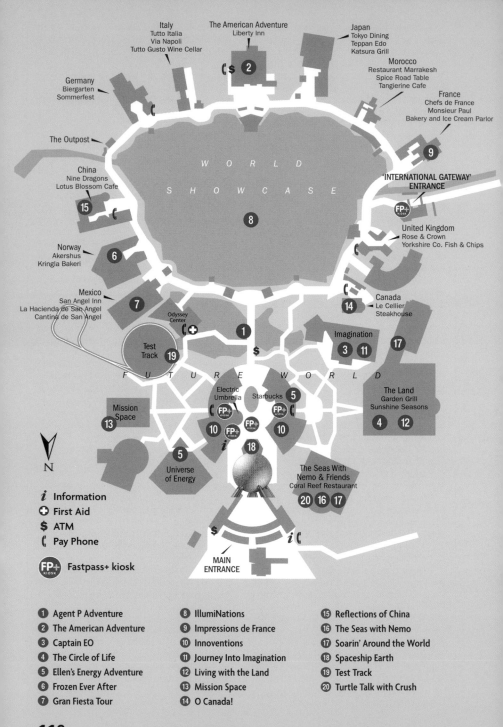

Italy
Tutto Italia
Via Napoli
Tutto Gusto Wine Cellar

The American Adventure
Liberty Inn

Japan
Tokyo Dining
Teppan Edo
Katsura Grill

Morocco
Restaurant Marrakesh
Spice Road Table
Tangierine Cafe

Germany
Biergarten
Sommerfest

France
Chefs de France
Monsieur Paul
Bakery and Ice Cream Parlor

The Outpost

'INTERNATIONAL GATEWAY'
ENTRANCE

China
Nine Dragons
Lotus Blossom Cafe

W O R L D

S H O W C A S E

United Kingdom
Rose & Crown
Yorkshire Co. Fish & Chips

Norway
Akershus
Kringla Bakeri

Canada
Le Cellier
Steakhouse

Mexico
San Angel Inn
La Hacienda de San Angel
Cantina de San Angel

Odyssey
Center

Imagination

Test
Track

The Land
Garden Grill
Sunshine Seasons

F U T U R E   W O R L D

Mission
Space

Electric
Umbrella

Starbucks

Universe
of Energy

The Seas With
Nemo & Friends
Coral Reef Restaurant

N

i Information

✛ First Aid

$ ATM

(Pay Phone

FP+ Fastpass+ kiosk
KIOSK

MAIN
ENTRANCE

1 Agent P Adventure
2 The American Adventure
3 Captain EO
4 The Circle of Life
5 Ellen's Energy Adventure
6 Frozen Ever After
7 Gran Fiesta Tour

8 IllumiNations
9 Impressions de France
10 Innoventions
11 Journey Into Imagination
12 Living with the Land
13 Mission Space
14 O Canada!

15 Reflections of China
16 The Seas with Nemo
17 Soarin' Around the World
18 Spaceship Earth
19 Test Track
20 Turtle Talk with Crush

Attractions at a Glance

Five-star attractions ★★★★★

Agent P's World Showcase Adventure. ✔ Funny interactive scavenger hunt triggers special effects, stars "Phineas and Ferb" characters. World Showcase.

The American Adventure. ✔ Film and Audio-Animatronics figures tell the story of this country. World Showcase.

UPDATED! Soarin' Around the World. ✔ FastPass+ Simulated hang-glider trip will change from a California trip to one that travels the world, with high-definition video. The Land pavilion, Future World.

Turtle Talk with Crush. FastPass+ An interactive show with real-time conversations between the audience and the animated sea turtle from the 2003 film "Finding Nemo." The Seas pavilion, Future World.

Four-star attractions ★★★★

NEW! Frozen Ever After. FastPass+ When the kingdom of Arendelle holds a Winter Festival in the summer, everyone breaks into song. A dark boat ride gives you a tour. Norway pavilion, World Showcase.

IllumiNations. ✔ FastPass+ Nightly fireworks and laser show portrays abstract history of the world. Explosions, fire may scare youngsters. World Showcase.

Impressions de France. 1980s film celebrates the art, landscape and music of France. France pavilion, World Showcase.

Living with the Land. ✔ FastPass+ Indoor boat ride through greenhouses full of real, amazing plants, aquaculture tanks. The Land pavilion, Future World.

Mission Space. FastPass+ Flight simulator takes you to Mars. The original ride achieves intense G forces by spinning in a NASA-style centrifuge; a milder version does not spin. Not for those with claustrophobia or spinning problems. Min. height 44 in. Future World.

O Canada. Comedian Martin Short hosts funny CircleVision 360 film about Canada. Canada pavilion, World Showcase.

Test Track. ✔ FastPass+ You design a car then virtually test it on a real track; speeds reach 65 mph. Min. height 40 in. Future World.

Three-star attractions ★★★

Gran Fiesta Tour. Bizarre, confusing, insulting, addicting Mexican boat ride stars 1944 Disney film's "The Three Caballeros." Mexico pavilion, World Showcase.

Innoventions. Corporate exhibits showcase new technologies. A Raytheon Sum of All Thrills exhibit lets guests design, then ride a virtual coaster atop a robotic arm (min. height 48 in). Future World.

The Seas with Nemo & Friends pavilion. ✔ FastPass+ Calm dark ride retells story of 2003's "Finding Nemo"; leads to stale exhibits of wonderful sealife. Future World.

Spaceship Earth. ✔ FastPass+ Slow-moving dark ride uses Audio-Animatronic characters to show history of communications. Better than it sounds. Future World.

Two-star attractions ★★

The Circle of Life. Dated, faded film uses stars of 1994's "The Lion King" to preach environmental protection. The Land pavilion, Future World.

Ellen's Energy Adventure. Before she was Dory, comedian Ellen DeGeneres apparently would do anything for a buck, including being a corporate shill for Exxon, the one-time sponsor of this elaborate 45-minute infomercial that extolls fossil fuels. Includes some realistic dinosaurs. Future World.

One-star attractions ★

Captain EO. FastPass+ Woefully indulgent space adventure stars Michael Jackson at his most Wacko Jacko; produced by George Lucas at a time when common sense escaped him. Originally produced for this theater in 1986, its value today is only historic. Imagination pavilion, Future World.

Journey Into Imagination... with Figment. FastPass+ Mischievous dragon Figment interrupts goofy Eric Idle's tour of a stuffy Imagination Institute. Even Figment fans don't like it, but young children might. Imagination pavilion, Future World.

Reflections of China. Circular film shows a selective culture, geography and history of China. China pavilion, World Showcase.

Disney's best pizza. Charred crusts of imported caputo flour, true-Italian toppings and dedicated Italian cooks make the pizzas at Via Napoli mama-mia marvelous.

Restaurants and food

Table service. There are only two poor restaurants at Epcot, a price-gouging princess buffet and a sad Chinese spot.

★★ **$$$$ Akershus Royal Banquet Hall.** Disney princesses come to your table at this bustling Princess Storybook Dining Experience. Breakfast is American, served family-style: all-you-can-eat but brought to your table. Lunch and dinner are three-course Norwegian buffets. Appetizers such as sliced peppered mackerel (fish jerky) are acquired tastes, but the lamb stew and kjøttkake meatballs will seem familiar to anyone raised on hearty American fare. Kids can choose from hot dogs, pasta, pizza and grilled chicken. The room is noisy. The last lunch and dinner seatings often have walk-up tables available. *Five characters may include Ariel, Belle, Jasmine, Snow White, Princess Aurora (Sleeping Beauty), Mulan, Cinderella, Mary Poppins. Norway pavilion. Breakfast 8 a.m.–11 a.m., $47 (children $28). Lunch 11:55 a.m.–3:30 p.m., $50 (children $29). Dinner 4:55 p.m.–8:40 p.m., $55 (children $30). Seats 255.*

★★★★ **$$$$ Biergarten.** A live band rolls out a barrel full of polkas at this Oktoberfest buffet, waltzes too, stopping now and then to demonstrate some strange instrument or lead a toast—"Tiki toki, tiki toki, HOY HOY HOY!" Best bets on the buffet include potato leek soup, beef rouladen and pork schnitzel (the last two at dinner only). Skip the seafood. Beer choices include light and dark Spaten, Becks and Franziskaner Hefe-Weisse. The dining room simulates a medieval Rothenburg courtyard at night; the moon and stars glow overhead. Unless you're a party of eight you'll share your table with others, sharing toasts and conversations whether you want to or not. Young waiters wear traditional Bavarian tracht wear—green lederhosen shorts, white shirts, green suspenders, little black hats and teeny weeny little ties. *Germany pavilion. Band performs a 20-minute set hourly. Lunch noon–3:45 p.m., $28 (children $15). Dinner 4 p.m.–9 p.m. (last show 8:05 p.m.), $39 (children $19). Seats 400.*

★★★ **$$$$ Chefs de France.** Generous with cream and cheese, this sophisticated spot offers everything from sandwiches to seafood. Good appetizers include lobster bisque. Big kids will love the adult menu's mac and cheese (lunch only), made with cream and gruyere. For dessert the signature créme brulee is rich and silky. Tile floors and tin ceilings are nice but noisy. Founded by acclaimed French chefs Paul Bocuse, Gaston Leôtre and Roger

Under the sea. Sharks, rays and sea turtles swim past diners at the Coral Reef restaurant, which looks into the huge saltwater aquarium of The Seas pavilion.

Vergé, managed today by Paul's son Jerome. *France pavilion. Lunch noon–3 p.m., $15–$30 (children $9–$10). Dinner 5 p.m.–9 p.m., $19–$33 (children $9–$10). Seats 266.*

★★★★★ ✔ $$$$ **Coral Reef.** You eat fish while you watch fish at this dimly lit romantic yet family-friendly hidden treasure, where a long glass wall looks into The Seas aquarium. The signature appetizer is a creamy lobster bisque; entrees are consistently good. Brushed-metal tables are trimmed in light woods. Arrive at 11:30 a.m. and you may be able to walk right in; otherwise book lunch two weeks early; dinner at least 60 days out. When you arrive ask for an aquarium-front table on the floor; it's worth a longer wait. Amazed by the sharks, turtles and other sealife swimming inches away from them, tired children may forget they're tired. *The Seas pavilion. Lunch 11:30 a.m.–3:30 p.m., $12–$33 (children $9–$11). Dinner 4 p.m.–8:50 p.m., $20–$33 (children $9–$11). Seats 275.*

NEW MEALS! ★★★★ ✔ $$$$$ **Garden Grill.** Serving breakfast, lunch and dinner as of November 8, 2015, this often-overlooked country restaurant offers Disney's most unusual character meals. Perched on the top floor of The Land pavilion, the circular Garden Grill is built like a merry-go-round, its open dining balcony slowly rotating around its kitchen once every two hours. Tables overlook the indoor portion of the Living with the Land attraction, which includes a realistic rainforest and other landscapes. As you dine, cartoon chipmunks Chip 'n' Dale, "farmer" Mickey Mouse and Pluto mosey up to say hi and sometimes sit a spell. Thanks to the restaurant's small size you see the characters often, maybe three times each if you stay an hour. Food is served "family style," which means servers bring big platters and bowls to your table for your party to share, and replenish them as often as you like. Breakfast includes typical eggs, bacon and Mickey waffles but also a signature item unique to this spot, Chip's Sticky Bun Bakes. Lunch and dinner feature typical sliced beef and turkey, but also a Farmer's Salad that uses vegetables grown in the Living with the Land greenhouses. Ask to sit on the balcony's outside ring and you'll get another benefit—your booth's high-backed seats will block your family's view of the rest of the restaurant, making each character's stop at your table a delightful surprise as you won't see him coming. *The Land pavilion. Breakfast 8 a.m.–10:30 a.m., $30 (children $18). Lunch 11:30 a.m.–3 p.m., $35 (children $20). Dinner 4 p.m.–8 p.m., $45 (children $21). Seats 150.*

★★★★ ✔ $$$$ **La Hacienda de San Angel.** This inviting waterfront restaurant offers

French find. Open only at dinner, Monsieur Paul offers Epcot's only true gourmet meals. It's run by Jerome Bocuse as a tribute to his father, Paul, a French Legion of Honor winner for his black-truffle soup.

authentic Mexican fare and tasty drinks. Best bets include the fresh salsas, creative appetizers and flavorful on-the-rocks margaritas—of which six varieties were developed with an expert mixologist. A tequila ambassador helps guests choose a flight from among 17 choices. The restaurant emulates a cozy hacienda, with original artwork and unusual blown-glass light fixtures. Oversized windows provide a good view. *Mexico pavilion. 4 p.m.–9 p.m., $24–$59 (children $9–$10). Seats 250.*

★★★ $$$$ **Le Cellier.** The toughest Epcot reservation to nab, this low-ceilinged, stone-walled eatery resembles a chateau wine cellar. Alberta-beef steaks are aged 28 days. Other entrees include fish, seafood, chicken and sandwiches. Made with Moosehead beer, a cheddar-cheese soup makes a nice makeshift dip for complimentary soft breadsticks. *Canada pavilion. 11:30 a.m.–9 p.m., $28–$50 (children $8–$15). Seats 156. A Disney Signature Restaurant.*

★★★★★ ✓ $$$$$ **Monsieur Paul.** Can you imagine? Being awarded your nation's highest honor because of the quality of your soup? That's what happened to French chef Paul Bocuse in 1975, who was placed into the French Legion of Honor after he created a black truffle soup for a state dinner hosted by President Valéry Giscard d'Estaing. Once you taste it, the award will make sense. Crowned with a pastry dome to retain its truffle flavor, the soup exhales a steaming cloud of pungent vapor when its crust is pierced, then proceeds to soak its pastry into its broth, which hides a meticulous mix of carrots, chicken, duck, foie gras and, of course, black truffles, direct from the ground beneath French oak and

hazelnut trees. Incredibly, that magnifique creation is available here, along with many of Bocuse's other achievements, thanks to the oddity of Bocuse (along with friends Gaston Leôtre and Roger Vergé) setting up the restaurants of the France pavilion in 1982, and the luck that they're managed today by his son Jerome, who has recently refocused this smaller one into a tribute to his father.

And a fine tribute it is, as nearly everything here is much the same as that soup—an exquisite, heartfelt offering that you'd never expect to find in a theme park, with a depth of flavor in its sauce only the French seem to understand. Friendly yet distinctly formal, the white-tablecloth, truly gourmet Monsieur Paul expects its diners to dress up (though no dress code is enforced) and children to be well-behaved. As you arrive, tuxedoed French servers line up to greet you, each offering a cordial bonsoir ("good evening"). Of course it's all very expensive, but portions are reasonable and overall a dinner here is worth every penny. In fact some items are actually bargains. In France the truffle soup is 85 euros, about $93. Here it's $29. *On the second floor of the France pavilion, above Chefs de France. 5:30 p.m.–9 p.m., $39–$44 (children $13–$16). A four-course, prix-fixe meal is $89 without wine. Seats 120. A Disney Signature Restaurant.*

★★ $$$$ **Nine Dragons.** Nearly everything at this tired restaurant lacks imagination and punch. There are some high points, including good teas and light desserts. Direct from China's National Guest House, a tiny cucumber stack appetizer is an indulgence. Greens, yellows and blues highlight a serene decor; window tables make for good

Paul Bocuse

Top chefs. Friends Paul Bocuse, Gaston Leôtre and Roger Vergé at the ground-breaking of Epcot's French pavilion. The three chefs opened and oversaw the pavilion's restaurants.

people-watching. *China pavilion. Noon–9 p.m., $13–$19 (children $8–$10). Seats 300.*

★★★ $$$$ **Restaurant Marrakesh.** Though it sounds exotic, there is nothing scary about Moroccan cuisine. Ingredients are the same as those in American cooking, and flavors are mild. The lamb shank couscous is like your mom's pot roast, complete with roasted carrots and meat that falls off the bone, but tossed in light fluffy wheat instead of potatoes. Lunch includes beef and fish dishes and a prix-fixe meal for $20; dinner adds sampler platters. Of course, mom's meals probably didn't include a belly dancer. Here, one shimmies in front of a small band (on the hour from 1–8 p.m. except for 4 p.m.), her moves more graceful than sexy. Children can join in. Ceilings are intricately decorated; walls are covered in tiles. Since Moroccan food is unfamiliar to many Americans, this is the least crowded Epcot eatery. Ask to sit by the dance floor. *Morocco pavilion. Lunch 11:30 a.m.–3:30 p.m., $16–$23 (children $8). Dinner 3:30 p.m.–9 p.m., $22–$30 (children $8). Seats 255.*

★★★★ ✔ $$$$ **Rose & Crown Dining Room.** It's not the fanciest food in Epcot and probably a little too hearty, but every time we eat here we want to come back. Maybe it's the menu, which includes some of the most deliciously creamy potato soup we've ever had. Maybe it's the servers, a young bunch who exude British charm. Maybe it's the little covered patio, which on a nice day is one of Disney's best outdoor dining spots. The menu includes British entrees such as bangers and mash (good) and shepherd's pie (better) and a good selection of British beers. *United Kingdom pavilion. Noon–3:30 p.m., $16–$29 (children $9). Dinner 4 p.m.–9 p.m., $16–$32 (children $9). Seats 242.*

★★★ $$$$$ **San Angel Inn.** Good choices include signature tortilla soup and a steak that tastes like it's straight off a backyard grill. Sitting on padded chairs and benches around a lantern-lit table, you dine in a faux moonlit courtyard. In the distance is a rumbling volcano that, depending on your margarita intake, may appear to be the most realistic effect Disney has ever created. The restaurant is run by the Debler family, the proprietors of the namesake Mexico City restaurant. *Mexico pavilion. 11:30 a.m.–9 p.m., $18–$25 (children $9–$11). Seats 156.*

REVISED MENU! ★★★★★ ✔ $$$$ **Spice Road Table.** Cursed with an accurate but ultra-unclear name—its dishes aren't hot, they're seasoned, with spices from the Mediterranean, Middle East and North Africa—this little waterfront restaurant

Upscale Mexican. Run by a Mexican family sincerely devoted to its craft, La Hacienda de San Angel creates modern recipes that add zest to typical entrees and zip to margaritas.

often sits almost totally empty. And that's a shame, since it's one of Epcot's best places to eat. A fusion of flavors, each of its dishes wakes up your taste buds yet is perfectly balanced. Best bets include the creamy brie fondue served with apricots, walnuts and rosemary bread; the perfectly crusted tender rack of lamb (the most expensive item on the menu at only $30); unusual flash-fried hummus; for dessert either crème brûlée-style saffron lemon custard or a nuanced sampling of tasty baklavas; and drinks that include iced mint tea, a juicy watermelon drink, first-rate sangria and interesting Mediterranean beers and Moroccan wines. A three-hose hookah highlights the decor of the small dining room; an outdoor patio is nicely shaded. The restaurant's Moroccan wait staff is attentive and friendly; ambient acoustic music adds to the relaxed vibe. As for issues, its small tables are placed close together, so when it does fill up it's overcrowded. A step above the pavilion's other dining choices, Spice Road is a joint effort of Disney and its Moroccan management; the difference is obvious. Reservations usually aren't needed until after 7 p.m. Note: The restaurant's original "small-plate" menu was replaced in 2015. *Morocco pavilion. 11:30 a.m.–9 p.m., $22–$30. Seats 172.*

★★★ $$$$ **Teppan Edo.** An entertaining tableside chef may juggle knives or make a "smoking Mickey train" out of onion stacks in these stunning red-and-black dining rooms. Using a grill set into your table, the chef's hands fly fast as they slice, dice and stir-fry your choice of beef, seafood or chicken. You share your table with other guests. *Japan pavilion. Noon–9 p.m., $17–$30 (children $9–$14). Seats 192.*

★★★★ ✔ $$$$ **Tokyo Dining.** With good food, nice atmosphere and great service, this is what a World Showcase restaurant is supposed to be—a non-threatening way to experience a foreign cuisine. Traditional entrees include a tender beef teriyaki and light shrimp tempura. A sushi menu has 50 selections. For dessert, the green tea pudding melts in your mouth. Diffused lighting, dark tables and a tile floor create a peaceful decor. The friendly staff bows to you at every opportunity. *Japan pavilion. Noon–9 p.m., $16–$32 (children $12). Seats 116.*

★★★★★ ✔ $$$$$ **Tutto Italia.** This is the best Italian spot on Disney property, thanks to its imported pastas and delicate sauces. Meat and fish entrees are good too, though sides are $10. Entree salads use ingredients like asparagus, curly endive and fava beans. As you arrive, don't let the formal maitre'd

© Disney

An undiscovered gem. Also overlooking the World Showcase lagoon, Spice Road Table serves seasoned dishes using spices from the Mediterranean, Middle East and North Africa.

fool you; the young Italian wait staff is friendly. An elegant decor has dark woods. *Italy pavilion. Lunch 11:30 a.m.–3:30 p.m., $17–$29 (children $10). Dinner 4:30 p.m.–9 p.m., $23–$30 (children $10). Seats 300.*

★★★★★ ✔ **$$$$ Via Napoli.** Disney's best pizza place, this one may be the most satisfying restaurant in Epcot; in 2015 TripAdvisor named it one of the Top 3 pizza spots in Orlando. Its true-Italian toppings and flavorful flaky crusts are worth every penny it charges, which is about twice as many as your neighborhood Pizza Hut. The flavorful, charred pizza crusts are made from caputo flour imported from Naples. Individual pizzas are large enough to share if you add an appetizer. We like the classic margherita pie, but love the decadently creamy paccheri pasta. Ask to sit in the breezy main dining room; it's so relaxing you'll lose track of time. Just don't plan on any quiet conversations; its tile floors and open wood-and-plaster ceilings create quite a din. *Italy pavilion. 11:30 a.m.–9 p.m., $18–$28 (children $9). Seats 400, including 24 at a community table.*

Counter service. Our two top choices: Sunshine Seasons and Katsura Grill.

★★ **$$ Electric Umbrella.** Basic eatery has lackluster atmosphere. Burgers, chicken and salads. *Innovations Plaza, Future World. $9–$11 (children $6). 11 a.m.–9 p.m. Seats 426.*

★★★ **$ Starbucks Fountain View.** This standard Starbucks includes pastries and breakfast sandwiches; many coffee options. *Innovations Plaza, Future World. 9 a.m.–9 p.m. $4–$5. Seats 68 outside.*

★★★★★ ✔ **$$ Katsura Grill.** Comfortable spot serves subtle teriyaki dishes that appeal to all ages; its udon noodle soup is even better. *Japan pavilion. 11 a.m.–9 p.m. $8–$13. Seats 60 inside, 34 outside.*

★★★★ ✔ **$$ Kringla Bakeri Og Kafe.** Tiny spot offers fresh pastries and sandwiches. *Norway pavilion. 11 a.m.–9 p.m. $6–$8 (children $5). Seats 50, outdoor but shaded.*

★★★ **$ La Cantina de San Angel.** Sitting lakeside along the promenade, this fast-food spot sells empanadas, nachos, tacos, churros, margaritas and beer. *Mexico pavilion. 11 a.m.–9 p.m. $8–$12 (children $5).*

★★★★★ ✔ **$ La Cava del Tequila.** This bustling little bar serves over 200 tequilas, and has eclectic margaritas. A great escape from theme-park madness. *Mexico pavilion. Noon–9 p.m. $8–$50. Seats 30.*

★★★★ ✔ **$ L'Artisan Des Glaces.** Tiny parlor scoops up artisanal ice cream and sorbet. *France pavilion. Noon–9 p.m. $4–$10. Seats 24 outside.*

A unique caramel shop. German cooks make Werther's caramel popcorn throughout the day at Epcot's Karamell-Küche shop, the only freestanding Werther's shop in the world.

★★★★ ✔ **$ Les Halles Boulangerie & Patisserie.** The only World Showcase counter-service spot open before 11 a.m., this bakery serves pastries, quiche, sandwiches. *France pavilion. 9 a.m.–9 p.m. $7–$11. Seats 64.*

★★ **$$ Liberty Inn.** Ho-hum burgers, chicken, hot dogs; also a kosher meal. Nondescript atmosphere has nice air conditioning. *The American Adventure pavilion. Noon–9 p.m. $8–$11 (children $6). Seats 710.*

★★ **$ Lotus Blossom Cafe.** Egg rolls, chicken and stir-fry meals lack flavor. *China pavilion. 11 a.m.–9 p.m. $7–$12 (children $7). Seats 106 on covered patio.*

★★★ **$ Sommerfest.** Bratwurst, frankfurters, Reubens and other hearty fare, all begging to be washed down with beer. *Germany pavilion. 11 a.m.–9 p.m. $4–$9. Seats 24 on covered, sheltered patio.*

★★★★★ ✔ **$ Sunshine Seasons.** Excellent food court serves freshly prepared grilled meats (try the pork chop), noodles, salads, sandwiches, soups. Breakfast too. *The Land pavilion, Future World. 9 a.m.–9 p.m. $5–$13 (children $6–$7). Seats 707.*

★★★★ ✔ **$$ Tangierine Cafe.** Tasty chicken and lamb platters; a pastry counter serves assorted baklava, tea, liqueur coffees and beer. *Morocco pavilion. 11 a.m.–9 p.m. $9–$15 (children $8). Seats 100.*

NEW! ★★★★ ✔ **$ Taste Track.** Specialty grilled cheese sandwiches draw a crowd to this nondescript stand in front of Test Track; each comes with a side salad or tomato bisque soup. Other items on its debut menu include a chicken salad sandwich, craft beer. *Future World. 11 a.m.–7 p.m. $8–$10 (children $6). No seats; 6 stand-up tables; benches nearby.*

★★★★ ✔ **$$$ Tutto Gusto Wine Cellar.** This tiny spot resembles a wine cellar with its brick arches, wood beams and stone walls and floors. Its menu features small plates of cheeses, mini-panini, pasta and seafood and nearly 200 Italian wines—a nice way to get a taste of Italy without breaking the bank. *Italy pavilion. 11:30 a.m.–9 p.m. $9–$18. Seats 96.*

★★★ **$ Yorkshire County Fish Shop.** This walk-up window serves only fish and chips; which pale next to those at Cooke's of Dublin at Disney Springs. *United Kingdom pavilion. 11:30 a.m.–9 p.m. $9. Seats 30 outdoors.*

Fun find sweets and treats. Meticulous research by the author's daughter has found a treasure trove of treats at the World Showcase pavilions:

Canada. ❶ Pure maple-syrup lollipops at the Trading Post shop ($3). ❷ Tossed in cinnamon sugar, cronuts (croissant doughnuts, $4) are nearby at the Refreshment Port.

Funnel cakes. Once a Christmas novelty sold at church bazaars, the treats are cooked-to-order at the American Adventure pavilion, topped with apples, chocolate or ice cream.

United Kingdom. ❸ Cadbury dairy milk chocolate candy bars at the Tea Caddy ($4). Smoother and creamier than our Hershey's brand, Cadbury is a favorite chocolate in the U.K.; the bar melts quickly in the Florida heat.

France. ❹ The bakery's créme brulee ($5); top it off with a little cream and sugar, stir it up and head off to heaven. ❺ Also good: the ice cream shop's chocolate macaroon ice cream sandwich ($4). ❻ Wine flights at the wine shop give you three two-ounce pours ($9).

Morocco. ❼ The walnut baklava from the bakery case of the Tangierine Café ($3); almond and cashew varieties are also good.

Japan. ❽ Each piece of sweet watermelon Botan rice candy has a melt-in-your-mouth wrapper; an eight-piece package ($1) comes with a colorful little sticker that's awesomely odd—for example, a smiling diva pickle wearing high-heels and lipstick. ❾ Also good: packages of creamy Tirol green tea chocolates with rice cake fillings ($3) ❿ and semi-hard Sakuma strawberry milk candy ($4).

The American Adventure. ⓫ A warm funnel cake topped with a slab of ice cream (overpriced at $9) at Funnel Cakes, a small stand in front of the pavilion.

Italy. ⓬ A Baci Perugina hazelnut chocolate fortune ball ($1), sold at La Bottega. Each ball has a different fortune inside.

Germany. ⓭ A freshly-made Werther's caramel apple oatmeal cookie ($5) at the Karamell-Küche shop. As wide as a large grapefruit, it's drizzled with fresh Werther's caramel, and easily broken apart to share. ⓮ You also can't go wrong with some fresh Werther's caramel popcorn.

China. ⓯ Check out the White Rabbit creamy candy, which tastes like chewy vanilla taffy. Each piece is shaped like a little Tootsie Roll, and has an edible inner wrapping made from a transparent sheet of rice. One bag ($6) holds a few dozen individually wrapped pieces.

Norway. ⓰ Made of almonds, Marabou chocolate and a brittle toffee center, sweet Daim ("Dime") candy bars ($3) are lusciously sweet. ⓱ Another must is the bakery's school bread ($3), a sweet cardamom bun that's been filled with vanilla cream custard and topped with toasted coconut and sugar crystals.

Mexico. ⓲ Indulge in Glorias, a creamy goat's milk candy that's made with pecans. This subtle, creamy treat can get sticky once unwrapped. Packages of five pieces ($6) are sold inside the pyramid but get moved around; you may have to ask for them to find them.

See also **Restaurant Policies** in the chapter **Walt Disney World A–Z.**

A bold choice. A trio of guests take photos of each other outside the gift shop in front of the Mexico pavilion. Few people buy its large sombreros, but many try them on.

Shops and merchandise

In Future World. The main Epcot souvenir store, **MouseGear** (★★★ ✔, Innoventions Plaza) is a huge place with all kinds of Disney stuff both routine and special. For the most part, however, it does not stock items sold in the World Showcase pavilions. Other Future World shops include **After Market** (★★★, at the Test Track exit) which stocks automotive merchandise and Test Track souvenirs; **The Art of Disney** (★★★, along the left side of Spaceship Earth), a gallery of lithographs, oils, figurines; the **Soarin' gift counter** (★★★, The Land pavilion), which, since it's the sign-up spot for Disney's Behind the Seeds greenhouse tour, sells horticulture items; and **Club Cool** (★★★★ ✔, Innoventions Plaza), a Coca-Cola shop known throughout the Disney universe not for its routine Coke merchandise, but rather its unlimited free samples of foreign soft drinks. The best ones—Bibo from South Africa, Fanta Pineapple from Greece. The worst: Beverly, a bitter Italian soda Disney has slipped in as a joke. It's not a soft drink, but rather an aperitif.

World Showcase pavilions. Though most of these pavilion's more touristy items come from China, each of them also stocks at least some things from the country it represents.

★★ **Canada.** Two connected stores offer little authentic Canadian merchandise, though Northwest Mercantile sells real maple-syrup treats and dreamcatchers, and The Trading Post offers Canadian books and a silly moose-antler hat. **Fun find:** The small Goofy lumberjack plushie.

★★★ **United Kingdom.** Half a dozen pretty little shops offer a variety of merchandise from the U.K. The Crown & Crest specializes in family name and coat of arms items as well as Guinness souvenirs. Lords and Ladies stocks fine silver jewelry and "Downton Abbey" merchandise. The Queen's Table sells "Keep Calm and Carry On" items. As its name suggests, The Sportsman's Shoppe stocks sports apparel; rugby, soccer and tennis shoes; balls; and sports books. The Tea Caddy offers many varieties of Twinings tea, plus fine bone china, teapots, biscuits and British candies. Though it used to sell toys, The Tin Soldier now offers Beatles, Rolling Stones and Monty Python merchandise. **Fun find:** Quirky Dr. Who and Mr. Bean T-shirts.

★★★★ ✔ **France.** Small Guerlain Paris offers limited-edition fragrances, some

From France. Saida Dubois readies her French pavilion stands early one morning. A resident of the village of Troyes, she came to Epcot through Disney's Cultural Representative Program.

in signature bee bottles, all very French. Cosmetics can be applied on the spot. Brands at Plume et Palette include Annick Goutal, Chanel and Dior. Tiny boutique Parfums Givenchy is the only place in the United States with the full line of Givenchy perfume; each year it has a U.S. exclusive. A cozy store that channels a homey village kitchen, L' Esprit de la Provence sells cookware, cookbooks and kitchen items. Aux Vins de France sells wines by the glass or by the bottle. Skip Souvenirs de France; its faux French souvenirs come from China. **Fun finds:** A top-seller in France, Guerlain's La Petite Robe Noire ("little black dress," $75 for 1.6 ounces) starts with a base of vanilla, patchouli, smoked tea and musk, then brings out notes of lemon, almonds, anise, roses, even raspberry macaroons and licorice. Yet it's subtle. Another find: the parasols on the promenade, hand-painted by young French artists. Little girls love them.

★★★★★ ✔ **Morocco.** Five open-air shops run independently of Disney make this pavilion's shopping the most unique at Epcot. An open-air alley the Marketplace in the Medina has seagrass baskets, ceramic-topped tables and two strange drums: ceramic tam-tams covered in camel skin, and open-top darboukas with flounder-skin bottoms. Adjacent Tangier Traders has traditional caftans,

gandouras and other robes and wraps, as well as handmade leather slippers. The Brass Bazaar stocks handmade brass plates and platters as well as packaged couscous, spices, wooden cookware and rosewater bottles. Casablanca Carpets offers rugs but also lamps that filter their light through henna-dyed lamb skin, incense holders, leather pouf chairs and colorful sequined pillows. Out front, the open-air Souk-Al-Magreb ("The Flea Market of Northern Africa") offers a mix of merchandise from the other shops. **Fun find:** Aromatic bowls and boxes made out of thuya, a burled-root wood grown only in Morocco.

★★★★★ ✔ **Japan.** A 10,000-square-foot Mitsukoshi store overflows with merchandise. The largest area has Pokémon plush, figurines and cards; Hello Kitty items; and quirky toys. An entertaining Pick-A-Pearl station draws big crowds, as shoppers select their own oyster and keep whatever pearl is discovered inside for $17. A second zone bridges Japanese and Western cultures with glass-bead jewelry, sandals, Mikimoto pearl jewelry and creative fashion apparel. Also for sale are bonsai trees, silk kimonos, lanterns, rice paper and tatami mats. In back, chopsticks, porcelain dishes, teas and sweets fill the shelves. **Fun find:** Sake by the glass, at the little bar at the back of the store.

Norwegian perfume. A small Geir Ness boutique in the Norway pavilion offers the designer's acclaimed Laila perfume and Geir for Men cologne. Ness himself appears at the store every now and then.

★ **The American Adventure.** The small Heritage Manor Gifts sells patriotic apparel and books, most of which come from China. Some fancy packaged foods are American. Out front, a wood cart sells T-shirts.

★★★ **Italy.** Two stores offers interesting Italian merchandise. Il Bel Cristallo has an eclectic collection of Murano glass, jewelry, fragrances, and Puma sportswear; in a smaller room an artisan creates papier-mâché, fabric Carnivale masks in front of you. Across the plaza, La Bottega sells wine by the bottle or glass, Perugina candy and Christmas ornaments. **Fun find:** Delicate Murano Christmas ornaments. Each is unique.

★★★★ **Germany.** Eight stores and one promenade stand line a central courtyard. Masculine Das Kaufhaus sells apparel, backpacks, soccer balls and sandals. Children's items at Der Teddybar include Steiff bears, Schleich toys, Playmobil sets, plushies, Snow White costumes and customized Engle-Puppen dolls. Christmas shop Die Weihnachts Ecke sells handmade Steinbach nutcrackers. Worth visiting for the aroma alone, Old World German caramel shop Karamell-Küche is an Epcot treasure. Young German bakers make treats before your eyes. Arribas Brothers store Kunstarbeit in Kristall sells lovely crystal jewelry, personalized glassware, Swarovski crystal pins and collectible figurines. Stein Haus offers intricate beer steins. More are at Volkskunst, as are Schneider cuckoo clocks, glassware, pewter and Troika watches. Egg artist Jutta Levasseur often works in a corner. Weinkeller serves wines and schnapps by the bottle or glass. On the promenade, the Glaskunst stand personalizes glass figures, frames, glassware and steins.

Fun find: Classic glass pickle ornaments, at the Christmas shop.

★★ **China.** The spacious House of Good Fortune department store carries a variety of interesting merchandise, but it's been redone recently to focus on apparel, both traditional Chinese clothing and modern T-shirts. Other choices include incense, jewelry, accessories and housewares. A separate children's area stocks panda-themed clothing, toys and stuffed animals. **Fun find:** Personality-filled marionettes, at a stand in front of the pavilion.

★★★ **Norway.** The Puffin's Roost sells "Frozen" merchandise, troll figurines, stylish if pricey Norwegian apparel from brands Helly Hansen and Dale of Norway, and crisp Laila perfume and Geir for Men cologne—creator Geir Ness appears at the store every now and then. For the young, young at heart or anyone who is "drinking around the world," there are silly plastic Viking helmets—all with horns, some with braids. **Fun find:** The small Donald Duck Viking plushie.

★★★★ ✔ **Mexico.** The large, dim Plaza de los Amigos sits inside the pyramid and offers a huge variety of merchandise, including blankets, books, candy, crystal, glassware, ceramic piggy banks, piñatas, fleece ponchos, salsa, sombreros, and tequila. A small table in the corner holds the Animalés Fantasticos Spirits in Wood artisans and their exquisite handmade wooden animals. Out front, an outdoor stand offers huge colorful sombreros; it seems everyone stops to pose in one. **Fun find:** Authentic Day of the Dead T-shirts, inside the pyramid.

See also **Shopping Policies** in the chapter **Walt Disney World A–Z.**

Micaela Neal

IBM room. A Spaceship Earth scene imagines a 1960s computer room with its programmers. The slow-moving ride uses 22 dioramas to portray the history of communications.

Spaceship Earth

Slow ride through history is cooler than it sounds

★★★★ ✔ FastPass+ This huge silver sphere is more than just the park icon. It's also a ride—a trip back in time through the history of communications. Starting with prehistoric cave-dwellers and continuing through the Renaissance, Dark Ages and early uses of telegraphs, telephones and computers, nearly two dozen dioramas, four dozen Audio-Animatronic figures depict communication advances through history, explained by the calm narration of Dame Judi Dench.

A four-seat ride vehicle takes you slowly through each scene. At one point, you travel through a 1960s IBM computer room where two programmers watch over a huge reel-to-reel mainframe; a young female tech sports a miniskirt and giant Afro. Another scene shows a 1976 Silicon Valley garage where a young man—Steve Wozniak, maybe?—creates the first personal computer.

The ride turns interactive as it nears its finish. Using a touchscreen in your vehicle you choose how you'd like to live or work in the years ahead, then see your future come to life, your face atop an animated body. A large post-show area features interactive exhibits that showcase Siemens, the ride's sponsor.

Tips. *When to go:* After 8:30 p.m. there's no wait. *For couples:* This is Disney's best ride for snuggling; it's dark, slow and has bench seats.

Fun facts. ❶ Engineer R. Buckminster Fuller coined the phrase "Spaceship Earth." His 1963 treatise, "An Operating Manual for Spaceship Earth," argued that all the world's peoples must work together as a crew to guide our planet's future. ❷ Science-fiction author Ray Bradbury ("Fahrenheit 451") helped design the attraction. ❸ The caveman is speaking a Cro-Magnon language. ❹ The cave drawings are based on images found

Average wait times

9am	10am	11am	Noon	1pm	2pm	3pm	4pm	5pm	6pm	7pm	8pm	9pm
5m	15m	25m	35m	25m	10m	20m	25m	20m	20m	15m	15m	5m

Text along right margin: 1939 World's Fair: LOC. Unisphere: Flapane at Italian Wikipedia. Epcot: Micaela Neal

Similar spheres. From top, left to right: The Perisphere icon of the 1939 New York World's Fair; its slow-moving indoor ride; the 1964 World's Fair Unisphere; Epcot's Spaceship Earth.

in the Salon-Niaux cave in Ariége, France. ❺ The Egyptian hieroglyphics reproduce actual Middle Eastern drawings. ❻ The pharaoh's words come from a real letter.

Fun finds and Hidden Mickeys. ❶ A placard on the right of the computer room reads "Think," the IBM slogan that inspired Apple's "Think Different." ❷ The radio station's call letters "WDI" refer to Walt Disney Imagineering. ❸ Your work future will predict "a great big beautiful tomorrow," the theme song of the Carousel of Progress. ❹ Mickey's three circles appear as parchment ink blots made by a sleeping monk and ❺ bottle rings on the table of the first Renaissance painter.

Building the ball. A 180-foot-high geodesic sphere, Spaceship Earth was built over 26 months, without scaffolding or supports.

Two balls in one. First, over 100 steel pilings were pounded into the ground, to depths of 150 feet. Three pairs of angled legs were placed on top, themselves topped with a six-sided platform about 45 feet off the ground. Secured on that platform, adjustable cranes built a circular frame around themselves, using hundreds of metal-strut triangles. After an outside crane hoisted the pre-constructed top, workers secured rubber-coated panels to the triangles, creating a giant waterproof black ball. Finally, a separate, decorative

outer sphere was added, set off 2 feet from the inner black ball by 4-inch aluminum pipes. It's made up of 11,324 triangles of Alucobond, a rustproof material made of plastic bonded to anodized aluminum. The building weighs 16 million pounds. That's 158 million golf balls.

Doesn't drip water. Spaceship Earth does not drip water: a 1-inch gap between each triangle flows rainwater into two interior gutters. They drain through the ball's support legs into canals that run alongside the park.

A World's Fair homage. Spaceship Earth is similar to the icons of the New York World's Fairs of 1939 and 1964. The first one featured the 180-foot-tall Perisphere, which inside held a slow-moving ride that showed Democracity, a "perfectly integrated garden city" from the year 2068. The 1964 icon was the Unisphere, a 140-foot open-grid Earth that symbolized global interdependence. It's still standing.

Key facts. *Best for:* Adults. *Duration:* 14 min. Allow up to 45 min. for post-show activities. *Capacity:* 38 (2 per seat). *Queue:* Outdoor, partially covered. *Debuted:* 1982, revised 1994, 2008. *Access:* Must be ambulatory. Stops intermittently to load mobility-impaired guests. Vehicles offer a choice of narration languages—English, French, German, Japanese, Portuguese and Spanish. *Disability services:* Audio Description. *Location:* Future World.

Timeless message. A dad and daughter stroll past a recent IBM exhibit in Innoventions West, which lately has been closed for renovations.

Innoventions

Corporate exhibits offer fun diversions, change often

★★★ ✓ These two buildings—Innoventions East and West—house sponsored displays with games or activities. Some are fun—the Sum of All Thrills exhibit especially so—but it's hard to feel you're on vacation while a big IBM logo stares you in the face. Note: At press-time Innoventions West was closed, so only exhibits in Innoventions East appear below.

NEW! Colortopia. A Glidden Paint press release promises a "highly interactive color experience" where "guests will encounter unique interactions through fun and surprising hands-on activities" with this exhibit "for all ages" that pairs "the magic of the park experience with the magical role color plays in our lives." Well, that nails it down. Colortopia is scheduled to open in the fall of 2015. It replaces the Test the Limits Lab, a Underwriters Laboratories exhibit that had been a fixture of Innoventions since 2003.

Habit Heroes. Florida Blue Cross teaches healthy living superhero style.

Take a Nanooze Break. Easy to miss, this small place to relax is presented by Cornell University and National Science Foundation.

Sum of All Thrills. This Raytheon physics-based exhibit is the only Innoventions ride. After designing a roller coaster, jet plane or bobsled track, you experience it virtually in a small capsule that moves atop a robotic arm.

StormStruck. This Federal Alliance for Safe Homes exhibit compares how different homes fare during a hurricane.

Tips. *When to go:* For Sum of all Thrills, before 11 a.m. or between 2 and 3 p.m.

Key facts. *Best for:* Families. *Duration:* Avg. 20 min. *Debuted:* 1994, revised 2009. *Access (Sum of All Thrills):* Height min: 48 in., wheelchair and ECV users must transfer; Audio Description. *Location:* Future World.

Average wait times (Sum of All Thrills)

9am	10am	11am	Noon	1pm	2pm	3pm	4pm	5pm	6pm	7pm	8pm	9pm
0m	5m	10m	20m	30m	10m	10m	20m	25m	20m	n/a	n/a	n/a

Mine! Mine! Audio-Animatronics gulls outside the Seas pavilion squawk just as they do in "Finding Nemo." The voice is that of the movie's director, Andrew Stanton.

The Seas with Nemo & Friends

Underrated pavilion displays sealife, has talking turtle

★★★ ✔ Themed to the 2003 Pixar film "Finding Nemo," this two-story pavilion surrounds guests with marine life real and animated. Visitors enter the pavilion on "clam-mobiles"—three-seat ride vehicles which pass animated dioramas of Nemo and his pals, who appear at one point to swim in the aquarium itself.

Interactive show. Thanks to some hidden cameras, real-time animation techniques and an improv performer backstage, children have real-time conversations with the animated surfer-dude sea turtle at **Turtle Talk with Crush** (★★★★★ ✔ FastPass+), using a huge video screen that resembles a viewing window into an ocean. He addresses his subjects individually by name ("Elizabeth, your polka-dot shell is totally cool!"), asks specific questions ("Austin, is that your female parental unit in the fourth row? She's a total babe!") and reacts to their responses. His facial expressions are spot-on—and priceless. During the show, Crush also works in some turtle trivia and conservation tips, and welcomes blue tang Dory, who can speak whale perhaps a little too well.

Seating is on backless benches; young children can sit up front on the carpeted floor. The show's queue area holds jellyfish, stingrays, eels and fish from the Great Barrier Reef. Getting a Fastpass for the show guarantees you entry, but no special seating.

Crush mostly talks to children who sit down front, but sometimes seeks out guests along the theater's center aisle. To have him talk with your child, have your child sit in the front row and wear a funny hat. If your child is in a wheelchair and would like to be near the screen, ask a cast member to arrange it before the show begins. *Duration:*

Average wait times (Turtle Talk with Crush)

9am	10am	11am	Noon	1pm	2pm	3pm	4pm	5pm	6pm	7pm	8pm	9pm
5m	5m	15m	15m	15m	10m	10m	10m	10m	10m	10m	10m	n/a

Dancing with a dolphin. The author's daughter rocks back and forth with one of the pavilion's bottle-nose dolphins. Below, guests ride clam-mobiles to enter the pavilion; a live chat during Turtle Talk with Crush.

© Disney

© Disney

12 min; shows every 20 min. Capacity: 210. Queue: Indoor, air-conditioned. Access: Guests may remain in wheelchairs, ECVs. Reflective captioning, assistive listening; Audio Description. Debuted: 2004.

Exhibits. The Seas pavilion holds many marine creatures, some in the main aquarium, others in smaller tanks in side rooms.

Nemo & Friends. This room displays live versions of many "Finding Nemo" stars, including clownfish, blue tangs, Moorish idols and cleaner shrimp. Tanks also hold eels, frogfish, venomous lionfish, seahorses and live coral.

Bruce's Shark World. A re-creation of the film's sunken submarine has interactive displays and photo props, educating kids about the threats sharks face.

Caribbean aquarium. On the second floor, this huge saltwater aquarium simulates a coral reef. It's filled with blacknose, brown and sand tiger sharks; some angelfish, cobia, snapper and tarpon; schools of lookdown; sea turtles; and a few rays. Lined with floor-to-ceiling windows, an observation tunnel extends into the tank. Divers unload food

pouches while a presenter adds educational trivia at 10 a.m., 1 p.m. and 3:30 p.m. A side area holds a bachelor herd of dolphins—Rainer (born in 1986), Calvin and Kyber (1997) and Malabar (2001). Huge bars keep the mammals in their area; otherwise they "play" with the fish. Stop by the dolphin tank at 10:45 a.m., 2:15 p.m. or 4:15 p.m. to watch trainers conduct identity-matching, rhythm-identification or echolocation research.

Aquaculture. This upstairs room holds coral and cuttlefish, as well as endangered species such as giant clams and clownfish.

Manatee aquarium. Guests watch endangered Florida sea cows munch lettuce heads from above the surface on the second floor or through a first-floor underwater window. Docents give talks twice an hour.

Fun find. ❶ As you pass by her in your clam-mobile on your way into the pavilion, "Finding Nemo" sea star Peach desperately clings to the aquarium glass as fish around her continue to sing the theme song "Big Blue World." "Hey wait! Take me with you!" she begs. "It's a nice song but they just never stop! Never, never, ever, ever, ever!"

© Disney

Flying high. Soarin' flies guests high literally and virtually. Rising 40 feet in front of a concave screen, riders appear to glide 800 feet above sites such as the Golden Gate Bridge.

Soarin' Around the World

Updated hi-def hang-gliding trip gives you an amazing ride

UPDATED! ★★★★★ ✔ FastPass+ This virtual hang-gliding experience really does give you the feeling of flight. Exhilarating but not scary, it's a smooth, fun trip everyone will love. This year it will add a third theater, get higher-definition digital screens and projection systems, and its journey will change from one over California to one that travels the world.

An impractical fantasy. After you board a multi-seat "hang glider," you lift up to 40 feet into an 80-foot projection dome. From all sides your vision fills with natural landscapes and man-made wonders—in the old film places like El Capitan and the Golden Gate Bridge, in the new one landmarks such as Monument Valley and the Great Wall of China—as you live the fantasy of hang-gliding directly over them. Your glider tilts as it travels, your legs dangling free underneath. Hidden fans, odorizers and surround-sound speakers add to the experience. The films are shot using cameras mounted on the front of helicopters that mimic a hang glider's sways and swoops.

Tips. *When to go:* Immediately as the park opens or anytime with a Fastpass. *Where to sit:* Top-row center. Ask for Row 1, Gate B.

Fun finds. ❶ The entire attraction resembles an airport. Cast members dress as airline employees, the gift stand is a ticket counter, the walkway a concourse, its boarding areas gates. The theater has runway lights, its gliders navigation lights. ❷ Cast members may refer to your flight as "No. 5-5-0-5," a nod to the ride's opening date of May 5, 2005.

Key facts. *Best for:* All ages. *Duration:* 5 min. *Capacity:* 174 per theater. *Queue:* Indoor. *Restraint:* Seat belt. *Debuted:* 2005. *Access:* Height min: 40 in. Wheelchair and ECV users must transfer. *Disability services:* Handheld captioning. *Location:* The Land pavilion.

Average wait times

9am	10am	11am	Noon	1pm	2pm	3pm	4pm	5pm	6pm	7pm	8pm	9pm
5m	55m	90m	65m	50m	60m	80m	50m	60m	60m	50m	40m	20m

A fragrant float. The Living with the Land boat ride travels through greenhouses filled with exotic plants, as well as an aquaculture hut where fish swim in elevated glass tanks.

Living with the Land

Slow boat ride takes compelling trip past exotic plants

★★★★ ✓ FastPass+ This indoor boat ride presents a subject that's usually dull as dirt—agricultural science—in an entertaining way. A calm trip through four working greenhouses, it's filled with weird plants and odd growing techniques; you can often smell the leaves and fruit.

Crops include hanging bananas, coconuts, papayas, 3-foot winter melons and 500-pound Atlantic giant pumpkins; enormous nine-pound lemons and jackfruit weigh down their branches. Many plants hang from strings or trellises, naked roots in the air. Some grow on overhead conveyor belts, touring their greenhouses like suits in a dry cleaner. You're bound to see a Mickey-shaped cucumber, pumpkin or watermelon, each grown in a specially shaped plastic mold. An aquaculture quonset hut has catfish, sturgeon, shrimp, eels, even young alligators, easy to

see in elevated glass tanks. Its red light keeps its animals calm and reduces algae growth. The ride begins with a journey through faux rainforest, desert and farm habitats; some with Audio-Animatronic animals.

Tips. *When to go:* There's no line before 10 a.m. *Where to sit:* In the front row.

Key facts. *Best for:* All ages. *Duration:* 14 min. *Capacity:* 20 per boat. *Queue:* Indoor. *Debuted:* 1982; revised 2009. *Access:* ECV users must transfer. Handheld captioning. Audio Description. *Location:* The Land pavilion.

Nearby movie. Though it stars Timon and Pumbaa from "The Lion King," **The Circle of Life** (★★) is dated, blurry and preachy. *Duration:* 13 min. *Capacity:* 482. *Queue:* Indoor. *Debuted:* 1995. *Access:* Guests may stay in wheelchairs, ECVs. Handheld, reflective captioning; assistive listening. *Location:* Just above Living with the Land.

Average wait times

9am	10am	11am	Noon	1pm	2pm	3pm	4pm	5pm	6pm	7pm	8pm	9pm
5m	5m	10m	10m	10m	10m	10m	10m	10m	10m	10m	n/a	n/a

Figment's home. Annoyed by a stuffy tour of the Imagination Institute, dragon Figment hijacks your ride vehicle and takes you to his home, which is upside down.

Journey Into Imagination with Figment

There's never a wait at this, the lamest of all Disney rides

★ A tongue-in-cheek open-house tour of a stuffy Imagination Institute, this slow-moving dark ride stops at various labs, where ever-practical Institute director Dr. Nigel Channing ("Monty Python" alum Eric Idle) tries to demonstrate how he's studying a particular human sense so he can "capture and control" imagination. Trouble is he's always interrupted by Figment, a little dragon who ends up hijacking the tour to his upside-down house, to show how imagination can come "home" when it sees things from new perspectives.

Though the ride may appeal to kids, it's a long way from Disney's best. It does have, however, one great effect: in a cage past the Sight Lab, a huge butterfly appears to disappear as you pass it.

Epcot's own character. And just who, you may ask, is Figment? In Disney's original Journey Into Imagination ride (1983–1999), he was the creation of Dreamfinder, a jolly wizard-like scientist. Composed of elements that Dreamfinder found in his travels—the horns of a steer, the snout of a crocodile and the delight at a child's birthday party—he

was voiced by Billy Barty, a little person who landed many movie roles, most infamously when he was 9 as a baby who escapes from his stroller in the pre-code "Gold Diggers of 1933."

Fun Finds and Hidden Mickeys. ❶ The entranceway includes the office doors of Wayne Szalinski, the subject of the former adjacent movie Honey, I Shrunk the Audience, **❷** 1997's "Flubber" inventor Phillip Brainard **❸** and Dean Higgins, the principal in 1969's "The Computer Wore Tennis Shoes," **❹** and a page for Merlin Jones, the chimp teacher in 1965's "The Monkey's Uncle." **❺** Red tennis shoes sit outside the ride's computer room, a second nod to the 1969 film. **❻** Mickey-eared headphones sit in the Sight Lab, on top of a wheeled table. **❼** Mickey appears as two carpets and a toilet seat in Figment's bathroom.

Key facts. *Best for:* Kids. *Duration:* 6 min. *Capacity:* 224. *Queue:* Indoor. *Fear factor:* The last room has a sudden flash. *Debuted:* 1983, revised 1998, 2001. *Access:* Guests may remain in wheelchairs, ECVs. *Disability services:* Handheld captioning, Audio Description. *Location:* The Imagination pavilion.

© Disney

Retread Ruler. Michael Jackson knows how to defeat evil sorceress Anjelica Huston. Just turn her black-and-white world to color—and rehash all of his dance moves from "Thriller."

Captain EO

Big names produced this self-indulgent drivel

★ And you thought Jar Jar was bad. Developed by "Star Wars" creator George Lucas and directed by Francis Ford Coppola—yes, the guy who helmed "The Godfather"—this 1986 3-D musical film stars singer Michael Jackson at his most Wacko. Though it may be diverting for those wearing very rosy nostalgic glasses, for anyone else the show just lays down and wallows in numbing '80s excess.

The story is set in space. When Jackson, aka Captain EO, and an oddball puppet crew discover a colorless planet ruled by an evil sorceress (Oscar-winner Anjelica Huston) and her forces of darkness, he knows just what to do: use the power of music, dance and light to transform his crew into musicians and musical instruments, which will turn the black-and-white land into a world of color. Huston's minions defect to Jackson's side, and everyone grooves in a boogie wonderland.

Even before you see Captain EO, you've seen it all before—the same "Thriller"-style dance moves and overdone military fashion from Jackson, the same robots and Death Star trench George Lucas used in "Star Wars."

It's hard to believe the combined talents of Coppola, Jackson and Lucas came up with such self-indulgent drivel. Perhaps all three were at a point in their careers when no one ever told them "No." It's all such shame. With all his oddities, Jackson is such an easy target to mock, but at his best the guy could really sing, and had groundbreaking dance moves.

When it debuted in 1986, the film was accompanied by special effects which were groundbreaking for its time. Lasers appeared to shoot over the audience, creating impacts on the theater walls; smoke and fog rolled out at key moments; a field of stars filled the air. Unfortunately, none of these are still around.

Tips. *When to go:* Anytime. It'll be just you and crickets. *Where to sit:* In the center of a middle row, to keep the 3-D effects in line.

Key facts. *Best for:* Jackson fans. *Duration:* 17 min. *Capacity:* 570. *Queue:* Indoor. *Fear factor:* None. *Debuted:* 1986, reintroduced 2010. *Access:* Guests may stay in wheelchair ECVs. *Disability services:* Handheld, reflective captioning; assistive listening. *Location:* The Imagination pavilion.

The Exxon Experience. Disney's Universe of Energy pavilion holds Ellen's Energy Adventure, an elaborate oil-company presentation about the importance of oil.

Ellen's Energy Adventure

An Exxon lesson about the importance of Exxon

★★ A dated attraction that has dinosaurs, a funny comedian and a skewed corporate view of the "Universe of Energy." What is... Ellen's Energy Adventure! Based on the game show "Jeopardy," this lengthy presentation about energy (originally sponsored by Exxon) is highlighted by a slow-moving tram ride past Audio-Animatronic dinosaurs. Created back when the average price of a gallon of gasoline was $1.30, the show totally ignores the problems of fossil fuels. There's no mention of the Middle East, no talk of global warming, oil spills or fuel efficiency.

Tips. *When to go:* Anytime; there is never a wait. *Where to sit:* In the pre-show, stand in the center of the room to have a proper view of the wide screens. In the ride vehicle, sit in the left-hand car, on the right side of the row, halfway back. You'll get close to the dinosaurs and get a good view of the video screens. You'll also be able to see more of the show, since the left car leads the others. *For families:* The show's dark Big Bang section, its oil-rig segment and its explanation of fusion could frighten young children.

Fun finds. ❶ After Jeopardy's Alex Trebek praises Ellen for her "first correct response!" her lips don't move as she yells "Freeze!" ❷ Bill Nye's lips stay shut when, in front of a solar mirror, he says "All right." ❸ Michael Richards, who played Kramer in "Seinfeld," cameos as a caveman who discovers fire.

Key facts. *Best for:* Seniors. *Duration:* 45 min. (new shows every 17 min.). *Capacity:* 582. *Queue:* Outdoor, unshaded. *Fear factor:* The portrayal of the Big Bang is loud. *Operating hours:* Park open–7 p.m. *Debuted:* 1982, updated 1996. *Access:* ECV users must transfer. *Disability services:* Assistive listening, handheld captioning. *Location:* Future World.

Average wait times

9am	10am	11am	Noon	1pm	2pm	3pm	4pm	5pm	6pm	7pm	8pm	9pm
10m	10m	10m	10m	10m	10m	10m	10m	10m	10m	10m	n/a	n/a

Mild or wild. Guests choose from two versions of Disney's space-flight simulator Mission Space; the original intense adventure or a mild alternative. Crowds are often light.

Mission Space

Its G-forces make you feel like an astronaut. Or feel sick.

★★★★ FastPass+ So intense it includes motion-sickness bags, this flight simulator offers realistic sensations of space flight. It's set in the year 2036, when you and other astronauts are training for a mission to Mars. But as soon as you start, everything goes wrong.

The ride comes in two variations. The "Orange" one is a NASA-designed G-force creator that discreetly is a rapidly rotating centrifuge with capsules on its spokes. It gives you a true sense of a real rocket launch but can also make you dizzy, nauseated or worse. A "Green" variation is the same thing but doesn't spin, giving you the same ride without the G-forces. An elaborate post-show area has games, kiosks and a toddler area.

Tips. *When to go:* Not after a meal, anytime but meal times to avoid a long wait. *How not to get sick on the Orange ride:* Stare straight at the video screen without glancing around.

Fun finds and Hidden Mickeys. ❶ The queue room is bordered by a 35-foot Gravity Wheel, a prop from the year-2000 Disney live-action film "Mission to Mars." ❷ The wheel's hub includes the logo for Horizons, the previous ride at this site. ❸ Mickey's three-circle shape appears in the courtyard as craters on the moon near the Luna 8 site and as tiles in the patio, and in the queue as craters on Mars on monitors above desks.

Key facts. *Best for:* Teens. *Duration:* 6 min. *Capacity:* 4 per vehicle. *Queue:* Indoor. *Fear factor:* Intense sensations. *Restraint:* Seat belt. *Debuted:* 2003. *Health advisories:* Guests should be free from claustrophobia; motion sickness; pregnancy; high blood pressure; heart, back or neck problems. *Access:* Height min. 44 in. Wheelchair and ECV users must transfer. *Disability services:* Activated video captioning. *Location:* Future World.

Average wait times

9am	10am	11am	Noon	1pm	2pm	3pm	4pm	5pm	6pm	7pm	8pm	9pm
10m	10m	15m	10m	20m	10m	15m	10m	20m	20m	15m	20m	20m

TT for Test Track. The entrance to the latest version of Test Track, where you create a virtual car onscreen and then track its performance as you race through a proving ground.

Test Track

You design your car (in a sense) at this confused attraction

★★★★ FastPass+ Revised in 2012, Test Track is now more than a ride. Before boarding, you build your own car using a touchscreen, picking its color, shape, graphics, accessories and strongest attribute—capability, efficiency, responsiveness or power. But then, no matter how you've designed your car—regardless if you've made a sleek silver sports sedan or a hot-pink bulgemobile with a giant spoiler and solar panels on its hood—your ride experience is always exactly the same; your design choices making no difference to what your actual car looks like or how it behaves at all.

It's hard not to feel let down by that, and makes the experience not one you'll be dying to repeat. Your virtual design is run through the ride's computers at least, so as you ride an in-dash video screen shows you how your car would perform if it was on the track, and how it would compare to the designs created

by the other passengers who ride with you. The track itself offers little to look at, mostly lots of long horizontal light strips that seem straight out of Disney's 1980s movie "Tron."

Setting aside all that, the ride itself is the same thrill it's always been—once your open-topped car gets outside it reaches 65 mph. With 34 turns but no drops or loops, its mile-long course is ideal for those who like speed but hate all the up-and-down stuff.

A post-show has activities linked to your virtual car (one lets you make a commercial for it); additional screens give you the chance to make more designs.

Tips. *When to go:* First thing in the morning; if you can't use the Single-Rider line or a Fastpass. *Where to sit:* For the most legroom sit in the middle of your seat, with another rider on each side of you. *Tips for families:* Help your young children design their cars;

Average wait times

9am	10am	11am	Noon	1pm	2pm	3pm	4pm	5pm	6pm	7pm	8pm	9pm
5m	40m	80m	80m	30m	30m	50m	40m	40m	30m	50m	60m	50m

Concept cars. Sponsor General Motors has placed a few design studies inside the Test Track building, in a section of the waiting line labeled the Chevrolet Design Studio.

it's a little complex. If you're with a friend or spouse, or have older children, don't pitch in on a design together, instead build two different cars, so you can virtually race them against each other. To get two screens, tell the cast member outside the design studio that each of you want to make a car. *About the Single-Rider line:* If you use it you won't design a car, but rather pick from eight pre-made vehicles.

Fun facts. ❶ The first ride in this building was General Motors' World of Motion, which opened with the park in 1982. The pavilion has always been sponsored by GM, even during its recent bankruptcy. ❷ With a top speed of 65 mph, Test Track is the fastest attraction at Walt Disney World.

Hidden Mickeys. In the Standby queue, the three-circle shape of Mickey Mouse appears on two photo collages on the right side of the walkway. ❶ First in a collage of designers, to the left of the drawing hand of a man wearing glasses and writing with a marker, ❷ and second in a collage which shows people drawing concept art, above a vertical white dashed line.

Key facts. *Best for:* Older children, teens, car enthusiasts. *Duration:* 5 min. for the ride. Allow 1 hr. if you add every post-show experience. *Capacity:* 192 (6 per two-row car). *Queue:* Indoor. *Fear factor:* Intense for those scared by speed. *Restraint:* Seat belt. *Weather issues:* Closed during thunderstorms. *Debuted:* 1999, revised 2012. *Health advisories:* Guests should be free from motion sickness; pregnancy; high blood pressure; heart, back or neck problems. *Access:* Height min. 40 in. Must be ambulatory. *Location:* Future World.

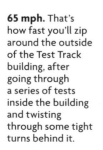

65 mph. That's how fast you'll zip around the outside of the Test Track building, after going through a series of tests inside the building and twisting through some tight turns behind it.

The World
Showcase

The global village

Originally planned to be a park of its own, Epcot's World Showcase has an odd shape. It's round—a wide walkway dotted with clusters of buildings that circle a man-made lake. Meant to be sort of a permanent international fair, it calls those clusters pavilions, devotes them to the architecture, culture and cuisine of particular countries, and staffs them with young people from those countries—more than a thousand cast members in all.

Empty lots. Though the area was designed to hold up to 20 pavilions, it has only 11, resulting in large wooded gaps throughout the circle. Pavilions representing Israel, Spain and Equatorial Africa were announced in the 1980s but later scrapped.

Two entrances. The World Showcase is connected to Future World on its south side and has a secondary entrance on its west side (the "International Gateway") between the pavilions that represent the United Kingdom and France. Landscaped walkways lead to a large hotel area that includes Disney's BoardWalk Inn, Yacht and Beach Club and the Walt Disney World Swan and Dolphin; water taxis serve those resort hotels as well as Disney's Hollywood Studios theme park.

About this section. The following reviews focus on ways to enjoy the pavilions without spending additional money; for detailed restaurant, food and shopping information check out this chapter's "Overview" section.

Canada

The grounds of this 3-acre pavilion are dominated by Disney's French Gothic Hotel du Canada, a miniature version of Ottawa's Chateau Laurier. The forced-perspective facade sits behind a flower garden that's inspired by the Butchart Gardens in Victoria. Out front, a native village is represented by a log cabin, a trading post and some totems (carved by a Tsimshian Indian in 1998, the one on the far left shows the Raven folk bird releasing the sun, moon and stars from a carved cedar chest). Up the steps, a stone building reflects the British influence on Canada's East Coast. The back of the pavilion

World Showcase pavilions. This page, from top: Canada, United Kingdom, France, Morocco, Japan. Opposite page: The American Adventure, Italy, Germany, Norway, Mexico. Previous page: China.

recalls the Canadian Rockies—a 30-foot waterfall flows into a stream; an opening to a mine shaft (the theater entrance) is trimmed with shoring and Klondike equipment.

Entertainment. Now this is different. Two-man lumberjack teams compete against each other in the Paul Bunyan Lumberjack Show (★★★★ ✔). Feats include wood chopping, sawing, axe throwing and log rolling, and change with every show. Corny jokes often fall flat, but everything else is so unique it doesn't matter. *15-min. shows hourly noon–7 p.m. daily. Promenade ("Mill") stage.*

Movie. You stand up to watch O Canada, an entertaining travelogue starring comedian Martin Short that's projected onto nine screens that wrap completely around you. Rocky crags, waterfalls and other sights surround you as you fly past them. One of two remaining CircleVision 360 films, it's like Soarin' without the ride. *15 min. Continuous shows. Capacity 600. Covered outdoor queue. Guests may stay in wheelchairs, ECVs. Reflective captioning, assistive listening, Audio Description. Debuted 1982, revised 2012.*

Restaurants and food. There's one food choice, steakhouse Le Cellier.

See review at **Restaurants and Food.**

Shops and merchandise. Two connected stores offer Canadian-themed merchandise.

See reviews at **Shops and Merchandise.**

Fun fact. ❶ Developed in the 1950s by video engineer (and original Mickey Mouse animator) Ub Iwerks, Disney's CircleVision 360 theaters use nine projectors to display video from a nine-lens camera onto nine screens. Why nine? Because the concept only works with an odd number—each projector sits in a gap between two screens. Epcot has two such theaters, here and in the China pavilion.

Fun find and Hidden Mickeys. ❶ Along the promenade, an odd carved bird head is split in two, with a hole for you to stick your face through. ❷ Along the pavilion entrance, two Mickeys hide under the top set of hands of the left totem; ❸ another hides in the ends of wine bottles behind the Le Cellier check-in counter.

United Kingdom

Each building in this sprawling pavilion represents a different period in U.K. history. Along the promenade, the brick turrets and medieval crenelation of the Sportsman's Shoppe mimic Henry VIII's 16th-century Hampton Court. Its white-stone side is Abbotsford, the 19th-century Scottish estate where Sir Walter

Strong-arm tactics. Lumberjacks compete at the Canada pavilion.

Scott wrote novels. Across a street is the 16th-century thatched-roofed cottage of Anne Hathaway, the wife of William Shakespeare. Farther down the street sits a half-timbered 15th-century Tudor leaning with age, a plaster 17th-century pre-Georgian, a stone 18th-century Palladian and a home built of angled bricks. Alongside the lagoon, the Rose

& Crown Pub is divided into three styles—a medieval rural cottage, a 15th-century Tudor tavern and an 1890s Victorian bar.

Entertainment. Performing on the sidewalks of the pavilion, Scottish folk group the Paul McKenna Band (★★★★★ ✔) seems too good for a stage—its musicianship too expressive, its adventurous arrangements too tight, its lead singer's lilt too nuanced to be experienced from more than a few

Fooling your eye. Disney's architectural tricks make the small shops of its U.K. pavilion appear tucked beneath towering townhomes.

feet away. Formed a decade ago, the fiery five-piece band has appeared on the BBC, toured throughout Europe and been honored at multiple festivals in its home country. The New York Times calls it "the best folk band to have come out of Scotland in the last 20 years." Unfortunately, the band's stay at Epcot lasts only through 2015; after that it heads back to Europe. At press time Disney had not announced a replacement. *15-min. shows hourly noon–7 p.m. Wed.–Sun. Sidewalks.* Cover band The British Revolution (★★★★ ✔) takes Baby Boomers back in time with hits of the Beatles, Clash, Led Zeppelin and The Who. *20-min. shows hourly 3 p.m–9 p.m. daily. Back green stage.* Late in the day, a piano player (★★★★ ✔) adds life to a hidden corner of the Rose & Crown Pub. Alas, only 12 seats can see her. *45-min. shows hourly 5 p.m.–9 p.m. daily. Back corner.*

Restaurants and food. The U.K. pavilion has two dining options: the relaxed Rose & Crown Dining Room and the Yorkshire County Fish Shop, a small walk-up window that sells fish and chips.

See reviews at **Restaurants and Food.**

Shops and merchandise. Half a dozen pretty little shops offer Twinings tea, bone china, Beatles-themed gear and other items.

See reviews at **Shops and Merchandise.**

Fun finds and Hidden Mickeys. ❶ To the right of the pavilion, three red phone booths make great photo props. ❷ Along the promenade, the three-circle Mickey shape is formed by a soccer ball, a football and a racket on the sign for the Sportsman's Shoppe.

France

You approach the Paris of La Belle Époque ("the beautiful time" from 1870 to 1910) on a replica of the Pont des Arts footbridge. Once over it you enter a small village, its three-story facades topped with copper and slate mansard roofs, many with chimney pots. A rear shop is based on the 1850 iron-and-glass Les Halles fruit and vegetable market. Towering off in the distance is the Eiffel Tower, with a period-correct tawny finish. Disney built the one-tenth-scale replica using Gustave Eiffel's blueprints.

Entertainment. A wine steward and a Serveur Amusant ("amusing server") (★★★★) mime a balancing act with a table and chairs. *20-min. shows hourly noon–5 p.m. Fri.–Tue. In front of Chefs de France.*

Movie. Lovely travelogue Impressions de France shows off stunning visuals, from mountain peaks to huge castles to icons such as Notre Dame. Produced more than 30

A French tease. Posters promoting impressionistic art shows paper the columns in front of the France pavilion, though no such exhibits have ever appeared there.

years ago it has a timeless feel, its evocative imagery accompanied by classical music. Yet there's no sense of humor. Early on its narrator intones "My Frahnce awakens with the early dawn." Well, duh. The pretty theater has small seats; women larger than a size 16 won't be comfortable. *18 min. Continuous shows. Capacity 325. Indoor queue. Guests may stay in wheelchairs, ECVs. Reflective captioning, assistive listening. Debuted 1982.*

Restaurants and food. Fully realized in terms of dining choices, the pavilion includes an ice cream parlor (L'Artisan Des Glaces,, a bakery and sandwich shop (Les Halles Boulangerie & Patisserie, a sophisticated cafe (Chefs de France) and a true gourmet restaurant (Monsieur Paul).

See reviews at **Restaurants and Food.**

Shops and merchandise. You'll find three quality French items here: fragrances, cosmetics and wine; each in its own shop. All are very much worth a look.

See reviews at **Shops and Merchandise.**

Hidden Mickeys. ❶ In the courtyard, the three circles hide within metal tree grates; also in a bush in the fleur-de-lis hedge garden. ❷ In the film, Mickey appears at a wedding reception, as the silhouette of a Mickey Mouse doll in a second-floor window of a house behind the wedding party.

Morocco

Created and in part managed by the Kingdom of Morocco, this World Showcase pavilion is the most true to its country and the most exotic, with food, music and wares that are little-known in the West. Wafting incense will remind baby boomers of a head shop.

Meant to evoke a desert city, its buildings are made of brick, tan plaster and reddish sandstone. Like traditional Moroccan cities, the pavilion is divided into two sections, the ville nouvelle (new city) and the medina (old town). In front, the pavilion's new city recalls Casablanca and Marrakesh. It's anchored by the Koutoubia Minaret prayer tower. The medina of Fez lies in back, behind the 8th-century Bab Boujouloud Gate. On the left is the central courtyard of a traditional Moroccan home, complete with the sounds of the family. On the right is an open-air market, its bamboo roof lashed to thick beams. Restaurant Marrakesh is a Southern Moroccan fortress. Nearby is the Nejjarine Fountain. Rising above the old city is the Chellah Minaret, a 14th-century necropolis found in Morocco's capital city of Rabat.

Entertainment. Unless you speak Arabic or Berber you'll miss the message of B'net Al Houwariyate (★★★★ ✔), a female music and

Hey sister... go sister.... B'net Al Houwariyate invites women to join in as it sings (in Arabic and Berber) of the female condition. At right, a child mannequin seems unhappy with hers.

dance troupe from Marrakesh that, according to its press material, reflects "the female condition, above and beyond the stereotype, with emotion, humor and energy" as it "illuminates the stories and experiences of women in Morocco." (If only there was closed captioning!) The group's name translates to "the Daughters of the Berbers," an indigenous people who predate Morocco's European and Islamic cultures. The five women play, chant, sing and dance to native Moroccan music—mainly *al-aita,* a style popular with the country's Arabic poor, and *chaabi,* a modern pop mix of ancient Berber sounds with Flamenco rhythms. Instruments include iron castanets, oboe-like *rhaita* and Berber recorders played from open ends. Before coming to Disney the group performed at the Kennedy Center in Washington D.C. *25-min. shows hourly 1–8 p.m. Wed.–Sun. Promenade stage.*

Exhibit. Traditional accessories, jewelry and clothing are displayed in Moroccan Style: The Art of Personal Adornment (★★★). Heavily tiled and molded, the exhibit's Gallery of Arts and History is easy to overlook from outside. It's to the left of the pavilion's front courtyard, behind closed doors. Once you're inside, look up. The ceiling is gorgeous.

Restaurants and food. A belly dancer shimmies at the fine Restaurant Marrakesh;

dishes are mild. Tastier entrees draw inspiration from five countries at the excellent Spice Road Table, currently one of the authors' favorite World Showcase restaurants. Tasty chicken and lamb platters highlight fast-food Tangierine Café, which also has a bakery.

See reviews at **Restaurants and Food.**

Shops and merchandise. Five open-air shops offer Moroccan apparel, belly-dancing outfits and trim pieces for all ages, home furnishings and other items.

See reviews at **Shops and Merchandise.**

Fun finds and Hidden Mickeys. ❶ Each of the pavilion's intricate tiled rooms has at least one tiling mistake. Moroccan artists created deliberate flaws to reflect the Muslim belief that only Allah creates perfection. ❷ Seen from across the lagoon—specifically from the right of the Mexico pavilion—the Morocco pavilion appears to include a tall reddish building behind it. Actually, that's The Twilight Zone Tower of Terror at Disney's Hollywood Studios, which shares a Spanish influence. ❸ Mickey's shape is formed by brass plates on a door of the Souk-Al-Magreb shop, ❹ as a window in the dome of a minaret on the backdrop in Aladdin and Jasmine's indoor meet-and-greet area; Mickey is in the upper right-hand segment, next to a small ladder.

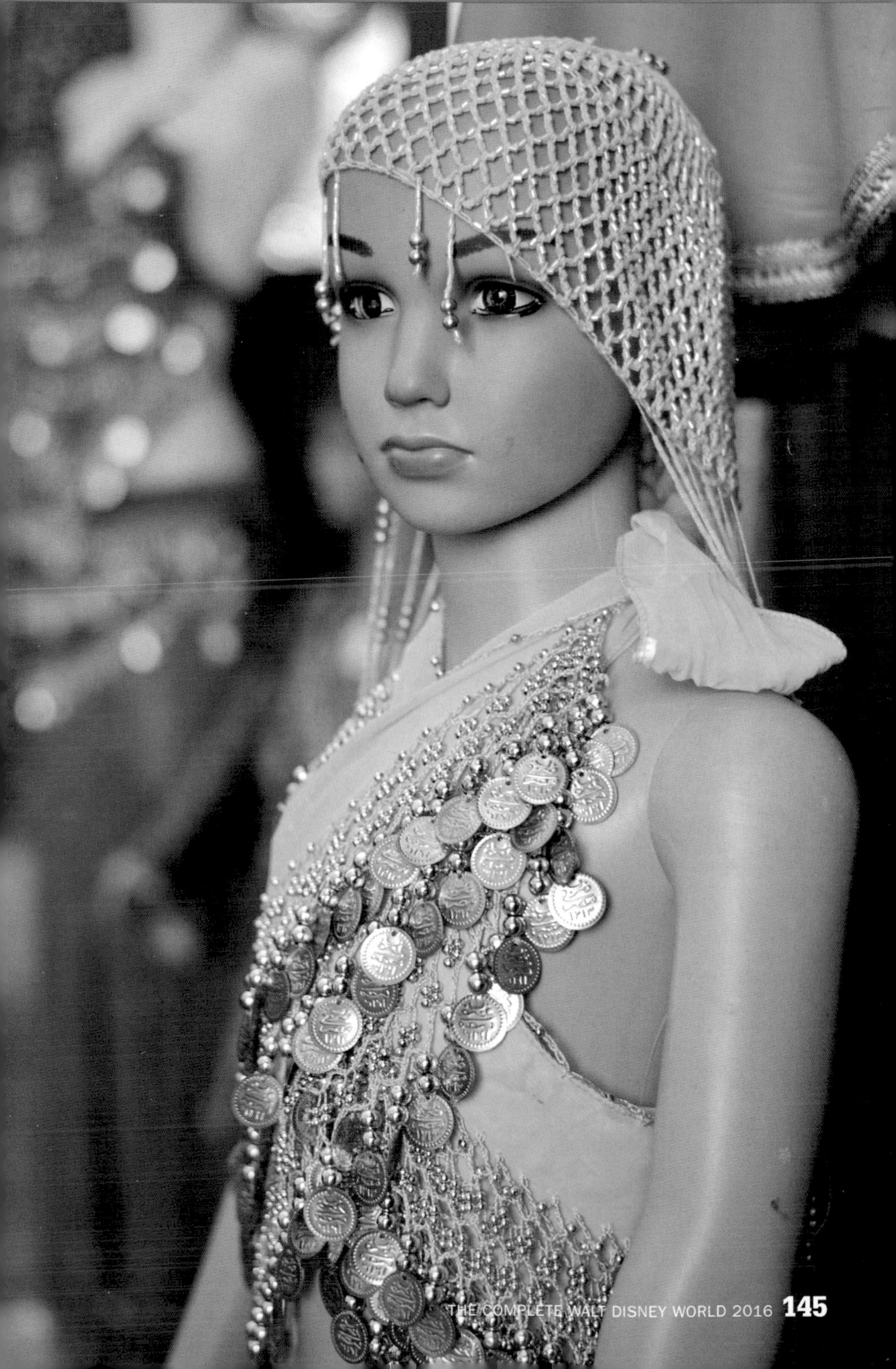

Hidden path. A group of friends crosses a small creek as it heads to the popular Katsura Grill. Unseen by most visitors, the Japan pavilion's back gardens are behind its pagoda.

Japan

This pavilion is run by the Mitsukoshi company, Japan's oldest retail business. An 83-foot pagoda recalls the 8th-century Horyuji Temple in Nara. Its five stories represent the five elements of creation—earth, water, fire, wind and sky. A hill garden's evergreens symbolize eternal life, its rocks the longevity of the earth and its koi-filled water the brief life of animals and man. In the garden, the rustic Katsura Grill is modeled on Kyoto's 16th-century Katsura Imperial Villa. The structure on the right houses the store and restaurants, and recalls the ceremonial Shishinden Hall of the 8th-century Gosho Imperial Palace at Kyoto. In back, a (shallow!) 17th-century wood-and-stone Nijo castle houses sculptures of mounted samurai warriors. A moat fronts the Shirasagijo (White Heron) castle, a 14th-century fortress.

Entertainment. An intense drumming trio, Matsuriza (★★★★ ✔) pounds out propulsive beats on huge hand-made instruments. *20-min. shows hourly noon–7 p.m. Wed.–Sun. On the pagoda, maybe in front of it.*

Exhibit. Spirited Beasts: From Ancient Stories to Anime Stars (★★★) explores the connection between ancient myths and modern media. Filled with about 100 objects, displays showcase creatures from Japanese folklore that have inspired anime characters. Look for Kappa the water sprite, the basis for Pokémon Golduck. The exhibit's Bijutsu-kan Gallery is at the back of the pavilion.

Restaurants and food. Peaceful, polite Tokyo Dining offers a traditional menu and sushi; tableside hibachi chefs entertain at Teppan Edo. Best value: the teriyaki dishes and noodle soups at fast-food Katsura Grill.

See reviews at **Restaurants and Food.**

Shops and merchandise. A Mitsukoshi department store overflows with Japanese items, from toys to kimonos to sake.

See reviews at **Shops and Merchandise.**

Hidden Mickeys. ❶ In metal tree grates in the courtyard and ❷ as the center of a koi-pond drain cover near a bamboo fence.

American Adventure

The attraction is first-rate, the entertainment too, but otherwise this pavilion is a real letdown. There's so much to our country—so much culture, cuisine, geography, so many types of people—you'd think a Disney pavilion about it would be overflowing with creative displays and things to do. Well, no. In fact there's really no pavilion here, instead just a show and an amphitheater. And that's

Meeting of the minds. Robotic versions of Benjamin Franklin (left) and Mark Twain discuss U.S. history atop the Statue of Liberty during the American Adventure theatrical show.

The American Adventure

Elaborate American history lesson is thoughtful, inspiring

★★★★★ ✔ This elaborate theatrical show embraces the triumphs of the United States and the optimism of its people, but doesn't shy away from its flaws and challenges. Ben Franklin and Mark Twain tell the American story from the Pilgrims through World War II, with help from George Washington, Thomas Jefferson, Will Rogers, Rosie the Riveter and other Audio-Animatronic figures. Film segments, a combination of photos and paintings, pan across scenes in the way later made famous by documentarian Ken Burns.

Included are moments from our past both sterling and shameful. Chatting with Franklin, Twain says, "You Founding Fathers gave us a pretty good start… [but then] a whole bunch of folks found out that 'We the People' didn't yet mean all the people." Subsequent scenes portray slavery and the persecution of Native Americans.

At the end Franklin quotes Thomas Wolfe. "So, then, to every man his chance… the right to live, to work, to be himself, and to become whatever thing his manhood and his vision can combine to make him."

Fun facts. ❶ Hidden from view, the show's staging system is a mechanical marvel, a mass of wiring and cables just beneath the audience sight line. Underneath it a 175-ton scene changer wheels in 13 different sets.

Hidden Mickey. ❶ As three rocks at the beginning of the first film in the show, behind and to the right of a kneeling Pilgrim woman.

Key facts. *Best for:* Ages 10+. *Duration:* 30 minutes. Typically shown every 45 minutes. *Capacity:* 1,024. *Queue:* Indoor. *Debuted:* 1982, revised 1993, 2007. *Access:* Guests may stay in wheelchairs, ECVs. Audio Description, assistive listening, reflective captioning. *Location:* American Adventure pavilion.

Average wait times

9am	10am	11am	Noon	1pm	2pm	3pm	4pm	5pm	6pm	7pm	8pm	9pm
n/a	n/a	15m	20m	20m	20m	20m	20m	20m	20m	20m	20m	n/a

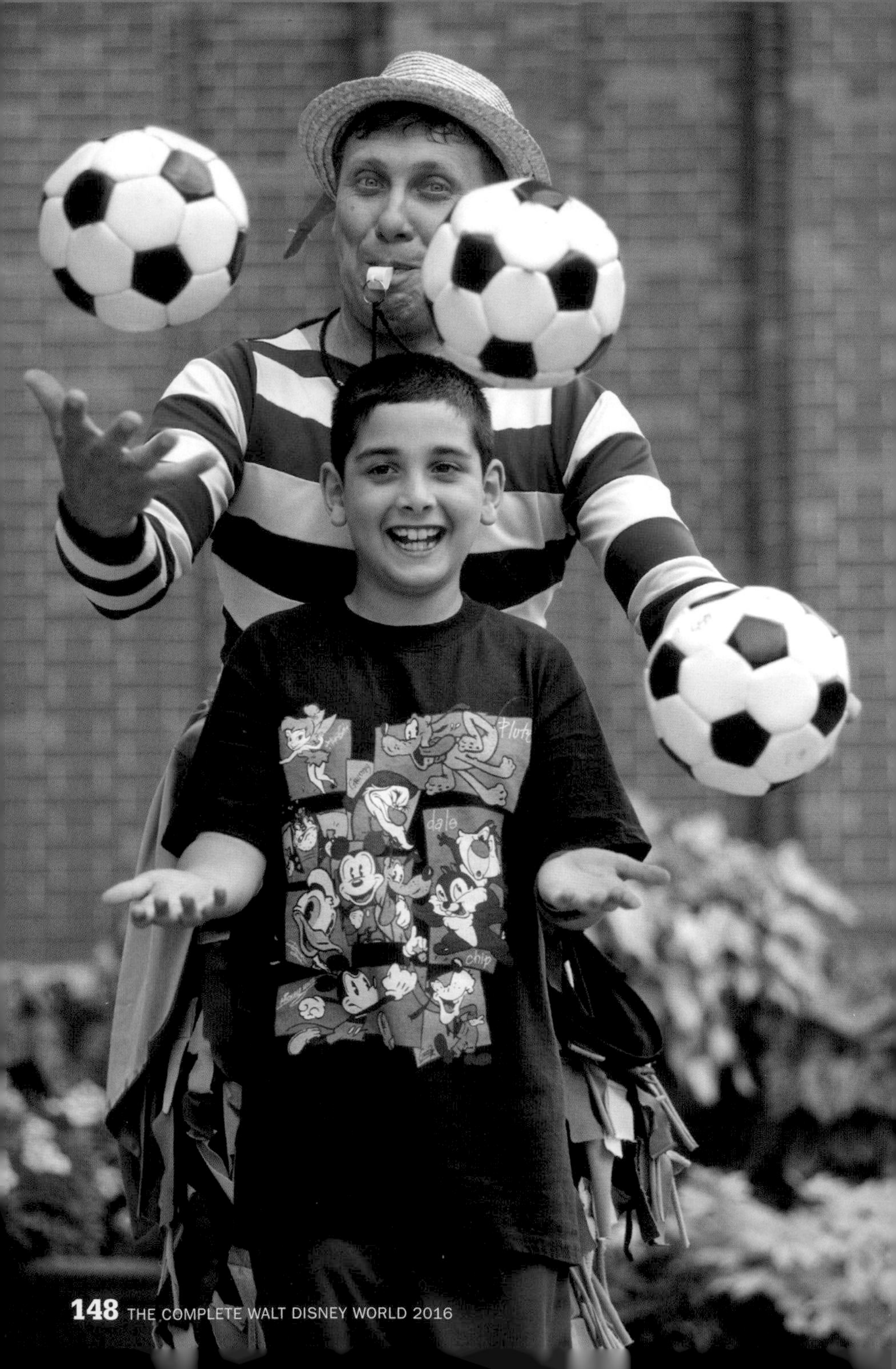
Pluto
dale
chip

Don't stop believin'. Despite its cheesy name, the top-notch American Music Machine harmonizes a quality pop set list. At left, Italy's Sergio juggles around an audience "volunteer."

such a wasted opportunity, especially since Disney gets so many international visitors. English-Georgian architecture recalls the look of many Colonial buildings built just before and after the Revolutionary War.

Exhibit. Re-Discovering America: Family Treasures from the Kinsey Collection (★) displays art and a few slave- and oppression-related artifacts from a black family—a bill of sale for a slave sold in 1832, a 1930 steel plaque from the American Beach Negro Ocean Playground. Pre-recorded narrators such as Diane Sawyer and Whoopi Goldberg intone on the concepts of Belief, Courage, Heritage, Hope and Imagination, but unfortunately it all comes off as pompous and dull, as the exhibit has too few items for its space and its art (the work of "genius") is routine. *Lobby.*

Entertainment. "Dream On"... "California Dreaming"... "Dream a Little Dream of Me"... "Teenage Dream"... the hits just keep on coming from the American Music Machine (★★★★★ ✔), which despite its cheesy name is a talented a cappella ensemble in which every member has an extreme range and terrific control. Led by the beatbox sounds of a vocal percussionist, the five-person group belts out a mash-up of American pop tunes, more than 30 in 20 minutes, a tour of Top 40 history that all ages will love. Its

harmonies were created by Tim Cook, the vocal arranger of the television series "Glee." *20-min. shows hourly noon–6 p.m. Wed.–Sun. America Gardens Theatre.* The pavilion's original a cappella group, The Voices of Liberty (★★★★★ ✔) performs traditional tunes such as "America the Beautiful" with a delicate passion. Rotunda shows are best, as the singers stand close to the audience. *15-min. shows hourly noon–5 p.m. Mon.–Tue. America Gardens Theatre; hourly 11 a.m.–5 p.m. Wed.–Sun. America Adventure rotunda.*

Restaurants and food. Decent treats are at Funnel Cakes and other stands out front; otherwise its ho-hum fast food at Liberty Inn. See reviews at **Restaurants and Food.**

Shops and merchandise. Small Heritage Manor Gifts has patriotic apparel and books. See reviews at **Shops and Merchandise.**

Fun facts. ❶ One of the few Disney buildings that use *reversed* forced perspective, the pavilion appears to be just three stories tall though it rises more than 70 feet. ❷ Its 110,000 hand-formed bricks were laid with an old-fashioned one-then-a-half technique.

Italy

One of the most attractive World Showcase facades, a Venetian entrance area disguises

Tiny train. Just a few inches tall, a locomotive chugs around a miniature German train village that's complete with its own people and trees. Behind it is the main pavilion's restroom.

the fact that this take on Lo Stivale ("the boot") is nothing but shops and restaurants. With the World Showcase lagoon acting as the Adriatic Sea, a waterfront area includes Venetian bridges, gondolas and striped pilings. The pavilion itself is a town square. Two freestanding columns recall 12th-century monuments; one topped by the guardian of Venice, the winged lion of St. Mark the Evangelist; the other's crowned by St. Theodore, the city's former patron saint who's shown killing a dragon, the act that gave him the courage to declare himself Christian. The 10th-century Campanile bell tower dominates the skyline, though this version's just 100 feet tall, less than a third the height of the real one; gold-leafed ringlets decorate an angel on top. Lining the plaza is the 14th-century Doge's (leader's) Palace; its first two stories resting on realistic marble columns that front leaded-glass windows, its third floor tiled and topped by marble sculptures, statues and filigree; a stairway and portico reflect Verona. The La Bottega shop is a Tuscany homestead; a sculpture of Neptune and his dolphins recalls Bernini's 1642 fountain in Florence and the Trevi fountain in Rome.

Entertainment. Funnyman mine Sergio (★★★★ ✔) pulls children into his shows as he juggles soccer balls. If your child wants

to be in the show, have him or her wear a distinctive hat or outfit, smile and catch the tireless performer's eye. *20-min. shows hourly noon–7 p.m. Sun.–Thr. Plaza at promenade.* In medieval times, standard-bearers were soldiers who led their units into battle carrying distinctive flags, designed to easily be spotted and recognized by the troops behind them during the heat of a battle. Simple commands were conveyed by pre-arranged signals, such as lifting the flags up and down or swaying them back and forth. Over time these routines grew more elaborate, as honor guards turned them into spectacles of color and precision. Formed in the small Italian town of Sansepolcro in 1953, Sbandieratori Di Sansepolcro (★★★★★ ✔) keeps alive its country's version of the art, using hand-painted flags and matching tunics and tights to recall the geometric patterns of its town's most illustrious citizen, Renaissance painter Piero della Francesca. Supporting trumpeters and drummers round out the act. The group appeared in the 2003 film "Under the Tuscan Sun." This offshoot came to Epcot in 2014. *15-min. shows hourly 1–7 p.m. Daily. Plaza.*

Restaurants and food. Fine Tutto Italia is an expensive treat; Via Napoli is Disney's best pizza place; expect to pay twice that of your local Pizza Hut and be glad you did.

Africa? Yes... but no. Village Traders, a small shop between Germany and China, was planned to be part of an Equatorial Africa pavilion. Today it offers items from other Epcot spots.

Tutto Gusto Wine Cellar serves small plates along with 200 varieties of wine.

See reviews at **Restaurants and Food.**

Shops and merchandise. Two stores offer Italian jewelry, fragrances, wine (by the bottle or glass), Perugina candy.

See reviews at **Shops and Merchandise.**

Germany

Like its Italian neighbor, Disney's Germany is little more than shops and food spots. Worse, there's no free entertainment.

An outdoor plaza is nicely detailed. Its centerpiece is a sculpture of the patron saint of soldiers, St. George, shown slaying a dragon during a trip to the Middle East. A clock comes to life at the top of each hour with a three-minute animated display. The facade of the Das Kaufhaus shop was inspired by the Kaufhaus, a 16th-century merchants' hall in the Black Forest town of Freiburg. Three statues on its second story recall the rule of the Hapsburg emperors. The pavilion's rear facade combines the looks of two 12th-century castles, the Eltz and the Stahleck.

Restaurants and food. An oompah band entertains at the boisterous Biergarten, an indoor Oktoberfest-style buffet; wursts and beer can be found at Sommerfest, an outdoor stand hidden behind the Biergarten entrance; worth visiting for the aroma alone is caramel shop Karamell-Küche.

See reviews at **Restaurants and Food.**

Shops and merchandise. Steiff bears, Schleich toys, Steinbach nutcrackers... there's plenty of authentic German fare here, spread among eight connected shops.

See reviews at **Shops and Merchandise.**

Fun finds and Hidden Mickeys. ❶ If you've got children, make sure you stop at the miniature outdoor train village to the right of the pavilion. A walkway leads over track tunnels and alongside the little town, which has its own wee little live landscape. Four working trains roam out over the rivers and through the woods, each on its own track. During some holidays the village is decorated for the season; at Christmas some of its homes are topped by snow and have wreaths on their doors, some of the tiny trees have lights. The village participates in Epcot's Flower and Garden Festival each spring, with its own streetside banners and flower pots. ❷ You'll find Mickey's three-circle shape in the center of the crown of the left-most Hapsburg emperor statue on the second story of Das Kaufhaus. ❸ A small Mickey figurine often hides in the train village, usually perched in a window of a hilltop castle.

China

Global communist superpower? There's no hint of *that* China in this pavilion, which serves up a version of its country in which no one makes iPhones and Chairman Mao never ruled. The pavilion is run by a Chinese company—a fact that should make it stand out but somehow just makes it bland.

Its highlight is its landscaping and architecture, a Disney-created salute to a century of colorful designs and styles. Out front, a Suzhou-style pond garden symbolizes nature's order and discipline; keeping with Chinese custom, it appears old and unkempt. Alongside the lagoon, pockmarked boulders demonstrate a tradition of designing surprising views in landscapes by creating holes in waterside rock formations.

Behind a triple-arched gate sits the Hall of Prayer for Good Harvests, the circular main building of Beijing's 1420 Temple of Heaven, a summer retreat for emperors. Its rotunda columns and beams allude to the cycles of nature; a floor stone is cut into nine pieces, as in China nine is a lucky number.

Along the main walkway are facades of an elegant home, a school house and stores that reflect European influences. The gallery building has a formal saddle-ridge roof line.

Entertainment. The six 18- to 21-year-old adults that make up the Jeweled Dragon Acrobats (★★) perform feats of agility, balance and strength. But the pace is slow—sometimes it seems you're watching little more than a warm-up for a yoga class—and for the most part the performers simply balance things on their heads or feet then present themselves for applause. Ta da! *20-min. shows hourly 3–8 p.m. Daily. Courtyard, moved inside Hall of Prayer in bad weather.*

Exhibit. The terra cotta "spirit army" found in the tomb of China's first emperor Qin Shi Huang (259–210 B.C.) is re-created at Tomb Warriors—Guardian Spirits of Ancient China (★★★★). The largest archeological find in the world, the actual 22-square-mile site contains 8,000 full-size statues arranged in military formations; here an army of 200 half-size reproductions offers a sense of the real thing. The exhibit also includes two dozen small tomb artifacts from the Han, Six, Sui and Tang Dynasties (through 906 A.D.). It's in the Gallery of the Whispering Willow, in the center of the pavilion.

Movie. An actual piece of communist propaganda, the CircleVision 360 Reflections of China reflects reality like a fun-house mirror, blatantly excluding segments of Chinese history and culture to show you the most serene and trouble-free country on earth. You stand up for your indoctrination, as the images project all around you on a circular screen; one scene was filmed by a camera hanging from a banking helicopter. *20 min. Continuous shows. Capacity 200. Indoor queue. Guests may stay in wheelchairs, ECVs. Reflective captioning, assistive listening, Audio Description. Debuted 1982, revised 2003.*

Restaurants and food. Sadly, both table-service Nine Dragons and fast-food Lotus Blossom Cafe are forgettable.

See reviews at **Restaurants and Food.**

Shops and merchandise. The spacious House of Good Fortune focuses on apparel, and has a separate children's area.

See reviews at **Shops and Merchandise.**

Fun fact. ❶ Though she did not provide the singing voice of Mulan in Disney's 1998 movie "Mulan," pop star Christina Aguilera recorded a version of the song shortly thereafter, using the China pavilion as the backdrop for its video. Her take reached number 15 on the Adult Contemporary chart and led to her first record contract.

Fun find. ❶ Wild giant bullfrogs hide under lily pads in the pond, and sometimes poke their heads above water.

Norway

Despite all the chatter about its new ride and meet-and-greet, there's more to this pavilion than its tie-ins to "Frozen." Specifically, there's stuff about… Norway! At the entrance is a replica of the tiny 13th-century Gol Church of Hallingdal, a Stave church that played a key role in the country's movement to Christianity. Other facades recall cottages of the island communities of Alesund, the seaside town of Bergen and the rural valley of Setesdal. The bakery has a sod roof, a traditional way to insulate Setesdal homes still used today. The pavilion's restaurant and rear facade re-create Akershus, a 14th-century Oslo castle and fortress.

Exhibit. A small museum-style exhibit inside the Stave Church, Norsk Kultur: Creating the World of Frozen (★★★) displays traditional Norwegian clothing, musical instruments, furniture and artifacts that

Jeweled Dragon Spooler. A performer at the China pavilion.

© Disney

Name that tune. In this Disney concept art, Queen Elsa serenades Frozen Ever After riders as they sail into her ice castle, using her powers to make snow flutter around them.

Frozen Ever After

High-tech Maelstrom makeover focuses on characters, music

NEW! ★★★★ ✔ Fastpass+ You knew this was coming. It won two Oscars. It's the most popular Disney movie ever, the top-grossing animated film of all time. And lately, when little girls are dressing up as princesses at Disney World, they're Anna and Elsa way more often than Cinderella or Snow White. So now Disney is premiering its first ride based on "Frozen." Here at Epcot, in the Norway pavilion. It replaces Maelstrom, an aging boat ride and travelogue movie that focused on Norwegian mythology.

Scheduled to open in May 2016, the ride will use the same boats and waterway as Maelstrom, but everything along its banks will be new. Audio-Animatronic characters will incorporate projectors behind their faces, much like the dwarfs seen on Magic Kingdom's Seven Dwarfs Mine Train. They'll appear in scenes that show the kingdom of

Arendelle holding a Winter Festival in the middle of summer—since, you know, its queen has the power to pull off things like that. And just what will those faces do? Sing! Goofy snowman Olaf, Princess Anna, iceman Kristof, reindeer Sven… they all break into song. Topping off the tour is, of course, Queen Elsa. Floating into her ice castle, you'll watch her belt out the Academy-Award winning "Let It Go" as you're surrounded by swirling snow. If you've seen the movie you'll know all the songs but not all the lyrics, as movie composers Robert Lopez and Kristen Anderson Lopez have added a few new ones to match the attraction's storyline.

A celebration of "Frozen" characters, the ride will also include Grandpappy Troll, and from the 2015 short "Frozen Fever," once-evil snowman Marshmallow and those cute little Snowgie babies. The waiting line will

Average wait times (estimated)

9am	10am	11am	Noon	1pm	2pm	3pm	4pm	5pm	6pm	7pm	8pm	9pm
5m	45m	85m	85m	35m	35m	55m	45m	45m	35m	55m	65m	55m

On the move. Shown here in Magic Kingdom's Fairytale Hall, Princess Anna (left) and Queen Elsa will be greeting guests in the Norway pavilion starting in mid-2016.

pass Wandering Oaken's Trading Post and Sauna, where the owner will sporadically clear the steam off a window and utter a hearty "yoo-hoo!"

Controversy. Does Frozen Ever After belong in the Norway pavilion? Perhaps not. Until now the pavilions of the World Showcase have focused on real countries; indeed that's the whole point of the place. But the ride isn't. Like its movie, it's set a fictional world, the kingdom of Arendelle. However, the Frozen story is based on the region of the world that includes Norway—Scandinavia. In fact, it's a version of "The Snow Queen," a fairy tale written in 1845 by Danish author Hans Christian Andersen, the same guy who wrote the fable "The Little Mermaid."

In truth, Disney has been putting non-authentic elements into the World Showcase for years. A few years ago it placed Aladdin and Jasmine into Morocco with no uproar at all (like "Frozen," the movie "Aladdin" takes place in a fictional world, the city of Agrabah) and that pavilion has always featured at least one belly dancer, even though that form of entertainment comes from Egypt. Only a few fans complained a few years later when Disney updated the ride in its Mexico pavilion with an overlay featuring the title characters of its "Three Caballeros" movie,

the leader of which (José Carioca) is a dapper Brazilian parrot. Most World Showcase merchandise comes from China.

And though Disney doesn't acknowledge it, many of its World Showcase entertainers don't come from the countries they represent. Those amusing waiters at France? They're Russian. The Canadian lumberjacks? All the way from Kissimmee, the Orlando suburb right next door to Disney.

Despite all that, Epcot traditionalists will still probably hate Frozen After Ever (there's always the anti-princess angle), but fans of the movie will certainly enjoy it.

Character greeting. Anna and Elsa greet guests too, in a large new building— the "Royal Sommerhus." It's the first new structure in the World Showcase in ages.

Tips. Book Fastpasses for both the ride and the character greeting unless you plan to arrive first thing in the morning. Expect long lines all day, as the popular Princess Storybook character meal is right next door.

Key facts. *Best for:* Frozen fans. *Duration:* 4 minutes. *Capacity:* 192. *Queue:* Indoor. *Fear factor:* Often dark, with one scary moment. *Debuted:* 2016. *Access:* Wheelchair and ECV users must transfer. Assistive listening, reflective captioning. *Location:* Norway pavilion. *Scheduled to open:* May 2016.

Confident horn. Members of Mariachi Cobre perform at the Mexico pavilion. Walt Disney World's best live band, the 11-piece group has been at the pavilion since its opening day.

relate to Disney's 2013 movie "Frozen." A female figure wears an outfit similar to Anna's. Some items date back to the 1200s.

Restaurants and food. It's a princesspalooza at the Akershus Royal Banquet Hall, a character buffet that includes Norwegian cuisine. Sandwiches and treats are at Kringla Bakeri Og Kafe.

See reviews at **Restaurants and Food.**

Shops and merchandise. The Puffin's Roost sells Frozen items, Norwegian apparel and perfume and silly viking helmets.

See reviews at **Shops and Merchandise.**

Mexico

It's margaritaville! Young adults in particular enjoy this pavilion's Cinco de Mayo atmosphere. Everyone likes the music, most like the shopping and tasty dining experiences. The bulk of the pavilion is inside what appears to be the ancient Aztec pyramid of serpent god Quetzalcoatl. Inside, an "outdoor" market recalls the town of Taxco during its peak silver-mining days in the 16th-century. Outside, a café looks similar to the 17th-century Mexico City's San Angel Inn, a restaurant run by the same family who operates the eateries here.

Entertainment. The best live band at Disney, the outstanding Mariachi Cobre

(★★★★★ ✔) is a staple of Epcot, an example of the nuanced culture of our southern neighbor and its beautiful music that too often gets overlooked today. The 11-piece group features confident trumpets, violins and vocals, which are backed up by the wonderful sound of harmonizing guitars. Together for 44 years, the band has played with (and recorded with) Julio Iglesias and Linda Ronstadt, and has been appearing at Epcot since the park's opening day. Three members have been with it since its formation; eight have been part of it since its park debut. The coauthor of this book tries to photograph the group yearly but always fails; there seems to be no way to visually capture the spirit of its songs. *25-min. shows hourly 11 a.m.–5 p.m. Daily (marimba trio Tues–Wed.) Promenade next to gift stand, moved inside pyramid in bad weather.*

Restaurants and food. Choose from modern Mexican fare at waterside La Hacienda de San Angel or traditional choices in the pyramid's San Angel Inn (both good but pricey). For fast-food its the waterside La Cantina de San Angel; for tequilas it's back inside to the tiny bar La Cava del Tequila.

See reviews at **Restaurants and Food.**

Shops and merchandise. The indoor Plaza de los Amigos offers many Mexican items.

See reviews at **Shops and Merchandise.**

Animation art © Disney

Birds of a feather. The Three Caballeros—Donald Duck, Panchito Pistoles and José Carioca—perform in the Gran Fiesta Tour, a dark boat ride themed to Mexican culture.

Gran Fiesta Tour

Wacky overlays to boring boat ride create one strange trip

★★★ Fastpass+ A mutant freak of an attraction, this slow-moving dark boat ride tours the cultural history of Mexico while simultaneously reveling in the antics of the Three Caballeros—Brazilian parrot José Carioca, Mexican charro rooster Panchito Pistoles and Don Juan Donald Duck—who are about to serenade the masses of Mexico City. Only they can't, as Donald has gone off sightseeing and spied some señoritas who have stolen his heart. Will José and Panchito find him in time? You won't care, as the frolicsome fowls only appear in video clips, which are set within unrelated three-dimensional scenes of pyramids and temples. In the middle of it all is a doll-filled Day of the Dead celebration straight out of It's a Small World.

In other words, this is one messy muddle of an attraction, a cheap update of the El Rio Del Tiempo, an original Epcot ride which may have been dull but was at least coherent. There's rarely a wait unless a Brazilian tour group shows up. (And then—¡ay caramba!)

Come here, my little enchilada. Donald Duck is a wild-eyed skirt chaser in 1944's "The Three Caballeros," the weirdest animated musical the Walt Disney company has ever made. Combining morphing sugar-rush animation with a storyline that redefines Donald as an unfettered philanderer, its Mexican segment sends the trio off on a flying serape tour of the country, where the duck goes ga-ga for dozens of live-action human women, at night hitting the clubs as he tries to kiss a few.

Key facts. *Best for:* Tequila'd adults. *Duration:* 8 minutes. *Capacity:* 250. *Queue:* Indoor. *Debuted:* 1982, revised 2007. *Access:* ECV users must transfer. Handheld captioning. *Location:* Mexico pavilion.

Average wait times

9am	10am	11am	Noon	1pm	2pm	3pm	4pm	5pm	6pm	7pm	8pm	9pm
n/a	0m	0m	0m	0m	0m	0m	5m	5m	0m	0m	0m	n/a

Finding Perry. Sign-up carts for Agent P's World Showcase Adventure are near the United Kingdom (above), Italy and Norway pavilions and on the Future World Odyssey Bridge.

Agent P's World Showcase Adventure

'Phineas and Ferb' fans will love this scavenger hunt

★★★★★ ✔ This interactive game uses refurbished cell phones and hidden special effects to channel the comic sensibility of "Phineas & Ferb," the Disney Channel animated series about two brothers and their pet platypus, Perry. As fans of the show know, Perry has an alter ego as a secret agent—Agent P—and a nemesis—Dr. Doofenshmirtz, a bumbling mad scientist who for years has been out to take over his tri-state area. But now he has bigger plans. Off on a vacation to Epcot and its World Showcase, now he wants to take over the world. And what's worse, Agent P can't stop him. It's up to you.

As you sign up for the game, you become an agent of OWCA (the Organization Without a Cool Acronym) and are sent to a World Showcase pavilion to foil the scientist's plans. You receive instructions by using a FONE (Field Operative Notifications Equipment), which helps you defeat Doofenschmirtz as you bring elements of the surroundings to life.

Fans of the show will love it. Its silliness breaks up the seriousness of the World Showcase and gives children something to do.

Where to sign up. There are four spots; one on the wide footbridge that connects Future World to the World Showcase, three others on the World Showcase walkway. The mission you get depends on where you sign up. *Odyssey Bridge:* You'll be sent to Mexico, Norway or the U.K. *United Kingdom pavilion:* The U.K., France, Japan, Mexico or Norway. *Norway pavilion:* Mexico, Norway or China. *Italy pavilion:* Germany or Japan. When you finish one mission, you can do another one.

By the way, you choose your agent name. When the author plays, she's Agent J.

Tips. *When to play:* During the summer right when the park opens at 11 a.m., before the weather gets too hot or rainy.

Fun fact. ❶ "Phineas & Ferb" creators Dan Povenmire and Jeff "Swampy" Marsh spent many days at Epcot brainstorming ideas for the game and scouting locations.

Key facts. *Best for:* Phineas & Ferb fans. *Length:* Allow 25 min. *Capacity:* 100. *Hours:* 11 a.m.–8:15 p.m. *Debuted:* 2012. *Access:* Guests may stay in wheelchairs, ECVs. *Location:* Various World Showcase pavilions.

Today's world: chaos. That's one way to read the fiery finale of IllumiNations, which abstractly portrays the history of the world from the dawn of time to the present.

IllumiNations

Spectacle trumps storytelling in nightly fireworks finale

★★★★★ ✔ FastPass IllumiNations sets its sights high: to tell the history of Earth without narration. Synchronized to a symphonic score of world music, the nightly fireworks and special-effects extravaganza uses the entire World Showcase to do that, though its points are so abstract you almost have to know them ahead of time to realize what they are. Strobe lights flash, laser beams dance, pavilions light up and fireworks burst, a rotating Earth glides across the lagoon and shows moving images on its continents. It's a confusing experience—but still one that shouldn't be missed.

Tips. *When to go:* Nab a spot 20 to 30 minutes before 9 p.m., the show's nightly start time. *Where to watch it:* You'll need a Fastpass for the best viewing spot—between the two gift shops at World Showcase Plaza. From there you'll see the show's symmetry as its designers intended; you'll also be close to Epcot's front exit so you'll be ahead of the masses when it ends. *For families:* Whisper to your children what the images are that appear on the globe; they change quickly.

Fun facts. ❶ Two-thousand eight-hundred fireworks launch from 750 mortar tubes in 34 locations; some explode 600 feet overhead. ❷ Wrapped in more than 180,000 LEDs, the 28-foot steel globe was the world's first spherical video display. ❸ The pavilions are outlined in 26,000 feet of lights. ❹ The Morocco pavilion does not participate in the show since some of its buildings represent religious structures. ❺ The show's music supervisor was Hans Zimmer, the composer for the 1994 Disney movie "The Lion King." ❻ Nineteen torches around the lagoon symbolize the first 19 centuries of modern history. The 20th torch, the one in the globe, represents our current one (don't do the math on that; it's not good).

Key facts. *Best for:* Anyone ages 5+ who likes loud noises. *Duration:* 14 minutes. *Fear factor:* Loud, bright explosions and fire (the authors' daughter hated this show when she was little). *Weather issues:* Cancelled during thunderstorms. *Debuted:* 1988; revised 1997, 1999. *Access:* Guests may remain in wheelchairs, ECVs. *Location:* On and above World Showcase Lagoon.

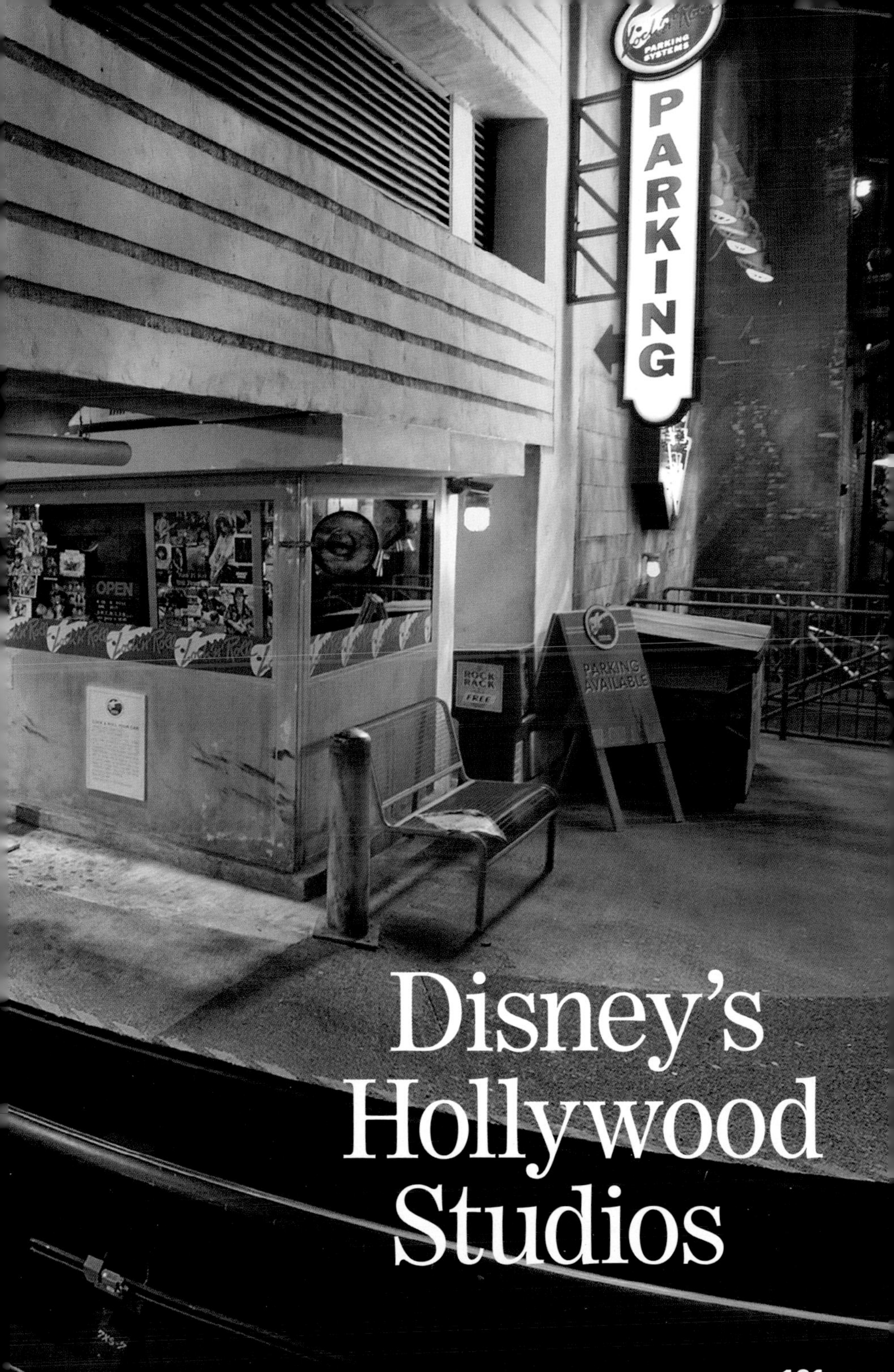

PARKING

Rock Roll
PARKING
SYSTEMS

OPEN

ROCK
RACK
FREE

PARKING
AVAILABLE

Disney's Hollywood Studios

Disney's tribute to Tinseltown

Over the next few years Disney will transform large sections of this park into Star Wars and Toy Story lands—for complete information on all that's coming see the What's New section of the front of this book. In the meantime, this park still offers much to enjoy, even though there's not much here. A love letter to show business focus on movies and television shows, and has something for every age. Fans of old-style glamour encounter Humphrey Bogart and James Cagney at the Great Movie Ride; a Star Tours ride delights fans of the Force. Animation buffs get experiences based on "Frozen" and "Toy Story." Television is represented by the ride's signature thrill ride, The Twilight Zone Tower of Terror.

Best of the park. Disney's Hollywood Studios has **exhilarating thrill rides**—Rock 'n' Roller Coaster Starring Aerosmith and the Twilight Zone Tower of Terror both hurl you through the dark in ways that surprise you. It has a **sense of humor.** Many of its experiences put a smile on your face—its Citizen of Hollywood street performers, its

hilarious Dr. Bunsen Honeydew and Beaker at Jim Henson's MuppetVision 3-D, its sarcastic servers at the 50's Prime Time Café. Its **preschooler show** Disney Junior Live on Stage speaks directly to young children without being condescending. And finally, **it won't wear you out.** Unlike most Disney parks, the Studios doesn't make you spend all day on your feet. It's quick to get around, and offers many ways to sit down and relax.

Worst of the park. For those visiting in 2016 the upcoming expansions don't mean much; what does is that right now **there's not much here.** Over the last few years the park has lost its parade, its outdoor street show, its Studio Backlot Tour, its Magic of Disney Animation, its Legend of Captain Jack Sparrow show; rumor is that One Man's Dream will be closing soon, too. Over the next couple of years more things may leave too, including much of Streets of America. The park's iconic giant sorcerer's hat is gone too, though that's not a bad thing—it restores the original view down Hollywood Boulevard.

Picturesque Echo Lake honors Echo Lake Park in Los Angeles, an on-location setting for many early movies. At left, Sunset Boulevard. Previous spread: Rock 'n' Roller Coaster.

Getting oriented. Disney's Hollywood Studios is divided into five themed areas:

Animation Courtyard. Its entrance arch is modeled on the Paramount Studio gate; inside is a soundstage plaza and a former working studio of Disney Feature Animation.

Echo Lake. This picturesque spot recalls Echo Lake Park in downtown Los Angeles, where 1920's silent movie czar Mack Sennett shot many of his Keystone Comedies.

Hollywood and Sunset Boulevards. The front of the park channels Old Hollywood. Its architecture and street entertainment embody Los Angeles during the glory days of Tinseltown—the 1920s through the 1940s.

Pixar Place. Styled after Pixar's headquarters in Emeryville, Calif., this small, busy spot holds one of Walt Disney World's most popular attractions—the high-tech shooting gallery Toy Story Mania. Green Army Men patrol the street and pose for photos.

Streets of America. This former backlot area is dominated by New York Street, a 500-foot Beaux Arts thoroughfare based on the Big Apple's West 40th Street. A crossing street recalls San Francisco.

Where to meet characters. About 20 Disney characters appear at the park. It's the only place to meet "Monsters Inc." characters Mike and Sulley, "Cars" characters Lightning McQueen and 'Mater, and Disney Junior stars such as Doc McStuffins.

Buzz Lightyear. Woody's Picture Shootin' Corral, Pixar Place.

Chip 'n Dale. Central plaza in front of the Chinese Theater, Hollywood Blvd.

Daisy Duck. Central plaza in front of the Chinese Theater, Hollywood Blvd.

Doc McStuffins. Animation Courtyard; Play 'N Dine character meals, Echo Lake.

Donald Duck. Central plaza in front of the Chinese Theater, Hollywood Blvd.

Goofy. Central plaza in front of the Chinese Theater, Hollywood Blvd.

Green Army Men. Pixar Place.

Handy Manny. Play 'N Dine character meals at Hollywood & Vine, Echo Lake.

Jake. Animation Courtyard; Play 'N Dine character meals, Echo Lake.

Lightning McQueen. Team McQueen Headquarters, Streets of America.

'Mater. Team McQueen Headquarters, along the back side of Streets of America.

Mickey Mouse. Near Studio Catering Co. (in his Sorcerer's Apprentice garb).

Mike Wazowski. Streets of America, across from the playground.

Minnie Mouse. Main plaza in front of the Chinese Theater, Hollywood Blvd.

Popular Pixar Place is modeled after the headquarters of Pixar Animation Studios in Emeryville, Calif., which uses the same brick. At right, the Twilight Zone Tower of Terror.

Phineas and Ferb. Near Mama Melrose's Ristorante Italiano, Streets of America.

Pluto. Central plaza in front of the Chinese Theater, Hollywood Blvd.

Sofia the First. Animation Courtyard; Play 'N Dine character meals, Echo Lake.

Sulley. Streets of America, across from the playground.

Woody. Woody's Picture Shootin' Corral, Pixar Place.

See also the chapter **Characters.**

Street performers. The park has a terrific improv troupe and a fine rock 'n' roll band:

★★★★★ ✔ **Citizens of Hollywood.** Impersonating showbiz stereotypes with unfettered glee, this improv troupe roams the park's Old Hollywood area as the living, breathing residents of a 1940s Tinseltown. The cast includes directors, divas, heartthrobs, has-beens, wannabes, starlets, inept public works employees, a card shark, even a caterer. Most skits include audience "volunteers." To be chosen for one, wear something colorful, stand in front, smile and make eye contact with the performers. *20- to 30-min. shows. Hollywood and Sunset Boulevards.*

★★★★★ ✔ **Mulch, Sweat and Shears.** Driving its pickup truck and trailer onto the Streets of America, this landscape crew transforms itself into a band ready to "Rake 'n' Roll." Tapping into their engine's battery for power, wannabe comedian and ladies man Morris Mulch and his group crank out classic tunes and medleys, grabbing female audience members to join in on cow bells and air guitars. Because of its Disney location, the band changes some lyrics; a line from the Eagles' "Life in the Fast Lane" becomes "They had one thing in common, they were good... at sports!" *30-min. shows. Streets of America, also Hollywood Boulevard.*

If it rains. With its small size and plethora of indoor things to do, the park is easy to enjoy during a shower. There are many stores and dining spots to duck into, the new Star Wars Launch Bay has no restrictions how long you stay there. The stunt shows and playground close due to rain; nightime show Fantasmic is cancelled when lightning is nearby.

Family matters. All of the park's thrill rides have height minimums—48 inches for Rock 'n' Roller Coaster Starring Aerosmith, 40 inches for Twilight Zone Tower of Terror as well as the Star Tours motion simulator. Three other attractions may be too much for toddlers: Fantasmic (it has explosions, fire and villains), The Great Movie Ride (gunshots, fire,

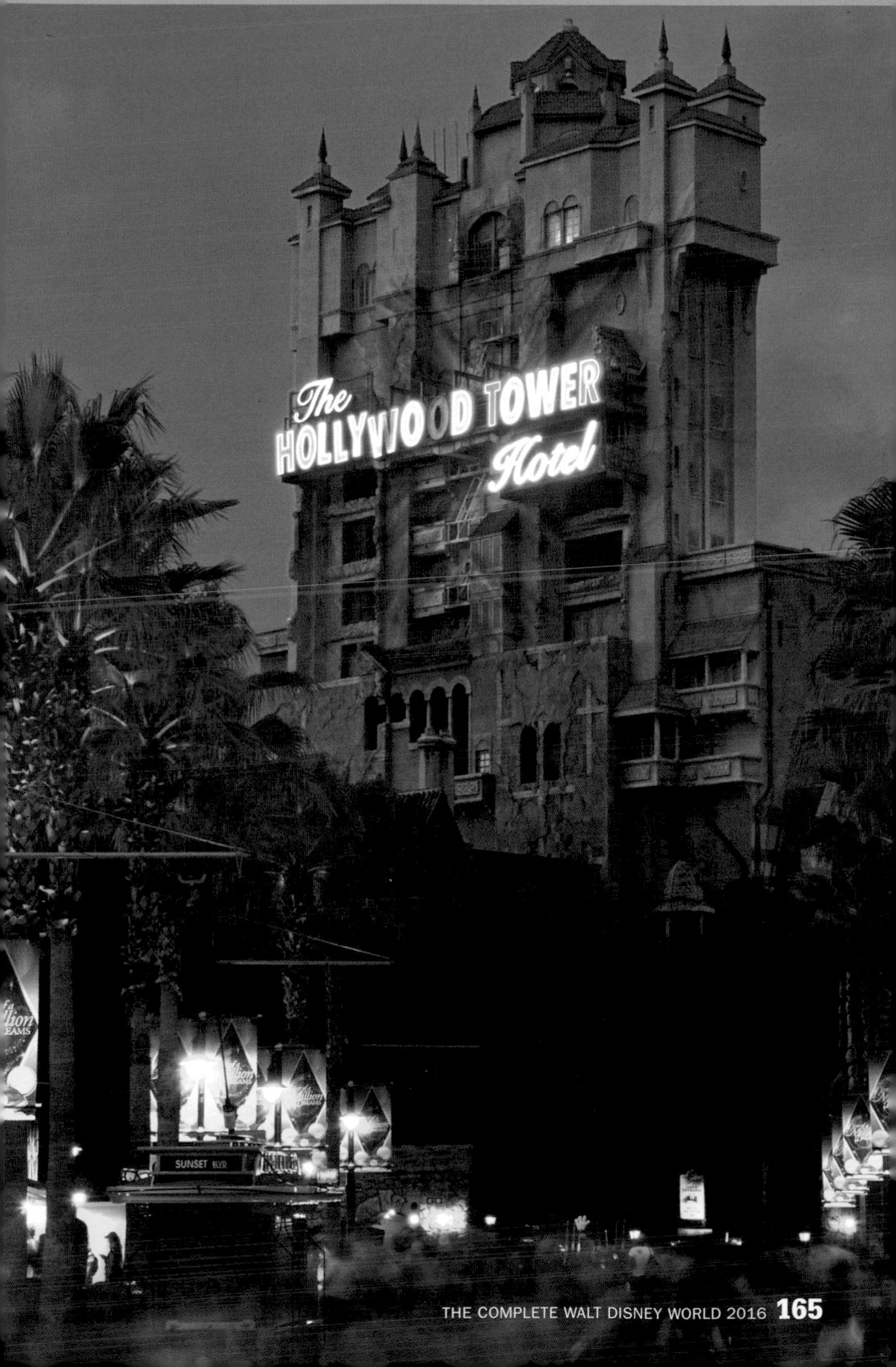
The
HOLLYWOOD TOWER
Hotel
SUNSET

Micaela Neal

Jedi Training Academy. Guided by a Jedi Master, younglings use "training" light sabers to duel Darth Vader or other villains. The show will be refreshed with new characters in 2016.

an alien, the Wicked Witch) and Voyage of the Little Mermaid (its Ursula makes many little ones cry). Every restaurant offers a children's menu. Disney Junior characters appear at Hollywood & Vine for breakfast and lunch.

Fun finds and Hidden Mickeys. Lots of little details and in-jokes are scattered around the park's grounds and in its shops. ❶ On Hollywood Boulevard, offices above an entrance to the Keystone Clothiers shop include one for tailor Justin Stitches. ❷ In Echo Lake, "We've Finished Some of Hollywood's Finest" is the motto of acting-and-voice studio Sights and Sounds. Located behind Keystone Clothiers, it's run by master thespian Ewell M. Pressum, voice coach Singer B. Flatt and account exec Bill Moor. ❸ Nearby are the dental offices of C. Howie Pullum, Ruth Canal and Les Payne. ❹ Crates to the left of Min & Bill's snack stand refer to the films "Casablanca," "Citizen Kane," "Gone With the Wind" and "It's a Wonderful Life." ❺ On Sunset Boulevard, an office above the Reel Vogue store is home to the union the International Brotherhood of Second Assistant Directors (say it slowly: IBSAD), which has the motto "We're Standing Behind You." During the Great Depression, Second Assistant Director was a mercy title given to

go-fers, who were often told "Get coffee and stand behind me." On the Streets of America, ❻ a back corner of the Stage 1 Co. Store includes the Muppet lockers and Happiness Hotel front desk from 1981's "The Great Muppet Caper." Nearly two dozen silly signs in the shop include one over a doorway that reads "Absolutely no point beyond this point." ❼ Sharp eyes can spot the three-circle-shape of the head of Mickey Mouse in the Cover Story store on Hollywood Boulevard, in the black decorative molding below the second-floor windows; ❽ along Sunset Boulevard as impressions on the curbs that read "Mortimer & Co. Contractors 1928" (a reference to Walt Disney's original name for Mickey, who Disney created in 1928); ❾ in Echo Lake as washers used to secure tops of coffee tables in the Tune-In Lounge; ❿ on the Streets of America outside the Stage 1 Co. Store as purple paint drips on a recessed light under a bronze lion head and ⓫ inside the store as green drips on a wood bureau shelf, ⓬ also Mickey's red shorts hang above the check-in desk of the Happiness Hotel.

Architecture. The front of the park re-creates the look of Los Angeles during the mid-20th century. The turquoise entrance structures and their white-ringed pylons

© Disney

New Star Wars attractions for 2016. Though the park's Star Wars land won't be finished until 2018, a new Star Wars Launch Bay previews the area and new Star Wars movies, and offers character meet and greets. Starting in mid-2016, a summertime Season of the Force fireworks spectacular will be set to an iconic Star Wars score.

reflect 1935's Art Deco Pan Pacific Auditorium, a sports and music hall.

Hollywood Boulevard. This dreamlike, 500-foot version of the iconic Tinseltown thoroughfare has 15 facades that are modeled on actual structures in Los Angeles. A Crossroads of the World gift kiosk is a replica of a Streamline Moderne stand at the 1937 Crossroads of the World shopping center. Sid Cahuenga's is a tribute to 1930s and 1940s Craftsman bungalows that became Hollywood tourist shops. The Disney & Co. store brings back a Hollywood veterinary clinic and the black-marble-and-gilt Security Pacific Bank building, itself a copy of L.A.'s Richfield Oil Building, whose black and gold trim represented the "Black Gold" of the oil industry. Keystone Clothiers includes facades of Hollywood's Max Factor Building and Jullian Medical Building.

The right side of the street is equally inspired. The photo center is a clone of The Darkroom, a 1938 Hollywood photo shop known for its front window trim that looked like a giant camera. Celebrity 5 & 10 evokes an Art Deco building that once housed a J.J. Newberry five and dime. Finally, the Hollywood Brown Derby is modeled from the 1929 second location of the famous restaurant, a legendary dining spot for movie stars.

Inside the various buildings is a ceiling lover's paradise. Cover Story's film-roll theme recalls Frank Lloyd Wright.

At the end of the road is a full-scale model of Grauman's Chinese Theatre. The front is designed from the same blueprints as the 1927 building and has most of the original's trim and detailing. The only real difference: this one has its ticket booth off to the side.

Echo Lake. This area recalls Echo Lake Park in Los Angeles, where 1920s silent-movie czar Mack Sennett shot many of his Keystone Comedies. Two snack stands re-create that era's programmatic architecture—a tramp steamer is Min & Bill's Dockside Diner; an apatosaurus is Dinosaur Gertie's Ice Cream of Extinction, a tribute to 1914 cartoon star Gertie the Dinosaur that includes her footprints in the walkway. Nearby Hollywood & Vine restaurant evokes a cafeteria that stood on North Vine, near the actual Hollywood Blvd.

Sunset Boulevard. The Disney version begins with a replica of the 1940 Mulholland Fountain in Griffith Park. On your left, the Colony Sunset shop is New York City's Colony Theatre as it appeared in 1928, when it

Demanding your approval, the improvisational Citizens of Hollywood appear in the park's Old Hollywood areas as its living, breathing residents. Skits include audience "volunteers."

premiered the first Mickey Mouse sound cartoon, "Steamboat Willie." The Sunset Ranch Market recalls the 1934 Los Angeles Farmers Market where Walt Disney often had lunch. On the right, the Legends of Hollywood store has the facade and corkscrew tower of the 1938 Academy Theater. The Once Upon a Time shop is a dead ringer for the 1926 Carthay Circle Theatre, which hosted the premiere of "Snow White and the Seven Dwarfs" in 1937.

The entrance to Fantasmic's Hollywood Hills Amphitheater draws its design from the Ford Amphitheater in the Hollywood Hills. The stone entranceway to The Twilight Zone Tower of Terror replicates the Hollywood Gates, the 1923 entrance to the Hollywoodland real-estate development. The Hollywood Tower Hotel recalls the Spanish Revival look of the 1902 Mission Inn in Riverside, Calif.

Animation Courtyard, Pixar Place. The buildings and soundstages at the rear of the park have the look of those at the Walt Disney Studios in California. Pixar Place is styled after the headquarters of that animation studio in Emeryville, Calif.

A real studio. Originally both a theme park and a working studio, what was first called Disney-MGM Studios opened as a production facility in 1988, then to the public on May 1,

1989. An old-fashioned Hollywood gala, its Grand Opening aired as a two-hour special on NBC-TV. On hand were many Hollywood legends, including Lauren Bacall, George Burns, Audrey Hepburn and Bob Hope. "Welcome to the Hollywood that never was and always will be," Disney CEO Michael Eisner proclaimed.

Hit me Justin, one more time. Real movies and television shows were produced at the park for years. In 1988 the films "Ernest Saves Christmas" and "Newsies" were shot on the backlot (todays Streets of America), two years later so was the Warren Beatty/Madonna vehicle "Dick Tracy." Soundstages hosted shows such as "Ed McMahon's Star Search," in which a 10-year-old Britney Spears and 11-year-old Justin Timberlake both appeared on and lost, and the 1989–1994 Disney Channel program "The New Mickey Mouse Club," which starred young Spears and Timberlake as well as fellow preteens Christina Aguilera, Ryan Gosling and Keri Russell.

Meanwhile, in the building that today hosts the Star Wars Launch Bay, a Disney animation studio (Walt Disney Feature Animation Florida) produced sequences of 1991's "Beauty and the Beast" and later entire films including 1998's "Mulan" and 2002's "Lilo & Stitch." But after the flop of its 2004 movie "Home on the Range,"

© Disney

Britney, Christina, Justin... none of them were famous when they worked at the park, the child stars of a version of the Mickey Mouse Club that aired from 1989 through 1995. Also featuring Ryan Gosling and Keri Russell, the show was taped in front of a live audience in the building that today houses Toy Story Mania.

Disney management decided to downsize and eventually close the animation studio, as well as everything else. Today, no television or motion-picture work is done at the park.

Know before you go. Need some cash? A stroller? Help with MyMagic+? Here you go:

ATMs. The park has two: There's one outside the entrance on the left, another inside the Toy Story Pizza Planet Arcade.

Baby Care Center. Located on your left as you enter the park, right beside the Guest Relations office, this indoor spot has changing rooms, nursing areas, a microwave and a playroom. It sells diapers, formula, pacifiers and over-the-counter meds.

FastPass+ kiosks. Cast members help you book and modify Fastpasses at these walk-up touchscreens. You'll find them at Sid Cahuenga's One-of-a-Kind shop, at the corner of Hollywood and Sunset, at Jim Henson's MuppetVision 3-D and Toy Story Mania, and on Sunset Boulevard next to The Twilight Zone Tower of Terror.

First aid. An indoor clinic is beside Guest Relations next to the Baby Care Center. Registered nurses treat minor emergencies. They call EMTs for serious issues.

Guest Relations. Located at the entrance to the park on the left, this office has walk-up windows outside the touchpoints, a walk-in lobby just inside. Cast members answer general questions, make dining reservations, exchange currency, hand out maps and times guides for all Disney World parks, and store items found in the park that day.

Locker rentals. They're inside the park at Oscar's Super Service ($7 a day, $5 deposit).

MyMagic+ Service Center. Inside Sid Cahuenga's One-of-a-Kind shop, cast members answer questions about MyMagic+ services: the My Disney Experience website and app, the MagicBand ticketing system and the FastPass+ attraction-reservation service.

Package pickup. Anything you buy in the park can be sent to the park entrance for you to pick up later at no charge; allow three hours. Packages can also be delivered to Disney hotels or shipped nationally.

Parking. $17 a day per car. Free for Disney hotel guests and annual passholders.

Stroller rentals. Oscar's Super Service rents single strollers for $15 a day ($13 length of stay), doubles for $31 ($27 length of stay). Get replacements at Tatooine Traders.

Disney transportation. Boats go to Epcot and Epcot resorts. There's direct bus service to all other Disney resorts, theme parks and Blizzard Beach; but not to ESPN Wide World of Sports, Disney Springs or Typhoon Lagoon.

Wheelchair and scooter rentals. Available at Oscar's Super Service. Wheelchairs $12 a day, $10 a day length of stay. Four-wheel electric scooters $50 a day, $20 deposit.

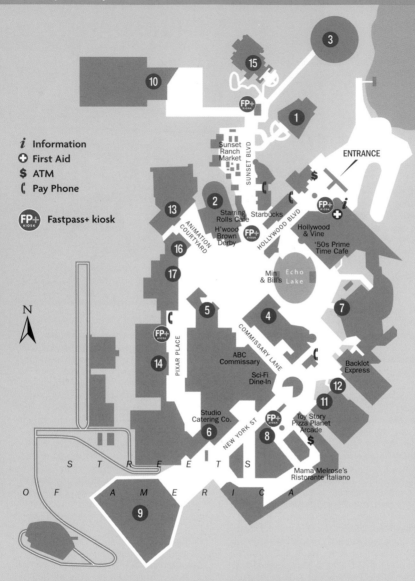

i **Information**

✚ **First Aid**

$ **ATM**

℘ **Pay Phone**

FP+ **Fastpass+ kiosk**

ENTRANCE

Sunset Ranch Market

SUNSET BLVD

Starring Rolls Cafe

Starbucks

H'wood Brown Derby

HOLLYWOOD BLVD

Hollywood & Vine

'50s Prime Time Cafe

ANIMATION COURTYARD

Min & Bill's

Echo Lake

COMMISSARY LANE

N

PIXAR PLACE

ABC Commissary

Sci-Fi Dine-In

Backlot Express

Studio Catering Co.

NEW YORK ST

Toy Story Pizza Planet Arcade

Mama Melrose's Ristorante Italiano

S T R E E T S

O F   A M E R I C A

1. **Beauty and the Beast—Live on Stage**
2. **Disney Junior—Live on Stage**
3. **Fantasmic!**
4. **For the First Time in Forever**
5. **The Great Movie Ride**
6. **"Honey, I Shrunk the Kids" Playground**
7. **Indiana Jones Epic Stunt Spectacular**
8. **Jim Henson's MuppetVision 3-D**
9. **Lights Motors Action**
10. **Rock 'n' Roller Coaster Starring Aerosmith**
11. **Star Tours**
12. **Star Wars: Jedi Training Academy**
13. **Star Wars Launch Bay**
14. **Toy Story Mania**
15. **The Twilight Zone Tower of Terror**
16. **Voyage of the Little Mermaid**
17. **Walt Disney: One Man's Dream**

Attractions at a Glance

Here's a quick look at the attractions at Disney's Hollywood Studios, each of which is reviewed in detail later in this chapter. Each attraction is rated from one to five stars (★); a checkmark (✔) indicates an author favorite. The Fastpass+ logo (FastPass+) appears if the attraction can be reserved in advance.

Five-star attractions ★★★★★

Beauty and the Beast Live on Stage. ✔ FastPass+ Stage musical is fun, moving. Sunset Boulevard.

Disney Junior Live on Stage. FastPass+ Lively puppet show stars Disney Junior characters. Disney's best preschooler attraction. Animation Courtyard.

Rock 'n' Roller Coaster Starring Aerosmith. ✔ FastPass+ Dark coaster corkscrews, goes upside down, blares rock. Height min. 48 in. Sunset Boulevard.

UPDATED! Star Tours. ✔ FastPass+ Wacky thrills aboard a Star Wars ship; routes vary with each ride, there are new ones for 2016. High-tech 3-D simulator can cause motion sickness. Height min. 40 in. Echo Lake.

UPDATED! Star Wars: Jedi Training Academy. ✔ Kids volunteer to learn light saber techniques, duel villains. Echo Lake.

Toy Story Mania. ✔ FastPass+ Shoot at targets and rack up a high score in this ride-through series of 3-D video games starring "Toy Story" characters. Pixar Place.

The Twilight Zone Tower of Terror. ✔ FastPass+ Out of control elevator falls and ascends 13 stories in an unpredictable pattern. Sudden, swift drops and lifts. Height min. 40 in. Sunset Boulevard.

Four-star attractions ★★★★

ENHANCED! The Great Movie Ride. ✔ FastPass+ Indoor tram ride tours classic film scenes which robotic characters bring to life. Turner Classic Movies sponsorship has improved its queue, added Robert Osborne as its narrator, refreshened its film-clip finale. Hollywood Boulevard.

Indiana Jones Epic Stunt Spectacular. FastPass+ Physical stunt show based on 1981's "Raiders of the Lost Ark." Echo Lake.

Jim Henson's MuppetVision 3-D. ✔ FastPass+ Kermit stars in this dated but funny movie, which tours a 3-D lab. Streets of America.

Walt Disney One Man's Dream. ✔ Walt Disney and Disney Company memorabilia and artifacts in a museum-style setting; a short biographical film narrated by Walt himself. To the left of Animation Courtyard.

Three-star attractions ★★★

Fantasmic. FastPass+ Evening spectacle stars Mickey Mouse. Characters, lasers, dancing fountains, water screens, fireworks, loud noises, bright flashes, scary villains abound. Sunset Boulevard.

NEW! For the First Time in Forever. FastPass+ Former seasonal "Frozen" sing-along has all the hits, but characters Anna and Elsa are only on stage for a few minutes.

Voyage of the Little Mermaid. FastPass+ Musical stage show tells Ariel's story with puppets, a live singer, special effects and too much video. Animation Courtyard.

Two-star attractions ★★

'Honey, I Shrunk the Kids' Playground. Soft-floored outdoor play area has tunnels, oversized props; it's based on 1989's "Honey, I Shrunk the Kids" film. Streets of America.

Lights, Motors, Action Extreme Stunt Show. FastPass+ Outdoor automotive stunts create faux action-movie scenes. You sit on bleachers far from the action. Loud, often boring. Streets of America.

Decked out with old knickknacks, formica tables and vinyl chairs, seating areas at the 50's Prime Time Café recall vintage dinettes. Black-and-white televisions play old sitcom clips.

Restaurants and food

Table service. A quick summary: The best food at this park is at the Brown Derby (but it's pricey), the most relaxing spot is at Mama Melrose's, the most fun the 50's Prime Time Cafe. The best fast food: ABC Commissary. The author's top eats: the Brown Derby Cobb salad; the Prime Time fried chicken.

★★★★★ ✔ $$$ **50's Prime Time Cafe.** This retro experience is a hoot; servers hassle diners who don't keep their elbows off the table or eat their vegetables. Stage-set dinettes may remind baby boomers of grandma's house. Formica tables, sparkly vinyl chairs and black-and-white table TVs create a surreal atmosphere. The menu is comfort food—fried chicken, meatloaf, pot roast—and it's good. No reservations? Sit at the bar. *Echo Lake. Lunch, dinner. 11 a.m.–park close, $14-$24 (children $9). Seats 225, 14 at the bar.*

★★★ $$$ **Hollywood & Vine.** At dinner this crowded, noisy buffet serves a wide variety of meats, seafood and side dishes, some quite good. Unfortunately, it smells a little greasy, and the carpet is often spattered with the meals and muddle of those before you. For the price you can do a lot better. The experience at breakfast and lunch is very different—a character buffet that stars Disney Junior's Doc McStuffins, Handy Manny, Jake from "Jake and the Never Land Pirates" and Sofia from "Sofia the First." These popular characters not only greet their young fans, they also sing, dance and play with them, with a human host acting as emcee. Ironically, the experience is not very well known, so kids often get to spend an enormous amount of time with the characters. The uninspired breakfast buffet has a standout—Mickey Mouse-shaped waffles. *Echo Lake. Breakfast 8–11:20 a.m., $27 (children $15). Lunch 11:40 a.m.–2.25 p.m. $34 (children $18). Dinner 3:30 p.m.–30 minutes before park close, $34 (children $17). Seats 468.*

★★★★★ ✔ $$$$$ **Hollywood Brown Derby.** With some of the best food of any Disney restaurant, this fine-dining spot offers steaks, seafood and other American classics that are reworked to a modern, yet never trendy, standard. As a Disney Signature Restaurant, the Derby's food is consistently excellent, providing a great break from the theme-park grind. Especially good: the original Hollywood Derby Cobb salad in all its chopped authenticity, and the light, tart grapefruit cake. New for 2016 are a burger, noodle bowl and other less-expensive options at lunch. The elegant eatery faithfully re-creates the 1929 second location of the

Tinseltown landmark; to fully enjoy it take time to check out its details — its hat-shaped brass table-side lamps, its gorgeous four-table Bamboo Room in the back corner (ask nicely when you check in and the host or hostess may let you sit there), and especially all the celebrity caricatures on the walls. Those in black frames are re-creations of portraits of original Derby diners that once hung on the walls of the original restaurant. Those in gold frames are of singers and musicians of the era who had million-selling recordings. *Hollywood Boulevard. Lunch, dinner noon–park close, $16–$47 (children $6–$14). Seats 224, 40 in the outdoor lounge.*

★★★★ ✔ $$$$ **Mama Melrose's Ristorante Italiano.** Traditional Italian cuisine gets a California twist at this comfortable eatery, which is hidden in a back corner of the park. It's so relaxing you may need a nap afterward. Mama's is best for families and couples who need a break and want comfort food. The signature dish is chicken alla parmigiana; other choices include seasonal pastas, brick-oven flatbreads, even a steak. Portions are generous. Resembling a converted warehouse, the dining room has open ceilings strung with Christmas lights, brick walls covered with Californian and Italian pop-culture relics, and wood floors. Mismatched light fixtures add to the eclectic look. *Streets of America. Lunch, dinner. Noon-one hour before park closing. $15–$33 (children $9). Seats 250.*

★★★ $$$$ **Sci-Fi Dine-In Theater.** This starlit indoor dining room channels a 1950s drive-in theater, with a huge silver screen that shows trailers from kitschy sci-fi flicks such as "The Cat Woman from Mars" as well as odd newsreels, intermission bumpers and space-age cartoons. Sound comes from actual drive-in speakers mounted to booths; some servers roller skate. Diners sit two abreast in miniature versions of 1950s Chevy and Pontiac convertibles. Unfortunately, the tight row seating makes it tough for families to talk, and a pricey menu overhypes its food. If you go stick to the hamburgers and milkshakes, and make sure you ask for a car when you check in; otherwise you may get a plain-Jane patio table at the back at the room. *Streets of America. Lunch, dinner. 11 a.m.–park close. $14–$32 (children $9). Seats 252.*

Counter service. The park's fast-food doesn't match up well with its table-service choices. Your best bet is the ABC Commissary; avoid the Toy Story Pizza Planet Arcade.

★★★ ✔ $ **ABC Commissary.** Live palms, cushioned booths and chairs, unobtrusive lighting and soft carpet make this the park's most comfortable fast-food spot. The only downside: Ceiling-mounted televisions play ABC-TV promos on a short loop, over and over, ad infinitum. Food is mostly fine but forgettable—burgers, sandwiches, occasionally a good specialty. Outside seating provides nice people-watching, although in the summer even a covered umbrella is too hot. *Commissary Lane. Lunch, dinner. 11 a.m.–park close. $7–$12 (children $5–$6). Seats 562 indoors, 128 outdoors.*

★ $ **Backlot Express.** This faux prop warehouse offers lackluster burgers, hot dogs, grilled sandwiches and salads. None of the choices match up to the quality of the food at the ABC Commissary. Open ceilings and concrete floors add to the "warehouse" feel of the place, which almost always has at least a few empty tables. The condiment and self-serve fountain drink areas are sticky and not very well maintained. Real Hollywood clutter crowds the walls and corners—thousands of authentic movie and television props, gadgets and trivial-but-fascinating down-and-dirty junk (for example, call sheets from the "Cheers" television series and Bennie the Cab stunt car from 1988's "Who Framed Roger Rabbit." Outside seating is mostly under umbrellas; several tables offer good viewing of the adjacent Jedi Training Academy shows. *Echo Lake. Lunch, dinner. 11 a.m.–8 p.m. $7–$11 (children $5–$6). Seats 330 indoors, 270 outdoors, mostly covered.*

★★ $ **Min & Bill's Dockside Diner.** You'll swear this outdoor counter-service spot is a boat. There it is, apparently floating on Echo Lake. The menu transforms often, at press time it offered a frankfurter in a pretzel roll, an Italian sandwich using French bread, a turkey leg and two good gourmet macaroni and cheese options—one featuring buffalo chicken and crumbled blue cheese and the other featuring barbecued pulled pork and crispy onions. *Echo Lake. Lunch, dinner. 10 a.m.–park close. $8–$12. Seats 140.*

★★ $ **Starbucks Trolley Car Cafe.** Newly opened in 2014, this Starbucks has the same menu as every other one; there's nothing Disney about it. Breakfast sandwiches and pastries are good, but coffee is the star. *Hollywood Boulevard. Breakfast, lunch, dinner. Park hours. $4–$5. No seating.*

★★★ ✔ $$$ **Starring Rolls Cafe.** Laughably small, this combination bakery and sandwich

The outdoor snack bar Min & Bill's Dockside Diner appears to be a boat floating on palm-lined Echo Lake. It's an homage to the 1930 Academy Award-winning film "Min and Bill."

shop is packed during meal times, with a line spilling out the door. Seating is outdoors, mostly under umbrellas. The cafe is recessed down a few steps, so a small wall separates diners from passersby. Breakfast offers fresh pastries, bagels and muffins. Lunch is either a generous ham or turkey sandwich from the kitchens of the adjacent Brown Derby or fresh sushi from the Japan pavilion in Epcot. The excellent food can be trumped by the problem of having to eat outdoors; the Florida weather doesn't always cooperate. *At the corner of Hollywood and Sunset Boulevards. Breakfast, 9–11:30 a.m., $3–$6. Lunch, 11:30 a.m.–4 p.m., $6–$11 (children $5). Seats 60, mostly covered.*

★★ $$ **Studio Catering Co.** The menu gets made over about once a year at this covered concrete patio, the closest sit-down food spot to Toy Story Mania. Usually it's not that good; always the metal tables and chairs are uncomfortable—the chairs' seats angle back, forcing you to lean back. *Streets of America. Lunch, dinner. 11:30 a.m.–7 p.m. $7–$10 (children $5–$6). Seats 498 (328 covered).*

★★★ ✓ $ **Sunset Ranch Market.** Sitting alongside bustling Sunset Boulevard, this outdoor food court can be a pleasant spot to people-watch. Delighted screams from the nearby Twilight Zone Tower of Terror fill the air. Food ranges from nondescript burgers and turkey legs to tasty barbecue and hand-dipped ice cream. *Sunset Boulevard. Breakfast, lunch, dinner. Park open–park close. $8–$15 (children $5–$6). Seats 400.*

★★ $ **Toy Story Pizza Planet Arcade.** The pizza is ho-hum at this combination arcade and pizza parlor; side salads come drenched in Caesar dressing; kids choose from a mini chicken sub or a cheese pizza the size of a hockey puck. Open ceilings and tile floors add to the arcade din. Sit on the second floor for the quietest experience or if you want to charge your phone; there are plenty of outlets. The place looks nothing like the Pizza Planet from "Toy Story." *Streets of America. Lunch, dinner. 11 a.m.–90 minutes before park close. $8–$11 (children $6). Seats 472 indoors; 112 outdoors, mostly covered.*

Snacks. Re-creating the atmosphere of a small bookshop café, the **Writer's Stop** (★★★★ ✓) offers freshly baked goods, coffee and frozen drinks. Try the cream-cheese-filled carrot cake cookie for an indulgent treat. A tiny spot next to the Sci-Fi Dine-In, it has four small tables. In Echo Lake, **Peevy's Polar Pipeline** (★★★) serves up frozen soft drinks behind the Keystone Clothiers shop.

See also **Restaurant Policies** in the chapter **Walt Disney World A–Z.**

Despite its marquee, Legends of Hollywood has everything for the film fan only if that film is "Frozen." Its Streamline Moderne facade recalls a 1930s Los Angeles movie theater.

Shops and merchandise

An odd mix. The Studios seems to lack focus with its shopping—though most of the park is themed to Old Hollywood there's no shop that sells nostalgic merchandise. The better shops are listed below.

★★★ **Adrian & Edith's Head to Toe.** It will only take 10 or 15 minutes to personalize a Mickey ear hat at this small shop. Choose from dozens of styles; the basic embroidery uses black, gold or dark pink thread; a fancier version offers more choices. Towels can be personalized, too. Built as a candy shop, the store has the black and white tile common in confectioneries. Tailoring and sewing equipment line upper shelves. *Hollywood Blvd.*

★★★★ ✔ **Animation Gallery.** This store's walls and shelves are covered with original art and prints, along with figurines, Walt Disney World Collectibles (coins, medallions, gold-plated tickets), Precious Moments works, Disney by Britto artwork and posters. A Disney artist draws and paints before your eyes; when he's done you can buy the results. Light classical versions of Disney songs fill the air. *Animation Courtyard.*

★★★ ✔ **Gem Creations.** Every hand-crafted necklace and bracelet is unique at this tiny covered open-air stand; the artist—the owner, the woman behind the counter—is an independent entrepreneur, not a Disney employee. *Echo Lake.*

★★★ **In Character.** This open-air shop offers Disney princess costumes and accessories, but not for every princess. Belle costumes are at Once Upon a Time (see below). *Animation Courtyard.*

★★★ **It's a Wonderful Shop.** Oddly, this Christmas shop doesn't have a Christmas theme. Instead, it looks like a prop warehouse, with all sorts of gewgaws on the walls. Merchandise includes ornaments, stockings and nutcrackers. A snowman in front of the store makes a good spot for a Christmas-in-July photo. *Streets of America.*

★★★★ ✔ **Keystone Clothiers.** Men, women and juniors will find fashionable apparel and accessories in this upscale boutique. *Hollywood Blvd.*

★★★★ **Once Upon a Time.** This children's shop has stylish kids' apparel, Belle costumes and accessories, casual shoes, costume jewelry, plush and toys. An homage to Hollywood's legendary Carthay Circle theater, its interior has an ornate arched ceiling and maroon velvet drapes. The radio

Tatooine Traders. The exit to the Star Tours ride, this gift shop holds a plethora of Star Wars stuff. The desert planet of Tatooine is the home of Anakin and Luke Skywalker.

broadcast of the 1937 premiere of "Snow White and the Seven Dwarfs"—which was held at the actual Carthay Circle—fills the air. *Sunset Blvd.*

★ **Reel Vogue.** Formerly Villians in Vogue, this store now is simply a generic Disney souvenir shop. *Next to Sunset Ranch Market, Sunset Boulevard.*

★★★★★ ✔ **Rock Around the Shop.** Slash as a Mickey Mouse doll? Guitar-shaped purses? Guitar-pick earrings? This Rock 'n' Roller Coaster shop has 'em, as well as Aerosmith items and a surprising variety of fashionable shirts for juniors. Wood floors, open ceilings and exposed lighting recall a backstage area, as do display stands that look like instrument cases and trunks. *At the exit to Rock 'n' Roller Coaster Starring Aerosmith, Sunset Blvd.*

★★★★ ✔ **Stage 1 Company Store.** This faux prop storage room was originally a Muppet shop, and the back half still is— though Phineas and Ferb items have also crept in, as those characters meet fans right outside. The front is a children's shop, with infantwear, children's wear and costumes that will transform your little girl into Minnie Mouse or Tinker Bell. *Streets of America.*

NEW! **Star Wars Launch Bay.** This Star Wars movie-and-park-land preview center will offer a selection of Star Wars merchandise, perhaps somewhat different than that of Tatooine Traders. *Animation Courtyard. Opens late 2015.*

★★★ ✔ **Sweet Spells.** Bakers create candies, caramel apples and cookies in front of you at this small confectionery, which also sells packaged treats. *Sunset Blvd.*

★★★★★ ✔ **Tatooine Traders.** Drool you will over this store's "Star Wars" stuff—from its "Build Your Own Lightsaber" station to its Yoda backpacks to its Droid Factory to its Stormtrooper helmets. Star Tours souvenirs include toy Starspeeders and action figures. *At the exit to Star Tours, Echo Lake.*

★★★★★ ✔ **Tower Gifts.** The gift shop of the Hollywood Tower Hotel, AKA The Twilight Zone Tower of Terror—Tower Gifts has fancy carpet, plaster walls with arches and elaborate ironwork. Keeping with its theme, it offers items from the hotel: door hangers, room key chains, front-desk bells, bathrobes, towels, mugs and glassware, all with the Hollywood Tower Hotel logo. Off in a corner is merchandise related to the 1993 movie "The Nightmare Before Christmas" and the Magic Kingdom ride The Haunted Mansion. *At the exit to the Tower of Terror, Sunset Boulevard.*

See also **Shopping** in the chapter **Walt Disney World A–Z.**

We'll always have Paris. Audio-Animatronic figures depict Humphrey Bogart bidding goodbye to Ingrid Bergman in "Casablanca" during The Great Movie Ride.

The Great Movie Ride

TCM tie-in refreshes this elaborate tribute to classic films

ENHANCED! ★★★★ ✔ FastPass+ Gene Kelly "Singin' in the Rain," Humphrey Bogart reminding Ingrid Bergman that "we'll always have Paris," all those nearly naked showgirls twirling on that tiered Tower of Beauty in "Footlight Parade"—OK, so you may not recognize everything you pass, but even so, this indoor tram-trip is still worth your time. A robotic tribute to Tinseltown, it takes you through soundstage sets that depict nearly every type of movie, with actors represented by robotic figures who sing, swing, fly, cower, sneer and threaten. A new Turner Classic Movies sponsorship has refreshed the attraction's queue (it's much better), added TCM's Robert Osborne as the tram's pre-recorded narrator and updated its film-montage finale.

The ride's entrance facade is a reproduction of Grauman's Chinese Theatre, a famous Hollywood landmark. Like its inspiration, the Disney building's plaza is filled with real celebrity handprints, more than 100. Front and center is the work of Warren Beatty, nearby are those of Bob Hope, Jim Henson (who brought Kermit), Dustin Hoffman and Robin Williams (who brought their kids), George Burns, Tony Curtis and George Lucas.

Tips. *Where to sit:* Ask a boarding attendant for the second row of the first car of your tram, right behind its driver. When it's hijacked, the villain will be right there with you.

Key facts. *Best for:* Seniors, movie buffs. *Duration:* 22 min. *Capacity:* 560. *Queue:* Indoor. *Fear factor:* There are faux gunshots, sometimes fire. The "Alien" creature threatens you, as does the Wicked Witch, who looks real from a distance. *Debuted:* 1989. *Access:* ECV users can stay in their vehicle. *Disability services:* Assistive listening, handheld captioning. *Location:* Hollywood Boulevard.

Average wait times

9am	10am	11am	Noon	1pm	2pm	3pm	4pm	5pm	6pm	7pm	8pm	9pm
5m	15m	30m	25m	15m	15m	15m	15m	15m	5m	20m	20m	5m

© Disney

'Let it go.' Princess Anna (right) and sister Queen Elsa lead the audience in singing the signature tune from the popular 2013 movie "Frozen" during For the First Time in Forever.

For the First Time in Forever

A half-hour show stars Anna and Elsa—for five minutes

NEW! ★★★ **Fastpass+** You only get about 5 minutes with the characters you came to see in this video-heavy "Frozen Sing-Along Celebration." It stars not Princess Anna and Queen Elsa, but instead two newly-appointed Arendelle historians, who retell the "Frozen" story. The princess, queen and Kristoff make brief appearances, but for the most part it's the narrators on stage, cracking lame jokes and making you wish they weren't there.

Their narration is punctuated by musical clips from the film. The audience is encouraged to sing along, but no one needs persuading; the crowd—mostly children—raises the roof as it sings its heads off. Lyrics appear on the screen karaoke-style, but only a few people seem to need them.

The clips are shown on enormous screens in high-definition, and their sound quality is crisp and clear. You'll be reminded why you liked the movie in the first place.

Instead of using excerpts from all the film's songs, the show features only its most popular tunes in their entirety. They're all here, including "Do You Want to Build a Snowman?" "For the First Time in Forever" and Olaf's hilarious "In Summer." Finally, Queen Elsa belts out "Let It Go" joined by her sister, and when they do they're accompanied by swirling Disney snow—only soap bubbles, of course, but it's a breathtaking moment.

The show plays in the Hyperion Theater, formerly the Superstar Television Theater, home to the American Idol Experience.

Tips. *When to go:* See the first show of the day or get a Fastpass. *Where to sit:* As close to front center as you can get. Fastpass holders get preferred seating near the stage. *For families:* This cool, dark theater is a great place to breastfeed, and the half-hour show gives you the time.

Fun finds. ❶ Anna throws a snowball at Kristoff near the end of the show.

Key facts. *Best for:* Children, "Frozen" fans. *Duration:* 30 min. *Capacity:* 1,040. *Queue:* Outdoor, covered. *Showtimes:* Scheduled performances; 9 or 10 shows daily. *Debuted:* 2014. *Access:* Guests may remain in wheelchairs, ECVs. *Disability services:* Assistive listening. *Location:* Echo Lake.

Indiana Jones battles a bad guy in the Indiana Jones Epic Stunt Spectacular, a display of physical stunts that retells the story of the 1981 movie "Raiders of the Lost Ark."

Indiana Jones Epic Stunt Spectacular

Witty, fast-paced special-effects show is visibly dated

★★★★ FastPass+ Basically unchanged since its debut in 1989, this outdoor stage show is still entertaining and often funny, especially if you've never seen it before. Fireballs, gunshots, spears, swords, a great big boulder and a muscle-bound Nazi threaten Indiana Jones and his girlfriend Marion, as Disney actors re-create physical stunts from the 1981 movie "Raiders of the Lost Ark." Between scenes you'll learn how backdrops can be quickly set up and dismantled, how heavy-looking props can be feather-light, and how stunt actors fake a punch. For flavor, Disney pretends the show is a real film shoot. Mock cameramen peer through mock cameras; a fake director barks out fake directions.

Tips. *Which show to see:* Either the first one or the last, when crowds are typically light and it's easy to get a good seat. The best show is at dusk, when fiery explosions pop against the sky. Avoid afternoon shows in the summer, when the poorly ventilated seating area can feel like a sweatbox. *Where to sit:* Front row center. The left side of the theater is set aside for Fastpass holders, who enter the theater early. *How to be in the show:* A few minutes before the show begins, a "casting director" chooses a handful of adults to be "extras" in the show. If you're seated close to the front, and jump up, wave and scream with wild abandon, you'll likely get picked.

Fun finds. ❶ To the left of the entrance, a British archeologist has dug a hole and lowered himself down into it. Pull on his rope and he'll get irritated ("I say! Stop mucking about up there!"). ❷ The sidecar motorcycle is a duplicate of the one Harrison Ford commandeered in the 1989 movie "Indiana Jones and the Last Crusade." It even has the same front-fender license number: WH38475.

Key facts. *Best for:* Adults. *Duration:* 30 min. *Capacity:* 2,000. *Queue:* Outdoor, covered. *Fear factor:* Fire, simulated gunfire, explosions may upset toddlers. *Showtimes:* Scheduled performances, typically starting at 11:30 a.m. *Weather issues:* Canceled during rain. *Debuted:* 1989. *Access:* Guests may stay in wheelchairs, ECVs. *Disability services:* Assistive listening, handheld captioning, Audio Description. *Location:* Echo Lake.

© Disney

A podrace through the desert canyons of Tatooine is one of many possible journeys on Star Tours, a 3-D motion simulator that varies its flight with every ride.

Star Tours

High-tech simulator offers thrilling, randomized adventures

UPDATED! ★★★★★ ✔ FastPass+ Taking off on a tourist trip where everything goes wrong, you'll be immersed in the Star Wars universe by this 3-D motion simulator. Even the waiting line is fun. You'll want to go on it multiple times, as its scenes and destinations change with each flight. You might head to Tatooine, Coruscant, Naboo, or even a Death Star, may be stopped by Darth Vader or receive a hologrammed message from Princess Leia ("Help me, Star Tours, you're my only hope!"). New scenes will be added in 2016.

Tips. *When to go:* Early, then again after lunch. *Where to sit:* In the middle of a center row, for the best 3-D experience and to avoid nausea. Avoid the front row; the visuals may be skewed. *For families:* Pose your kids on a Speeder bike across from the ride entrance. *How to understand the ride:* Watch the queue and boarding videos; they set up the plot.

Fun finds and Hidden Mickeys. ❶ The queue rooms are filled with references to the Star Wars films. ❷ Outside the attraction, Mickey's three-circle shape appears as moss high on a tree trunk just below the Ewok village platform. ❸ In the queue an R-2 droid adjusts satellite dishes on its head, which for a moment look like Mickey ears.

Key facts. *Best for:* Children, teens, adults. *Duration:* 7 min. *Capacity:* 240 (6 40-seat simulators). *Queue:* Indoor. *Fear factor:* Skittish children may be startled by some effects. *Restraint:* Seat belt. *Debuted:* 1989 (Disneyland 1987), redone 2011. *Health advisories:* Riders should be free from motion sickness; pregnancy; high blood pressure; heart, back or neck problems. *Access:* Height min. 40 in. Wheelchair, ECV users must transfer. *Disability services:* Assistive listening, handheld captioning. *Location:* Echo Lake.

Average wait times

9am	10am	11am	Noon	1pm	2pm	3pm	4pm	5pm	6pm	7pm	8pm	9pm
10m	10m	20m	20m	10m	10m	10m	10m	10m	10m	10m	10m	10m

No cheap 3-D tricks. Though Kermit says his show will not stoop to any, Fozzie Bear soon guides a remote-control cream pie over its audience. The pie ends up, of course, on Fozzie.

Jim Henson's MuppetVision 3-D

Silly film is a classic, despite two weak characters

★★★★ ✔ FastPass+ Chaos reigns as Kermit the Frog attempts to demonstrate the latest invention of Dr. Bunsen Honeydew in this 3-D movie, which showcases the inspired humor and attention to detail of the late Jim Henson. Miss Piggy stars in two musical numbers, both of which go haywire. In the process, guests get squirted with water, showered with bubbles and caught in a crossfire of cannonballs.

Though it includes two of Henson's least appealing characters—Bean Bunny and Waldo C. Graphic—the attraction has a timeless charm. Digitally restored in 2010, the film and its pre-show video are bright and clear. The pre-show takes place in a prop warehouse filled with real Muppet memorabilia.

Tips. *When to go:* In the middle of the day, when the lines are long at other attractions, and the cool theater will feel especially refreshing. *Where to sit:* In the center of a middle or back row. The film will be in great focus, and the 3-D effects will really pop. Avoid the first few rows. The film will seem blurry as the red and green images separate when viewed too closely, and some effects won't make sense without an audience in front of you. *For families:* Don't be afraid that your young children could be startled by the 3-D effects. Unlike some 3-D films, this one uses the technology to make you smile, not jump.

Key facts. *Best for:* Anyone ages 5 and up. *Duration:* 25 min. including pre-show. *Capacity:* 584. *Queue:* Indoor, air-conditioned; also rarely used shaded outdoor area. *Fear factor:* The film has no startling or frightening images. *Debuted:* 1991, restored 2010. *Access:* Guests may remain in wheelchairs, ECVs. *Disability services:* Assistive listening, reflective and activated video captioning, Audio Description. *Location:* Streets of America.

Average wait times

9am	10am	11am	Noon	1pm	2pm	3pm	4pm	5pm	6pm	7pm	8pm	9pm
5m	5m	5m	5m	5m	5m	5m	5m	5m	5m	5m	5m	5m

Little girls race around a huge can of Play-Doh in the "Honey, I Shrunk the Kids" playground. A cushy ground makes falls relatively painless. Other props include a sneezing dog.

'Honey, I Shrunk the Kids' Playground

Small dated playspace has 'shrunken' decor that kids love

★★ Too cramped, too small, and too sweaty on hot days, this outdoor play space is nevertheless fun for young children, as it lets them pretend they're the size of bugs, wandering in a suburban backyard. Towering blades of grass shade climb-through ant tunnels and super-sized plants, insects and toys. Unfortunately, it's all packed into just a sliver of space, and is never updated. The playground is based on Disney's 1989 movie "Honey, I Shrunk the Kids," but children don't have to know the film's plot to enjoy it.

On most days the area stays pretty cool. Electric fans create a breeze, water areas spray and mist guests and, unlike the asphalt and concrete walkways everywhere else in the park, the playground's cushy floor doesn't retain heat. Water fountains are scattered throughout.

Tips. *When to go:* Late in the afternoon, ideally about an hour before sunset. Your children will be ready to burn off some energy. Use your morning for attractions that will be impossibly crowded later. *Other tips:* Photograph your kids with some of the props:

a giant spiderweb, atop fiddlehead ferns, posing with a huge ant. Because of its many nooks and crannies, the playground makes it tough to keep track of your children. There's only one exit, however, and it's always monitored by a Disney cast member.

Fun finds. The playground has three hidden interactive features. ❶ As you enter, look to your left for a leaky garden hose, which occasionally squirts water on unsuspecting heads. In-ground squirters are nearby. ❷ Walk up to the top of the back wall to find the nose of a huge dog. It sniffs you, then sneezes. ❸ Look behind the entranceway, to the right of the dried bubble gum, to discover the Sound Steps, three-inch-high cut grass stalks that make noise when you step on them.

Key facts. *Best for:* Young children. *Duration:* Allow 30 min. *Capacity:* 240, including parents. *Operating hours:* Park open–dusk. *Weather issues:* Closed during rain. *Debuted:* 1990. *Access:* Guests may remain in wheelchairs, ECVs. *Location:* Just off New York Street, Streets of America.

Great balls of fire. A car jumps toward the audience during the finale of Lights, Motors, Action. Other highlights include choreographed chase scenes using cars and motorcycles.

Lights, Motors, Action

Loud automotive stunt show isn't worth your time

★★ FastPass+ Cars and motorcycles fly through the air—for a few seconds—in this loud outdoor stage show, as stunt drivers demonstrate how Hollywood chase scenes are created. Little boys will like it, as will fans of the 2002 movie "The Bourne Identity," from which the show is obviously inspired. But unfortunately you sit far from the action, and there are boring delays between each stunt. "Cars" star Lightning McQueen (a real car) appears during a silly bit with his friend Mater, who pops up on a video screen.

Tips. *When to go:* See the first show of the day, especially during the summer. Later shows often get rained out. Arrive about 30 minutes before showtime to get a decent seat. *Where to sit:* If you have a choice, take a center seat about 10 rows up. *For families:* Skip this one. It'll take over an hour of your time, and there's a good chance your kids will be fussy and bored during the bulk of the show. If you do go, talk to your children about the gunplay in this show. It's casual, deadly and not played for laughs, and in today's world that deserves a conversation.

Fun facts. ❶ Each car has a 2-stroke, 150-hp engine with four forward and four reverse gears, which lets it reach the same speed in either direction. ❷ Each car weighs 1,300 pounds, less than half that of a similar production vehicle. ❸ The "live" video was filmed before the show opened in 2005.

Fun finds and Hidden Mickeys. ❶ On the background facade a coffee shop is named the Cafe Fracas, the "restaurant of the noisy rumpus." ❷ Mickey's classic three-circle shape is formed by a gear and two circular belts inside a window of a motorcycle shop. ❸ A full-figure Mickey appears in the window of the Antiquites Brocante ("Secondhand Antiques") shop.

Key facts. *Best for:* Young boys. *Duration:* 33 min. *Capacity:* 5,000. *Queue:* Outdoor, shaded. *Showtimes:* Scheduled performances; two to three daily. *Weather issues:* Cancelled during rain. *Debuted:* 2005, Disneyland Paris 2002. *Access:* Guests may remain in wheelchairs, ECVs. *Disability services:* Assistive listening. *Location:* Streets of America.

Riders don 3-D glasses as they travel through Toy Story Mania, a series of virtual shooting arcades. The game take place in the Toy Story world, under Andy's bed.

Toy Story Mania

Quick 3-D midway games are easy to play, tough to master

★★★★★ ✔ FastPass+ This ride will be getting a third track in 2016, which is good, because though this series of virtual midway games is certainly fun it's not worth waiting hours to experience. You don 3-D glasses and then sit side-by-side with a partner in a moving vehicle, stopping in front of each game for about 45 seconds to pitch baseballs at flying plates, shoot darts at dinosaur balloons, even hurl eggs at scurrying animals. The games are easy to play and rewarding whether you score high or low; when you hit an object, the illusion is often enhanced by a real blast of air or spritz of water. The games are hosted by an assortment of "Toy Story" characters, including Woody and Buzz Lightyear.

The standby queue winds past a huge robotic Mr. Potato Head, who interacts with people in line thanks to a wealth of phrases pre-recorded by the voice of the character, comedian Don Rickles. He occasionally sings a song, or takes off his hat or ear.

Tips. *When to go:* Immediately after the park opens; anytime with a Fastpass. *For families:* A small child can ride on your lap as long as his or her legs fit under the lap bar.

Hidden Mickey. ❶ In the boarding area on a wall mural, as frames on the box this "toy"— a Toy Story Midway Games Playset—came in.

Key facts. *Best for:* Children, teens, adults. *Duration:* 7 min. (game play 5 min.). *Capacity:* 108 (2 per vehicle). *Queue:* Indoor, overflows into uncovered outdoor area. *Restraint:* Lap bar. *Debuted:* 2008, revised 2010. *Health advisory:* Vehicles move in a jerky, funhouse fashion. *Access:* Offline loading area for disabled guests, into vehicles equipped with guns that have buttons as well as pull strings. ECV users must transfer. *Disability services:* Closed captioning. *Location:* Pixar Place.

Average wait times

9am	10am	11am	Noon	1pm	2pm	3pm	4pm	5pm	6pm	7pm	8pm	9pm
30m	75m	80m	80m	60m	55m	65m	65m	65m	50m	50m	65m	45m

You've got a friend in... your partner!

BY MICAELA NEAL There are three keys to getting a high score on Toy Story Mania: Shoot constantly (your cannon can fire six objects per second), know where the high-value targets are, and... teamwork! To get a top score, work together with the person sitting next to you. That way, the two of you can hit multiple targets simultaneously, which will reveal hidden levels of the game.

GAME BOOTH	HIGH-VALUE INITIAL TARGETS	HOW TO REVEAL BONUS TARGETS
HAMM AND EGGS	❶ A 500-pt horse is in the barn doorway. ❷ Green ducks in the lake are 500 pts. ❸ A 500-pt squirrel runs up both sides of the screen. ❹ Three gophers repeatedly pop up along the bottom. The brown ones are 500 pts; the grays 1000. ❺ Animals in the tree are 1000 pts each. A 1000-pt goat peers out of the barn window. A 1000-pt mouse skitters along its roof.	❶ Hit the mouse (see Tip 5 at left) and the barn will rotate to reveal its interior, which is filled with 2000-pt rats. Hit every rat and 1000-point rats appear in the grass. ❷ Hit the fox on the henhouse (in the bottom left corner) and three hens will scurry out of it. The first is worth 1000 pts; the second 2000 pts; the third 1000 pts. ❸ Hit the 500-pt donkey that walks along the hills and the animal will turn and run the other way as a 2000-pt target.
REX AND TRIXIE'S DINO DARTS	❶ 500-pt targets are in the lava, on eggs at the bottom left, held by two red dinos at the bottom center and tied to a blue stegosaurus and red raptors in back. ❷ A blue dino on the right chews 1000-pt targets, others tie to a back pink bronto. ❸ Pterodactyls hang from the sky with 500- and 1000-pt targets.	**Team up with your partner** to hit the lava flows until the volcano erupts. Then hit the two meteors on the left and right of the volcano three times each (the last two meteors, worth 500 pts each, must be hit within one second of each other). This will cause three large comets (spheres formed by 1000-pt balloons) to crash into the screen.
GREEN ARMY MEN SHOOT CAMP	❶ Helicopters hover with plates worth 1000 pts. More 1000-pt plates appear within the mass of plates and are carried by trucks along the bottom. ❷ Airplanes tow plates worth 2000 pts. Others are tossed up on either side of the mountain.	**Team up with your partner** to simultaneously hit the two 2000-pt plates that are tossed up from the sides of the mountain (see note at left) at the same time. Doing so will open the mountain and reveal a tank that shoots plates toward you worth 5000 pts each.
BUZZ LIGHTYEAR'S FLYING TOSSERS	❶ Meteors near the sides are 500 pts. ❷ Rockets are 1000 pts. ❸ Jetpack aliens are worth 2000 pts. ❹ Aliens at the top corners of the screen are 5000 pts.	**Team up with your partner** to simultaneously hoop all of the aliens in the central rocket to launch it and reveal a huge robot. When its mouth opens, toss rings into it to score, if you reveal it early enough, up to 2000 pts per toss.
WOODY'S ROOTIN' TOOTIN' SHOOTIN' GALLERY	All initial targets are worth 100 pts each.	❶ Each 100-pt target triggers a series of bonus targets worth up to 1000 pts each. ❷ As your vehicle moves from screen 1 to 2 (or from screen 2 to Woody's Bonus Roundup), hit two 100-pt or 500-pt targets close together to reveal a 2000-pt target.
WOODY'S BONUS ROUNDUP	The second-to-last mine cart on each track is always worth 2000 points.	❶ Hit 1000-pt targets above the carts by 2 bats to wake them and reveal 5000-pt targets. ❷ Hit all of the carts on a track and the last one will be worth 5000 pts. ❸ The final target is worth 2000 pts if you hit it often enough.

Spoonmen. A colorful stage musical, Beauty and the Beast Live on Stage retells Disney's take of the fairy tale. Above, spoons-turned-chefs welcome Belle to dinner in "Be Our Guest."

Beauty and the Beast Live on Stage

Nearly as old as time, musical stage show still enchants

★★★★★ ✔ FastPass+ As good as ever after more than two decades of performances, this lavish stage show re-creates the spirit of Disney's 1991 movie by focusing on its musical numbers. Choreographed productions of "Belle," "Gaston," "Be Our Guest," "Something There," "The Mob Song" and the title song are thoroughly entertaining, as they form a condensed account of the tale as old as time. Leads Belle and villain Gaston speak and sing live, other characters rely on audio from the film. Like the movie, the show manages to be both funny and touching. Colorful costumes and creative lighting lend a true theatrical feel.

The supporting cast is a delight. Portraying villagers and castle attendants, unheralded performers faint, fight, jump, kick, swoon, twirl and waltz, often with skill usually seen only in Broadway performances.

Tips. *When to go:* See the first show of the day; it's generally the least crowded. During the summer avoid shows after noon; the theater is covered but otherwise open to heat, humidity and blowing rain. *Where to sit:*

As close to front-row center as you can. This means getting a Fastpass, as this area is set aside for Fastpass holders until right before the show starts. You'll see every expression on the performers' faces, details such as the sequins on the ball gowns, and be able to fully enjoy the show's many symmetrical dance numbers. *While you wait:* There's no pre-show, but unlike most Disney theaters, this one allows you to bring in food, and return and come back to your seat as often as you wish before showtime. If you get there early enough, and if someone in your group can hold your seat, consider leaving to take a restroom break, or even to bring back food. Decent barbecue and hand-scooped ice cream is sold at the Sunset Ranch Market, which is right out in front. *For families:* Talk with your children afterward about the strong message of the story, which is that what matters about a person is what they are like inside, not how they look. *For birthday girls:* If you have a little girl celebrating a birthday, she may be able to get a velvety faux rose presented to her by Belle and the

A most peculiar mademoiselle. At right, village girls dismiss Belle. Below, Gaston explains how "it's not right for a woman to read"; villagers prepare to storm the castle with the rally cry "Kill the beast!"

prince at the end of the show. Talk with a cast member at the show entrance ahead of time, preferably in the morning, to set this up.

Fun fact. ❶ "The Mob Song" includes a quote from Shakespeare. As he rallies villagers to kill the Beast, Gaston commands "Screw your courage to the sticking place," the phrase Lady MacBeth uses to urge her husband to kill Duncan.

Fun finds. Thirty television stars have left impressions at the theater, in a small plaza with a fountain just behind the rear bleachers. ❶ "Star Trek's" Scotty, James Doohon, added "Beam Me Up." ❷ "Jeopardy" host Alex Trebek wrote "Who is Alex Trebek?" Also here, the prints of: ❸ Morey Amsterdam from "The Dick Van Dyke Show," ❹ Imogene Coca from "Your Show of Shows," ❺ Bob Denver from "Gilligan's Island," ❻ June Lockhart from "Lassie," ❼ George Wendt from "Cheers," ❽ even journeyman actor Martin Mull. Most prints are from the early 1990s, made during ceremonies during the park's "Star of the Day" events. ❾ During the show, keep an eye on Gaston, especially during the "Belle" and "Gaston" songs. He struts

onstage, makes the village girls swoon and admires himself in any reflection he can find. After the finale, when the whole cast comes onstage to bow, he stays perfectly in character, often flexing his biceps as he winks and flashes the "call me" sign at female members of the crowd. ❿ The show begins with a pun: a ringing bell. ⓫ The Theater of the Stars stage arch resembles the one at the famous Hollywood Bowl in Los Angeles. ⓬ The arch lights up during some of the songs.

Key facts. *Best for:* Anyone ages 5 and up. *Duration:* 25 min. *Capacity:* 1,500. *Queue:* Outdoor, unshaded. *Fear factor:* Little ones may be disturbed during the ominous "Mob Song" and just afterward as Gaston stabs the Beast (the violence is not graphic). *Showtimes:* 5 or 6 scheduled shows daily. *Weather issues:* If it's raining bring your umbrella or poncho if you plan to get there early. The waiting area is simply a sidewalk. When it's hot beat the heat by using a Fastpass. *Debuted:* 1991, latest revision 2001. *Access:* Guests may remain in wheelchairs, ECVs. *Disability services:* Assistive listening, Audio Description. *Location:* Sunset Boulevard.

A vintage Cadillac, mounted upside-down on a headstock of an electric guitar—tops off the entrance gate to G-Force Records and Rock 'n' Roller Coaster Starring Aerosmith.

Rock 'n' Roller Coaster Starring Aerosmith

Rocketing launch highlights thrilling dark coaster

★★★★★ ✓ FastPass+ You go upside down twice on this dark, indoor roller coaster. The beginning is the scariest part: a powered launch that hurls you forward to a speed of 57 mph in just 2.8 seconds, then zooms through a half-mile of twists and turns, two loops and a tight corkscrew. A true rush, the ride recreates a frantic Los Angeles freeway trip: As Aerosmith rock music pounds from speakers surrounding your seat in what looks like a Cadillac convertible limousine, you pass through two famous L.A. landmarks, the iconic "Hollywood" sign and the huge doughnut that in real life promotes Randy's Donuts near the Los Angeles airport.

"Make it a super stretch." The grins begin as you enter the building, the headquarters of mythical "G-Force Records." Step through the lobby and you're off on a time-warp to the 1970s. Along the walls are displays of real vintage recording and playback gear. Soon you come to Studio C, where you find the rock band Aerosmith (via video) mixing the rhythm tracks to their new number, "Walk This Way." Suddenly the guys have to leave; they're late for a show. But no worries: since the band members "can't forget our fans," they offer you—and everyone in line—backstage passes to their show. As the manager phones for a car she counts the crowd, then tells the limo company "We're going to need a stretch. In fact, make it a super stretch."

You're then ushered into a grimy back alley, where up pulls your ride. Moments later Aerosmith's Steven Tyler is screaming out a countdown, then a rubber-burning start

Average wait times

9am	10am	11am	Noon	1pm	2pm	3pm	4pm	5pm	6pm	7pm	8pm	9pm
5m	20m	70m	70m	40m	40m	40m	30m	30m	30m	50m	40m	40m

squeals you off into the darkness. Eventually you arrive at the backstage entrance of an L.A. arena, where a red carpet leads to (a video of) the band performing on stage.

Tips. *When to go:* During the first hour; you'll be able to ride it again before the hour's up. Later, use the Single-Rider line or get a Fastpass, though if you do you'll bypass the lobby. *Where to sit:* For the most intense launch, ask for the front row. It will only add a couple of minutes to your wait, and it's worth it for its great view and most surprising ride—front-row passengers never know what scenery is coming up, as it lights up just as they reach it. Riders with long legs should ask for an odd-numbered row; those seats have far more legroom. Riders who use the Single-Rider line are not allowed to choose their seat. *For families:* Your child shouldn't be afraid to ride; the coaster starts fast but is always very smooth. Though children may have no idea who Aerosmith is, that won't diminish their fun. The thrills stand on their own. *Other tips:* In the pre-show room, stand to the left to be first in line when the door opens.

All-American Rock 'n' Roll. Known for its driving riffs and suggestive lyrics, Aerosmith formed in Boston in 1970. Its raunchy swagger, highlighted by Steven Tyler's prancing stage antics, drew comparisons to the Rolling Stones; Tyler and Stones singer Mick Jagger even looked similar. Early hits included 1975's "Walk This Way," which like the Stones' earlier "Satisfaction" used a groove so strong the words didn't matter. Aerosmith also created rock music's first power ballad, adding strings to 1973's piano-based "Dream On." Plagued by drug abuse in the late 1970s, the band got back on track in 1986, when Tyler and lead guitarist Joe Perry appeared on rap group Run D.M.C.'s cover of "Walk This Way." The video became an MTV staple. Later hits include "Love in an Elevator" and "Livin' on the Edge."

Fun facts. ❶ Unlike a regular coaster, the ride doesn't start off with a lift hill. Its launch is powered by a magnetic linear induction system imbedded in the track. Vehicles accelerate by being quickly pushed and pulled from one hidden magnet to another. An earlier, more primitive linear induction system powers Magic Kingdom's PeopleMover ride. ❷ When Disney agreed to the deal to feature Aerosmith on the ride, initially the company couldn't reach frontmen Steven Tyler and Joe Perry. Unbeknownst to Disney execs, the two were vacationing with their families at the time… at Walt Disney World.

Fun finds and Hidden Mickeys. ❶ The columns in the lobby mimic guitar necks, complete with frets and strings. ❷ The first display case holds a 1958 Gibson Les Paul Standard guitar ❸ as well as a disc cutter, a device that "cut records" by etching sounds from a mixing console onto a master disc. ❹ Record players in the second case range from a 1904 external-horn Edison Fireside to ❺ a 1970s Disc-O-Kid. ❻ Put your ear to doors marked "Studio A" or "Studio B" to hear Aerosmith rehearsing. ❼ Concert posters in the next room include one for a 1973 show from Aerosmith's first national tour, as the opening act for the New York Dolls. It's midway down on the right. ❽ An MC5 poster includes a still-visible marijuana leaf that Disney has covered with a small American flag. ❾ As you stand in the alley, signs to the rear of the G-Force building indicate that repair work has been done by Sam Andreas and Sons Structural Restoration, the garage is run by Lock 'n' Roll Parking Systems and that its dumpster is owned by the Rock 'n' Rollaway Disposal Co. ❿ A glass case displays rates for Wash This Way Auto Detail. ⓫ Limo license plates sport messages such as 2FAST4U and H8TRFFC. ⓬ The disc jockey heard on the car radio is longtime Los Angeles rock jock Uncle Joe Benson. ⓭ As you leave the ride, an Aerosmith concert video loop shows in front of you occasionally shows Tyler screaming "Rock 'n' Roller Coaster!!!" ⓮ Mickey appears twice on the building's sign. Tyler's shirt has Mickey silhouettes and ⓯ the boy wears mouse ears. ⓰ The three-circle shape also appears as tile pieces in a beige section of the foyer's floor mosaic, ⓱ as a distorted carpet pattern in the first display room, ⓲ as cables on the recording-studio floor, ⓳ on the registration stickers of the limos' rear license plates and ⓴ as the "O" in the phrase "Box #15" on an exitway trunk.

Key facts. *Best for:* Children, teenagers, adults. *Duration:* 1 min. 22 sec. *Capacity:* 120; 5 24-seat vehicles seated 2 across. *Queue:* Indoor, air-conditioned; overflows into shaded outdoor area. *Single-rider line:* Often available. *Fear factor:* Very fast start, darkness, speed. *Restraint:* Shoulder harness. *Top speed:* 57 mph. *Track:* Standard steel, 3,403 feet, max. height 80 feet. *Debuted:* 1999. *Health advisories:* Guests should be free from motion sickness; pregnancy; high blood pressure; heart, back or neck problems. *Access:* Height min. 48 in. Wheelchair and ECV users must transfer. *Location:* Sunset Boulevard.

Beware. Guests enter The Tower of Terror through the grounds of the Hollywood Tower Hotel. Supposedly abandoned since 1939, the hotel has a "Keep Out" sign on its gate.

The Twilight Zone Tower of Terror

Disney's best thrill ride randomizes drops, psychs you out

★★★★★ ✔ FastPass+ You plummet—and soar—up to 130 feet aboard a pitch-black freight elevator in this fully realized thrill ride. The falls, the lifts, the special effects... they're all unpredictable, as a computer randomly freestyles each ride individually. Loaded with special effects and superb detailing, the dark, creepy experience appeals to nearly everyone except those with an intense fear of falling.

From the moment you walk through its entranceway, Disney has designed the attraction to freak you out. It's set in what appears to be an abandoned hotel, its lobby covered in cobwebs. You stop in a spooky library, then head to an unwelcoming basement where a rusty service elevator creaks as its doors shut... only to open a moment later as the elevator stops at a floor with ghosts, then close again as it heads up to a

nonexistent 13th floor where things really start to get creepy. And then, just when you realize you're about to fall, there's just the right amount of perfectly timed... silence.

A 'somewhat unique' story. Meant to recall the eerie style of "The Twilight Zone," the experience is even more fun if you know its story. According to Disney lore, the extravagant 12-story Hollywood Tower Hotel opened in 1917 as a gathering place for Tinseltown elite. Two decades later, on Oct. 31, 1939, the hotel hosted a Halloween party in its rooftop lounge. But at precisely 8:05 p.m. a huge lightning bolt hit the building, dematerializing two elevator shafts and the wings they supported. Among the victims were five people riding in an elevator — a child actress with her nanny, a young Hollywood couple and a bellhop.

The hotel stood deserted for decades, and now has mysteriously reopened, just in

Average wait times

9am	10am	11am	Noon	1pm	2pm	3pm	4pm	5pm	6pm	7pm	8pm	9pm
10m	20m	30m	30m	30m	30m	20m	20m	20m	10m	30m	10m	20m

time for your visit. As you arrive to check in, a bellhop asks you to wait in the library, where immediately the power goes out but a black-and-white TV comes on, showing the start of the 1960s television show, "The Twilight Zone." As host Rod Serling describes a "somewhat unique" story about a maintenance service elevator, he adds, "we invite you, if you dare, to step aboard. Because in tonight's episode, you are the star."

Boarding the hotel's service elevator, you enter that episode yourself, traveling past strange images as you journey to a mysterious 13th floor. Once there, your cab unexpectedly moves forward, its doors slam shut and soon you're tossed — violently — up, down — down, up — up, up, down.

Every ride is different. Occasionally other doors open, revealing the open sky and the theme park down below. Those five victims from 1939 may appear again, or rain may fall, or an odd smell may waft around you. Finally the madness stops, and you calmly arrive in the basement. "The next time you check into a deserted hotel," Serling you, "make sure you know just what kind of vacancy you're filling. Or you may find yourself a permanent resident of… 'The Twilight Zone.'"

Tips. *When to go:* To avoid a long wait, ride the Tower of Terror before 10 a.m. or use a Fastpass to go later in the day. *Where to sit:* For the most unobstructed view of the effects, ask to sit in the center of the elevator's front row. As you line up at the boarding area, tell the attendant you'd like the last spot in Row 2. If you plan to ride but are uneasy about the drops, ask to sit at the end of one of the rows of seats. In the boarding area, that corresponds to the first spot in any of the six rows. Your seat will be against a side wall and have a handle to hold onto. *Children's issues:* This is one scary ride. Although its ascents and drops are smooth, Disney's mind games are intense, especially for younger riders who have never been in such a believable artificial environment. When the dim elevator shaft turns black and silent just before it pitches up or down, even some adults find the tension hard to bear.

Fun facts. ❶ While planning the ride Disney considered a variety of themes. One idea featured actor Mel Brooks as a madman hotel owner who chased guests into an elevator. Another had actors filming a horror movie, with a walk-through segment narrated by Vincent Price. ❷ When Serling speaks on the television, you're actually

watching him introduce a 1961 "Twilight Zone" episode, "It's a Good Life." He originally said "This, as you may recognize, is a map of the United States," though on the video the camera cuts away as he pronounces the word "map" and you hear him say "maintenance service elevator." ❸ Since Serling died in 1975, and there was never a "Twilight Zone" episode about a Hollywood Tower Hotel, his lines are voiced by impersonator Mark Silverman. ❹ The elevators have four loading areas but only two exits. The initial four shafts merge into two paths on the top floor. ❺ The cast members' break room is between the drop shafts. When you scream, they hear you. "It's very difficult to relax," one tells us. ❻ The ride's engines are at the top and bottom of the shafts. Each develops 110,000 foot-pounds of torque, uses regeneration for deceleration control and is 35 feet long, 7 feet wide, 12 feet tall and weighs 132,000 pounds. ❼ The Tower is 199 feet high, just a foot short of requiring aircraft warning lights. ❽ In 1993 as it was being built, the Tower was struck by lightning.

Fun finds and Hidden Mickeys. ❶ To the right of the lobby's reception desk, an American Automobile Association plaque honors the hotel's "13-diamond" status. A real award, it was presented by the AAA when the ride opened in 1994. ❷ Abandoned items at the desk include a fedora, topcoat, folded newspaper, open registration book, alligator-skin luggage and mail-slot mail and messages. ❸ A bag, cane and white fedora lean against the concierge desk. ❹ A poster at the concierge desk promotes a show by Anthony Freemont, the name of a 6-year-old boy in a 1961 "Twilight Zone" episode ("It's a Good Life") who uses telepathic powers to terrorize his neighbors. ❺ On a table to the left rest a diamond ring, white glove and two glasses. Next to it is a champagne bucket. A mah-jongg game is in progress on another table. Tea has just been served to the players; a cart holds cups ready for pouring, roses and a newspaper. ❻ Another teacup rests on the end table in front of a fireplace; a goblet and small plate sit on a table to the right. ❼ In the library, the footage of Serling has been altered to remove a cigarette from his right hand. ❽ The little girl sings the nursery rhyme "It's Raining, It's Pouring" on the video, and later on the fourth floor. ❾ The bookcases hold such items as the devil-headed "Ask Me a Yes or No Question" fortune-telling machine seen in the 1960 Twilight Zone episode "Nick of Time" (a

Screams of delight. Riders sit in a falling hotel service elevator on The Twlight Zone Tower of Terror. Then they're jerked up again, and fall a second time, a third, maybe even a fourth. Each ride has an unpredictable pattern.

story of a man unable to make decisions from himself) and ⑩ the tiny silver robot featured in the 1961 episode "The Invaders" (a tale of a farm woman who kills what appear to be small invading aliens). ⑪ In the boiler room, though the service elevators' tracking dials only go to "12," their arrows go to an unmarked "13." ⑫ As your elevator doors close in front of you, a hint at your destination—a "1" on the left door and a "3" on the right—disguises itself as a "B," the elevator's letter. ⑬ A small inspection certificate on the interior wall of the elevator is signed by "Cadwallader," a jovial character in the 1959 episode "Escape Clause" who secretly is the devil. ⑭ Dated Oct. 31, 1939 (the day of the infamous lightning strike), the certificate has the number 10259, a reference to the date "The Twilight Zone" series premiered: Oct. 2, 1959. ⑮ When your elevator stops to unload, you sit next to a basement storage area that includes a "Special Jackpot $10,000" slot machine from the 1960 episode "The Fever" (a story of a talking slot machine that drives a tightwad crazy) ⑯ and two ventriloquist dummies used in 1962's "The Dummy" (a dummy switches places with his human owner) as well as 1964's "Caesar and Me" (a

ventriloquist uses his cigar-smoking dummy to commit crimes). ⑰ In the basement, the clock in the basement office is stuck on the time 8:05, the moment of the lightning strike. ⑱ Up in the far top left corner of the office is a small silver spaceship, the home to the library's "Invaders" robot. ⑲ The bulletin-board notes to the right of the basement office seek finders of items such as "Pocket watch, sentimental value, broken crystal" a reference to the 1963 episode "A Kind of Stopwatch" (in which a bank robber stops time forever when he breaks an unusual timepiece). ⑳ The hotel gift shop's outdoor display windows are still decorated for the Halloween of 1939, the night of the mythical lightning strike. ㉑ As for Hidden Mickeys, you'll find the first one in the lobby, as a pair of folded wire-rim glasses on the concierge desk (the temples form Mickey's face, the eye rims make his ears). ㉒ The sheet music to the 1932 ditty "What! No Mickey Mouse?" is in the left library, on a bookcase directly in front of the entrance door. ㉓ The little girl in the TV video is holding a 1930s Mickey Mouse doll. ㉔ In the boiler room, Mickey's three-circle shape appears as large, round ash doors beneath a fire box on a brick furnace (on your right just after you've entered the room), and ㉕ as water stains just to the left of a fuse box on the boiler room's left wall, just past the spot where the queue divides. ㉖ Mickey also hides up on the 13th floor, in the center of the star field as it comes together to form a pinpoint.

The Science of Spooky. Hidden behind all the theming is a unique mix of innovative engineering, classic special effects and modern math. Combining three distinct ride systems, the mechanics of the attraction represent a novel achievement of applied science. Its "elevator" goes up, moves forward, then plummets down and soars up a second shaft, all in one seamless experience.

An elevator. The first system is obvious: an elevator. When you leave the boiler room, you're in a standard, 50-foot elevator shaft, with sliding doors and two stops.

A pallet driver. The second system kicks in at the top of the shaft. As your car (an independent vehicle, which rode up the shaft in a cage) moves forward, it's using the technology of a self-guided pallet driver, an automated machine used by companies such as Amazon.com and Anheuser-Busch to move inventory through large warehouses. Controlled by an unseen computer, it rolls on wheels and gets its power from an on-board battery.

A second cage. The third system is Disney's own. Once your cabin enters the drop shaft, it's silently locked into a second cage that is tightly suspended on looped steel cables. Pulled by high-speed winches and motors, the cage "falls" faster than the pull of gravity (you reach 37 mph in just 1.5 seconds, about a quarter of a second faster than if you were falling freely) and shoots up with similar speed. The result: though you never actually fall and are never truly free of the ride's grasp, you feel completely out of control.

Basic effects. Though often stunningly realistic, most of the elevator effects are created by simple, time-tested methods.

At your first stop, a long corridor filled with translucent people, disappearing windows and sudden star fields is really a shallow area filled with transparent screens, which show images from hidden projectors. Though it looks far away and 8 feet tall, the end of the hall is actually just a few feet in front of you, and only 4 feet high.

Once your elevator moves forward, mirrors on the floor and ceiling make it seem those planes have disappeared. The characters to your side are simply independently moving plastic cutouts, split down the middle to make them look warped. In front of you, the changing star field comes from synchronized fiber-optic lights built into the doors to the final drop zone.

Random drops. Each ride is different, as a computer system chooses the particulars of your fall using a random-number generator based on modulo functions—calculations that search for two numbers that, when divided by a third number, have the same remainder. The attraction has a reprogrammable ride system. "We can reinvent the experience as often as we want," says Imagineer Theron Skees. "We can add effects, change timing sequences and alter the way the elevator moves."

Transcendental TV. "There is a fifth dimension beyond that which is known to man... a middle ground between light and shadow, between science and superstition... it is an area which we call The Twilight Zone." Also with a four-note theme song ("do-do-do-do, do-do-do-do..."), those classic words welcomed viewers to "The Twilight Zone," an imaginative CBS television anthology that aired from 1959 to 1964. Placing ordinary people into extraordinary situations, the episodes often had mind-bending twists, with confused characters in unfamiliar, sometimes supernatural surroundings. Host Rod Serling created the show after getting fed up with censorship hassles at his job as a writer of the dramatic series "Playhouse 90." Though "The Twilight Zone" was twice popular as today's "Big Bang Theory" (each episode was watched by about one in 10 Americans), Serling had to fight hard to keep it on the air. In the pre-cable world of the 1960s, an audience that size was considered pitiful. Though the show made him a giant in the TV industry, Serling stood only 5-foot-5 and weighed just 137 pounds. A chronic smoker, he died from complications of heart surgery in 1975, at age 50.

Key facts. *Best for:* Teenagers, adults. *Duration:* 4 min. *Capacity:* 84 (4 21-seat elevators). *Queue:* Indoor, air-conditioned; overflows into shaded outdoor queue. *Fear factor:* Nerve-wracking. *Restraint:* Seat belt. *Debuted:* 1994, last revision 2002. *Health advisories:* Guests should be free from motion sickness; pregnancy; high blood pressure; heart, back or neck problems. *Access:* Height min. 40 in. Wheelchair and ECV users must transfer. *Disability services:* Handheld captioning. *Location:* Sunset Boulevard.

"I want more!" She's got gadgets and gizmos aplenty, whosits and whatsits galore—but that's not enough for teenage Ariel in the stage show "Voyage of The Little Mermaid."

Voyage of the Little Mermaid

Grainy video mars stage show with lively singer, puppets

★★★ **FastPass+** Sweet but not sappy, this indoor stage show tells an abridged version of Disney's 1989 movie "The Little Mermaid" with live performers, puppets and video clips. A misty high-tech theater creates the sensation of being underwater, as you watch a rollicking blacklight rendition of "Under the Sea," a Broadway-quality Ariel longing to be "Part of Your World" and Ursula the Sea Witch singing "Poor Unfortunate Souls." At the end the mermaid grows her gams and hugs her honey. The only downer: an abundance of large-screen video that is distinctly low-res.

Tips. *When to go:* Before noon or after dark. First thing in the morning the theater is only half full. *Where to sit:* In the center, two-thirds back. You'll see many cool effects on the theater's ceiling and walls. *For families:* Don't sit in the front three rows; small children can't see onto the elevated stage.

Fun fact. ❶ One of the show's original Ariels was Leanza Cornett, who went on to become the 1992 Miss Florida, the 1993 Miss America and a host of many television shows.

Fun find. ❶ A wooden replica of P.T. Barnum's 1842 "FeeJee Mermaid" hides in the lobby above the theater's right entrance door as one of Ariel's treasures. Half dead monkey, half dried fish tail, Barnum's version convinced many that mermaids were real.

Key facts. *Best for:* Children. *Duration:* 17 min. *Capacity:* 600. *Queue:* Outdoor, shaded; indoor lobby. *Fear factor:* Some little ones cry when they see Ursula, a 12-foot-tall robotic octopus with glowing eyes. *Showtimes:* Continuous shows; first one typically before 10 a.m. *Debuted:* 1992. *Access:* Guests may stay in wheelchairs, ECVs. *Disability services:* Assistive listening, reflective captioning. *Location:* Animation Courtyard.

Average wait times

9am	10am	11am	Noon	1pm	2pm	3pm	4pm	5pm	6pm	7pm	8pm	9pm
0m	20m	25m	25m	30m	25m	20m	25m	25m	15m	20m	15m	10m

© Disney

A live host chats with Jake the Never Land Pirate during Disney Junior Live on Stage. The puppet show features stars from other Disney Junior shows too, including "Sofia the First."

Disney Junior Live on Stage

Quality preschooler puppet show delights families

★★★★★ **FastPass+** In this lively puppet show, Mickey Mouse and other stars of Disney Junior television shows teach children how to solve everyday problems, doing it in a way that has them bouncing, dancing and singing along. Updated in 2013, the current version features characters from the programs "Mickey Mouse Clubhouse," "Doc McStuffins," "Jake and the Never Land Pirates" and "Sofia the First." The plot? When Mickey and his friends want to throw Minnie a surprise birthday party, they decide to take in some stories from the other shows to get ideas, all of which involve teamwork.

Production values are the equal of any Disney show. The puppets are articulated, the sound is crisp, and hundreds of tiny overhead spotlights ensure everything is lit. Human host Casey addresses her young audience as equals, and bounces into it to meet some children face-to-face. Kids sit on a flat, carpeted floor, which makes it easy for them to be part of things. The semicircular stage curves into the seating area, so even if you arrive at the last minute you'll still be close to the action.

Tips. *When to go:* See the first show of the day. The crowd will be small, and both the performers and the young crowd will be fresh. If you have a Fastpass you enter the theater first and get your choice of places to sit. *Where to sit:* In the middle of the theater, where young ones are close to the stage but can still see onto it. Avoid the first three rows; since the stage is elevated, little ones who sit that close often can't see the characters. A couple of benches in the back of the theater can hold leftover grandparents. *Need a bathroom?* Doors at the far right of the theater lead to the restrooms of the Hollywood Brown Derby.

Fun find. ❶ The stage has a hidden sliding walkway that allows the host to magically walk on the same floor as the puppets.

Key facts. *Best for:* Young children. *Duration:* 22 min. *Capacity:* 600. *Queue:* Outdoor, shaded. *Operating hours:* 8–12 shows daily. *Debuted:* 2001, last revision 2013. *Access:* Guests may remain in wheelchairs, ECVs. *Disability services:* Assistive listening; handheld and reflective captioning. *Location:* Animation Courtyard.

Baby boat. Just a few inches tall, a model boat awaits guests in this 1954 hand-built concept for Disney's Jungle Cruise ride. The piece is often displayed at Walt Disney: One Man's Dream.

Walt Disney: One Man's Dream

See this nice gallery while you can; its days may be numbered

★★★★ ✔ A salute to the life and dreams of Walt Disney, this multimedia gallery combines memorabilia exhibits with a short film. The attraction has 400 artifacts in its collection, though many are rotated on and off display. One of the most interesting is the robotic Abraham Lincoln figure that starred in the 1964-65 New York World's Fair. Here shown without clothing (or skin!) Honest Abe has a control board next to him with buttons that read "elbow" and "finger."

Other pieces include the desk Disney used as a Missouri second-grader (with his initials "WD" carved into it) and his studio desk from the 1930s. His hand in theme-park history is well represented. Built by Disney himself in 1949, a hand-wired wooden diorama displays early ideas for multiple-room attractions such as Snow White's Scary Adventures. Nearby, a "Dancing Man" electronic marionette tested figure-movement techniques that led to the development of Audio-Animatronic robots. Display cases hold tabletop models used to create the first Jungle Cruise and Peter Pan's Flight rides. Another display portrays the creation of It's a Small World. A simulated TV studio shows Disney filming a video he used to interest investors in his ultimate, unfulfilled dream: the Experimental Prototype Community of Tomorrow, or EPCOT.

A 200-seat theater shows a moving biographical film. Narrated by Disney himself through audio clips, the inspirational 16-minute movie is surprisingly straightforward.

Tips. *When to go:* During the hottest part of the day, when this calm, cool spot is especially refreshing. It's also a great spot to get out of the rain. *For young adults:* Watch the movie. Disney offers some good advice about the important of failing when you're young.

Key facts. *Best for:* Adults. *Duration:* Allow 35 min. total, the movie is 16 min. *Capacity:* 200. *Operating hours:* Park hours; the movie plays continuously. *Debuted:* 2001, revised 2010. *Access:* Guests may remain in wheelchairs, ECVs. *Disability services:* Assistive listening, reflective and handheld captioning, Audio Description. *Location:* Behind the Great Movie Ride, just to the left of the Animation Courtyard.

Mickey Mouse wields a magical sword in the evening spectacle Fantasmic. Using a variety of scenes and many Disney characters, the multimedia show tells a story of good versus evil.

Fantasmic

Kitschy spectacle offers eye-popping way to cap your day

★★★ FastPass+ Held in an open-air amphitheater, this lavish evening spectacle includes boats, cannons, characters, fireworks, fountains, laser beams, music, smoke, water screens and before you can say "great balls of fire!" one of those, too. It tells a story of good versus evil, as Mickey Mouse dreams of animals and princesses but also of scheming villains. Most of it takes place on a 60-foot-tall mountain that's ringed by a narrow lagoon.

Though confusing, the show is a visual delight. It begins as Mickey, dressed as the Sorcerer's Apprentice from the 1940 movie "Fantasia," conducts water fountains like instruments in an orchestra. As his powers increase, he imagines flowers and animals that perform a version of "I Just Can't Wait to be King" from the 1994 film "The Lion King."

Mickey's dream becomes a nightmare as a video version of Monstro the whale (1940's "Pinocchio") lunges at the audience and the amphitheater turns dark. Live-action villains include Gov. Ratcliffe (1995's "Pocahontas"), the Evil Queen (1937's "Snow White and the Seven Dwarfs"), Jafar (1992's "Aladdin") and Maleficent (1959's "Sleeping Beauty") who transforms into a fire-breathing dragon.

All ends well, of course. A boat parade includes Ariel (1989's "The Little Mermaid"), Belle (1991's "Beauty and the Beast") and Snow White. The finale is a now-you-see-him, now-you-don't, now-you-do Mickey farewell.

A snack bar sells hot dogs and other snacks. Souvenir hawkers roam the stands.

Tips. *When to go:* If there are two shows see the second one; it will be much less crowded. Arrive an hour early for the first show, 30 minutes early for the second. *Where to sit:* As close to front row center as possible. If you get a FastPass you'll sit just left of center. Front rows can get misted with water.

Key facts. *Best for:* Disney enthusiasts. *Duration:* 25 min. Capacity: 9,900 (6,900 seats). *Queue:* Outdoor, uncovered. *Fear factor:* Loud noises, bright flashes, fiery water. *Weather issues:* Cancelled during rain. *Debuted:* 1998 (Disneyland 1992). *Access:* Guests may stay in wheelchairs, ECVs. *Disability services:* Assistive listening, reflective captioning. *Location:* Sunset Boulevard.

Disney's Animal Kingdom

THE COMPLETE WALT DISNEY WORLD 2016 **199**

A fully realized theme park

Nature lovers will adore this sophisticated theme park. Themed to animals and their environments, its attractions include a roller coaster through the Himalayas, stage shows based on two of Disney's best animal-themed movies, and a truck ride into a wildlife savanna. The park is also a zoo, with 250 species of exotic animals displayed in lush natural habitats. Many are either endangered or the biggest, smallest or most colorful of their kind. Accredited by the Association of Zoos and Aquariums, Animal Kingdom conducts animal research and breeds endangered species. As a zoo, it's the most popular one in the United States.

Best of the park. The only Disney World park that's less than 25 years old, Animal Kingdom has no wide expanses of concrete, no cheesy fast-food spots, no aging restrooms or embarrassingly dated attractions. On a nice day, just wandering around it can be fun. Particular highlights include: A giraffe—or a rhino, or an ostrich—may come right up to your truck on the open-air truck ride

Kilimanjaro Safaris, as you meander through 110 acres of simulated African habitat brimming with free-roaming animals; new twilight trips debut in 2016.... Just a few feet away from you, two groups of **gorillas** examine you with eyes and expressions that are oh-so-human on the Pangani Forest Exploration Trail. One group's a family, with a massive silverback, motherly females and wrestling youngsters; the other a bachelor troupe... The self-guided nature of the park's animal attractions gives it a **slower pace** and invites you to relax... It has two **great live shows:** Festival of the Lion King invigorates you with acrobats, a fire dancer, creative costumes and great music; Finding Nemo: The Musical re-imagines its film using huge puppets and live singers... With a backward plunge followed by an 80-foot drop, **the Expedition Everest roller coaster** takes you on a unique high-speed adventure.

Worst of the park. Some traditional theme-park fans hate this park, and their most common complaints are worth noting. First, there's **the walking.** It's a half-mile

The Discovery River (left) meanders through the park. Above: the new open plaza in front of the Tree of Life. Previous spread: a fire-baton twirler at the Festival of the Lion King.

from the front of the park to the back of it, and a half-mile from the left side to the right. Attractions are often far apart, with large gaps of open space between them. Altogether the park covers 500 acres, five times that of Magic Kingdom... You spend a lot of time outside in **the heat,** which can be challenging between April and October, when the Central Florida weather is especially hot and humid... Though this will change when the Pandora section of the park opens, right now it has **a lack of rides.** There are only six. By comparison, Epcot has 9, Magic Kingdom 23... Excluding fast-food spots there's a real **lack of restaurants.** There are only three, and they consist of a character buffet and two non-Disney eateries, one of which is outside the park entrance.

Getting oriented. Animal Kingdom is divided into six themed areas:

The Oasis. These shady walkways connect the park's entrance to its central hub, bordered by creatures in natural habitats.

Discovery Island. The hub of the park is a lush tropical circle that's wrapped by a river. It's home to most of the park's restaurants and shops, each of which is decorated in a creative and colorful Caribbean theme.

The Tree of Life. Pathways on the island wind through the roots and up to the trunk of this unusual park centerpiece. With a tapestry of more than 400 animals sculpted into its gnarled roots, trunk and thick branches, the fantastical African baobab is meant to symbolize the grandeur of nature and embody the idea that all life is interconnected. A main branch resembles the upturned trunk of an elephant; it's to the left of a bald eagle. The new front viewing area is framed by animals emerging from roots, including an armadillo, crocodile and Komodo dragon. The back of the tree, seen from a path along the Discovery River as well as the walkway between Africa and Asia, includes a rearing horse and a herd of wildebeests running up the trunk. The tree stands 145 feet high; its concrete trunk 50 feet wide at its middle, 170 feet wide at its base. A dozen large fiberglass branches and about 8,000 smaller ones hold 103,000 plastic leaves.

Africa. The heart of the park, this area is home to the East African port town of Harambe. Weathered from decades of rain and sand storms, the old gold and ivory trading post struggles to establish a new economy based on ecotourism.

Asia. Also wrestling with economic issues is this mythical kingdom of Anandapur and its mountainside village of Serka Zong.

DinoLand U.S.A. This tongue-in-cheek land's stuffy Dino Institute pokes fun at the

Not behind bars. Animals often stand, sit or perch only a few feet from guests. Above a scarlet macaw in the Oasis. At right, a Patterson's eland on a Kilimanjaro Safaris savanna.

dryness of 1970s scientists, while its adjacent DinoRama takes on tacky roadside tourist traps and traveling carnivals.

Rafiki's Planet Watch. A train takes you from Africa to this conservation-oriented land, which includes the park's working veterinary facility, animal- and nature-focused exhibits and a petting zoo.

Where to meet characters. More than a dozen Disney characters appear at the park. It's the only place to meet Rafiki, Russell and Dug, or Tarzan.

Baloo. Upcountry Landing, off the walkway between Asia and Africa.

Chip 'n Dale. Conservation Station courtyard, Rafiki's Planet Watch.

Daisy Duck. Across from the Creature Comforts Starbucks, Discovery Island; Donald's Safari meals, Tusker House, Africa.

Donald Duck. On the Cretaceous Trail (with Duckasaurus Donald, his own creation), DinoLand U.S.A. Also at Donald's Safari meals, Tusker House, Africa.

Goofy. Across from the TriceraTop Spin ride at DinoLand U.S.A., he poses with Pluto in front of a giant postcard. Also at Donald's Safari character meals, Tusker House, Africa.

King Louie. Upcountry Landing, off the walkway between Asia and Africa.

Mickey Mouse. Adventurers Outpost, Discovery Island. Dressed in safari gear, Mickey poses with Minnie Mouse in front of a giant park map. Actual photos of Mickey and Minnie in Africa, Nepal, Tibet and the Himalayas in these outfits decorate the queue. Mickey's also at Donald's Safari character meals, Tusker House, Africa.

Minnie Mouse. Adventurers Outpost, Discovery Island

Pluto. DinoLand U.S.A. Service Station.

Pocahontas. Character Landing, between Discovery Island and DinoLand U.S.A.

Rafiki. At Conservation Station, Rafiki's Planet Watch.

Russell and Dug. At Dug & Russell's Wilderness Explorers Club House, a sheltered area near the entrance to It's Tough to Be a Bug, Discovery Island. While you're there bark into a "Bark-O-Lator" and then learn what you just said in dog language.

Tarzan. On a Discovery Island trail (often by Galapagos tortoise).

See also the chapter **Characters.**

Street performers. Frankly, these acts are all terrific. World-music musicians never fail to impress, neither does a performance artist.

★★★★★ ✔ **Burudika.** This wonderful Afropop band performs engaging rhythmic

The Adventurers Outpost is home to Mickey and Minnie Mouse, who greet guests and pose for photos in front of a huge map—which has a Hidden Mickey on its lower left corner.

music that's subtly complex. 30-min. shows. In front of Tusker House, Africa.

★★★★★ ✔ **Chakranadi.** This sitar-tabla duo performs haunting instrumentals, evocative music you rarely hear live. 30-min. shows. Near the Yak & Yeti Restaurant, Asia.

★★★★★ ✔ **DiVine.** Covered in realistic leaves, fruit, flowers and vines, this sinuous stilt-walker blends into the foliage. Many visitors walk right past her. 20-min. shows. On the walkway between Africa and Asia.

★★★★ ✔ **DJ Anaan.** A disc jockey spins catchy Asian pop tunes while two young women in colorful saris dance and encourage onlookers to join them. Channels the dance-fest finale of the movie "Slumdog Millionaire." 20-min. shows. Near Yak & Yeti, Asia.

★★★★ ✔ **Gi-Tar Dan.** This funnyman guitarist sings catchy animal songs to and with children, often weaving their names into the lyrics. 20-min. shows. Outside Conservation Station, Rafiki's Planet Watch.

★★★★★ ✔ **Tam Tam Drummers of Harambe.** Every show's a delight as this rousing native percussion quintet gives guests of all ages lessons in hip-shaking West African dances. About a dozen volunteers follow its leader's whistled cues, some quite skillfully. 15-min. shows, though some go longer. On a small stage in front of Tusker House, Africa.

If it rains. With its large size and many outdoor attractions, Disney's Animal Kingdom makes it tough to ignore the weather. No ride or show closes due to rain alone, but the Flights of Wonder bird show can be changed and shortened. Roller coasters Expedition Everest and Primeval Whirl temporarily close when lightning is in the area, as does The Boneyard playground, Kali River Rapids, TriceraTop Spin and the walking trails in Africa and Asia. Ironically, Kilimanjaro Safaris trips are actually better in the rain, as its savanna animals are usually more active.

Family matters. All of the thrill rides at Animal Kingdom have height minimums—40 inches for Dinosaur, 44 inches for Expedition Everest, 38 inches for Kali River Rapids and 48 inches for Primeval Whirl. The park offers one character meal, available for breakfast, lunch and dinner: Donald's Safari Dining at Africa's Tusker House, which stars Donald Duck, Daisy Duck, Mickey Mouse and Goofy. An excellent Wilderness Explorers program offers hands-on activities that are especially fun for children, who can earn badges at 31 stations spread throughout the park.

Fun finds and Hidden Mickeys. Disney really paid attention to detail in this park,

Come on up. Street performers often enlist audience volunteers. The Tam Tam Drummers of Harambe teach guests hip-shaking African dances, usually without saying a word.

creating immersive environments that are filled with extra touches you'd never expect. Besides the ones on attractions, examples include: *Africa:* ❶ The sounds of residents of a boarding house often can be heard behind the back door of the Tusker House restaurant. ❷ Sometimes there's knocking on a door: a landlady trying to collect back rent. *Asia:* ❸ Along the Maharajah Jungle Trek walking trail, an actual fertility urn sits in the aviary's entrance building. It's the tomb of Anantah, the first ruler of Disney's mythical kingdom of Anandapur. Anantah's ashes are said to be in the urn, which is carved in the shape of an abstract couple engaging in, um, fertility activity. ❹ Throughout the Asia section of the park, each Anandapur business displays a tax license featuring the fictional kingdom's king and queen. The bigger the license, the more taxes that business pays. *DinoLand U.S.A:* ❺ To the right of Chester & Hester's Dinosaur Treasures, two baby dinosaurs hide underneath the Cementosaurus folk-art sculpture. One is hatching. ❻ Four hanging signs above the Dinosaur Treasures entrance read, from one direction, "When in Florida... Be sure to... Visit... Epcot." ❼ Ambient music includes bone-themed country songs (played on radio station "W-BONE") such as "I Like Bananas Because They Have No Bones," a 1935 ditty by the Hoosier Hot Shots. Archeological and dinosaur references abound in the Restaurantosaurus fast-food eatery. Among the best: ❽ The shapes formed by greasy hand prints on the walls of the Quonset hut; the cans of Sinclair Litholine Multi-Purpose Grease and Dynoil ("keep your old dinosaur running") on the shelves of that room; ❾ the song titles in the Hip Joint rec room juke box (such as "Dust in the Wind"); ❿ posters in that room for bands Dinosaur Jr. and T Rex; and ⓫ the ambient music, which includes the 1988 Was Not Was hit "Walk the Dinosaur." *Hidden Mickeys:* The iconic three-circle head-and-ears silhouette of Mickey Mouse can be found throughout the park: ⓬ In Africa's Harambe Village, as a large shape of gray pavement behind the Fruit Market. ⓭ As a drain cover (marked with a "D") and two ear-shaped pebble groupings, to the left of the main entrance to Mombasa Marketplace, across from Tusker House. ⓮ As another drain cover (this one with the letter "S") and two pebble groupings in front of Tamu Tamu Refreshments, facing Discovery Island. ⓯ In Dinoland U.S.A. as cracks in the parking lot, to the right of Dinosaur Treasures. ⓰ On a Steamboat Willie cast member pin on the right of the

A sitar player performs evocative music as part of the instrumental duo Chakranadi in the Asia section of the park, near the Yak & Yeti restaurant.

fourth back hump of the Cementasaurus folk sculpture. ⑰ On Discovery Island in the Pizzafari restaurant, as an orange firefly in the nocturnal room, to the left of a large tiger, behind a frog.

Know before you go. Need cash? A stroller? Help with your Fastpasses? Here's where to find it:

ATMs. The park has two: There's one right at the entrance on the right, another outside the Dinosaur Treasures gift shop.

Baby Care Center. Situated behind the Starbucks on Discovery Island, this indoor spot has changing rooms, nursing areas, a microwave and a playroom. It sells diapers, formula, pacifiers and over-the-counter meds.

Disney transportation. Buses serve all Disney resorts and theme parks and Blizzard Beach; but there's no direct service to Disney Springs, Typhoon Lagoon or ESPN.

FastPass+ kiosks. Trained cast members help you book and reschedule Fastpasses at these walk-up touchscreens. Look for them on Discovery Island at the Island Mercantile and Disney Outfitters shops, in Africa at the entrance to the Kilimanjaro Safaris ride and in Asia at the entrance to Kali River Rapids.

First aid. A clinic is beside and behind the new Starbucks on Discovery Island, next to the Baby Care Center. Nurses treat minor issues, and call EMTs for emergencies.

Guest Relations. Located left of the park entrance, this office has walk-up windows outside the gate, a walk-in lobby inside. Cast members answer questions, make dining reservations, exchange currency, hand out maps and times guides for all Disney World parks, and store items found in the park that day.

Locker rentals. They're inside the park next to Guest Relations ($7 a day, $5 deposit).

MyMagic+ Service Center. Just inside the park entrance (to the right of the Guest Relations office), cast members answer questions about MyMagic+ services.

Package pickup. Anything you buy in the park can be sent to the park entrance for you to pick up later at no charge. Allow three hours. Packages can also be delivered to Disney hotels or shipped nationally.

Parking. $17 a day per car. Free for Disney hotel guests and annual passholders.

Stroller rentals. Just inside the park entrance on the right, Garden Gate Gifts rents single strollers for $15 a day ($13 length of stay), doubles for $31 ($27 length of stay). Get replacements at Mombasa Marketplace.

Wheelchair and scooter rentals. Garden Gate Gifts rents wheelchairs for $12 a day ($10 length of stay). EVCs are $50 ($20 deposit).

On the way. Debuting in 2016, a Rivers of Light nighttime spectacle (above) promises live music, floating lanterns and water screens. The following year brings forth Pandora, the park's fifth land (below), with mythical landscapes and experiences based on the film series "Avatar."

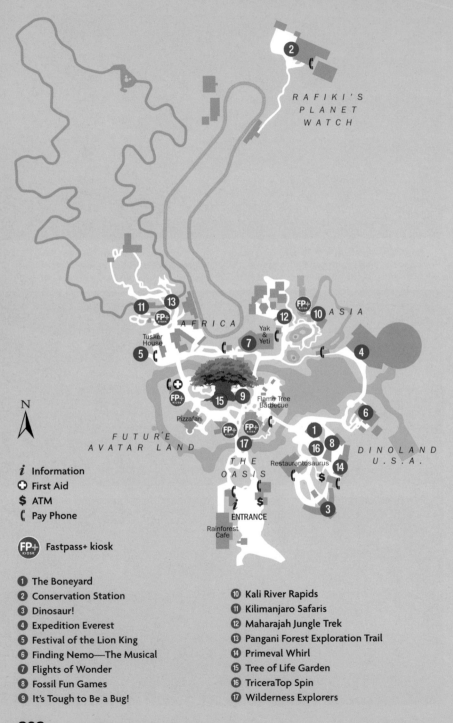

RAFIKI'S
PLANET
WATCH

AFRICA

ASIA

Yak
&
Yeti

Tusker
House

Flame Tree
Barbecue

Pizzafari

FUTURE
AVATAR LAND

DINOLAND
U.S.A.

Restaurantosaurus

THE
OASIS

N

i Information

✚ First Aid

$ ATM

(Pay Phone

FP+ Fastpass+ kiosk
KIOSK

ENTRANCE

Rainforest
Cafe

❶ The Boneyard
❷ Conservation Station
❸ Dinosaur!
❹ Expedition Everest
❺ Festival of the Lion King
❻ Finding Nemo—The Musical
❼ Flights of Wonder
❽ Fossil Fun Games
❾ It's Tough to Be a Bug!

❿ Kali River Rapids
⓫ Kilimanjaro Safaris
⓬ Maharajah Jungle Trek
⓭ Pangani Forest Exploration Trail
⓮ Primeval Whirl
⓯ Tree of Life Garden
⓰ TriceraTop Spin
⓱ Wilderness Explorers

Attractions at a Glance

Five-star attractions ★★★★★

The Boneyard. Dig-site playground has climbing zone, slides, sand pit and tunnels. Kids can trigger dinosaur roars and other special effects. DinoLand U.S.A.

Expedition Everest. ✔ FastPass+ This indoor-outdoor roller coaster is a runaway train which speeds into and out of a mountain, goes backward and zooms past an angry yeti. Smooth ride, high lift, one curving steep drop. Height minimum 44 inches. Asia.

Festival of the Lion King. ✔ FastPass+ Rousing in-the-round musical revue (shown at right) includes acrobats, fire-baton twirler, flying ballerina, many stilt walkers and talented live singers. Africa.

Finding Nemo—The Musical. ✔ FastPass+ Broadway-quality stage musical retells 2003's "Finding Nemo" with huge puppets and live singers. Dory is a hoot. DinoLand U.S.A.

Kilimanjaro Safaris. ✔ FastPass+ Bouncy open-air truck wanders 100-acre African forest and savanna; passes elephants, giraffes, lions, rhinos and many other rare species, all of which appear to be roaming freely. Africa.

Maharajah Jungle Trek. ✔ Pathway around and through a crumbling palace passes bats, tigers and other Asian animals, meanders through an aviary full of rare and exotic birds. Asia.

Pangani Forest Exploration Trail. ✔ Shady walkway roams past unusual African species. Includes a beautiful aviary and large gorilla habitat. Other animals include okapi, meerkats, monkeys. Africa.

TriceraTop Spin. Dumbo with four-seat dinosaurs, cheesy roadside carnival theme. DinoLand U.S.A.

Four-star attractions ★★★★

Dinosaur. ✔ FastPass+ You search for dinos in an open vehicle on this dark jerky ride, and barely miss a meteor shower. An intense, loud experience. Threatening dinosaurs chase you. Height minimum 40 inches. DinoLand U.S.A.

Flights of Wonder. ✔ Bird show presents a conservation message in a humorous, lightweight way. Includes about 20 species; some fly over the audience. Asia.

Kali River Rapids. FastPass+ Jerky, wet raft ride travels down a threatened rainforest river; riders often get soaked. Height minimum 38 inches. Asia.

Wilderness Explorers. ✔ Earn badges in this series of nature-themed activities, based on Russell's scouting experiences in the 2009 movie "Up." Earnest docents help you out. Very well done; includes an elaborate booklet. Park-wide.

Three-star attractions ★★★

Conservation Station. ✔ Animal-care facility has exhibits, presentations, veterinary center with viewable procedures. Petting zoo holds domesticated animals, mostly free-roaming, brushes provided. Inconvenient, accessible only by train. Rafiki's Planet Watch.

Fossil Fun Games. ✔ Winners of these midway games get stuffed-animal prizes. $4 to $5 per game. DinoLand U.S.A.

It's Tough to Be a Bug. Playfully sadistic 3-D movie displays insect survival skills. Stars characters from 1989's "A Bug's Life." Intense for preschoolers. Discovery Island.

Primeval Whirl. FastPass+ Kitschy spinning roller coaster takes you back in time, as cartoon-cutout dinosaurs warn "The End is Near." Jerky, with one slight-but-steep drop. Height minimum 48 inches. DinoLand U.S.A.

Tree of Life Garden. Narrow pathways wind through a lush tropical garden, alongside massive Tree of Life roots and waterfalls, past kangaroos and other exotic creatures. Discovery Island.

An indoor outdoor market. The colorful Tusker House serving area appears to be an outdoor area shaded by hanging blankets, with balcony shops overhead.

Restaurants and food

Animal Kingdom has the fewest restaurants of any Disney World theme park, but there is much to like. Below, each restaurant is rated from one to five stars (★); a five-star eatery fully lives up to its promise. A checkmark (✔) indicates one of the authors' personal favorites. The price of a typical adult entree is summarized by dollar signs as follows:

$ less than $10
$$ less than $15
$$$ less than $20
$$$$ less than $25
$$$$$ more than $25

Table service. A quick summary: The best food is at Yak & Yeti, for lunch or dinner. The best fast food is at Flame Tree Barbecue. The author's choice: Yak & Yeti's mahi mahi, with fried won tons for dessert.

★★★ $$$$ **Rainforest Cafe.** The atmosphere is the draw at this kid-friendly spot, where robotic elephants and gorillas come to life in a dense faux jungle. Huge aquariums hold exotic fish. Delivered by friendly servers, the food is fine, portions are generous. But it's all overpriced, because here you're paying not just for a hamburger, but also a hooting chimp. *Entrance plaza. Breakfast 8:30–10 a.m., $9–$6 (children $5–$7). Lunch and dinner 10 a.m.–park close, $13–$33 (children $7–$9). Seats 985 plus 72 at the bar. Run by Landry's; direct reservations at 407-938-9100.*

★★★★ $$$$$ **Tusker House.** Quality vegetarian dishes highlight these varied, well-prepared, but overpriced character buffets, all of which have a "Donald's Safari" name (i.e., "Donald's Safari Breakfast.") Breakfast is American fare; standouts at lunch and dinner include couscous, tabbouleh and salads; spit-roasted carving-station meats, stews and desserts are also pretty good. Greeting you as you dine are Donald Duck, Daisy Duck, Mickey Mouse and Goofy. The "Safari Orientation Centre" of the mythical Harambe Village, the dining area is lined with real African artifacts, faux maps and notices. *Africa. Breakfast 8 a.m.–10:30 a.m. $30 (children $17); lunch 11:30 a.m.–3:30 p.m. $37 (children $19); optional photo package. Dinner 4 p.m.–park close. $37 (children $19). Seats 1,206. Outdoor bar seats 256.*

★★★★★ ✔ $$$$ **Yak & Yeti.** Cool couples and families love the tasty Southeast Asian cuisine at this interesting restaurant, the only place inside Animal Kingdom where servers bring you your food. Crispy Mahi Mahi doesn't taste a bit fishy; its sweet and sour sauce is the best I've had. For an appetizer try the mild Ahi tuna, served with hot dipping sauce and sweet slaw. As for desserts, order the pineapple and cream cheese wontons—two honey-sauced skewers which you dip into vanilla ice cream—then resist the urge to lick your plate like a dog. Infused with flavor, mango iced tea is a perfect accompaniment. Other good food choices: pork egg rolls, seafood curry, baby back ribs and a Kobe beef burger. Kids pick from a mini burger, vegetable lo mein, chicken tenders or an egg roll. Portions are generous; service is on par with Disney spots. Relaxed dining areas offer lots to look at; a plethora of authentic Asian artifacts decorate walls and ceilings; chairs, drapes and light fixtures are totally mismatched. You can usually be seated immediately without a reservation before 11:30 a.m; ask to sit upstairs by the windows, overlooking the walkway below. *Asia. Lunch and dinner 11 a.m.–park close, $18–$29 (children $8–$9). Seats 250, 8 at the bar. Run by Landry's; direct reservations at 407-824-9384.*

Counter service. The top picks here: Flame Tree Barbecue (outside) and Pizzafari (inside). A basic walk-up window, Tamu Tamu has some tasty choices too.

★★★★★ ✓ **$$ Flame Tree Barbecue.** This outdoor restaurant specializes in smoked meats: chicken, ribs and pork. Each has the flavor you hope for: that savory taste that tells you it's straight out of an outdoor smoker. Chicken, ribs and pork are all so tender they nearly fall off their bones. Sides include delicious barbecue baked beans. Overall prices are a touch higher than the park's other fast-food spots but this place is still a relative value—you get more and better food, and if the weather's right a wonderful atmosphere. Looking for a bargain? Get the combo chicken and rib meal, $15 but big enough for two. Want all-white-meat chicken? Whenever we've asked it's no extra charge. On the downside, the weather's often not right, and on a hot or muggy day even Flame Tree's shaded waterfront tables—complete with nice views of the Expedition Everest mountain-scape—won't keep you from lusting after some air-conditioning. Also, of course, it's messy. Unlimited moist towelettes help. The children's menu offers only non-messy choices—a chicken sandwich, baked drumstick, hot dog or PB&J. Wherever you sit, note the subtle predator-and-prey theme. *Next to the entrance to DinoLand U.S.A., Discovery Island. Lunch,*

dinner 11 a.m.–park close. $7–$16 (children $5–$6). Seats 500 outside, mostly shaded from the sun and rain.

★★★★ ✓ **$$ Harambe Market.** It's a pity everything is overpriced, because the foods at these new walk-up stands are truly special. If only the servings weren't so small! Each of five windows offers a different item, each of which is inspired by an African street food. Choices include spice-rubbed karubi ribs; skewered chicken; curry-sausage corn dogs based on a type of South African sausage called a boerewors; and a shwarma flatbread sandwich. There are also African alcoholic drinks, wine, sangria, beer and fountain beverages such as Sparberry from Zimbabwe and Bibo from South Africa. It's all good, but if you come hungry you'll leave hungry. *Africa. $9–$14. 10:30 a.m.–one hour before park close. Seats 200 in outdoor seating, mostly covered.*

★★★★ ✓ **$ Pizzafari.** Yes! A Disney-run pizza spot that cares about its pizza! The individual pies here are head and shoulders better than those in other Disney parks, with evidence of actual herbs and spices in their sauces and preparation that included something more than just slapping it into a microwave oven. Other choices aren't bad either—a hot Italian deli sandwich and a Caesar salad with chicken. The sprawling eatery has several different dining rooms, each themed to a different type of animal. Beautiful murals, floor mosaics and ceiling art add to a clean, cool, relaxing feel that makes it tempting to stay here for hours. In fact, the authors often do just that. See that middle-aged couple, or that sweet college girl over in the corner, tapping away at their iPhones and laptop? That's us! *On the walkway to Africa, Discovery Island. Breakfast park open–10:30 a.m. $4–$9. Lunch and dinner 11 a.m.–park close, $10–$12 (children $5–$6). Seats 680.*

★★★ **$ Restaurantosaurus.** Tucked into a corner of DinoLand U.S.A., this place has a lavishly wacko theme — it's an old fishing lodge that's been converted into the dorm of the graduate students who work at the nearby Dinosaur Institute—i.e., the Dinosaur ride. Unfortunately, the food is also dorm-like: bland cheeseburgers, mac and cheese and such that make no impression on you at all. At least the soda refills are free, and there's a nice self-serve fixings station with grilled onions and mushrooms and runny gooey yummy fake cheese. The menu is priced OK if this is the kind of food you want. *Near TriceraTop Spin, DinoLand*

© Schussler Creative

Animal Kingdom food spots. Clockwise from top: the exterior of Africa's Tusker House restaurant, which hides its large size; an artifact-filled dining room inside Yak & Yeti; a Southeast Asian bus converted to an ice-cream stand; the new Harambe Market; a popcorn stand on Discovery Island.

© Disney

Some mischievous graffiti on the side of a DinoLand U.S.A. snack-stand cooler shows a dinosaur stealing a sip of Coca-Cola from a 1960s teenager.

U.S.A. Lunch and dinner 11 a.m.–park close, $9–$11 (children $7). Seats 750, including 104 outside in mostly shady areas.

★★★ $ **Starbucks Creature Comforts.** Opened in 2015, this Starbucks has the same menu as others, though its drinks don't come with straws (no park drinks do; it's to keep the animals from digesting them). Its earth-tone exterior has a coffee-bean theme. *Discovery Island. Park hours. $4–$5. No seating.*

★★★★ ✔ $ **Tamu Tamu.** This shady outdoor window couldn't be more unassuming; you'll have to look twice to find it. At press time, its menu was limited to three items: chicken curry, vegetarian curry and roasted chicken salad. Want an adult treat? Try the Dole Whip-like pineapple soft-serve topped with a pour of either dark or coconut rum. It's not real ice cream, but you won't care. Kids "Snack Packs" are collections of pre-packaged items such as yogurt, carrot sticks and goldfish crackers served with a drink. You'll have to look three times to find the seating area—it's behind the window, in a patio-like setting that's covered but not protected from rain. Tables often have vegetation on them courtesy of the surrounding trees. *Across from Tusker House, Africa. 10:30 a.m.–1 hour before park close. $9 (child Snack Pack $5). Seats 92 in outdoor covered seating.*

★★ $ **Yak & Yeti Local Food Cafés.** Next to Yak & Yeti, these walk-up windows offer Asian food court staples, none of which compare to what the restaurant serves. Nearby tables seem to be an afterthought. In the afternoon DJ Anaan may be playing his driving pop right next to you, which helps takes your mind off the fact that you've picked the wrong place to eat. *In front of Yak & Yeti, Asia. $9–$11, kids $5. 10:30 a.m.–one hour before park close. Seats 350 in outdoor covered seating.*

Snacks. The park has lots of little snack stands and carts serving up all the basics—popcorn, ice cream, gigantic turkey legs. Want something more memorable? Africa's **Kusafiri Coffee Shop and Bakery** (★★★★ ✔) serves freshly baked pastries, desserts, coffee and hot chocolate from a window adjacent to Tusker House. There's also the Amarula Schokoleti—hot chocolate with Amarula. Right in front of it is a stand selling fresh fruit. A very nice tea stand, the **Royal Anandapur Tea Co.** (★★★★★ ✔) offers a wider variety of hot individually brewed teas than you'd expect, as well as specialty and iced coffees and pastries. It's in Asia, across from the Yak & Yeti Restaurant.

See also **Food and Restaurants** in the chapter **Walt Disney World A–Z.**

Africa's Mombasa Marketplace sells distinctly non-Disney and non-brand items such as bamboo plants, Kenyan batik caftans, hand-carved figurines and henna body artistry.

Shops and merchandise

If you know where to look for it, Disney's Animal Kingdom is filled with merchandise you won't find anywhere else at Disney, sometimes anywhere else in the United States. The most unique shops are summarized below. They're rated from one to five stars (★); a checkmark (✔) indicates an author favorite.

★★★ **Bhaktapur Market.** Amazingly cramped, this small, open-air boutique sells authentic merchandise from Asia, much of it interesting kitsch. Run by the adjacent Yak & Yeti Restaurant, it's also stocked with Yak & Yeti souvenirs. *In front of Yak & Yeti, Asia.*

★★★★ **Chester & Hester's Dinosaur Treasures.** This rural gas station is run by amateur fossil hunters who have turned it into a tacky souvenir stand, decorating it with hundreds of cheap plastic dinosaurs. None of those, unfortunately, are for sale, but on the shelves are plenty of things for kids—Disney games, novelty hats, plush, sundries and Vinylmation figurines. *Across from Primeval Whirl, DinoLand U.S.A.*

★★★★ **The Dino Institute Gift Shop.** Resembling a museum gift shop, this classy store is decorated with fossils and paintings of dinosaur skeletons lit with track lighting. A giant sea turtle skeleton hangs from the ceiling. Dinosaur souvenirs and toys dominate the store, from apparel to plush, books to puppets. Check out the toy remote-control Time Rover from the ride. You can also purchase a souvenir ride photo. *At the exit to the Dinosaur ride, DinoLand U.S.A.*

★★★★ ✔ **Disney Outfitters.** This calm spot with its wood shelving, carved wooden animal statues and tile floors provides an appropriate setting for its high-end merchandise. Dooney & Bourke and Vera Bradley bags get their own featured displays, and you'll also find fashionable apparel for men, women, juniors, children and infants. Fine artwork is worth a look. The shop stays open up to an hour after park closing. *Across from Flame Tree Barbecue, Discovery Island.*

★★★★ ✔ **Mandala Gifts.** This teeny open-air store sells junior apparel and accessories, much of it nature-themed, little of it having anything to do with Disney. Included are colorful sundresses, short-shorts, scarves, costume jewelry and some cute straw hats. *In front of Yak & Yeti Restaurant, Asia.*

★★★★★ ✔ **Mombasa Marketplace.** For a real taste of Africa, check out this eclectic shop. Merchandise includes African books

With dried-yak-dung walls and firewood stored on its roof, Serka Zong Bazaar certainly looks different that most Disney gift shops. Inside are Expedition Everest souvenirs.

and cookbooks, bamboo plants and braided "money trees," batik caftans made in Kenya, beaded animal figurines, musical instruments and serious safari hats. The store's dark woods, plaster walls and authentic African table displays transport you to a different place. Artist Larry Dotson sells prints of Animal Kingdom scenes. Outside the shop an African artist carves figurines, canes and other works. There's a henna artist, too. *Across from Tusker House, Africa.*

★★★★ **Island Mercantile.** This place has a little of everything—everything you can find everywhere else at Disney. It's this park's version of The Emporium at Magic Kingdom, though it's much smaller and has a much better decor. Hanging from the ceiling are charming brightly painted wooden birds and butterflies that look like airplanes; nearby are beavers that look like saws. The shop also carries a wide range of Animal Kingdom apparel, backpacks, hats and souvenirs as well as toy binoculars and Expedition Everest T-shirts. Island Mercantile stays open up to an hour after park closing. *Next to the Oasis bridge, Discovery Island.*

★★★ **Rainforest Cafe Gift Shop.** This sprawling store sells mostly Rainforest Cafe items, but look closely and you'll find some stylish fashion apparel for women and juniors. A giant aquarium sits in the middle of the store; every now and then robotic animals on the walls and ceilings roar and hoot. The shop opens an hour before the park, and stays open two hours afterward. *Inside Rainforest Cafe, park entrance.*

★★★★ ✔ **Serka Zong Bazaar.** The high shelves of this big shop are jam-packed with gobs of authentic Asian artifacts and mountaineering gear; a huge clawed yeti figure rises from the center of the store. Things you can actually buy include Expedition Everest souvenirs (don't miss the adorable yeti plush and knit hats) and ride photos, as well as prayer flags from Tibet and books about the real Mt. Everest. Sometimes it has lovely Christmas ornaments created from air cylinders left behind on the mountain. *At the exit to Expedition Everest, Asia.*

★★★ **Ziwani Traders.** Fans of "The Lion King" will like lots of the merchandise here, which includes hard-to-find puzzles, Simba plush and original oil paintings. Decorated like a trading post and outfitting shop, the store has authentic safari gear on its out-of-reach high shelves and ceiling, including heavy-duty backpacks, canteens and lanterns. *Next to Mombasa Marketplace, Africa.*

See also **Shopping** in the chapter **Walt Disney World A–Z.**

A winding walkway leads to the indoor theater for It's Tough to Be a Bug, which is tucked inside the base of the icon of Disney's Animal Kingdom, the Tree of Life.

It's Tough to Be a Bug!

Witty 3-D film suffers from dated tech, frightening effects

★★★ FastPass+ "It was awesome!" said the 8-year-old girl, leaving the theater with her parents. "I hated it!" said the 7-year-old boy next to her, crying to his parents. Different children have different reactions to this sadistic 3-D movie, which demonstrates how insects defend themselves by pretending to torture its audience. Special effects make it seem like guests are sprayed with acid and attacked by poison quills. Two characters from the 1998 movie "A Bug's Life" appear in the theater as robotic figures—mild-mannered ant Flik (the host) and grasshopper villain Hopper. Once state-of-the-art, the show is blurry compared to modern 3-D efforts.

Tips. *When to go:* Anytime. There's no need to get a Fastpass; there are no seats set aside for Fastpass holders and they don't enter the theater early. *Where to sit:* In the center of a back row. Lean back to feel all the effects.

Fun facts. Character voices include those of ❶ Dave Foley (Flik), ❷ Cheech Marin (Chili) and ❸ Kevin Spacey (Hopper).

Fun finds and Hidden Mickeys. ❶ Outside the lobby a plaque honors Dr. Jane Goodall's work with chimpanzees. ❷ Lobby posters and ambient music recall previous shows such as "Beauty and the Bees" and "Little Shop of Hoppers." ❸ The theater is an anthill; its projection booth a wasp nest. ❹ As the show ends, fireflies swarm to exit signs. ❺ Mickey's three-circles appear as spots on a root in the lobby, to the left of the handicapped entrance.

Key facts. *Best for:* Older kids. *Duration:* 8 min. *Capacity:* 430. *Queue:* Outdoor, shaded. *Fear factor:* Intense, dark, menacing bugs. *Debuted:* 1998. *Access:* Guests may stay in wheelchairs, ECVs. *Disability services:* Assistive listening, reflective captioning, Audio Description. *Location:* Discovery Island.

Average wait times

9am	10am	11am	Noon	1pm	2pm	3pm	4pm	5pm	6pm	7pm	8pm	9pm
5m	5m	5m	10m	5m	5m	5m	5m	5m	5m	5m	n/a	n/a

A carved crocodilian emerges from an oversized root in the Tree of Life garden. Pathways pass habitats of kangaroos, Galapagos tortoises and other exotic creatures.

Tree of Life Garden

Tropical area has hidden walkways, cool animals, new bird show

★★★ The park centerpiece, this lush garden surrounds a massive man-made icon with exotic wildlife. Surrounding the Tree of Life, tropical hills are dotted with streams, grottos and waterfalls. Two walking paths are rarely crowded; wander down one and you'll have its peaceful environment almost all to yourself.

Garden area. This open spot directly in front of the Tree offers a good view of flamingos and whistling ducks (they hang out in a pond to the left); to the left is a shady otter habitat with an underwater viewing area.

Front trail. So hidden few guests notice it, a trail off the park's walkway to Africa leads to an up-close look at the kangaroo enclosure. It connects to the walkway to Asia behind the Wilderness Explorers Club House.

Back trail. Running along the Discovery River, this trail snakes past parrot, porcupine, stork and tortoise habitats.

Winged Encounters. A variety of endangered macaws fly freely over the island, landing on the bridge to DinoLand U.S.A that crosses the Discovery River. Avian experts answer questions. Training for the show, the birds take unannounced flights early some mornings. *10 min. Show times vary. Docent presentation in front of the Tree of Life; birds visible throughout the island. New in 2015.*

Tips. *When to go:* Early in the morning to see the animals at their liveliest. *For families:* Small children may have a hard time seeing the kangaroos. Their viewing spot sits behind a concrete wall that's about 4 feet tall.

Key facts. *Best for:* All ages. *Duration:* Allow 20 minutes. *Specs:* Garden area, 2 trails (1,680 ft.), 9 viewing areas, 15 species. *Debuted:* 1998. *Access:* Guests may remain in wheelchairs, ECVs. *Location:* Discovery Island.

See also **Animal Guide.**

Average wait times

9am	10am	11am	Noon	1pm	2pm	3pm	4pm	5pm	6pm	7pm	8pm	9pm
0m	0m	0m	0m	0m	0m	0m	0m	0m	0m	0m	n/a	n/a

A **"troop leader"** teaches a brother and sister the "W" sign of the Wilderness Explorers, preparing them for a day that will take them throughout Disney's Animal Kingdom.

Wilderness Explorers

All ages will enjoy this hands-on scavenger hunt

★★★★ ✓ You start off learning the Wilderness Explorer call: "The wilderness must be explored! Caw! Caw! Roar!" Then you go off to earn badges—stickers—at 31 stations scattered throughout the park by completing activities that teach you fascinating things about animals, nature and world cultures. Yes it can take forever—in fact, Disney assumes you'll take more than one day to complete everything—but assuming you've got that time there's no rush, and if you've got a child interested in these subjects it's a terrific bonding experience.

It's all wonderfully low-tech—there are no video screens, no hand-held gizmos, no special effects. Instead, Disney hands you a surprisingly nice handbook (which makes a wonderful free souvenir) and you and your child discover, sketch, explore and occasionally talk to real live people.

If you like to help your child earn scouting awards you'll love it, though so will nature lovers of any age. Even earning just a few badges is a great way to enhance your day. Wilderness Explorers is based on Russell's troop in the 2009 Pixar movie "Up."

Tip. *How to do it:* Get your handbook as soon as you enter the park, and earn your badges as you take in whatever rides, shows and animal exhibits you were already planning to see. For example, as you view the Pangani Forest animals you can earn a Ham Radio Badge, a Hiking Badge, a Birding Badge, a Tracking Badge and a Gorilla Badge.

Key facts. *Best for:* Families. *Duration:* Apx. 20 min. per badge. *Operating hours:* Park open–6 p.m. *Weather issues:* Closed in thunderstorms. *Debuted:* 2014. *Access:* Guests may stay in wheelchairs, ECVs. *Location:* Sign-up on bridge between Oasis, Discovery Island.

Average wait times

9am	10am	11am	Noon	1pm	2pm	3pm	4pm	5pm	6pm	7pm	8pm	9pm
0m	0m	0m	0m	0m	0m	0m	0m	0m	0m	0m	n/a	n/a

Micaela Neal

Wild animals. Creatively costumed dancers channel African animals as they dance and twirl within a few feet of audience members at the Festival of the Lion King.

Festival of the Lion King

In-the-round musical spectacle is Disney's best show

★★★★★ ✓ FastPass+ Fans of Disney's 1994 movie "The Lion King" will love this rousing musical spectacle. Filled with energized renditions of the best songs from the film, it combines the pageantry of a parade, the wit of a Catskills comedy revue and the emotions of a gospel revival. The show is presented in-the-round in an air-conditioned theater.

It begins with an evocative take on the film's opening scene, as animal-costumed dancers create an abstract sunrise to "The Circle of Life." Four singers bring in nearly 50 more performers, including Timon, the revue's wisecracking emcee. Parade floats roll in too; on one is Simba, on another Pumbaa.

From then on, singers, dancers, acrobats, stilt-walkers and giant puppets fill your field of vision. Acrobats fly through the air, a fire-baton twirler performs to "Be Prepared," a ballerina soars overhead to "Can You Feel the

Love Tonight?" A twirling finale becomes a kaleidoscopic circle of life.

Tips. *When to go:* Anytime, but with a Fastpass. You'll enter the theater before the rest of the audience and easily get a good seat. *Where to sit:* As close to the front as you can, as the performers come right up to the crowd. *For families:* Since the bleachers are shallow, small children often can't see if someone tall sits in front of them.

Key facts. *Best for:* All ages. *Duration:* 28 min. *Capacity:* 1,375. *Queue:* Indoor area spills into an outdoor covered line. *Showtimes:* Typically one per hour starting about 10 a.m. *Weather issues:* During a rain, the audience is held in the theater until the floats move backstage. *Debuted:* 1998. *Access:* Guests may stay in wheelchairs, ECVs. *Disability services:* Assistive listening, handheld captioning. *Location:* Africa.

Average wait times

9am	10am	11am	Noon	1pm	2pm	3pm	4pm	5pm	6pm	7pm	8pm	9pm
n/a	n/a	n/a	n/a	n/a	n/a	n/a	n/a	n/a	n/a	n/a	n/a	n/a

Open-sided safari trucks wind through a re-created savanna where free-roaming African animals forage for food. Giraffes often feed directly in the path of the trucks.

Kilimanjaro Safaris

Disney's largest attraction makes you forget you're in Florida

UPDATED! ★★★★★ ✓ FastPass+ A great zoological attraction, this open-air truck ride takes you through a seamless re-creation of African jungles and savannas that are filled with free-roaming wildlife. There are no visible fences, and many animals can come up to your vehicle. Creatures include crocodiles, elephants, giraffes, hippos, lions, rhinos, warthogs and many species of antelope. Rutted roads, creaky bridges and blind corners lend a sense of adventure.

The trip takes you through an African wildlife preserve, an effort by Disney's village of Harambe to replace its timbering economy with eco-tourism. Though drivers say the journey will take two weeks and cover 800 square miles, it's actually a 20–25 minute trip through about 100 acres. The ride will be extended for a new nighttime adventure in the spring of 2016, when you'll be able to travel through the savanna amid a magically extended orange glow of the setting sun.

Disney veterans may notice that the ride no longer has a storyline. There's no Big Red or Little Red elephants, the driver no longer speaks to a game warden in an overhead plane, the poachers have packed up and left.

Some of the animals have changed recently too. African wild dogs are now on the savanna, as are addax, hyenas, springboks and zebra. Thompson's gazelle and scimitar horned oryx are now only at Animal Kingdom Lodge. There are no longer impala (they didn't take well to the climate) or male greater kudu.

Tips. *When to go:* First thing in the morning through the standby line, when crowds are light and the animals are feeding. Another good time: during a shower, especially after a hot morning or afternoon. The animals will be especially active; elephants sometimes

Average wait times

9am	10am	11am	Noon	1pm	2pm	3pm	4pm	5pm	6pm	7pm	8pm	9pm
5m	30m	20m	40m	20m	40m	40m	60m	40m	30m	15m	15m	n/a

Micaela Neal

A safari truck cruises by a flock of flamingos. Below, a white rhino crosses the road. Animals always have the right-of-way; trucks are sometimes forced to stop and wait for them to move.

Micaela Neal

play in their pool when it rains. *Where to sit:* On the left of the truck for the best views, in front for the smoothest ride, in back to take photos because you can turn around and shoot behind you. Hold on tight to your camera, though—the back of the truck gets really bouncy. *For families:* Ask for the front row, and sit your child close to the driver for the most immersive experience. If your child asks the driver questions (especially about the animals), the driver will often speak directly with your child. Ask the cast member in the boarding area (the one who asks "How many?") to sit in the row you prefer; he or she will almost always be happy to accommodate you. Fastpass holders get no special seating.

Fun facts. ❶ Disney created the "muddy" road by coloring concrete to look like soil, then while it was still wet rolling truck tires through it and tossing in dirt, stones and twigs. ❷ The first hippo pool contains all males; the second females. ❸ There's a reason your driver says the termite mounds are "as hard as concrete." ❹ A pile of ostrich eggs is equally tough to crack. ❺ The acacia trees are actually Southern live oaks with their lower branches removed. ❻ The first baobab tree on the route isn't a tree at all. It's a storage shed. ❼ Kilimanjaro Safaris has the largest collection of Nile hippos and African elephants in North America. ❽ It's the largest Disney attraction in the world. The entire Magic Kingdom would fit inside it.

Fun finds and Hidden Mickeys. ❶ Posters for Big Red still appear in the queue office. ❷ Prehistoric drawings appear on a gate past the flamingos and on rocks to the right as you pass the lions. ❸ Just beyond the clay pits past a baobab tree, Mickey's three circles appear as a puffy spot between a split branch, opposite the main elephant area. ❹ They form the flamingo island ❺ as well as an indentation in a boulder on the right, just past that island but before the next gate.

Key facts. *Best for:* All ages. *Duration:* 22 min. *Capacity:* 36 guests per truck. *Queue:* Outdoor, covered. *Debuted:* 1998, revised 2013. *Health advisories:* Expectant moms should not ride. *Access:* ECV users must transfer. *Disability services:* Assistive listening, hand-held captioning. *Location:* Africa.

See also **Animal Guide**.

"Place of enchantment" in Swahili, Pangani lives up to its name. The self-guided walking tour wanders through lush jungles as it passes gorillas, hippos, meerkats and okapi.

Pangani Forest Exploration Trail

Enchanting walking trail passes gorillas, meerkats, hippos

★★★★★ ✔ Streams and waterfalls flow through the grounds of this self-guided tour of African animals, including gorillas, hippos and meerkats. The trail is shady, and benches are scattered throughout.

Presented as a series of research areas, the area has a scientific theme. A research station features naked mole rats, interactive displays and child-level cages and tanks that hold creatures kids find fascinating: plate-sized giant African bullfrogs, hissing cockroaches and dung beetles. Exhibits shed light on subjects as diverse as bushmeat hunting and baobab trees. One display recalls the African fable "When The Hippo Was Hairy." A 40-foot glass wall lets you view hippos underwater.

A suspension bridge and viewing island divide two large gorilla habitats. One holds a family (a silverback, two moms and five youngsters); the other a bachelor troupe.

Tips. *When to go:* In the morning; the hippo water is clear, the gorillas active. *For families:* Skip the bushmeat exhibit (just past the colobus monkeys); it shows animals killed for their meat. *What else to do:* Talk with the docents; they are full of fascinating stories.

Hidden Mickeys. ➊ In the research station on a backpack to the left of the naked mole rats and ➋ as the "O" in the word "Asepco" and two paper-reinforcement rings on a box of soap on a small ledge behind the desk lamp.

Key facts. *Best for:* All ages. *Duration:* Allow 30–45 min. *Specs:* 1 trail (2,100 ft), 9 viewing areas, 10 species plus aviary, indoor exhibits. *Operating hours:* Park open–dusk. *Weather issues:* Closed during thunderstorms. *Debuted:* 1998. *Access:* Guests may stay in wheelchairs, ECVs. *Disability services:* Audio Description. *Location:* Africa.

See also **Animal Guide.**

Average wait times

	9am	10am	11am	Noon	1pm	2pm	3pm	4pm	5pm	6pm	7pm	8pm	9pm
	0m	0m	0m	0m	0m	0m	0m	0m	0m	0m	0m	n/a	n/a

Animals are examined and sometimes operated on in front of guests at Conservation Station's veterinary care center. The procedures only take place in the morning.

Conservation Station

Isolated, engaging area has petting zoo, educational exhibits

★★★ ✔ This theme-free pavilion houses straightforward exhibits, a veterinary care center and a few character-greeting spots. A petting zoo sits next to it. The area is inconveniently located and much of what it offers can also be seen at many zoos. For what it is, though, it's well done. You can watch animals undergo medical procedures each morning, typically until noon. Vets explain what's going on while overhead cameras offer up-close views. About three animals are treated daily.

To get to the area you take a "Wildlife Express" train from the park's Africa area. Despite its name the train offers no wildlife views, just a few backstage pens used to house Kilimanjaro Safaris animals.

Tips. *When to go:* Arrive before 10 a.m. to see a procedure. *For families:* If you have young kids skip the video "Sharing the Planet." It shows a poached tiger, injured manatees and wolves being hunted. *For couples:* Lovebirds will enjoy the Song of the Rainforest exhibit. You enter a small booth, close the door and sit side-by-side on a bench. With a push of a button the lights go out and an audio show begins. It lasts six minutes.

Hidden Mickeys. ❶ As overlapping circles in tree grates. ❷ Throughout the entrance mural and the Song of the Rainforest display. ❸ As orange spots on the outdoor-stage wall. ❹ Often as a pattern on a sheared sheep.

Key facts. *Best for:* Children, adults, animal lovers. *Duration:* Allow 1.5 hrs. *Specs:* 49 species. *Operating hours:* 9:30 a.m.–dusk. *Weather issues:* Train closed during thunderstorms. *Debuted:* 1998. *Access:* Guests may remain in wheelchairs, ECVs. ECV users must transfer to a wheelchair to enter the petting zoo. *Location:* Rafiki's Planet Watch. See also **Animal Guide.**

Average wait times

9am	10am	11am	Noon	1pm	2pm	3pm	4pm	5pm	6pm	7pm	8pm	9pm
n/a	10m	10m	10m	10m	10m	10m	10m	10m	10m	n/a	n/a	n/a

Micaela Neal

Giving back. A crow returns a dollar to an audience volunteer during a performance of Flights of Wonder. The show takes place in an outdoor theater with a shaded seating area.

Flights of Wonder

Educational, comedic show with flying birds, green message

★★★★ ✔ Birds fly inches over your head in this entertaining live show, which demonstrates natural behaviors as it promotes the intrinsic value of these animals and the need to protect them. Altogether you'll see about 20 birds, including a bald eagle.

Though the subject is serious, the presentation is anything but. Just as it gets started, it's interrupted by a loony lost tour guide who wanders up on stage, flag in hand, in search of his group. You soon learn that he suffers from FOB — "fear of birds." As he faces his fears, you witness various up-close-and-personal flight demonstrations. The grassy natural stage features a backdrop of a crumbling stone building set in a shady grove.

A brief preshow in front of the theater features a great horned owl. When the show is over, handlers bring out a bird or two for a brief meet-and-greet session.

Tips. *When to go:* All shows are good. *Where to sit:* In the center, at the end of a front row. Birds will fly over your head (arrive 20 minutes early to be among the first people in the theater). *For families:* Want your child to be in the show? Sit front and center and have her wave wildly when the trainer asks for volunteers. Since the seating area is flat, small children should sit close to the stage.

Key facts. *Best for:* Children, adults, animal lovers. *Duration:* 25 min. *Capacity:* 1,150. *Queue:* Outdoor, shady. *Showtimes:* Scheduled performances mid-morning through mid-afternoon. *Weather issues:* Changed and shortened during rain, cancelled during lightning and thunderstorms. *Debuted:* 1998. *Access:* Guests may remain in wheelchairs, ECVs. *Disability services:* Assistive listening. *Location:* Asia.

See also **Animal Guide.**

Average wait times

9am	10am	11am	Noon	1pm	2pm	3pm	4pm	5pm	6pm	7pm	8pm	9pm
n/a	n/a	n/a	n/a	n/a	n/a	n/a	n/a	n/a	n/a	n/a	n/a	n/a

Churning waters splash riders on Kali River Rapids. The turbulent raft ride carries a conservation message, as key scenes depict the clear-cutting and burning of a rainforest.

Kali River Rapids

Wet, exhilarating raft ride condemns rainforest destruction

★★★★ FastPass+ This raft ride takes you down a turbulent jungle river that has many twists and turns and a 25-foot drop. Erupting springs, spraying water jugs and squirting statues ensure you get wet, maybe soaked. Each raft holds 12 people; nearby lockers (free to use for a short time) keep valuables dry.

The ride carries a strong conservation message, as it depicts the process of deforestation. Though it begins in a lush jungle, at the river's headwaters it shows the illegal operations of a logging business, clear-cutting a pristine section of a rainforest to harvest tropical hardwoods, setting ablaze wood that doesn't have commercial value.

Tips. *When to go:* In the heat of mid-afternoon when you'll welcome getting soaked, with a Fastpass so you can skip the long line. *For families:* Talk to your children about the ecological issues raised in this attraction. Deforestation and habitat loss are worthwhile topics, especially when you are surrounded by the species being threatened.

Fun finds. ❶ In the queue, Mr. Panika's Shop sells "Antiks Made to Order." ❷ King of Pop Michael Jackson is among the raft riders in a mural in the last queue room; he's at the top right of a raft with his hands raised. ❸ On the exitway, buttons on a footbridge shoot sprays of water on unsuspecting riders.

Key facts. *Best for:* Children, teens. *Duration:* 6 min. *Capacity:* 240 (20 12-person rafts). *Queue:* Outdoor, shaded. *Fear factor:* Bumpy, splashy, 1 steep drop *Restraint:* Seat belt. *Weather issues:* Closed during thunderstorms. *Debuted:* 1999. *Health advisories:* Guests should be free from motion sickness; pregnancy; high blood pressure; heart, back or neck problems. *Access:* Height min. 38 in. ECV users must transfer. *Location:* Asia.

Average wait times

9am	10am	11am	Noon	1pm	2pm	3pm	4pm	5pm	6pm	7pm	8pm	9pm
0m	5m	5m	30m	50m	80m	60m	60m	40m	30m	10m	n/a	n/a

Guests walk through the overrun grounds of a mythical ancient hunting lodge on this lovely trail, past a Komodo dragon, giant bats and playful tigers.

Maharajah Jungle Trek

Exotic trail has captivating bats, tigers, a Komodo dragon

★★★★★ ✔ Tigers, giant fruit bats and other exotic Asian animals line this shady winding walkway. Other animals include a Komodo dragon (the world's largest living lizard) and some unusual deer and cattle. A lush aviary is filled with beautiful birds. Docents are stationed at key viewing spots. Large overhead fans help keep you cool in the bat pavilion, the attraction's only indoor area. Some children are afraid of the bats, but there is no need to be. They're *fruit* bats.

The circular walkway winds through the ruins of a mythical hunting lodge, which, in one of Disney's best architectural efforts, has been taken over by the forces of nature. Trees have taken root within towers, bursting their seams from within. Birds have moved into the grand ballroom, which has lost its roof. Eventually, the story goes, the lodge was given to the local village, which uses it today as a wildlife refuge.

Tips. *When to go:* First thing in the morning (the bats are fed at 9:15 a.m., and the rest of the animals are alert and lively) or during a light shower (the tigers get playful). Avoid hot afternoons; the animals hide. *For families:* Kids will like spotting the shed antlers in the habitat just past the tigers. Eli, a male deer, grows new ones every four months.

Hidden Mickeys. ❶ At the second tiger viewing area, in the first mural on the right as swirls of water under a tiger. ❷ As a maharajah's earring in the first mural on your left.

Key facts. *Best for:* All ages. *Duration:* Allow 30 min. *Specs:* 1 trail (1,500 ft), 7 viewing areas, 14 species plus aviary. *Operating hours:* Park open–dusk. *Weather issues:* Closed during thunderstorms. *Debuted:* 1998. *Access:* Guests may stay in wheelchairs, ECVs. *Disability services:* Audio Description. *Location:* Asia.

See also **Animal Guide.**

Average wait times

9am	10am	11am	Noon	1pm	2pm	3pm	4pm	5pm	6pm	7pm	8pm	9pm
0m	0m	0m	0m	0m	0m	0m	0m	0m	0m	0m	n/a	n/a

Colorful prayer flags decorate the entrance to the Expedition Everest roller coaster. Its tea trains climb 200 feet to reach the top of Disney's "Forbidden Mountain."

Expedition Everest

Thrilling mountain coaster goes backward, angers Yeti

★★★★★ ✔ FastPass+ This smooth high-speed roller coaster climbs forward, zooms backward in the dark and takes some steep sweeping turns. What appears to be an old tea train zips you around, into and through a snow-capped mountain and narrowly escapes a snarling beast. Though you don't go upside down, your 4,000-foot journey climbs 200 feet, stops twice, takes an 80-foot drop and hits 60 miles per hour. It's a rush.

A monster myth. The coaster is even more fun if you know its story, which—if you look for it—is told by props in the standby queue. The tale starts in the 1920s, as tea plantations begin to flourish along the mountains of the mythical Asian kingdom of Anandapur. A steam train line is established to carry the tea to villages, where it is shipped to distant markets. Soon, however, strange track snaps appear, which force the trains to shut down.

Locals blame the British, claiming their attempts to reach the summit of nearby Mt. Everest has angered the Yeti, a creature they say guards the mountains. But today the rail line has reopened. Despite local protests, a bohemian American (known only as Bob) has restored the old tea trains for his Himalayan Escapes Tours and Expeditions, a new business which makes it easy for trekkers to get to Everest quickly. You're on his first train.

What could possibly go wrong?

Tips. *When to go:* At dusk or at night if you can, when the mountain is lit in eerie oranges and purples. *Where to sit:* Right in the front seat for the best view and mildest ride; in back for the wildest experience. *How to save time:* Use the single-rider line if you arrive during a busy time, don't have a Fastpass, don't mind riding by yourself and don't care where you sit. You'll get on right away.

Average wait times

9am	10am	11am	Noon	1pm	2pm	3pm	4pm	5pm	6pm	7pm	8pm	9pm
10m	15m	20m	35m	25m	35m	25m	20m	20m	15m	10m	n/a	n/a

Julie Neal

© Disney

The Expedition Everest coaster starts with a trip up a high mountain range and ends with an encounter with a Yeti. The ride is one of only a few at Disney with a single-rider entrance.

Hidden Mickeys. In the queue ❶ as a hat on a Yeti doll, ❷ bottle caps in a display of patches, ❸ a dent and two holes in the museum's tea kettle, ❹ and on the left wall after the museum (with a sorcerer's hat) as wood stains in a photo.

A closer look. Yetis are not real; scientists agree there is no credible evidence they exist. The Yeti legend, however, certainly exists. For centuries, Himalayans have told stories about a humanoid monster that fiercely guards the area around Mt. Everest. Reports increased in the 20th century, when Westerners began seeing an "Abominable Snowman." Interest peaked in 1960, when Sir Edmund Hillary's fact-finding trip to the peak brought trip-wire and time-lapse cameras, but found nothing.

The villain of 1964's stop-motion classic "Rudolph the Red-Nosed Reindeer" is a Yeti named Bumbles. The 2001 Disney/Pixar film "Monsters, Inc." includes an Abominable Snowman voiced by John Ratzenberger.

Key facts. *Best for:* Teens, adults. *Duration:* 3 min. *Capacity:* 34 per train (5 cars seat 6, last one seats 4) *Queue:* Indoor, outdoor, mostly covered. *Fear factor:* High lift, often dark, threatening monster, 1 steep drop. *Restraint:* Lap bar. *Top speed:* 60 mph. *Weather issues:* Closed during thunderstorms. *Debuted:* 2006. *Health advisories:* Guests should be free from motion sickness; pregnancy; high blood pressure; heart, back or neck problems. *Access:* Height min. 44 in. Wheelchair, ECV users must transfer. *Location:* Asia.

Julie Neal

Nine of ten riders agree: Expedition Everest's 80-foot drop is a highlight of their Animal Kingdom day. At top, the ride appears to come to an end as it reaches the top of a mountain.

© Disney

An angry carnotaurus threatens riders on Dinosaur. A hidden hydraulic system on the ride's Time Rover simulates the pitch, roll and yaw of a slippery trip through a primeval forest.

Dinosaur!

A carnotaurus stalks you in this bumpy, dark, scary ride

★★★★ ✔ FastPass+ Ferocious dinosaurs chase you in this tense dark ride. As your vehicle (a motion simulator on a track) careens through a primeval forest, asteroids rain from the sky, raptors threaten you, a carnotaurus chases you. Smoke cannons, strobe lights and loud sounds ratchet up the thrills.

The adventure begins at the stuffy Dino Institute Discovery Center, a 1970s-style museum. After a multimedia show explains that an asteroid shower wiped out dinosaurs long ago, the director announces that— thanks to a new time-traveling vehicle—you can safely travel back to that time yourself. But when her sneaky assistant reprograms your ride, all heck breaks loose. The attraction is based on the 2000 movie "Dinosaur."

Tips. *When to go:* Early, late or with a Fastpass. *Where to sit:* Ask for the front seat for the best view and most legroom.

Fun finds and Hidden Mickeys. ❶ A cast of the largest, most complete T-Rex ever found (Sue, South Dakota, 1990) stands in front of the ride. ❷ In the boarding area, red, yellow and white pipes are marked with the chemical makeups of ketchup, mustard and mayonnaise; a nod to McDonald's, the ride's original sponsor. ❸ Mickey's shape hides a mural in the first lobby, as marks on a tree trunk.

Key facts. *Best for:* Older children, teens, adults. *Duration:* 3 min, 30 sec. *Capacity:* 144 per hour. *Queue:* Indoor. *Fear factor:* Intense, loud, jerky, dark. *Restraint:* Seat belt. *Debuted:* 1998. *Health advisories:* Guests should be free from motion sickness; pregnancy; high blood pressure; heart, back or neck problems. *Access:* Height min. 40 in. Wheelchair and ECV users must transfer. *Disability services:* Assistive listening, video captioning. *Location:* DinoLand U.S.A.

Average wait times

9am	10am	11am	Noon	1pm	2pm	3pm	4pm	5pm	6pm	7pm	8pm	9pm
5m	10m	20m	20m	20m	20m	30m	20m	20m	15m	10m	n/a	n/a

© Disney

"Time machines" spin as they zig-zag down a narrow track on Primeval Whirl. The throwback coaster is the signature ride of Dino-Rama, Animal Kingdom's cheesy carnival.

Primeval Whirl

Cheap-thrill spinning coaster parodies the Dinosaur ride

★★★ FastPass+ A kitschy timetrip back to the days when dinosaurs became extinct, this quirky roller coaster combines the thrills of an old-school Wild Mouse with the spins of a Disney tea cup. Riders often feel like they are about to fall off its narrow track, as its wide cars whip around turns as they build speed.

According to Disney lore, Primeval Whirl is the work of local low-brows Chester and Hester, who wanted a time-travel ride for their Dino-Rama carnival to steal tourists away from the nearby Dino Institute. Each candy-colored car features the fins and chrome of a 1950s automobile and the huge reflectors of an old bicycle. On its dash sits an alarm clock, a clock radio and egg timer; lining the course are cartoon clocks, spinning vortices, dinosaur cut-outs warning "The End is Near."

Tips. *When to go:* Very early or late, so you don't have a long wait. *How to spin fast:*

Put the heaviest person in your group at one side. *For families:* If you have a child who's nervous about roller coasters, have them sit in the middle. *For couples:* The seats fit four, but are divided in the middle, leaving two cozy couple spots. You are jerked and thrown together throughout the ride. *Feel queasy?* Stare at the orange radio box in the center of the dash to keep your dizziness at bay.

Key facts. *Best for:* Children, teens. *Duration:* 2 min, 30 sec. *Capacity:* 104 on 2 tracks (4 per car). *Queue:* Outdoor, covered. *Fear factor:* Jerky, spins, 1 steep drop. *Restraint:* Lap bar. *Top speed:* 29 mph. *Weather issues:* Closed in thunderstorms. *Debuted:* 2002. *Health advisories:* Guests should be free from motion sickness; pregnancy; high blood pressure; heart, back or neck problems. *Access:* Height min. 48 in. Wheelchair and ECV users must transfer. *Location:* DinoLand U.S.A.

Average wait times

9am	10am	11am	Noon	1pm	2pm	3pm	4pm	5pm	6pm	7pm	8pm	9pm
5m	20m	20m	30m	30m	20m	20m	20m	20m	20m	10m	n/a	n/a

Underrated. TriceraTop Spin may not have the charm of Dumbo the Flying Elephant, but it does seat four and there's rarely a long line. A covered queue has fans to keep you cool.

TriceraTop Spin

A dino Dumbo, perfect for young families

★★★★★ Circling around a colorful spinning-top tin toy, you and up to three other passengers ride in a chubby triceratops that climbs, dips and dives at your command. Eye candy includes playful dinosaurs that pop out of the top, flying cartoon comets that circle around it and, at night, white light bulbs that line the hub and spokes. Manic banjo and fiddle music adds a wacky cornpone touch.

Though the ride lacks the charm of Magic Kingdom's Dumbo the Flying Elephant, it's easier to enjoy. There's never a long wait; in fact there's often no wait at all. And since each vehicle seats four, small families can ride together. Though Disney purists dismiss the ride as too cheesy, younger children will love it, and after all, cheesy is the point of the whole DinoRama area.

Tips. *When to go:* Anytime except the hottest part of the day, when the asphalt "parking lot" of this faux roadside carnival reflects just too much heat. *Where to sit:* In the front seat for the most legroom, in back to control the height of your dino. *For families:* TriceraTop Spin is the only ride at Disney's Animal Kingdom that is completely toddler friendly, with nothing scary and no height minimum. *For couples:* Don't ride this unless you're in the mood to touch each other; the cozy seats force riders to squeeze together.

Fun fact. ❶ The vehicles circle every 13 seconds. That's the same speed as Dumbo and Aladdin's Magic Carpets, half the pace of the rockets of Astro Orbiter.

Key facts. *Best for:* Children. *Duration:* 1 min., 30 sec. *Capacity:* 64 (4 per car, seated two across). *Queue:* Outdoor, covered. *Weather issues:* Closed during thunderstorms. *Debuted:* 2001. *Access:* ECV users must transfer. *Location:* DinoLand U.S.A.

Average wait times

9am	10am	11am	Noon	1pm	2pm	3pm	4pm	5pm	6pm	7pm	8pm	9pm
0m	0m	0m	0m	5m	5m	20m	10m	10m	5m	5m	n/a	n/a

No wait here. Part of a tongue-in-cheek "Dino-Rama" carnival, Disney's Fossil Fun midway games are often deserted late in the day. Behind them is the Primeval Whirl roller coaster.

Fossil Fun Games

Inexpensive, fair midway games that children can beat

★★★ ✔ These whimsical midway games reward winners with prizes. Compared to actual carnival games, they're easy. Three are designed specifically for children: the watergun Fossil Fueler, the ball-rolling racing derby Mammoth Marathon and the mallet-strike game Whac-A-Pachycephalosaur ("Whacky Packy" for short). Two others—a ball toss and basketball throw—require serious skill to win.

Tips. *Fossil Fueler:* To shoot straight, use your free hand to cradle the barrel of your gun. *Mammoth Marathon:* Ask for a practice ball before the race begins. Roll your balls slowly. *Whac-A-Pachycephalosaur:* Wait until you see a dino head pop up before you swing at it; don't try to anticipate.

Key facts. *Best for:* Families. *Duration:* 1 min. *Cost:* $3–4. *Players:* 1–10. *Weather issues:* Closed during thunderstorms. *Debuted:* 2002. *Access:* Players may remain in wheelchairs, ECVs. *Location:* DinoLand U.S.A.

Average wait times

9am	10am	11am	Noon	1pm	2pm	3pm	4pm	5pm	6pm	7pm	8pm	9pm
0m	0m	0m	0m	0m	0m	0m	0m	0m	0m	0m	n/a	n/a

The Boneyard playground entertains elementary-age kids with a towering maze of nets, slides and tunnels; preschoolers play in a fossil-filled sandy pit.

The Boneyard

Disney's best playground is themed to an archaeological dig

★★★★★ Geared for toddlers through elementary-school kids, this large outdoor playground is themed to be a dinosaur dig site. Two distinct areas are connected by an overhead footbridge. Highlights include a three-story tower of nets and slides and a sandy pit where kids dig for mammoth bones.

Extras include a maze of tunnels, walls embedded with dinosaur skeletons, climb-on bones and rocks, steep net and rope-climbing ramps and waterfalls just right to drench a young head. Mesh canopies filter the sun, and the flooring is a spongy material that stays cool and won't harm tumbling youngsters.

The playground offers plenty of spots for parents to get off their feet. Overhead fans keep things breezy. An abundance of nooks and crannies makes it easy to lose sight of your child, but there's only one exit, and its gate is always monitored.

Tips. *When to go:* Anytime. *Where to sit:* There are many places for parents to sit and relax, including multiple picnic tables and a ledge that surrounds the sandy dig area.

Fun finds and Hidden Mickeys. ❶ Notes sound when kids bang a "xylobone" in a wall near a Jeep. ❷ Nearby dino tracks trigger roars when kids step on them. ❸ Mickey's three circles appear at the entrance as a big stain under a drinking fountain, ❹ as a quarter and two pennies on a table in a fenced-off area on the second level by the slides ❺ and as a fan and two hardhats in a fenced-off area at the back of the mammoth-bone pit.

Key facts. *Best for:* Children. *Duration:* Allow 15–30 min. *Capacity:* 500. *Operating hours:* May open 1 hr. after park open. *Weather issues:* Closed in thunderstorms. *Debuted:* 1998. *Access:* Guests may stay in wheelchairs, ECVs. *Location:* DinoLand U.S.A.

Average wait times

9am	10am	11am	Noon	1pm	2pm	3pm	4pm	5pm	6pm	7pm	8pm	9pm
0m	0m	0m	0m	0m	0m	0m	0m	0m	0m	0m	n/a	n/a

After curious clownfish Nemo (left) defies his overprotective father in "Finding Nemo—The Musical," each takes off on a journey that teaches them to understand each other.

Finding Nemo—The Musical

The movie as a song-and-dance puppet show. And it works.

★★★★★ ✔ FastPass+ Shimmying sharks, body-surfing turtles and a bicycle-riding stingray star in this colorful, whimsical stage show, which re-creates the 2003 Pixar movie "Finding Nemo" as a musical. Nine songs tell the story with help from acrobats, dancers and huge mechanical puppets. Broadway-quality but for its length, the show is funny, touching and a visual treat.

Main characters are represented by live performers, who act out their roles while operating large puppet versions of themselves. Others are portrayed using a variety of puppetry styles, including bunraku, a Japanese form in which one huge puppet is operated by multiple puppeteers. The production takes place in the enclosed Theater in the Wild.

Tips. *When to go:* Get a Fastpass for this show; holders get to enter the theater 20 to 30 minutes before non-Fastpass holders, and take all the good seats. If you can't, arrive at least 30 minutes early; the last show of the day is usually the least crowded. Food is allowed in line but not inside the theater. *Where to sit:* In the middle of the auditorium to see the full spectacle, or along the center catwalk to be immersed in it.

Fun finds and Hidden Mickeys. ❶ Before the show begins, Nemo swims back and forth through oversized bubbles on the sides of the stage. ❷ Mickey's shape appears as three blue bubbles, two lit and one drawn, at the bottom left of the stage wall.

Key facts. *Best for:* All ages. *Duration:* 30 min. *Capacity:* 1,500. *Queue:* Outdoor, uncovered. *Operating hours:* Scheduled shows mid-morning to mid-afternoon. *Debuted:* 2007. *Access:* Guests may remain in wheelchairs, ECVs. *Disability services:* Reflective captioning. *Location:* DinoLand U.S.A.

Average wait times

9am	10am	11am	Noon	1pm	2pm	3pm	4pm	5pm	6pm	7pm	8pm	9pm
n/a	n/a	n/a	n/a	n/a	n/a	n/a	n/a	n/a	n/a	n/a	n/a	n/a

A male silverback western lowland gorilla along the Pangani Forest Exploration Trail.

Micaela Neal

Animal guide

By **Micaela Neal** Sure it's a theme park, but Disney's Animal Kingdom is also a zoo, the most popular one in the United States. Exotic animals are everywhere, often roaming freely in natural habitats. On the following pages, the location of each animal is abbreviated as follows:

- **AF** = Affection Section
- **AS** = Asia landscape
- **CS** = Conservation Station
- **DI** = Discovery Island
- **DL** = DinoLand U.S.A. landscape
- **FL** = Flights of Wonder
- **KS** = Kilimanjaro Safaris
- **MJ** = Maharajah Jungle Trek
- **OA** = Oasis
- **PF** = Pangani Forest Exploration Trail

Anteater. The 9-foot-long **southern giant anteater** (OA) is the world's largest anteater; its 2-foot-long tongue can lick up 30,000 ants a day. It has the largest claws of any mammal, and uses its huge bushy tail as a blanket.

Antelope. Domesticated by Egyptians as early as 2500 BC, the **addax** (KS) is critically endangered today. It has spiraling horns that grow up to 2 feet long, and tracks rainfall to find grazing spots... The **blackbuck** (MJ) can

run 50 miles per hour. In Hindu mythology, it transports moon goddess Chandrama. Males have ringed, spiraling horns; females smooth curved ones... Chocolate-brown with a purplish sheen, the **bontebok** (KS) is extinct in the wild. Like the blackbuck, both sexes have horns... Topped with twisting 5-foot horns, clashing **greater kudu** (KS) males can get stuck together and starve to death. Their horns are used to make Jewish shofars, blown at Rosh Hashanah... The 2,000-pound, 6-foot-tall **Patterson's eland** (KS) is the world's largest antelope, and is farmed like cattle in South Africa. Its sweet milk takes months rather than days to expire... Only older male **sable antelopes** (KS) are black ("sable"); females and young are reddish-brown. Its scimitar-shaped horns can kill lions. Adults rest in a ring around their young, horns out... The national animal of South Africa, the **springbok** (KS) can run 60 miles per hour and leap 13 feet. It's the most common prey of lions, making up 70 percent of caught meals... Despite its name, the shaggy **waterbuck** (KS) doesn't spend much time in water; it just hides there to escape predators. Its coat is water-repellant... The 8-foot-tall **western bongo** (KS) is the largest forest antelope. The name "bongo"—Swahili for "thirteen"—comes from the 13 white stripes on its sides. Its shyness earns it the nickname "Ghost of the

A male lion overlooks the Kilimanjaro Safaris savanna.

Forest"... The odd **white-bearded wildebeest** (KS) looks like a striped, hairy horse with a cow's horns. It was the partial inspiration for the Beast's face in Disney's 1991 movie "Beauty and the Beast." Herds of wildebeest migrate annually in the world's largest wildlife movement... The **yellow-backed duiker** (KS, PF) has a yellow patch on its rump that erects when alarmed. Duikers ("divers" in Afrikaans) are named for their habit of diving into underbrush when startled.

Bats. With a 6-foot wingspan, the **Malayan flying fox** (MJ) is the world's largest bat. It can eat its body weight in fruit and vegetation daily... With only a few hundred of its kind left in the wild, the **Rodrigues fruit bat** (MJ) struggles to survive on the Indian Ocean's tiny Rodrigues Island.

Beetles. The **dung beetle** (PF) rolls dung into balls. It was sacred to ancient Egyptians; they compared it to the god of the rising sun, who rolled the sun across the sky... The carnivorous but also edible **predaceous diving beetle** (CS) is served roasted and salted in Mexico, often with tacos... The iridescent, multicolored **rainbow scarab** (CS) is a North American dung beetle. The male has a curved, black horn.

Centipede. The carnivorous, 8-inch-long **giant desert centipede** (CS) has a painful, venomous "bite" that is actually a pinch.

Cockroach. The **Madagascar hissing cockroach** (PF, CS) hisses by forcing air through its abdomen breathing pores. Its docile nature makes it a common stand-in for more familiar species in films and television.

Cows. With horns 28 inches around, the **Ankole cow** (KS) has the world's largest horn circumference. Hollow and full of blood vessels, its horns keep it cool... A shy ox, the **banteng** (MJ) was the first endangered species to be successfully cloned... Descended from original Spanish stock left in the southern United States in the early 16th century, the rare **Pineywoods cow** (AF) has since bred without interference along the Gulf Coast.

Cricket. Named for its humped back, the **camel cricket** (CS) doesn't chirp, and in most places is considered a household pest.

Crocodilians. Growing up to 16 feet long, the **American alligator** (CS presentations) has 80 teeth, but usually won't eat animals larger than raccoons. Chirping, yellow-striped young grow to be solid gray-black. Adults bellow, unique for crocodilians... The **American crocodile** (DL) can grow to 18 feet and 2,000 pounds. A 2009 cold spell killed off 150 American crocs in Florida, including Wilma, a famous female on Sanibel Island, the author's hometown... The second largest crocodile at 20 feet long and 2,200 pounds, the **Nile crocodile** (KS) is the most prolific

A baby elephant and her mom roam the Kilimanjaro Safaris grasslands.

predator of humans among wild animals, and kills hundreds to thousands yearly. It can also take on giraffes, young hippos and elephants, and even lions.

Deer. Hunted throughout history for its hide, meat, and impressive antlers, only a few thousand **Eld's deer** (MJ) remain in a 15-square-mile Indian marsh. Its wide, spreadable hooves are perfect for wetland living... The small, exotic **Reeve's muntjac** (OA) is known as the "barking deer" for its danger-signaling call. Males have short antlers and large canine teeth for injuring enemies.

Donkey. According to Christian lore, Mary rode a **Sicilian miniature donkey** (AF) the night Jesus was born. A cross-shaped stripe lays over its back and shoulders. Brother and sister Jack and Jill have been at Animal Kingdom since the park opened in 1998.

Elephant. At 20 feet long and 14,000 pounds, the **African elephant** (KS) is the largest living land animal. Unlike Asian elephants, both sexes have tusks. Its vocalizations include low-frequency rumbles inaudible to people. It lives in matriarchal groups. During mating, the entire herd takes part in a noisy "mating pandemonium"—females and calves mill, circle, wave their trunks, and trumpet up to an hour.

Felines. The largest African predator, the **African lion** (KS) can run 37 miles per hour and leap 40 feet. Its roar can be heard five miles away. It's the most social big cat, forming prides of five to ten individuals; the females hunt while the dominant male defends the pride. It spends 20 hours each day sleeping... The endangered, 660-pound **Asian tiger** (MJ) is the world's largest cat. Its unique stripe pattern is on both its fur and its skin. It can walk silently, leap 30 feet, and drag 3,000 pounds. A group of tigers is called an "ambush"... Able to accelerate from 0 to 70 miles per hour in three seconds—the same rate as the Rock 'n' Roller Coaster at Disney's Hollywood Studios—the **cheetah** (KS) is the world's fastest land animal. It hunts by day, primarily by sight. While chasing prey, its long tail helps it balance and its doglike semi-retractable claws provide traction.

Fish. The **African cichlid** (PF) protects its young by hiding them in its mouth. It keeps water clear by feeding on hippo waste... Using primitive lungs, the eel-like **African lungfish** (PF) can breathe air. It uses its long, fleshy fins to plod through mud. Its ancestors developed true limbs and evolved into early land animals... At up to 10 feet long and 650 pounds, the **Paroon shark-catfish** (DI) is the largest scaleless freshwater fish. It has a shark-like dorsal fin... The chubby, herbivorous **tambaqui** (DI) looks like, and sometimes confused with, the smaller carnivorous piranha.

An Asian tiger slinks through its territory along the Maharajah Jungle Trek.

Frogs and toads. The plump **African bullfrog** (PF, CS) resembles "Star Wars" character Jabba the Hutt. It eats anything it can swallow, and has a painful bite... The largest native toad in the United States, the **Colorado river toad** (CS) is also the archetypal "psychedelic toad"—its venom contains potent hallucinogens and is illegal to possess... The world's most poisonous vertebrate, the **golden poison dart frog** (CS) has enough toxin to kill two bull elephants, or up to 20 humans. It appears to vibrate when it calls. Like all poison dart frogs, it loses its toxicity in captivity due to changes in its diet. Native South American people use poison from dart frogs to coat the tips of blow darts, hence the frogs' "poison dart" names... Named for the pattern on its back, the **hourglass tree frog** (CS) is the only vertebrate capable of laying eggs both on land and in water... The endangered **Puerto Rican crested toad** (CS) was thought to be extinct until 1967... The flat, aquatic **Surinam toad** (CS) looks like a mottled brown leaf. Its odd face has a triangular head and beady eyes, but no tongue or teeth. Young toads develop in pockets on a mother's back; 60-100 emerge as miniature adults.

Giraffes. The tallest land animal and the largest giraffe subspecies, the **Masai giraffe** (KS) is distinguished by jagged, irregular spots. Its strong kick can crush a lion's skull... The most common giraffe in captivity, the **reticulated giraffe** (KS) is distinguished by clear spots separated by a netlike ("reticulated") grid of white lines. Males fight by violently slamming their necks into one another.

Goats. The long flobby ears of the **Anglo-Nubian goat** (AF) earn it the nickname "Rabbit Goat"... With less than 300 remaining in the wild, the rare **Arapawa goat** (AF) descends from two goats released on Arapawa Island by Captain James Cook in 1773. Its face has distinctive black-striped markings. Males have wide, sweeping horns; females have short curved ones... The gentle **Nigerian dwarf goat** (AF) can be trained to use a leash. Its milk is used for cheese and making soap.

Gorilla. At up to 450 pounds, the **Western lowland gorilla** (PF) is the largest and most powerful primate. It's also the most populous gorilla species. A mature male has a silver back and is twice the size of a female. The gorilla has human-like fingernails and fingerprints. It's intelligent, able to learn sign language and can make and use tools. A herbivore, it's the least aggressive primate; its iconic chest-beating is just a display.

Hedgehog. The nocturnal **South African hedgehog** (CS presentations) rolls into a ball when threatened, exposing only its spiny back. Hedgehogs fight by butting heads.

Harmless to man, a Rodriguez fruit bat dines on a melon. Above, a slender-tailed meerkat.

Hedgehog tenrec. Despite looking like a hedgehog, the Madagascar-dwelling **hedgehog tenrec** (PF, CS presentations) is most closely related to two other equally-strange creatures: the golden mole and the elephant shrew. Unlike true hedgehogs, it's active during the day.

Hippopotamus. The most aggressive African animal, the **Nile hippopotamus** (KS, PF) grows up to 15 feet long and 8,000 pounds. It can outrun man and hold its breath for 12 minutes. During the day it rests underwater; at night it grazes on land. Its skin oozes a pinkish, moisturizing oil that acts as a sunscreen. The hippo's closest relatives are dolphins and whales.

Kangaroos. The largest marsupial and Australian mammal, the **red kangaroo** (DI) stands 7 feet and can jump 30 feet. It's farmed for its meat, which is eaten by people around the world, and for its hide, which makes the world's lightest, strongest leather... A nocturnal 'roo relative, the timid **swamp wallaby** (OA) defensively kicks and scratches the faces of predators. It can drink salt water when fresh isn't available... The least common kangaroo in United States zoos, the **Western grey kangaroo** (DI) has a face like a donkey. When threatened, it growls like a dog.

Katydid. At up to 6 inches with a 10-inch wingspan, the **Malaysian giant katydid** (CS)

is the world's largest katydid. It's bright green, camouflaged to look like a leaf.

Lemurs. One of five subspecies of the brown lemur, the **collared lemur** (DI) is distinguished by its reddish beard and orange eyes. It salivates on poisonous millipedes and rolls them between its hands before eating them, to remove toxins... The distinctive, golden-eyed **ring-tailed lemur** (DI) uses its tail as a flag to signal its location and warn of danger. Females are dominant.

Lizards. The slender **black tree monitor** (CS) uses its semi-prehensile tail for stabilization while climbing trees; its tail is two-thirds its full length. It can sense movement 800 feet away... The 4-foot **caiman lizard** (CS) is named for the raised scutes on its back that resemble those of the crocodilian caiman. Its scales are lime green; the more colorful male has a red head. Snails make up most of its diet... The colorful **emerald tree monitor** (MJ) is one of the few social monitor lizards. It removes the legs of stick insects before swallowing the bodies... At 10 feet long and 250 pounds, the **Komodo dragon** (MJ) is the world's largest lizard. Its venom, combined with 57 types of dangerous bacteria that thrive in its mouth, makes its bite deadly. A tenacious predator, it hunts monkeys, horses, smaller Komodo dragons and other animals; in 20 minutes

Micaela Neal

Micaela Neal

The rare okapi (lower right) combines the looks of the Masai giraffe and the zebra.

it can swallow a goat whole. It will eat dead animals too; it can smell them from six miles away. Sometimes, it digs up human bodies from graves and devours them. Intelligent and curious, it plays by sticking its head into boxes and shoes… A foot-long desert herbivore, the **ornate spiny-tailed lizard** (PF) has a turtle-like head and an armored tail. A gland around its nose excretes salt… Named for the horn-like scales on its nose, the 3-foot-long **rhinoceros iguana** (OA) lays some of the largest lizard eggs. A group of iguanas is called a "mess."

Mantids. Camouflaged to look like a brown, decaying leaf, the **Malaysian dead-leaf mantis** (CS) displays colorful wings when threatened… Named for its slender, violin-shaped prothorax, the **violin mantis** (CS) hunts flying insects.

Meerkat. A type of mongoose, the **slen-der-tailed meerkat** (PF) can kill striking cobras. It lives in multifamily burrows that divide duties among individuals; sentry duty is shared by rotating guards. A famous fictional meerkat is Timon, of "Lion King" fame.

Monkeys. The **Angolan black & white colobus monkey** (PF) is named "colobus"—from the Greek word for "mutilated"—because it has no thumbs… With a distinctive puffy crest of fur on its head, the endangered **cotton-top tamarin** (DI, CS) lives in family groups and

mates for life. Its sophisticated communication sounds like chirping… Named for its resemblance to German emperor Wilhelm II, the **emperor tamarin** (CS) sports a long, white, regal mustache… Endangered due to habitat destruction and illegal pet trading, the **golden lion tamarin** (CS) is named for its long, mane-like golden fur… The male **mandrill** (KS) is the largest and most colorful monkey; the more times he has mated, the more vividly colored he becomes. The mandrill is non-aggressive and social; it bares its massive canine teeth as a greeting, not a threat. It beats its hands against the ground when upset. Disney's famous mandrill is Rafiki, the wise shaman in "The Lion King"… The largest, loudest gibbon species, the **siamang** (AS) inflates its throat sac and produces a "hoot" that reaches 113 decibels, nearly as loud as jet aircraft at 100 yards… The territorial call of the **white-cheeked gibbon** (AS) is a crescendo of siren-like "whoops." Males and juveniles are black with white cheeks; females and newborns are blond.

Newt. The armored skull of the **emperor newt** (CS) looks like an emperor's crown. By expanding its rib cage, it triggers a release of poison from orange glands on its body. One newt has enough toxin to kill 7,500 mice.

Okapi. With a giraffe's body, face and ossicones mixed with a zebra's striped rear, the

Young male blackbucks spar in their habitat along the Maharajah Jungle Trek. Many Animal Kingdom creatures display similar natural behaviors, in full view of park visitors.

forest-dwelling **okapi** (KS, PF) is the nearest giraffe relative. It sleeps five minutes a day. Not identified as a species until 1900.

Otter. The world's smallest otter, the **Asian small-clawed otter** (DI) catches prey using its dexterous, non-webbed front paws, unlike other otters. It can stay underwater up to eight minutes. Very social, it loves to play tag and tug-of-war, and can juggle pebbles.

Pigs. With a name meaning "pig-deer," the male **babirusa** (OA) has strange, antler-like tusks that grow up through his muzzle and curl back toward his face. Genetically the animal is closer to a hippo than a pig... With less than 200 left in the wild, the **guinea hog** (AF) is unique to North America. The breed was brought to the United States on slave ships. Thomas Jefferson owned some guinea hogs in 1804... With a name meaning "fat and round," the **kunekune pig** (AF) (pronounced "cooney cooney") is the world's smallest and most sociable pig. A popular pet, it's as smart as a dog... The only grassland pig, the **warthog** (KS), is named for the male's warty facial growths. It defends itself with sharp 6-inch lower tusks and curved 2-foot upper tusks. Pumbaa from "The Lion King" is a warthog.

Rhinoceros. Actually gray, the **black rhinoceros** (KS) has a triangular upper lip used for grasping leaves and a horn up to 4 feet long. It can charge at 35 miles per hour... The largest, most social, and most numerous rhino species, the **white rhinoceros** (KS) weighs up to 5,000 pounds. Its name is a mistranslation of the Afrikaans "wijt" ("wide"), a reference to its broad, grazing mouth.

Rodents. The largest, heaviest African rodent, the **African crested porcupine** (DI)

An infant gorilla explores its Pangani Forest Exploration Trail habitat. Baby animals are commonplace at Animal Kingdom. Its most recent gorilla was born in August, 2014.

A Pineywoods cow contemplates approaching guests at the Affection Section petting zoo. The area keeps its larger animals behind fences, but lets smaller ones roam freely among visitors.

has a crest formed by erect quills; others rise when alarmed. It doesn't shoot its quills; though their barbed tips imbed themselves easily in flesh... The **four-striped grass mouse** (PF) builds a burrow system with runways leading to its regular feeding grounds... Neither a mole nor a rat, the pink, blind **naked mole rat** (PF) is related to the guinea pig. Teeth on the outside of its mouth allow it to dig without swallowing dirt. It is the only mammal that organizes itself into ant-like colonies led by a queen... The long-legged **Patagonian cavy** (OA) looks like a small deer that has the head of a rabbit. It can run 28 miles per hour and leap six feet.

Salamanders. The endangered, aquatic **axolotl** (CS) (ACK-suh-LAH-tuhl) can't breathe air. It was a staple in the diet of Aztecs... The colored glands of the **European**

fire salamander (CS) exude samandarin, a neurotoxin that causes muscle convulsions, hypertension and hyperventilation... With no hind legs, the eel-like **greater siren** (CS) is the most primitive living salamander. It intimidates predators with duckling-like cheeps... At 4 feet long, the aquatic, snake-like **two-toed amphiuma** (CS) is the longest salamander in the United States. It has two rows of razor sharp teeth, and a savage bite.

Scorpions. The aggressive **desert hairy scorpion** (CS) is the largest North American scorpion. It digs to find water... The tropical, docile **emperor scorpion** (PF, CS) is one of the largest scorpions, up to 8 inches long.

Sheep. The rare **babydoll sheep** (AF) originated in the United States in the 1980s. The two-foot-tall adult has fine wool in the class of cashmere... The oldest North American

Timid and shy, a South African hedgehog sits in the glove of a Conservation Station handler. Daily presentations include a variety of small creatures, most of which guests are allowed to touch.

Micaela Neal

Clockwise from top: A colobus monkey, cotton-top tamarin, mandrill and ring-tailed lemur.

sheep breed, the **Gulf Coast native sheep** (AF) was brought to the United States by Spanish colonists in the 1500s. It's now indigenous to portions of all Gulf Coast states... A breed of hair sheep, the **Katahdin sheep** (AF) has a woolless, smooth coat that doesn't need to be sheared.

Skinks. Named for its bright, curled tongue that startles predators, the **blue-tongued skink** (CS) stores food and water in its tail... The largest skink species, the tree-dwelling **prehensile-tailed skink** (CS) uses its tail to maneuver from branch to branch.

Snakes. Named for its tendency to curl into a ball when frightened, the **ball python** (CS presentations) is revered by the Nigerian Igbo people. If one is accidentally killed, the community will build it a coffin and have a

funeral... The **desert rosy boa** (CS) is one of few boas native to the United States. It moves with a slow, caterpillar-like motion... The large, angular snout of the **green tree python** (CS) has heat-sensing pits. The yellow hatchling turns green and nocturnal as an adult; the change may be overnight or take months... The **Kenyan sand boa** (PF) spends 80 percent of its life buried; it suffocates prey by dragging it under the sand. Its diet includes naked mole rats... The largest snake in Puerto Rico, the **Puerto Rican boa** (CS) hangs down in front of cave entrances to catch flying bats.

Stick Insects. Camouflaged to look like a prickly twig, the **giant spiny stick insect** (CS) travels in groups at night... Ten inches long and quite aggressive, the female **Malayan jungle nymph** (CS) lays the largest eggs in

Clockwise from top: A red kangaroo, a bontebok, a pair of Ankole cattle, a Patagonian cavy, a crouching cheetah, a banteng ox.

the insect world. She snaps her spiny back legs together like scissors.

Tarantulas. The burrow of the **Arizona blond tarantula** (CS) goes two feet straight down... The third largest tarantula, the **Brazilian salmon pink tarantula** (CS) is also known (correctly) as the "birdeater"... The aggressive **brown baboon tarantula** (CS) rears up and strikes down repeatedly when provoked. It is eaten by baboons... The agile **Indian ornamental tarantula** (CS) can catch flying insects in midair... A **Mexican red rump tarantula** (CS) stars in the 1955 sci-fi movie "Tarantula," in which a giant one terrorizes a desert... The bite of the **Mombasa starburst tarantula** (PF) can put you in the emergency room.

Tortoises and turtles. The primitive **Asian brown tortoise** (DL) provides more parental care than any other tortoise... The third-largest tortoise, the **African spurred tortoise** (KS queue) is named for its spurred back legs. It's regarded by some African cultures as a mediator between men and gods... The male **Eastern box turtle** (CS) has red eyes; the female has brown eyes... The tiny **Egyptian tortoise** (CS) is only 5 inches long... At 5 feet long, the **Galapagos tortoise** (DI) is the world's largest tortoise. It lives 150 years. Males "fight" by stretching their necks; the highest stretch wins... The endangered **gopher tortoise** (CS) digs deep burrows that it shares with other animals. These burrows can be 50 feet long and 10 feet deep. It lives

Micaela Neal

Micaela Neal

Clockwise from top: A Nile hippopotamus, a brilliant male caiman lizard, a Komodo dragon, a dark gray American crocodile, a pale gray Nile crocodile, an axolotl salamander.

in the southeast United States… The flat, pliable shell of the **pancake tortoise** (PF) lets it squeeze into tight openings. When threatened, it doesn't withdraw into its shell; instead it dashes for cover… The **South American yellow-footed tortoise** (CS) makes a sound like a baby cooing… Named for the web-like pattern on its shell, the **spider tortoise** (PF) is critically endangered.

Zebras. Black with white stripes, the **Grant's zebra** (KS) is the most abundant zebra. It "barks" instead of neighs. Members of a herd sleep in turns, so some are always alert… White with black stripes, the **Grevy's zebra** (PF) is the rarest and largest zebra; it's twice the size of the Grant's zebra. It brays like a donkey. A herd's foals are left in male-led

"kindergartens" while their mothers get water. It was used in circuses in ancient Rome.

Birds. Animal Kingdom has more than 140 species of exotic birds on display. Most make their home in the aviaries of the Pangani Forest Exploration Trail and the Maharajah Jungle Trek, though you'll also find them in the Oasis entrance area, along the Discovery Island trails, and beside the queue and in the habitats of the Kilimanjaro Safaris ride.

Barbet. Named for the thick bristles under its bill, the **bearded barbet** (PF) has a call that's a growling *scrawk*.

Cormorant. A skilled fisher, the **white-breasted cormorant** (KS) is also known by its unusual mating ritual—it courts by wrapping

Clockwise from top: A male babirusa, a white-bearded wildebeest antelope, a warthog, a white rhinoceros, a rhinoceros iguana, a Galapagos tortoise, a black rhinoceros.

its neck around a potential mate. A group of cormorants is called a "gulp."

Crow. The smart **pied crow** (FW) drops stones onto ostrich eggs to crack them open.

Doves and pigeons. Rare in zoos, the fig-eating **African green pigeon** (PF) also likes carrion and dried antelope blood... The **Bartlett's bleeding-heart dove** (MJ) is

All photos: Micaela Neal

An Nicobar pigeon (top), green-winged dove (above left) and African green pigeon (above).

named for the crimson patch on its breast, which looks like a bloody wound... Common in rainforests, the male **green-winged dove** (MJ) courts females by dancing and bobbing his head... A close relative to the extinct dodo, the **Nicobar pigeon** (MJ) has long hackles around its head that look like dreadlocks... The male **pied imperial pigeon** (MJ) displays by inflating his neck and hopping in place... The world's largest pigeon, the turkey-sized **Victoria crowned pigeon** (MJ) is named after Queen Victoria. It has an unusual booming call, and sports a lacy white-tipped crest.

Ducks. Actually a misnamed duck, the **African pygmy goose** (PF) is the smallest African waterfowl. Its favorite food is water lilies... The hot-headed **common shelduck** (OA) honks like a goose... A mother

Mandarin duck (MJ) coaxes her ducklings to jump to the ground from their tree hollow nest; she then leads the youngsters to water. A pair of Mandarin ducks are a traditional wedding gift in Korea... Used as a "guard dog" in its native Tibet, the **ruddy shelduck** (MJ) is large, loud and aggressive.

Eagles and hawks. The national symbol of the United States since 1782, the **bald eagle** (FW) is named using an older usage of the word "bald," which means "white headed." Its high-pitched chirps are often replaced by the more impressive cries of the red-tailed hawk in movies and television shows, most ridiculously in the tongue-in-cheek opening credits of the Comedy Central program "The Cobert Report." Some wild bald eagles nest near Disney property... Unlike other birds of

A **Mandarin duck** (above), turkey-sized Victoria crowned pigeon (top) and West African crowned crane (left).

prey, the **Harris hawk** (FW) hunts in coordinated groups, earning it the nickname "the wolf of the sky." It nests in saguaro cacti.

Goose. One of highest-flying birds, the **bar-headed goose** (MJ) migrates seasonally over the Himalayas.

Hoopoe. A relative of kingfishers, the **green wood hoopoe** (PF) climbs trees like a woodpecker.

Hornbill. Named for its loud call, the **trumpeter hornbill** (FW) sounds like a crying human child.

Junglefowl. The colorful **green junglefowl** (MJ) is metallic green, but many other colors too. Some of its feathers are bronze, and its comb and wattles are pastel blue, pink and purple.

Kingfisher. Using its large red and black bill, the **blue-breasted kingfisher** (PF) excavates nests in termite mounds.

Ostrich. At 8 feet tall, the **common ostrich** (KS) is the world's largest bird. Capable of reaching 45 miles per hour when it runs, it is the fastest two-legged land animal; kicks from its strong legs can kill a lion. Contrary to popular belief, an ostrich doesn't "hide" by sticking its head in sand; it just lays its head on the ground.

Owls. Named for the "horns" on its head (tufts of feathers), the **great horned owl** (FW) has golden eyes that are among the largest and most powerful in the animal kingdom... The rainforest-dwelling **spectacled owl** (FW postshow) sometimes hunts sloths. The female screams like a steam-whistle.

Partridge. The small, rotund **crested wood partridge** (MJ) uses its feet to probe for insects and seeds.

Parrots. Able to associate human words with their meanings, the intelligent **African gray parrot** (FW) develops a large vocabulary over its 50- to 70-year lifespan... The second largest macaw, the **green-winged macaw** (DI, FW) is twice the size of the similar-looking scarlet macaw... Named for its olive-green feathers that resemble Spanish army fatigues, the **military macaw** (OA) eats clay from riverbanks for nutrients... Only the male **plum-headed parakeet** (MJ) has a purple head; the female's is gray. The bird likes to mimic electronic tones... Better known as the "galah"—Australian slang for "loud-mouthed idiot"—the **rose-breasted cockatoo** (FW) has a puffy pink crest... The national bird of Honduras, the noisy **scarlet macaw** (OA, FW) has the longest tail feathers of any macaw.

Clockwise from top: A bearded barbet, two red-fronted macaws, and a green-winged macaw.

Peafowl. The sexes of the **Java green peafowl** (MJ) look similar, though only the male has a 6-foot tail. Known as the dragonbird, it hunts venomous snakes.

Pelican. Social, group-hunting **pink-backed pelicans** (KS) will reuse the same nests for years, until they collapse.

Pheasant. One of the largest pheasants, the male **great argus pheasant** (MJ) is over 6 feet long. It is named after the mythological Argus, the Greek hundred-eyed giant, for the eye-like pattern on its flight feathers.

Seriema. An odd terrestrial bird of prey, the **red-legged seriema** (FW) has long legs and can run 15 miles per hour. It kills its prey by slamming it repeatedly against the ground.

Songbirds. The **black-collared starling** (MJ) feeds by blindly probing dense vegetation with an open bill... The **chestnut-breasted malkoha** (MJ) is a large cuckoo that—unlike most cuckoos—builds its own nest and raises its own young... The male **fairy bluebird** (MJ) is iridescent blue and black; its call is a liquid, two-note *glue-it*... The usually timid **hooded pitta** (MJ) displays excitement by bowing, bobbing its head, flicking its wings and fanning its tail... Known for its acrobatic somersaults, the **racquet-tailed roller** (PF) is named for its teardrop-tipped double tail streamers... One of the first recordings of birdsong was of a **Shama thrush** (MJ), in 1889 on an Edison wax cylinder.

Swans. With the longest neck of any swan, the **black swan** (OA) has a loud, bugle-like call. It is featured on the flag and coat of arms of Western Australia... The **black-necked**

A pink-backed pelican feeds in groups by herding fish. Females reuse their nests for years until they fall apart. Below, a black swan and a black-necked swan.

All photos: Micaela Neal

swan (OA) is the largest South American waterfowl. Parents piggyback their young to keep them warm and safe from predators.

Toucan. With a huge bill making up a third of its length, the **toco toucan** (FW preshow) is the world's largest toucan. Sacred to South American natives, it's seen as a conduit between the living and spirit worlds.

Turacos. The world's largest turaco, the **great blue turaco** (PF) has tail feathers that are prized for making good luck talismans... The **white-bellied go-away bird** (PF) is named for its call, which sounds like *g'away*.

Wading birds: cranes. Distinguished by its halo-like golden crown and red-and-white face patch, the **East African crowned crane** (FW) stomps the ground to kick up insects... The world's tallest flying bird, the **Sarus crane** (MJ) is 6 feet tall and has an 8-foot wingspan. It's revered and considered a symbol of marital fidelity in India... Unlike the East African crowned crane, which has a white cheek with a red top, the **West African crowned crane** (DI, KS queue) has a red cheek with a white top. It trumpets loudly at sunrise... With only 5,000 left in the wild,

the **white-naped crane** (MJ) is the only crane with pink legs.

Wading birds: flamingos. A flamingo gets its pink color from its diet. It feeds by holding its head upside-down in the water to filter out food. A group of them is called a "flamboyance"... The world's largest and palest flamingo, the **greater flamingo** (KS) can live up to 75 years... The smallest, pinkest and most numerous flamingo, the **lesser flamingo** (DI) performs ritualized group displays of marching, head-flagging and wing salutes.

Wading birds: spoonbills. Disney often lets its spoonbills breed and raise their young in front of guests... When courting, the white **African spoonbill** (OA) clacks its bill... Often mistaken for a flamingo from a distance, the **roseate spoonbill** (OA) has vivid pink plumage that's tinged with red and orange.

Wading birds: storks. Named for Turkish Governor Bey El-Arnaut Abdim, the small **Abdim's stork** (DL) is seen as a harbinger of rain and good luck to native Africans... Though a young **painted stork** (DI) can loudly call to attract its parents, by 18 months it is practically voiceless. A threatened chick

All photos: Micaela Neal

Clockwise from top: A male taveta golden weaver, great blue turaco and East African crowned crane. Right (clockwise): A lesser flamingo, roseate spoonbill, painted stork, lappet-faced vulture, white stork, and African jacana.

disgorges its food and plays dead... Named for its bill, which is topped with a yellow saddle-like growth, the **saddle-billed stork** (DI, KS) is depicted in Egyptian hieroglyphics... The legend of storks bringing human babies to homes comes from the migration of the **white stork** (DI) from Africa to Germany every spring, a common time for human births. The bird nests on German chimneys.

Other wading birds. The oversized feet of the **African jacana** (PF) allow it to walk on water plants. Females are dominant, which is rare for birds... The neon-yellow-billed **black crake** (PF) pecks parasites off of hippos and warthogs... Named after the German "hammerkopf" ("hammerhead") because of

its odd-shaped head, the **hammerkop stork** (PF) is actually not a stork at all, and is more closely related to pelicans. It builds tree nests up to 4 feet across, which are strong enough to support a man's weight... Named for its distinctive yellow mask, the **masked plover** (MJ) has a small yellow claw hidden in each wing; a false myth says the claws inject venom. The bird sleeps for only a few minutes each day.

Vultures. The foul-smelling nest of the colorful **king vulture** (FW) wards off predators. In the Mayan calendar it represents the 13th day of the month... The most powerful, aggressive and widespread African vulture, the **lappet-faced vulture** (DI) will eat live prey. Skin folds (lappets) hang off its head.

Micaela Neal

Weavers. To compete for females, male **taveta golden weavers** (PF) build oval nests over water; a female chooses her mate based on how impressed she is by his nest-building efforts and abilities... The **white-headed buffalo weaver** (PF) is named for its tendency to follow African buffalo and eat the insects it disturbs.

Water Parks

Sunny and soaked. Giggles, laughs and squeals fill the air at Blizzard Beach and Typhoon Lagoon, Walt Disney World's two water parks. Close your eyes and you'll notice a unique serenade of happy people enjoying life. Why? Because it's just so much fun to play in water, especially with family or friends.

The United States has more than a thousand water parks, but few offer such an immersive experience as these two. Plastic culverts appear to be streams and rivers, their steel supports hidden under forested hills. An offbeat mix of pop songs fills the air. Everywhere you look is spic-and-span, and everywhere you go is family oriented.

How do the parks compare? Sunny and spacious, Blizzard Beach has longer and faster slides with many height minimums, a better preteen spot and a wackier theme. Shady and intimate, Typhoon Lagoon offers bigger waves, a better toddler spot and a wider variety of attractions, only two of which have height minimums.

Best reasons to go. Whether it's a multi-person tube slide, a side-by-side mat race or simply a makeshift Monkey in the Middle game in a pool, Disney's water parks offer many ways for you to interact with your partner, children or friends... Disney's lazy rivers let you drift away in dappled shade, and there's hardly ever a wait... The scariest attraction in all of Walt Disney World is Summit Plummet at Blizzard Beach. The most fun? For many, it's the wave pool at Typhoon Lagoon... Unlike the passive "here we are now entertain us" attractions common in theme parks, water-park experiences often demand you get off your rear end and actually do something. Such as swim, slide, splash, snorkel or surf.

Worst aspects of the parks. The food. Except for some creative snacks, the food at Disney water parks is overpriced and

Sandy beach. The authors' daughter soaks up the sun in front of Melt-Away Bay at Disney's Blizzard Beach water park.

uninspired... The lines. If you don't plan your day right, long waits for the water slides can definitely put a damper on your fun... The stairs. Tummy not toned? Butt not buff? You'll be huffin' and puffin' as you climb Disney's many hot, sunny stairways.

Planning your day. Regardless of whether you visit Blizzard Beach or Typhoon Lagoon, be prepared for a day that wears you out. Though both parks are smaller than any Disney theme park and require less walking, their attractions are much more physical. Queue lines often wind up stairs, sometimes in direct sun. What's more, you'll be outside all day. At either park, the only indoor spots are the restrooms and the gift shop.

Cooler days. Colder days can be more enjoyable; except for the 70-degree pools of Typhoon Lagoon's Shark Reef, all of Disney's water-park water is heated to 80 degrees.

Tickets. As of August 2015, an adult ticket to either park costs $58. Children ages 3–9 pay $50. Those under 3 are admitted free.

If you already have a ticket to a Disney theme park, you can use it to get into a water park by upgrading it with what Disney calls the Water Park Fun & More option. Allowing you unlimited visits to both water parks for the duration of your theme-park ticket, it adds $64 to the cost of a one-day Magic Kingdom ticket, $72 to a longer Magic Kingdom ticket, and $72 to any other theme-park ticket regardless of length. Water park annual passes cost $110 for adults, $90 for children. Most prices are discounted for Florida residents and members of the military.

See also **Tickets** in the chapter **Walt Disney World A–Z**

What to bring with you. We say travel light—just a cap or hat, wallet or purse, sunscreen and swimsuit (Disney does not allow suits with rivets, buckles or exposed metal; or string-back or thong suits). Consider rash guards to protect skin from burns and scrapes, especially for children. A towel is a must, but you can rent one for $2. Want to bring more? Disney will let you haul in a cooler, food, small toys, strollers, towels and

At the surf pool. Despite their family focus, Disney's water parks are a haven for teenagers. Blizzard Beach has thrilling slides; Typhoon Lagoon the largest surf pool in the United States.

wheelchairs, but not alcohol, boogie boards, glass containers, tubes or water toys.

How to avoid the crowd. The two most popular water parks in the world, Blizzard Beach and Typhoon Lagoon each attract about 8,000 visitors a day. Such a crowd often makes empty beach chairs tough to find, and creates lines for water slides that are just ridiculous. At a theme park few people would wait in line 40 minutes for a 10-second ride, but at a water park people do it every day. To avoid that crowd, follow these four steps:

First, arrive at your park before it opens. On the day you visit your water park, get there 45 minutes before it officially opens, which is typically 9 or 10 a.m. This gives you time to park, walk to the entrance, scan your ticket or MagicBand, and rent a locker and towels at a relaxed pace, while still staying ahead of the masses (at both water parks, the entrance usually opens 15 minutes early).

Snare your chairs, then hit the slides. You'll have your choice of chairs, including some by the pool and others back in the shade. Waiting lines at the slides will be short or nonexistent, so you'll do them all before noon.

Do pools and rivers after lunch. Same for playgrounds. They all get crowded on busy days, but none of them ever have lines.

If there's a storm, wait it out. Most guests will leave, unaware that in Florida a thunderstorm usually lasts no more than an hour, and is almost always followed by a clear sky. Once it appears you'll have your park almost all to yourself.

Sitting down. Each park has hundreds of beach chairs and their use is complimentary. But those in good spots get taken very early.

Seats for sale. Want to pay for a spot? You can. Both parks rent reserved covered patios or decks, but they cost a pretty penny—$325 a day for up to 6 guests ($175 after 2 p.m.) with additional guests (up to 10) $25 each. For that you get 6 cushioned chairs including 2 lounge chairs, a table, a cooler stocked with water, a locker rental, towels, refillable soft-drink mugs and an attendant who stops by every 20 minutes. Though way overpriced, these spots can be handy for families with very young or elderly members. They often sell out in the summer. To reserve one call 407-939-7529 up to 90 days in advance.

Best seats. The best spot at Blizzard Beach is patio No. 4, a secluded, shady alcove near the chairlift, preteen area and toddler zone. The best spots at Typhoon Lagoon are cabanas No. 2, which is very shady, next to a large strangler fig and overlooks that park's

Toboggan Racers. Guests race each other on several slides. Regardless of skill or strategy, the heaviest rider usually wins.

lazy river; and No. 3, a wood deck under a large umbrella that sits on the bank of the river and has a nice view of the surf pool. For $55 you can reserve a much smaller spot— two lounge chairs, a small table and a beach umbrella. These usually aren't conveniently located, and offer no real views.

Drinking up. Addicted to caffeine? Disney sells a refillable soft-drink mug at both water parks for $10.75. It's good for just one day, but can be renewed for another day for $6.50. Want alcohol? Both parks sell beer and mixed drinks, but with no all-you-can-drink option.

Seasonal closures. Both parks close for annual maintenance. Typhoon Lagoon usually shuts down in November and December, Blizzard Beach in January and February.

What if it rains? If lightning is within five miles of a Disney water park it will close its rides and clear its pools. The attractions reopen afterward.

Rain checks. If the attractions are closed for 30 minutes or more, a guest who has been inside a park less than four hours can get a rain check good for a future entry anytime within the next year; all members of that party then have to leave. Rain checks are issued from the park's Guest Relations stand or any ticket booth. Disney will not issue a rain check if the park entry was with a previous rain check.

Family matters. Almost nowhere offers a better place for families to bond than a Walt Disney World water park. There are, however, a few issues parents should be aware of.

Age restriction. Visitors under the age of 14 must be accompanied by an older guest to enter either park.

Life jackets. Disney offers use of standard life jackets at no charge. The parks do permit guests to bring in water wings, even though those swimming aids are easy to puncture.

Lost children. Easy to identify by their distinctive uniforms and name tags, water park staffers and life guards ("cast members") take lost children to marked areas (usually picnic tables) at the front of each park. To avoid losing their children, some families arrange before their visit to meet in a specific spot at a specific time just in case family members lose track of each other.

Rafts and toys. Neither water park allows guests to bring in rafts or other air-filled toys. The parks provide rafts, tubes and mats at rides that are designed for them.

Swim diapers. Infants and toddlers who are not potty-trained are required to wear plastic swim diapers. Gift shops sell them.

The view from the beach. Summit Plummet rises high above Melt-Away Bay, a swimming pool that appears to be created by streams of melting snow. Bobbing waves wash through it.

Blizzard Beach

Sunny park has many thrilling slides, inspired preteen spot

A metling ski resort. A towering ski jump, snow-covered ski slopes and a mountainside chairlift create the illusion that this whimsical water park is a melting snow-ski resort. But hiding within it is a hot-weather haven, an assortment of pools and slides that the whole family can love. Carved out of a forest of pine trees, Blizzard Beach is within walking distance of Disney's Coronado Springs Resort, about a mile from Disney's Animal Kingdom theme park. Disney's Winter Summerland miniature golf course sits right in front of it, off the same parking lot. The second-most-popular water park in the world, Blizzard Beach attracts nearly 2 million guests a year.

Attractions. Blizzard Beach has two intense body slides, two tube slides and two mat slides. There's also a bobbing wave pool, a family raft ride, a lazy river, a toddler area and a great preteen spot. Below, each attraction is rated from one to five stars (★) based on how well it lives up to its promise. A checkmark (✔) indicates an author favorite.

★★★★ ✔ **Cross Country Creek.** Lined with evergreens, this shady floating stream circles the park as it flows under bridges, over springs, past a squirting snowmaking machine and through a cave with dripping water that's icy cold. Seven entry points offer complimentary tubes. Photopass photographers stand in the water. *25 min (roundtrip). 3000 ft, 15-ft wide, 2.5-ft deep, max speed 2 mph. Fear factor: None.*

★★★ **Downhill Double Dipper.** You'll drop down a short tunnel, drop down again, then shoot through a curtain of water... all as you race against someone next to you in these steep, enclosed tube slides. Alpine cowbells cheer you on as you leave the gate; a finish-line scoreboard flashes your time. Thrill-seeking youngsters love it. Pull up on your tube handles just before the catch pool to fly across the water. *6 sec. 230 ft, 50-ft drop, max speed 25 mph. Fear factor: You feel out of control. H eight min 48 in.*

★★★ ✔ **Melt-Away Bay.** Nestled against the base of Mt. Gushmore, a 90-foot snow-capped peak, this swimming pool appears

Short and sweet. Despite leaving his gate seven-tenths of a second later, a boy still beats her girlfriend in a race down the Downhill Double Dipper, Disney's fastest tube slide.

to be created by streams of melting snow. Bobbing waves wash through the pool for 45 minutes of every hour; a sandy sunbathing beach lines one side. The pool's shallow beachside entry makes it easy for young children to enter it. *Unlimited time. 1 acre. Fear factor: None.*

★★★★ ✔ **Runoff Rapids.** Banked curves make riders feel like bobsledders on these three banked tube slides. Two open slides allow two-person tubes; an enclosed one-person slide is inside a dark plastic pipe that's lit by pin lights, which gives it a Space Mountain effect. Reached by a back-of-the-park climb up 127 steps, Runoff Rapids is worth every huff and puff. *600 feet. Fear factor: Enclosed tube may feel claustrophobic.*

★★★★★ ✔ **Ski Patrol Training Camp.** This inventive collection of experiences for preteens is a gem. At Fahrenheit Drop, kids hold on to a sliding T-bar that drops them into an 8-foot pool. The ride has two bars, which move over the water at different heights. At the Thin Ice Training Course, overhead rope grids help kids hang on as they walk over slippery floating "icebergs." As for tube slides, Snow Falls has wide ones for the timid, Cool Runners has short bumpy ones. A short enclosed body slide, Frozen Pipe Springs plops riders out a few inches above its pool.

Children can see each ride before choosing it. *Unlimited time. Fear factor: None.*

★★★★ ✔ **Slush Gusher.** Looking like a gully covered in slushy snow, this steep body slide starts off slow but gives fully grown riders some airtime off its second drop; the heavier the rider, the wilder the flight. A viewing area at the end has covered bleachers. Visible from most of the park, Slush Gusher is easy for children to evaluate ("I am definitely doing that!") before they get in line. *2 drops. 11–13 sec. 250 ft, 90-ft drop, max speed 50 mph. Fear factor: Scary after the second drop. Height minimum 48 in.*

★★★★ ✔ **Snow Stormers.** You lie face-first and speed down S-curves on these fast high-banked mat slides, three side-by-side courses that make it easy for family or friends to race each other. To win your race, keep your elbows on your mat and your feet up. As you careen up corners water splashing in your face makes it tough to see; a horizontal line on the wall helps you keep your bearings. *15–20 sec. 350 ft. Fear factor: Fast, disorienting.*

★★★★★ ✔ **Summit Plummet.** The scariest ride in all of Walt Disney World, this very steep 12-story body slide is Disney's true tower of terror. Lying down at the top of what looks like a ski jump, you cross your arms and feet then push yourself over the edge.

She's not chicken. Though her boyfriend backed out moments earlier, a teenage girl braves Summit Plummet; a guy gets airborne on Slush Gusher, a snow-gully body slide.

The sky and scenery blur as you fall; the water around you roars as you splash down. The impact can send much of your swimsuit where the sun never shines; wear a T-shirt or rash guard to avoid stinging your skin.

One of the tallest and fastest slides in the United States, Summit Plummet has no exit stairway; those who chicken out at the last second squeeze back down the crowded entrance steps in what cast members privately refer to as the "walk of shame." The launch tower rises only 30 feet above Mt. Gushmore and just 120 feet over the park, but it seems much taller. The fall is so intense even some of its designers don't care for it. During its construction, Disney Imagineer Kathy Rogers "made the mistake of going up the stairs and looking down. I thought, 'There's no way I'd put my body in there!' I did it once and said, 'Done!'"

It's easy to determine if Summit Plummet is a ride you can handle, as it's viewable from throughout the park. Is your child going, but you're not? There's an observation deck and viewing area at the end of the slide; a display shows rider speeds. *9–10 sec. 360 ft, 66-degree 120-ft drop, max speed 60mph. Fear factor: All of it. Height min: 48 in.*

★★★★★ ✔ **Teamboat Springs.** Nowhere else at Disney do so many families have such a good time together—all ages laugh and smile on this, the world's longest family raft ride. Sitting in a raft the size of a plastic kiddie pool, up to 8 people slide down a high-banked course together, spinning on tight curves which toss them up on steep walls. Thirty holes in each raft's bottom edge make sure derrieres get soaked; a 200-foot ride-out area passes under a dilapidated roof that's dripping cold water. There's often a minimum of four riders per tube, so smaller groups sometimes ride together. *2 minutes. 1,200 feet. Fear factor: Rough ride; unavoidable water sprays.*

★★ **Tikes Peak.** Gentle slides, rideable baby alligators and an ankle-deep squirting "ice" pond highlight this unshaded preschooler playground. Though much of it is paved concrete, there is a fountain play area, a little waterfall and a scattering of sand boxes, as well as lawn chairs, chaise lounges and picnic tables. Still, there are few ways for parents and children to spend time together. Children should wear water shoes; the pavement can get very hot. *Unlimited time. Fear factor: None. Height maximum: 48 inches for slides.*

Headed high. A chairlift makes it easy to reach the top of the park's Mt. Gushmore; tubers take it easy on Cross Country Creek, a shady lazy river.

★★★★ ✓ **Toboggan Racers.** Inspired by amusement-park gunnysack slides, this straight, 8-lane mat slide races guests down its two dips face first. Since multiple riders go at once, whole families and large groups of friends can compete against each other. More joyful than scary, Toboggan Racers is fun for all ages. To go really fast, push off the starting line quickly then slightly lift the front of your mat so it doesn't plow in the water. Regardless of technique, the heaviest rider usually wins. *10–20 sec. 250 ft. Fear factor: None.*

Characters. Goofy often greets guests next to the park's Lottawatta Lodge fast-food spot and sometimes wanders nearby walkways. He's usually out for 30 minutes at a time. Expect the shortest lines late in the afternoon.

Food. Three Blizzard Beach fast-food spots and two seasonal ones offer hamburgers, hot dogs, sandwiches, salads and personal pizzas ($8–11). Snack stands sell hot mini donuts, cotton candy, funnel cakes, ice cream treats, nachos and snow cones. Other spots have coffee, tea, pastries, beer and rum drinks. Have a sweet tooth? If they're fresh, get the hot mini-donuts. Disney will let you bring a cooler and food into the park, but not glass containers or alcohol.

Shopping. Located in the park's Alpine Village entrance area, the Beach Haus stocks a decent selection of beachwear, swimwear and sportswear from Billabong, Oakley, O'Neill, Quiksilver, Roxy and Speedo. Across from the park's changing rooms, the Shade Shack sells beach towels and sundries while North Pearl offers Japanese akoya pearls in their oysters (5–10 millimeters, $16), pearl settings and pearl jewelry.

Fun finds. Barrels of "Instant Snow" (from the Joe Blow Snow Co.) line the walkways to Slush Gusher, Summit Plummet and Teamboat Springs; authentic snow-making equipment (from the Sunshine State Snow Making Co.) sits alongside Cross Country Creek and the queue for Toboggan Racers… A beach chair with an umbrella and a skier with a leg cast are depicted in the "ancient" drawings inside the Cross Country Creek cave; the Northern Lights shine through the cave's ceiling. For more fun finds see our companion book, "The Complete Walt Disney World Fun Finds & Hidden Mickeys."

Little squirts. A preschooler plays on a squirting alligator at Tikes Peak; a pre-teen swings over swaying icebergs at the Ski Patrol Training Camp.

Key facts. *ATM:* At the Guest Relations kiosk at the park entrance. *Cooler policy:* Coolers with up to two wheels are allowed. Blizzard Beach does not store medication coolers. *First aid:* To the right of the Beach Haus gift shop, in the Alpine Village entrance area. *Guest Relations:* A kiosk just outside the park entrance. *Life jacket use:* Complimentary. At Snowless Joe's, Alpine Village. *Lockers:* Rented at the Beach Haus and Snowless Joe's in Alpine Village ($8–$10 per day plus $5 deposit; stands typically open 15 minutes before the stated park opening time). Lockers are located next to Snowless Joe's, near the Ski Patrol Training Camp, and alongside the Downhill Double Dipper. *Lost*

Blizzard Beach average wait times

ATTRACTION	9A	10A	11A	Noon	1P	2P	3P	4P	5P	6P	7P	8P
Chair lift	0	5	10	20	25	25	20	15	15	10	10	5
Downhill Double Dipper	0	5	5	10	10	15	20	15	10	15	5	5
Fahrenheit Drop	0	5	5	5	5	5	10	10	10	5	5	5
Runoff Rapids	0	0	10	15	15	15	15	15	15	15	15	5
Slush Gusher	0	5	15	20	25	20	25	10	15	20	10	5
Snow Stormers	0	0	10	10	15	15	15	15	15	15	15	5
Summit Plummet	0	5	20	30	40	35	35	20	30	25	20	10
Teamboat Springs	0	5	10	20	30	25	25	10	20	15	10	5
Thin Ice Training Camp	0	5	5	5	5	5	10	10	10	5	5	5
Toboggan Racers	0	5	5	10	10	10	15	10	10	15	5	5

Wait times: averages of random days, summers 2011–15

Relaxing, racing. A raft the size of a kiddie pool spins down curves and up banks on the 1,200-feet-long Teamboat Springs. Below, two teens compete on Toboggan Racers; the park closed to new visitors on a busy summer day.

children: Taken to a marked, staffed table in Alpine Village, on the walkway between the changing rooms and Lottawatta Lodge food spot. There's sometimes a sandwich board there that reads "Lost Children." *Lost and Found:* At the Guest Relations kiosk, outside the park entrance. *Parking:* Free. *Phone number:* 407-560-3400. *Strollers and wheelchairs:* Allowed but not available for rent. The park's sandy areas are tough to wheel through. *Towel rentals:* At the Beach Haus and Snowless Joe's, Alpine Village ($2 each). *Disney transportation:* Disney buses shuttle guests to Blizzard Beach from all Disney-owned hotels, the Walt Disney World Swan and Dolphin and Disney's Animal Kingdom theme park. Officially there is no service from Blizzard Beach to other parks or Disney Springs, but all buses that stop at Animal Kingdom also stop at Blizzard Beach.

Let's build a ski resort. Disney's history books tell of a freak snowstorm that hit central Florida in the mid-1990s. And of how, mesmerized by the snow, the company's "imagineers" had a brainstorm—"Let's build a ski resort!"

Just a few days later, they had done just that. They built a small mountain and topped it with a ski jump as well as bobsled, slalom and sledding runs. And they had finished things off with an adjacent Alpine Village, complete with a hotel and—of course—a large gift shop.

When the snow stopped they realized the foolishness of their efforts—they were, you know, in the Sunshine State—but before the imagineers could go drown their sorrows they spotted a lone alligator, still blue from the cold, which had somehow strapped on a pair of skis and was careening down their ski jump. Flying wildly through the air, this giddy "Ice Gator" landed on their restrooms, crashed into their gift shop, and emerged with a smile.

Watching him, the imagineers realized that their failed ski resort would make a great water park. They quickly reconfigured the ski jump as a body slide, redid the ski runs into mat and tube slides, and turned a convenient creek into a lazy river.

Naming its new creation Blizzard Beach, Disney opened it to the public. On April Fools Day, 1995.

Calm. Before the waves begin, the Typhoon Lagoon surf pool is a calm, peaceful spot perfect for anyone wanting to take an easy dip in the water...

Typhoon Lagoon

Laid-back shady park has something for everyone

Storm-struck tropics. With an atmosphere that's one part Hawaii and two parts "Gilligan's Island," Typhoon Lagoon is a shady, silly escape. Thorough landscaping immerses guests in a tropical environment. Located along the eastern side of Disney World property, the 61-acre park is located across the street from Disney Springs, within easy access of Interstate 4. Typhoon Lagoon is the most popular water park in the world, drawing more than 2 million visitors a year.

Attractions. Below, each attraction is rated from one to five stars (★) based on how well it lives up to its promise. A checkmark (✔) indicates an author favorite.

★★ **Bay Slides.** These two short children's body slides are in the calm left corner of the surf pool, an area called Blustery Bay. One slide is uncovered with a few gentle bumps; the other has a 4-foot tunnel. Though kids disappear on the walkway up to the slides parents have no need for concern; its 10 steps lead only to the slides. *10 sec. 35 ft, max speed 7 mph. Fear factor: None. Height max: 60 in.*

★★★★★ ✔ **Castaway Creek.** Lined with palms, this shady lazy river circles the surf pool. Expect to get misted, drizzled on and, as you float into a cave, maybe completely drenched. Shoreline sights include three crashed boats and the Ketchakiddee Creek playground; the Mt. Mayday Trail suspension bridge crosses high above you. The creek splits in two for a short distance. There's never a wait, though the creek gets crowded on summer afternoons. *25 min (round trip). 2,100 ft, 15-feet wide, 3-ft deep, max speed 2 mph. Fear factor: None.*

★★★★★ ✔ **Crush 'n' Gusher.** Powered by water jets as well as gravity, these three flumes have both lifts and dips, just like roller coasters. The wildest one, Pineapple Plunger has three short tunnels and two peaks. Coconut Crusher has three tunnels of various lengths. A slightly longer track, Banana Blaster includes one long and two medium-length tunnels, but only has two-person rafts. To stay in control, push your feet down into the front of your tube. For a wilder time, lift your feet up. Riding Pineapple Plunger? Lean

Crazy. ... but once its waves start (each with a mighty "WHUMPH!") the pool becomes chaotic, and ideal for guests who long to be hit by walls of rushing water.

back to catch some air. Ride together if there are no more than three people in your group; in general the more people on a tube, the faster and more fun it is.

The attraction is meant to be the hurricane-ravaged remains of the Tropical Amity (say it slowly) fruit-packing plant. The flumes are its spillways, which cleaned fruit before it was shipped. Aptly named Hideaway Bay, the attraction's 5-acre setting is tucked behind Typhoon Lagoon's main locker area. Besides the flume rides, it includes a shallow gradual-entry swimming pool lined with beach chairs and chaise lounges—a perfect place for parents and toddlers to play. *30 sec. 420 ft, max speed 18 mph. 2-, 3-person tubes. Covered queue. Fear factor: Chaotic, disorienting; few visual reference points. Height min 48 in.*

★★ **Gangplank Falls.** Though it doesn't last long, this big-tube slide has its moments, as riders go under waterfalls and through a small cave. The rafts hold four, maybe five people. To make Gangplank Falls worthwhile, ride it early or late in the day, when there's little or no wait. *30 sec. 300 feet, avg speed 7 mph. 4-person rafts. Fear factor: Rough ride; unavoidable water sprays.*

★★ **Humunga Kowabunga.** Did Bart Simpson name these three identical enclosed body slides? Maybe so; they are his type of thing: short, steep, straight dark drops. A shady viewing area lets Homer and Marge types watch others whoosh into the run-out lanes. *7 sec. 214 ft, 60-degree 50-foot drop, max speed 30 mph. Fear factor: Scary but brief. Height min 48 inches.*

★★★ **Keelhaul Falls.** Tubes slowly build speed on this short gentle C-curve, the park's tamest full-size tube slide. Heavier guests glide up the side of the slide just before it ends. *50 sec. 400 feet, avg speed 6 mph. Fear factor: None.*

★★★★★ ✔ **Ketchakiddee Creek.** This large and elaborate geyser-and-volcano area is a kiddie water park all its own. For tiny tots a 100-foot palm-lined tube slide has three little dips; a surrounding area offers bubbly small fountains and ankle-deep streams and pools. More adventurous toddlers hurl themselves down two slip 'n' slides (cushy 20-foot mats with 20-degree drops) while older kids battle each other at the S.S. Squirt, an oversized sand sculpture with swiveling water cannons. Nearby water hoses shake, shimmy and squirt atop a 12-foot-tall Blow Me Down boiler. The area has shady chairs and picnic tables; many families build sand-castles. Crowds often pack Ketchakiddee Creek in the afternoon, as Disney doesn't enforce its posted rule that children who play

Peaceful paradise. Lush landscaping surrounds Castaway Creek, a palm-lined lazy river that takes floaters on a tropical journey around the park.

here be shorter than 48 inches. *Unlimited time. 18 activity spots. Fear factor: None. Height max 48 in for slides.*

★ **Mayday Falls.** A triple vortex, this swervy "white water" tube slide triple vortex can spin you around, but it's not as much fun as it should be. Since its water is just an inch or two deep and its bottom is rippled concrete, the ride pounds your rear end like some sadistic fitness machine. There's one small waterfall. *30 seconds. 460 feet, average speed 10 mph. Fear factor: Rough ride.*

★★★ **Mount Mayday Trail.** Hidden at the back of the park, this fern-and-hibiscus-lined scenic walkway goes over a suspension bridge high above Castaway Creek, then winds up Mount Mayday to the impaled Miss Tilly shrimp boat. There's nothing to do, but it is pretty. Tiny streams splash over the walkway, which begins at the entrance to the Gangplank Falls tube slide (look for the sign) and ends at the top of the Humunga Kowabunga body slide. The trail is usually vacant even on the most crowded days, as few visitors know it's here. *Fear factor: None.*

★★★★★ ✔ **Shark Reef.** You look down on tropical fish as you swim over an artificial reef in this chilly saltwater snorkeling pool. Sights include "smiling" rainbow parrotfish, Dory-esque blue tangs, rays and

(quite passive) little leopard and bonnethead sharks. Hold still as you float to have the fish come close to you. For the most time above the reef take the scenic route, in the uncrowded water away from the overturned tanker. A resting area sits in the middle of the pool. Want to watch someone else snorkel? Do it underwater, through the windows of a real capsized tanker. *Unlimited, though swimmers are not allowed to reverse their course. Fear factor: Cold saltwater. Complimentary use of masks, snorkels, life vests, changing areas and outdoor showers.*

An optional Supplied Air Snorkeling experience (Reef Adventure, ★★★★★ ✔) includes use of an air tank, regulator, flippers and instruction and usually takes place away from the crowd. It's run by the National Association of Underwater Instructors. Fees go to a conservation program. *30 minutes. Ages 5 and up, $20. Late April to late August).*

★★★★ ✔ **Storm Slides.** Winding down a steep wooded hill, these shady, high-banked body slides are long and curvy. Each of the three offers a different experience: Jib Jammer is totally open to the sky; Rudder Buster has a small tunnel; Stern Burner includes a longer, dark tunnel. Don't want to ride? You can wait for those who do on unshaded bleachers at the catch pool. 25

Fish spotters. Shark Reef snorkelers swim and float in a crystal-clear, cold saltwater pool past a (real) overturned tanker. The water is filled with fish, rays and small passive sharks.

seconds. 300 feet, maximum speed 20 mph. Fear factor: May frighten young children.

★★★★★ ✓ **Surf Pool.** Body-surfable waves sweep down this large pool, making it a popular teen hangout as well as a fun spot for families. Few people body surf but many gather to be knocked around by the waves, the height of which varies throughout the day. A chalkboard in the front of the pool shows the daily schedule. *Unlimited time. Waves 2–6 feet. Fear factor: Waves intimidate, can topple you even in shallow areas. Young children should stay with parents.*

The 2.5-acre area resembles a tropical cove, with a real sandy beach, bubbling "tide pools" and an artificial sand bar about 50 feet "offshore." The 115-by-395-foot wave pool is the largest in North America in terms of guest capacity, water volume and wave height. Waves are created in the closed-off deep end of the pool, as 12 backstage collection chambers repeatedly push 80,000 gallons of water through two underwater doors.

Surfing lessons are often held in the pool early in the morning, before the park opens. See also **Sports and Recreation** in the chapter **Walt Disney World A–Z.**

Characters. Lilo and Stitch (from the 2002 movie "Lilo & Stitch") greet parkgoers until 4 p.m. in front of the Singapore Sal's gift shop. They do not appear together, but rather alternate for 20 minutes at a time. Expect the shortest lines after 3 p.m.

Food. Typhoon Lagoon fast-food spots sell fish, hamburgers, hot dogs, small pizzas, salads, sandwiches, fried shrimp and turkey legs ($8–$11). The Leaning Palms fast-food counter has the greatest variety.

Snack stands have cotton candy, funnel cakes, hot mini donuts, nachos, pretzels, smoothies and faux ice cream. The hot mini-donuts are an indulgent treat. Other stands offer coffee, tea and pastries; a converted scooter truck serves beer and mixed drinks.

The park has two picnic areas, though you can set up a meal virtually anywhere. Disney will let you bring a cooler and food into the park, but not glass containers or alcohol.

Shopping. Located near the park entrance, Singapore Sal's gift shop has beach towels, sundries, swimwear and a good selection of young-adult apparel from Billabong, Oakley, O'Neill, Quiksilver and Roxy (the authors' daughter shops here for her college clothes). At Shark Reef, a Pearl Factory stand sells Japanese akoya pearls in their oysters (5–10mm, $16), pearl settings and jewelry.

Splashes and squirts. New Jersey's Amanda Mathus, 14, braces for the splash on the Stern Burner Storm Slide. Dads join in water-cannon fun at Ketchakiddee Creek.

Fun finds. Nautical flags hanging above the park entrance spell out "WELCOME TO TYPHOON LAGOON." Discreetly hanging to their right, other flags spell out "PIRANHA IN POOL"... Feel sadistic? In front of the Happy Landings snack bar, the props of outboard motors waiting to being serviced can be aimed at passing floaters on Castaway Creek, and can squirt them with water... Long-forgotten Typhoon Lagoon mascot Lagoona Gator lives in the Board Room, a shack in front of the surf pool. Look inside to find a

poster for the movie "Bikini Beach Blanket Muscle Party Bingo," a flyer for a concert by The Beach Gators ("So cold blooded, they're hot!"). For more fun finds see our companion book, "The Complete Walt Disney World Fun Finds & Hidden Mickeys."

Key facts. *ATM:* At Singapore Sal's gift shop, near the park entrance. *Cooler policy:* Coolers with up to two wheels are allowed. Typhoon Lagoon does not store medication coolers. *First aid:* Behind the Leaning Palms

Typhoon Lagoon average wait times

ATTRACTION	9A	10A	11A	Noon	1P	2P	3P	4P	5P	6P	7P	8P
Crush 'N Gusher	0	5	10	10	10	10	15	15	15	10	10	5
Gangplank Falls	0	5	20	30	40	35	35	20	30	25	20	10
Humunga Kowabunga	0	0	5	5	5	10	15	15	15	10	5	5
Keelhaul Falls	0	0	10	10	10	15	15	15	15	15	15	5
Mayday Falls	0	0	10	15	15	15	15	15	15	15	15	5
Shark Reef	0	0	10	10	10	10	15	10	15	10	5	5
Storm Slides	0	5	5	10	10	10	15	10	10	15	5	5

Wait times: averages of random days, summers 2011–15

All smiles. At right, a young boy enjoys the Mayday Falls tube ride. Below, Keelhaul Falls is the park's tamest full-size tube slide, while the family-style Gangplank Falls has rafts that hold up to five people.

fast-food restaurant. *Guest Relations:* A kiosk just outside the park entrance. *Life jacket use:* Complimentary. At Singapore Sal's and High 'N Dry Towels, both near the park entrance. *Lockers:* Rented at Singapore Sal's near the park entrance ($8–$10 per day plus $5 deposit), which typically opens 15 minutes before the official park opening time. Most lockers are nearby; some are at Shark Reef. *Lost children:* Taken to Safe Harbor, a staffed area outside of Singapore Sal's gift shop, near the park entrance. There's sometimes a sandwich board there that reads "Lost Children." *Lost and Found:* At the Guest Relations kiosk, outside the park entrance. *Parking:* Free. *Phone number:* 407-560-7223. *Strollers and wheelchairs:* Allowed but not available for rent. The park's sandy areas are tough to wheel through. *Towel rentals:* At Singapore Sal's, near the park entrance ($2 each). *Disney transportation:* Disney buses shuttle guests to Typhoon Lagoon from all Disney resort hotels. Before 10 a.m. the buses drop off guests at Typhoon Lagoon and then continue to Disney Springs; after 10 a.m. they stop first at Disney Springs.

There is no direct bus service between Typhoon Lagoon and any Walt Disney World theme park.

A topsy-turvy tropical playground. According to Disney lore, the Placid Palms resort was built on Florida's volcanic Atlantic coastline, in a tranquil Florida valley alongside a Florida mountain. Right. Anyway, over the years the valley experienced a few tremors and rumblings but overall remained, well, placid. Then in 1955, Hurricane Connie struck the Placid Palms head-on. The storm impaled a shrimp boat on the volcano, destroyed an adjacent fruit processing plant, blew in crates of fireworks from a nearby island (where at the time a Mr. Merriweather Pleasure put on a nightly fireworks show) and cut off the harbor from the Atlantic, trapping saltwater fish at a reef. Despite these setbacks, Placid Palm managers remained totally cool. Grabbing some sign paint, they renamed their place the Leaning Palms and re-opened it as a topsy-turvy playground: a water park. Typhoon Lagoon opened on June 1, 1989.

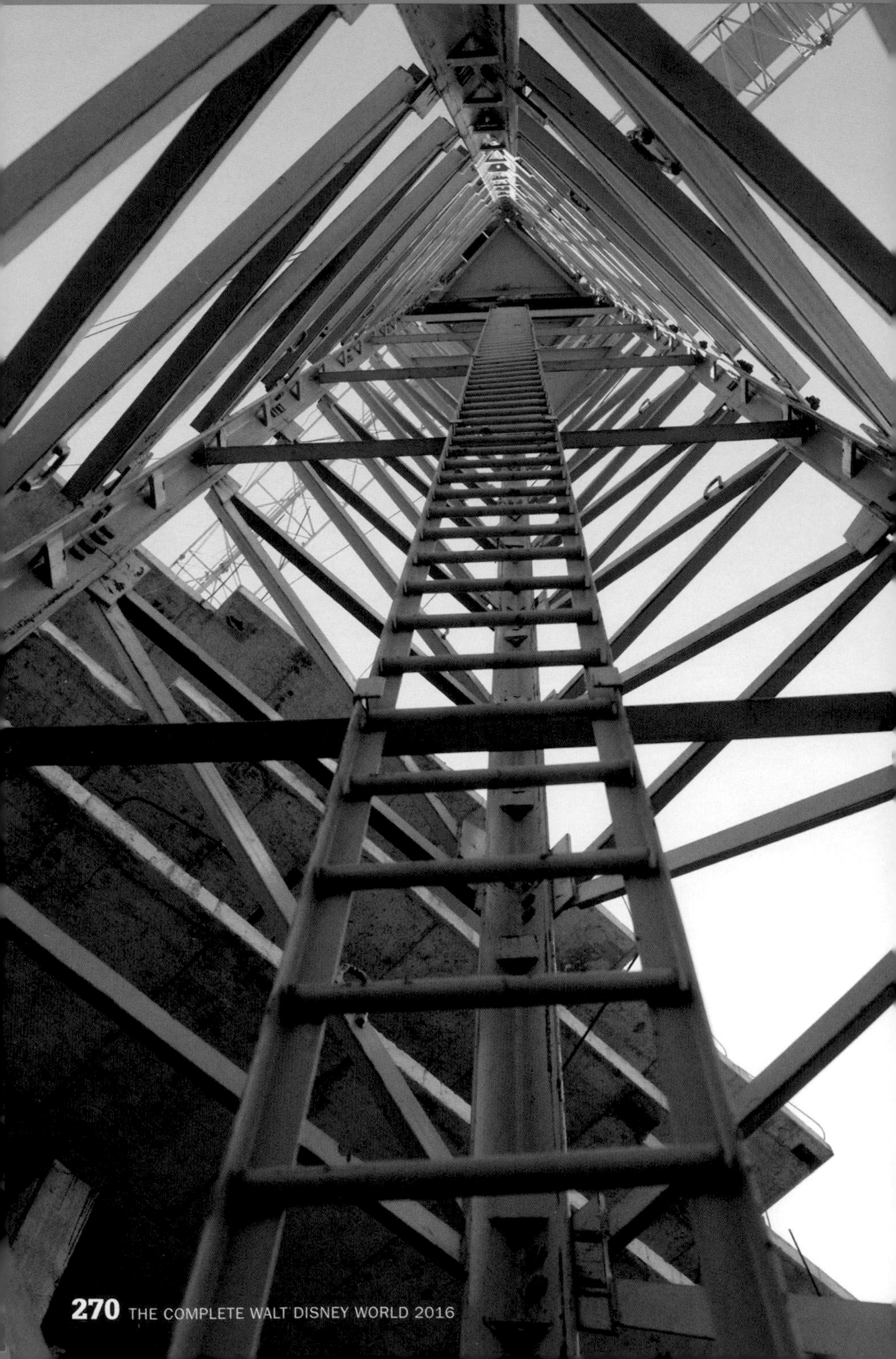

Disney Springs

A whole new world. Eighteen million a year. That's how many visitors Disney is hoping come each year to this reimagined and greatly expanded dining, shopping and entertainment complex, which for the last few decades was known as Downtown Disney. Eighteen million. That's 50,000 a day. Project managers say it's costing the company $350 million, for which it's getting a million-square-foot development with its own dedicated highways, bus lanes, pedestrian bridges and parking garages that finally end the problem of finding an open space. When finished—the official done-date is August 16, 2016, though at press time that was starting to look iffy—Disney Springs will have 150 retailers and restaurants, the latter of which will include 10,000 dining seats.

Decidedly more refined than other Disney shopping efforts, the new complex will offer a diverse mix of what Disney describes as "premium, affordable luxury and fast fashion" retailers and "sophisticated dining diversions" designed to appeal to young singles and conventioneers as well as the traditional Disney family crowd.

Four neighborhoods. Basically a huge outdoor mall, Disney Springs will consist of four connected "neighborhoods."

Town Center. The heart of the project, this main area will look like a small Florida town from the 1920s, its tree-lined walkways paved with sea shells, its buildings reflecting the Mediterranean Revival, Craftsman and industrial architecture of the period. Flowing through the area will be streams fed from convincing artificial springs, which at night will be lit by floating lights. Set behind a large central depot for Disney buses, Town Center will include 10 performance stages, allowing for lots of live entertainment, and be anchored by a small indoor mall.

Totally new from the ground up, Town Center is being built on land that was last used for bus stops and parking lots, stretching from the existing Planet Hollywood restaurant to the World of Disney store.

Other areas. Another new section, the Landing sits behind Town Center on the site of the former Pleasure Island, and includes a mix of waterfront bars and restaurants. Downtown Disney's old Marketplace and West Side areas stay put, with minor updates.

Highways, bridges and parking spaces. Out front, infamously gridlocked Buena Vista Drive has been completely redone, with a central dedicated bus lane and 10 lanes for automobile traffic. Three new pedestrian bridges span the new road, as does a bridge for an entirely new highway that leads directly to Disney Springs from Epcot Center Drive and Interstate 4. Replacing parking lots that held 1,500 cars, two new parking garages hold four times that many.

Best of Disney Springs. If it lives up to its promise, Disney Springs will be the most creative and entertaining shopping area in Central Florida, perhaps in the entire state. By design, every new restaurant serves good food and every new shop is a good one—either an unusual one-of-a-kind place, the flagship location of a chain, or at least one that offers something different from others in its chain. Young adults will love the area, with its modern stores such as Uniqlo, lively street entertainment and spirited nightspots such as STK Orlando and the Edison.

Worst of Disney Springs. *I'm melting! I'm mellllting!* You'll feel like the Wicked Witch of "The Wizard of Oz" if you're here on a summer afternoon, as yet again Disney's California designers have created an area that would be ideal for their state but is so unsuited for Florida; our summer heat and humidity will broil these sun-soaked walkways every May through September. There are other issues, too. Most of the new places offer only pricey goods and grub, as Disney continues to skew upscale. Except for a Walt Disney-themed restaurant in the Landing the new areas lack much of a traditional "Disney" feel, as nearly every eatery and shop comes from an outside business. Finally, when complete the entire Disney Springs area may simply be too big—too exhausting to fully enjoy in one visit, too impossible to track down all the spots that would most appeal to you, too easy to get lost in its meandering design.

Bus drop. For those arriving by bus, the entrance to Disney Springs will be at Town Center. A "Waterworks" fronts the area, behind it walkways meander though a huge outdoor space.

Know before you go. The following information is accurate as of August, 2015:

ATMs. The Marketplace has three ATMs: near Tren-D, Ghirardelli and inside World of Disney. The West Side has two: at the House of Blues Co. Store and near the Characters in Flight balloon. Disney will add more ATMs into The Landing and Town Center.

First aid. For now at the Marketplace aspirin and Band-Aids are sold at World of Disney and the stroller and wheelchair rental counter; in the West Side at DisneyQuest Emporium and the Cirque du Soleil box office.

Guest Relations. A new office will open in Town Center in mid-2016. Until then it's in the Marketplace *(adj to Arribas Bros., 8:30a–11p Sun–Thr, to 11:30p Fri, Sat)* and on the West Side *(DisneyQuest Emporium 9a–11:45p).*

Mailbox. In the Marketplace, next to the fountain in front of World of Disney.

Parking. Free. Two garages hold 6,000 vehicles. Open spaces are remarkably easy to find, thanks to a series of electronic signs. One at the entrance of each garage shows you the number of open spots inside it by floor; signs inside lead you to those floors, the rows where those spots are and the spaces themselves. There's a parking lot at the west end of the complex, near the Cirque du Soleil theater and House of Blues complex.

Valet parking. In front of the Cirque du Soleil theater *($10 2 hrs, $20 day, after 1:30p).*

Stroller rentals. Soon in Town Center, for now at the Marketplace by Once Upon a Toy; on the West Side at DisneyQuest Emporium *(single $15/day, double $31, plus $100 dep).*

Disney transportation. Buses serve all Disney hotels *(initially noon–mid at the Marketplace, changing mid-2016 8a–2a at Town Center).* Boats shuttle guests from Old Key West, Port Orleans and Saratoga Springs to The Landing, docking between Jock Lindsey's Hangar Bar and Paradiso 3, and from one side of Disney Springs to the other *(9a–1:30a).* The new Marketplace dock is tough to find, hidden behind Rainforest Cafe on a walkway to Saratoga Springs.

Wheelchair and scooter rentals. Soon at Guest Relations at Town Center, for now only at the Marketplace next to Once Upon a Toy and at the West Side at the DisneyQuest Emporium *(wheelchairs $12 day, ECVs $50 day, each w/ $100 deposit).*

About this chapter. The upcoming reviews and descriptions are based on information available as this book went to print in August, 2015; the authors live just a few miles from Disney Springs and stopped by it daily for months (we know that West Side Starbucks

© Disney

Indoor market. As this concept art shows, Town Center will include both indoor and outdoor areas, with small flowing waterways everywhere. It should open by August, 2016.

well). Some places are reviewed in two categories; most often because it's a restaurant that switches to a clubby atmosphere at night or an entertainment spot that includes a restaurant.

Town Center

Shops and merchandise. The dominant retail area of Disney Springs, Town Center will consist of primarily large stores focused on national and international brands.

NEW! Edward Beiner. Miami-based store promises "the world's most original, authentic and innovative designer, fashion and high-performance eyewear" for "today's aspiring lifestyle-oriented customer"—from brands such as Cartier, Chanel and Tom Ford.

NEW! Lilly Pulitzer. Colorful Palm Beach womenswear, beachwear and resort wear from this popular designer name.

NEW! L'Occitane en Provence. French body, face, fragrance and home products.

NEW! Pandora. Quality charm and bead bracelets; fine, costume jewelry; creative, colorful Disney items.

NEW! Tommy Bahama. Island-inspired sportswear and swimwear for men and women, often in eclectic prints.

NEW! UGG. U.S. producer of Australian-style boots that became trendy in the '90s due

to their comfy twin-faced sheepskin. Today's brand also includes slippers, shoes, blankets, apparel, home furnishings and handbags.

NEW! Uniqlo. Town Center will be home to the flagship store of this fast-growing Japanese clothier. Uniqlo ("YOU-nee-klo") sells low-cost but "highly finished" quality-fabric shirts, jeans and other basics that come in few styles but a stunning array of colors. Expect some unique Disney styles.

NEW! Zara. Town Center will also include the flagship store of this popular chic clothing shop, which specializes in knockoffs of the absolute-latest designer styles for adults and children. The Spanish-based chain is known for needing just one week to develop an item, produce it and get it into its stores, as well as pulling it just one week later if it doesn't sell.

And maybe.... Other retailers rumored to be a part of Town Center when it opens are Apple, Anthropologie, Cole Haan, Dior, Free People, Paul Frank, Japan's Superdry and London's Topshop/Topman. Also in the works is a major makeup store.

Restaurants and food. As of presstime only a couple eateries have been announced so far for this all-new area, but so far so good.

NEW! Chef Art's Florida Fish Camp. Expect amazing Southern seafood and probably fried

© Disney

Great boats, good food, dumb prices. The waterfront Boathouse is overpriced, but its spectacular collection of boats out back makes it tough to pass up. Maybe just a drink...

chicken at this celebrity-chef restaurant. It's the brainchild of Chef Art Smith, a two-time recipient of the James Beard Award whose resume includes the founding of such acclaimed eateries as the Southern Art & Bourbon Bar in Atlanta. Smith has plenty of ties to the Sunshine State—a Florida native, he completed a culinary internship at Walt Disney World while a student at Florida State; later he was the personal chef to two Florida governors. *In the Springs area of Town Center, behind T-Rex. Opens late spring 2016.*

REDONE! Planet Hollywood Observatory. On the drawing board for years, a major makeover of the world's most popular Planet Hollywood is finally here, and promises to bring this oh-so-'90s icon into the modern world. Oddly, it'll do that by going back in time, becoming a 1920s Observatory straight out of the machine-age of star travelers such as Buck Rogers and Flash Gordon. Outdoor changes include a dining terrace, an outdoor bar and live entertainment; inside the restaurant's open dining room will take on the look of a planetarium, with stars and constellations on its ceiling. Remaining will be Planet Hollywood's displays of movie memorabilia, including the blue gingham dress worn by Judy Garland in 1939's "The Wizard of Oz." As for the food, it will probably stay under-rated

and pretty good. On board for sure will be the signature Chicken Crunch appetizer, a recipe from cofounder Demi Moore that's secretly coated in crushed Cap'n Crunch. The restaurant will re-open mid-2016. *Lunch, dinner. 11a–mid (summer 11a–2a). $14–$30 (children $8). Seats 720. Info: 407-827-7827.*

Counter service. Blaze will be a lifeline— an affordable, air-conditioned oasis of good food with lots of places to sit.

NEW! Blaze Pizza. Three minutes is all it takes to cook a pizza at this innovative eatery. Just like at a Subway or Moe's, you direct your pizza makers as they move down an assembly line, building your thin-crust pie to your specifications. It's then flash-fired in an open-flame oven for 180 seconds. Other offerings include salads, blood-orange lemonade and s'mores pies. This Blaze will be larger than others, the chain's 5,000-square-foot flagship. *11-inch pies $5–$10. 40 toppings. Seats 200. Opens mid-2016.*

NEW! Sprinkles. Homemade cookies, cupcakes and slow-churned ice cream. In front of the shop, a Cupcake ATM dispenses boxed treats 24 hours a day. *In the Springs area of Town Center, behind T-Rex. Opens early 2016.*

And maybe.... Rumored eateries for Town Center include Argo Tea, Shake Shack and a chocolate shop.

Entertainment. Take yourself higher, then dance to the music. (Sly Stone, you kids you.)

NEW! World of Coca-Cola. The world's most famous soft drink gets the royal treatment at this three-story complex (which may not actually be named World of Coca-Cola), which celebrates its history, taste and cultural significance. Based on a similar spot in Atlanta, expect a huge collection of Coke memorabilia, a bottling line, a chance to taste-test over a hundred Coca-Cola products from around the world. Beverages will be served on a rooftop patio. *Between Planet Hollywood and STK Orlando. Opens mid-2016.*

★★★★★ ✔ **Street performers.** Bands and musicians perform near the Boathouse and The Edison. Performance times vary by day and time of year. No charge.

The Landing

Pleasure Island reborn. Sitting on the same land as Disney's old Pleasure Island nightclub district, The Landing completely reimagines the space as the active waterfront of Disney's 1920s Florida town, one focused mainly on shops and restaurants. Yet there's still nightlife here, most notably at The Edison but also at restaurants such as STK Orlando and Morimoto Asia that turn clubby at night. Electronic ambient music is shared with the adjacent West Side.

Shops and merchandise. Small boutique shops fill these retail spaces, which are meant to complement the surrounding restaurants and nightlife.

NEW! APEX by Sunglass Hut. This modern sunglass store has an environmental simulator that lets you compare polarized to non-polarized lenses and check out a pair of glasses in different light conditions and wind speeds; standing in front of it is a great way to cool off from the heat. A Build-Your-Own-Oakleys station lets you mix and match lenses, frames, icon and ear socks. Brands include Oakley, Ray-Ban, Maui Jim.

NEW! The Art of Shaving. High-end shaving supplies and grooming products. Barber Spa indulgences include the Royal Shave, which starts off with a hot towel and protective oil; follows with hot shaving cream, a traditional straight razor, a shave with the grain then against, a second hot towel with lemon oil, an after-shave mask of minerals and oils to deep-clean your pores, a cold towel with lavender oil, a hydrating toner and after-shave balm. *Haircut $40. Shave $35–$55. Both $55–$80. Appts (407) 560-8320.*

NEW! Chapel Hats. Cute fashion-forward yet retro hats for women, men and children, including beanies, berets, cadets, cloches, drifters, fedoras, fascinators, top hats. Ideal for cosplay at The Edison. Vintage tin ceiling.

NEW! Erwin Pearl. Quality enamel and semi-precious fashion jewelry and accessories marked by style, creativity, sometimes whimsy. Exclusive Van Gogh collection includes beautiful purses, scarves, watches.

NEW! Havaianas. Brazilian brand is the original rubber flip-flop. Colorful, sometimes pricey styles for both sexes, all ages. Make-your-own station. A competitor to Sanuk.

NEW! Sanuk. Lightweight casual shoes and squishy comfortable flip-flops, some made from the same foam as yoga mats. Funky but functional; adored by wearers. A competitor to Havaianas.

NEW! The Ship's Store. Nautical-themed apparel, mugs, board games, sunglasses, watches. Boat, outboard-motor models; cute rubber ducks are priced beyond retail. Blue-blood vibe. At The Boathouse restaurant.

Shop for Ireland. Small store has unusual mix of Irish apparel, cookbooks, infantwear, mugs, music. At Raglan Road.

NEW! Sound Lion. Hi-tech headphones, docking stations, ear buds, speakers as well as "education in digital music applications that improve the listening lifestyle." Included is a Skull Candy store-within-a-store; other brands include Beats by Dre, Sennheiser. Everything can be tested, clerks are willing to open any box. Known for its customer service and matching the prices of its competitors.

Restaurants and food. Lots of new places to eat here, most of them priced at the top of the food chain. Meanwhile, the best value is at tried-and-true Cookes of Dublin.

NEW! ★★★ $$$$$ The Boathouse. A first-class decor and friendly servers can't overcome the sinking feeling you get at this lakeside tourist trap. Though its dining areas are filled with antique outboard motors and other eclectic and fascinating nautical items, you pay through the nose to sit by them. Its $50 steaks come with nothing—no salads, no sides. An ear of corn is $8; a kids fruit cup $10. High-quality seafood and ambitious finishes are wasted in entrees that are often too salty, too small or too bland. If you go, afterward take a walk out on the dock; the historic boats back there are beautifully restored.

© Disney

Tony toppers. Fashionable boutique Chapel Hats carries fashion-forward fedoras and other hats for women, men and children, many with a distinctive retro flair.

11a–11p, $19–$62 (children $10). Meals for two $60–$135, raw bar $4–$100. Bar menu to 2a, $15–$29. Uses 2 credits on the Disney Dining Plan. Seats 600. Direct reservations, information at 407-939-2628 (939-BOAT).

★★ **$$$$$ Fulton's Crab House.** A terrific exterior and interior decor belie the fact that this onetime standout is past its prime. Tired seafood dishes seem stuck in the '70s, unaware of modern places like Morimoto Asia and Chef Art's Florida Fish Camp just a few steps away. On the plus side, you'd never guess this 20,000-square-foot steamship isn't the real thing. From the outside it looks just like an old paddlewheeler (except for the, *ahem,* absence of paddlewheel) and inside its narrow halls, creaky floors and wooden ceilings suggest a long life on the water. Actually it was built by Disney as a restaurant and despite appearances is not floating. If you do eat here, ask to sit in of the semicircular Constellation Room on the second deck; its ceiling glows blue at night. *Lunch $11–$29 (children $8–$14) 11:30a–4p. Dinner $25–$65 (children $8–$14) 4–11p. Seats 660 (24 outside). Direct reservations: 407-934-2628.*

NEW! ★★★★★ ✔ **$$$$$ Morimoto Asia.** Expect unusual entrees including unequaled seafood dishes, fantastic sushi, a trendy atmosphere and ridiculous prices at this Asian fusion restaurant, assuming it's anything like others run by "Iron Chef" star Masaharu Morimoto (the current Morimoto in New York City; the earlier Morimoto XEX in Tokyo). In other words: perhaps your best meal ever, at a price you'll long to forget. A two-story layout includes terraces, a grand hall, private rooms and waterside seating. An exhibition kitchen showcases Asia's dining traditions, including street-food stalls, Peking Duck carving and dim sum. The restaurant will be managed by the Patina Restaurant Group, which also runs the eateries in Epcot's Italy pavilion. *Opens late 2015.*

EXPANDED! ★★★★ ✔ **$$$$ Paradiso 37.** A loud yet laid-back vibe combines with good burgers, fries, burritos and guacamole to make this waterside spot a better value than the nearby Boathouse, and a better choice than STK Orlando or Morimoto Asia unless you're just out to go big. Its menu represents the street food of the 37 countries of the Americas—in other words the street food of Miami, where the owner is from. Options include Chilean salmon and an outstanding little appetizer: Central American "crazy corn," roasted on the cob and covered in cheese. A bar reps 37 tequilas including some at $50 a shot. Paradiso doubled its seating in 2015, adding more outdoor dining and a new outdoor stage. *$14–$38 (children $8) 11:30a–12p, to 1a Thr–Sat. Seats 500 (inc 200 outside, 20 at bar). Live entertainment nightly 6:30p–11p. Direct reservations 407-934-3700.*

★★ **$$$$ Portobello.** This lovely little hideaway doesn't totally disappoint, though you'll find better Italian spots in the theme parks. OK entrees sound better than they taste; many lack flavor, sandwiches have lots of bread. Service is sometimes sharp, sometimes sloppy. Decor is very Italian; seating is comfortable and spacious. *Lunch 11:30a–3:45p $9–$19 (children $5–$11). Dinner 4–11p $10–$29 (children $5–$11). Seats 414, inc 86 outside. Direct reservations: 407-934-8888.*

★★★★★ ✔ **$$$$ Raglan Road.** Why go someplace more expensive? Raglan Road gives you everything you'd hope for at a vacation restaurant—unique food, memorable atmosphere, fine service—at a price way less than all of the new places surrounding it. This isn't an aspiring lifestyle-oriented-upscale-concept tourist trap, this is the real thing, a real Irish restaurant run by real Irish people who know Irish food and drink and know how to serve it. Its master chef is Kevin Dundon, the proprietor of Ireland's Dunbrody Country House Hotel and Restaurant, where he also runs a cooking school. He's cooked for many celebrities in his career, including Queen Elizabeth and singer Bono. His experience shows: Raglan Road's food is a step beyond tradition—pub classics have distinctly gourmet touches. The decadent bread pudding—big enough to share—comes with creamers of butterscotch and creme anglaise. Guinness is on tap; other choices include an ample selection of other beers and ales, and a mead that tastes like warm alcoholic honey. The antique decor includes two 130-year-old bars from Ireland with traditional leaded-glass dividers. Ask to sit in the loud main room to see the Irish dancers and band. *Lunch 11a–3p $15–$26. Dinner 3–11p $15–$29 (children $7–$14). Live band, table step-dancers evenings Mon–Sat Two outdoor bars. Children welcome. Seats 600, inc 300 outside. Direct reservations: 407-938-0300*

NEW! **STK Orlando.** This clubby chophouse chain is known for its swanky atmosphere, loud music, knowledgeable servers and exorbitant prices. Nationwide the average tab per person is $127—the price of a prime seat at La Nouba. Expect superior steaks, salads and sides, from menus where everything is a la carte, even sauces; steaks come in small, medium and large. Opened late 2015 in the space that once held the famed Comedy Warehouse, it's the only Disney Springs spot with rooftop dining. *$25–$75. Opens 2016.*

Counter service. Three distinct choices here, all worth considering:

★★★★★ ✔ **$ Cookes of Dublin.** Flaky and hot. That's what you'll get at this authentic Irish hole-in-the-wall, whether you order the hand-battered fish and chips or the comforting beef and lamb pie. Other choices include battered sausages, burgers and salads. Everything's "almost-to-order" so expect a short wait. The tiny spot is run by Raglan Road, which it butts up against. Stop by during an off time to have a shot at a table. *11a–11p. Seats 33, addl stand-up tables.*

NEW! ★★★★ **$ Erin McKenna's Bakery NYC.** This place is a dream for people with dietary restrictions; everything is gluten-free, soy-free, dairy-free and egg-free, and sweetened with unprocessed sugar or agave. Staff are happy to meet particular needs. Cookies, cupcakes, doughnuts and other goodies are baked throughout the day. Unfortunately, the only place to sit is on a bench out in the heat. *10a–11p. Pastries $2–$5. No seating.*

NEW! ★★★★ ✔ **$ Tea Traders Café.** Tea lovers will feel like kids in a candy store here. Unusual selections include frozen teas as thick as milkshakes, spiked teas and baked treats made with tea leaves. Brews use ingredients from gardens around the world, hand-blended and freshly prepared. Daily hands-on brewing demonstrations and traditional Chinese tea ceremonies entertain; if you're a tea novice helpful staff will offer suggestions and free samples. Teas served at counter or to go. Also packaged teas, teapots, accessories. *10a–11p Sun–Thr, 10a–11:30p Fri–Sat. Teas $4–$9, pastries $1–$2. Seats 6 at bar.*

NEW! ★★★★ ✔ **$ Vivoli il Gelato.** A real Italian family runs this gelataria, the manager of this shop does not speak English. The original Florence-based store has been selling gelato since 1932; today it's a landmark in Italy. The family's recipes have been passed down through the years, and are still used today in both Florence and here. Quality gelato is made using real Florida fruit and cocoa powder, hazelnuts and pistachios imported from Italy. The best flavor is the creamy riso (rice pudding), the owner's favorite. On hot days there's a long line to order, but it moves quickly. *10a–mid. Gelato and sorbetto $5–$7; sundaes, floats, shakes $10; other snacks $5–$8. 20 flavors; servings come in 3 cup sizes or a cone. No seating.*

Flirty flappers. Cabaret girls will shake up Disney Springs entertainment at The Edison, a 1920s nightclub that should be nearly identical to its popular Los Angeles namesake (above).

Bars, clubs and entertainment. The Edison and STK Orlando may become huge hits; there's nothing like either of them in Central Florida.

NEW! ★★★ Boathouse boat tours. It's a car! It's a boat! Oh my God it's sinking! With you riding shotgun and up to two of your friends or family members in the back seat, a trained captain splashes a rare Amphicar into the lake behind Disney Springs, then as you putt through the water with him for 20 minutes tells you the history of this bizarro 1960s German convertible (long story short: it bombed, as it sat so low in the water that it couldn't stop even small waves from splashing over its sides). Similar tours are available on replicas of a 40-foot 1969 Italian water taxi and an itsy-bitsy 19th-century steamboat. The Amphicar tour is the most authentic; the steamboat tour romantic, but all are pricey for what you get. *10a-10p weather permitting. Amphicar $125 for up to 3 adults or 2 adults and 2 small children. Water taxi $75 per person (children under age 13 $50). Steamboat tour for 2 $150. Taxi, steamboat tours inc chocolate-covered strawberries, champagne toast, live music. Walk-up reservations avail. 407-939-2628. The Boathouse restaurant.*

NEW! The Edison. Dames and daddies will get reckless with their credit cards at what promises to be a swell take on a power plant in the 1920s—the era that gave birth to the blind date, Tin Pan Alley and, of course, Mickey Mouse; the first decade to emphasize youth culture. Stunningly swanky, the speakeasy-themed club will flicker filament lamps and silent films on very dark walls, and have cabaret girls, contortionists, DJs, jazz combos and palm readers performing under very tall ceilings. Further reasons why it will seem like everyone in Orlando has gotten there ahead of you: its many nooks, crannies and long leather sofas; its friendly gangsters and busy flappers who fix up and hand over fancy hootch and giggle water as well as over-styled yet nifty nibbles (you may need your flashlight app to read the menus); and, wheeling a trolley of absinthe, a roving Green Fairy who will definitely not be Tinker Bell. Similar to The Edison nightclub in Los Angeles, this one will have the same dim lighting and Industrial Gothic mechanics, but with additional themed areas such as a Telegraph Lounge, Patent Office and waterfront patio and perhaps more emphasis on food. Sure it'll cost you a few clams, and there are sure to be long waits for saps and Dumb Doras who don't make reservations, but if you want to have a drink or two at a place you'll remember, this joint should be the bee's knees. Dieselpunk cosplayers may get dolled up for the occasion; nearby Chapel Hats (see) has perfect fedoras and fascinators. *Opens late summer 2016.*

NEW! Jock Lindsey's Hangar Bar. It's got an odd little premise—that it's owned by Jock Lindsey, the floatplane pilot who helped Indiana Jones escape from some angry natives at the beginning of 1980's "Raiders of the Lost Ark" and who kept in his plane his pet, a boa constrictor named Reggie ("there's a big snake in the plane, Jock!")—but this fun, kitschy lounge fully delivers on it. Much like the Trader Sam's Grog Grotto at Disney's Polynesian Village Resort, the bar looks as if its owner decorated it with his own memorabilia (in this case letters from Indy, maps, travel posters), serves heavily styled, humorously named snacks and drinks ("Rolling Boulder Meatballs," "Hovito Mojitos") and has hidden elements that come to life whenever someone orders an expensive drink; Reggie himself makes one such appearance. Expect to be wowed by the decor (ceiling fans resemble airplane props, a booth is a diving bell, the whole thing is a quonset hut), impressed by the offerings (the mojito uses pisco, a form of brandy), tempted by the souvenir glasses, and frustrated that the wait to get in on weekend nights may take an hour. *4p–mid, must be 21 after 8p; $9–$16 (no kids menu); drinks $8–$42. Seats 150 (82 outside on deck and dry-docked boat "Reggie"). No reservations.*

★★★★★ ✔ **Raglan Road.** Definitely not the place for a quiet evening, this dyed-in-the-wool Irish pub is busy, loud and awesome at night. A lively house band plays ballads, jigs and reels early, late sets get rowdy; energetic step dancers perform in front of the band and atop an old parson's pulpit in the middle of the room, occasionally with children from the audience. An ever-changing variety of Irish and European beers and whiskeys satisfies nearly everyone, though some of us go for the mead, an ancient sweet drink made from fermented honey. Make a reservation ahead of time to ensure a table; to get one that views the stage specifically ask for that when you check in and be willing to wait. *Main stage band 4p–1:30a Mon–Thurs, 7:30p–1:30a Fri–Sat, noon–4p and 7:30p–1:30a. Sun. Dancers on the hour 5p–10p, Sun noon–4p. Outdoor band on patio nightly. No cover. Restaurant seats 600; all ages. Direct reservations: 407-938-0300.*

NEW! STK Orlando. Forget the meat. After dark it's beefcake, cheesecake, booze and booty-shaking as the bar of this steakhouse becomes a youthful mecca of loud, laissez-faire extravagance. A DJ drops driving beats, friendly bartenders keep you hydrated, elevated dance areas urge you to show your stuff. Contrasts nicely with the retro Edison club right across the walkway. *Opens 2016.*

NEW! The Walt. This three-story eatery will celebrate Walt Disney, the man. Expect fascinating memorabilia everywhere. Known by Disney officials as "The Walt," it was awaiting its official name from Imagineering as this book went to press. You'll find it left of the Edison, near the balloon. *Opens mid-2016.*

★★★★★ ✔ **Street performers.** Bands and musicians perform near the Boathouse and the Edison. *Performance times vary by day and time of year. No charge.*

The Marketplace

The original Disney mall. When it opened in 1975 as the Lake Buena Vista Shopping Village, this 48-acre open-air shopping mall was intended to connect to the rest of Walt Disney World only by monorail. Charming for its day, its architecture recalled a Swiss village, with buildings covered in naturally stained rough-hewn beams and cedar-shake shingles—a trendy look in '70s California, where Disney's design team was based.

As its name changed over the years—to the Walt Disney World Village, then the Disney Village Marketplace and finally just the Marketplace—the area lost some of its charm; its planned monorail beams replaced by highways, its stained wood painted over in bright shades of orange, red and green.

For its Disney Springs incarnation the Marketplace isn't changing much. So far Disney has expanded its signature World of Disney store, added a walkway over its end of Village Lake that makes it easier to get around, built pedestrian bridges over adjacent roadways that makes the area easier to reach from nearby hotels, and updated its ambient music with new arrangements of Disney tunes. In 2016 the Marketplace woodwork will return to its original natural color scheme, and its bus depot will close.

Shops and merchandise. Unlike the other Disney Springs areas, the Marketplace is dominated by Disney shops selling Disney stuff. Also different: the carts and kiosks on its walkways, tempting you with everything from fancy soaps to yo-yos. It's anchored by the World of Disney, Disney World's largest store.

© Disney

Bridging the lake. A new brick-and-steel causeway connects one side of the Marketplace to the other. That's Fulton's Crab House behind it, then the Characters in Flight balloon.

Arribas Brothers. Hand-cut crystal, hand-blown glass and engraving. Artisans work in front of guests. New for 2016 is a huge blown-glass wall sculpture from St. Augustine artist Thomas Long. It's not for sale.

The Art of Disney. Collectible animation cels, attraction posters, Lenox china figurines, lithographs, paintings, quality art pieces.

Basin. The aroma intoxicates you inside this lovely shop, which offers items for the "shower, tub, sink and soul." Try out the salt and sugar scrubs in the handy sinks; shelves teem with all-natural massage and shampoo bars, bath bombs, body butters and lotions. Made in Orlando, fresh soaps come in many colors and scents.

Disney Design-A-Tee. Design a Hanes T-shirt using a touch screen. Choose from hundreds of Disney graphics; add 3 or 4 lines of text. Results look amateur.

Disney's Days of Christmas. Huge holiday shop has dated ornaments, figurines, Mickey-eared Santa hats, stockings; most with a stale 1990s design. Embroidery and engraving available.

Disney's Pin Traders. Small open-air shop filled with collectible pins. Limited variety.

Disney's Wonderful World of Memories. Scrapbooks, photo albums, frames. Small selection of good Disney books.

NEW! Florida Bath Co. An offshoot of Basin, this kiosk offers bath bars and lotions made from home-grown ingredients such as citrus oils and organic vegetable juices.

Ghirardelli. Candy, cocoa, fudge sauce, hot-chocolate mix. Free chocolate samples.

Happy Hound. Kiosk with custom collars and tags, outfits, toys; spills over onto the walls of a nearby store.

NEW! Icon Jewelry by Bico. Pewter jewelry from Australia based on universal symbols, enhanced with crystal, leather and rosewood. Customizable.

NEW! Kate & Leo. Charming child-focused cart has games, toys and art supplies, none of which need batteries.

Lefty's. Kiosk has products for left-handers; much like those at the signature Lefty's on San Francisco's Fisherman's Wharf.

The Lego Store. Part store, part playground, this crowded shop boasts the world's largest Pick-A-Brick wall, with 320 bins sorted by color and size. There's a huge variety of Lego collections, priced as little as $6. Indoor-outdoor play areas include tracks for kids to race vehicles they build. Giant creations outside the shop make good photo backdrops.

Little Miss Matched. For 'tween girls: cute, affordable, cheaply made mismatched socks in many colors, styles and lengths—liners, anklets, knee highs. Colorful clothing, accessories. One of 7 stores in the chain.

NEW! Marketplace Co-Op. Six boutiques make up this spot, which looks like a cooperative of small independent merchants but is actually a Disney testing lab for retail-shop concepts and products. None of the stores are necessarily permanent; Disney "reimagines" them whenever it sees fit. The current line-up: Cherry Tree Lane sells sophisticated women's accessories such as bags, jewelry, scarves, shoes; D-Tech on Demand offers personalized electronic accessories; Disney Centerpiece (the best co-op spot) sells odd home furnishings and housewares based on theme-park art, such as salt-and-pepper shakers that look like Adventureland trash cans; The Trophy Room sells sports apparel and collectibles; WonderGround Gallery stocks commissioned, original and limited-edition artwork inspired by Disney/Pixar films, characters and icons (new in 2015, it replaced the Beautifully Disney cosmetics shop); Zoey and Pickles offers apparel, shoes and accessories for "the up-and-coming fashionista"—in other words, a stylish young girl who's too young for the offerings at Tren-D.

Marketplace Fun Finds. Trite Disney crap, under big letters that spell out "F-U-N."

Mickey's Pantry. Mickey Mouse-styled housewares; non-Disney cookware, food, tableware, wine. A Spice and Tea Exchange area blends salts, sugars, spices and teas.

Once Upon a Toy. Ho-hum Hasbro store has theme-park items, Build-Your-Own Mr. Potato Head station. In the back room a giant toy train circles the ceiling.

Pearl Factory. Japanese akoya pearls in their oysters (6–9 mm, $16); settings, pearl jewelry. Not as fun as a similar counter in Epcot's Japan pavilion. One of 26 stores in California, Florida, Hawaii and Vegas.

Rainforest Cafe Retail Village. Every bit as inspired as its name, this restaurant shop has forgettable animal-themed apparel, plush, toys. Animated decor.

T-Rex Dino-Store. Dinosaur-themed children's apparel, toys; Build-A-Dino area. Outdoor play pit has faux fossils, sluice.

Tren-D. Interesting junior apparel from Disney, Billabong, Hurley, Roxy.

World of Disney. Department store has areas for Girls, Ladies and Juniors, Boys, Men, Infants, Hats and T-shirts, Housewares, Home Decor, Jewelry and Pins, Candy and Snacks, Souvenirs. Often too crowded for quality service; most items are also in park

gift shops. Expanding in 2016. Also includes a makeover salon, the Bibbidi Bobbidi Boutique. *Salon: Girls $55–$190 and up; boys $16. Ages 3–12. Allow 30–60 min. Reservations 407-939-7895 available 6 months in advance.*

Restaurants and food. Of the dozens of table-service restaurants at Disney Springs, know how many are in the Marketplace? Two. Just *two.* And in a way, they're the same place.

★★ **$$$$ Rainforest Café.** Fake robotic animals come to life every 22 minutes in a dusty faux jungle at this touristy eatery, sister restaurant to dino-centric T-Rex. Young kids love it, but it gets old quickly for their parents. The vast menu offers standard chain food that is neither exceptional nor awful. A giant Sparkling Volcano dessert will drown a family of four in chocolate. A volcano erupts every half hour from the roof; you can see its propane fire throughout Disney Springs. A quiet Lava Lounge behind the restaurant has its own menu as well as the full one; it doesn't require a reservation and provides nice views of the lake—with no robotic elephants. *11:30a–11p. Sun–Thr, to mid Fri, Sat. $13–$30 (children $7). Seats 575, inc 30 at outdoor waterfront bar. Direct reservations: 407-827-8500. No same-day reservations.*

★★★ **$$$$ T-REX.** Dinos and prehistoric beasts roar and move every 22 minutes at this lively eatery, reminiscent of its sister restaurant Rainforest Cafe. You choose from four distinct environments: a fiery volcano area, a glowing Ice Age cave, a jungle habitat and a calm ocean area (which comes complete with large aquariums that house saltwater fish and a bar that changes colors). No matter where you sit, it's loud and difficult to have a quiet conversation. Expect generous portions of typical American food from the extensive menu. A standout is an over-the-top dessert, Chocolate Extinction, which will feed the table. A Dino Dig area for kids includes a place to store shoes and clean up. *11a–11p. Sun–Thr, to mid Fri, Sat. $15–$35 (children $7–$8). Seats 626, inc 26 at bar. Direct reservations: 407-828-8739.*

Counter service. We know exactly one person who hates Earl of Sandwich. And a hundred who love it.

NEW! ★★★★ ✔ $ Dockside Margaritas. Florida rum, fruit and sugar cane make the potent potables at this shady spot special for those not from the Sunshine State. Despite its name most of its options aren't margaritas; mojitos, rum runners, fruit wine and local

Dockside Margaritas. A nice spot to relax after dark, this new waterfront bar includes a deck furnished with a handful of tables and chairs. There's a waterside counter 'round back.

beers dominate. Don't overlook its long waterside bar; you can't see it except from the water. *Drinks $7–$13 (non-alcoholic $5–$6). Nuts $4. 50 covered outdoor seats 50 inc 12 at bar.*

★★★★★ ✔ **$ Earl of Sandwich.** Hot crusty sandwiches and soothing soups make this fast-food spot the most popular at Disney Springs; its roast beef sandwich and tomato soup are legendary among Disney regulars. On the downside it's always crowded and finding an open table is sometimes a chore. Don't let the long line discourage you; it moves quickly. Prices are comparable to a Subway but here you get what signs claim is, only with a slight exaggeration, "the best hot sandwich in the world." The holiday sandwich, with turkey and dressing, is to die for. The original restaurant in the small Earl of Sandwich chain, this one is owned by the ancestors of John Montagu, the fourth Earl of Sandwich who in 1762 invented the sandwich. Decent breakfast is cheaper than the nearby Wolfgang Puck Express but not as good. *Breakfast 8:30a–10:30a $2–$5. Lunch, dinner 10:30a–11p $5–$6 (children $4). Seats 190, inc 65 outside.*

★★★ **$ Forty Thirst Street.** Along with Wetzel's Pretzels (see), this little smoothie stand sits right next to the Waterside Stage. *Smoothies $6. Spiced coffee $9.*

NEW! ★★★★ **$ Flour & Sugar.** Cookie kiosk offers flavors of the Sunshine State, such as coconut, key lime and strawberry, all fresh from Orlando's award-winning Iced Bakery. *$4, 6 for $18. Free samples.*

★★★★ **$$ Ghirardelli Soda Fountain.** Rich, house-made Ghiradelli chocolate is used to make the decadent desserts served at this ice cream parlor. It's hard to finish the massive sundaes, so plan to share. People flock here, so also be prepared to wait awhile to order. The interior looks like an old-fashioned ice cream counter and smells of heavenly chocolate. Finding a seat is a challenge. Inside tables are stalked by families trying to nab a spot, while outside areas are often hot enough to instantly melt your treat. *10:30a–11p Sun–Thu, 10:30a–mid Fri–Sat. Ice cream $5–$7, sundaes $10–$11, shakes $7–$9 (children $3–$7). 13 flavors of ice cream. Seats 88, inc 22 outside.*

★★★ **$ Goofy's Candy Company.** Fresh and create-your-own apples, cookies, other treats. Coffees, smoothies.

NEW! ★★★★ **$ Starbucks.** There's only one thing wrong with this walk-up stand— it's a walk-up stand. As such it pales to the Starbucks on the West Side. *Breakfast sandwiches $4–$5, lunch $5–$6. In front of World of Disney. No seating. Opens 7:30a.*

NEW! ★★★ $ Marketplace Snacks. Easy to overlook, this small stand's main benefit is its location—right next to the shady tables of Dockside Margaritas. Go ahead, sit there. Blame it on us. Decent wraps, overpriced hot dogs. *$8–$10. Beer, wine $7–$9. No seating.*

★★★ $ Wetzel's Pretzels. Small stand sells decent hand-rolled pretzels, hot dogs, lemonade. Next to the Waterside Stage. *$4–$7.*

★★★★ ✓ $$ Wolfgang Puck Express. Here's the Puck place you'll prefer—its food is at least as good as the other Disney Springs Puck locations but less expensive, prepared faster and there's never a wait to get seated. Best bets include the breakfast pizza, the barbecue chicken pizza, the salads and the chicken and butternut-squash soups. Everything's made-to-order, and it all comes with real cutlery on real plates, even though this is technically a fast-food place. Bring cash for a tip; though you order at a counter a server brings you your food and refills your drinks. *Breakfast 9a–11a, $10–$15 (no kids meals). Lunch, dinner 8:30a–10:30p $11–$20 (children $7–$8). Seats 184.*

Entertainment. Yes! Some things for your two-year-old! Don't overlook the fountain.

★★★★★ ✓ Street performers. On many evenings a DJ hosts a kids or adult dance party across from the World of Disney, street musicians perform near the entrance to T-Rex. *Performance times vary by day and time of year. No charge.*

★★★★ Kiddie rides. Hand crafted in Italy, the Marketplace Carousel is a small antique merry-go-round has 19 horses (originally with real horse hair) and two carriages. Painted murals above the horses depict the nearby landscape, a plain mural with red roses hides the three-circle shape of Mickey Mouse. Nearby is the Marketplace Express kiddie train, also another kid's favorite—a splash fountain made of three rings, another Hidden Mickey. *Carousel next to Earl of Sandwich, train across from Tren–D next to Disney Pin Traders. Fountain at entrance to pedestrian bridge to Hotel Plaza Blvd. Both 10a–11p, until 11:30p Fri, Sat. $2, children <42 in tall must be accompanied by adult who rides free. Cash, credit cards.*

West Side

Not much new. Chunks of abandoned elevated railways weave through the West Side walkway, the most obvious of very few changes to this area. The shady platforms provide a respite from the Florida sun; they were going to be perches for guests to look down on the area until budget and safety issues killed off that idea.

Shops and merchandise. Mostly budget-friendly shops offering a mix of odd items, with the occasional awesome shop tossed in.

Bongos Gift Shop. Cuban apparel, books, coffee, maracas, margarita glasses, mugs. Small shop inside Bongos Cuban Cafe sadly never seems to have any customers.

Cirque du Soleil Boutique. Stunning circus caps, apparel, figurines, masks, purses and scarves. La Nouba souvenirs. Crowded after shows. Next to the box office.

Curl by Sammy Duvall. Junior and adult beachwear, fashion apparel, hats, jewelry, purses, shoes, sunglasses, swimwear. The authors' 21-year-old daughter buys back-to-college clothes here. Billabong, Hurley, Oakley, Roxy brands.

DisneyQuest Emporium. Totally uninspired Disney merchandise shop.

D Street. The place to go for Vinylmation figures; it has more of them than anywhere else and there's always at least one that's just perfect for your cubicle. Also quirky Star Wars, Marvel T-shirts, accessories.

Fit2Run. Florida shop stocks athletic walking and running shoes, tech running apparel and accessories such as performance eyewear, tech socks, personal-training devices. Official running retailer of RunDisney.

House of Blues Company Store. This laid-back little shop's eclectic items at first glance seem unrelated to each other. But the blues CDs, cornbread mix, folk art, hot sauce and incense all share a through-the-roof quotient of cool. Funky skull-head T-shirts fit right in.

Memory Lanes. The Splitsville gift shop.

Orlando Harley-Davidson. Speaking of ho-hum, here's a motorcycle shop that's no bike, all shop. Heavy metal thunder? Only on display, for the kiddies to climb on.

Pop Gallery. Signed paintings, three-dimensional wall art, wild glass sculptures. Champagne bar. Next to Splitsville, right next to the parking garage.

Something Silver. Silver jewelry your 'tween can afford, in many styles from around the world. Odd little knickknacks too, like wristbands made from guitar strings for $1.

Sosa Family Cigars. Miami-based shop offers cigars mainly from the Dominican Republic that use Dominican and Nicaraguan

Above the crowd. A second-story Splitsville drinking and dining balcony overlooks the West Side walkway. Seen behind it is the House of Blues and Cirque du Soleil theater.

tobacco. Hand-rolling demonstrations. Adults can smoke.

NEW! Super Hero Headquarters. Toys, apparel and collectibles based on Marvel characters and movies.

NEW! United World of Soccer. Cleats, jerseys and other sports gear.

Restaurants and food. Best bets: The House of Blues restaurant and the Disney food trucks. There's a good Starbucks, too.

★★ **$$$$ Bongos Cuban Cafe.** Pop singer Gloria Estefan created this Cuban restaurant, but it hasn't held up nearly as well as "The Rhythm is Gonna Get You" or her other classic hits. If you've ever eaten Cuban food in Miami (or Havana) you won't be impressed with these bland dishes. Aside from the food, however, there is much to like. The architecture is unique—maybe the only building anywhere that's built around a three-story adobe pineapple. An evocative decor recalls Cuba during the 1940s and 1950s. A second-story patio is a great place to watch the dancing and enjoy the view over the lake and well as crowds down on the walkway below. The star of a pricey drink menu is a refreshing mojito. Gloria, come out of the dark, cook up some ropa vieja and save this place! *$16–$45 (children $6–$9). 11a–11p, 'til*

12p Fri, Sat. Seats 560 (60 outside, 87 bar). No reservations. 407-828-0999.

★★★★ ✓ **$$$ Crossroads at House of Blues.** Colorful folk art adds a funky, artistic vibe to the walls, ceilings, even the bathrooms at this quirky, casual spot, a bluesy bayou take on a Hard Rock Cafe. The food is authentic southern fare, with generous portions of everything from voodoo shrimp to spicy jambalaya to a melt-in-your-mouth jalapeño cornbread. Service is especially attentive and engaging. Dining rooms get louder as more young adults show up at night, with live music on weekends. *$12–$29 (children $7). 11:30a–11p Sun–Mon; 'til 12p Tue–Wed, 1:30a Thr–Sat. Seats 578 (158 outside, 36 outside bar). Brunch $34 (children $17); Sun 10:30a, 1p in Music Hall, 250 seats. No reservations. 407-934-2583.*

★★★ **$$$ Splitsville Luxury Lanes.** It's time to re-think bowling alley food. The fare at this retro spot is surprisingly high-quality, with huge portions and an extensive menu. Good choices include the juicy hamburgers, creative sliders and fresh sushi. Draft beer comes in an ice-cold goblet glass; cocktails are generous with alcohol. Servers are friendly and attentive. There are three distinct seating areas: indoors by the bowling, outside in front of the building and upstairs on a second-floor balcony. All three offer great people-watching, and usually live music to boot. *Mon–Wed 10:30a–1a, Thr–Fri 10:30a–2a, Sat 10a–2a, Sun 10a–1a. $12–$25 (children $7). Seats 450, including 50 outside.*

★★★ $$$$ **Wolfgang Puck Grand Café.** Wolfgang Puck fans will be disappointed by this one-time standout; over the years its small offerings have turned bland and pedestrian. Epcot's Via Napoli has much better pizza. Disney's Puck eateries have suffered since their namesake's 2002 split from his wife and business partner, Barbara Lazarof, and his sale of them to Levy's Restaurants, which also owns nearby Portobello and Fulton's Crab House. Lazarof personally decorated the Puck restaurants, giving them their eye-catching (if now dated) look. *Lunch 11:30a–4p $13–$29 (children $8–$9). Dinner 4p–10:30p Sun–Mon, to 11p Tue–Thr, to 11:30p Fri, Sat $13–$31 (children $8–$9). Weekend lunch serves dinner menu. Takeout window. Private room for groups. Seats 586, inc 30 at sushi bar. Direct res 407-938-9653.*

★★★ $$$$$ **Wolfgang Puck Dining Room.** It's past its prime. What used to be a special fine-dining experience is now less than memorable. The menu has a little of everything but nothing especially creative. Best choices are the steak and salmon, which are cooked spot-on. Portions are on the small side. The wait staff can be aloof, and aren't always attentive, although the hostesses are friendly. The ambience is quiet and relaxing, with lovely views of the lake. *6–9p Sun–Thr, 6–10p Fri–Sat. $25–$45 (children $10–$16). Seats 120. Direct reservations: 407-938-9653.*

Counter service and snacks. The new Starbucks is ideal early in the morning, the food trucks will surprise you, especially after dark when there's often a musician nearby.

★★ $ **Disney's Candy Cauldron.** Candied and caramel apples, chocolate-covered strawberries made in view; other treats. Decor recalls dungeon of 1937's "Snow White and the Seven Dwarfs."

★★★★ ✔ $$ **Disney food trucks.** Four trucks serve dishes influenced by recipes from particular Disney theme parks. Best bets include hand-dipped corn dogs in the spirit of those at Disneyland and butter chicken inspired by Disney's Animal Kingdom. At least two trucks can always be found in Exposition Park, where a small stage offers nightly entertainment. *12:30p–11p, $8–$14 (no kids menu). Hours vary based on crowds, weather. Seating varies by location. Exposition Park next to Bongos Cuban Cafe.*

★★★ $ **Häagen-Dazs.** This is just a typical Häagen-Dazs stand; the ice cream is as good as ever but it definitely isn't unique. There's no real seating; it can be tricky to find a nice spot to enjoy your treat before it starts to melt. *10:30a–11p. Ice cream $6–$7 (children $5); shakes $8; sundaes $7–$9 (children $6). 14 flavors. No seating.*

★★★ ✔ $ **The Smokehouse at House of Blues.** You'll have a magical experience for an affordable price if you stop by this take-out window at the right time. In the evenings, talented musicians play classic rock and blues from a patio nearby; lights strung over tables provide mood lighting. If you eat in the afternoon, it can be downright unpleasant: there's no entertainment, you sit out in the heat, and your only shade is from a few trees. The menu is Southern barbecue with sweet sauce; meats are smoked in the main House of Blues kitchen. Food comes in little cardboard boxes; it can be messy. *11:30a–10p, $7–$13 (children $7). No seating; outdoor, uncovered tables nearby.*

NEW! ★★★★★ ✔ $ **Starbucks.** The food is a cut above standard coffee-shop fare at this special Starbucks. Creative and tasty small plates, draft beers and a nice wine selection are available on the evening menu; the best bet here is the creamy truffle macaroni and cheese, which is topped with a light crunchy breading. The building's design has a lot of thought and detail put into it; eco-friendly touches include tables made from salvaged trees and a green roof made up of hundreds of living lemongrass plants. An interactive touchscreen "chalkboard" shows a live feed of guests; touch the screen and it switches to a live view of the Disneyland Starbucks. The building has its own Wi-Fi, which can be a lot more reliable than the widespread Disney network. Crowded after 10 a.m., often everyone seems to be under 30. *8a–mid, coffee beverages $3–$5; evening menu starting 4p, $3–$8 (no kids meals). Also pastries, all-day breakfast items. Rare coffees blends available from Reserve bar in dining area. Seats 60, inc 25 on patio.*

Bars, clubs and entertainment. This is where the authors go for movies; the parking is so convenient now for the Fork & Screen.

★★★ ✔ **AMC 24 Theaters.** Arrive early at the traditional multiplex of this modern movie palace; latecomers are forced into seats that are stupidly close to the screens. Auditorium No. 1 offers an Enhanced Theater

Powerful pipes. Rising on a tilted set piece as she stands behind its flower box, a singer belts out a tune during La Nouba. The Cirque du Soleil show has many memorable moments.

Experience, with a 20-percent larger floor-to-ceiling screen and 12-channel audio. A self-service concession area can slow you down as you enter. Separate Fork & Screen auditoriums offer a nicer way to catch a flick: in an comfortable reserved recliner, with a waiter who brings you food and drinks that are nothing to brag about but decent. Assume you'll be ordering during the previews, get your food in the opening minutes of the film, get the check halfway through and pay your bill before it ends. Servers aren't disruptive and never stand in front of you. Note: The Fork & Screen entrance is far removed from the main AMC entrance, close to the main entrance to the Orange (west) parking garage. *Multiplex $7–12 based on time of day (children ages 2–12 $9), 3-D movies $5–$6 addl; 16 theaters w stadium seating, 2 3-story theaters w balconies. Fork & Screen $10–$19 (children $10–$11); 6 theaters; patrons must be 18 years or older or accompanied by someone over 21. Tiny bar. Total seats 5,390. THX Surround Sound, Sony Dynamic Digital Sound. Listings 888-262-4386. Box office 407-827-1308.*

★★★ **Bongos Cuban Cafe.** This spacious Gloria Estefan-owned spot channels Havana (or at least Miami) on Friday and Saturday evenings, when its live band and dance floor attract a spirited adult crowd. Drinks are pricey, service is sound. *11:30p–2a. Restaurant capacity 560. All ages admitted. No cover. 407-828-0999.*

★★★ ✔ **Characters in Flight.** This 10-minute tethered balloon ride is pricey for what it is; a trip on the nearby Orlando Eye giant wheel is twice as long and costs as little as $2 more. This one's at Disney though, which means you get a 400-foot-high birds-eye view of Disney Springs and in the distance the rest of Walt Disney World; though you're stuck where you stand and can't move around. The balloon sways a little, but otherwise moves so slowly you barely feel it. Afternoon and evening flights are often cancelled by winds and weather. *8:30a–mid. $18 (children ages 3–9 $12); all ages $10 before 10a. 9 min. Children <12 years of age must fly with adult. Capacity: 30 when winds 0–3 mph, 20 3–12 mph, 10 12–22 mph. Does not fly in winds >22 mph. Weather refunds day of purchase only.*

★ **DisneyQuest.** Badly dated "high-tech" adventures from the 1990s lose out to purposefully retro arcade games from the 1980s inside this depressing 5-story building, where Disney is letting something that used to be great waste away. Wear-and-tear is everywhere; a once-Genie-hosted Cyrolator (all custom-voiced by the late Robin Williams) has been an ordinary elevator for years. If it's already included in your Disney tickets you can still have a blast with the right attitude, especially during bad weather, but if you have to pay extra for it you'll regret it; the games you can play at home have now surpassed nearly everything here. If you do go look for one great recent addition: pseudo-vintage Fix-It Felix cabinets (from the 2012 movie "Wreck-It Ralph") that are addicting to play. Closing soon, to be replaced by the NBA Experience (see). *11:30a–10p Sun–Thur, until 11p Fri–Sat. $45 (children ages 3–9 $39), includes unlimited play. Height min (in.): 51 CyberSpace Mountain, Buzz Lightyear's AstroBlaster; 48 Mighty Ducks Pinball Slam; 35 Pirates of the Caribbean. Children under 10 must be with an adult. No strollers. 2 counter cafes. Free coat check. Capacity 3,689. 407-828-4600.*

★★★★ **House of Blues Music Hall.** You might get squished like a sardine on the main floor, but there are no bad views from the balcony of this intimate two-story music venue, which offers great acoustics, good service and pricey drinks at a wraparound bar. It books a range of mainly blues and rock acts; both local wannabes and major stars perform close to the audience. A folk-art decor, hardwood floors and quality lighting add to the experience. A fun Gospel Brunch raises the roof on Sundays. The adjacent Crossroads restaurant (see) has acoustic acts at its outdoor bar, plugged-in shows late Thursday–Saturday. *Showtimes typ 7p–9:30p. Doors open 60m early weekdays, 90m weekends. $8–$95. All ages. Capacity 2000 (tables, stools 150; standing room 1,850). General adm; diners get priority. Outdoor bar shows 6p–11p, until 2a Thr–Sat. 407-934-2583 or hob.com.*

★★★★★ ✔ **La Nouba.** Amazing, beautiful, classy, cute, elegant, fantastic, funny, quirky and getting just a little dated, this European-style (i.e., animal-free) circus suffers only from its opening act's 1990s World Wide Web backdrop. Otherwise it's exactly what a modern circus should be: a sophisticated collection of highly skilled acrobats and jugglers presented in a purpose-built, acoustically superb arena. Most any seat offers a fine view; sitting in the front row helps you appreciate the complexity and skill of the acts. Though veteran Cirque du Soleil patrons may expect a bit less comedy and a bit more variety, for Cirque newcomers it's superb. Movie buffs will find references to 1997's "The Fifth Element" in La Nouba's odd music and warbling diva, and influences of 1998's "Dark City" in its looming cityscapes and unexpected moving floors. Art lovers will note homages to Calder and Matisse. Front-row center is Row A, Section 103, Seat 6. The highest prices are in the "Golden Circle," Rows E and F, Section 103, Seats 1 through 20. Designed specifically for a Disney audience, it's appropriate for children of any age who can sit still and appreciate it. *6p, 9p Tue–Sat. $59–$162 (children $48–$137). Seats 1671. 90m show, no intermission; arrive 30m early. Snack stand. Tickets avail 6 mo. early at cirquedusoleil.com or box office (11a–11p, until 9p Sun–Mon, 407-939-7600).*

NEW! NBA Experience. Interactive experiences, "immersive video productions," a restaurant and a store will make up this 2016 attraction, the replacement for DisneyQuest.

★★★ ✔ **Splitsville.** Despite its name and retro red-white-and-black color scheme, this impressive boutique bowling alley is definitely not your daddio's. Its 30 lanes aren't all side-by-side but rather are clustered in groups of four and six, spread out over two floors and surrounded by bars, dining tables, pool tables, a sushi bar and on some nights live entertainment. Short lanes and approaches wreck the games of serious bowlers, but others find the setup neat. Days skew to families, nights to adults, as a DJ spins upstairs and the five bars are often packed; business groups have loads of fun. A window runs the length of the first four lanes downstairs, putting those bowlers on display to outsiders. Prices are crazy—you pay by time, not by game, and the amount per person varies by the size of your group as well as the time you play. On average if everyone in your group is a fast bowler and doesn't take extra time to eat or drink, you'll spend about $20 per person for two games—about what adults pay at a standard bowling alley. If anyone takes their time, however, that price can easily double, and that's before factoring in food, drinks and a tip. Enticing servers take you to your lane and eagerly deliver anything you'd like. *10:30a–1a Mon–Wed; 10:30a–2a Thr, Fri; 10a–2a Sat; 10a–1a Sun. $12–$20 per person per session; sessions 60–90m based on size of party (children age 9 and under $7). 407-938-7467.*

★★★★★ ✔ **Street performers.** Live bands and solo musicians perform in front of the West Side Starbucks and in the Food Truck plaza on many evenings; Living Statues appear in front of the Cirque du Soleil theater. Performance times vary by day and time of year.

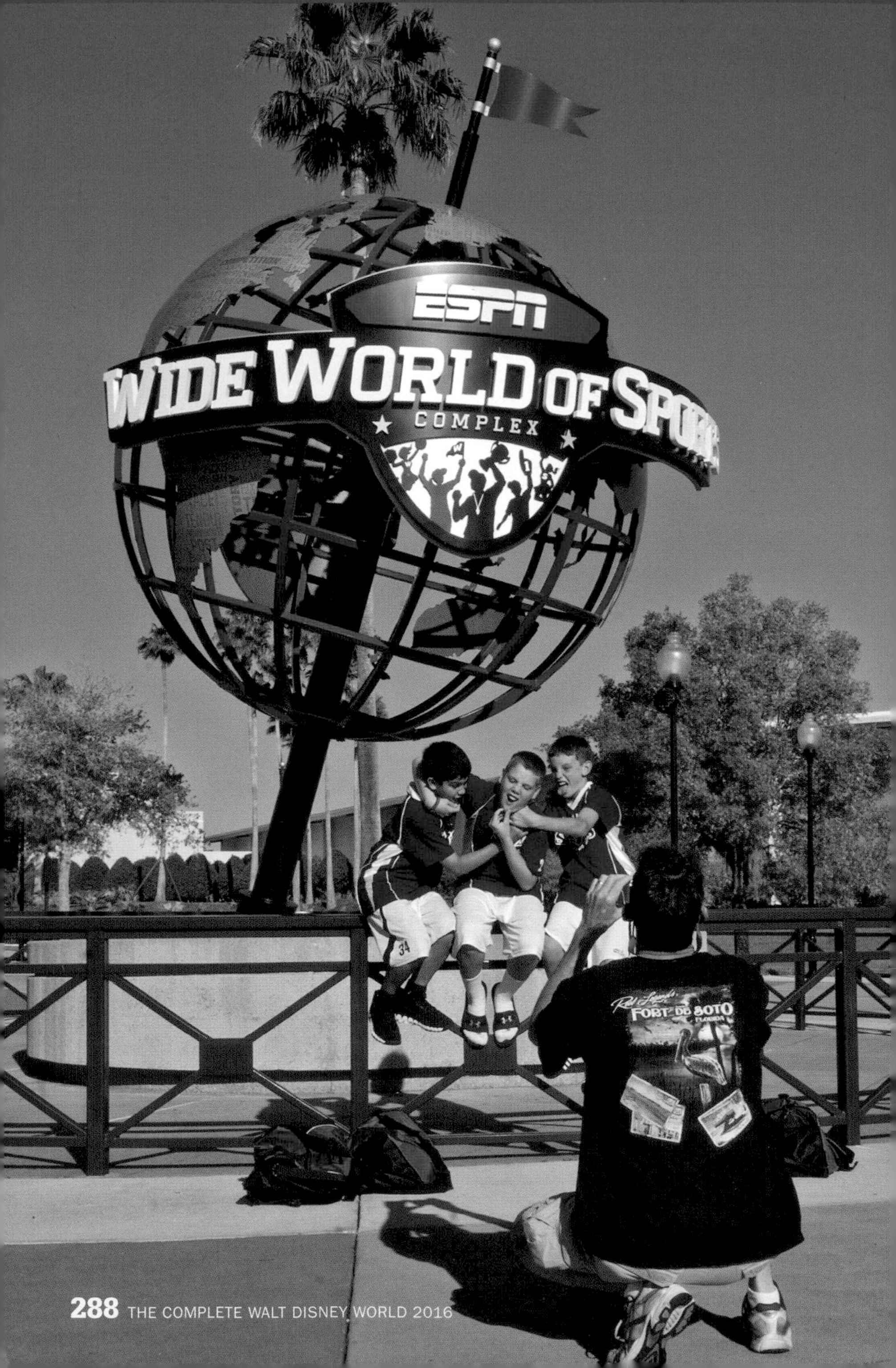
ESPN
WIDE WORLD OF SPO
COMPLEX
FORT DE SOTO

ESPN Wide World of Sports

A real Sports Center. One of the few places on Disney property that is not a tourist spot, the 230-acre ESPN Wide World of Sports complex (700 S Victory Lane, Lake Buena Vista FL 34747. 407-828-3267, live operator 407-939-1500, youth group information 407-939-4263; espnwwos.com) is the top youth sports center in the United States. Each year it hosts more than 100 events and attracts about 330,000 athletes and 1.5 million total visitors. Facilities include a baseball stadium, two field houses, 18 multipurpose fields, 16 baseball/softball fields, a track-and-field area and a 10-court tennis center.

Popularity. As of 2015 over 3 million athletes have competed at the complex, representing more than 231,000 teams. Larger events include the annual Disney Soccer Showcase, which draws more than 11,000 athletes and 660 teams. The complex is also a recruiting ground for colleges, as high school competitions such as the Disney Field Hockey Showcase attract hundreds of coaches.

Design. Built in 1996, ESPN Wide World of Sports features what Disney calls "Florida Picturesque" architecture—yellow Spanish-style buildings offset by blue and green accents. Its field area has shady walkways landscaped with palms and hardwoods on its left side, thanks to the triangular shapes of its baseball and softball fields, but few trees on its right side, where rectangular multipurpose fields often leave little extra space.

Video coverage. Roving ESPN production crews, robotic cameras and a 20-zone audio system capture the action at most events. About a dozen highlight and interview clips are produced daily, which air on video screens throughout the complex as well as on Disney hotel-room televisions. Major events are covered with up to seven cameras, two more than most ESPN college-football telecasts. Hidden within the grounds of the baseball stadium, a 2,500-square-foot production center includes two studios and eight edit bays. One of five ESPN distribution

'Now let's try a silly one.' Teammates pose at the entrance to the ESPN Wide World of Sports complex.

hubs in the United States, the complex is the anchor point to more fiber-optic cable than AT&T Stadium in Dallas.

Broadcast coverage. Over the past decade the various ESPN cable networks have aired over 2,000 hours of coverage from the Wide World of Sports complex, including on-location broadcasts of such shows as "Mike & Mike," "Baseball Tonight" and "Gruden's QB Camp." Online streaming service ESPN3 airs over 600 hours of events each year.

ESPN Innovation Lab. Located in a small building between the tennis center and Hess Convertible Fields 7 and 9, ESPN staffers develop broadcast technologies by using the sports complex as a real-world testing ground for the ESPN Emerging Technology Group. So far the results have included Ball Track, a Doppler-radar system that can continuously update the distance and height of a baseball in flight; ESPN Snap Zoom, a freeze-frame technology that zooms in on an area of a football play to provide more insight on the action; and the EA Virtual Playbook, which allows studio analysts to bring to life key match-ups, formations and game action with multi-dimensional animation. Unfortunately, the lab is closed to the public.

Venues. Consisting of eight distinct venues, the complex has an array of courts and fields.

Baseball Quadraplex. For baseball this is Disney's nicest place to play. It features four manicured fields, a half field for infield drills and various bullpens, batting tunnels and pitching machines. Center fields have batter's-eye backdrops. Field 3 has lights. A separate pitching area has 10 enclosed bullpens. The quad is used by pros during Atlanta Braves Spring Training, Gulf Coast League and Fall Instructional League seasons. *340-foot right- and left-field lines, 385-foot power alleys, 400-foot center field. Fields 2, 4 and 5 have small covered infield bleachers, Field 3 has small covered bleachers behind home plate. No concession stand. Restrooms, pay phones, souvenir kiosk.*

Champion Stadium. This double-decker ballpark hosts amateur competitions as well as Atlanta Braves Spring Training games.

Jostens Center. One of two field house, it's large enough to hold two inline hockey rinks, six basketball courts or a dozen volleyball courts

Most seats are in direct sun; a few are under a balcony. Wide concourses create a pleasant atmosphere, but the stadium lacks the intimate feel found at other Florida Spring Training sites. Concession stands offer sandwiches, hot dogs, snacks, soft drinks, and beer. A general-admission grass berm beyond left field seats 2,000. *340-foot right- and left-field lines, 385-foot power alleys, 400-foot center field. 9,500 seats, 80 percent behind infield. Four sky boxes; two open-air suites with patios. Concession stands, carts, restrooms throughout. Gift shop.*

Hess Sports Fields—Baseball. Four large diamonds (Fields 21–24) sit at the far right of the complex. A lack of landscaping creates a hot, sunny environment for spectators. All fields have lights and bullpens, with batting tunnels nearby. *355-foot maximum right- and left-field lines, 489-foot maximum center field. Small 3-row infield bleachers may be tented. No concession stand, snack tents may be set up. Soft-drink machine. Restrooms nearby.*

Hess Sports Fields—Convertible Fields. Spread throughout the complex, these 13 huge rectangles can host football, lacrosse, soccer and similar sports. Features vary. *Specs:* Next to the Baseball Quadraplex, Fields 7 and 9 lack scoreboards, though Field 7 has a coaching tower. Behind the HP Field

House, Fields 16 and 17 include lights for night play, as do adjacent Fields 18 and 19. Next to the Jostens Center, Field 20 has no scoreboard. Note: Because of their proximity to the complex entrance plaza, Fields 19 and 20 have ambient music: a soundtrack of upbeat pop tunes. Most fields are crowned with 1-degree slopes. *Fields 7 and 9 lack spectator seating; share a concession stand, restrooms. Field 16 has a small shaded bleacher area. Fields 17 and 18 have large sections of covered stadium seats; have concession stands and restrooms nearby. Field 19 lacks spectator seating; has concession stands and restrooms nearby. Field 20 has no spectator amenities.*

HP Field House. With high arches and trusses reminiscent of a 1950s field house, the main arena at this 165,000-square-foot facility can host a variety of multi-court events. Two auxiliary courts sit upstairs. The bottom floor has locker rooms, a workout area and pro memorabilia cases. *Next to Champion Stadium. 5,500 stadium seats; top row 35 ft. high. Auxiliary courts have 6-row bleachers. Concession stands sell sandwiches, hot dogs, snacks, soft drinks, no beer. Wetzel's Pretzels stand at aux. courts. Restrooms. No gift shop. Back patio overlooks Hess Field 17.*

Jostens Center. This indoor arena has all of its competition area in one space. It can

HP Field House. A main arena holds 5,500 spectators, and be divided into multiple courts. With the highest row of seats only 35 feet above the court, everyone gets a good view.

be divided into two inline hockey rinks, six basketball courts or a dozen volleyball courts. Locker rooms are available. *5-row bleachers line two sides. Concession stand, Wetzel's Pretzels stand on second level. Restrooms on both levels. Adjacent to souvenir shop, ESPN Wide World of Sports Grill.*

Diamondplex Softball Complex. Six fields can accommodate fast-pitch softball, slow-pitch softball or youth baseball. A central tower at the main quad has a concession stand, as well as areas for scorekeepers and officials. All fields have lights and bullpens, with batting tunnels nearby. *Fields 10 and 11 maximum dimensions: 275-foot right-, left- and center-field lines. Quad fields (12, 13, 14 and 15) maximum dimensions: 305-foot right-, left- and center-field lines. Fields 10 and 11 have small covered bleachers behind home plates. Quad fields have small covered infield bleachers. Concession stand sells sandwiches, hot dogs, snacks, soft drinks, beer. Restrooms, pay phones. Souvenir kiosk nearby.*

Tennis Center. These 10 clay courts, which include a stadium court, once hosted the U.S. Men's Clay Court Championships. All courts are in direct sun; seven have lights. *Stadium court elevated bleachers seat 1,000. No amenities, though food and souvenir carts may be set up for events. The back side of the*

adjacent ESPN Innovation Lab has a concession stand that, if open, sells sandwiches, hot dogs, snacks and soft drinks; nearby are soft-drink machines, restrooms, pay phones.

New Balance Track and Field Complex. This 400-meter polyurethane area meets the standards of the International Association of Athletics Federations, the sport's governing body. It has nine 48-inch lanes, double straightaways, three shot-put rings, two discus/hammer rings, a javelin runway, two high-jump pits, two interior horizontal-jump runways and two pole-vault zones. An adaptable cross-country course is adjacent. *Large covered bleachers. No concession stand. Adjacent restrooms.*

Events. The complex hosts more than 100 amateur competitions a year, which include 11,000 individual games and contests and athletes from more than 70 countries. Many are sponsored by the Amateur Athletic Union (AAU) (407-934-7200, aausports.org), which has its headquarters on Disney property near Disney Springs. Signature events include:

Disney Spring Training. A pre-season warm-up for high-school and college teams, this spring festival includes baseball, softball, lacrosse, and track and field tournaments. Typically 150 to 200 teams participate.

Champion Stadium. Fans await the start of an Atlanta Braves Spring Training game. The Braves take on other Grapefruit League teams each February and March.

Cheerleading World Championships. The Super Bowl of cheerleading, this April event usually includes more than 8,500 cheerleaders; 100 teams from 40 countries.

AAU Boys National Basketball Championships. High-school players compete in this July showcase.

Old Spice Classic. A NCAA Division I basketball tournament, this bracket-format event features 12 games in three days in November. Each team competes in one game per day.

Pop Warner Super Bowl. After advancing through regional contests, 64 youth football teams compete in these December championships. Divisions consist of Jr. Pee Wees (ages 8–11 years), Pee Wees (9–12 years), Jr. Midgets (10–13 years) and Midgets (11–15 years).

Pop Warner National Cheer & Dance Championships. Held during the Pop Warner Super Bowl, this December event brings together about 500 cheer and dance squads. Teams compete in the same age ranges as the football players as well as by squad size (Small and Large) and three skill categories (Novice, Intermediate and Advanced).

Disney's Soccer Showcase. A series of three top-level national events, this huge fall festival typically features more than 600 teams (about 10,000 athletes) in divisions from U11 to U18. Athletes in divisions U15 through U18 first compete in a September Qualifier. The top two finishers in each group advance to the main event in December; winners are guaranteed a spot in the top flight. For divisions U11 through U14, Disney's Junior Soccer Showcase offers national competition over Thanksgiving weekend. The Showcase is open to state-cup or higher level teams. About 800 college coaches attend.

Braves Spring Training. After two weeks of workouts, the Atlanta Braves play a 15- or 16-game Spring Training schedule at Champion Stadium in late February and March. Grapefruit League competitors include the New York Yankees, Boston Red Sox and St. Louis Cardinals. Disney characters often appear during the games; afterward, children can run the bases.

Tickets (ranging from $18 for general admission lawn seats to $54 for lower-level reserved seats; $3 additional day of game; group tickets and multi-game packages available) are sold at Ticketmaster (800-745-3000; ticketmaster.com) and the complex box office (prerecorded 407-828-3267; live voice 407-939-1500 or 407-939-4263) starting the first week in January. Games against the most popular teams—such as the Yankees, Red Sox and Cardinals—often sell out.

Open to all visitors at no additional charge, Braves workouts and practices take place in the stadium and at the Baseball Quadraplex. Major league players leave at the end of March; minor leaguers (the "Baby Braves") stay through April. Except for autograph hounds the workouts draw few fans.

Policies and resources. The complex includes food spots, gift shops, a Welcome Center and some procedures and practices:

Admission. Though courts and fields are open only to participating groups, the public is welcome as spectators. Admission for amateur events is $17 for ages 10 and above, $12 for ages 3–9. Length-of-event tickets are often available. Walt Disney World annual passholders get in free. Professional events are ticketed separately.

© Disney

Youth sports. High school volleyball players take over the HP Field House each June for the Amateur Athletic Union National Championships.

ATM. There's one, outside the gates by the ESPN Clubhouse store. A portable ATM is set up in Champion Stadium for Braves games.

Coolers. Each guest may bring in one cooler of up to one gallon for personal use. A coach can bring in one cooler of up to five gallons for team use. No coolers are allowed in the Jostens Center.

Credentials. Athlete and coach credentials are distributed to teams at registration. To get them, each team must have paid its tournament entry fee and submitted waivers for each athlete and coach. A coach can pick up credentials for an entire team. Credentials provide admission to specific areas on specific dates.

Driving directions. *From the north:* Take the Florida Turnpike to Interstate 4, head west to Osceola Parkway West (exit 65). Turn left at stoplight onto Victory Way. *From the southwest:* Take Interstate 4 east to Osceola Parkway West (exit 65). Turn left at stoplight onto Victory Way. *From the southeast:* Take the Florida Turnpike north to Exit 249 (Osceola Parkway West), go about 10 miles, turn left onto Victory Way.

Equipment drop off. For some events (including those at the softball complex) teams can drop off equipment at a spot alongside the parking lot, where it's loaded onto a motorized cart and taken to the appropriate venue. A team representative must accompany it. Team members themselves must walk to their fields.

Family matters. Parents wanting to watch their child compete will find shaded bleachers at most outdoor venues, and either bleachers or stadium seats at most indoor spots. Nursing mothers will find the best indoor options to be various nooks and crannies in the HP Field House and Jostens Center, or, on uncrowded days, a back table at the ESPN Wide World of Sports Grill (although none of these three spots allow strollers). Moms might find it tough to nurse in Champion Stadium; the baseball park has few private spots beyond restrooms, especially out of the heat.

First Aid. During events, trainers in marked tents aid injured athletes. Non-athletes needing over-the-counter pain medications, bandages or other basic supplies should contact a Disney cast member. The entrance gift shop sells these items.

Food. Concession stands dot the grounds; temporary carts offer snacks and beverages on event days. Guests can place advance orders for boxed meals, bulk beverages and snacks to be delivered to particular fields; items range from $8 sandwiches

Other spots. A Welcome Center offers event schedules, books restaurants and provides general Disney information. Below, the ESPN Clubhouse Shop and the ESPN Innovation Lab.

to $20 pizzas. Officially only visitors with special dietary needs (i.e., medical conditions, religious doctrines) may bring food into the complex, however this rule is often not enforced. No glass bottles or alcoholic beverages can be brought into the complex, though many concession stands sell beer.

★★★ $$ **ESPN Wide World of Sports Grill.** This American fast-food spot has you order at a counter but delivers your food to your table. The menu has chicken wings, individual pizzas, salads and sandwiches; best bets are the roast beef and blackened fish sandwiches. Soft drinks are refillable. A photo prop looks like a "SportsCenter" set. Seven huge high-def screens show popular sports channels as well as, sometimes, events going on within the complex. More TVs are at the separate bar, which serves liquor as well as beer and wine. *Across from Champion Stadium, next to the Jostens Center. 10:30 a.m.–7 p.m.; on slow days will close early or have limited menu. Lunch, dinner: $8–$13, Seats 350, 48 in bar.*

Getting around. This place is huge! Larger than most Disney theme parks, the 220-acre complex requires a lot of walking to get around, especially to reach its back areas. The hike from the parking lot to the Softball Complex is seven-tenths of a mile, which at a leisurely pace takes about 15 minutes.

Lockers, equipment storage, showers. The complex has no public lockers or storage. The HP Field House and the Jostens Center have team locker rooms with showers.

Parking. General parking is free; valet parking is available for some events for $10 to $20, depending on the event. The small parking lot often fills to capacity; overflow parking is available on grassy areas behind it and on the median of Victory Way, the road that leads to the complex. Late arrivals for Spring Training games may walk almost a mile to Champion Stadium.

Park tickets. The Welcome Center sells all types of Disney World park tickets, including a specially priced ticket that's available only to visitors to the ESPN complex. A "1-Day After 2 p.m." ticket provides admission to any one Disney World theme park for $74; a similar "1-Day After 1 p.m." for water parks is $32. The tickets are valid only on the day of purchase. (Prices as of August 2015.)

ESPN crews. An on-site ESPN production center mixes feeds from field reporters as well as 42 robotic cameras to generate coverage of events. Results appear on video displays throughout the grounds.

Pets. Except for service animals, no animals are allowed on the grounds.

Restrooms. Facilities are available at, or near, all competition venues.

Shops. The ESPN Clubhouse Shop offers ESPN, sports-team and complex apparel and other merchandise, as well as a small selection of collapsible chairs, sunglasses and umbrellas. The shop has two locations: at the complex entrance and inside Champion Stadium. Next to the ESPN Wide World of Sports Grill, a Custom Tee Center booth customizes event T-shirts. Souvenir kiosks are often set up at event venues.

Strollers. Strollers are allowed in most areas of the complex, but prohibited inside the HP Field House, Jostens Center and ESPN Wide World of Sports Grill. Stroller parking is available outside of those venues. The complex does not rent strollers.

Transportation. Complimentary bus service is available from Disney's All-Star Resort, Caribbean Beach Resort and Pop Century Resort. Buses run from one hour prior to the complex opening to 11 p.m. or closing time (whichever is later) on days when events are taking place, as well as every Thursday through Monday from 5 p.m. to 11 p.m. These buses arrive on the hour and the half-hour. Buses may not be able to accommodate all teams and equipment.

Welcome Center. Located between the HP Field House and Jostens Center, a small Welcome Center offers event schedules and provides general Disney World information. It also sells theme-park, water-park, DisneyQuest and La Nouba tickets; makes Disney dining reservations; and helps with transportation issues.

Wheelchair rentals. No wheelchairs are available for rent, though a limited number of complimentary wheelchairs is available at the Welcome Center, for use only at the complex. A photo I.D. is required.

Wi-Fi. Free though unreliable, Disney Wi-Fi is available throughout the complex.

Weather. When lightning or other severe weather threatens, Disney halts all outdoor ESPN events at least temporarily. The Weather Channel web site (weather.com) offers current Walt Disney World conditions and forecasts.

Accommodations

A decision. As the most popular vacation destination on the planet, Walt Disney World has no shortage of places to stay. Disney itself owns 20 resort hotels, all with architecture, decor and landscaping that immerse you in a unique experience. Combined, these places can hold 126,000 people. More than a dozen other hotels at Disney are managed by outside companies, such as Hilton and Starwood. This chapter reviews all of them, and includes details you won't find anywhere else.

But does it matter? Since you can instantly find the cheapest spot for any day of the year at TripAdvisor or other online sites, can't you just book that one and be done with it? Since any Disney spot will give you a decent place to crash, why put more effort into this?

Frankly, maybe you shouldn't. Unless you've got children, will be driving to Disney or renting a car, or have a big sense of adventure. If any of those things are true, you should take your time with this. Here's why:

It's a great big class-defined tomorrow. Since Disney groups its hotels by price (see below), it inadvertently tends group its hotel guests by income. Wealthier folks fill the Grand Floridian resort; middle-class families gather at Caribbean Beach; paycheck-to-paycheck types stay at an All-Star resort. Fight this trend and you'll be surrounded by people who may not be much like you. Of course this should be a good thing—different people coming together to realize there's so much that they share that it's time they're aware It's a Small World After All—but in reality that's a ride in *Fantasy*land. In real life it means little girls from working families at the Grand Floridian who can't understand why they can't go to its pricey princess tea; little boys from tony homes at the Pop Century resort who think their dad's a dweeb because he's like the only one without a tattoo; young families at an All-Star resort who just don't be comfrtable being continually surrounded by lively teenage girls, most of whom only speak Portuguese.

Perfect for couples. The entrance to a garden suite at Disney's BoardWalk Inn.

To avoid these issues, stay at a Disney Moderate hotel. These places draw the most middle-class crowds, and book few youth groups except over Spring Break.

"Hey there honey..." Another crowd that can affect your stay: Conventioneers. The lifeblood of the Walt Disney World Swan and Dolphin, these business travelers make up a good percentage of the crowd at any Disney hotel with a convention or conference center—the BoardWalk, Contemporary, Coronado Springs and Yacht and Beach Club. Except for the fact that these folks dress in suits instead of T-shirts and shorts, they're often just as rowdy as those teenagers after their sessions are done for the day, and they can all legally drink and many have expense accounts that let them wine, dine... and flirt with your underage daughter to their heart's content. To avoid these problems stay at a Disney hotel that has no business facilities—any Value, any Moderate except Coronado Springs, any Deluxe that's not the BoardWalk, Contemporary or Yacht and Beach Club.

Moderate or Deluxe? Trying to decide between these two hotel types? If you're with children, we say go Moderate. Of course the Deluxe Resorts are plush, spacious and elegant; their rooms are larger, their linens more plush, their restaurants far better. But they also have smaller fast-food spots, fewer swimming pools, and parking options that require you either to pay $20 a day for valet service or, in most cases, hike a literal half-mile to get from your "self-service" spot to your room—a major headache if you are carrying sleeping toddlers or in the midst of one of Central Florida's frequent downpours. Moderate Resorts, on the other hand, are set up so you can park right next to your building, sometimes right outside of your room.

$100 a night for a tent? What a deal! Seeking a truly memorable stay? Have a sense of adventure? Consider camping at Fort Wilderness. And don't just camp, do it up—set up an open canopy over your picnic table and BBQ grill, pop up one tent for your adults and separate little ones for each of your kids, string Christmas lights all over everything then kick back for a week

© Disney

Pick your price. Standard rooms from Disney's three price categories. Top: the Moderate Port Orleans Riverside. Above left: the Deluxe Contemporary. Above right, the Value Art of Animation.

of family bonding like you've never thought possible. And trust us, you'll fit right in. There's a whole Disney camping cult that does exactly this. Don't have a tent? Disney will rent you one and set it up free of charge.

Disney hotel categories. Disney groups its 20 hotels into four groups by room rate—and therefore by their amenities, room size and how many people those rooms will hold.

Value resorts. (Disney's All-Star, Art of Animation, Pop Century). These huge motel-like complexes hold Disney's least expensive rooms. Most sleep four. All-Star Movies and Art of Animation also offer family suites. Amenities are limited, but do include swimming pools, playgrounds and food courts.

Luggage service is hourly. Oddly, the Values are the only Disney hotels that have obvious Disney themes; many buildings are trimmed with props that recall Disney movies.

Moderate resorts. (Disney's Caribbean Beach, Coronado Springs, Fort Wilderness, Port Orleans). These large complexes have geographical themes, larger rooms, elaborate pools and in most cases table-service restaurants. Most rooms have queen beds. Amenities include on-site recreation.

Deluxe resorts. (Disney's Animal Kingdom Lodge, BoardWalk Inn, Contemporary, Grand Floridian, Polynesian Village, Wilderness Lodge, Yacht and Beach Club). Serious architecture and lush landscaping distinguish these top-of-the-line hotels. Rooms are large;

Big deals. Some DVC timeshare units don't become available for nightly rentals until the last minute, which can make them bargains on online booking sites. Day-before rates can be less than half that of a Deluxe hotel room. Options include studio villas (above, at the Beach Club), 1-bedroom villas (left, at the BoardWalk) and Grand Villas (top, at Kidani Village).

most sleep five. Amenities include fine restaurants, club levels and valet parking.

Deluxe Villas. (Disney's Old Key West and Saratoga Springs; sections of Animal Kingdom Lodge, Beach Club, BoardWalk, Contemporary, Grand Floridian, Polynesian Village, Wilderness Lodge). These Disney Vacation Club (DVC) timeshare studios, suites and condos are available nightly as ownership usage permits.

Disney hotel benefits. Staying anywhere on Disney property is convenient—it's easy to get to a park early in the morning and to return to your hotel for a midday break. Benefits of a Disney-owned hotel include:

Extra Magic Hours. Each day, at least one Disney park offers extended hours for guests staying at Disney-owned hotels, opening one hour early or staying open up to two hours late. Water parks also participate.

Land of giants. A jumbo jukebox at the All-Star Music Resort. Other huge props include a towering Sheriff Woody at All-Star Movies and monstrous megaphones at All-Star Sports.

Complimentary transportation. Disney boats, buses and monorails take you to all theme and water parks as well as Disney Springs at no additional charge.

Unique extras. Every resort hotel offers pin trading in its lobby or a gift shop, complimentary swimming pool activities such as children's pool parties and Movies Under the Stars nightly (a rotating collection of Disney films). All pools also offer complimentary use of children's life jackets. New for 2016, all laundromats accept credit cards.

Magical Express. This complimentary bus service shuttles guests between the Orlando International Airport and Disney-owned resort hotels. In most cases users can bypass baggage claim, as Disney itself picks up luggage from the airlines and delivers the bags to its hotels. In addition, many guests can check their baggage for the return flight at their Disney resort. Magical Express is only available to guests using certain commercial airlines and staying at Disney resort hotels.

MagicBand. This wristband acts as a room key, park ticket and charge card. Each Disney hotel guest, including each child, gets one with their reservation packet or at check-in.

Package delivery. Anything a Disney hotel guest buys at a Disney theme park can be delivered to their hotel free of charge.

Guaranteed admission. If they have tickets, Disney resort guests are guaranteed entry into Disney theme parks, even, in most cases, when those parks are officially filled to capacity. Visiting at Christmas, the Fourth of July or another peak period? This matters.

Special deals. Disney resort guests can prepay for their meals through the Disney Dining Plan and get preferred tee times and discounts at Disney's four golf courses.

About the following reviews. Hotels and restaurants are rated from one to five stars (★) for quality and value. A checkmark (✔) indicates an author favorite. Also for restaurants, the price of a typical adult dinner entree is summarized by dollar signs—$ for less than $10; $$$$$ for more than $25. Room rates do not include resort tax (13.5 percent at the All-Star Resorts; 12.5 percent at all other hotels). All Disney hotel addresses are in the city of Lake Buena Vista, Florida, ZIP code 32830.

Abbreviations. The Location section of each listing abbreviates the areas of Disney World as follows: MK for Magic Kingdom, EP for Epcot, DHS for Disney's Hollywood Studios, DAK for Disney's Animal Kingdom, BB for Blizzard Beach, TL for Typhoon Lagoon, DS for Disney Springs and ESPN for the ESPN Wide World of Sports complex.

★★★ ✔ **Disney's All Star Resorts.** For years we've given these places bad reviews. We said the rooms were too small, the food was too bland and the architecture was way too hideous. And now we've changed our minds. The rooms are still puny, but they're very clean. The remodeled food courts look nice, and their food can be—yes, we're going to say it—delicious, at least at lunch and dinner. As for architecture, for the most part it's still a sad joke, the ugliest Disney buildings in Florida. So three stars and a check, for the cheapest place on Disney property.

Built to compete with the rash of discount motels on nearby U.S. 192 (most of which have since fallen into disrepair), each hotel is laid out like a typical motel complex, but on a giant scale. A central building holds the registration area, food court and bus station, and fronts the main pool.

Three-story lodging buildings spread out from there. Each is coated with bright paint; stairwells and elevator entrances are hidden by larger-than-life icons—either Disney film characters (All-Star Movies), musical instruments (Music) or sports gear (Sports)—and roofs are topped with related things such as stars, musical notes, sports pennants or sayings. They're nearly all gaudy and garish, though all of its detail does make it easy to find your room ("Remember dear, we're just under the blue flag and the giant "30-15" sign, left of the pink tennis racket"). Landscaping is generous, as the resort was built in a palm-and-pine forest and has many additional trees and shrubs.

Highs. Good rates; large swimming pools; All-Star Music's family suites have decent furnishings that make them a bargain compared to those at Art of Animation. All rooms are near parking lots. Except at breakfast, the food courts are pretty good these days, much better than most park fast-food spots and the McDonald's that sits next door. Pools are nice for the price too, with colorful fountains.

Lows. No table-service dining; garish theming; unshaded and crowded bus stops; small guest rooms; crowded food courts especially in the morning. Youth groups such as marching bands and soccer teams often stay here, giving the resorts a teenage vibe that may be too much for families.

Rooms. Modestly decorated rooms have cheery colors, tasteful art and honey faux woods. All-Star Music has family suites. *Rooms: 260 sq ft. Sleep 4. Two double beds. Accessed by outdoor walkways. Suites: 520*

Spring break at the All-Star. To test the theory that Disney's Value Resorts are awful places to stay when they're filled with young people, the authors of this book stayed at the All-Star Sports Resort during the peak of the most recent Spring Break, the week before Easter in 2015.

And by stay, we mean *stay.*

For seven straight days we never left, remaining at the resort all day long, every day, walking through the grounds and both pool decks every morning, noon and night to eat every one of our meals at the All-Star Sports food court.

And here's what it was like: Yes, the entire place was full of high schoolers and college kids. Cheerleaders. Lacrosse teams. Spring breakers.

And yes, they did clash, visually at least, with the young families there. And some of those families did have that deer-in-the-headlights look as they roamed the grounds, wondering where the families went in this supposed family mecca.

But it wasn't loud. The food courts were packed with young people, but they were always in such a hurry to get somewhere—to the parks, to their game, to their buses—that they never stayed very long, and never had any loud conversations.

And it wasn't rowdy. At the pools a few pale girls in bikinis laid out nervously on the chaise lounges and a few pasty shirtless guys pretended not to look at them. But the pools themselves were too filled with the sounds of Disney lifeguards hosting kiddie games for anything even slightly wild or crazy to take place.

However, the high school seniors who filled all of the other rooms in our giant-tennis-racket building did gather outside it every morning at nine ("All right then! Everyone to Epcot!!!"), and thanks to the four chatty girls staying next to us, as the week went we learned through our wall which guys in their class were totally hot and totally not in vivid giggly detail. (Hey Tyler R., if you would just shave that stupid mustache...)

But we were only paying $120 a night, half the rate of anywhere else. Our room was clean and easy to work in; we wrote much of this chapter there. The food at breakfast was fair, but the lunch and dinner items were really good. Overall it suited our needs perfectly.

© Disney

Animals on parade. A rare okapi roams the savanna of Disney's Animal Kingdom Lodge. Other species on display include bongo, giraffe, impala, kudu, ostrich and waterbuck.

sq ft. Sleep 6. 1 king bed, 1 sleeper-sofa double bed, 2 single beds convert from chair and ottoman, kitchenette, 2 full baths.

Swimming pools. Each complex has two themed swimming pools, a large one with a kiddie pool behind its central hall and a second pool nestled within some outlying lodging buildings. None of the pools have slides, but central ones have fountains that shoot water over swimmers' heads. Some of the pools have interesting shapes—the main one at All-Star Music looks like a guitar.

Restaurants and food. Each resort has a food court (★★★ $$ 6:30a–11p; seats 500), bakery, convenience store and small bar open to its main pool. Room service (pizza, salads, desserts) is 4 p.m. to midnight.

Other amenities. Arcade, mile-long jogging trail, playground. Laundromat, laundry service. Shop with groceries. Organized children's activities posted on boards at main swimming pools each morning.

Disney transportation. Buses serve parks and Disney Springs but not the ESPN complex. You wait for your bus in the sun.

Location. Southwest Disney, near Animal Kingdom. Distance to (in miles): MK 5, EP 5, DHS 3, DAK 1, BB 1, TL 4, DS 4, ESPN 3. Movies 1901 W. Buena Vista Dr., Music 1801 W. Buena Vista Dr., Sports 1701 W. Buena Vista Dr., 32830.

Key facts. Disney Value resorts with clustered buildings; 5,740 rooms, 298 suites, 246 acres. Built: Sports, Music 1994; Movies 1999. Phone: Movies 407-939-7000; Music 407-939-6000; Sports 407-939-5000. Fax: Movies 407-939-7111; Music 407-939-7222; Sports 407-939-7333. Check In 3p, Out 11a.

Rates. Rooms: Rack $85–$192, discounted to $77. Suites: $212–$394, discounted to $194.

★★★★★ ✔ **Disney's Animal Kingdom Lodge.** A giraffe may wander behind your balcony at this African-themed complex. With many rooms overlooking wildlife savannas, it consists of two distinct spots—the original Lodge, now called Jambo House, and Kidani Village, a newer timeshare complex next door. At Jambo House, 19 interconnected buildings arc into a 33-acre savanna. Kidani Village is surrounded on three sides by a 13-acre savanna; its interior areas less elaborate than Jambo House. Which one should you pick? Jambo House. It's a fully realized resort with comfortable rooms, first-class dining and a nice swimming pool. Not at all a village, Kidani Village is one very long building with a parking garage underneath. Its guests take a bus to Jambo House to eat breakfast.

Highs. Roaming wildlife, superb restaurants, all rooms are easily accessible, good

'Round-the-clock refreshment. Guests relax early one morning at the Animal Kingdom Lodge swimming pool, which is open 24 hours a day.

pools, child-care center onsite, Kidani's larger suites are stunning.

Lows. Pricey. Distant location. Most standard rooms sleep four, not five.

Rooms. Rooms have multicolored fabrics and dark wood furniture handcrafted in Africa. Ground-level rooms have patios; others have balconies which extend 4 feet. Most overlook wildlife savannas, though some face the pool or parking lot. Club level available. Jambo House suites are at prime locations at the end of animal trails. Some have pool tables. Kidani Village has 492 Disney Vacation Club villas; Jambo House has 109. Kidani Village hallways were renovated in 2015 to make them brighter. *Rooms: 340 sq ft. Sleep 4. Two queen beds, or one queen plus bunk beds, small refrigerator. Suites sleep 4–9 in 1-, 2- and 3-bedroom units. DVC villas sleep 4–12 in studio, 1-, 2- and 3-bedroom units.*

Swimming pools. Open 24 hours, the large Jambo House pool has a 67-foot water slide and a zero-entry gradual ramp. Nearby are a kiddie pool, two hot tubs, a shady playground and a flamingo habitat. The Kidani Village pool complex has a winding slide, hot tub and 4,200-square-foot kiddie play zone.

Restaurants and food. The resort has three restaurants, a fast-food cafe and two lounges. Room service is 6 a.m. to midnight.

★★★★★ ✔ $$$$$ **Boma.** This wonderful buffet combines American comfort food with non-threatening African options. The buffet area resembles an outdoor market, with each serving station its own hut or makeshift stand. Several seating areas sit under thatched ceilings with hand-cut glass and tin fixtures. *Breakfast 7:30a–11a, dinner 4:30p–9:30p. Seats 400. Jambo House.*

★★★★ ✔ $$$$$ **Jiko.** Relaxing and romantic, this African-fusion jewel has the largest selection of South African wine in the United States. Hanging from the ceiling, sculpted kanu birds fly over diners to bring them luck. Representing a sunset, a back wall slowly changes color. *5:30p–10p. Seats 300. Jambo House. A Disney Signature Restaurant.*

★★★★★ ✔ $$$$ **Sanaa.** Serving Indian-inspired East African cuisine with dishes both spicy and mild, this colorful dining room comes with an added bonus: diners near windows watch exotic animals roam a savanna. The bread service is a must. A stylized decor recalls an African marketplace; lights that resemble ripe fruit hang from abstract acacia trees. *Lunch 11:30a–3p, dinner 5p–9p. Seats 124, 24 in lounge. Kidani Village.*

★★★★ ✔ $$ **The Mara.** A relaxed fast-food spot serving American/African options. A small store has fruit, snacks, South African

Radiator Springs redux. A sign for the Cozy Cone Motel twirls in the "Cars" section of Disney's Art of Animation Resort. Behind it a lodging building disguises itself as a mountain range.

wines. Cartoons play on televisions. *7a–11:30p, bakery opens 6a. Seats 250. Jambo House.*

Other amenities. 24-hour animal viewing, night-vision animal spotting, arcade, nightly campfire, culinary tours and wine tastings, playground, poolside crafts. Afternoon, after-dark truck safaris into hotel savannas (extra charge). Business center. Laundromat, laundry service, massages, shops. Kidani Village: BBQ pavilion; basketball, shuffleboard, tennis courts; community hall with children's activities, books, games. Many organized children's activities (daily, some with fee) including African cultural programs, arts and crafts, cookie decorating. face painting, pool games.

Disney transportation. Buses shuttle guests to parks and Disney Springs, as well as between Jambo House and Kidani Village.

Location. Southwest Disney, near Animal Kingdom. Distance to (in miles): MK 6, EP 5, DHS 3, DAK <1, BB <1, TL 5, DS 5, ESPN 9. 2901 Osceola Parkway, 32830.

Key facts. Disney Deluxe resort with two lodges, animal savannas; 762 rooms, 19 suites, 708 villas, 74 acres. Built: Jambo House 2001, Kidani Village 2009. Phone: 407-938-3000. Fax: 407-938-4799. Check In 3p, Out 11a.

Rates. Rooms: Rack $320–$675, discounted to $199. Suites: $928–$2433, discounted to $652. Villas: $421–$1750, discounted to $325.

★★★ ✔ **Disney's Art of Animation Resort.** This Value complex is much like the Pop Century one next door. Though it has its own entrance, it uses the land and some of the buildings originally meant to be a second phase of that complex. As a result, it's landscaped and decorated in much the same fashion, with brightly colored motel-style buildings that are trimmed with gigantic icons that hide outdoor stairwells and elevator banks. But unlike those at Pop Century, these buildings and trim pieces are done more tastefully, so they're easier on your eye. Most actually look good. A central building holds the resort's registration area, food court and bus station, and fronts the main pool. Parking lots surround the complex on three sides; in back is a large retention pond and a footbridge to Pop Century.

Art of Animation has four sections, each one based on a Disney or Pixar movie—"Cars," "Finding Nemo," "The Lion King" (all family suites) and "The Little Mermaid" (standard rooms). Many families will love the look; the Cars area is especially well done. Rooms, however, are small, and even the suites have some fiberboard furnishings.

Highs. Affordable room rates, nicer and newer than other Value resorts, the closest hotel to the ESPN complex.

Look at this stuff, isn't it neat? A giant Ariel hides an elevator bank in "The Little Mermaid" section of the resort, the only section with standard hotel rooms.

Lows. Small standard rooms, no table-service restaurant, in-your-face decor.

Rooms. Art of Animation rooms have vivid color schemes and are boldly decorated with characters from recent Disney and Pixar films; furniture is painted in a vibrant mix of bright colors. Carpet patterns in the hotel's Cars suites have a yellow-gold Southwest coloring with large logos from that movie's locales; Finding Nemo suites recall waving seagrass; Lion King ones use browns and greens; Little Mermaid room furnishings use seashell patterns. *Rooms: 260 sq ft. Sleep 4. Two double beds. Accessed by outdoor walkways. Suites: 565 sq ft. Sleep 6. 1 queen bed, 1 sleeper-sofa double bed, 1 dining-table double bed, kitchenette, 2 full baths. Suites accessed by indoor hallways.*

Swimming pools. The resort has three pools, all with adjacent kiddie pools. At the main pool, characters from the 2003 movie "Finding Nemo" can be heard under the water. The largest swimming pool at Disney that's not in a water park, the Nemo pool also has a zero-entry side that makes it easy for toddlers and disabled guests to enjoy, a nearby kiddie splash zone and a pool bar.

Restaurants and food. An attractive food court (★★★ ✔ $$ 6a–11p; seats 650) has choices beyond standard fare; lunches and dinners include Mongolian barbecue. Nearby is a bakery, convenience store. Room service (pizza, salads, desserts) is 4 p.m. to midnight.

Other amenities. Arcade, beach, playgrounds. Learn-to-draw-a-Disney-character lessons. Laundromat, laundry service. Shop with groceries. Running trail (1.29 mi). Children's activities: Organized pool activities are posted at the main pool each morning; afternoon Pixel Parade in lobby.

Disney transportation. Buses shuttle you to parks and Disney Springs, but not to the ESPN Wide World of Sports complex.

Location. South Disney close to Interstate 4, near Hollywood Studios and the ESPN Wide World of Sports complex. Distance to (in miles): MK 6, EP 5, DHS 3, DAK 4, BB 4, TL 2, DS 3, ESPN 2. 1850 Century Dr. 32830.

Key facts. Disney Value resort with clustered buildings; 864 rooms, 1120 suites, 65 acres. Built: 2012. Phone: 407-938-7000. Fax: 407-938-7070. Check In 3p, Out 11a.

Rates. Rooms: Rack $109–$199, discounted to $90. Suites: $269–$457, discounted to $249.

★★★★★ ✔ **Disney's BoardWalk Inn.** Disney cut no corners when it built this hotel, a re-creation of the golden days of Atlantic City. Everything has the look of a community that has grown over time—"newer"

Surrey with fringe on top. A family pedals a rented bicycle surrey down the lakefront promenade that lines Disney's BoardWalk Inn, passing its shops and restaurants.

structures appear unrelated to "older" ones; mom-and-pop shops are tucked into residential buildings. A wide lakeside promenade includes a dance hall and dueling-piano bar. Surrounded by water on three sides, the property includes timeshare units and a conference center. Most rooms spread out among interconnected buildings; some overlook the lake, most face landscaped areas or pools.

Highs. Good dining variety, quality; within walking distance of Hollywood Studios and the back entrance to Epcot; evening boardwalk entertainment; lovely lakeside setting.

Lows. No restaurants are within the hotel interior; there's no Disney transportation to the main entrance of Epcot unless it's raining.

Rooms. Colorful period decor creates an immersive experience. Beds have plush mattresses on wood frames. Bathrooms have marble sinks. A club level is available. Two-story garden suites have individual front lawns with white picket fences. *Rooms: 385 sq ft. Sleep 5. 2 queen beds, sleeper sofa, small refrigerator. Suites sleep 4–9 in 1-, 2-, 3-bedroom units. DVC villas sleep 4–12 in studio, 1-, 2-, 3-bedroom units. Villas refurbished in 2015.*

Swimming pools. The Luna Park swimming pool area features a 200-foot red slide that looks like a 1920s wooden roller coaster, with small dips, sweeping turns and, at its

exit, the mouth of a giant clown head. Nearby is a kiddie pool, playground and sunny hot tub. Two quiet pool areas are somewhat shady—the Villas one (refurbished in 2015) is nicely landscaped with a large grill; a smaller one at the Inn has fewer trees, no grill.

Restaurants and food. The BoardWalk offers a variety of good dining choices, though it doesn't have an indoor fast-food spot. Room service is available 24 hours a day at the Inn; 6 a.m. to midnight at the Villas.

★★★ ✔ $$$ **Big River Grille & Brewing Works.** Sporting Disney World's only micro brewery, this classy little franchise also offers down-to-earth food and free Wi-Fi. The food—grilled meats, seafood, pasta, sandwiches—and the prices are reasonable. Small gunmetal tables make it noisy when crowded. It serves dinner later (to 11p) than most Disney restaurants. Equipped with two televisions, the small bar can be a less-crowded sports-bar alternative to the nearby ESPN Club. *11:30a–11p. Seats 190, including 90 outside.*

★★★ $$ **ESPN Club.** This casual, noisy eatery combines a sports bar with a second room that hosts radio-style talk shows. It has 123 television monitors. Weekends can be packed. Basic bar chow includes burgers, hot dogs, ribs, steaks. *11:30a–11p Seats 450.*

Super slide. The BoardWalk's Luna Park swimming pool features a 200-foot slide that channels a 1920s wooden roller coaster, exiting through the mouth of a giant clown.

★★★ $$$$$ **Flying Fish Cafe.** Cramped, bright and loud, the poor atmosphere at this pricey seafood spot interferes with its quality food. A show kitchen boosts the noise. Sit in the back for the calmest experience. Good bets include calamari, crab cakes, scallops, steak, or the six-course prix-fixe Chef's Wine Tasting Dinner. *5:30p–10p. Seats 193. A Disney Signature Restaurant.*

NEW! ★★★★ ✔ $$$$$ **Trattoria al Forno.** Want Italian but don't want to spend *una fortuna?* Here's your place—the fourth Italian restaurant in the Epcot area; the only one operated by Disney and the least expensive of the bunch. Breakfast choices include waffles with mascarpone cheese; dinner is dominated by pasta and pizza but also includes a signature chicken parmigiana and a whole roasted fish—a holdover from this restaurant's previous life as Cat Cora's Kouzzina (yay!). The tiramisu is luscious but tiny; about four bites and you're done. An Italian wine list offers 60 varieties, half available by the glass; grappas, Italian liqueurs and Italian beers round out the bar menu. Four distinct dining areas portray areas of a fictional family's home as they slowly convert it into a restaurant: their humble kitchen, formal dining room, stately living room and cozy brick-walled den. All overlook the actual restaurant's massive exhibition kitchen. *Breakfast 7:30a–11a., $7–$13 (children $6). Dinner 5p-10p, $17–$37 (children $9). Seats 232.*

★★★ $ **BoardWalk Bakery.** Pick up fresh-baked pastries and treats at this walk-in spot; also hot breakfast sandwiches, cold lunch ones. *6:30a–varies. No seating.*

★★★★ $ **Seashore Sweets.** Hand-scooped ice cream, fudge, packaged candy. Walls lined with portraits of every Miss America. *10:30a–11p. No seating.*

Other amenities. Arcade, BBQ grill, bike and surrey rentals, fitness center, lighted tennis courts. 2 nightclubs including Jelly Rolls piano bar. Laundromat, laundry service. Shop with groceries. Conference center (9,600 sq ft, ballroom, 14 breakout rooms). Business center. Children's programs: Organized activities (daily, some have a small fee) include arts and crafts, pool games.

Disney transportation. Boats sail to Epcot, Hollywood Studios; buses serve other parks and Disney Springs. When boats can't operate (i.e., during lightning), buses serve all parks.

Location. Central Disney, in between Hollywood Studios and Epcot. Distance to (in miles): MK 4, EP <1, DHS <1, DAK 4, BB 4, TL 4, DS 2, ESPN 4. 2101 N. Epcot Resorts Blvd., 32830.

Key facts. Disney Deluxe resort with interconnected buildings; 378 rooms, 20

Palms aplenty. Centertown, the amenities center for Disney's Caribbean Beach Resort, holds its restaurant, food court and gift shop.

suites, 533 villas, 45 acres. Built: 1996. Phone: 407-939-5100. Fax: 407-939-5150. Check In 3p (Villas 4p), Out 11a.

Rates. Rooms: Rack $381–$1087, discounted to $256. Suites: $1468–$3202, discounted to $554. Villas: $369–$2551, discounted to $256.

★★★ ✔ Disney's Caribbean Beach Resort.

A nice mix of value and convenience, Caribbean Beach is a good choice for families who want a resort-hotel experience but don't want to bust their bank account. There's nothing truly Caribbean here, but look beyond that and there's lots to like. Disney's second largest hotel complex, this 200-acre resort is wrapped around a 42-acre man-made lake and landscaped with palms and native pines. Colorful metal-roofed lodging buildings cluster into six self-contained "villages," each of which has its own parking lot. A dining, shopping and recreation center, Old Port Royale, is centrally located. Footbridges over the lake lead to Caribbean Cay, a flowery one-acre island dotted with benches and hammocks.

Highs. Decent rates; convenient to all Disney parks, Disney Springs and ESPN; comfortable rooms near parking lots; tropical landscaping lends a distinct vacation feel.

Lows. Dining facilities are weak and too limited, especially at breakfast; many lodging buildings are far from bus stops; superficial Caribbean theming; childish room decor, especially in pirate-theme rooms. Check-in counters and the main concierge center are at the Custom House, a building along the entranceway far from other areas.

Rooms. All are specifically themed, most in a Finding Nemo trim; some in a cheesy pirate theme with molded-plastic beds that resemble ships, dressers that look like crates and skull-and-sword bathroom drapes. *Rooms: 314 sq ft. Sleep 4. 2 queen beds, small refrigerator. Some pull-down wall beds. Accessed by outdoor walkways. Renovated 2015.*

Swimming pools. The main pool sits in a stone fort. Cannons spray swimmers; a small slide has a 90-degree turn. Nearby is a kiddie pool, hot tub and a small water playground with mini-slides, fountains and a barrel that dumps water from above. Calm basic pools sit within each lodging area.

Restaurants and food. A comfortable restaurant serves overpriced dinners; a comfy food court serves lame food all day long (★★ $$ 6:30a–11p; seats 500). There's also a bakery and small convenience store. Room service (pizza, salads, desserts) is available 4 p.m. to 11:30 p.m.

★★ $$$$ Shutters. This little spot is often among the worst of Disney's hotel eateries;

Playing pirate. The main swimming pool at Caribbean Beach winds through a stone fort. Quiet pools sit within each of the resort's clustered lodging areas.

most of its American/Caribbean fare is over-priced. That said, it's also an entry-level job for Disney chefs, who sometimes create fine dishes here before moving on. The decor is bland, but tables are big and chairs wide and padded. *5p–10p. Seats 132.*

Other amenities. Arcade, beach, bike and boat rentals, campfire, guided fishing trips, hammocks, picnic area, sand volleyball court, surrey rentals, walking trail. Some lodging areas (Barbados, Jamaica, Trinidad, Old Port Royale) have playgrounds. Laundromat, laundry service. Small shop with groceries. Complimentary children's arts and crafts, beach and pool activities, daily dance party; pontoon-boat pirate adventure (extra $).

Disney transportation. Bus stops throughout the complex serve the parks, Disney Springs and the ESPN complex. A separate bus circles within the resort.

Location. Central Disney near Hollywood Studios. Distance to (in miles): MK 5, EP 4, DHS 3, DAK 5, BB 3, TL 1, DS 2, ESPN 3. 900 Cayman Way, 32830.

Key facts. Disney Moderate resort with clustered buildings; 2,112 rooms, 200 acres. Built: 1988. Phone: 407-934-1000. Fax: 407-934-3288. Check In 3p, Out 11a.

Rates. Rack $162–$331, discounted to $136.

★★★ **Disney's Contemporary Resort.** One of Walt Disney World's original hotels, this 1971 property has an indoor monorail station, comfortable rooms and a character meal, but yet fails to deliver a magical experience—much of it seems more like an office building than a hotel. It consists of a 15-story A-frame, a nondescript wing, a convention center and the timeshare Bay Lake Tower. It's the only hotel within walking distance to Magic Kingdom. As for being contemporary, each room has its own computer, but the rest of the resort channels a coldhearted office complex from the 1970s. Ceilings are often acoustical tile. A restricted Disney Vacation Club property, Bay Lake Tower looks modern, though some of its interior areas seem cheap and too angular. It also has its own recreation area and a rooftop lounge with an outdoor deck.

Highs. On the monorail route, within walking distance to Magic Kingdom, big comfortable rooms, extensive water recreation, lakeside. Great views from higher floors.

Lows. An abundance of glass, carpet and sprayed plain concrete lends a cold corporate feel. Restaurants are pricey, fast-food weak.

Rooms. Most have an Asian decor; a club level is available. A concierge lounge has seasonal and organic foods; yoga and spa sessions available. *Rooms: 394 sq ft. Sleep 5. 2*

Pick your pool. A winding pool at Disney's Contemporary Resort sits behind its signature 15-story A-frame. A nearby second pool is perfectly round, and gets deeper in its center.

queen beds, daybed, small refrigerator. Suites sleep 4–8 in 1-, 2-bedroom units. DVC villas sleep 4–12 in studio, 1-, 2-, 3-bedroom units.

Swimming pools. The main pool has a 17-foot-high spiraling slide, a large central fountain and a row of smaller sprays. A second pool sits next to the lake. It's round, and gets deeper in its center. Cabana tents are available for rent (407-939-7529; 407-824-2464 same-day). Nearby are a beach volleyball court and a kiddie pool area with a splash pad and water cannons. A Bay Lake Tower pool includes a zero-entry side and a 20-foot-high spiraling slide wrapped in a glass block. Near it are a hot tub, Mickey-shaped kids fountain, shuffleboard and bocce ball courts and a BBQ pavilion with shaded picnic tables.

Restaurants and food. The Contemporary has three restaurants, a character buffet and a fast-food spot. Room service is 24 hours.

★★★★★ ✓ $$$$$ **California Grill.** Superb New American and Japanese fare is matched by a stunning view atop the resort's A-frame. Expect exquisite sushi. Diners can watch Magic Kingdom's Wishes fireworks show from inside or on rooftop walkways, with the show's music audible. Recently remodeled, the restaurant's stylish decor uses honey woodwork. *5:30p–10p. Seats 156. A Disney Signature Restaurant.*

★★ $$$$$ **Chef Mickey's.** This busy character meal features Mickey Mouse as a chef; Minnie Mouse, Donald Duck, Goofy and Pluto as cooks. Unfortunately, characters often spend little time with each diner. *Breakfast 7a–11:30a. Dinner 5p–9:30p. Seats 405.*

★★★★ ✓ $$$$ **The Wave.** This upscale American eatery serves fresh, healthy food in recipes that blend flavors to create unique tastes. The open dining room has a sophisticated decor but no windows. Hidden; often not crowded. *Breakfast 7:30a–11a, lunch noon–2p, dinner 5:30p–10p. Lounge noon–mid. Seats 222 plus 100 in lounge.*

★ $$ **The Contempo Cafe.** Though it has a great location in the middle of the A-frame atrium, this fast-food spot offers little to recommend it. Its food is uneven, its electronic ordering irritating. Watching the monorail trains pass by is fun. *6a–10p. Seats 112.*

Other amenities. Arcades; beer tastings, boat rentals; campfire; guided fishing trips; tennis, beach volleyball courts; water sports. Fitness center, hair salon, laundromat, laundry service. Convention center (120,000 square feet, 4 ballrooms, 1,600-square-foot stage, 33 breakout rooms). Business center. Children's arts and crafts, beach and pool activities. Bay Lake Tower Community Center has board games, shuffleboard, DVD

Night lights. Disney's Mexican-themed Coronado Springs Resort is anchored by its dining, shopping and convention complex, which sits on a 15-acre lake.

rentals. The Electrical Water Pageant passes behind the hotel between 10:05 and 10:25 p.m.

Disney transportation. Monorail trains serve Magic Kingdom, Epcot, the Grand Floridian and Polynesian Village. Boats head to Wilderness Lodge and Fort Wilderness. Buses run to Hollywood Studios, Animal Kingdom, water parks and Disney Springs.

Location. Northwest Disney near Magic Kingdom. Distance to (in miles): MK <1, EP 4, DHS 4, DAK 7, BB 5, TL 6, DS 7, ESPN 7. 4600 N. World Dr., 32830.

Key facts. Disney Deluxe resort with A-frame, wing and separate DVC wing; 632 rooms, 23 suites, 295 villas, 55 acres. Built: 1971. Phone: 407-824-1000. Fax: 407-824-3539. Check In: 3p. (Bay Lake Tower 4p). Check Out: 11a.

Rates. Rooms: Rack $356–$1000, discounted to $269. Suites: $1066–$3483, discounted to $895. Villas: $444–$2923, discounted to $370.

★★★ ✔ **Disney's Coronado Springs Resort.** This sprawling Spanish Colonial convention complex offers a quality place to stay at a decent price, even if you're not there on business. It consists of an amenities and convention center and three distinct lodging areas, all of which circle around a 15-acre lake. Rooms and suites are grouped into an urban-styled Casitas area near the

convention center; a Ranchos section that has an American Southwest landscape of sagebrush, cactus and gravel; and a Cabanas area decorated like Mexico's Gulf Coast. It's Disney's only mid-priced convention property.

Highs. Family-friendly despite convention location, many rooms near parking lots, excellent swimming and recreation complex. Tropical landscaping is well-maintained.

Lows. Little Disney feel. Dining options are only fair. Rooms can be far from the convention area, a pain for business travelers.

Rooms. A modern Mexican decor combines dark woods with blue, green and yellow fabrics; club-level rooms have DVD players. Most rooms are close to parking lots. *Rooms: 314 sq ft. Sleep 4. 2 queen beds, small refrigerator. Accessed by outdoor walkways. Renovated 2015–2016.*

Swimming pools. With old-fashioned swing sets, treasures buried in the sand and a sneaky spitting jaguar next to a winding swimming-pool slide, children may never realize they're at a convention hotel if they hang out at Coronado's large outdoor recreation complex. Adjacent to the Ranchos area, it includes a large swimming pool, kiddie fountain pool, 22-person hot tub, sand volleyball court and indoor arcade. Smaller quiet pools are located in each lodging area.

Modern Mexican. The Casitas area of Disney's Coronado Springs Resort reflects the country's urban areas. Spanish Colonial buildings sit among palms and low hedges.

Restaurants and food. The Disney touch is absent at the Coronado's dining choices, which are run by an outside company. A small lounge is geared to expense accounts. Room service is available 7 a.m. to 11 p.m.

★★★ $$$$ **Maya Grill.** Breakfast dishes at this American-Latin eatery include a Kobe brunch burger and Huevos Rancheros. Meats, Tex Mex platters dominate lunch and dinner. An open kitchen has a wood-burning oven. *Breakfast 7a–11a, dinner 5a–10p. Seats 220.*

★★ $$ **Pepper Market Court.** Mall-quality American/Mexican dishes disappoint, but the atmosphere is nice. As you get your own food but not your drinks, there's an automatic 10 percent service charge. *Breakfast 6a–10:30a; lunch, dinner 11a–11p. Seats 420.*

★★ $ **Café Rix.** This small spot serves pastries, sandwiches, gelato. *6:30a–mid. Seats 50.*

Other amenities. Arcades; beach; bike, boat, surrey rentals; nightly campfire; fitness center; guided fishing trips; hammocks; mile-long running trail. Hair salon with facial, hand and foot treatments; nail salon. Laundromat, laundry service. Shop with groceries. Convention center (220,000 square feet, ballroom, exhibit hall, 45 breakout rooms). Business center. Organized children's activities (daily, some have small fee) include arts and crafts, pool games.

Disney transportation. Buses serve parks and Disney Springs.

Location. Next to Disney's Western Way entrance, near Hollywood Studios. Distance to (in miles): MK 4, EP 3, DHS <1, DAK 2, BB <1, TL 3, DS 4, ESPN 5. 1000 W. Buena Vista Dr., 32830.

Key facts. Disney Moderate resort with buildings in three areas; 1,877 rooms, 44 suites, 125 acres. Built: 1997. Phone: 407-939-1000. Fax: 407-939-1001. Check In 3p, Out 11a.

Rates. Rooms: Rack $167–$338, discounted to $140. Suites: $401–$1357, discounted to $351.

★★★★ ✓ **Disney's Fort Wilderness Resort & Campground.** Almost everything you could hope for in a campground except way more expensive, Fort Wilderness offers a wonderful family-friendly experience. Lined with creek-like canals and nestled alongside a 450-acre natural lake, it's a huge swath of land tucked into a thick pine forest and, in some areas, a drained cypress wetland. Three roads branch off into 28 loops, each of which is lined with either cabins or campsites. In back, a Settlement area includes a restaurant, general store, music hall and marina, from which boats ferry you to Magic Kingdom. Though shuttle buses circle the complex, many guests rent electric carts to get around. Staying either in

Campground carts. Many families rent electric carts to get around Disney's Fort Wilderness Resort & Campground, as its common areas don't have parking lots.

a tent, RV or rustic cabin, you'll feel removed from civilization, and will certainly bond with your family.

Highs. Relaxed wooded setting, wide variety of outdoor recreation, only Disney campsite, pets welcome in some spots.

Lows. Pricey campsites; cabins can be chintzy. Complex transportation to parks, other Disney areas. Limited dining options.

RV campsites. The resort offers three different types of campsites for recreational vehicles. Full-Hookup Sites—in other words, standard sites—(10-by-60 feet) allow for both an RV and tent. Preferred Sites (also 10-by-60) allow for an RV and up to two tents, and are near the Settlement area of the resort, which has its restaurant, entertainment halls and boat dock. Premium Sites (18-by-60) are spacious but allow for only an RV.

Tent campsites. The same size as most RV sites (10-by-60 feet), these spots accommodate up to either two tents or a pop-up van and one tent. A tents-only Creekside Meadow is reserved for camping groups of 20 or more, and has no hookups.

Campsite amenities. Except for Creekside Meadow, all RV and tent sites include a paved pad; cable TV, electric, Internet, water and sewage hookup; a BBQ grill; and a picnic table. All sites are near air-conditioned

24-hour comfort stations with private showers, ice dispensers, laundromats and vending machines. All camping areas are connected by paved walkways to recreation areas and shuttle-bus stops. Buses circle through the resort from about 8a until around midnight, depending on the hours of the theme parks.

Cabins. Faux log cabins sit mostly within a pine and palm forest in the front half of the large resort; some are in a drained cypress wetland. Exteriors have wood decks, picnic tables and BBQ grills; interiors have rustic Western themes and roughhewn furniture. *504 sq ft. Sleep 6. Living room with Murphy bed, kitchen, bath, bedroom with 1 double and 2 bunk beds, deck, picnic table, outdoor grill. Vaulted ceilings, daily housekeeping.*

Swimming pools. A large main pool has a water slide, hot tub, children's splash zone and nearby playground. A smaller quiet pool sits in the center of the cabin area.

Restaurants and food. Fort Wilderness dining choices include a buffet restaurant and two dinner shows. There's no fast-food restaurant or food-delivery service.

★★★★ $$$$ **Trail's End Restaurant.** Though the price is a might steep at this down-home eatery its food is good; potatoes are creamy, vegetables have flavor. Breakfast and dinner buffets serve fried chicken and other comfort

Home sweet home. Don't have a tent? Disney will rent you one this size and set it up for you at no charge. A 10-by-60-foot campsite includes a picnic table, grill and full hook-ups.

food; lunch is a la carte. A take-out counter has sandwiches, salads, pizzas; there's a tiny bar. *7:30a–2p, 4:30p–9:30p. Take-out noon–2p. Seats 192, 6 at bar. The Settlement.*

★★★ $$$$$ **Hoop-Dee-Doo Musical Revue.** This rootin' tootin' dinner show has been performed 35,000 times since 1974. Most children love its six exuberant performers and its rat-a-tat jokes, though the songs and skits aren't anything special—expect a lot of "So, where're ya from?" Vittles include all-you-can-eat pails of fried chicken and ribs, "fixin's" and unlimited draft beer and wine. Tables are reserved; book one near the stage and the corny cowpokes and cowgals will come right to your table. *2-hr shows at 5, 7:15, 9:30p. Tues–Sat. Seats 360. Pioneer Hall.*

★★★ $$$$$ **Mickey's Backyard Barbecue.** With Mickey Mouse, Minnie Mouse, Goofy and Chip 'n Dale on hand to dance with diners, this old-fashioned country show is fun for children. Held in a large outdoor pavilion, it includes a live country band, a trick roper and a big ol' dollop of 1950s-style patriotism. A so-so buffet offers pork ribs, chicken, corn on the cob, watermelon and beer. Diners share long tables. Arrive early; those in first sit next to the dance floor. *2-hr shows at 6:30p. Thr, Sat except in Jan, Feb. Seats 300. The Settlement.*

Other amenities. Arcade, archery instruction, beach, bike rentals, dog park, golf cart rentals, picnic areas, playgrounds, Segway tour, stable, surrey rentals, walking trail, watercraft rentals. Basketball, horseshoes, tennis, tetherball, volleyball courts. Cane-pole fishing, guided fishing trips. Carriage, wagon, trail, pony rides. Laundromat. Two stores with groceries, camping supplies. Children's programs: Arts and crafts, pool activities; outstanding down-home campfire/movie with live entertainer, Chip 'n Dale. The Electrical Water Pageant passes behind the campground between 9:45 and 10:05 p.m.

Disney transportation. Buses serve parks, Disney Springs; a separate one circles within the resort. Boats serve Magic Kingdom.

Location. Northwest Disney. Distance to (in miles): MK 2, EP 4, DHS 4, DAK 6, BB 4, TL 6, DS 6, ESPN 6. 3520 N. Ft. Wilderness Trail, 32830.

Key facts. Disney Moderate resort; 784 campsites, 409 cabins, 740 acres. Built: 1971. Phone: 407-824-2900. Fax: 407-824-3508. Check In 3p, Out 11a.

Rates. Cabins: Rack $299–$500, discounted to $235. Full-hook-up campsites: Rack $69–$129. Preferred campsites: Rack $79–$140. Premium campsites: Rack $85–$145. Tent campsite: Rack $50–$107, optional tent rental $30 per day (includes set-up and breakdown,

A bygone era. A father plays with his son on the beach behind Disney's Grand Floridian Resort & Spa. The resort recalls fabled Sunshine State retreats of the late 19th century.

must be arranged at least 1 hr. before sundown). Cots $5 per night. Campfires allowed; firewood $25 1/2 bin; $50 full bin. Max. 10 people per campsite. Group camping areas $10 per person, min. 20 people. Pets (up to 4) $5 per night in select cabins and climate-controlled RVs only. To arrange tents or group camping call 407-939-7807. Note: Campsites are rarely listed in TripAdvisor or other booking sites, and therefore rarely discounted. To book one go to disneyworld.com or call 407-939-7429.

★★★★★ **Disney's Grand Floridian Resort.** The signature Walt Disney World resort, the Grand Floridian lives up to its promise, even if its formal nature seems out of place next to the world's most popular theme park. With its gabled roofs and miles of moldings, scrolls and turnposts, its genteel lodging buildings bring the Sunshine State's short-lived Victorian era back to life, as does its landscape of canary palms, Southern magnolias and formal gardens. In the evenings, the main building's five-story atrium features a grand pianist and retro live orchestra. Compared to the nearby Polynesian Village, the Grand is more beautiful but less charming, has ritzier food choices but smaller rooms.

Highs. On the monorail loop, comfy rooms, top-notch dining, lakeside, adjacent wedding pavilion, unique children's programs.

Lows. Very expensive, more formal than fun, the self-parking lot is ridiculously far off.

Rooms. A Victorian decor uses light woods and fabrics, ceiling fans and marble sinks. A club level is available. *Rooms: 440 sq ft. Sleep 5. 2 queen beds, some daybeds, small refrigerator. Suites sleep 4–8 in 1-, 2-bedroom units. Rooms refurbished in 2015; suites 2016. Villas sleep 5–12 in studio, 1-, 2-, 3-bedroom units.*

Swimming pools. A calm swimming pool sits in a central courtyard, surrounded by a kiddie pool and hot tub. A second beachside pool, however, is the family favorite. It has a swerving 181-foot slide that takes 12 seconds to travel, as well as a 20-foot waterfall, a zero-entry side for toddlers and wheelchair guests and an Alice in Wonderland water play area. Cabanas are available for rent (407-939-7529 in advance, 407-824-2464 same-day).

Restaurants and food. Options include three high-roller restaurants and two relative bargains. Room service is 24 hours a day.

★★★★★ ✔ $$$$$ **1900 Park Fare.** These joyous character meals are the best at Walt Disney World. Breakfast stars Mary Poppins, Winnie the Pooh and Alice in Wonderland ("little kids call me Alison," one of the Alices

Luxurious lobby. Victorian flair fills the Grand Floridian's five-story atrium lobby. Two stained-glass domes filter natural light through its ceiling.

told us). At dinner it's Cinderella as well as what amounts to a comedy troupe—bickering stepsisters Anastasia and Drizella and step-mother Lady Tremaine. Prince Charming's on hand too, gallantly kissing the hands of any females who offer them. Varied buffet choices are delicious. The elegant dining room has a vintage amusement park theme. *Breakfast 8a–11:30a, dinner 4:30p–8:30p. Seats 270.*

★★★★ ✔ **$$$$$ Cítricos.** Lit with a yellow glow, this Mediterranean gem doesn't have the view of Narcoossee's or the glam of Victoria & Albert's, but does offer the most relaxed setting of any Disney Signature restaurant. Tall windows overlook the resort's main pool and marina. *5:30p–10p. Seats 190. A Disney Signature Restaurant.*

★★★★ ✔ **$$$$ Grand Floridian Café.** This relaxing American spot features quality entrees, floral wallpaper and thick carpeting. Sunny at breakfast. *7a–2p; 5p–9p. Seats 326.*

★★★★★ ✔ **$$$$$ Narcoossee's.** Expensive yet pretension-free, this circular building over the Seven Seas Lagoon is the author's choice at Disney for fine seafood, though its wood floors and peaked ceilings make it almost too noisy. At night ask for a windowside table for a perfect view of Magic Kingdom's fireworks show, which reflects in the water. *5:30p–10p. Seats 270. A Disney Signature Restaurant.*

★★★★★ ✔ **$$$$$ Victoria & Albert's.** For an evening to remember this AAA Five-Diamond gourmet restaurant is worth its cost; it may give you the best meal you've ever had. A seven-course dinner is matched to your personal taste. A four-hour Chef's Table option includes more courses, a kitchen tour and a chat with the cooks. *Two dinner seatings. Formal dress. Jackets required for men; loaners available. No children under age 10. Seats 90, including 10 at Chef's Table.*

★★★★ **$$ Garden View Tea Room.** This tiny, elegant spot overlooks lovely outdoor gardens. English tea sandwiches, scones, tarts, teas and specialty coffees are served on flowery china. *2p–6p. Seats 80.*

★★ **$ Gasparilla Grill and Games.** Good fast food in a noisy arcade. *24 hrs. Seats 150.*

★★★★ **$$$ Mizner's Lounge.** Hidden behind the lobby's orchestra stand, this second-floor retreat pours high-end ports, cognacs and scotches into classic highballs. Upmarket appetizers tempt. *4:30p–mid. Seats 30.*

Other amenities. Arcade, beach, boat rentals, fireworks cruise, nightly campfire on beach, guided fishing trips, tea parties, tennis courts and clinics, walking trail. Daily Changing of the Guard at 4:30 p.m. Hair salon, laundromat, laundry service. Full spa. Adjacent Wedding Chapel.

Twilight twinkles. The Conch Flats community hall at Disney's Old Key West Resort includes a restaurant, gift shop and a small marina, which rents a variety of watercraft.

Shop with groceries. Convention center (40,000 square feet, 2 ballrooms, 16 breakout rooms). Business center. Children's programs: Pontoon-boat pirate adventure; complimentary pool activities. The Electrical Water Pageant passes behind the hotel between 9:15 and 9:35 p.m.

Disney transportation. Monorail trains serve Magic Kingdom, Epcot; Contemporary, Polynesian Village resorts. Buses head to Hollywood Studios, Animal Kingdom, water parks, Disney Springs. Boats go to Magic Kingdom; Wilderness Lodge and Fort Wilderness resorts.

Location. Northwest Disney, near Magic Kingdom. Distance to (in miles): MK 1, EP 4, DHS 4, DAK 7, BB 5, TL 7, DS 7, ESPN 7. 4401 Grand Floridian Way, 32830.

Key facts. Disney Deluxe resort with clustered buildings; 842 rooms, 25 suites, 147 villas, 40 acres. Built: 1988. Phone: 407-824-3000. Fax: 407-824-3186. Check In 3p, Out 11a.

Rates. Rooms: Rack $517–$3166, discounted to $342. Suites: $1362–$3458, discounted to $915. Villas: $569–$1659, discounted to $449.

★★★★ Disney's Old Key West Resort.
Visitors from Southwest Florida (and perhaps the Keys) will feel right at home amid the Olde Florida facades, swaying palm fronds

and falling pine needles of this DVC village, the original Disney Vacation Club community. Spacious villas offer views of woods, canals or the Lake Buena Vista golf course. Lodging buildings combine clapboard siding with shuttered windows, gingerbread accents and tin roofs, clustering into villages along three roadways. Near the entrance is a food, shopping and recreation center.

Highs. Spacious villas, expansive closet space, good restaurant, parking within steps of each villa, palm-filled tropical landscaping.

Lows. Pools are small, simple and few for a property this size; limited dining options don't include an indoor fast-food spot.

Villas. Most have a tropical color scheme with hardwood floors and granite countertops. Each has a balcony or patio. The units are notable for their size; some bedrooms are so big that even with two queen beds they look empty. *Studios: 376 sq ft; sleep 4. 1-bedroom 942 sq ft; sleep 4. 2-bedroom 1,333 sq ft; sleep 8. 2-story 3 bedroom 2,202 sq ft; sleep 12. Accessed by outdoor walkways.*

Swimming pools. The main pool, at Conch Flat Community Hall, has a water slide that looks like a giant sandcastle. A faux lighthouse stands nearby, also close is a kiddie pool, playground and hot tub. Three quiet pools sit among the villages.

Heigh Ho, Heigh Ho. It's off to work maids and lifeguards go early one morning at Disney's Polynesian Village Resort. Disney World's first hotel, the large complex is still a guest favorite.

Restaurants and food. A small restaurant is the only indoor place to eat. Room service (pizza, salads, sandwiches, desserts) is available from 4 p.m. to midnight.

★★★ ✔ $$$$ **Olivia's Cafe.** Jimmy Buffett would fit right in at this Keys-inspired eatery; its menu a mix of standard American fare and regional dishes heavy on shrimp, conch and accents such as mango glazes. A homey decor includes a tin ceiling and mismatched padded chairs. *7:30a–10p. Seats 156, inc. 22 outside.*

★★ ✔ $ **Good's Food To Go.** This outdoor counter offers burgers, hot dogs, salads and sandwiches. *11:30a–10p. No seating.*

★★★ ✔ $$$ **Gurgling Suitcase.** Full-service bar decked out with license plates, patches and family pics of DVC members. *Indoor, outdoor seating. 11:30a–mid. Seats 75.*

Other amenities. Arcade; bike, boat and surrey rentals; campfire; Community Center rents DVDs; fitness center; guided fishing trips; marina; playground. Basketball, shuffleboard, volleyball courts; 3 tennis courts, 2 lighted. Laundromat, laundry service. Shop with groceries. Children's programs: Arts and crafts, pool activities, sandcastle building.

Disney transportation. Boats go to Disney Springs; Port Orleans French Quarter and Riverside, Saratoga Springs. Disney buses shuttle guests to all theme parks, water parks and Disney Springs. A separate shuttle circles within the resort.

Location. East Disney, between Disney Springs and Port Orleans French Quarter. Distance to (in miles): MK 4, EP 2, DHS 3, DAK 5, BB 4, TL 2, DS 2, ESPN 3. 1510 N. Cove Rd., 32830.

Key facts. Disney Deluxe Villas resort with clustered buildings; 761 villas, 74 acres. Built: 1991. Phone: 407-827-7700. Fax: 407-827-7710. Check In 4p, Out 11a.

Rates. Studios: Rack $327–$484, discounted to $229. Villas: $452–$1920, discounted to $316.

★★★★★ ✔ **Disney's Polynesian Village Resort.** Walt Disney World's original family resort, the Polynesian offers the definitive Disney vacation: a room at a themed, world-of-its-own hotel that's just a short glide on a monorail from the Magic Kingdom. The 12-building complex is themed to the South Seas, with many palms, waterfalls and torch-lit walkways. A central building holds the resort's front desk and concierge, restaurants, bar, shops and monorail station. The resort was transformed in 2015, as it reverted to its original name (restoring the word "Village"), redid its parking lot, motor lobby, indoor lobby and main swimming pool complex, opened a unique new bar, converted

© Disney

Sweeping space. Totally redone in 2015, the Polynesian's lobby no longer has its signature central waterfall, but does offer a more spacious area that can handle a crowd.

some hotel rooms to timeshare units and built new "bungalows" that sit out over the water. The "Poly" has a unique claim to fame: it's where, in 1974 while visiting with his children, John Lennon signed the legal documents that officially dissolved The Beatles.

Highs. Distinctive laid-back child-friendly attitude, beautiful rooms, tropical landscaping, wacky 1960s American Tiki culture, fun swimming pool, unique spirited bar.

Lows. Expensive. Grounds are spread out in a confusing fashion; it's easy to get lost.

Rooms. Hand-carved furniture, batik-print fabrics and dim lighting create a unique decor. A club level is available. *Rooms: 415 sq ft. Sleep 5. 2 queen beds, some daybeds, small refrigerator. Suites: Sleep up to 9.*

Villas. New in 2015, 20 bungalows sit just off the beach. Each has a living room, two bedrooms, two baths, a full kitchen and an array of Disney-style tropical touches and playful modern artwork. Most unique: a furnished private back deck with a plunge pool (think hot tub, without the heat or bubbles) and speakers that sync to the soundtrack of the visible Wishes fireworks show at Magic Kingdom. Former standard rooms in three older buildings (Rapa Nui, Tahiti and Tokelau) are now studios, the largest at Disney. *Bungalows sleep 8, include 1 king*

bed, 1 queen bed, queen-sized sleeper sofa, 2 pull-down bunk beds, stacked washer and dryer. Studios sleep 5, include queen bed, queen sleeper, kitchenette.

Swimming pools. Completely redone in 2015, the central Lava swimming pool is nestled against a simulated volcano, itself now slightly shorter so 'Ohana diners can see Cinderella Castle. Kids love standing underneath its waterfall, taking repeat trips down its slide—a slippery two-story tunnel with squirting water and eerie colored lights—and listening closely to hear the pool's underwater music. A zero-entry gradual ramp provides access for toddlers and disabled guests. Nearby is a hut tub and a new Kiki Tikis Splash Play area, a water playground for children 48 inches and under. Larger and more elaborate than water playgrounds at other Disney hotels, it includes buckets that douse kids, two slides, and playful tikis that spit and spout water. Tucked in to a lodging area, a smaller East pool is rarely crowded.

Restaurants and food. There's a little of everything, and it's pretty good. Room service is available 6:30 a.m. to midnight.

★★★★ ✔ $$$$ **Kona Café.** The best mid-priced restaurant on the monorail loop, this one-time coffee shop today serves first-rate

Get your hands up. Girls from the audience get a quick hula lesson during the Polynesian's Spirit of Aloha dinner show, which features a song-and-dance tour of the South Seas.

Pan-Pacific American meals. Tables and booths sit in a subdued, carpeted decor open to the lobby. The authors eat here often. Kona coffee is available. *7:30a–3p, 5–10p. Seats 163.*

★★★ $$$$ **'Ohana.** Highlighted by fresh coconut-pineapple bread, this breakfast is one of Disney's most popular character meals. Lilo, Stitch and Mickey Mouse lead kids in a maraca-shaking parade hourly. Come hungry for dinner, when skewers of Polynesian-flavored meats and seafood are grilled over a fire and continually delivered to your table. Children participate in coconut races and hula contests. *7:30a–11a, 5p–10p. Seats 300.*

★★★ $$ **Captain Cook's Snack Co.** A well-done variety of American fast food, flatbreads and stir-fry, plus Dole Whip soft-serve faux ice cream. Nice dining area. *6:30a–11p. Seats 150.*

NEW! ★★★★★ ✓ $$$ **Trader Sam's Grog Grotto.** First, the bad news. The rum drinks average $20, and they're a little light on the rum. There may be a wait to get in, and when you do get in it's up to you to find a seat. Party of 4? Well, there's a stool over there, a chair over here, and perhaps that couple way in the back could scooch over a bit. Now the good news: this is a fantastic place, you'll definitely remember your time here, the unique "small plates" food items are often really good, drinks start at $8, until 8 p.m.

your kids can come in with you, and there's no cover. In other words, go.

Supposedly owned by the "head sales-man" seen on the Jungle Cruise ride in Magic Kingdom's Adventureland, this very Disneyfied little rum bar is decorated with items that he's collected on his world travels, including Uh-Oa, the Audio-Animatronic "tiki goddess of disaster" who once lorded over the Magic Kingdom's Enchanted Tiki Room, a giant clam named Shelly, and of course, shrunken heads. These items come to life when patrons order certain drinks, and with the place nearly always full that means every few minutes. (Disneyphiles should search the walls for the hidden Orange Bird, or the reference to Tiki Room bird Rosita.)

Servers (who are, in keeping with the Jungle Cruise theme, "skippers") add to the fun. Depending on what drink order he or she gets, Skipper Dan might open fire at "the hippos in the trees"; Skipper Britney may don a snorkel and mask and start swimming around the tables; Skipper Dylan may suddenly shout out a joke ("Why are pirates called pirates? They just arrgh!"). Ambient music includes the theme from the 1960s television series "Hawaii 5-0," the iconic 1963 Chantays surfer instrumental "Pipeline" and Don Ho's brain-dead 1966 ditty "Tiny

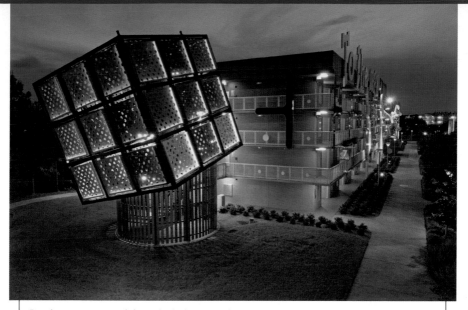

Pop icons. A giant Rubik's Cube hides a circular stairway at Disney's Pop Century Resort. Other step screens include a behemoth-sized bowling pin and an elephantine 8-track tape.

Bubbles"—which actually sounds pretty good after a couple of those $20 drinks.

A relaxing outdoor patio serves the same drinks and food but lacks the wacky atmosphere. It does, however, offer a view of the Magic Kingdom fireworks show, with its audio piped in. *4p–mid; must be 21 after 8p. Seats 51 inside, 82 outside.*

★★★ $$$$$ **Spirit of Aloha.** A dancing, drumming and musical tour of Hawaii, New Zealand, Samoa, Tahiti and Togo, this venerable dinner show features skimpy traditional costumes and lots of moving bodies. The story of a native girl returning to her roots has a corny first half with sitcom-style skits. Toward the end, children are invited onstage to learn the hula. The meal is an all-you-can-eat feast of uninspired meats. Service is perfunctory. If you go, splurge for the front-of-the-house seats; if you sit in back you may have a hard time hearing. *Prepaid only. 2-hour shows Tue–Sat at 5:15p, 8p. Seats 420.*

★★★★ ✔ $$$ **Kona Island.** In the morning this stand next to Kona Café serves pastries; in the afternoon it's a sushi bar with alcoholic beverages. *6:30a–4p, 6p–10p. Seats 16.*

Other amenities. Arcade; beach; boat and surrey rentals; campfire; guided fishing trips; hula dancing lessons; 1.5-mile walking trail. Laundromat, laundry service.

Evening torch-lighting ceremony has a fire-baton twirler. A musician often entertains in the lobby. Playground. Children's arts and crafts, beach and pool activities. Lilo's Playhouse childcare center (ages 3-9) offers dress-up, crafts, storytelling; decor inspired by Little Golden Books. The Electrical Water Pageant passes behind the hotel between 9 and 9:20 p.m.

Disney transportation. Monorail trains go to Magic Kingdom, Epcot; Contemporary, Grand Floridian resorts. Buses serve other parks, Disney Springs; boats Magic Kingdom.

Location. Near Magic Kingdom. Distance to (in miles): MK 1, EP 4, DHS 4, DAK 6, BB 5, TL 6, DS 6, ESPN 7. 600 Seven Seas Dr., 32830.

Key facts. Disney Deluxe resort; 497 rooms, 5 suites, 380 villas, 39 acres. Built: 1971, updated 2015. Phone: 407-824-2000. Fax: 407-824-3174. Check In 3p, Out 11a.

Rates. Rooms: Rack $429–$1143, discounted to $300. Suites: $1059–$3306, discounted to $557. Villas: $439–$878, discounted to $230. Bungalows: $2272–$3535, discounted to $1184.

★★★ ✔ **Disney's Pop Century Resort.** Children will know they are someplace special if you stay here. Though meant to appeal to nostalgic adults, this bright and bold resort looks—at least to young eyes—like a kid

The surreal seventies. Other strange sights at Pop Century include a massive Mickey Mouse telephone and a freakish foosball field. Words behind them ask "What's Your Handle?"

designed it. Everywhere you turn is a spirit of poster-paint art. Grouped into five sections, the lodging area is a collection of four-story motel buildings, each a poster-paint collage that recalls a particular decade of American popular culture, from the 1950s to the 1990s. Gigantic props such as 41-foot Rubik's Cubes and 65-foot bowling pins hide stairwells; roofs are lined with giant catchphrases such as "Do the Funky Chicken." A front complex includes a food court, arcade, gift shop, the bus stop and the main swimming pool.

Highs. Large colorful pools, a fun theme for those old enough to remember the 60s and 70s. Relatively bargain rates.

Lows. Small rooms, popular with youth groups, no restaurant, long lines at food courts, lame breakfasts, crowded bus stops.

Rooms. They're cheaply decorated; in each a curtain hangs between the beds and bathroom vanity. Rooms in the 1960s buildings ($10–$22 surcharge) are closest to the front complex; 1950s rooms are almost as convenient. *260 sq ft. Sleep 4. 2 double beds. Accessed by outdoor walkways.*

Swimming pools. The resort has three themed pools, each with an adjacent kiddie pool. The 1960s Hippy Dippy pool has four giant metal flowers that spray swimmers; the kiddie pool has a flower shower. The 1950s pool is shaped like a bowling pin. A 1990s computer pool (a rectangle) has a spongy keyboard deck. A Goofy water-jet fountain sits between the 1960s and 1970s areas.

Restaurants and food. A food court (★★★ $$ 6:30a–mid; seats 650) offers classic and modern choices, ambient music is vintage Top 40. Nearby is a bakery, convenience store and little bar open to the main pool. Room service (pizza, salads, desserts) is 4 p.m. to midnight.

Other amenities. Arcade, beach, playground, 1.29-mile Memory Lane walking/running trail lined with signs that track key pop-culture events from 1950 to 1999. Laundromat, laundry service. Shop with groceries. Organized children's activities are posted on a poolside board each morning; kids join food-court cast members to do the Twist daily at 8 a.m., march to the Mickey Mouse theme at 2 p.m. and do the Hustle at 6 p.m.

Disney transportation. Buses serve parks, Disney Springs; but not the ESPN complex.

Location. Near Hollywood Studios, ESPN. Distance to (in miles): MK 6, EP 5, DHS 3, DAK 4, BB 4, TL 2, DS 3, ESPN 2. 1050 Century Dr., 32830.

Key facts. Disney Value resort with clustered buildings; 2,880 rooms, 177 acres. Built: 2003. Phone: 407-938-4000. Fax: 407-938-4040. Check In 3p, Out 11a.

Rates. Rack $95–$210, discounted to $85.

Delicate details. Pastel colors, wrought-iron railings and mansard roofs recall classic New Orleans architecture at Disney's Port Orleans French Quarter Resort.

★★★ ✔ **Disney's Port Orleans Resorts.** Though Disney lumps them together as if they're similar, these two side-by-side resorts are quite different. Representing New Orleans, the smaller Port Orleans French Quarter (★★★) has tree-lined walkways that look like narrow streets, lots of wrought-iron railings and some intimate gardens. Its pool area is themed to a Mardi Gras parade; the food court looks like a warehouse for Mardi Gras parade props. Representing the plantation country of the Old South, the sprawling Port Orleans Riverside (★★★★ ✔) has four distinct lodging areas, a restaurant and a better food court. Three recall the look of Southern plantations, their white-columned buildings set within shady live oaks, magnolias and other hardwoods. One (Alligator Bayou) symbolizes more primitive areas, with walkways that meander through unkempt landscapes of palmettos and pines.

Highs. The French Quarter landscape is intimate, especially around its hot tub and kids playground; all of its rooms are close to the fast-food court and pool; and parking is convenient. The Riverside area offers way more amenities including a restaurant and multiple pools, as well as convenient parking and rooms that sleep five. Both areas are often available online at bargain rates, as

they're usually the last Disney hotels to fill up—not because they're bad but because to Disney neophytes they seem so far off the beaten path, set as they are in an area few guests ever see.

Lows. French Quarter has no restaurant, poor food, its nola theme is often cheaply tacked on. At Riverside, getting to your room can be quite a hike if you don't have a car.

Rooms. Those in the French Quarter have cherry woods, purple and gold bedspreads and gold carpet. Riverside rooms vary; most have cherry woods and tapestries while those in Alligator Bayou have backwoods hickory furnishings and quilted bedspreads. Riverside also offers 512 somewhat cheesy Royal Guest Rooms, decorated with Disney characters, themed fabrics and headboards embedded with fiber-optic fireworks. *Rooms: 314 sq ft. Most sleep 4, Alligator Bend rooms have trundle beds, sleep 5. 2 queen beds, small refrigerator. Accessed by outdoor walkways.*

Swimming pools. A huge dragon winds through, and forms the slide of, the French Quarter's Doubloon Lagoon pool; an alligator jazz band dances through its grounds. At Riverside, a large Ol' Man Island recreation area includes a swimming pool with the most waterfalls of any Disney hotel spot; a swerving slide dribbles water on those who

Peaceful havens. Calm "quiet" swimming pools sit within most of the clustered lodging areas of Disney's Moderate Resorts. This one's at the Port Orleans Riverside Resort.

go down it. There's also a hot tub and kiddie pool. Five peaceful quiet pools sit between the Riverside lodging sections.

Restaurants and food. French Quarter has a food court. Riverside has a restaurant and a food court. Room service (pizza, salads, desserts) is available 4 p.m. to midnight.

★★★ ✔ $$$$ **Boatwright's Dining Hall.** This underrated table-service restaurant serves decent Southern dishes, though actual Southerners may find them bland. A 46-foot boat hangs above the dining room; ship-building tools adorn walls. Faux-wood tables sit on tile floors; a back room has a fireplace. *5p–10p. Seats 206. Riverside.*

★ $ **The Sassagoula Floatworks & Food Factory.** With a name that long you'd think there'd be something special here, but this food court is one of Disney's worst. What's good: made-to-order beignets. *6a–mid. Seats 550. French Quarter.*

★★ $ **Riverside Mill.** Resembling a cotton mill, this spacious American food court features a large water wheel with working gears. *6a–mid. Seats 550. Riverside.*

Other amenities. Arcade, campfire, playground. Bike, boat, surrey rentals; guided fishing trips, cane-pole fishing. Carriage rides (same-day reservations at 407-824-2832). Laundromat, laundry service. Shop with

groceries. Children's programs: Pontoon-boat pirate adventure; pool activities.

Disney transportation. Buses run to parks, Disney Springs. Boats serve Disney Springs; Old Key West, Saratoga Springs; shuttle between French Quarter and Riverside.

Location. Northeast Disney, near Disney Springs. Distance to (in miles): MK 4, EP 2, DHS 4, DAK 6, BB 4, TL 2, DS 2, ESPN 4. French Quarter 2201 Orleans Dr., 32830; Riverside 1251 Riverside Dr., 32830.

Key facts. Disney Moderate resorts with clustered buildings; French Qtr. 1,008 rooms, 90 acres; Riverside 2,048 rooms, 235 acres. Built: French Qtr. 1991, Riverside 1992. Phone: French Qtr. 407-934-5000; Riverside 407-934-6000. Fax: French Qtr. 407-934-5353; Riverside 407-934-5777. Check In 3p, Out 11a.

Rates. Rack $162–$326, discounted to $147.

★★★★ **Disney's Saratoga Springs Resort.** This equestrian-themed DVC condo complex is the only Disney-owned resort with a golf course. It offers tranquil grounds, good food, a full-service spa and upscale suites. Lodging buildings cluster into five sections that horseshoe (see what we did there?) around a recreation center. Located behind Disney Springs, Saratoga Springs is as far away as you can get from a Disney theme

A calm place to stay. A mom and her daughters wander to breakfast on a distant walkway at Disney's Saratoga Springs Resort. Trim landscaping and fountains keep ponds in shape.

park and still be at a Disney resort. Despite its name, there are no springs, nothing New York and no horses. Considered part of Saratoga Springs only because it's right next door, an unrelated Treehouse Villas hideaway is nestled into a pine forest; its 60 stand-alone octagons are elevated 10 feet off the ground.

Highs. Tranquil, upscale villas adjacent to parking lots; great fitness center and spa; direct golf-course access.

Lows. The resort's theme and its villa's interior decor will be of little interest to children—it looks like a nice apartment complex. Theme parks are relatively distant; there's no room service; the main swimming pool is small and therefore often crowded.

Villas. All have large, masculine furniture; larger units add whirlpool tubs; Grand Villas two-story living rooms. Rustic-chic Treehouse Villas have cathedral ceilings, granite countertops. *Sleep 4–12 in studio, 1-, 2-, 3-bedroom units.*

Swimming pools. The main pool has a 126-foot slide between cascading waterfalls, an interactive fountain area and a zero-entry gradual ramp. It often shows Disney movies at night; you float while you watch. Nearby is a kiddie pool, two playgrounds, two hot tubs and a sand volleyball court. A Paddock-area pool has a water slide, zero-entry ramp,

splash zone and hot tub. The other two lodging areas have quiet pools, each with a hot tub and barbecue area.

Restaurants and food. There's a restaurant, a food court and a counter-service grill at The Paddock pool. Saratoga Springs has no room service; grocery delivery is available.

★★★★ ✔ **$$$ Turf Club Bar & Grill.** This manly steak place feels like a country club; you can shoot billiards while you wait for your table. Balcony tables overlook the golf course and Disney Springs. *Noon–9p. Seats 146, inc. 52 outside.*

★★★ ✔ **$$ Artist's Palette.** Padded booths highlight its nice dining area, but this fast-food's tiny order counter creates long lines. A shop has limited groceries. *11a–11p. Seats 112.*

Other amenities. Arcades, bike rentals, nightly campfire, Community Center with DVD rentals, fitness center, guided fishing trips, surrey rentals. Basketball, shuffleboard courts, full-service spa, 2 lighted tennis courts, two walking trails. Lake Buena Vista 18-hole golf course. Laundromat, laundry service. Shop with groceries. Children's programs: Arts and crafts; ceramic, canvas, plaster painting activities (extra charge); pool activities.

Disney transportation. Buses serve all parks and Disney Springs; a separate shuttle

Beep, beep. A golf cart heads off to the Lake Buena Vista course on a Saratoga Springs path. Saratoga Springs is the only Disney-owned resort where golfers can start a game.

circles within the resort (Treehouse Villas guests transfer at the main resort's Springs and Grandstand stops). Boats serve Disney Springs; Old Key West, Port Orleans resorts.

Location. East Disney, across a small lake from Disney Springs. Distance to (in miles): MK 5, EP 3, DHS 4, DAK 6, BB 4, TL 2, DS 2, ESPN 4. 1960 Broadway, 32830.

Key facts. Disney Deluxe Villas resort with clustered buildings; 828 villas, 65 acres. Built: 2004. Phone: 407-827-1100. Fax: 407-827-1151. Check In 4p, Out 11a.

Rates. Studios: Rack $327–$484, discounted to $229. Villas: $452–$1920, discounted to $316. Treehouses: $727–$1224, discounted to $508.

★★★★★ ✔ **Disney's Wilderness Lodge.** A dead ringer for one of those rustic park service lodges in the American West, this secluded resort is nestled in a forest along 450-acre Bay Lake. The complex consists of a central eight-story lodge and three wings, one of which is a DVC timeshare property. The lobby features a three-sided stone fireplace, the layers of which illustrate the geological history of the Grand Canyon. The fourth-floor indoor balcony has cozy sitting areas and front and back porches. The fifth floor has a small back balcony. A simulated indoor hot spring in the lobby creates a

stream that appears to flow outside and into the swimming pool.

Highs. Stunning lobby; quality dining and amenities; comfortable, easily accessible rooms; pleasant boat ride to Magic Kingdom; nice pool; quiet atmosphere; great views; child-care facility; convenient self-parking.

Lows. Most rooms sleep 4, unlike most Disney hotels at this price point.

Rooms. Decorated with Native American and wildlife motifs, with vibrant quilts, plaid drapes, Mission-style furniture and hand-crafted embellishments. Beds have padded headboards topped with carved upper panels. A club level is available. *Rooms: 344 sq ft. Sleep 4. 2 queen beds, small refrigerator. Villas: Studio, 1-, 2-bedroom units sleep 4 to 8.*

Swimming pools. Portrayed as part of a mountain stream, a large swimming pool features a curving slide that sprays riders with mist. Nearby are two tubs (one hot, one cold), a kiddie pool, a new-for-2015 aquatic play area and a geyser that erupts hourly. The Villas area has a smaller quiet pool with four bubbling "springs" and a 15-person whirlpool.

Restaurants and food. The Lodge has two restaurants and a fast-food spot. Room service is 7 a.m. to 11 a.m. and 4 p.m. to midnight.

★★★★ ✔ **$$$$$ Artist Point.** Foodies love the inspired entrees at this Pacific-Northwest

The Natural Northwest. Disney's Wilderness Lodge channels the historic lodges and rugged landscapes of the most famous U.S. national parks.

restaurant; its L-shaped dining room relaxes with blond and cherry woods, landscape murals and a soaring ceiling. Large windows view the resort's courtyard, pool. *5:30p–9:30p. Seats 225. A Disney Signature Restaurant.*

★★★ ✔ **$$$$ Whispering Canyon Cafe.** "So what'll it be, buckaroos?" Brusque servers highlight this tasty barbecue spot. All-you-can-eat skillets are pricey, many good choices are not. A retro cowboy decor is somehow tasteful. *7:30a–2:30p, 5p–10p. Seats 281.*

★★ **$$ Roaring Fork Snacks.** This noisy fast-food eatery serves grilled foods, pizza, salads, sandwiches. *6a–11p. Seats 250.*

Other amenities. Arcade; beach, bike, boat and surrey rentals; nightly campfire, movie at main pool. Fitness center, guided fishing trips, lobby tour, paved wilderness trail leads through undeveloped area to Fort Wilderness, it's ideal for jogging. Segway tour (extra charge). Community Center. Cub's Den childcare center. Laundromat, laundry service. Organized free children's activities, 2:30 p.m.–4 p.m. The Electrical Water Pageant passes behind the hotel between 9:35 and 9:55 p.m.

Disney transportation. Buses serve all theme and water parks and Disney Springs. Boats serve Magic Kingdom; Contemporary, Fort Wilderness resorts.

Location. Northwest Disney, southeast of Magic Kingdom. Distance to (in miles): MK 1, EP 3, DHS 4, DAK 6, BB 5, TL 5, DS 5, ESPN 7. 901 Timberland Dr., 32830.

Key facts. Disney Deluxe resort with lodge, two wings, DVC building; 701 rooms, 27 suites, 136 villas, 65 acres. Built: 1994. Phone: 407-824-3200, Villas 407-938-4300. Fax: 407-824-3232. Check In 3p (Villas 4p), Out 11a.

Rates. Rooms: Rack $289–$998, discounted to $202. Suites: $966–$1746, discounted to $515. Studios: $374–$582, discounted to $299. Villas: $512–$1416, discounted to $409.

★★★★★ ✔ **Disney's Yacht and Beach Club Resort.** These side-by-side Deluxe resorts share Disney World's best hotel swimming complex. They also have a lovely lakeside setting, comfortable rooms that are easy to get to and good food at all price levels. The oyster-gray Yacht Club has a clapboard exterior like those of formal oceanfront hotels common in New England in the 19th century. Inside, it's the look of old money—gold-fringed drapes, oak floors, antique chandeliers and lots of brass. Cast members dress in navy blue blazers. Behind the Yacht Club is a lighthouse marina. The pale-blue-and-white Beach Club strikes a more whimsical look, with stick-style

Cultured Club. A manicured back lawn highlights the genteel grounds of Disney's Yacht Club resort. A sand volleyball pit marks the rear area of the more casual Beach Club .

buildings that recall wooden seaside cottages. Inside it's nouveau riche—crisp colors and natural French limestone floors open up its lobby. Behind the Beach Club is a white-sand beach. The Beach Club is adjacent to the back (World Showcase) entrance to Epcot.

Highs. Within walking distance to Epcot and Hollywood Studios as well as evening entertainment at the BoardWalk; lovely lakeside setting; has the best Disney swimming complex; good food at all price levels.

Lows. Expensive. Limited fast food. No fair-weather transport to the front of Epcot.

Rooms. Nautical motifs have white furniture. A club level is available. Suites share the salty theme, as do Beach Club villas. *Rooms: 381 sq ft. Sleep 5. 2 queen beds, some daybeds, small refrigerator. Suites: Sleep 4–8. Villas: Studio, 1-, 2-bedroom units sleep 4–8. All rooms and suites refurbished in 2015.*

Swimming pools. Looking like a Nantucket lagoon, the spawling 3-acre Stormalong Bay is a miniature water park. It includes a meandering central pool, lazy river, shallow inlet with a real sandbar, a shady hot tub and an assortment of fountains, waterfalls and bridges. A spiral staircase on a life-sized simulated shipwreck leads to a 300-foot slide—starting off in a dark tunnel (the inside of the ship's fallen mast), it enters daylight

at a rocky outcropping; riders get showered by two waterfalls before splashing into the central pool. A large kiddie pool has overhead sprinklers and a sandy play spot; a second kiddie pool on the pirate ship has a tiny slide.

Restaurants and food. Offerings include a steakhouse, soda shop, good character meal and lounges. A gift shop has a fast-food counter. Room service is available 24 hours.

★★★★ ✔ **$$ Beaches & Cream.** Gigantic sundaes are the draw at this old-fashioned soda shop, a tiny spot with just three booths, six small tables and a few bar seats. Burgers and other sandwiches are good; the claim to fame is a ridiculous Kitchen Sink sundae served literally in a kitchen sink. A classic jukebox offers free plays; a tin ceiling has a tray center with elaborate moldings. *11a–11p. Take-out counter. Seats 48. Beach Club.*

★★★ ✔ **$$$$$ Cape May Café.** This relaxed buffet has the only Disney-operated character breakfast not in a park or on the monorail loop; small parties often don't need reservations. Characters are Donald Duck, Goofy and Minnie Mouse; breakfast has Mickey-face waffles; the clambake-dinner standout is carved-to-order top sirloin. Subdued lighting and seagull sounds make the café a pleasant place to end a day. *Breakfast 7:30a–11:30a, dinner 5p–9p. Seats 235. Beach Club.*

Winding waterway. A lazy river circles three-acre Stormalong Bay, a small water park which the Yacht and Beach Club share. The toppled past of shipwreck adds a 300-foot slide.

★★★★ ✔ **$$$$ Captain's Grille.** This nice restaurant makes a sincere effort to be a destination eatery though no one considers it that; the Yachtsman Steakhouse is next door. Decor is 1930s New England, with good lighting, padded chairs and gleaming brass. *Breakfast buffet 7:30a–11:30a, lunch 11:30a–2p, dinner 5p–9p. Seats 280. Yacht Club.*

★★★★★ ✔ **$$$$$ Yachtsman Steakhouse.** Disney's best steakhouse hits the trifecta—exceptional food, attentive service and a welcoming atmosphere. Top-notch steaks are large, better than the more-expensive Shula's at the nearby Walt Disney World Dolphin. The simple dining room has honey-colored wood, leather and brass; half on a wood floor; half on carpet. A glass wall lets you watch your steak be prepared. *5:30p–10p. Seats 286. A Disney Signature Restaurant. Yacht Club.*

★★★ **$ The Beach Club Marketplace.** The back of this general store offers pastries, salads, sandwiches and soups; a small area sells fruit and snacks. *7a–10p. Seats 48 on tables in the hall and on a nearby patio.*

Other amenities. Arcades, beach, bike and boat rentals, boat rides, nightly campfire, DVC Community Center with DVD rentals, fireworks cruises, guided fishing trips, walking trail. Changing of the Guard each afternoon. Sand volleyball, croquet, tennis courts. Hair salon, health club, laundromat, laundry service. Shop with groceries. Conference center (73,000 square feet, 2 ballrooms, banquet space for 3,000, 21 breakout rooms), business center. Children's programs: Pontoon-boat albatross adventure; complimentary arts and crafts, ceramics (extra charge), beach and pool activities.

Disney transportation. Buses serve Magic Kingdom, Animal Kingdom, water parks and Disney Springs. Boats serve the back entrance of Epcot and Hollywood Studios; except when lightning is in the area, then buses run to the front of those parks.

Location. Central Disney, next to the back entrance of Epcot. Distance to (in miles): MK 5, EP back entrance <1 front entrance 4, DHS 2, DAK 5, BB 3, TL 3, DS 3, ESPN 5. Beach Club 1800 Epcot Resorts Blvd., Yacht Club 1700 Epcot Resorts Blvd., 32830.

Key facts. Disney Deluxe resort with adjoining buildings; 1,197 rooms, 112 suites, 208 villas, 30 acres. Built: 1990. Phone: Beach Club: 407-934-8000. Villas: 407-934-2175. Yacht Club: 407-934-7000. Fax: Beach Club: 407-934-3850. Yacht Club: 407-934-3450. Check In 3p, Out 11a.

Rates. Rooms: Rack $356–$944, discounted to $249. Suites: $654–$3340, discounted to $649. Studios: $369–$611, discounted to $269. Villas: $535–$1359, discounted to $390.

© Disney

Circle Vision. A porthole-like opening heightens the nautical feel of a Beach Club balcony, which overlooks the lawns and walkways of its waterfront area.

★★★★ ✔ **Walt Disney World Swan and Dolphin.** If you have a choice where you stay on an Orlando business trip, choose here. Giant swan statues, huge fish figurines, a towering triangular roof—the architecture of these adjacent convention resorts is one-of-a-kind, and they're right in the middle of Walt Disney World. They're the signature properties of Starwood Resorts, the company that operates Sheraton and Westin properties. The smaller Swan is quiet and intimate, the larger Dolphin boisterous and bubbly.

Designed by architect Michael Graves, the hotels feature playful "entertainment" architecture. Seen together, abstract designs on the back of the buildings define the Dolphin as a tropical mountain surrounded by huge banana palms, its waterfall splashing into the lagoon between the structures and then onto the Swan, which is painted as if it's a huge sand dune. Interiors are classy and modern.

Highs. Central Disney location, first-class pool complex, adjacent miniature golf course, classy restaurants, Disney World's only karaoke bar, the most popular place for Starwood Preferred Guests to redeem their Starpoints.

Lows. No Disney spirit. Convention atmosphere may clash with family needs.

Rooms. Pale woods, floral carpeting, maple bureaus, Westin Heavenly® Beds. Club level

available. Refurbished 2014–2016. *Rooms: 360 sq ft. Sleep 5. Dolphin king or 2 double beds, Swan king or 2 queens. Suites sleep 5 to 10.*

Swimming pools. An elaborate swimming area (5 pools, 5 hot tubs, kiddie pool) arcs between the resorts. A meandering Grotto pool has a waterfall and slide; tiny waterfalls splash near a volleyball net that extends over a narrow area. A circus-themed beach area has two volleyball nets, a basketball court and a boat-like playground piece with covered slides. Children will like finding a statue of a seal that sprays water from its nose.

Restaurants and food. Seven restaurants, a sushi bar and plenty of lounges offer lots of variety. Room service 8 a.m. to midnight.

★★★ ✔ **$$$$$ Bluezoo.** Seafood dishes are geared toward corporate and special-occasion diners. Supervised by infamous celebrity chef Todd English. *5p–10p. Seats 400. Dolphin.*

★★ ✔ **$$$$$ The Fountain.** This small cafe and ice-cream counter sits just inside the Dolphin's back entrance. Kids will insist on its PB&J milkshake. *11a–11p. Seats 58. Dolphin.*

★★★ **$$$ Fresh Mediterranean Market.** Mediterranean breakfasts and lunches in a light, airy atmosphere with nice outdoor views. *7:30a–3p. Seats 264. Dolphin.*

★★ **$$$$ Garden Grove Cafe.** American breakfast and lunch, themed buffet dinners.

A point for professionals. A palm-lined walkway connects the The Walt Disney World Swan to its sister Dolphin resort. The two Starwood hotels cater to convention guests.

Indoor park-like setting has tall domed ceiling, 25-foot tree. Weekend character meals. *6:30a–3p, 5:30p–10p. Seats 150. Swan.*

★★★★★ **$$$$$ Il Mulino.** An offshoot of the famed NYC restaurant. Serious Italian. Live music Fri, Sat. *5p–10p. Seats 224. Swan.*

★★★★★ ✔ **$$$$ Kimonos.** Japanese sushi bar decorated with kimonos. Nightly karaoke. *5p–mid. Seats 105. Swan.*

★★★ ✔ **$$ Picabu.** Buffeteria is hidden down a maze of hallways but worth finding. Its food is decent, its prices fair, its dining room comfortable. *24 hrs. Seats 140. Dolphin.*

★★★ **$$$$$ Shula's.** Indulgent expense-account steakhouse owned by the famed Miami Dolphins coach. Masculine decor with memorabilia. *5p–10p. Seats 215. Dolphin.*

Other amenities. Arcades, beach, swan pedal-boat rentals, fitness centers, 4 tennis courts. Hair salon, laundromat, laundry service, massage services, spa. Fantasia Gardens miniature golf across street. Huge convention center (254,000 sq. ft., 9,600-sq.-ft. ballroom, 3 other ballrooms, exhibit hall, 84 breakout rooms). Business centers. Child-care facility.

Disney transportation. Boats to Epcot and Hollywood Studios, buses to Magic Kingdom, Animal Kingdom, water parks and Disney Springs. When boats can't operate (i.e., during lightning), buses take their place.

Location. Central Disney near Hollywood Studios, Epcot. Distance to (in miles): MK 4, EP <1, DHS <1, DAK 4, BB 4, TL 4, DS 2, ESPN 4. Dolphin 1500 Epcot Resorts Blvd., Swan 1300 Epcot Resorts Blvd., 32830.

Key facts. 2,265 rooms, 191 suites, 87 acres. Built 1990. Dolphin 407-934-4000, Swan 407-934-4499. Fax: Dolphin 407-934-4884, Swan 407-934-4710. Check In 3p, Out 11a.

Rates. Rooms: Rack $299–$594, discounted to $149. Suites: $390–$1440, discounted to $190.

★★★★★ **Four Seasons Orlando.** Far from the crowds within Disney's uber-luxe Golden Oak residential community, the Four Seasons features Spanish Revival architecture and lush grounds with mature live oaks, cypress stands and nearly a thousand palms.

Rooms. Oranges and teals accent contemporary white furnishings. Bathrooms have marble tubs, in-mirror televisions, Bose surround-sound audio. Large balconies. *Rooms: 500 sq ft. Sleep 4. King bed with queen-size sleeper or 2 double beds. Suites sleep 2 to 4.*

Key facts. Southeast of Magic Kingdom, beyond Fort Wilderness. 10100 Dream Tree Blvd., Golden Oak FL 32836. 375 rooms, 68 suites, 26.5 acres. 4 restaurants, lounges. Elaborate 5-acre swimming area with lazy river, water cannons. Beach volleyball,

© American Q

A flatbed of food. A cherry-red 1951 Ford pickup serves as a buffet line at American Q, a barbecue restaurant inside the B Resort & Spa. Skewered meats are carved at your table.

climbing wall. Outdoor movie nights. Arcade, basketball, fitness center, 3 Har-Tru tennis courts. Massage services, sauna, steam room, full-service spa with 18 treatment rooms, yoga. Tranquilo golf course (formerly Disney's Osprey Ridge) with pro shop, golf instruction, driving range, putting green, club rental and on-site restaurant. Child-care facility, teen center. Buses shuttle to Magic Kingdom twice an hour, other Disney parks once an hour. Built 2014. Check In 4p, Out noon. Phone: 407-313-7777. Fax: 407-313-8500.

Rates. Rooms: Rack $549–$830, discounted to $366. Suites: $695–$12000, discounted to $545.

★★★★ **Shades of Green.** Exclusively for active and retired members of the U.S. military and accompanying families and friends, this relaxed resort is the only Armed Forces Recreation Center in the continental United States. Comparable in many ways to a Disney Deluxe resort it has full-service restaurants and a great location, but lacks distinctive grounds, architecture or interiors. Bargain rates are about a third what Disney would charge. Built in 1971 as the Disney Golf Resort, Shades of Green sits next to the Palm, Magnolia and Oak Trail golf courses. Huge rooms feature light oak woods. *Rooms: 455 sq t, sleep 5, 2 queen beds, small refrigerator,* *daybed, balcony or patio. Suites sleep 6 to 8. Reservations: 888-593-2242. Hotel direct: 407-824-3400. Fax: 407-824-3665.*

Rates. Based on rank (lower ranks=lower rates): Rooms $98–$148. Suites $262–$394.

Disney Springs hotels. Situated at the northeast corner of Disney, these independent hotels lack the ambience of Disney spots but often have rooms available when other properties are full. Developed in the 1970s as Disney's Hotel Plaza, the properties were later known as the Downtown Disney hotels. They share a shuttle bus to the Disney parks.

★★★★ **B Resort & Spa.** Huge rooms set this modern-themed spot apart from its competition; they're the largest of any Disney Springs hotel. Some have kitchenettes, wet bars, bunk beds. *Rooms, suites sleep 5, 2 double beds, pillow-top mattresses, sleeper.*

NEW! ★★★★★ ✔ $$$$ **American Q.** Sincere effort shines through at barbecue spot. Cooking methods honor the time-tested techniques of the distinctive styles of Kansas City, Memphis, St. Louis, South Carolina and Texas. Sourced from Florida farms, quality beef and pork comes grass-fed and hormone-free and is smoked daily. Rounding things out are top-notch sauces—the Carolina one is *perfection*—as well as awesome appetizer

Swine Candy, a big grab of thick bacon strips that have been roasted in molasses and spices. As for drinks, the Caribbean Passion Picante cocktail—a blend of vodka, cinnamon, chili sauce, mango and passionfruit—has just the right balance of sweet and heat. You dine either buffet style or a la carte. Inspired by Brazilian rodízo steak houses, the buffet gives you your fill of nine different meats, carved at your table by attentive servers. Going a la carte saves you money, and includes entrees that aren't part of the buffet like tender St. Louis spare ribs. Chandeliers made from mason jars light the casual dining room; its centerpiece is a cherry-red '51 Ford flatbed that holds the buffet's sides. *Breakfast 7a–11a, buffet $18 (children $9), a la carte $6–$17 (no kids menu). Dinner 5p–10p, buffet $35 (children $10), a la carte $16–$43 (children $3–$8). Children's price applies only to kids shorter than "seven chickens" (4ft 7in); kids 5 and under eat free. Bar 2p–mid Mon–Fri, noon–mid Sat–Sun. Happy hour (half off drinks) 4p–7p. Seats 200, inc 11 at bar and 40 in semi-private dining room. Direct reservations (407) 827-3080.*

Key facts. 394 rooms, 23 acres. 17 stories. 1905 Hotel Plaza Blvd., 32830. Swimming pool. fitness center, full-service spa. Business center, laundromat, meeting rooms, mini-mart. Formerly the Royal Plaza. Phone: 407-828-2828. Check In 4p, Out 11a. Rates: Rooms: Rack $105–$195, discounted to $90. Suites: $185–$205, discounted to $149. $20 daily resort fee.

★★★ **Best Western Lake Buena Vista.** 321 rooms, 4 suites, 12 acres. 2000 Hotel Plaza Blvd., 32830. Rooms and suites sleep 4–5, 2 queen beds, balconies or patios. Cherry-walnut furniture, granite counter tops, Italian tile bathrooms. 2 restaurants, snack bar, Pizza Hut Express. Swimming pool, kiddie pool. Arcade, child-care service, fitness center, playground, tennis courts. Business center, car-rental counter, laundromat. Garden gazebo. Lakefront. Phone: 407-828-2424. Fax: 407-827-6390. Check In 3p, Out 11a. Rates: Rooms: Rack $85–$149, discounted to $66.

★★★★ **Buena Vista Palace and Spa.** Huge 1970s complex, 890 rooms, 124 suites, 27 acres. 27 stories. 1900 Buena Vista Dr., 32830. Rooms sleep 4, 2 queen beds, balconies or patios, refrigerator. Suites sleep 4–8. 2 restaurants, Sunday Disney character breakfast, mini-mart. 3 swimming pools, hot tub. Arcade, fitness center, playground, sauna, full-service spa (407-827-3200). Basketball, tennis, volleyball courts. Business center, car-rental counter, convention center, laundromat, laundry services, salon. Phone: 407-827-2727. Fax: 407-827-3136. Check In 4p, Out 11a. Rates: Rooms: Rack $89–$170, discounted to $74. Suites: $145–$499, discounted to $109.

★★★ **Doubletree Guest Suites.** The only all-suite hotel at Disney. 229 suites, 7 acres. 7 stories. 2305 Hotel Plaza Blvd., 32830. Suites: Sleep 6, 1 or 2 bedrooms, Sweet Dreams bedding, microwave, refrigerator, 2 TVs, bathroom TV-radio. 1 restaurant, mini-mart. Swimming pool, kiddie pool, hot tub. Fitness center, playground, pool table, tennis courts. Business center, car-rental counter, child-care service, laundromat, laundry services, meeting rooms. Phone: 407-934-1000. Fax: 407-934-1015. Check In 4p, Out 11a. Rates: Suites: Rack $115–$429, discounted to $99.

★★★ **Hilton.** The most upscale Disney Springs hotel. 704 rooms, 110 suites, 23 acres. 10 stories. 1751 Hotel Plaza Blvd. 32830. Rooms sleep 4, 2 double beds, mini-bar. Suites sleep 4–6. Club level. 7 restaurants inc. Benihana, Disney character breakfast Sunday (no reservations); mini-mart. 2 swimming pools, kiddie pool with spray area. Arcade, fitness center, golf pro shop, pool table. Business center, car-rental counter, child-care services, concierge, cyber cafe, laundromat, salon. Phone: 407-827-4000. Fax: 407-827-3890. Check In 3p, Out 11a. Rates: Rooms: Rack $95–$340, discounted to $79. Suites: $155–$360, discounted to $119.

★★★ **Holiday Inn.** 323 rooms, 1 suite, 10 acres. 14 stories. 1805 Hotel Plaza Blvd., 32830. Rooms: Sleep 4 to 5, 2 queen beds, sleeper, pillow-top mattresses, small refrigerator, work desk. Restaurant. Zero-entry pool with whirlpool. Business center, health club, laundromat, laundry services. Phone: 407-828-8888. Fax: 407-827-4623. Check In 4p, Out 11a. Rates: Rooms: Rack $109–$205, discounted to $89.

★★★ **Wyndham Lake Buena Vista.** A favorite of British guests, formerly the Regal Sun and the Grosvenor. 619 rooms, 7 suites, 13 acres. 19 stories. 1850 Hotel Plaza Blvd. 32830. Rooms: Sleep 4, 2 queen beds. Suites: Sleep 4–6. Restaurant; English pub; Disney character breakfast Tuesday, Thursday, Sat. 2 swimming pools, kiddie pool, water playground for children. Fitness center, playground. Basketball, shuffleboard, tennis, volleyball courts. Business center, car-rental counter, currency exchange, laundromat, laundry services, meeting rooms. Phone: 407-828-4444. Fax: 407-828-8192. Check In 3p, Out 11a. Rates: Rooms: Rack $75–$155, discounted to $64. Suites: $435–$529, discounted to $349.

Characters

Real celebrities. Although some fantasy-free adults may not see them as such, Disney's walk-around characters are *real* to many visitors, especially children—that's not a sweaty young woman in a fur suit, *that's Pluto!!!* Dozens of Disney stars appear in shows and parades and personally greet guests at theme parks, water parks and resort hotels.

Character types. Disney has two types of walk-around characters, "face" and "fur." Face characters, such as Cinderella, appear in a costume that shows the face of the performer, who talks to and interacts with guests in character. Fur characters, such as Pluto, appear in a complete costume that includes an oversized head. Most of them don't speak, and interact with guests purely through mime. However, fur character Mickey Mouse does speak at Town Square Theater in Magic Kingdom. His mouth moves and when you talk to him, he often talks back.

Meet-and-greet lines. Most characters pose for photos and, in most cases, sign autographs at designated locations, many of which draw long lines. Guests with autograph books should bring a pen or, better, a Sharpie marker. Some characters don't sign because of costume limitations. It's fine to hug, kiss or pat characters, but not to give them gifts. A PhotoPass photographer is often on hand, although guests are welcome to take photos themselves, or have the PhotoPass photographer take a photo for them with their camera or phone.

How to help your child interact. Though face characters rarely intimidate children, the fur folks, with their cartoonishly large heads, sometimes do. To help your child feel comfortable, talk with her beforehand so she knows what to expect. For meet-and-greet lines, buy her an autograph book to give her something to focus on besides the face-to-fur encounter. When it's her turn don't push her; the characters are patient and are trained to be sweet. Approach a character from the front. Fur characters in

One mean mother. Cinderella's stepmom Lady Tremaine rarely smiles.

particular often cannot see guests standing behind or beside them.

Character meals. A handful of Disney buffet and table-service restaurants offer "character meals," in which an assortment of characters come up to each table to greet guests as they eat. Each theme park has at least one character-meal restaurant, as do many Disney resort hotels.

How to find a character. Though the following Character Guide lists the official locations of characters, they often show up other places. To learn where, ask any Disney cast member. They can usually find out.

Character guide. More than 70 Disney characters greet guests at Disney World parks and resort hotels. Here's a list of the ones who appear most often, and where you're most likely to find them:

Aladdin. Arab "street rat," star of 1992's "Aladdin." Wins love of princess Jasmine after learning to be true to himself. *Magic Kingdom:* At Magic Carpets of Aladdin, Adventureland. *Epcot:* Morocco pavilion.

Alice. Star of 1951's "Alice in Wonderland." Curious, proper British girl dreams of non-sensical Wonderland. The park character has confided to the authors that many young girls confuse her name, thinking it's "Allison Wonderland." *Magic Kingdom:* Mad Tea Party, Fantasyland. *Epcot:* Tea garden, U.K. pavilion; Akershus Royal Banquet Hall meals (often), Norway pavilion. *Grand Floridian Resort:* 1900 Park Fare breakfast; Wonderland Tea Party, Garden View Tea Room.

Anastasia and Drizella. Squabbling step-sisters to Cinderella in 1950's "Cinderella," daughters of Lady Tremaine. Redhead Anastasia is spiteful and graceless; brunette Drizella disorganized. *Magic Kingdom:* Great wall, Fantasyland. *Grand Floridian Resort:* 1900 Park Fare dinner.

Anna and Elsa. Loving sisters in 2014's hit "Frozen." Redheaded younger Anna is the optimistic, fearless, awkward princess of Arendelle. Older platinum blonde Queen Elsa is more quiet and reserved, and can magically conjure snow and ice. Anna wears her blue embroidered dress; Elsa her silver

Mickey Mouse

Minnie Mouse

and blue gown. *Magic Kingdom:* Princess Fairytale Hall, Fantasyland. *Epcot:* Norway pavilion starting May 2016.

Ariel. Rebellious redheaded teen mermaid, star of 1989's "The Little Mermaid." "Sick of swimmin,'" loves all things human. Falls in love with Prince Eric. Best friend is a fish, Flounder. Wears a seashell bikini top as mermaid, a turquoise gown as a human (though it's pink in the film). *Magic Kingdom:* Ariel's Grotto, Fantasyland; Cinderella's Royal Table breakfast, lunch (often), Cinderella Castle. *Epcot:* Akershus Royal Banquet Hall meals (often), Norway pavilion.

Aurora. Blameless blond princess of 1959's "Sleeping Beauty" awakened from Maleficent's cursed coma by Prince Phillip's kiss. Also known as Briar Rose. Pink gown. *Magic Kingdom:* Town Square, Main Street U.S.A.; Cinderella's Royal Table breakfast, lunch (often), Cinderella Castle. *Epcot:* France pavilion fragrance garden; Akershus Royal Banquet Hall meals (often), Norway pavilion. *Grand Floridian Resort:* My Disney Girl's Perfectly Princess Tea Party, Garden View Tea Room.

Baloo. Happy-go-lucky, lazy bear in 1967's "Jungle Book" teaches "man-cub" Mowgli how to relax, live in wild. Loves to scratch

back on trees, eat fruit. *Magic Kingdom:* Move It! Shake It! Dance & Play It! Street Party, Cinderella Castle hub. *Disney's Animal Kingdom:* Upcountry Landing, on trail off Asia-Africa walkway.

Beast. Selfish prince is transformed by sorceress into a hideous creature in 1991's "Beauty and the Beast." Has face of wildebeest; tusks of boar; mane of lion; body of bear; legs, tail of wolf. Transforms back into prince after learning to be kind and earning love of Belle. *Magic Kingdom:* Be Our Guest at dinnertime to greet diners.

Belle. Heroine of 1991 Disney movie "Beauty and the Beast," in which the brunette bookworm falls in love with her beastly captor. Stands up for herself. Wears golden gown or modest blue dress with a white apron. *Magic Kingdom:* Enchanted Tales with Belle, Fantasyland; Cinderella's Royal Table, Cinderella Castle. *Epcot:* France pavilion promenade; Akershus Royal Banquet Hall meals (often), Norway pavilion.

Buzz Lightyear. Confident, macho "Toy Story" space ranger is Sheriff Woody's best friend. *Magic Kingdom:* Alongside the Carousel of Progress, Tomorrowland. *Disney's Hollywood Studios:* Woody's Picture Shootin' Corral, Pixar Place.

Micaela Neal

Cinderella

Micaela Neal

Tinker Bell

Captain Hook. Dastardly, melodramatic nemesis of Peter Pan and captain of the Jolly Roger pirate ship in 1953's "Peter Pan." Perpetually exasperated with incompetent first mate Mr. Smee. Has a hook in place of his left hand, which was cut off in a fight with Peter; the hand was eaten by a crocodile, which has hunted the Captain ever since. *Contemporary Resort:* Pirates & Pals Fireworks Voyage.

Chip 'n Dale. Playful, fast-talking chipmunks from 1940s–1950s cartoons. Nearly twins, though smarter, sneakier Chip has small black nose that resembles a chocolate chip, while goofier Dale has a large red nose and two separated buck teeth. *Magic Kingdom:* Rivers of America Crossing, Liberty Square; Move It! Shake It! Dance & Play It! Street Party, Cinderella Castle hub. *Epcot:* Walkway behind Innoventions West. Garden Grill during breakfast, lunch and dinner, The Land pavilion. *Disney's Hollywood Studios:* Central plaza, Hollywood Blvd. *Disney's Animal Kingdom:* Conservation Station courtyard, Rafiki's Planet Watch. *Fort Wilderness Resort:* Mickey's Backyard Barbecue, Chip 'n Dale's Campfire Sing-A-Long. *Walt Disney World Swan:* Garden Grove dinner (Fri).

Cinderella. The definitive rags-to-riches heroine, upbeat blonde saved by Prince Charming from life of stepmother servitude in 1950's "Cinderella." Friend to animals, especially Gus, Jaq and other castle mice. Lives in Cinderella Castle with her prince; wears light blue gown at Disney though in the movie it's white. *Magic Kingdom:* Princess Fairytale Hall; Cinderella's Royal Table, Cinderella Castle. *Epcot:* Akershus Royal Banquet Hall meals (often), Norway pavilion. *Grand Floridian Resort:* 1900 Park Fare dinner.

Country Bears. The stars of the attraction Country Bear Jamboree square-dance with guests in the Frontierland Hoedown Happening street show. *Magic Kingdom:* Outside the attraction, Frontierland.

Daisy Duck. Donald Duck's impatient, sassy girlfriend; she appeared with him in a series of 1940s–1950s cartoons. Likes shopping, flowers. Best friend of Minnie Mouse. *Magic Kingdom:* Pete's Silly Sideshow, Storybook Circus, Fantasyland. *Epcot:* Entrance Plaza. *Disney's Hollywood Studios:* Central plaza, Hollywood Blvd. *Disney's Animal Kingdom:* Across from Creature Comforts Starbucks, Discovery Island; Donald's Safari meals, Tusker House, Africa.

© Disney

Ariel

Micaela Neal

Gaston

Doc McStuffins. The star of the Disney Junior show "Doc McStuffins," 7-year-old African-American girl pretends she's a doctor like her mom, "cures" her toys. *Disney's Hollywood Studios:* Animation Courtyard; Play 'N Dine character meals, Echo Lake.

Donald Duck. He's rude, he's crude, he doesn't wear pants. He shouts, pouts and loses his temper at the drop of a pin. He likes to be mean. Yet who doesn't love Donald Duck, a character who responds to life the way we want to, but rarely dare? Created in 1934 as a foil for Mickey Mouse, Donald soon emerged as Disney's most popular star. The "duck with all the bad luck" is known for his "hopping mad" boxing stance, a leaning, jumping posture with one arm straight, the other twirling like a windmill. *Magic Kingdom:* Pete's Silly Sideshow, Storybook Circus, Fantasyland; Move It! Shake It! Dance & Play It! Street Party, Cinderella Castle hub. *Epcot:* Mexico pavilion (in garb from 1944's "The Three Caballeros"). *Disney's Hollywood Studios:* Central plaza, Hollywood Blvd. *Disney's Animal Kingdom:* On the Cretaceous Trail, DinoLand U.S.A.; Donald's Safari meals, Tusker House, Africa. *Beach Club Resort:* Cape May Café breakfast. *Contemporary Resort:* Chef Mickey's meals.

Duffy the Disney Bear. According to Disney Merchandise lore—yes, there is such a thing—Duffy is the teddy bear Minnie Mouse made for Mickey to take on his travels, and is named for the duffel bag Mickey uses to carry him. Exists only as merchandise; has no cartoon or film credits. *Epcot:* World Showcase Friendship Ambassador Gazebo, in front of the Disney Traders East gift shop.

Eeyore. Gloomy plush donkey from 1960s "Winnie the Pooh" shorts used to create the 1977 movie "The Many Adventures of Winnie the Pooh." Speaks in depressed monotone. Devoted to friends. His tail—tied with a pink bow—often falls off. *Magic Kingdom:* Crystal Palace meals, Main Street U.S.A.; The Many Adventures of Winnie the Pooh, Fantasyland.

Fairy Godmother. This absent-minded fairy helps Cinderella go to the ball in 1950's "Cinderella." Rotund, grandmotherly, uses wand to make magic with a "Bibbidi, bobbidi boo!" *Magic Kingdom:* Cinderella Castle fountain, Fantasyland.

Frozone. Superhero name of Lucius Best, a confident speed-skater and best friend to Mr. Incredible in 2004 Pixar film "The Incredibles." Can freeze moisture in air, make snow. *Magic Kingdom:* #INCREDIBLESSuperDanceParty, Tomorrowland.

Merida

Snow White

Gaston. Vain, flirty handsome he-man villain of 1991's "Beauty and the Beast" often flexes his biceps, stares at his own reflection. Believes every female he meets is in love with him. *Magic Kingdom:* Outside Gaston's Tavern, Fantasyland.

Genie. Witty, fast-talking blue genie in 1992's "Aladdin" channels his voice talent, the late great Robin Williams. Can reshape his body. Grants Aladdin three wishes. *Magic Kingdom:* Magic Carpets of Aladdin, Adventureland (occasionally); Move It! Shake It! Dance & Play It! Street Party, Cinderella Castle hub.

Goofy. Good-hearted country simpleton appeals to your inner idiot. Clumsy and gullible, has hard time concentrating. Has bad posture, ill-fitting clothes, big stomach yet always mugs for camera (just like, ahem, many husbands). Has many physical characteristics of a dog; was first known as Dippy Dog in a few 1930s cartoons. Later hosted series of "How To" cartoon sports parodies; in 1950s was oddly transformed into suburban everyman, the sometimes-earless human George Geef. *Magic Kingdom:* Pete's Silly Sideshow, Storybook Circus, Fantasyland; Move It! Shake It! Dance & Play It! Street Party, Cinderella Castle hub.

Epcot: Character Spot, Innoventions Plaza. *Disney's Hollywood Studios:* Central plaza, Hollywood Blvd. *Disney's Animal Kingdom:* DinoLand U.S.A. Service Station; Donald's Safari meals, Tusker House, Africa. *Blizzard Beach:* On the walkway that circles the park. *Contemporary Resort:* Chef Mickey's meals. *Fort Wilderness Resort:* Mickey's Backyard Barbecue dinner show. *Beach Club Resort:* Cape May Cafe breakfast. *Polynesian Village Resort:* 'Ohana breakfast. *Walt Disney World Swan:* Garden Grove breakfast (Sat, Sun), dinner. *Buena Vista Palace:* Watercress Cafe breakfast (Sun). *Four Seasons Orlando:* Ravello breakfast (Thur, Sat).

Green Army Men. Molded-plastic "Toy Story" soldiers have green mesh over faces; don't speak. Humorously mime guard duties. *Disney's Hollywood Studios:* Pixar Place.

Handy Manny. Star of Disney Junior TV show "Handy Manny," bilingual Hispanic handyman Manny Garcia uses talking tools. *Disney's Hollywood Studios:* Play 'N Dine character meals, Echo Lake.

Jack Sparrow. Snarky scoundrel has flexible morals and a love of rum in the "Pirates of the Caribbean" films (2003-2011). Has evaded capture for years by talking his way out of trouble. Lost his ship, the Black Pearl, after

Belle. The "Beauty and the Beast" heroine occasionally strolls through the promenade of Epcot's France pavilion, delighting guests who recognize her, confusing those who don't.

being betrayed by his mutinous first mate Hector Barbossa. *Magic Kingdom:* Captain Jack's Pirate Tutorial, Adventureland.

Jake. Fearless, enthusiastic leader of the Never Land Pirates, from Disney Junior's "Jake and the Never Land Pirates." *Disney's Hollywood Studios:* Animation Courtyard; Play 'N Dine character meals, Echo Lake.

Jasmine. Spirited 16-year-old princess in 1992's "Aladdin." Long black ponytail. Wears aqua bedlah with pouffy pants. Has pet tiger. *Magic Kingdom:* Magic Carpets of Aladdin, Adventureland; Cinderella's Royal Table breakfast, lunch (often), Cinderella Castle. *Epcot:* Morocco pavilion; Akershus Royal Banquet Hall meals (often), Norway pavilion.

Jessie. Plucky yodeling "Toy Story" cowgirl. Woody's exuberant friend; has crush on Buzz Lightyear. *Magic Kingdom:* Splash Mountain exit courtyard, Frontierland.

King Louie. Orangutan from 1967's "Jungle Book" plays practical jokes, kidnaps boy Mowgli to learn about fire and therefore learn to be like a human. *Magic Kingdom:* Move It! Shake It! Dance & Play It! Street Party, Cinderella Castle hub. *Disney's Animal Kingdom:* Upcountry Landing, on trail off Asia-Africa walkway.

Lady Tremaine. Imperious, belittling stepmom in 1950's "Cinderella" treats Cinderella as servant. Mother of Anastasia, Drizella. *Magic Kingdom:* Outside Cinderella Castle, Fantasyland. *Grand Floridian Resort:* 1900 Park Fare dinner.

Lightning McQueen. Hotshot star of "Cars" movies. Was arrogant; now bighearted, loyal. Best friends with 'Mater. *Disney's Hollywood Studios:* Team McQueen Headquarters, Streets of America.

Lilo. Lonely 7-year-old Hawaiian orphan of 2002's "Lilo & Stitch." Loves Elvis Presley, surfing. Adopts alien as pet, names it Stitch. Lives with older sister, Nani. *Polynesian Village Resort:* 'Ohana breakfast. *Typhoon Lagoon:* Near High 'N Dry Towels.

Mad Hatter. Manic milliner confuses Alice during "unbirthday" party in 1951's "Alice in Wonderland." Lisps; channels voice actor Ed Wynn. Tall green hat bears "10/6" (ten shillings, six pence) price tag. *Magic Kingdom:* Mad Tea Party, Fantasyland. *Grand Floridian Resort:* 1900 Park Fare breakfast; Wonderland Tea Party, Garden View Tea Room.

Marie. White French kitten in 1970's "The Aristocats" thinks girls are better than boys; bosses two brothers. Wears pink bows. Often very glad to meet you. *Magic Kingdom:* Town Square, Main Street U.S.A. *Epcot:* France pavilion (sporadically).

Crazy canines. Pluto and Goofy mug for the camera as a group of girlfriends take turns posing with them in DinoLand U.S.A., a section of Disney's Animal Kingdom.

Mary Poppins. Magical nanny teaches uptight family to enjoy everyday life in 1964's "Mary Poppins." Proper, kind, thinks for herself, flies with umbrella. *Magic Kingdom:* Town Square, Main Street U.S.A. *Epcot:* Tea garden, U.K. pavilion; Akershus Royal Banquet Hall meals (often), Norway pavilion. *Grand Floridian Resort:* 1900 Park Fare breakfast.

'Mater. Rusty good ol' boy tow truck in 2006 film "Cars." Prankster, Lightning McQueen sidekick. *Disney's Hollywood Studios:* Team McQueen Headquarters, Streets of America.

Merida. Flame-tressed Scottish princess determined to be in charge of her own fate in 2012's "Brave." Loves archery. Wears dark green gown. *Magic Kingdom:* Fairytale Garden, Fantasyland.

Mickey Mouse. Based in part on silent-film star Charlie Chaplin, debuted in 1928 as underdog who dreamed big. Looks are based on his predecessor, Oswald the Lucky Rabbit. Originally named "Mortimer" Mouse. His optimistic attitude was perfect antidote to 1930s Great Depression; at many theaters, the name "Mickey Mouse" would be in larger letters on marquee than stars of feature. In 1933 received 800,000 fan letters (more than any live-action Hollywood star); President Roosevelt later began showing Mickey cartoons at the White House. Happy-go-lucky, said to be Walt Disney's alter ego. World's most recognized and celebrated cartoon character, Americana pop-culture icon, corporate symbol. During World War II symbolized can-do spirit of U.S. Banned in Nazi Germany in 1933, the Soviet Union in 1936, Yugoslavia in 1937, Italy in 1938; in 1960s was embraced by counterculture as symbol of mischievous rebellion. *Magic Kingdom:* Town Square Theater; Move It! Shake It! Dance & Play It! Street Party, Cinderella Castle hub. *Epcot:* Character Spot, Innoventions Plaza; Garden Grill dinner, The Land pavilion. *Disney's Hollywood Studios:* Near Studio Catering Co. (as Sorcerer's Apprentice). *Disney's Animal Kingdom:* Adventurers Outpost, Discovery Island; Donald's Safari meals, Tusker House, Africa. *Contemporary Resort:* Chef Mickey's meals. *Fort Wilderness Resort:* Mickey's Backyard Barbecue dinner show. *Polynesian Village Resort:* 'Ohana breakfast. *Four Seasons Orlando:* Ravello breakfast (Thur, Sat).

Mike Wazowski. One-eyed green monster likes to get laughs in "Monsters, Inc." films. Emotional, overconfident; Sulley's best friend, roommate. *Disney's Hollywood Studios:* Streets of America, across from playground.

Smooching the street rat. Jasmine surprises Aladdin with a kiss. The sweethearts greet guests together in Magic Kingdom's Adventureland and at Epcot's Morocco pavilion.

Minnie Mouse. Mickey Mouse's girlfriend. Flatters, swoons over her main squeeze. Quick-witted; energetic; loves animals, cooking and gardening. Can play harmonica, guitar, piano. In early cartoons she has a temper: slaps Mickey after he forces her to kiss him in 1928's "Plane Crazy" then jumps out of their open-cockpit airplane; smashes a lamp on Mickey's head when he pulls her nose in 1930's "The Cactus Kid"; when she mistakenly thinks Mickey has given her a bone for a present in 1933's "Puppy Love" kicks him out of her house and sobs "I hate him! I hate all men!" Has old flame (suave, tap-dancing Mortimer) in the 1936 cartoon "Mickey's Rival"; has children in 1933's "Mickey's Steam Roller." As portrayed in 1928 cartoon "The Gallopin' Gaucho," Mickey and Minnie first meet in an Argentine bar. When Minnie, a flirty tavern dancer, bats her eyes at Mickey, a cigarette-smoking outlaw(!), he watches her dance, chugs a beer, then grabs her for a dramatic tango. Later, he rescues her from a kidnapper. Walt Disney originally voiced both Mickey and Minnie Mouse. *Magic Kingdom:* Pete's Silly Sideshow, Storybook Circus, Fantasyland; Move It! Shake It! Dance & Play It! Street Party, Cinderella Castle hub. *Epcot:* Character Spot, Innoventions Plaza. *Disney's Hollywood Studios:* Central plaza,

Hollywood Blvd. *Disney's Animal Kingdom:* Adventurers Outpost, Discovery Island; Donald's Safari meals, Tusker House, Africa. *Beach Club Resort:* Cape May Cafe breakfast. *Contemporary Resort:* Chef Mickey's meals. *Fort Wilderness Resort:* Mickey's Backyard Barbecue dinner show. *Buena Vista Palace:* Watercress Cafe breakfast (Sun). *Hilton Orlando Lake Buena Vista:* Covington Mill breakfast (Sun). *Four Seasons Orlando:* Ravello breakfast (Thur, Sat).

Mister Incredible. Frustrated claims adjuster, super-strong Bob Parr is devoted dad, superhero who misses his glory days in 2004 Pixar movie "The Incredibles." *Magic Kingdom:* #INCREDIBLESSuperDanceParty, Tomorrowland.

Mrs. Incredible. Quick-witted mother, wife, superhero in "The Incredibles," Helen Parr's stretching ability gives her superhero name Elastigirl. *Magic Kingdom:* appears in the #INCREDIBLESSuperDanceParty, Tomorrowland.

Mister Smee. Comical, bumbling first mate to Captain Hook is the friendliest of the pirates in 1953's "Peter Pan." *Contemporary Resort:* Pirates & Pals Fireworks Voyage.

Mulan. Star of 1998's "Mulan"; brave Chinese girl pretends to be boy, joins army to take frail father's place. Quick-witted,

Mary Poppins. The nanny poses for a practically perfect iPad photo at Epcot's U.K. pavilion. She also appears in character meals at Epcot and the Grand Floridian, and at Magic Kingdom.

strong, saves China. *Epcot:* China pavilion formal gardens; Akershus Royal Banquet Hall (often), Norway pavilion.

Penguins. Dancing Jolly Holiday waiters in 1964's "Mary Poppins." *Magic Kingdom:* Town Square, Main Street U.S.A. (often with Mary).

Peter Pan. Confident preteen boy of 1953's "Peter Pan" vows to never grow up. Loves adventure, fights pirates, flies with pixie pal Tinker Bell. *Magic Kingdom:* Near Peter Pan's Flight, Fantasyland. *Contemporary Resort:* Pirates & Pals Fireworks Voyage.

Phineas and Ferb. Stepbrothers Phineas Flynn and Ferb Fletcher concoct imaginative projects over their summer vacation in the Disney Channel animated comedy series "Phineas and Ferb." Talkative optimist Phineas has eyes outside his head; quiet brainiac Ferb has a tree-trunk body and green hair. Pet platypus Perry rarely appears at Disney. *Magic Kingdom:* Move It! Shake It! Dance & Play It! Street Party, Cinderella Castle hub. *Disney's Hollywood Studios:* Near Mama Melrose's Ristorante Italiano, Streets of America.

Piglet. Stuffed pig faithful to Pooh in 1977's "The Many Adventures of Winnie the Pooh." Small, shy, fearful. *Magic Kingdom:* Crystal Palace meals, Main Street U.S.A.; The Many Adventures of Winnie the Pooh, Fantasyland.

Pluto. Pet dog of Mickey Mouse; gangly yellow hound is only Disney Fab Five character who doesn't walk upright (except, of course, at theme parks). Licks, sniffs, romps and runs in a fashion recognizable to dog lovers everywhere; a favorite of children. Wears collar with nametag. Always thinking, known for his vivid expressions. First appeared in 1930 cartoon "The Chain Gang" as an unnamed bloodhound, then briefly was Minnie's pet, named Rover. He has spoken two lines total: in 1931 short "Mickey Steps Out" did an impersonation of Al Jolson's famous moment in 1927 talkie "The Jazz Singer," kneeling to proclaim "Mammy!" In 1931's "The Moose Hunt," Pluto looked into Mickey's eyes and whispered "Kiss me!" Named for the now-demoted planet. *Magic Kingdom:* Town Square, Main Street U.S.A. *Epcot:* Entrance Plaza; Garden Grill dinner, The Land pavilion. *Disney's Hollywood Studios:* Central plaza, Hollywood Blvd. *Disney's Animal Kingdom:* DinoLand U.S.A. Service Station. *Contemporary Resort:* Chef Mickey's meals. *Polynesian Village Resort:* 'Ohana breakfast. *Walt Disney World Swan:* Garden Grove breakfast (Sat, Sun), dinner. *Buena Vista Palace:* Watercress Cafe breakfast (Sun). *Hilton Orlando Lake Buena Vista:* Covington Mill breakfast (Sun).

Fairy Godmother   **Rafiki**   **White Rabbit**

Pocahontas. Brave, noble Native American teenager loves nature, animals (especially raccoon best friend Meeko) and English captain John Smith in 1995 Disney movie "Pocahontas." Spreads message of preserving, honoring nature. Has long straight black hair. *Disney's Animal Kingdom:* Character Landing, Discovery Island.

Prince Charming. Handsome, quiet, well-mannered royal meets, loses, re-meets and finally rescues the original rags-to-riches girl in 1950's "Cinderella." *Grand Floridian Resort:* 1900 Park Fare dinner.

Rafiki. Wise shaman mandrill (with a baboon's tail) advises Simba's father Mufasa in 1994's "The Lion King." Carries gourd-topped walking stick; lives in baobab tree. *Disney's Animal Kingdom:* Conservation Station, Rafiki's Planet Watch.

Rapunzel. Spunky artistic teen princess with 70 feet of golden hair, star of 2010's "Tangled." Locked in tower for years, seeks escape with help from charming, handsome bandit Flynn Rider. Magical hair has healing powers. Wears purple gown. *Magic Kingdom:* Princess Fairytale Hall, Fantasyland.

Russell and Dug. Stars of 2009's "Up," Wilderness Explorer scout Russell is a young boy intent on earning badges; dog Dug can talk but has trouble paying attention because—squirrel! *Disney's Animal Kingdom:* Dug & Russell's Wilderness Explorers Club House, near the entrance to It's Tough to Be a Bug, Discovery Island.

Snow White. Gentle young princess whose jealous stepmother repeatedly tries to kill her because of her beauty in 1937's "Snow White and the Seven Dwarfs." Befriends, mothers seven dwarfs; saved from death by "love's first kiss" from a prince. White skin, raven-black hair. Has the most colorful princess gown; yellow skirt, white collar, blue bodice with red trim. *Magic Kingdom:* Town Square Theater porch, Main Street U.S.A.; Cinderella's Royal Table meals (often), Cinderella Castle. *Epcot:* Germany pavilion wishing well; Akershus Royal Banquet Hall meals (often), Norway pavilion.

Sofia the First. Wide-eyed young girl learning how to live like a princess, from the Disney Channel show "Sofia the First." *Disney's Hollywood Studios:* Animation Courtyard; Play 'N Dine character meals, Echo Lake.

Stitch. Mischievous alien in 2002's "Lilo & Stitch," known initially only as Experiment 626. Escapes from space prison to Hawaii, where he is adopted, named, by Lilo. Loving but has bad-boy behavior; picks nose, burps. *Magic Kingdom:* Carousel of Progress, Tomorrowland; Move It! Shake It! Dance & Play It! Street Party, Cinderella Castle hub. *Typhoon Lagoon:* Near High 'N Dry Towels. *Polynesian Village Resort:* 'Ohana breakfast.

Sulley. Calm, good-natured giant monster James P. Sullivan in "Monsters, Inc." movies. Has blue fur, purple spots, horns. One-eyed Mike Wazowski is best friend, roommate. *Disney's Hollywood Studios:* Streets of America, across from the playground.

Tarzan. Wild, loinclothed man raised by a gorilla troop swings on vines through the jungle in 1999's "Tarzan." Signature yell is a fierce, challenging yodel. Falls in love with British explorer Jane Porter. As in movie, at the park does not wear a shirt. *Disney's*

Tiana   **Lilo**   **Donald Duck**

Animal Kingdom: Discovery Island Trail (often by the Galapagos tortoise).

Tiana and Prince Naveen. Stars of 2009's "The Princess and the Frog." Disney's first African-American princess, Tiana is an aspiring New Orleans restaurant owner who falls in love with funny, carefree, jazz-loving Prince Naveen. In a twist on the classic fairytale, when she kissed the frog prince she was turned into a frog herself. Tiana wears a pale green gown inspired by bayou elements. *Magic Kingdom:* Tiana's Garden Glen, behind Ye Olde Christmas Shoppe, Liberty Square.

Tigger. Ebullient, optimistic stuffed toy tiger in 1977's "The Many Adventures of Winnie the Pooh" loves to bounce. Tells Pooh false rumors about honey-stealing "heffalumps and woozles." Proud to be "onliest" tigger in the Hundred-Acre Wood. *Magic Kingdom:* Crystal Palace meals, Main Street U.S.A.; The Many Adventures of Winnie the Pooh, Fantasyland. *Epcot:* The Toy Soldier, U.K. pavilion. *Grand Floridian Resort:* 1900 Park Fare breakfast.

Tinker Bell. Feisty, jealous pixie loyal to Peter Pan in 1953's "Peter Pan," jealous of Wendy. Jingles when moving; flies using magic pixie dust. Has talent for fixing things, hence "tinker" name. Dresses in bright green leaves. *Magic Kingdom:* Town Square Theater, Main Street U.S.A.

Tweedledee, Tweedledum. Plump twin brothers in 1951's "Alice in Wonderland" dress identically. Always odd, sometimes menacing, often finish each other's sentences. *Magic Kingdom:* Mad Tea Party, Fantasyland (occasionally).

Wendy. In 1953's "Peter Pan," the eldest Darling child is growing out of her childhood, is caring, sensible. Wears nightgown. Loves to tell stories. Close to Peter Pan; Wendy is the object of Tinker Bell's jealousy. *Magic Kingdom:* Near Peter Pan's Flight, Fantasyland (occasionally).

White Rabbit. Nervous, worried rabbit continually declares that he's late in 1951's "Alice in Wonderland." Carries giant watch; wears waistcoat, glasses. Alice follows him down rabbit hole to Wonderland. *Magic Kingdom:* Mad Tea Party, Fantasyland, often with Alice or Mad Hatter.

Winnie the Pooh. Gentle, lovable stuffed bear in 1977's "The Many Adventures of Winnie the Pooh." Loves honey; fears heffalumps and woozles (Tigger's words for elephants and weasels) will steal it. Best friends Christopher Robin, Piglet. *Magic Kingdom:* Crystal Palace meals, Main Street U.S.A.; The Many Adventures of Winnie the Pooh, Fantasyland. *Epcot:* The Toy Soldier, U.K. pavilion. *Grand Floridian Resort:* 1900 Park Fare breakfast.

Woody. Practical, good-natured, old-fashioned cowboy sheriff doll in Pixar's "Toy Story" trilogy. The favorite toy of his owner Andy, a boy growing out of childhood. Has pull-string on back. Best friends with former rival Buzz Lightyear. Girlfriend is Bo Peep, a porcelain lamp base. Named for Woody Strode, an actor who appeared in 1939's "Stagecoach" and other classic Westerns. *Magic Kingdom:* Splash Mountain exit courtyard, Frontierland. *Disney's Hollywood Studios:* Woody's Picture Shootin' Corral, Pixar Place.

Walt Disney World A–Z

Airports. Orlando has two main commercial airports. Most U.S. airlines fly into the huge Orlando International Airport, while some international carriers use the smaller Orlando Sanford International airport.

Orlando International. Located 19 miles to the east of Walt Disney World, Orlando International Airport is one of the busiest airports in the United States. It handles 35 million passengers a year, an average of 97,000 people a day. At just over 23 square miles, it's the third largest airport in the country behind Denver and Dallas.

Orlando International's hub-and-spoke layout features a large central terminal that's connected by elevated trains to four remote concourses. The terminal is divided into two sides ("A" and "B") and has two lobbies. The east end is topped with a Hyatt Regency hotel that wraps around a tall atrium; the west end is overlooked by a Chili's Too restaurant.

The airport "MCO" IATA code refers to its former life (1940–1976) as McCoy Air Force Base, a Strategic Air Command installation. During the 1962 Cuban Missile Crisis, McCoy was the primary forward operating base for U.S. U-2 reconnaissance aircraft. Today's terminal opened in 1981; the last gate opened in 2000 (One Jeff Fuqua Blvd., Orlando, 32827; 407-825-2001; orlandoairports.net).

Arrivals and departures. Real-time information is available over the phone and on the airport's home page (orlandoairports.net). Arriving and departing flights: 407-825-8463.

Cabs and shuttles. Mears Transportation (407-423-5566) will take you to Walt Disney World by taxi ($55–$65), 4-person town car ($80–$90), 8-person van ($80–$90) or shuttle bus ($22 one-way per adult, $17 one-way child; $36 round-trip per adult, $27 round-trip child).

See also **Transportation.**

Chapel. Open to all faiths, the airport chapel is just past the west security checkpoint (Gates 1–59). Any passenger with a boarding pass is welcome. Catholic mass is held Sundays at 8:15 a.m. and noon.

Checking in. The Greater Orlando Aviation Authority says to arrive two hours before a domestic departure; three hours before an international one.

Child ID cards. In general children under age 18 are not required to have photo identification for U.S. domestic flights. Airlines have more specific requirements.

Getting to Disney. The simplest route (25 minutes) is to take the airport's South Exit road 4 miles to Florida 417 (a toll road), go west 13 miles to Osceola Parkway (Exit 3), then head west again 2 miles.

Highway tolls. Two toll booths sit between Disney and the airport on Florida 417; each requires a toll of $1.25, cash only. Vehicles enrolled in Florida's SunPass/E-Pass program are charged automatically and don't have to stop.

Internet access. Complimentary Wi-Fi is available in all public areas. Several kiosks offer wired connections.

Lost and found. You'll find this office (7 a.m.–10 p.m., 407-825-2111) in Terminal B, across from the food court.

Magical Express. This Disney service will handle your bags for you and shuttle you to your Disney resort at no charge.

See also **Magical Express.**

Operating hours. The airport is open 24 hours a day. Each airline within it sets its own hours of operation.

Paging. This system (407-825-2000) lets you page airport visitors at no charge.

Parking. Parking lots ($10–$25 daily, 407-825-8463; orlandoairports.net/ops/parking) accept cash, credit cards and SunPass/E-Pass transponders. Valet parking services can include auto detailing.

Rental cars. The airport is the largest rental car facility in the world. Most car rental companies are located in a parking garage adjacent to the terminal. Rental counters are on both sides of the terminal on the Ground Transportation level.

See also **Transportation.**

Restaurants and food. The airport has many fast-food spots. The main terminal has a food court with 10 quick-service counters (including McDonald's and Carvel

Winter Summerland. Cinderella Castle is a snowy obstacle on the miniature golf course.

Ice Cream) and each of the four concourses has at least seven more. The airport has five table-service restaurants, three in the terminal (Chili's Too, Fox Sports Grill, Romano's Macaroni Grill) and two in the Hyatt (Hemisphere, a steak and seafood spot; and McCoy's Bar and Grill, which serves pizza, pasta and sushi).

Shopping. The airport has 30 stores in its main terminal, including shops from the Kennedy Space Center, SeaWorld, Universal Studios and, of course, Walt Disney World. Located in both terminal lobbies, two Disney stores stock popular Disney World merchandise, sell theme-park tickets and ship items purchased on Disney property. Disney's EarPort (407-825-2339) is in the East hall; The Magic of Disney (407-825-2370) is in the West.

Orlando Sanford International. Forty-eight miles from Disney, this airport (IATA code "SFB") serves 5,000 passengers a day. It began as a World War II Naval Air Station (1200 Red Cleveland Blvd., Sanford 32773; 407-322-7771; orlandosanfordairport.com).

Major airlines. Primarily British carriers, they include Allegiant (702-505-8888), ArkeFly (855-808-4015), Icelandair (800-223-5500), Monarch (44-0-1582-398-036), SST (407-288-8820), Thomas Cook (44-0-870-750-0512) and Thomson (44-0-871-231-4691).

Getting to Disney. The simplest route (50 minutes): Head south on Florida 417 (a toll road) 16 miles to Florida 408, go west 8 miles to Interstate 4, then south 16 miles.

Airlines serving the Orlando International Airport	
Aer Lingus	800 474-7424
AeroGal	00571 414 71 85
AeroMexico	800 237-6639
Air Canada	800 247-2262
Air Transat	877 872-6728
AirTran	800 247-8726
Alaska Airlines	800 252-7522
American Airlines	800 433-7300
Avianca Airlines	800 284-2622
Azul Airlines	844 499-2985
Bahamas Air	800 222-4262
British Airways	800 247-9297
CanJet Select Airlines	800 809-7777
Caribbean Airlines	800 920-4225
Copa Airlines	800 359-2672
Delta Airlines	800 221-1212
Frontier Airlines	800 432-1359
GOL	55 11 5504 4410
JetBlue Airways	800 538-2583
Lan Airlines	866 435-9525
Lufthansa	800 645-3880
Magni Charters	800 201-1404
Miami Air Intl	305 871-3300
Norwegian Airlines	800 357-4159
Silver Airways	800 229-9990
Southwest Airlines	800 435-9792
Spirit Airlines	800 772-7117
Sun Country Airlines	800 359-6786
Sunwing Airlines	800 761-1711
TACA Airlines	800 400-8222
TAM Airlines	888 235-9826
Thomas Cook	0844 879 8407
United Airlines	800 241-6522
U.S. Airways	800 428-4322
Virgin America	877 359-8474
Virgin Atlantic	800 862-8621
Volaris	866 988-3527
West Jet	800 538-5696

Alcohol. Guests cannot bring alcoholic beverages into any Walt Disney World theme or water park, though those of legal age can carry open containers of purchased alcoholic beverages (drinks served in restaurants, however, cannot be taken elsewhere). All Disney theme parks serve alcohol, though the Magic Kingdom only offers it on the dinner menu of its Be Our Guest restaurant. There are no liquor stores on Disney property, though hotels and theme-park gift shops sell beer, wine and liquor. It is illegal to carry open containers of alcohol in a car or public area in Central Florida. The legal age to purchase and consume alcohol in Florida is 21.

AA meetings. Friends of Bill W. Orlando (Alcoholics Anonymous) meet Monday through Saturday at 8 a.m. at the Community Presbyterian Church at 511 Celebration Ave. in Celebration, a community that's right next to Walt Disney World on the other side of Interstate 4. Meetings are also offered at 7 p.m. Wednesdays and Saturdays at 215a Celebration Blvd. in Celebration, in the North Village Meeting Room by the pool.

Birthdays. Walt Disney World offers many ways to help celebrate a birthday.

Balloons and buttons. Concierge staff at Disney hotels can often have balloons delivered to a room or a restaurant. Available free at theme-park Guest Relations locations, personalized Happy Birthday buttons cue cast members to recognize celebrants.

Cakes. All Disney table-service restaurants except Victoria & Albert's offer 6-inch birthday cakes with no advance notice ($21, chocolate or vanilla, serves 5). Plan ahead and Disney's Cake Hotline will let you choose your filling, icing and personalized decorations (407-827-2253, cakes $32 and up, 48 hrs. notice). Most hotel restaurants offer Mickey Mouse-shaped cakes through room service or guest services ($48, serves 12).

Cruises. You can watch Magic Kingdom's Wishes fireworks or Epcot's IllumiNations from a pontoon boat. One-hour trips include snacks and drinks ($275 for up to 8 people on 21-foot boat; $325 for up to 10 people on 25-foot boat. $25 additional for decorative banner and balloons). Cakes are available through Disney's Cake Hotline (see above). Reservations available 180 days in advance at 407-827-2253; 2-day cancellation policy.

Flowers and gifts. Disney Floral & Gifts (407-827-3505, disneyflorist.com) delivers adult and child arrangements, baskets and other presents throughout Disney property.

Goodie bags. Standard bags contain a party hat, game, coloring book and crayons; deluxe bags add a magnet activity set and Mickey-shaped straw (407-939-3463).

Goofy telephone call. Goofy will call your Disney hotel room with a free birthday greeting (407-824-2222).

Parties. At Disney Springs, the Goofy's Candy Company store offers kids celebrations themed to Goofy or Cinderella. They include balloons, favors, treats, drinks and games, and extra goodies for the birthday child. ($350 for up to 12 guests; $25 for additional guests up to 20. Ages 3 and up. 90 minutes. Reservations available 90 days in advance at 407-939-2329.)

Room decorations. Disney Floral & Gifts will decorate your Disney room in a personalized birthday theme (407-827-3505).

Children's services.

As you might guess, Disney offers many special services for kids.

Baby Care Centers. Located in each theme park, these quiet, air-conditioned spots are designed for parents with infants or toddlers. They have private nursing rooms with rocking chairs; changing rooms with tables and unisex bathrooms; feeding areas with high chairs and kitchens with microwaves, ovens and sinks; lounges with televisions, chairs and sofas; and playrooms. The centers sell baby food, diapers, formula, juice, pacifiers and over-the-counter medications.

Magic Kingdom's Baby Care Center is next to the Crystal Palace restaurant. Epcot's is in the Odyssey Center building, between Test Track and the World Showcase. The Hollywood Studios Baby Care Center is next to that park's Guest Relations office; the one at Animal Kingdom is tucked behind the Starbucks on Discovery Island.

Babysitters. Disney works with in-room childcare provider Kids Nite Out (407-828-0920, kidsniteout.com) to supply babysitting and childcare for kids ages 6 weeks to 12 years, including those with special needs. Caregivers bring toys, activities, books, games and arts and crafts. Rates start at $18 per hour with a 4-hour minimum, plus a $10 transportation fee.

Childcare centers. Five Disney-owned hotels offer an evening childcare center: Disney's Animal Kingdom Lodge, Beach Club, Grand Floridian, Polynesian Village and Wilderness Lodge. Each has a secure room staffed by adults and stocked with arts and crafts, books, games, toys and videos ($11.50 per hour per child, 2-hour minimum, includes dinner 6–8 p.m. Children must be toilet trained, no pull-ups, 4–12 years old. 4 p.m. [sometimes 4:30 p.m.] to midnight. 407-939-3463. Reservations required). The Walt Disney World Dolphin has Camp Dolphin ($10 per hour per child, 2-hour minimum, includes dinner 6:30–7:30 p.m. Ages 4–12, must be toilet trained, no pull-ups. 5:30 p.m.–midnight. 407-934-4241. Reservations required).

Child swap. This complimentary, unpublicized service allows you and your spouse to enjoy a ride even if you have a child who can't (or doesn't want to) ride who you don't want to leave unattended. To use it, tell a cast member at the ride's entrance of your situation, then you or your spouse gets in line while the other waits with your child and gets a Fastpass-like ticket to ride later. If the attraction does not offer Fastpasses you, your spouse and your child wait in line together. You ride while your spouse stays with your child, then your spouse rides.

Discounts for children. Disney World offers reduced prices for children ages 3 to 9 for park tickets (slightly), food and dining plans and paid-recreation options. Older children are charged adult rates. Children younger than age 3 are admitted free into Disney theme and water parks. Children are also charged less for the Disney Dining Plan.

See also **Disney Dining Plan, Tickets** and **Sports and Recreation.**

Equipment rentals. Disney has the basics, such as cribs, rollaway beds and strollers. Outside companies rent those items and more, and often handle delivery and pickup.

Getting in early. The crowd on Main Street U.S.A. is relatively light on Extra Magic Hour mornings, when even the most popular rides have little or no wait for at least the first hour.

Cribs and rollaway beds. Disney resorts offer free use of Pack 'n Play Playard cribs; request one when you make a reservation. Rollaway beds typically incur an extra fee ($20 to $30). All About Kids (800-728-6506, 407-812-9300, all-about-kids.com) and Baby's Away (888-376-0084, 407-334-0232, babysaway.com) rent standard cribs.

Strollers. You can rent strollers at each theme park and at Disney Springs (see theme-park and Disney Springs chapters for locations). Single strollers rent for $15 a day; double strollers $31 a day. For multiple-day rentals, consider a length-of-stay stroller rental. You pay once, wait in line less and save some money ($2 a day for single strollers, $4 a day for doubles). Made of molded plastic, Disney's strollers are not designed for infants. For an infant stroller, contact Baby's Away (407-334-0232), Kingdom Strollers (407-674-1866), Magic Strollers (866-866-6177) or Orlando Stroller Rentals (800-281-0884).

Other equipment. Baby's Away and All About Kids rent car seats, high chairs, playpens and the like. Most local car-rental companies offer infant or child safety seats ($7–$15 per day) with advance notice.

See also **Rental Cars** under **Transportation**

Face art. Scattered throughout Disney are artisans offering personalized creations.

Caricaturists. These artists offer their services in all theme and water parks, at most Disney-owned hotels and at Disney Springs. Finished portraits come with storage tubes. Prices range from $18 to $99, based on the number of people in the work and whether it includes color.

Face painters. Children (and adults) can get their faces painted for $12 to $18 at all Disney World theme parks, Disney Springs and on the boardwalk at Disney's BoardWalk Resort. Some park stands offer themed designs, for example animal styles at Disney's Animal Kingdom or Star Wars makeup at Disney's Hollywood Studios.

Silhouette artists. Artists cut profiles of children or adults out of paper in Magic Kingdom (on Main Street U.S.A. and in Liberty Square), Epcot (the France pavilion) and at Disney Springs (The Marketplace). Prices start at $9.

Infant care. Diaper-changing stations are in men's and women's restrooms throughout Disney World. Moms can nurse babies anywhere on Disney property without hassle.

Lost children. Lose your child? Tell the closest Disney cast member. They'll instantly spread the news throughout the park, and advise you on what to do next. Typically cast members who encounter lost children take them to the park's Baby Care Center. Some parents introduce their children to a cast member first thing when they arrive at a theme park, and point out the worker's distinctive name tag. Other parents use a permanent marker to write their cell-phone number on the child's arm.

Makeover salons. Disney offers two distinct types of fantasy salons:

Bibbidi Bobbidi Boutiques. Little girls turn into princesses and pop stars at these female-focused salons. There are two of them: in Magic Kingdom inside Cinderella Castle and at Disney Springs inside the World of Disney store. Three packages are available: Crown ($60 for a hairstyle, shimmering makeup, nail polish, sash and purse), Courtyard ($95, adds a sparkling Bibbidi Bobbidi Boutique T-shirt and tutu to the Crown package) and Castle ($195 and up, adds a costume and photo session with prints to the Courtyard package). There's a Knight Package for boys ($19 for hair gel, hair confetti and a toy sword and shield). Ages 3 and up. Reservations can be made up to 180 days in advance: 407-939-7895.

Pirates League. This Magic Kingdom salon transforms adults and children into swashbucklers, swashbucklerettes and mermaids. Packages ($30–$75) include facial effects, a reversible bandana, a false earring and eye patch, a sword, a temporary tattoo, a pirate coin necklace, an official pirate name and a personalized oath. Costumes, headwear and photo packages are also available. Participants can join an Adventureland Pirate Parade daily at 4 p.m. (Ages 3 and up. At the exit of Pirates of the Caribbean. Reservations up to 180 days in advance: 407-939-2739.)

Restaurants. Most Disney eateries offer kids' menus and high chairs. Only one excludes children: Victoria & Albert's at the Grand Floridian. Expense-account spots outside Disney often aren't child-friendly.

Convention facilities. Six hotels on Walt Disney World property— the Disney-owned BoardWalk, Contemporary, Coronado Springs, Grand Floridian and Yacht Club and Starwood's Walt Disney World Swan and Dolphin—have convention and conference centers (the largest convention facility is at the Dolphin; its Atlantic Hall consumes 60,000 square feet). Attendees get discounted room rates, deals on golf (20 percent off greens fees; free golf club rentals, range balls and transportation) and theme-park tickets.

See also **Tickets.**

Crowd patterns. In general Disney's theme parks are the most crowded whenever schools in the United States are not in session. During peak periods the wait times at major attractions can exceed three hours, and reservations for popular Fastpass+ times and restaurants are often booked solid at least a month in advance.

Least crowded times of year. The day after Labor Day (the slowest day of the year) until Epcot's Food & Wine Festival and mid-January through the first week in February.

Most crowded times of year. The week between Christmas Day through New Year's Day and Independence Day weekend; also

Height minimums

Magic Kingdom

The Barnstormer	40 in.
Big Thunder Mountain Railroad	40 in.
Seven Dwarfs Mine Train	38 in.
Space Mountain	44 in.
Splash Mountain	40 in.
Stitch's Great Escape	40 in.
Tomorrowland Speedway, solo	54 in.
To ride as a passenger	32 in.

Epcot

Mission Space	44 in.
Soarin'	40 in.
Sum of All Thrills (Innoventions)	48 in.
Test Track	40 in.

Disney's Hollywood Studios

Rock 'n' Roller Coaster	48 in.
Star Tours	40 in.
The Twilight Zone Tower of Terror	40 in.

Disney's Animal Kingdom

Dinosaur	40 in.
Expedition Everest	44 in.
Kali River Rapids	38 in.
Primeval Whirl	48 in.

Blizzard Beach

Chairlift	32 in.
Downhill Double Dipper	48 in.
Slush Gusher	48 in.
Summit Plummet	48 in.

Typhoon Lagoon

Crush 'n' Gusher	48 in.
Humunga Kowabunga	48 in.

DisneyQuest

Buzz Lightyear's AstroBlaster	51 in.
CyberSpace Mountain	51 in.
Mighty Ducks Pinball Slam	48 in.
Pirates of the Caribbean: Battle for Buccaneer Gold	35 in.

the Spring Break period (typically from the third week of March through the third week of April), holiday weekends, Presidents' week, Marathon Weekend.

Least crowded time of day. First two hours of the day; last hour of the evening.

Most crowded time of day. Afternoons.

At Disney's water parks, typically the hotter the weather, the larger the crowd.

Disability services. Disney offers a variety of services for guests with hearing, mobility, visual or other disabilities.

Disability Access Card. A replacement for Disney's old Guest Assistance Card as well as its former heavily abused policy that guests in wheelchairs and scooters always bypassed waiting lines, this small folded card is for those who are unable to withstand extended waits at attractions due to a disability. At each ride or show, showing the card lets a guest schedule a return time comparable to that attraction's current wait time, and if the guest runs late it's OK. At least that's the official policy. In reality, cast members at an attraction often have the ability to let a Disability Access Card holder enter it immediately through its Fastpass+ line, at their discretion—which lets Disney treat more seriously impaired guests with more appropriate compassion.

The card is available at Guest Relations locations. A doctor's note isn't required, but users must have their photos taken. The card is valid for up to 14 days.

Cognitive services. Disney publishes a complimentary pamphlet—Disney's Guide for Guests with Cognitive Disabilities—that's filled with tips. It's available online (at disneyworld.disney.go.com/guest-services/guests-with-disabilities) and in person at Guest Relations locations.

Hearing services. Disney's Handheld Device (yes, that's the name) is a wireless gadget roughly the size of a smart phone. It amplifies the audio at some stationary attractions, turns on captions on some pre-show video screens (single-button activators are also available for this), and displays captions at narrated moving attractions. Available at each park's Guest Relations location, Disney's Handheld Device costs nothing to borrow but requires a $25 daily deposit.

Reflective captioning. At many theatrical attractions, cast members can supply handheld acrylic panels that reflect captions from an LED display on a back wall.

Guest Assistance Packets. Available at many attractions, each packet consists of a three-ring binder which holds a script of the ride or show, a flashlight, a pen and a small pad of paper for cast members to use to communicate with any guest who has trouble hearing.

Sign language. Live interpreters typically translate live shows at Magic Kingdom on Mondays and Thursdays, Epcot on Tuesdays and Fridays, Disney's Hollywood Studios on Sundays and Wednesdays and Disney's Animal Kingdom on Saturdays. Cast members with sign language abilities wear identifying pins. For a schedule of interpreted shows call 407-824-4321.

TTY telephones. Pay phones with amplified handsets and Text Typewriters are located throughout the parks.

Mobility services. Disney rents mobility scooters (which the company calls "Electric Conveyance Vehicles," or ECVs) and wheelchairs. Both are available on a first-come, first-served, same-day basis (no reservations are accepted) and neither requires any proof of need. Disney's wheelchairs and ECVs may not be transferred from park to park, but the deposit ticket from a first rental will let you rent additional wheelchairs or ECVs on the same day at other Disney theme parks.

Mobility scooters. Disney rents ECVs for $70 a day which includes a $20 deposit. Arrive early to rent one; popular with obese as well as disabled guests, they sell out quickly. The maximum weight allowed is 450 pounds. You can bring your own scooter into any park.

Wheelchairs. Disney rents wheelchairs for $12 a day ($10 for multiple-day rentals). The maximum weight is 350 pounds. Identified by blue flags, parking-lot wheelchairs are free to use. Personal wheelchairs can be used anywhere on Disney property.

Rental locations. Magic Kingdom rents wheelchairs at the Wheelchair Rental Shop at the park entrance, and offers replacements at Buzz Lightyear's Space Ranger Spin, Castle Couture and the Frontierland Trading Post. Epcot has rentals at its front and back entrances; replacements at the Germany pavilion's Karamelle-Kuche shop. Disney's Hollywood Studios rents chairs at Oscar's Super Service just inside its gate, and has replacements at the Tatooine Traders and Writer's Stop shops. Disney's Animal Kingdom has rentals at Garden Gate Gifts and replacements at the Mombasa Marketplace store at the back of the park.

Disney Springs rents chairs at its Stroller Shop next to the Once Upon a Toy store and at the DisneyQuest Emporium—Disney Springs chair rentals require a $100 deposit. All wheelchair shops also rent ECVs. Wheelchairs are complimentary at Walt Disney World resort hotels with a $315 refundable deposit, though availability is limited.

Strollers as wheelchairs. Disabled children in strollers can get wheelchair benefits if their parents pick up a special tag at any Guest Relations location.

Transferring. Some park attractions require wheelchair and ECV users to transfer to a ride vehicle. Disney cast members are not allowed to lift guests.

Off-property rental companies. You cannot reserve a wheelchair or ECV in advance from Disney, but you can from Apple Scooter (800-701-1971), Best Price Mobility (866-866-3434), Buena Vista Scooter Rentals (866-484-4797), CARE Scooter Rentals (800-741-2282) or Scooterbug (800-726-8284).

Zero-entry pools. Nine Disney resort hotels have zero-entry swimming pools, one side of which gradually slopes into the water so guests in appropriate wheelchairs can roll into it—the Art of Animation, Caribbean Beach, Contemporary (behind Bay Lake Tower), Grand Floridian, Polynesian Village, Saratoga Springs and Yacht and Beach Club resorts, and both the Jambo House and Kidani Village areas of Animal Kingdom Lodge.

Visual services. Visually impaired guests can take advantage of four Disney resources:

Audio Description. Disney's Handheld Device provides audio descriptions of some attractions (see previous page).

Audiotape guides and tours. Audiotapes orient guests to a park. Tape tours offer routes, provide distances between attractions and recommend stopping spots. Free at Guest Relations locations with a $25 deposit.

Braille maps. Each park has a stationary Braille map with raised graphics to highlight landmarks and attractions.

Handheld braille guide. Each park has handheld braille guides which describe attractions, restaurants and shops. Free at Guest Relations locations with a $25 deposit.

Parking. Each park has a designated handicapped parking area. Courtesy trams do not serve this area, as they do not accommodate wheelchairs or ECVs.

Restrooms. All Disney restrooms have wheelchair-accessible stalls. Companion restrooms are throughout Disney property.

Service animals. Trained and leashed (or harnessed) service animals are welcome throughout Disney property, and can go on most attractions with their owners. Each park has designated potty break spots. If you have a service animal, you will most likely enter attractions through an alternate entrance, usually the Fastpass+ entrance.

Transportation. Most Disney buses and all monorail trains can accommodate wheelchairs and mobility scooters. Buses use a 30-by-48-inch lift; monorail trains use portable ramps. Some ferry boats accept chairs and scooters depending on water conditions.

Theme park guides. For each of its parks Disney publishes a complimentary Guide for Guests with Disabilities, which has in-depth information and a detailed map. All Guest Relations locations distribute all four guides.

Disney Dining Plan. Disney hotel guests and Disney Vacation Club members can add this prepaid meal plan (which can include recreation options) to their park-ticket purchase. Over a hundred restaurants participate. Five packages are available:

Basic Plan. Provides a table-service meal, a fast food ("quick-service") meal and a snack per each nightly stay and a refillable drink mug for use at your resort.

Deluxe Plan. Provides three daily table-service (or fast food) meals, two snacks and a refillable drink mug.

Quick-Service Plan. Provides two fast food meals and one snack per day, again with a refillable drink mug.

Premium Plan. Provides three daily table-service (or fast food) meals, two snacks and a refillable drink mug for use at your resort. Other perks include unlimited use of many recreation options, vouchers to the Cirque du Soliel show La Nouba, unlimited use of child-care facilities and select theme-park tours. Requires purchase of at least a one-day park ticket. Buy it six months early to cherry-pick your recreation times.

Platinum Plan. Same as the Premium Plan except with still more extras, such as an itinerary planning service, a spa treatment and a fireworks cruise.

How the plans work. You can use Disney Dining Plan meal and snack credits in any combination during your stay. For example, you can eat all table-service meals one day, all fast-food meals the next, and nothing but snacks the day after that. If one person in your party uses up his or her plan, others can continue to use theirs. Disney defines a breakfast meal as one entree and one beverage; or a combo meal and a beverage or juice. Lunch and dinner are defined as one entree, one dessert and one beverage; or a combo meal, dessert and beverage.

To use the plan, present your MagicBand to a cashier or server. Food usage is tracked electronically; balances are available on each food receipt. Nearly every Disney-owned restaurant participates in the Dining Plan, as do snack locations such as food carts and sweet shops. Tips are not included; neither are alcoholic beverages, some bottled drinks, souvenir mugs, or snacks and beverages from recreation-rental counters.

Key conditions. Each Disney Dining Plan has four key conditions:

It is sold per party, not per person. If one person in your group buys a Dining Plan, everyone else in your group must too. The only exception: children under age 3. They can eat from an adult's plate.

Kids are kids. When their parents are using a Dining Plan, children 3–9 must order from a kid's menu when one is available. Likewise, those children over 9 years of age must order from adult menus.

Some restaurants take two credits. These include Disney Signature restaurants, dinner shows and Cinderella's Royal Table at Magic Kingdom. Room-service meals at Disney Deluxe Resorts charge two credits, too.

Leftover credits have no value. Just like those magical accoutrements of Cinderella, unused Dining Plan meals and snacks expire at midnight on your checkout date.

Getting your money's worth. If you take advantage of it, the Dining Plan will give you great food and memorable meals. Handle it poorly, however, and your magical vacation can include a frustrating waste of time and resources. Here are four keys to getting the most for your money:

Don't overestimate your hunger. When determining which plan to purchase, keep in mind that it's tough to eat enough food to justify three table-service meals a day. It's also difficult to dine at more than one Signature restaurant a day, as each takes awhile to fully experience.

Use your credits efficiently. Except for those at Signature restaurants, the plan considers nearly all table-service meals equal. In most cases, dining with a princess, Mickey Mouse or Lilo and Stitch at an all-you-can-eat feast uses no more credits than getting a hamburger and fries at Magic Kingdom's Plaza Restaurant.

Know where the deals are. Though your plans will charge you the same amount—one credit—for most meals, some restaurants give you more for it. Great breakfast buffets include Boma at Animal Kingdom Lodge and the 1900 Park Fare character meal at the Grand Floridian Resort. For lunch, try Coral Reef at Epcot or Sanaa at Disney's Animal Kingdom Lodge (ask for a table by a window). For dinner, consider Boma, 1900 Park Fare, Spice Road at Epcot or Raglan Road at Disney Springs. Good quick-service choices include Sunshine Seasons at The Land pavilion and Earl of Sandwich and Wolfgang Puck Express at Disney Springs.

Make your reservations way early. Disney restaurants book to capacity sometimes months early, especially for the most popular dining times. Make reservations as early as possible to ensure you can dine at places, and times, that best suit your needs.

Extra Magic Hours. Each day at least one Walt Disney World theme or water park opens an hour early, or stays open two hours late, for those guests staying at Disney-owned resorts, the Walt Disney World Swan and Dolphin, Shades of Green or the Disney Springs Hilton. Residents of Disney's Golden Oak subdivision also qualify. To take advantage of an extra morning hour, simply arrive at the designated park's entrance with a valid park ticket or MagicBand wristband. During evening hours, you'll be asked to scan your MagicBand at each attraction. Note: On a day when a park offers an Extra Magic Hour in the morning, that park will be more crowded than usual later, during its regular hours.

Floral services. Disney Floral & Gifts (407-939-4438, 8 a.m.–6 p.m. daily, disney-florist.com) sells floral arrangements, gift baskets, balloons, fruit, liquor and plants, each with as much, or little, Disney theming as desired. Delivery is available at Disney theme parks, resorts and Disney Springs. A Disney Dream Makers division can decorate your room before arrival or for special occasions; the new Star Tours Adventure Pack includes a light saber and other "Star Wars"-inspired goodies. The Disney Event Group has arrangements for business gatherings (407-939-7129, disneymeetings.com); Disney's wedding planners help with bridal displays (407-939-4610, disneyweddings.com).

Groceries. Many Disney resorts have shops that offer groceries. Stores in resorts that offer suites and kitchen facilities have the best variety. Outside of Disney, many supermarkets are just a few miles away:

Gooding's supermarket. Close to Disney in the Crossroads Shopping Center; prices are 20–25 percent higher than Publix.

Publix supermarkets. Four locations are near Walt Disney World—at the Celebration shopping center Water Tower Place (29 Blake Boulevard; 321-939-3100), at 2915 Vineland Road (407-396-7525) at 7640 W. Sand Lake Road (407-226-3315) and at 7524 Dr. Phillips Blvd. (407 226-9884) (the last one one of the best Publix in Florida, with an expansive deli and even a cooking school). Florida's most popular supermarket chain, Publix has decent prices, a wide variety of two-for-one items and, at the Celebration and Dr. Phillips Blvd. locations, a spot to sit down to eat. For what it's worth, it also treats its employees pretty well.

Whole Foods. A short drive from Disney property at Interstate 4 and Sand Lake Road; this pricey market offers quality natural and organic groceries. Its produce department has more than 75 locally grown types of fruits and vegetables. An indoor-outdoor dining area offers a convenient spot to chow down on to-go items (8003 Turkey Lake Road, Orlando 32819; 407-355-7100).

Winn-Dixie supermarket. Two locations are near Disney, at 11957 S. Apopka-Vineland Road (407-465-8600) and 7840 W. Irlo Bronson Highway (U.S. 192) (407-397-2210).

Grocery delivery services. Two companies deliver groceries to Disney hotels. Note: The Walt Disney World Swan and Dolphin does not allow grocery deliveries.

Gardengrocer.com. This national delivery service offers 4,700 products. Local categories include "park essentials," baby care, natural and organic fresh produce and household products (866-855-4350, gardengrocer.com, minimum order $40, delivery fee $12, orders over $200 delivered free).

Whole Foods. The Orlando Whole Foods Market offers delivery to Walt Disney World, though it does not have an online ordering system (407-355-7100, no minimum order, delivery fee $30. 48 hours notice required).

Gasoline stations. Three Speedway (formerly Hess) stations sit on Disney property, all open 24 hours with self-serve gasoline and a convenience store. Prices are not inflated; in fact, a gallon of gas is often a nickel or dime per gallon cheaper inside Disney property than outside it.

Magic Kingdom. On the parking-lot exit road, next to the AAA Car Care Center (1000 W. Car Care Drive, 32801; 407-938-0143).

Disney's Hollywood Studios. Corner of Buena Vista Drive and Epcot Resorts Boulevard. Car wash available (300 East Buena Vista Drive, 32801; 407-938-0151).

Disney Springs. Directly across the street, under a towering sign that reads "Gas" (1475 Buena Vista Drive, 32801; 407-938-0160).

For Orlando-area gasoline prices over the past 48 hours see orlandoairports.net/transport/gas_prices.htm.

Gay and lesbian travelers. Gay and lesbian adults of all ages come to Walt Disney World during the first week in June for Gay Days (407-896-8431, gaydays.com); many wear red shirts in a sign of celebration and solidarity. Disney does not sponsor the event. GayCities Orlando (orlando.gaycities.com) and Gay Orlando (gayorlando.com) have lists of LGBT-friendly Orlando accommodations, bars and restaurants. The event was once controversial, though has been more accepted by straight guests and families in recent years.

Guest Relations. Each Disney theme and water park — and Disney Springs — has at least one Guest Relations office. Disney staffers make dining reservations, upgrade park tickets, sell annual passes, check on lost items (for items lost the same day) and provide answers to general questions. Free guidemaps and Times Guides for all the Disney World parks are available. Disabled guests can pick up park-specific guides for guests with disabilities, get a DAS card and/or borrow Disney's Handheld Device. International visitors can pick up complimentary Attraction Translation Devices and guidemaps in German, Japanese, Spanish and Portuguese as well as exchange currency. Many staffers are multilingual.

Each theme park has a walk-up Guest Relations window outside its entrance, and at least one location inside. Magic Kingdom's Guest Relations spot is at City Hall. Epcot has an indoor office to the left of Spaceship Earth. Guest Relations at Disney's Hollywood Studios sits beside Sid Cahuenga's shop. Disney's Animal Kingdom's location is just inside the entrance on the left.

Disney Springs has two Guest Relations offices. The Marketplace office is next to the Arribas Brothers shop. The West Side location is at the DisneyQuest gift shop. A new Guest Relations office will open in the Town Center section of Disney Springs in 2016.

Highways. Two major limited-access highways border Walt Disney World.

Interstate 4. The main drag through Central Florida, Interstate 4 runs along the southeastern edge of Disney, connecting it to Orlando (18 miles northeast) and Tampa (53 miles southwest). Technically the highway runs east to west, but through the Orlando area it often aligns more north and south.

Florida 429. This toll road runs along the southwestern edge of Disney property, and makes for a handy shortcut for those coming from the north on Florida's Turnpike. Taking it saves about a half-hour compared to continuing on the turnpike into Orlando, and gives you a drive through farmland and orange groves instead of congested urbania. To use Florida 429, take the turnpike south to Exit 267A, then head southeast on 429 11 miles to Exit 8, which leads to Disney's Western Way entrance. Tolls vary from $1.25 to $1.50. At Mile Marker 13 you can glimpse, way off to your left, Cinderella Castle, Space Mountain, the Contemporary Resort, Spaceship Earth and the Walt Disney World Dolphin Resort. Seeing that view at night can be stunning.

Holidays. Disney is especially busy during holiday periods—the days that surround Martin Luther King Jr. Day, Presidents Day, Good Friday, Easter, Memorial Day, Independence Day, Thanksgiving and the week between Christmas and New Year's Day.

Crowds. Airline seats and hotels book early. Theme parks are packed.

Costs. Room rates will be at their most expensive (nightly rates can go up more than $100), as will meals at many restaurants. Disney often temporarily increases the prices at its buffet restaurants during these times (typically $4 for adults, $2 for children) and charges a premium for its dining plan.

Hours. Disney theme parks have extended hours, and are often open late into the night.

Festivities. Depending on the holiday, Disney schedules additional activities and entertainment, and decorates the entrances to its theme parks and hotel lobbies.

Restrictions. Seasonal annual passes often cannot be used during holiday periods.

On peak days, neither can the Tables in Wonderland restaurant discount card.

International travelers. Wireless "Ears to the World" headsets ($100 deposit) provide translation of Disney attraction audio into French, German, Japanese, Portuguese or Spanish. Other Disney services include multilingual theme-park guidemaps, restaurant menus and tours. Multilingual cast members have nametags with gold badges.

Internet access. Disney offers free Wi-Fi in all its theme parks, water parks and hotels, as well as at Disney Springs and the ESPN Wide World of Sports complex. It usually works.

Theme and water parks, Disney Springs. You can access Disney's free wireless network under the name "Public Space Guest WiFi (Disney)." Covered carriers include AT&T, MetroPCS, Sprint, T-Mobile and Verizon. Expect service to be spotty.

Hotels. Disney hotels offer complimentary in-room wireless Internet access. You can access the free network under the name "In-Room Guest WiFi (Disney)." For in-room wired high-speed access, each room comes with a Local Area Network (LAN) cable to attach to a laptop. Most common areas will also have free Wi-Fi, including arcades, bus stops, convention areas, the main pool, the lobby, bus stops and restaurants.

Many non-Disney resorts also offer in-room wired access; some do so free of charge.

Business centers. Internet-connected computers ($10 for 15 minutes or $40 an hour; $1 per page to print. 9 a.m.–4 p.m.) are available at Disney's Animal Kingdom Lodge as well as its Beach Club, Contemporary, Coronado Springs, Grand Floridian and Yacht Club hotel.

ESPN Wide World of Sports. This complex offers free Wi-Fi throughout its grounds, although it can be unreliable.

Outside Disney. Wireless Internet access is available free of charge in all public areas of the Orlando International Airport. Several kiosks offer wired Internet connections in addition to standard dial service provided via RJ-11 jacks in pay phones.

The Osceola County Public Library has free Internet access; the closest branch to Disney is the West Osceola branch in Celebration (1134 Celebration Boulevard, 34747, 407-742-8888, Mon–Sat 10 a.m.–7 p.m.). For a list of free-Wi-Fi businesses check wififreespot.com or openwifispots.com.

Lockers. You can rent a multi-use, key-operated locker to store belongings at each theme park, inside the entrance. You pay $7 a day plus a $5 deposit, for a locker 11 inches tall by 9 inches wide by 16 inches deep. For a larger locker (17.5 inches tall by 12 inches wide by 16 inches deep), you pay $9 a day. When visiting more than one park in one day, return your locker key to get your deposit back, then present your receipt (and another deposit) at any subsequent park to get a locker there at no additional charge.

You can rent single-use, coin-operated lockers at the bus information booths at Epcot, Disney's Hollywood Studios and Disney's Animal Kingdom. You pay $1; and must use quarters.

Lost and found. At Disney theme parks, water parks and Disney Springs, you can check on items lost that same day at Guest Relations. Disney hotels have internal lost and found offices; you should check with the concierge desk. ESPN Wide World of Sports holds lost items at its Welcome Center.

After one day items move to the Theme Park Lost and Found office (407-824-4245, 9 a.m.–7 p.m. daily, shipping at no charge), located at the former Magic Kingdom kennel next to the Transportation and Ticket Center. It keeps most items 30 days. Cameras, credit cards, prescription eyeglasses, purses and wallets are kept 90 days; hats, strollers and sunglasses just one week.

If you've lost your purse and it had, say, a wallet and iPhone inside, ask Lost and Found to check for all three items. Sometimes only one item is found—for example, your iPhone but not the purse it was in. (Magic Kingdom 407-824-4521, Epcot 407-560-6646, Disney's Hollywood Studios 407-560-3720, Disney's Animal Kingdom 407-938-2785, Blizzard Beach 407-560-5408, Typhoon Lagoon 407-560-6296, Disney Springs 407-828-3150, ESPN Wide World of Sports 407-541-5600.)

Magical Express. This bus transportation and luggage delivery service is complimentary if you are staying at a Walt Disney World resort. To be more specific, if you are bound for a Disney-owned hotel traveling via commercial airline to the Orlando International Airport you can skip the airport's baggage claim area and take a shuttle bus to your hotel, where your bags then "magically" appear. When it's time to return home, if you are traveling on a participating airline you can check your bags for your flight at your hotel. Then you simply board a bus back to the airport. If you are planning to spend your entire vacation at Disney World, Magical Express makes traveling to Walt Disney World cheaper, and eliminates the need to rent a car. The service carries over 2.2 million passengers a year.

Eligibility. You can use the service if you are staying at any Disney-owned resort. Guests of the Walt Disney World Swan and Dolphin, Shades of Green and Disney Springs hotels are not eligible.

Booking. You can reserve the service when booking your Disney hotel accommodations, or anytime at least 10 days before your trip at 866-599-0951.

Arrivals. Upon landing, go directly to the Magical Express Welcome Center (on Level 1 at the B side of the terminal) to check in and board your shuttle bus. Luggage is delivered to your hotel within three hours after resort check-in for flights arriving between 5 a.m. and 10 p.m. daily. For later arrivals you collect your luggage at baggage claim, bring it to the Welcome Center yourself and carry it into the resort with you. International guests always claim their own baggage.

Departures. As your vacation draws to a close, you'll receive a Magical Express Transportation Notice advising you of the time you are scheduled for a bus ride back to the airport. With some airlines—Airtran, Alaska Airlines, American Airlines, Delta Air Lines, JetBlue, Southwest, United and US Air—you can check your bags and get boarding passes at your hotel, eliminating those chores at the airport. You will need to stop by your hotel's Resort Airline Check-In Desk three hours prior to your flight time. You'll need to show a valid government-issued photo I.D. and your Disney MagicBand.

Maps. Though the maps in this book should suffice for many planning needs, larger and more detailed ones are available free from Disney in advance of your visit.

Customized maps. You can create free customized maps of all Disney World theme parks at customizedmaps.disney.go.com. Choices include a map of the entire property. The full-color maps can be printed, or Disney will mail 14-by-20-inch copies free of charge. Allow two to four weeks for delivery.

For Disney hotel guests. If you are making a reservation to stay at a Disney-owned hotel, you can request a map of the grounds.

It shows lodging areas with room numbers, restaurants, shops, pools, smoking areas, recreation locations and transportation. Also available: a set of Disney's theme-park guide maps that are distributed in the parks.

Medical services. If you need medical care at Disney World, it's close at hand; either right on Disney property or just a few minutes away. Every theme and water park has a first aid station manned by registered nurses who can handle minor medical incidents and contact the proper emergency personnel for more serious matters. Disney resort hotels can arrange in-room appointments and prescription deliveries. Doctors, dentists and a major hospital are all within 5 miles.

Automated External Defibrillators. Walt Disney World has installed 700 Automated External Defibrillators (AEDs) throughout its property. Designed to aid a person suffering from cardiac arrest, an AED is easy to use even without training. When the device is used, it automatically calls 911 and gives responders its location.

Dental services. The Celebration Dental Group provides standard and emergency care (Florida Hospital at Celebration Health, 400 Celebration Place, Celebration 34747; 407-566-2222).

Equipment rentals. Outside companies rent portable commodes, crutches, nebulizers, oxygen, scooters (electric conveyance vehicles), walkers and wheelchairs. Contact Apria Healthcare (407-291-2229 or 800-338-1640, after hours 407-297-0100, apria.com), Care Medical Equipment (407-856-2273 or 800-741-2282, caremedicalequipment.com), Turner Drugs (407-828-8125, turnerdrug.com) or Walker Mobility (407-518-6000 or 800-726-6837, walkermobility.com).

See also **Pharmacies**

Hospital. Florida Hospital at Celebration Health is just three miles from Walt Disney World, across Interstate 4 (400 Celebration Place, Celebration 34747; 407-303-4000, emergencies 407-303-4034).

In-room care. For a non-emergency appointment contact Centra Care (407-238-2000), Doctors on Call (407-399-3627) or EastCoast Medical (407-648-5252).

Paramedics. Available on Disney property through Disney's Reedy Creek Emergency Services (407-560-1990 via Disney Security).

Pharmacy. Turner Drugs (just across Interstate 4 from Disney at 1530 Celebration Boulevard, Celebration 34747; Monday–Friday 9 a.m.–7 p.m., Saturday–Sunday 9 a.m.–5 p.m.; 407-828-8125, fax 407-828-8027; turnerdrug. com) delivers prescription and over-the-counter medications to the concierge desks of all Disney resort hotels; drivers ask the desk to notify recipients immediately. Through an arrangement with Disney, Turner Drugs will charge an order to a guest's Disney room account (deliveries $5, Monday–Friday 8 a.m.–9 p.m., Saturday–Sunday 8 a.m.–7 p.m.).

Vision services. The closest optometrist to Disney is Celebration Eye Care, which is five miles away (741 Front Street, Celebration 34747; 407-566-2020; celebrationeyecare.com).

Walk-in clinics. No appointment is necessary for Family Medicine of Celebration, which focuses on children. It's staffed with pediatric physicians and has a separate waiting room for children and their families. The lobby in its building has a combination drug and convenience store. A small playground sits outside (1530 Celebration Boulevard, Celebration 34747. Monday, Tuesday, Friday 8 a.m.–5 p.m.; Wednesday 7 a.m.–7 p.m.; Thursday 8 a.m.–4 p.m.; 407-566-0404; familymedicinecelebration.com).

Florida Hospital's Centra Care Walk-In Urgent Care Clinic offers free transportation from Walt Disney World to its location near Disney Springs (12500 S. Apopka Vineland Road, Orlando 32836. 8 a.m.–midnight. Monday–Friday, 8 a.m.–8 p.m. Saturday–Sunday. 407-934-2273. Book appointments online at centracare.org).

Money. Nearly every restaurant, snack stand and shop at Disney accepts credit and debit cards as well as cash. You'll need cash for tips, highway tolls, pressed-coin machines, single-use lockers, some taxi and limo services and parking fees at Disney theme parks.

ATMs. Chase Bank automated teller machines are located in each Disney theme and water park, at Disney Springs, at the ESPN Wide World of Sports complex and at all Disney resort hotels. The machines accept cards from the Cirrus and Plus systems. Withdrawals using out-of-state cards, or cards from a bank other than Chase, incur surcharges of $1.50 to $2.50.

Magic Kingdom. ATMs are located by the lockers at the main entrance, City Hall, the Adventureland / Frontierland breezeway, near the Pinocchio Village Haus restrooms and at the Tomorrowland Arcade.

Epcot. Both entrances have ATMs, as well as at the American Adventure restrooms and the Future World bridge.

Disney's Hollywood Studios. ATMs are located outside the entranceway, outside the Keystone Clothiers shop and inside the Toy Story Pizza Planet Arcade.

Disney's Animal Kingdom. At the park entrance and outside the Dinosaur Treasures gift shop in DinoLand U.S.A.

Disney Springs. The Marketplace has ATMs near the Tren-D store, next to the Ghirardelli shop and inside the World of Disney. On the West Side, an ATM sits outside the House of Blues Company Store.

Banks. Many banks nearby Walt Disney World offer full services.

Bank of America. In the community of Celebration, 5 miles from Disney World (700 Celebration Ave., Celebration 34747; Monday–Thursday 9 a.m.–5 p.m., Friday 9 a.m.–6 p.m., Saturday 9 a.m.–1 p.m.; 321-939-7677).

SunTrust. Across from Disney Springs (1675 E Buena Vista Dr, Lake Buena Vista 32830; Monday–Thursday 8 a.m.–5 p.m., Friday 8 a.m.–6 p.m.; 407-828-6103). Two SunTrust banks are in Celebration, across Interstate 4 from Disney World: downtown (650 Celebration Ave, Celebration 34747; Monday–Thursday 9 a.m.–4 p.m., Friday 9 a.m.–6 p.m.; 407-566-2265) and in the Water Tower Shoppes along U.S. 192 (74 Blake Blvd, Celebration 34747; Monday–Thursday 9 a.m.–4 p.m., Friday 9 a.m.–6 p.m.; 321-939-3970).

Wells Fargo. Near International Drive, 6 miles from Disney (7740 W Sand Lake Rd, Orlando 32819; Monday–Friday 8 a.m.–6 p.m., Saturday 9 a.m.–2 p.m.; 407-649-5800).

Credit and debit cards. Disney accepts American Express, Diners Club, Discover, Japan Credit Bureau (JCB), MasterCard and Visa cards, even at snack stands.

Currency exchange. Foreign currency can be exchanged for U.S. dollars at the Orlando International Airport, main bank branches, theme park Guest Relations locations and Disney resort hotel concierge desks.

Disney Dollars. This whimsical scrip is accepted at all Disney World theme parks and Disney-owned resorts and gift shops. Popular as on-property currency as well as souvenirs, the dollars are sold at Guest Relations locations, Disney hotel concierge desks and the World of Disney store at Disney Springs. Denominations are $1, $5 and $10; the exchange rate is always $1 for $1. Disney issues new designs nearly every year.

Gift cards. Disney gift cards can be used for purchases throughout Walt Disney World. The cards have no fees and don't expire, and can be ordered online in $25 increments up to $150 plus denominations of $200, $250, $300 and $500. Choose from hundreds of designs, or personalize a card using a photograph. Disney Dollars purchases are not eligible (disneygiftcard.com).

Gratuities. Tips often will be refused by Disney concierge staff and other cast members; guests can express appreciation for cast-member service by emailing wdw.guest. communications@disney.com; comments can boost a career. Gratuities are accepted by Magical Express bus drivers, housekeeping staff, restaurant servers, valets, and the non-Disney concierge staff at the Walt Disney World Swan and Dolphin Resort and Disney Springs hotels. An 18 percent tip is automatically added to the bill on room-service orders at Disney hotels, with use of a Tables in Wonderland discount card, for restaurant parties of six or more and at prepaid eateries and dinner shows. Gratuities are not automatically included in the Disney Dining Plan, so please tip accordingly.

Rental cars. Renting a car requires a major credit card or debit card with major-credit-card backing. Using a debit card will require a deposit (usually $200–$300) that will be credited back to the user's account a week or so after the car is returned.

Traveler's checks. Nearly any Disney expense can be paid for with a traveler's check. SunTrust Bank is the closest full-service bank that sells, replaces and redeems traveler's checks. For refunds on lost or stolen checks call American Express (800-992-3404). Instead of traveler's checks, Thomas Cook now sells Prepaid Currency Cards (800-287-7362).

Wire transfers. The Disney Springs SunTrust Bank (see above) handles wire transfers. Winn-Dixie (7840 W. Irlo Bronson Hwy; 8 a.m.–10 p.m. daily; 407-397-2210) offers Western Union (800-325-6000) transfers.

Obese visitors. Guests of nearly all shapes and sizes can experience just about all Walt Disney World has to offer with no problem, as long as they heed Disney's medical advisories and use common sense.

Bench seats. On some attractions an obese person should take a bench seat alone to fit comfortably. To make this easy, when a cast member at the loading area asks how many

Parking tram. Shuttles transport theme-park visitors to and from parking lots. Distinctive driver shades and large rear-view mirrors have earned the vehicles the nickname "Flying nuns."

are in your party, say "1" and then the number of the rest of your party, such as "and 3."

Getting around. Probably the biggest challenge for an overweight guest is handling all the walking at Disney. The typical theme-park guest easily ends up walking miles a day, which can be tough for anyone who isn't fit. Therefore have a good plan, pace yourself and take breaks. Disney rents Electric Conveyance Vehicles (ECVs) and extra-wide wheelchairs at its theme parks and at Disney Springs. EVCs often sell out early on crowded days.

Lap-bar rides. Many rides have lap-bar restraints a guest controls by pulling down until the lap bar fits snugly. When two people share a restraint, an obese person should not share a seat with a small or skinny person. The lap bar will stop and lock based on the large tummy, leaving the smaller person relatively unrestrained.

Recreation. *Epcot's DiveQuest:* Disney supplies wetsuits for guests scuba diving at the Seas pavilion up to size 5X. *Horseback riding:* The weight limit at Fort Wilderness is 250 pounds. *Parasailing:* Guests taking flight at Disney's Contemporary Resort should weigh no more than 330 pounds.

Restaurants. Many Disney eateries use chairs with armrests, which can prove problematic for obese guests. Hostesses can usually supply chairs without arms.

Seatbelt rides. Pull the seat belt out all the way before sitting down. Hold it out while you sit, then fasten the buckle. Ask a family member to help attach the buckle if needed. Disney cast members aren't allowed to help anyone who struggles to buckle belts.

Shopping. Many shops sell large-sized Disney T-shirts, up to 3X. The three stores with the most variety are the Emporium at Magic Kingdom, MouseGear at Epcot and World of Disney at Disney Springs. These stores commonly stock T-shirts, sweatshirts and jackets in sizes up to 4X and sometimes 5X. For details contact Disney Merchandise at 800-328-0368.

Spas. The Grand Floridian and Saratoga Springs spas supply robes in sizes up to 5X.

Theater seats. For attractions with armrests, obese guests may find it easier to sit on the front edge of a seat and then slide back, or sit sideways and then turn to squeeze in. Some theaters have narrow seats; the narrowest are those at Epcot's France pavilion.

Water parks. The weight limit to ride the Blizzard Beach chair lift is 375 pounds.

The independent website allearsnet.com has a terrific section for obese guests. Search "WDW at Large" and "At Large" trip reports.

Parking. Disney charges a fee for most visitors to park at its theme parks. Daily rates are $17 for cars, motorcycles or taxis; $18 for campers; $21 for buses and tractor-trailers. The fee allows self-parking at all four park lots for that day. Disney resort hotel guests and annual passholders don't pay to park. If you are a Tables in Wonderland cardholder you can park free, too; you receive a parking refund at a Guest Relations location with a table-service dining receipt.

Except for Magic Kingdom, all theme-park parking is just outside the main entrance to its park. The large Magic Kingdom lot is located a mile away at the Transportation and Ticket Center; after parking guests take either a monorail or a ferry to the park.

Parking is free at Disney water parks and Disney Springs. Most parking is complimentary at the ESPN Wide World of Sports complex, though premium spots may cost $5.

Hotel parking. Every Disney-owned hotel provides complimentary parking to guests staying at it or coming to shop or dine. Shades of Green charges $5 for parking, the Walt Disney World Swan and Dolphin Resort charges $16 for overnight self-parking, $26 for overnight valet parking, $10 per exit for day self-parking, $15 per exit for day valet parking. Valet parking is available at all Disney Deluxe Resorts and Disney Springs for $20 daily not including gratuity; your hangtag gives you free valet parking at any other Disney hotel that same day. Valet parking is complimentary for Tables in Wonderland cardholders with dining reservations and guests with a current handicap license plate or tag.

Pets. Bringing Spot or Fluffy with you to Disney? You have a few options for pet care.

At Disney resorts. Campers at Disney's Fort Wilderness Resort & Campground may keep their pet with them for $5 per day at select locations. Other Disney resort hotels permit service animals, but not pets.

Best Friends Pet Care Kennel. Located on Disney property across from the Port Orleans Resorts, this 50,000-square-foot facility is well maintained and lets dog owners spend time with their pet unleashed in a grassy backyard that has a water-play area. Billing itself as a "luxury pet resort," Best Friends refers to many of its 200-plus spaces as "suites" and "condos" since they are divided into multiple spaces, even though many are no larger than a cage. Some spots include controlled access to small outdoor areas. Dog facilities also include 14 "vacation villas" (6-feet by 7-foot rooms with raised bedding and flat-screen televisions) and four larger rooms marketed as "VIP suites." All dogs and cats must be at least 4 months old.

Birds are housed in an area with hamsters, guinea pigs, rabbits, ferrets and other pocket pets (owners supply cages, supplies and food). No primates or venomous pets are allowed.

Optional services include daytime boarding; activities such as nature walks, grooming and playgroups; and pampering such as ice-cream treats and bedtime stories. (Dogs: overnight $41–$89, daycare $34–$89; optional services $5–$22. Cats: overnight $28–$40, daycare $26–$35; optional services $3–$8. Small animals: overnight $11–$25. Across from Disney's Port Orleans Resort at 2510 Bonnet Creek Parkway, Lake Buena Vista 32830; 407-209-3126; wdw.bestfriendspetcare.com).

Bass Pet Resort. Check out this quality kennel for a less-expensive alternative to Best Friends. It's where the authors board their dog. (Dogs: overnight $23 and up, daycare $14 and up. Cats: overnight $13 and up. A short drive from Disney property off Highway 192 at 1043 S Bass Rd, Kissimmee 34746; 407-396-6031; www.basspetmotel.com).

Laws. It's illegal to leave a pet in a car in Florida with the windows up; the heat makes it dangerous for the animal, as temperatures can rise to unbearable degrees quickly.

Photography. Whether it's one in your phone or a fancy DSLR, a camera can capture spontaneous moments that create treasured memories. Consider giving your children their own cameras and perhaps bringing waterproof models for swimming pools and water parks. Whatever shots you snap, take turns being the photographer; if mom takes all the pictures none will include mom.

Nikon picture spots. These locations offer photogenic, iconic backdrops for your shot, such as Magic Kingdom's Cinderella Castle or Epcot's Spaceship Earth.

Selfie sticks. As of 2015 selfie sticks are no longer allowed in any Walt Disney World theme or water park.

Photographic services. Disney offers various photo services in its parks, hotels, restaurants and at Disney Springs:

Makeover salons. Some packages at the Bibbidi Bobbidi Boutique salons and Pirates League include photos (407-939-7895).

See also **Children's Services.**

Rewarding lines. Most of Disney's most popular rides have indoor waiting lines which are heavily decorated, such as this one for Toy Story Mania. Some have interactive elements.

PhotoPass. With this service Disney photographers take shots of your group throughout Disney World, but you pay for only those images you choose, if any. Photographers are stationed many places, including most theme-park icons and character spots, ready to link images of your group to a free credit-card-size PhotoPass card or to your MagicBand. You can view and purchase each shot at park Camera Centers or online, up to 45 days from when it was taken.

PhotoPass is not a replacement for taking your own photos, as photographers shoot only posed shots at specific locations. Besides, any Disney cast member will always take a photo of your group with your own camera free of charge (a courtesy that Disney does not publicize). If you do use the PhotoPass service, write down your card's 16-digit ID number and save it—if you lose your card you won't lose track of your images (single downloads $15, Memory Maker unlimited photo package $149 if arranged in advance, Archive Disc $169; 407-560-4300; disneyphotopass.com).

Disney Fine Art Photography & Video. Disney offers professional-quality packaged portrait sessions. Guests choose locations, themes and wardrobe, then pose at picturesque settings. Sessions last 20 minutes to an hour, and include a disc with 60 to 100 images. (Sessions: $150–$350; print packages: $75–$285; book up to 30 days in advance; 407-934-4004; disneyeventphotography.com/portraits).

Restaurant souvenir photos. Diners at the following locations can buy photos Disney will insist be taken before entering the dining area or tableside: Chef Mickey's (Contemporary Resort), Cinderella's Royal Table (Cinderella Castle, Magic Kingdom, photo charges included in meal price), Hoop-Dee-Doo Revue Dinner Show and Mickey's Backyard Barbecue (Fort Wilderness Resort & Campground), 'Ohana (Polynesian Village Resort), Planet Hollywood (Disney Springs), Princess Storybook Dining (Akershus, Norway pavilion, Epcot, photo charges included in meal price), Spirit of Aloha Dinner Show (Polynesian Village Resort).

Thrill-ride souvenirs. On some rides an automated camera takes a photo of you on the attraction then an exitway gift shop offers it to you either as a print or digital download. Prints are approximately $20; digital images are included on the Memory Maker package and the Disney PhotoPass Archive Disc (see above). Magic Kingdom: Buzz Lightyear's Space Ranger Spin, Space Mountain, Splash Mountain. Epcot: Test Track. Disney's Hollywood Studios: Rock 'n' Roller Coaster

Starring Aerosmith, The Twilight Zone Tower of Terror. Disney's Animal Kingdom: Dinosaur, Expedition Everest.

Pin trading. In 1999 Disney World began the tradition of collectible-pin trading. Many visitors exchange pins with each other, but most trading is between guests and cast members who wear pin-filled lanyards; those with green lanyards only trade with kids. Each park sells pins, which range from $8 to $35.

Postal services. Access to the U.S. Postal Service is available throughout Walt Disney World and the surrounding area.

Sending mail. *Magic Kingdom:* Guests can drop stamped mail in old-fashioned letter boxes at the park entrance next to the Newsstand gift shop and on Main Street U.S.A. (postmarks read "Lake Buena Vista" not "Walt Disney World"). *Epcot:* Camera Center, Spaceship Earth, Future World; also in an old mailbox in front of the American Adventure pavilion in the World Showcase. *Disney's Hollywood Studios:* Oscar's Super Service, entrance plaza. *Disney's Animal Kingdom:* Garden Gate Gifts, entrance plaza. *Nearby U.S. Post Offices:* Celebration: 610 Market Street, downtown, 407-566-1145, 9 a.m.–4 p.m., Saturday 8:30 a.m.–2 p.m. Full-service facility. Find other post offices at 800-275-8777, usps.com.

Stamps. *Magic Kingdom:* Newsstand, entrance plaza. *Epcot:* Camera Center, under Spaceship Earth. *Disney's Hollywood Studios:* Oscar's Super Service, entrance plaza. *Disney's Animal Kingdom:* Garden Gate Gifts, entrance plaza. *Disney hotels:* Main gift shops. *Disney Springs:* Guest Services, Marketplace. *Outside Disney:* U.S. Post Offices (see above).

Receiving mail. *Disney resort hotels:* You can receive letters, packages and postcards if you are staying at any Disney resort. Mail should include your arrival date if the item will be received before you check-in. *Non-Disney hotels:* Nearly all convention hotels in the area accept mail for guests, as do some other properties. Contact the particular hotel. *General Delivery:* You can receive mail care of General Delivery at most major post offices. You must first complete an application in person and show two forms of ID and a temporary local address. The application is valid for 30 days. Mail is held for up to 15 days.

See also **Shipping.**

Pregnant visitors. If you are an expectant mom, Walt Disney World can be a fun and safe place. Although roller coasters are off limits, there are numerous character greetings, fireworks, parades, shows, swimming pools and gentle rides that are easy for moms-to-be to enjoy. Of course, you should check with your doctor first, heed Disney's advisories and use common sense.

Attractions to avoid. You should consider avoiding rides that have sudden stops or drops, rough motion, spinning or require significant exertion. At Magic Kingdom, avoid Astro Orbiter, The Barnstormer, Big Thunder Mountain Railroad, Mad Tea Party, Seven Dwarfs Mine Train, Space Mountain, Splash Mountain, Swiss Family Treehouse (lots of steps) and Tomorrowland Speedway. At Epcot, skip Mission Space, Sum of all Thrills (an Innoventions exhibit) and Test Track. At Disney's Hollywood Studios stay away from Rock 'n' Roller Coaster, Star Tours and Twilight Zone Tower of Terror. At Disney's Animal Kingdom, avoid Dinosaur, Expedition Everest, Kali River Rapids, Primeval Whirl and Kilimanjaro Safaris (the bumpy ride is smoothest for those who sit in the front row). At Disney's water parks, don't ride any slides, and stay out of Typhoon Lagoon's wave pool when the big waves are in effect.

Water. It's important for everyone to stay hydrated while outdoors in Florida, but even more vital for expectant moms. You can bring water into Disney World theme parks (though not in glass containers or rolling coolers) and get free ice water (on request) from any counter-service restaurant. Water fountains dot each park.

Snacks. To ward off morning sickness, carry some light snacks, such as granola bars, crackers or fruit. It's fine to bring in food to a theme park as long as there are no glass containers. Each park has a variety of snack stands, some of which sell fresh fruit.

Baby Care Centers. All theme parks have Baby Care Centers which serve pregnant guests. Quiet air-conditioned spots offer a relaxing way to get off your swollen feet.

See also **Children's Services.**

Disney resort hotels. Staying at a hotel on Disney property—especially one on the monorail loop—will make it more convenient for you to return to your room for an afternoon rest. Housekeeping can provide extra pillows for additional support. Many Disney resorts have great swimming pools, a fact which can be especially important if you are pregnant; the buoyancy of the water can help take strain off your aching back.

Shopping. A few park stores carry unique (and usually high quality) infant apparel and other merchandise. Magic Kingdom: The Emporium, Hundred Acre Goods. Epcot: MouseGear, Showcase Station East Port. World Showcase has some hard-to-find goodies such as Steiff teddy bears (Germany pavilion) and puffin plushies (Norway pavilion). Disney's Hollywood Studios: L.A. Cinema Storage, Stage 1 Co. Store. Disney's Animal Kingdom: Island Mercantile.

Queues. One of the down sides to Disney is that you commonly have to wait in long lines for attractions, as the number of people who can fit into Disney's rides and shows at any one time is far less than the number it allows in its parks. For example, the attraction capac at Magic Kingdom is about 9,750, though on average that park contains about 30,000 guests and will let in at least twice that many.

Wait times. A sign at each attraction displays its current wait time. At many rides, an easy way to avoid that wait is to use Disney's free Fastpass+ reservation system.

See also **Children's Services** and **My Magic+ and Fastpass+** at the front of this book.

Single Rider lines. Three attractions have a third entrance. If you don't mind experiencing a ride by yourself, a Single Rider line is an easy way to lessen the time you have to wait. During peak periods, using one can cut your wait time by at least 30 minutes. You'll find Single Rider lines at Test Track in Epcot, Rock 'n' Roller Coaster Starring Aerosmith at Disney's Hollywood Studios and Expedition Everest at Disney's Animal Kingdom. There's also one at the Blizzard Beach chair lift.

How they work. When ride operators can't fill a vehicle from the regular line without breaking up a group, they take a guest from a Single Rider line. Groups can wait in that line together but will be split up. Riders cannot specify where they sit.

Quinceañera celebrations. Disney offers Latina teens ways to mark their 15th birthdays. Prices vary (321-939-4555).

Refurbishments and rehabs. For operational updates call 407-824-4321 or check online at disneyworld.com.

Restaurant policies. Disney-operated eateries share many policies and procedures.

Children's meals. Available throughout Disney theme parks and hotels, Disney Kids' Picks meals come with unsweetened applesauce, baby carrots or fresh fruit (your choice of two) and a beverage of low-fat milk, juice or water (french fries, a cookie and soft drinks can be substituted). Less than 35 percent of a Kids' Picks meal's calories come from fat.

Discounts. The Tables in Wonderland discount card ($100–$125 annually, available to annual passholders and Florida residents only, 407-566-5858, weekdays 9 a.m. to 5 p.m.) saves its holder and up to nine guests 20 percent off food and beverage during non-holiday periods at most Disney table-service restaurants, Value Resort food courts and some other spots. An 18 percent gratuity is added.

Annual passholders. Those with yearly park tickets typically save 10–20 percent off lunch or dinner at these locations: *Magic Kingdom:* Tomorrowland Terrace. *Epcot:* Biergarten, Nine Dragons, Restaurant Marrakesh, San Angel Inn, Teppan Edo, Tokyo Dining, Tutto Italia. *Disney's Hollywood Studios:* Disney's Hollywood & Vine. *Disney's Animal Kingdom:* Rainforest Café, Yak & Yeti. *Disney Springs:* Ghirardelli Soda Fountain, House of Blues, Paradiso 37, Planet Hollywood, Portobello Trattoria, Rainforest Café, T-REX Café, Wolfgang Puck Café (as well as some new places). *Disney resorts:* Sanaa (Animal Kingdom Lodge), ESPN Club (BoardWalk), The Wave (Contemporary), Trail's End (Fort Wilderness), Grand Floridian Café (Grand Floridian), Olivia's Café (Old Key West), the Turf Club (Saratoga Springs), Whispering Canyon Café (Wilderness Lodge) and Captain's Grille (Yacht & Beach Club).

Website. The Disney World site (disneyworld.com) often offers dining deals under a "Special Offers" link on its home page.

Dress codes. Most Disney restaurants have a dress code equal to that of the theme parks. With the exceptions of Cinderella's Royal Table, the Hollywood Brown Derby and Le Cellier, Disney Signature Restaurants have a business casual dress code—for men jeans, dress shorts, dress slacks or trousers and a shirt with a collar or T-shirt underneath; for women jeans, dress shorts or a skirt with a blouse or sweater, or a dress; not permitted are cut-offs, men's caps or hats, swimsuits, swimsuit cover-ups, tank tops or torn clothing. Victoria & Albert's requires jackets for men; dresses or dressy pants suits for women.

Gastric-bypass surgery guests. These guests can present a weight-loss-surgery card (issued by their doctor or hospital) to a server to pay the child price for an adult meal at buffets, or to possibly order from a kids menu at non-buffet meals.

Gratuities. Disney adds an automatic 18 percent gratuity to dining bills for parties of 8 or more. In general, tip 15–20 percent for good service; 10 percent for mediocre.

Reservations. Having a dining reservation is often a must at Disney, even for restaurants in your hotel. The best eateries often book to capacity far in advance, especially for popular dining times. During peak periods many don't accept walk-up diners regardless of how long a guest is willing to wait.

Reservations can be made 180 days in advance (190 days for Disney resort guests) at 407-939-3463, at disneyworld.com and at most restaurant check-in counters and resort concierge desks. Dinner shows and dining at Cinderella's Royal Table require payment up front; refunds are possible if bookings are cancelled 24 hours in advance. All Disney restaurants require a credit card to hold a reservation; you may be charged a $10-per-person fee if you fail to show up or cancel a reservation at least 24 hours in advance.

Plan to arrive at least 5 minutes before your reservation time. Your party will be seated at the next available table that can accommodate it. Most Disney restaurants will hold your reservation for 15 minutes.

Cinderella's Royal Table inside Magic Kingdom's Cinderella Castle is the toughest reservation to nab. It often books in full on the first day of availability. Other hot spots: Be Our Guest (Magic Kingdom), California Grill and Chef Mickey's (Contemporary Resort), Le Cellier (Epcot) and Victoria & Albert's (Grand Floridian Resort). The most popular reservation time is 7 to 8 p.m. To eat during that hour book your table at least a week early, especially for a party of six or more.

Special diets. No-sugar, low-fat, low-sodium, vegetarian or vegan diets can be met at table-service restaurants by telling a reservation clerk, host or server. Dinner shows need 24 hours notice. With three days notice, Disney restaurants can meet needs such as allergies to gluten or wheat, shellfish, soy, lactose or milk, peanuts, tree nuts, fish or eggs. Many counter-service restaurants offer gluten-free, low-fat and vegetarian options. No Disney restaurant serves food with added trans fats or partially hydrogenated oils.

Glatt kosher meals are available at most full-service restaurants with 24 hours notice at 407-939-3463. Requests require a credit-card guarantee and have a 24-hour cancellation policy. Kosher fast-food is always available—without notice—at Cosmic Ray's Starlight Café (Magic Kingdom), Liberty Inn (Epcot), ABC Commissary (Hollywood Studios), Pizzafari (Animal Kingdom) and the food courts at the All-Star, Caribbean Beach, Pop Century and Port Orleans Riverside resorts. Disney's kosher food is prepared in Miami.

Shipping. You can ship items either from Disney or from nearby shipping centers.

At Disney hotels. Ask the front desk or concierge for instructions. Some resorts have a business center or desk with shipping supplies. Expect to pay a handling fee.

Shipping luggage to a hotel can often be cheaper than checking it as airline baggage. Send packages in enough time so they arrive a couple of days early; use FedEx or UPS for the most reliable service. To be sure the hotel will hold your package until your arrival, address the shipping label as follows:

Guest's name (same as on reservation)
c/o Name of hotel
Hold for guest arrival on (date)
Reservation (number)
Hotel street address
City, FL Zip Code

At theme parks. Package Pickup can deliver purchases made in that park to any Disney-owned hotel or, via UPS or FedEx, any domestic or international address.

At Disney Springs. Stores can deliver purchases to Disney resorts or ship them elsewhere via UPS or FedEx.

Key FedEx and UPS locations. FedEx and UPS offices dot the area between Disney and the Orlando airport. Here are three:

Closest FedEx to Disney. Near Disney Springs, open 24 hours (12181 South Apopka Vineland 32836; 407-465-0085).

FedEx with the latest hours. At the Orlando International Airport, open to 8:30 p.m. Monday–Friday (10445 Tradeport Drive 32827; 855-596-6421).

Closest UPS Store to Disney. Behind the Orlando Premium Outlet Mall, 8 a.m.–7 p.m. Monday–Friday, 9 a.m.–5 p.m. Saturday, noon–5 p.m. Sunday (8131 Vineland Avenue 32821; 407-465-1700).

See also **Postal Services.**

Shopping. Walt Disney World has hundreds of stores, selling everything from hand-rolled cigars to the largest selection of Mickey

Wishful thinking. Known as the "World's Largest Orange," giant half-orange Eli's Orange World sells and ships Florida citrus. It's just a few miles south of Disney on U.S. 192.

Mouse merchandise in the world. Non-Disney apparel is sold at Magic Kingdom's Sunglass Hut, Disney Springs, Disney Deluxe resorts, Epcot's World Showcase and water parks. Ralph Lauren men's dress shirts are at the Commander's Porter shop at Disney's Grand Floridian Resort (9 a.m.–10 p.m.). To order Disney merchandise call 800-328-0368, online visit disneystore.com.

Disney return policy. Disney-owned stores will accept returns on merchandise within 90 days of purchase with a valid receipt. Items that cannot be returned include those marked "as is" or "all sales final," original artwork, fine jewelry and special orders. If you return an item without a receipt you'll receive credit based on the item's selling price at the time of the return. Some stores on Disney property—including many in Epcot's World Showcase and at Disney Springs—are not run by Disney; return policies at these shops vary. In most cases, Disney Stores across the U.S. accept returns of items bought at Disney-owned Disney World stores with a valid receipt.

Nearby retailers. *Apple Store:* Mall at Millenia, 4200 Conroy Road 32839; 16 miles from Disney, 407-241-5400. *Barnes & Noble:* 7900 West Sand Lake Road 32819, 7 miles from Disney. 407-345-0900. *Best Buy:* 4155 Millenia

Boulevard 32839; 16 miles from Disney. 407-248-2439. *Eli's Orange World:* 5395 W. Irlo Bronson Memorial Highway (U.S. 192) 34746; 3 miles from Disney. 800-531-3182. *Orlando Premium Outlet Mall:* 8200 Vineland Avenue 32821 at I-4 exit 68; 5 miles from Disney. 407-238-7787. *Target:* 4750 Millenia Plaza Way 32839; 16 miles from Disney. 407-541-0019.

Smoking. Florida law requires that all restaurants in the state be smoke-free. Smoking is allowed in freestanding bars that earn less than 10 percent of their income from food.

Disney theme parks have designated smoking areas. All Disney hotel rooms, balconies and patios are smoke-free (a $250–$500 "room recovery fee" is charged to guests who smoke); smoking is permitted at Fort Wilderness campsites and on cabin porches. All shops are non-smoking except Disney Springs's cigar shop. No tobacco products are sold in the parks, but are available (but not displayed) at hotel gift shops and Disney Springs. Hess stations sell them openly.

Spas. Disney has three full-service spas. All offer aromatherapy, exercise facilities, facials, manicures and pedicures, massages and child services. Robes and slippers are provided for body treatments.

Star Wars Weekends. A storm trooper escorts a girl and her brother down one of the Streets of America during a Star Wars weekend at Disney's Hollywood Studios.

Mandara Spa. At the Walt Disney World Dolphin, this Asian-inspired spa has two indoor gardens. Services include cellulite treatments and stone therapies (407-934-4772).

Senses Spa. This Grand Floridian spa offers a massage followed by a cocoon-like body wrap, a lavender facial and a pedicure with a hot-stone massage that uses honey lavender botanical oils. A second Senses at Saratoga Springs offers bamboo fusion massages, blueberry facials and a pedicure with a blueberry sugar scrub, hydrating masque and warm paraffin treatment (407-939-7727).

Special events. Disney holds unique parties, weekends and festivals year-round.

Epcot International Flower & Garden Festival. Disney's most elaborate one-park event, this 75-day garden party includes seminars, demonstrations and celebrity guest speakers, as well as character topiaries, a butterfly house with a live caterpillar and chrysalis exhibit and 30 million flowers. Themed weekends celebrate art, insects and Mother's Day. Concerts feature 1960s and 1970s acts. Vendor booths line walkways. *The first week in March through mid-May. Included in park admission. 407-934-7639.*

St. Patrick's Day. Special events mark this Irish holiday at two Disney locations: the Raglan Road restaurant at Disney Springs and the United Kingdom pavilion at Epcot's World Showcase. *Epcot events included in park admission.*

Easter Weekend. Outfitted in colorful homemade gowns straight out of the Old South, teenage Azalea Trail Maids from Mobile, Ala., greet guests along Magic Kingdom's Main Street U.S.A. and lead its Easter Day parade. At Epcot, children hunt for Easter eggs. Some Disney hotels offer egg decorating, egg hunts and characters in Easter costumes. *Park events included in park admission.*

Star Wars Weekends. This Hollywood Studios fan-fest includes celebrity motorcades, Q&A and autograph sessions (Mark Hamill appeared in 2014), roving characters and unique merchandise. Some guests wear costumes. Get there when the park opens to take advantage of all the activities and be greeted at the entrance by wisecracking stormtroopers. With the new series of Star Wars movies now being released, expect larger crowds than ever before. Mid-May through the first week of June. Included in park admission. Details at 407-827-2799.

Gay Days. Tens of thousands of gay adults congregate at Disney during the first week in June; many wear red shirts in solidarity.

Morbid makeup. Cast members at the Haunted Mansion display ghostly makeup—complete with cobwebs—at Mickey's Not-So-Scary Halloween parties.

Groups gather at each park on a particular day. Disney does not sponsor the event but subtly condones it; recently its bakery cases have offered rainbow-colored cupcakes. *First week in June. gaydays.com, 407-896-8431.*

Sounds Like Summer Concert Series. Cover bands perform tunes from Elton John, The Supremes, others. Three shows nightly at Epcot's America Gardens amphitheater. June–August. Included in park admission.

Independence Day Weekend. A spectacular Magic Kingdom fireworks show surrounds guests watching from Main Street U.S.A. Disney's Hollywood Studios has fireworks too. Historic characters share their stories at Epcot's American Adventure pavilion. Included in park admission.

Night of Joy. Live concerts by contemporary Christian artists highlight this Magic Kingdom event. Most rides are open. *Early Sept. $59 1 night; $108 2 nights. nightofjoy.com.*

Epcot International Food & Wine Festival. This two-month festival celebrates international food and drink. More than two dozen World Showcase booths sell small portions of ethnic and regional dishes. Each booth typically offers three food items and an alcoholic beverage. Events include cooking demonstrations, pricey dinners and wine seminars. Free Eat to the Beat concerts feature vintage pop acts such as Rick Springfield and Wilson Phillips. Included in park admission. *Mid-Sep–mid-Nov. Details at disneyworld.com/foodandwine or 407-939-3378.*

Mickey's Not-So-Scary Halloween Party. Disney World's most festive events, these parties are perfect for children, teens, young adults… people of any age who can appreciate clean campy fun. Focused on themes such as "The Nightmare Before Christmas" and The Haunted Mansion, the Magic Kingdom bash includes a unique parade, a special fireworks show, a new stage show, two dance parties and many character meet-and-greets. Dressed as candy makers, cast members hand out candy throughout the park.

Attendance is limited to 25,000 people—a third of Magic Kingdom's capacity. Though mos rides are open, few of them have long lines, and nothing is very crowded except the first parade and some of the character-greeting spots, as many characters are wearing Halloween costumes themselves or aren't seen at other times of the year.

Dates. The parties are held several nights a week throughout September and October. Each one runs from 7 p.m. until midnight.

Tickets. Adults $62–$77, children ages 3–9 $57–$72 (parties closest to Halloween cost more), children under age 3 admitted free of

Cosplay fun. Friends dressed as Giselle (from Disney's 2007 movie "Enchanted") and Raggedy Ann pose with the park's Anastasia (a stepsister of Cinderella) at a Halloween party.

charge. Nontransferable, nonrefundable. $6 advance-purchase discount often available, small discounts for annual passholders and Disney Vacation Club timeshare owners. Not included in any other Disney ticket. Available at 407-939-5277, disneyworld.com, Walt Disney World Guest Relations, Guest Services and Ticketing locations.

Tips. If you go to one of the parties there are four key things you should know:

Buy your tickets early. Especially for a weekend night in October. Those sell out.

Wear a costume. Many people do, adults as well as children. Young adults and families often go all out. Many outfits are homemade and elaborate; some are bizarre. Once the author spotted a group of younger men dressed as masculine versions of Disney princesses, then a group of older men who had transformed themselves into dolls from It's a Small World.

Get there early. At 4 p.m, as early as your ticket will let you in. You'll have three extra hours to explore Magic Kingdom at no extra charge. Some partygoers come early just to get in line to meet popular characters such as Jack and Sally or the Seven Dwarfs, each of whose lines start to form about 5:30 p.m. Once the party begins, the wait to meet these stars can be two or three hours.

Stay late if you can. Until midnight. The party really picks up after the fireworks show, as much of the crowd leaves. Lines for rides dwindle down to nothing, and good viewing spots for the second parade are easy to find even right before it starts. During the last hour of the party, cast members handing out candy get more generous and the character dance parties get more fun, as teens and young adults show up as well as families.

Christmas. Even the most diehard Scrooge will warm up to Disney in November and December. Most theme parks offers special entertainment, and elaborate holiday decor seems to be everywhere.

Magic Kingdom. Hands down this park has the most Christmas spirit; its Main Street U.S.A. decorations are so iconically American you'll swear they're straight from your childhood. Santa Claus appears just inside the entrance. At night, Cinderella Castle appears covered in glowing icicles.

Epcot. Forget Future World, the holiday mood here is all at World Showcase. Each pavilion has at least one holiday story-teller; most are excellent. The American Adventure pavilion also hosts the Candlelight Processional, a first-rate (and extremely popular) retelling of the birth of Jesus.

Very Merry marching men. Toy soldiers from 1961's "Babes in Toyland" march in the Magic Kingdom Christmas parade.

Disney's Hollywood Studios. The front of the park brings back the look of an Old Hollywood Christmas, with tinsel-heavy decorations and witty Citizens of Hollywood sketches. The back holds Disney World's best Christmas attraction, the Osborne Family Spectacle of Dancing Lights.

Disney's Animal Kingdom. There's not much spirit here, though some characters wear seasonal outfits.

Mickey's Very Merry Christmas Party. On many evenings Magic Kingdom hosts this festive extra-charge event, which is worth its additional fee. There's a lot to see and do, including exclusive shows and parades, a Christmas-themed fireworks display, two character dance parties and over two dozen character meet-and-greets. Many regular park attractions are also open, and Disney hands out complimentary hot chocolate and cookies throughout the park. Attendance is limited to 25,000 people.

Dates. Early November until the week before Christmas. Each party runs from 7 p.m. until midnight.

Tickets. Adults $67–$71, children ages 3–9 $62–$66 (parties closest to Christmas cost more) for tickets bought in advance, children under age 3 admitted free (prices for 2014). Same-day tickets up to $9 more.

Nontransferable, nonrefundable. Small discounts for annual passholders and Disney Vacation Club members. Not included in any other Disney ticket. Available at 407-939-5277; disneyworld.com; Guest Relations, Guest Services and Ticketing locations.

Tips. *When to buy your tickets:* Early. Many parties sell out, sometimes even the first one. *When to arrive:* At 4 p.m. Your party ticket is good at that time, so you'll have three hours to explore the park before the party starts. *How long to stay:* Until midnight. During the last two hours of the party, the lines for its attractions, characters, and complimentary hot chocolate and cookies nearly go away, but the dance parties get more crowded, and therefore more fun. *When to ride Jingle Cruise:* Late, after its lines die down. It's very popular, especially right at 7 p.m.

Note: For the last two weeks in December the party's fireworks, parade and shows become part of the regular Magic Kingdom day, so you can see them then without paying extra. But the crowds are awful then, so it's harder to enjoy yourself.

New Year's Eve. Magic Kingdom, Epcot and Disney's Hollywood Studios ring in the new year with special fireworks, complimentary party hats and noise makers. Many restaurants have special menus. New Year's

Jolly Saint Goofy. Santa Goofy hams it up as he greets guests in the DinoLand U.S.A. section of Disney's Animal Kingdom.

Eve events are extremely crowded. Events are included in regular admission. *Dec. 30-31.*

Sports and recreation. The best choices here: The free campfire and movie at Fort Wilderness, DiveQuest scuba diving, the Winter Summerland miniature golf course, the surfing lessons at Typhoon Lagoon and parasailing behind the Contemporary resort.

Archery. Fort Wilderness offers archery lessons followed by target practice. Children's bows are small; left-handed bows are available; arrows have rounded tips. *Check in at Bike Barn. $39, 90 min, Thurs–Sat 2:45p. Ages 7 and up. 10 students per class. Reservations taken 90 days early at 407-939-7529.*

Bicycle and surrey rentals. Nine Disney hotels rent bikes and/or multi-seat surreys: BoardWalk, Caribbean Beach, Coronado Springs, Fort Wilderness, Old Key West, Port Orleans, Saratoga Springs, Wilderness Lodge and Yacht and Beach Club (bikes only) *Bikes $9 hr, $18 day; surreys $20–$22 30 min.*

Boat charters. The Pirates and Pals Fireworks Voyage views Magic Kingdom's Wishes from a pontoon boat hosted by a pirate storyteller. Characters greet you afterward *$59 adults, $34 children 3–9. Fri–Mon, nightly over holidays. Contemporary Resort marina. 407-939-7529.* You can charter

your own guided pontoon boat to Wishes or IllumiNations with up to 9 friends. *$275–$325. 1 hr. Snacks. Wishes: Contemporary, Grand Floridian, Polynesian Village, Wilderness Lodge marinas. Illuminations: Yacht Club dock. 407-939-7529.* Or charter the Grand 1, a 52-foot Sea Ray yacht that cruises Seven Seas Lagoon and Bay Lake. *$744 for 1 hr, $1,116 90 min, $1,488 2 hrs, up to 18 people. Includes captain, deckhand. Food, butler opt. Grand Floridian marina. 407-824-2682.*

Boat rentals. Disney World has the world's largest fleet of rental boats. Boats vary by marina; for details call 407-939-7529.

Two-seat canoes and kayaks. *$6.50 30 min, $11 hr.*

Two-seat outboards. Sea Raycers. *$32 30 min, $45 hr. Ages 12–15 may drive with a licensed driver. Height min 60 in. Weight max per boat 320 lbs.*

Center-console outboards. *17-ft Boston Whaler Montauks, $45 30 min. Capacity 6.*

Pedal boats. *$6.50 30 min. Swan and Dolphin Resort swan boats $12–$14 30 min.*

Personal watercraft. 3-seat Sea-Doos at Sammy Duvall's Watersports Centre, Disney's Contemporary Resort. *Non-guided rides $80 30 min, $135 hr. 1-hr morning group rides into Seven Seas Lagoon $135. Max 3 riders per vehicle, max combined weight 400 lbs.*

For kids. Children roast marshmallows at a Chip 'n Dale campfire at Fort Wilderness; the authors' daughter about to release a bass she caught on the Seven Seas Lagoon.

Pontoon boats. *21-ft SunTrackers. $45 30 min. Capacity 10.*

Sailboats. *12-ft Sunfish $2 hr, 13-ft Hobie Cat $25 hr. Operator must be 16, have valid driver's lic.; renters must be 18. 407-939-0754.*

Campfires. Held often at a small outdoor amphitheater at the Fort Wilderness Resort and Campground, Chip 'n Dale's Campfire Sing-a-Long is a charming, throwback event that doesn't even cost anything. It includes a marshmallow roast, 30-minute sing-a-long with the two chipmunks (sit on the benches down front to meet one up close and personal) and a movie. A snack bar sells s'mores kits, marshmallows and sticks (Free. Schedule: 407-824-2727). Port Orleans Riverside offers a campfire sing-a-long (without a movie) seasonally. Other campfire activities are held seasonally at 11 other resorts—Animal Kingdom Lodge Jambo House, Animal Kingdom Lodge Kidani Village, the Beach Club, BoardWalk, Caribbean Beach, Contemporary, Coronado Springs, Old Key West, Polynesian Village, Port Orleans French Quarter, Saratoga Springs and Wilderness Lodge.

Carriage and wagon rides. Available at the Fort Wilderness, Port Orleans Riverside and Saratoga Springs resorts, horse-drawn carriages hold four adults or a small family. *$45 per carriage. 25 min 5:30–10p, those under 18 must ride with adult; reservations accepted 90 days in adv at 407-939-7529; same-day bookings at 407-824-2832. Fort Wilderness has 32-passenger wagons. Firework-view rides available. Pioneer Hall. $8 adults, $5 children 3–9, under 3 free. 45 min. 7, 9:30 p.m. Children under 11 must ride with adult. Walk-ups only. Group rides with 24 hrs notice at 407-824-2734.*

Diving and snorkeling. Guests scuba dive in a 5.7-million-gallon saltwater aquarium as part of Disney's DiveQuest experience, held at Epcot's The Seas pavilion. The tank has more than 65 species, including sharks, rays and sea turtles. *$175, 40 min. in water, 3-hr experience. Includes gear, lockers, showers, mini tour. Park admission not required. Optional video. Up to 12 divers per group. Ages 10 and up; those under 12 must dive with adult. Open-water certification req. Information at 407-939-8687.* The Epcot Seas Aqua Tour puts you in the tank with scuba-assisted snorkel (SAS) equipment. *$140, 30 min in water, 2.5 hrs total. Inc. instruction. Park admission not required. Ages 10 and* up; under 18 must dive with adult. *407-939-8687.* Proceeds from the experiences go to the Disney Worldwide Conservation Fund.

Dolphins in Depth. You'll spend a half-hour in knee-deep water with Epcot's bottlenose dolphins, learn about their anatomy and behavior and watch biologists do research. Individual instruction; interaction not guaranteed. Proceeds go to the Disney Wildlife Conservation Fund *$194, 3 hrs. Includes T-shirt, photo with dolphin, refreshments, use of wetsuit. No swimming. Park admission not required. Ages 13 and up. Those under 18 must be with adult. 407-939-8687.*

Fishing. Catching a fish is almost a certainty at Walt Disney World, as all fishing areas are stocked (with bass, bluegill and catfish), all fish must be released and only a handful of anglers are fishing at any one time.

Guided excursions. Guests routinely catch largemouth bass weighing 2 to 8 pounds on these guided pontoon-boat trips. Most trips catch five to 10 fish; guests average a few fish per hour. Bay Lake and Seven Seas Lagoon are teeming with bass; the largest fish (up to 14 pounds) are in the Crescent and Village lakes. *$235–$270 2 hrs, $455 4 hrs, addl hrs $110. Up to 5 guests. Inc. bait (shiners additional), guide, equipment, refreshments, digital camera. No license req.* Trips on Bay Lake, Seven Seas Lagoon, Crescent Lake, Village Lake and the Coronado Resort's Lago Dorado leave early and mid-morning, early afternoon. *407-939-2277. Reservations taken 2 wks in advance.*

Shoreline fishing. At the Fort Wilderness and Port Orleans Riverside resorts. *Cane poles $4 30 min, $9 day, 4–6 pole package $14 30 min, $28 day. Rods $6 30 min, $13 a day. Bait inc. No license req. 7a–3p. Fort Wilderness 407-824-2900, Riverside 407-934-6000.*

Golf. Grouped into three facilities, Walt Disney World's five golf courses offer different experiences. There's the long course, the short course, the flat course, the water course, and the child-friendly 9-hole. Home to alligators, deer, egrets, herons, otters and the occasional bald eagle, each course is designated as a wildlife sanctuary by the Audubon Cooperative Sanctuary System. All but the Lake Buena Vista course roam away from civilization. Greens have ultra-dwarf TifEagle Bermuda grass, which offers a true, fast roll. All Disney courses are run by Arnold Palmer Golf Management.

The best months to play are September, April and May, when the weather is nice and good tee times are easy to book. Build extra time into your round, as the pace may be slower than you expect.

Lake Buena Vista course. Disney's least forgiving course has narrow, tree-lined fairways and small greens. Play demands accuracy on tee shots and approaches. Errant shots can hit windows. Signature hole No. 7 has an island green; No. 18 is a 438-yard dogleg to the right. Ten holes have water hazards. You tee off at Disney's Saratoga Springs Resort then weave through Old Key West's lodging areas. *Yardage: 5,204–6,802. Par: 72. Course rating: 68.6–73.0. Slope rating: 122–133. Designer: Joe Lee. Year open: 1972. At the Saratoga Springs Resort.*

Magnolia course. How's that shoulder turn? It needs to be efficient on this long-game course, a rolling terrain amid more than 1,500 magnolia trees. The Magnolia has elevated tees and greens and 97 bunkers, the most of any Disney course. Greens are quick. Host to the final round of a PGA Tour stop for four decades, it's tested most top-name pros *Yardage: 5,232–7,516. Par: 72. Course rating: 69.4–76.5. Slope rating: 125–140. Designer: Joe Lee. Year open: 1971. Across from Disney's Polynesian Village Resort.*

Oak Trail course. A walking course, the 9-hole Oak Trail is nice for a quick nine, getting some practice, or introducing a child to the sport. With small greens and two good par 5s, the course requires accuracy with short irons. The longest hole, the 517-yard No. 5, has a double dogleg. Water hazards cross three fairways. Most greens and tees are elevated. The scorecard lists separate pars for children 11 and under and for those over 12. Golf shoes must be spikeless; tennis shoes are permitted *Yardage: 2,532–2,913. Par: 36. Course rating: 64.6–68.2. Slope rating: 107–123. Designer: Ron Garl. Year open: 1980. Next to Shades of Green, across from Disney's Polynesian Village Resort.*

Tranquilo course. Once known as Disney's Osprey Ridge, these links have been converted into a course for the Four Seasons hotel with just a few modifications. Set within beautiful rolling terrain, this challenging course winds through dense vegetation, oak forests and moss hammocks. More than 70 bunkers, mounds and a meandering ridge provide obstacles, banking and elevation changes. Some tees and greens are 20 feet above their fairways. Another challenge:

the course often has swirling winds. One bit of relief: fairway waste bunkers have hard sand, so you can play out of one with a more-normal swing *Yardage: 5,402–7,101. Par: 72. Course rating: 69.5–74.4. Slope rating: 123–131. Designer: Tom Fazio. Year open: 1992. Just east of Fort Wilderness.*

Palm course. Pretty palms. Ugly hazards. This course has both. Water hazards line seven holes and cross six. Shorter and tighter than the nearby Magnolia, the Palm course has a few long par 4s and a couple of par 5s that can be reached in two using a fairway wood. The large, elevated greens can be maneuvered with good lag putting. Save a sprinkle of pixie dust for hole No. 18; a long par 4 that was rated as high as fourth toughest hole on the PGA Tour. The Palm is rated one of Golf Digest's Top 25 Resort Courses *Yardage: 5,311–6,957. Par: 72. Course rating: 69.5–73.9. Slope rating: 126–138. Designer: Joe Lee. Year open: 1971. Next to Shades of Green, across from Disney's Polynesian Village Resort.*

Golf fees and policies. Greens fees: 18-hole courses $55–$195 cart included; 9-hole Oak Trail course $38, $20 for under 18. Proper golf attire required. 18-hole courses have putting greens, driving ranges. Free transportation from Disney-owned resorts. Reservations available 90 days in advance for Disney resort guests, 60 days other players. Cancellations require 48 hours notice. $50 Florida resident Annual Golf Membership saves up to 60 percent on greens fees after 10 a.m. for a member and up to three guests. Additional summer savings. Golf equipment is available for rent, including TaylorMade clubs for men and women ($15–$50). Adidas shoe rental $10 per pair; free for resort guests. Range balls $7 per basket. Oak Trail pull carts $6. *407-939-4653, disneygolf.com.*

Golf lessons. Choose from 30-minute tune-ups, 1-hour lessons, half-day or full-day golf schools, video analysis, group lessons, on-course playing lessons, and Callaway and TaylorMade club fittings. *$50–$150, 45-minute lesson for a single golfer $75, $50 ages 17 and under. Palm/Magnolia facility. PGA pros give lessons. All ages, skill levels. Individual lessons, clinics: 407-454-5096. Florida-resident Annual Golf Membership saves 20 percent.*

Horseback riding. Guides lead small groups down shady pine and palmetto trails at the Fort Wilderness Resort & Campground. Excursions start at the Tri-Circle D Livery at the resort's entrance. Early birds see wildlife such as snakes and deer. *$46, 45 min. Daily starting at 8:30a. Ages 9 and up. Height min 48 in. Max. weight 250 lbs. Closed-toe shoes required; no sandals or flip-flops. No trotting. Req. reservations available 30 days in advance at 407-939-7529.* Smaller children can take a short pony ride at the resort's petting farm; a parent walks the pony along a path. *$5, cash only. Ages 2 and up. Maximum height 45 inches. Maximum weight 80 pounds. 10 a.m.–5 p.m. daily. 407-824-2788.*

Marathons. A pair of running events—a 26.2-mile full marathon and a 13.1-mile half marathon—highlight Disney's Marathon Weekend (the first weekend in January). The full route goes through all four theme parks. Typically more than 30,000 athletes compete. Some runners dress as princesses in the Princess Half Marathon (mid-February) which winds through Magic Kingdom and Epcot. Many other races are held, too. *Details at rundisney.com or 407-938-3398.*

Miniature golf. Two themed complexes on Disney property make it easy to take a break from theme-park activities. *$14 adults, $12 children. 10 a.m.–11 p.m. Last tee time 30 minutes before close. Second rounds half-price if same day or next day. In-person same-day reservations accepted. 407-939-7529.*

Fantasia Gardens. Across the street from the Walt Disney World Swan and Dolphin, this two-course complex (407-560-4753) is busy at night, when tee-time waits can be an hour. Splashing brooms and dancing-ostrich topiaries line a Gardens course themed to Disney's 1940 movie "Fantasia." A Fairways course replicates real links with long fairways, sandy bunkers, roughs and undulating hills. The Gardens course closes at 10:30 p.m.

Winter Summerland. Next to Blizzard Beach, these two courses (407-560-7161) are often deserted at night. Themed to the activities of elves who, as the story goes, vacation here (Santa bought them the course as a respite from their duties at the North Pole), the courses are dotted with tiny elf trailers and Christmas decor. Getting a hole-in-one is easy, as greens often funnel into cups. Way more fun than Fantasia Gardens.

Surfing lessons. Know how to swim? In good shape? If so, then you are almost guaranteed to learn how to ride the crest of a wave at the Craig Carroll Surfing School. It holds instruction at dawn in the surf pool of Typhoon Lagoon, before the water park opens to the public. Conducted on dry land, a step-by-step introduction teaches you the basics, then you get in the surf pool and attempt to ride wave after wave after wave. After each try, Carroll critiques you from the lifeguard stand and an instructor in the water gives additional advice. Waves average about 5 feet for adults; half that for children.

About 70 percent of all students succeed; females tend to do better. "Girls don't think as hard about it, and try to do exactly what you say," Carroll explains. "Boys tend to think it's a macho thing." *$165. Must be 8 yrs or older, strong swimmer. Most students have never surfed. Days, hours vary with season. 2.5-hr lesson includes 30 mins on land, 2 hrs in water. Surfboards provided. Spectators permitted. Maximum 12 students per class; sessions sell out quickly. Reservations accepted 90 days in advance at 407-939-7873.*

Tennis. Disney has 34 lighted courts for recreational use, all at hotels. Use is complimentary for hotel guests, from 8 a.m. to 10 p.m. on a first-come, first-served basis. Courts are at Bay Lake Tower at Disney's Contemporary Resort, Kidani Village at Disney's Animal Kingdom Lodge, BoardWalk Inn and Villas, Old Key West Resort, Saratoga Springs Resort, the Yacht and Beach Club Resorts and the Walt Disney World Swan and Dolphin. Group and private lessons available at Bay Lake Tower, Kidani Village, BoardWalk, Saratoga Springs and the Yacht and Beach Club Resorts *$90 per hour, 321-228-1146.*

Water sports. At Disney's Contemporary Resort at Sammy Duvall's Watersports Centre (407-939-0754). A legendary skier himself, Duvall has won 80 pro championships.

Parasailing. Soaring hundreds of feet above the 450-acre Bay Lake beneath an open parachute, you get a birds-eye view of Disney World. You don't get wet; you take off and land on the boat. *Single riders $95 for 8–10 min at 450 ft; $130 for 10–12 min at 600 ft. Tandem riders $170 for 8–10 min at 450 ft; $195 for 10–12 min at 600 ft. Weight per flight 130–330 lbs.*

Other water sports. Kneeboard, wakeboard or go tubing or water-skiing behind a MasterCraft inboard. Friendly instructors are patient, especially with kids. *Per boat: $85 30 min, $165 1 hr, $135 per addl hr; water-skiing approximately $20 addl. Up to 5 skiers. Inc. equipment, driver, instruction. Extra charge*

if picked up from Fort Wilderness, Grand Floridian, Polynesian or Wilderness Lodge.

Taxes. Two types of taxes are relevant to most Disney visitors:

Hotel taxes. All area hotels charge both sales tax and a 6-percent resort tax on rooms.

Sales taxes. Nearly all of Walt Disney World sits in Orange County, where the sales tax rate is 6.5 percent. A portion of Disney property is in Osceola County, which has a sales tax of 7 percent. This area includes Disney's All-Star Resorts and the ESPN Wide World of Sports complex.

Telephone services. Although no cell-phone towers stand on Disney property, recent technology from AT&T has greatly enhanced the network experience at the resort. Miniature concealed antennas both indoors and out have greatly boosted cellular coverage. The distributed-antenna system (DAS) is the largest network of its kind in a single location in the world. All Disney parks can still have weak cell-phone service on their most crowded days; reception can be especially spotty before or after parades or fireworks, when usage is at its peak. A particularly bad area is The Seas pavilion in Epcot.

Cell-phone stores. Good locations relatively close to Walt Disney World include:

AT&T. Across from Celebration Avenue on U.S. 192. (6081 West Irlo Bronson Memorial Highway 34747; 407-396-2888. 10 a.m.–9 p.m. Monday–Thursday, 10 a.m.–7 p.m. Friday, 10 a.m.–9 p.m. Saturday, noon–6 p.m. Sunday), 4 miles from Disney.

Sprint. Next to WalMart on a service road alongside Interstate 4 (8910 Turkey Lake Road 32819; 407-351-5155; 10 a.m.–8 p.m. Monday–Friday, 10 a.m.–7 p.m. Saturday, noon–5 p.m. Sunday), 7 miles from Disney.

Verizon Wireless. Near North John Young Parkway at 1340 West Osceola Parkway #101 34741; 407-343-0516; 9 a.m.–9 p.m. Monday–Saturday, 11 a.m.–6 p.m. Sunday, 12 miles from Disney.

Disabled guests. Telecommunications Devices for the Deaf (TDD) are available at Guest Relations offices in the theme parks and Downtown Disney. Many pay phones are equipped with amplifying headsets.

Local calls. Callers must include the area code—"407" for all Disney numbers—in all local calls. It is not necessary to dial "1" first.

Hotels. Area hotels often add a hefty service charge on telephone calls made from a room phone. Check the information card near the phone for a list of costs involved.

Pay phones. Pay telephones are still found in all Walt Disney World theme parks, Disney Springs and Disney hotels. Local calls, including calls within Disney, cost 50 cents.

Prepaid phone cards. Private prepaid phone cards are sold at Disney World gift shops and Guest Relations offices. Outside Disney they're available at convenience stores, supermarkets and pharmacies.

Theme park policies. Walt Disney World has specific policies regarding park closures, dress codes, and what you can—and can't—bring into a theme park, though they aren't heavily publicized and enforcement can vary.

Dress codes. As family-oriented spots, the Disney parks have long had a policy of refusing, or revoking, admission to anyone who its managers deem is inappropriately dressed, especially if another guest complains and the offender refuses suggestions to comply. In the case of an offensive T-shirt, a wearer may simply be asked to turn it inside-out. Other unacceptable attire includes clothing that is too transparent, excessively torn or exposes inappropriate portions of the body (i.e., string bikini tops), and adult clothing that can be viewed as a costume (though costumes are allowed during some special events such as Mickey's Not-So-Scary Halloween Party). Children under age 10 can wear costumes at Disney any day of the year. All visitors must wear shirts and shoes. Women may wear bikini tops if they're covered by other clothing. Guests in formal wedding attire are "discouraged" from entering the parks.

Items allowed in theme parks. You can bring a lot into a Disney World theme park:

Coolers. Those that don't have wheels and are smaller than 24 inches long by 15 inches wide by 18 inches high are OK. (This isn't true at Disney's Animal Kingdom theme park, however, which prohibits all coolers except for those needed for medications.)

Food. You are welcome to bring in any snacks, foods or beverages (except alcoholic) that do not require heating and are not in glass containers.

Medications. You can bring in any necessary medications. Medication coolers may be stored in a locker or at Guest Relations.

Umbrellas. Most any umbrella is allowed.

Items not allowed in theme parks. Just have to bring that folding chair? Sorry. Other prohibited items include alcoholic beverages, glass containers (excluding baby food jars and perfume bottles), oversized items (strollers larger than 36-by-51 inches; backpacks or coolers larger than 24-by-15-by-18 inches), pets (service animals are OK), pulled items such as children's wagons, weapons, or wheeled items (inline skates, skateboards, shoes with built-in wheels, wheeled backpacks and coolers) except ECVs, strollers and wheelchairs.

At Disney's Animal Kingdom. For the safety of the wildlife, balloons, coolers and plastic drink lids and plastic straws (even those little straws that come attached to juice boxes) are not permitted.

Operating hours. Park operating hours vary throughout the year; the hours listed below are the most common:

Magic Kingdom. The world's most popular theme park is typically open 9 a.m.–10 p.m. It can, however, open as early as 7 a.m. and close as late as 4 a.m. Magic Kingdom's operating hours have the greatest variance of any Disney World theme park.

Epcot. 9 a.m.–9 p.m. Future World is open 9 a.m.–9 p.m., though some minor attractions may close at 7 p.m. World Showcase is open 11 a.m.–9 p.m.

Disney's Hollywood Studios. 9 a.m.–7 p.m.

Disney's Animal Kingdom. 9 a.m.–5 p.m.

Water parks. 10 a.m.–5 p.m.

For more information call 407-824-4321 or see disneyworld.disney.go.com/calendars.

Park closures. During peak periods the Disney theme parks can fill to capacity and close as early as 10 a.m. to additional guests, even to those who have valid tickets. Closures for capacity are easy to predict—they typically occur only on obviously busy days such as Independence Day and the week between Christmas Eve and New Year's Eve. Disney closes its parks in five distinct phases:

Phase 1. The park stays open to any additional guest who has purchased a park ticket, though Disney stops ticket sales at that park.

Phase 2. Open to only those additional guests who have multi-day park passes or are staying at a Disney-owned resort.

Phase 3. Open to only those additional guests who are using the last day of a multi-day pass or staying at a Disney-owned resort.

Phase 4. Open to only those additional guests who are staying at a Disney resort.

Phase 5. No additional entry available.

Before employing the steps above, occasionally the Magic Kingdom will first close its parking lot to new cars, then stop using

Disney transportation (monorail, buses, boats) to shuttle in new guests.

If you are already in a Disney theme park when it closes for capacity, you are not asked to leave. But if you leave one park to head to another one, you're taking a risk that you'll get locked out of both. Because of its expansive lawns and other open areas, Epcot rarely closes. To learn if a Disney theme park is currently closed, call 407-824-2222.

Tickets. Though Disney World's unconventional Magic Your Way ticketing concept is promoted as a way to let you create a ticket that matches your particular needs, it's also so complicated that, at first glance, it can seem impossible to understand. In a nutshell, Disney's plan lets you tailor tickets to include from one to 10 days of theme-park visits, and then add options such as the ability to visit more than one park a day or spend time at Disney's water parks. Other possible add-ons include a pre-paid dining plan (the Disney Dining Plan), itself with various options including recreation activities. To further complicate matters, Disney offers annual passes, and Florida residents get benefits like discounted tickets and the option of payment for passes in monthly increments.

Single-day tickets. There was big news in 2015: the price of a one-day ticket to a Disney theme park topped $100. Expect it to continue to increase faster than inflation. At press time a single-day ticket to Magic Kingdom costs $105 for adults, $99 for children ages 3 to 9. A ticket to Epcot, Disney's Hollywood Studios or Disney's Animal Kingdom costs $8 less.

Multi-day tickets. Multi-day tickets for adults start at $91.67 a day for three days, which adds up to $275; the child's price is $256. For four days, it's $76.25 a day for adults ($305 total); $71.25 for children ($285 total). The more days the ticket includes, the cheaper it is on a per-day basis.

For more ticket prices or to buy tickets from the Disney company, go to disneyworld.disney.go.com/tickets or call 407-934-7639, from 7 a.m. to 10 p.m. Eastern time.

Base tickets and options. The basic theme-park ticket—the "base ticket"—provides admission to one Disney theme park per day, and is good for up to 10 days. The days the ticket is used do not need to be consecutive, but it expires 14 days after its first use. Base tickets have three options:

Park Hopper. This option lets you visit more than one theme park in the same day.

The price ranges from $50 to $64, depending on the number of days on your ticket. Practical benefits include the ability to go to one park during the day then another at night to see its fireworks show, sample parks during a short visit and revisit favorite attractions. A downside: Disney's Fastpass+ policies make it tough to book Fastpasses at more than one park a day.

Water Park Fun & More. This adds admission to Disney World's two water parks, DisneyQuest, the ESPN Wide World of Sports complex and/or rounds of golf at Disney's 9-hole Oak Trail golf course or Disney's two miniature golf courses. The Water Parks Fun & More surcharge is $64 for a one-day Magic Kingdom ticket; $72 for a one-day ticket to one of the other Disney World theme parks; $64 for any multi-day ticket. The number of admissions the option provides varies by how long the base ticket is good for. Regardless of how long you stay, if you use this option at least twice during your visit it pays for itself.

No Expiration. This add-on is no longer available as of February, 2015.

See also **Disney Dining Plan.**

Theme-park annual passes. An annual pass ($654) includes admission to the four theme parks, plus free theme-park parking and discounts on dining, entertainment and merchandise. A Premium option ($779) adds admission to water parks, DisneyQuest and the ESPN Wide World of Sports complex. Seasonal passes are available. Florida residents, members of the U.S. military and Disney Vacation Club members pay less.

Monthly payments. Floridians can buy annual passes and pay for them monthly, without interest, with a down payment of $110. The down payment and first monthly payment are made at the time of purchase.

Discounts and upgrades. Disney offers discounts for Florida residents and members of the U.S. military. Purchased tickets can always be upgraded, but not downgraded.

Water park tickets. The basic ticket provides admission to either Blizzard Beach or Typhoon Lagoon, and is good for 1 day. The price is $58 for an adult, $50 for a child. For unlimited admission for both Blizzard Beach and Typhoon Lagoon for one year, the price is $110 for an adult, $99 for a child. A 1-day ticket can be upgraded toward the purchase of a water-park annual pass on the same day.

DisneyQuest tickets. A basic ticket provides admission for 1 day: $48 for an adult, $42 for a child.

Racy ride. Monorail trains serve the Contemporary Resort (above), the Grand Floridian and Polynesian Village hotels, Magic Kingdom, Epcot, and the Transportation and Ticket Center.

Tours. Organized tours offer a closer look at Disney World. Unless indicated below, tours are for guests ages 16 and older. Those that go backstage do not allow photography. Photo IDs are required. To book a tour listed below except a VIP tour call 407-939-8687.

Backstage Magic. View backstage creative and technical operations at all four theme parks. *$249, lunch included, park adm. not req. 7 hrs. Mon–Fri.*

Backstage Tales. Animal Kingdom tour visits behind-the-scenes animal-care areas. *$90, park adm. req. 3 hr, 45 min. Mond, Wed, Thr, Fri at 8:30a, 1p. Ages 12 and up.*

Behind the Seeds. A backstage look at the greenhouses of Epcot's Land pavilion. *$20 adults, $16 children 3–9, park adm. req. 1 hr. Daily. All ages.*

BoardWalk Ballyhoo Guided Tour. A guide takes you through Disney's BoardWalk Inn, explaining its architecture and history. *Free. 45 min. 9a Wed–Sat. All ages.*

Disney's Family Magic Tour. This Magic Kingdom scavenger hunt captures a dastardly villain; it's a skip (literally) through the park. *$34, park adm. req. 2 hr. Daily. All ages, best for ages 4 to 10.*

ESPN Wide World of Sports Tour. An guided inside look at the large athletic complex. *On busy days. Free. 1 hr. All ages.*

Holiday D-Lights. Tours the backstage decorations shop, Magic Kingdom's Main Street U.S.A., Osborne Dancing Lights at Disney's Hollywood Studios; includes seats for Epcot's Candlelight Processional, light buffet. *$209, no park adm. req. 4.5–5 hrs. Mon, Wed. 4p. Late Nov–Dec.*

Keys to the Kingdom. Guides discuss Magic Kingdom's history, philosophies; travels into its underground Utilidor. Disney World's most popular tour. *$79, includes lunch, park adm. req. 5 hrs. Daily.*

The Magic Behind Our Steam Trains. Shows how Magic Kingdom's antique steam trains are prepped for daily operation; also discusses Walt Disney's love of trains. An author favorite. *$54, park adm. req. 3 hrs. Mon–Thr, Sat. Ages 10 and up.*

UnDISCOVERed Future World. You'll learn of Walt Disney's planned Experimental Prototype Community of Tomorrow, visit Epcot's Future World pavilions and go backstage. *$64, park adm. req. 4 hr. Mon, Wed, Fri.*

The Ultimate Day for Young Families. Designed for families with kids under age 10, this "VIP Tour Experience" gives you a tour of a dozen of Disney's best family attractions. *$299. 6–7 hr. Tues, Fri, Sun; 8:10a. Park adm. required, guests under 18 must be accompanied by an adult. Table-service lunch inc.*

The Ultimate Day of Thrills. Another "VIP Tour Experience," this one takes you on 11 Disney thrill rides, including Expedition Everest, Space Mountain and the Twilight Zone Tower of Terror. *$299. 6–7 hr. Tue, Fri, Sun; 8:15a. Height min. 48 in., park adm. required, guests under 18 must be accompanied by an adult. Table-service lunch inc.*

VIP Tours. Your group gets its own guide, who uses your custom itinerary. *$315–$380 per hr, min. 6 hrs, park adm. required. Daily. All ages. 407-560-4033.*

Walt Disney: From Marceline to the Magic Kingdom. Explores how Walt Disney was motivated to achieve his dreams. Stops at Magic Kingdom attractions that had their start at 1964 World's Fair. *$30, park adm. req. 3 hr, Mon, Wed–Fri.*

Wild Africa Trek. Small groups take guided treks through the forest and savanna of the Kilimanjaro Safaris at Disney's Animal Kingdom. Includes winding remote pathways, life-line lean over a cliff to watch hippos as they are fed lettuce, swaying footbridge high over Nile crocodiles, memorable open-air truck ride through the savanna area, stop at covered viewing area stocked with fresh snacks. *Price varies by season; apx. $190–250 per person, park adm. req. 3 hr. Multiple times daily. Ages 8 and up. Max. 12 guests per trek. Inc. photographer.*

Wilderness Back Trail Adventure. You'll ride a rugged Segway X2 two-wheeled self-balancing vehicle down shady Fort Wilderness trails. *$95. 2 hr. Tues–Sat; 8:30, 11:30a. Min. weight 100 lbs, max 250. Same-day walk-up reservations at Fort Wilderness marina.*

Yuletide Fantasy. Explores the holiday decorations of Magic Kingdom, Epcot and a few Disney resort hotels. *$89, late Nov–Dec, park adm. not req. 3 hr. Mon–Sat.*

Transportation. Though many guests get around Disney World's 47-square-mile property in cars, there are many other options.

Disney buses. A huge fleet of diesel buses connects Disney's resorts with all theme and water parks and Downtown Disney, and also between some parks. Buses typically arrive every 20 to 30 minutes, from one hour before park opening until one hour after closing.

Though the buses run from theme park to theme park, and from any theme park to Blizzard Beach, they do not go from all theme parks to Downtown Disney or Typhoon Lagoon, and serve ESPN Wide World of Sports only from Disney's All-Star, Caribbean Beach and Pop Century resorts. There is also no official bus service between resort hotels, though hotels in the same area often share the same buses.

Except during thunderstorms, buses do not run from the Epcot resorts (BoardWalk, Yacht and Beach Club, Walt Disney World Swan and Dolphin) to Epcot or Disney's Hollywood Studios. Guests at those resorts travel to those parks via ferry boat or on foot. Guests enter Epcot through the park's rear International Gateway entrance into World Showcase.

Disney monorails. These electric trains connect Disney's Transportation and Ticket Center (TTC) with Magic Kingdom and the Contemporary, Grand Floridian and Polynesian Village resorts. A separate line runs to Epcot. Operating hours vary.

Disney boats. Ferries connect Magic Kingdom with the TTC and the hotels on Seven Seas Lagoon and Bay Lake; Epcot and Hollywood Studios with hotels in between those parks; and Downtown Disney with Port Orleans, Old Key West and Saratoga Springs. For transportation details call 407-939-7433.

Rental cars. Orlando is the largest rental-car market in the world. At the Orlando International Airport most major rental companies have their cars in an adjacent parking garage. Rental-car counters are located on the Ground Transportation Level (Level 1) of each side of the terminal.

If you're already at Disney, the most convenient place to rent a car may be Disney's Car Care Center at the exit of the Magic Kingdom parking lot. A counter (407-824-3470) offers Alamo and National vehicles and provides shuttle service to guests at all Disney hotels. Satellite desks are at the Walt Disney World Dolphin (407-934-4930) and the Buena Vista Palace (407-827-6363). Four other hotels on Disney property have car-rental counters: the Downtown Disney Hilton (Avis, 407-827-2847), Doubletree Guest Suites (Budget, 407-827-6089), Wyndham (Dollar, 407-583-8000) and Shades of Green (Hertz, 407-938-0600).

You'll pay a 6 percent sales tax, a $2.05 daily "road impact fee" and a 10 percent surcharge to the Greater Orlando Aviation Authority.

Taxicabs and town cars. Taxicabs, town cars and other vehicles are available for travel around Disney and the surrounding area. Mears Transportation—the largest transportation operator in the area, and the only contracted provider for Disney—has the most choices. *24-hr reservations 407-423-5566,*

Rainy day stroll. A spring shower brightens the colors of the flower garden at Epcot's Canada pavilion. Disney averages 51 inches of rain a year, mostly in the spring and summer.

taxicab mearstransportation.com; vehicles with child seats available on request.

Taxis. Mears taxis (pickup 407-422-2222 or 407-699-9999), operate under the Yellow Cab, Checker Cab and City Cab brands. Transportation within Disney property should cost $15–$30; the fare for traveling between the Orlando International Airport and Disney is typically $65–$75. For groups of 5 to 8 people, vans charge $90–$100. Non-Mears "gypsy" cabs lurk in the area, and may have unpredictable rates and may take only cash.

Town cars. Many upscale resorts in the area have Mears town cars available 24 hours a day. Airport service includes a driver who will meet a guest at baggage claim, and transportation in a luxury sedan to the guest's resort; the fare to Disney is typically $90–$100 for up to four passengers.

Airport shuttle service. Mears offers group transportation from the Orlando International Airport to Disney-area resorts. Passengers wait on a bus or van at the airport until the vehicle is full. On the return trip, shuttle passengers are picked up three to four hours before their flight times. Fares: One-way: $22 adult, $17 child. Round trip: $36 adult, $27 child. Children under 3 ride free.

Vehicle charters. Mears has 55-passenger buses, 25-passenger mini-buses, 11-passenger vans and 8-passenger limos. For current fares see mearstransportation.com.

See also **Airports.**

Weather. Florida's subtropical climate creates mild winters but summers that are hot and humid. Between May and August Disney guests can get exhausted with little effort, as the sun rises almost straight up in the sky. Temperatures in that direct heat usually are about 12 degrees warmer than those in the shade, and can easily reach 100 degrees. Afternoon heat indexes usually exceed 105 degrees. Brief afternoon thunderstorms are common. Overall, July is the hottest month at Disney, January the coolest. August is the wettest month, December the driest.

Current forecast. The Weather Channel provides a specific current forecast for Walt Disney World. Visit weather.com and search for "Disney World." There's also one available by phone, from the independent Disney Weather Hotline at 407-824-4104.

Hurricanes. Though hurricanes often strike the Florida coast, the risk of one hitting Disney is low, as the resort sits in the middle of the state—since the power of a hurricane is generated by being over water, its intensity lessens upon landfall and usually dissipates quickly. Three hurricanes, however, came close to Disney World in 2004. Disney closed its parks and golf courses for those storms, but kept its hotels open. The eye of Hurricane Charley passed just a few miles south.

Florida's hurricane season is June through November. Disney allows you to cancel hotel reservations without penalty whenever the National Hurricane Center issues a hurricane warning for the Orlando area (or a guest's place of residence) within seven days of your scheduled arrival date. If you're at Disney when a hurricane approaches, take it seriously and follow Disney's advice.

Rain gear. Disney sells clear plastic ponchos throughout its property; children and adult sizes cost about $8.50. Umbrellas are also available. Small collapsible ones go for about $15; large golf umbrellas are $43.

Weather refunds. There are no refunds at Disney World for bad weather. Disney theme parks stay open, rain or shine; water parks offer rain checks in some circumstances.

Weddings. Up to a dozen couples tie the knot at Walt Disney World every day. Sound strange? Actually, there's a lot to recommend it. Disney has unrivaled facilities for a family gathering, good year-round weather, a quality honeymoon spot and a one-stop Fairy Tale Weddings division. Most weddings are performed at Disney's Wedding Pavilion next to the Grand Floridian Resort and Spa. Several hotels—including the BoardWalk, Polynesian Village, Wilderness Lodge and Yacht Club—also host ceremonies.

Planning. Named after funnyman Martin Short's wedding planner in Disney's 1991 movie "Father of the Bride," Franck's Bridal Studio can arrange accommodations, cakes, flowers, music, photography and rehearsal dinners. It's next to the wedding pavilion.

Costs. Disney offers three wedding packages, which vary based on the number of guests and level of services. The average Disney wedding costs $31,000 and includes 100 people. Prices start at $2,495.

For more information call 321-939-4610 or go online to disneyweddings.com.

Honeymoons. Disney planning services includes an on-line registry (407-939-7776, disneyhoneymoonregistry.com), which lets couples create a wish list for their trip and have family and friends contribute. More honeymoon help is available at 800-370-6009 or online at disneyhoneymoons.com.

Wi-Fi. Disney provides complimentary wireless Internet access throughout its property, though it is often slow on crowded days and reception can be poor. For answers to technical issues, call Disney for assistance at 407-827-2732.

See also **Internet access.**

Youth groups. Disney World offers various activities and competitions for youth groups of 10 or more. Participants get discounted group rates for both accommodations and theme-park tickets. Opportunities include:

Disney Performing Arts OnStage. This audition-based program invites community groups and middle- and high-school students to perform at Disney year round. Instrumental and vocal groups participate, as do dance ensembles (instrumental groups 866-242-3617, vocal 866-578-4823, dance 866-578-4827). Optional performance workshops are available (866-578-4830).

Festival Disney. Held each spring, this educational experience is open to middle-school, junior- and senior-high school concert bands, jazz ensembles, marching bands, orchestras, vocal ensembles, show choirs and auxiliary units. No audition is required; directors choose either competitive or non-competitive adjudication options. Performances take place at Disney's Saratoga Springs Resort, Disney's Hollywood Studios and Downtown Disney (877-939-6884).

Disney Youth Education Series (YES). These programs give elementary through high school students real-world learning experiences at Disney theme parks. Hands-on courses focus on Leadership & Careers, Arts & Humanities, Physical Sciences and Natural Sciences.

Walt Disney World weather			
Month	Avg high	Avg low	Rain
Jan	72	48	2.4 in.
Feb	73	49	2.7 in.
Mar	77	53	3.3 in.
April	82	58	3.0 in.
May	87	64	3.8 in.
June	90	70	6.0 in.
July	93	72	6.6 in.
Aug	92	72	7.3 in.
Sept	90	71	6.0 in.
Oct	84	65	3.2 in.
Nov	79	57	2.4 in.
Dec	73	50	2.2 in.

Telephone Directory

Area Code 407 unless indicated

AUTOMOBILE RENTALS
Alamo Car Care Center.....................................824-3470
  Buena Vista Palace 827-6363
Avis Disney Springs Hilton 827-2847
Budget Doubletree Guest Suites......................827-6089
Dollar Wyndham 827-8324
Thrifty WDW Dolphin...934-4930

AUTOMOBILE SERVICES
Car Care Center 824-0976
  After hours...824-4777

BANKING SERVICES
Suntrust Disney Springs 828-6103

BUSINESS SERVICES
Disney Event Group Bus. gatherings...........939-7129
Disney Institute 566-2620
Disney Professional Seminars 824-7997

CONVENTION PLANNING
Disney convention centers 321 939-7129
WDW Swan and Dolphin 934-4290

DISABILITY SERVICES
Sign-language show schedule 824-4321
  Special requests 939-7807
TDD numbers Disney information 827-5141

ENTERTAINMENT
AMC Theater Disney Springs 827-1308
  Movie listings...888 262-4386
Atl Braves Spring Training Box office 939-4263
Atlantic Dance Hall BoardWalk Resort 939-2444
Chip 'n Dale's Campfire Movie schedule ..824-2727
Cirque du Soleil La Nouba Disney Sp.......939-7600
House of Blues Disney Springs 934-2583
Jellyrolls BoardWalk Resort...........................560-8770
Raglan Road Disney Springs 938-0300
Splitsville Disney Springs...............................938-7467

FLORISTS
Disney Floral & Gifts 827-3505
  Disney Dream Makers 939-4438
  Convention services..827-1266
  Wedding services................................321 939-4610

GASOLINE STATIONS
Speedway Disney Springs 938-0160
  Epcot Resort Area..938-0151
  Magic Kingdom...938-0143

GENERAL INFORMATION
Disney Springs 939-6244
Poison Control Center 800 222-1222
Time and temperature 646-3131
Walt Disney World Community relations 828-3453
  Customer service (live operator)...................824-2222
  Golden Oak Realty..939-5577
  Hotel reservations 939-7429
  Merchandise guest services.................877 560-6477
  Recreation reservations 939-7529
  Restaurant cancellations 939-2625
  Restaurant reservations 939-3463
  Technical support...939-7765
  Theme-park ticket sales 939-7429
  Vacation package booking 939-7675
  Walt Disney World Travel Co.............................939-6244
  For United Kingdom visitors 939-7718
  If calling from the U.K............................087 0242 4908
Weather Three-day Disney forecast..............824-4104

HAIR SALONS AND BARBER SHOPS
Bibbidi Bobbidi Boutique 939-7895
Harmony Barber Shop Magic Kingdom......824-6550
Ivy Trellis Salon Grand Floridian Resort......824-1679
Periwig's Yacht Club Resort...........................934-3260
The Salon WDW Dolphin.................................934-4772

HOTELS AND RESORTS
B Resort and Spa Disney Springs...............828-2828
Best Western Disney Springs.........................828-2424
Buena Vista Palace Disney Springs 827-2727
  The Spa 827-3200
Disney's All-Star Resorts
  All-Star Movies...939-7000
  All-Star Music..939-6000
  All-Star Sports...939-5000
  Lost and found...939-6882
Disney's Animal Kingdom Lodge 938-3000
  Lost and found...938-4778
  Simba's Cubhouse childcare center 938-4785
  Sunrise Safari / Sunset Safari 938-4755
  Zahanati Fitness Center....................................938-4715
Disney's Art of Animation Resort 938-7000
Disney's BoardWalk Inn and Villas 939-5100
  Lost and found...939-5116
  Muscles and Bustles Health Club 939-2370
Disney's Caribbean Beach Resort 934-3400
  Lost and found...934-3090
Disney's Contemporary Resort 824-1000
  Lost and found...283-3659
  Olympiad Fitness Center...................................824-3410
Disney's Coronado Springs Resort 939-1000
  La Vida Health Club..939-3030

Lost and found...939-3070
Disney's Fort Wilderness Resort 824-2900
  Campfire movie schedule.................................824-2727
  Electric cart rental 824-2742
  Group camping..938-3398
  Horseback riding...824-2900
  Lost and found..824-2726
  Pony rides 824-2788
Disney's Grand Floridian Resort 824-3000
  Ivy Trellis Beauty Salon 824-1679
  Lost and found..824-2988
Disney's Old Key West Resort 827-7700
Disney's Polynesian Village Resort 824-2000
  Lost and found..824-2192
  Lilo's Playhouse childcare center..................939-3463
Disney's Pop Century Resort 938-4000
  Lost and found..934-3090
Disney's Port Orleans Resorts
  French Quarter...934-5000
  Riverside 934-6000
Disney resort hotels Reservations 939-7429
  Photography sittings 824-1700
Disney's Saratoga Springs Resort 827-1100
  Lost and found..827-4942
Disney Vacation Club 800 800-9100
  Sales information..566-3100
Disney's Wilderness Lodge Resort 824-3200
  Cub's Den childcare center............................824-1083
  Lost and found..824-4751
  Sturdy Branches Health Club..........................939-2370
  Wilderness Lodge Villas 938-4300
Disney's Yacht and Beach Club Resort
  Beach Club 934-8000
  Beach Club Villas..934-2175
  Sandcastle Club childcare center 934-6290
  Yacht Club 934-7000
  Periwig's Beauty Salon....................................934-3260
  Ship Shape Health Club..................................934-3256
Doubletree Guest Suites Disney Springs.. 934-1000
Four Seasons Orlando 877 970-8117
Hilton Disney Springs 827-4000
Holiday Inn Disney Springs............................828-8888
Shades of Green 824-3600
Walt Disney World Swan & Dolphin ...934-4000
  Camp Dolphin childcare center......................934-4000
  The Salon..934-4772
Wyndham Disney Springs...............................828-4444

KENNELS
Best Friends Pet Care Center........877 493-9738

LOST AND FOUND
Disney Central Lost and Found 824-4245

Disney parks Animal Kingdom 938-2785
  Disney's Blizzard Beach...................................560-5408
  Epcot...560-6646
  Magic Kingdom...824-4521
  Disney's Typhoon Lagoon 560-6296
  Disney's Hollywood Studios............................560-3720
Disney Springs 828-3150
ESPN Wide World of Sports 541-5600

PHOTOGRAPHY SERVICES
Disney Photographic Services 827-5099
PhotoPass 560-4300

POLICE
Orange County Sheriff 254-7000
Osceola County Sheriff 348-2222
Walt Disney World Security 560-7959
  Urgent matters..560-1990

RECREATION
Boat rentals 939-7529
Camping Groups 938-3398
Carriage rides 939-7529
Characters in Flight Disney Springs..........938-9433
DisneyQuest Disney Springs........................828-4600
ESPN Wide World of Sports 828-3267
  Live operator...939-1500
  runDisney 938-3398
  Youth group information.................................939-4263
Fishing Disney excursions 939-2277
Golf Disney tee-time reservations 939-4653
Horseback riding Fort Wilderness 824-2900
Marathons and foot races 938-3398
Miniature golf Fantasia Gardens..................560-4753
  Winter Summerland.......................................560-7161
Pony rides Fort Wilderness 824-2788
Reservations Disney recreation 939-7529
Splitsville Disney Springs..............................938-7467
Surfing lessons Typhoon Lagoon 939-7873
Tennis Reservations, lessons........................621-1991
Wagon rides 939-7529
Water Sports Sammy Duvall's......................939-0754

RESTAURANTS
American Q B Resort......................................827-3080
Big River Grille BoardWalk Resort.............560-0253
The Boathouse Disney Springs....................939-2628
Bongos Cuban Cafe Disney Springs 828-0999
Crossroads House of Blues Disney Sp 934-2583
Disney restaurants Reservations 939-3463
  Dietary requests 824-5967
  Tables in Wonderland discount card 566-5858
Earl of Sandwich Disney Springs.................938-1762

Erin Mckenna's Bakery NYC Disney Sp ... 938-9044
ESPN Club BoardWalk Resort........................ 939-1177
Fresh WDW Dolphin.. 934-1609
Fulton's Crab House Disney Springs.......... 934-2628
Garden Grove WDW Swan........................... 934-1609
Ghirardelli Disney Springs............................ 934-8855
Haägen Dazs Disney Springs....................... 828-0257
Il Mulino WDW Swan..................................... 934-1199
McDonald's W Buena Vista Dr 939-0875
Paradiso 37 Disney Springs......................... 934-3700
Planet Hollywood Disney Springs 827-7827
Portobello Dsney Springs 934-8888
Raglan Road Disney Springs 938-0300
Rainforest Cafe Animal Kingdom................. 938-9100
  Disney Springs 827-8500
Shula's Steak House WDW Dolphin 934-1362
Starbucks Disney Springs West Side............ 560-0603
  Marketplace 560-0599
T-REX Disney Springs 828-8739
Todd English's bluezoo WDW Dolphin...... 934-1111
Vivoli il Gelato Disney Springs 828-8174
Wetzel's Pretzels Disney Springs 828-0256
Wolfgang Puck Cafe Disney Springs.......... 938-9653
Wolfgang Puck Dining Rm Disney Sp 938-9653
Wolfgang Puck Express Disney Springs.... 828-0107
Yak & Yeti Animal Kingdom 824-9384

RETAIL STORES

Apex by Sunglass Hut Disney Springs........ 560-8311
Arribas Bros. Disney Springs 828-4840
The Art of Shaving Disney Springs 560-8320
Basin Disney Springs 827-8080
  Grand Floridian 938-0355
Chapel Hats Disney Springs 801-8663
Curl Disney Springs.. 842-1302
Erwin Pearl Disney Springs 560-9942
Fit2Run Disney Springs.................................. 560-8333
Ghirardelli Disney Springs............................ 934-8878
Havaianas Disney Springs 560-8230
House of Blues Store Disney Springs 934-2583
The Lego Store Disney Springs.................... 828-0065
Little Miss Matched Disney Springs 938-9257
Orlando Harley-Davidson Disney Sp 938-0522
Pop Gallery Disney Springs 827-8200
Rainforest Cafe Store Disney Springs........ 827-8500
Sanuk Disney Springs..................................... 374-2447
Set the Bar Disney Springs 560-0590
Something Silver Disney Springs 828-8884
Sosa Family Cigar Co. Disney Springs...... 773-7412
Sound Lion Disney Springs............................ 560-8303
Sublime Gifts and Finds Disney Springs... 560-0580
Sunglass Icon Disney Springs...................... 827-0110
United World of Soccer Disney Springs.... 560-0605

SHIPPING SERVICES

FedEx S Apopka-Vineland Rd......................... 465-0085
UPS Vineland Ave 465-1700
U.S. Post Office Celebration 566-1145

SPAS

Mandara Spa WDW Dolphin.......................... 934-4772
The Spa Buena Vista Palace 827-3200
Senses Grand Floridian 939-2370
  Saratoga Springs 939-2370

SPECIAL EVENTS

Epcot Flower & Garden Festival 934-7639
Epcot Food & Wine Festival 939-3378
Mickey's Not-So-Scary Party 939-5277
Mickey's Very Merry Party 939-5277
Star Wars Weekends 827-2799

SPECIAL OCCASIONS

Cake Hotline Ordering 827-2253
Floral arrangements 321 939-4610
Honeymoons 800 370-6009
Quinceañera events 321 939-4555
Weddings 321 939-4610

THEME PARKS

Blizzard Beach Blizzard Beach Dr 560-3400
Capacity closures 939-4636
Disney's Animal Kingdom Osceola Pkwy . 939-5277
Disney's Hollywood Studios S Studio Dr . 939-5277
Epcot Epcot Center Dr 824-4321
Extra Magic Hours Schedule 824-4321
Magic Kingdom Seven Seas Dr.................... 939-5277
Refurbishments Schedule 824-4321
Ticket inquiries 566-4985
  Annual Passholder Hotline 827-7200
Ticket sales General 566-4985
  Convention attendees................................ 939-4686
Tours 939-8687
  VIP Tours 560-4033
Typhoon Lagoon E Buena Vista Blvd 560-4120

TRANSPORTATION SERVICES

Disney's Magical Express 866 599-0951
Mears Transportation Luxury sedans 423-5566
  Airport shuttles....................................... 423-5566
  Group transportation sales........................ 839-1570
  Taxicabs (Checker, City, Yellow Cabs)........... 422-2222
Walt Disney World Transportation 939-7433

YOUTH GROUPS

Disney Youth Programs 866 842-3340
Disney Performing Arts 800 359-0509

Index

About the authors

A FORMER WALT DISNEY WORLD concierge supervisor, Julie Neal is the author of "The Complete Walt Disney World" series of travel guides. As such she's spent over 2,500 days at Disney World not counting her time behind the desk. A roller coaster freak and a wildlife enthusiast, she lists Expedition Everest and the Pangani Forest Exploration Trail as her favorite Disney attractions. Her passions outside the world of theme parks include animal rights, reading and old movies.

Julie's husband Mike designed the book and took most of the photos for it. As it's been since he first rode it in high school, his favorite Disney attraction is Space Mountain, from the front seat. Outside of work his interests include cheeses, filmmaking and palm trees.

Julie and Mike live in Orlando with their daughter Micaela, who helps out in the family business when she's not scuba diving in the Caribbean or going to school at Florida State. She vets Julie's writing, takes photos of her own, and does the animal guide. Her favorite Disney attraction: Big Thunder Mountain Railroad.

The Neals share their home with the most important member of their family: Oliver, the world's most cuddly 85-pound rescue dog.